Compensation Management

SECOND EDITION

Dipak Kumar Bhattacharyya
Professor
Xavier Institute of Management, Bhubaneswar (XIMB)

Oxford University Press is a department of the University of Oxford.
It furthers the University's objective of excellence in research, scholarship,
and education by publishing worldwide. Oxford is a registered trade mark of
Oxford University Press in the UK and in certain other countries.

Published in India by
Oxford University Press
YMCA Library Building, 1 Jai Singh Road, New Delhi 110001, India

© Oxford University Press 2009, 2014

The moral rights of the author/s have been asserted.

First Edition published in 2009
Second Edition published in 2014

All rights reserved. No part of this publication may be reproduced, stored in
a retrieval system, or transmitted, in any form or by any means, without the
prior permission in writing of Oxford University Press, or as expressly permitted
by law, by licence, or under terms agreed with the appropriate reprographics
rights organization. Enquiries concerning reproduction outside the scope of the
above should be sent to the Rights Department, Oxford University Press, at the
address above.

You must not circulate this work in any other form
and you must impose this same condition on any acquirer.

ISBN-13: 978-0-19-945654-3
ISBN-10: 0-19-945654-2

Typeset in Baskerville
by Welkyn Software Solutions Pvt Ltd, Coimbatore
Printed at Repro India Limited

Third-party website addresses mentioned in this book are provided
by Oxford University Press in good faith and for information only.
Oxford University Press disclaims any responsibility for the material contained therein.

To
Sutapa, Sudip, and Tapodeep
for their patience while I was developing this manuscript

Features of

Learning Objectives
Learning objectives at the beginning of each chapter focus on learning and knowledge a reader should acquire by the end of the chapter.

Learning Objectives

After reading this chapter, you will be able to
- understand the term compensation from different perspectives
- analyse difference between wages and compensation
- study various principles of compensation/wage fixation
- examine theories of wage determination
- comprehend the basic dynamics of wage policy and objectives
- understand the various domains of compensation
- understand the concept of cost to company
- comprehend the terms pay grades and pay bands

OPENING CASE

Compensation Redesign at DeriPharma

Motivating and retaining good performers is an important priority for any organization. Companies cannot retain talent with high salaries alone. They also need to develop compensation packages that address the real and perceived needs of employees. It may include, among other things, making provisions for short-and long-term incentives, stock options, assistance in

Opening Case
Chapter-opening cases highlight the importance of the topic on which the chapter is based.

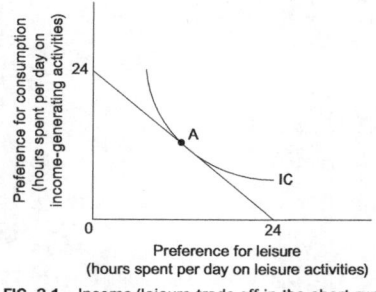

FIG. 3.1 Income/leisure trade-off in the short run

Figures and Tables
Figures and tables illustrate the topics discussed in the chapter.

TABLE 4.4 Turnover per Employee for BHEL and ONGC

Year	BHEL (₹ in crore)	ONGC (₹ in crore)
2007–08	0.49	1.860
2008–09	0.61	1.960
2009–10	0.74	1.880
2010–11	0.93	2.060
2011–12	1.00	2.336

the Book

SUMMARY

Organizations need to emulate best practices, continuously benchmark their compensation designs, and understand what works for them. Decisions on fixed and variable components of compensation need to be taken after considering numerous factors such as the nature of the job, company's business goals, product life cycle, performance management systems, etc. Choosing the right incentive plans is another important area of compensation design. There are various short-term and long-term incentive schemes that an organization can choose from. Taking into account its human resource strategy, the organization should choose an alternative which meet the cost–benefit test.

Summary
Summary at the end of each chapter draws together the main concepts discussed within the chapter, which helps a reader to reflect and evaluate important concepts.

Key Term

Compensation benchmarking It is an exercise to study the degree of competitiveness of an organization's compensation rate and policies with reference to industry standards.

Key Terms
Key terms explaining the important terms at the end of each chapter helps retain all the new concepts that a reader has learnt in the chapter.

Exercises

Concept Review Questions

1. Define the term 'executive compensation'. What are the important components of executive compensation?
2. Discuss different theories of executive compensation.
3. Discuss the salient features of employee compensation in India.
4. Write short notes on:

Critical Thinking Question

A manufacturing organization has to recruit a large number of both skilled and unskilled workers. These workers are easily available given the present economic conditions. Your company believes there is no need to pay the workers above the minimum wage set by the state government. However, you personally feel that since the company is capable of paying more (due to high

Exercises
Concept review questions test the level of understanding of core themes discussed in the chapter while critical thinking questions help develop further understanding of the concepts.

CASE STUDY: Retention Problems at IndiaRetail

Large organizations often face the challenges thrown by high attrition within a short span of time. It is not just limited to information technology enabled services (ITES). Sectors such as retail, banking, and automobiles also witness large scale movement of people. It is a challenge for the human resource (HR) managers of these sectors to retain employees using innovative compensation design. Considerations such as internal pay equity, loyalty, and commitment to the organization are often ignored by young executives. They prefer jobs that offer high compensation packages. So, high salaries are now considered the only way to retain talent.

With the entry of multinational companies (MNCs) and a positive economic growth, the problem of employee retention is of utmost concern to businesses in India.

Hemant Shukla was troubled while preparing the annual salary budget for his retail chain, IndiaRetail. The company had a presence in all the major metros. It had a 100 per cent growth on year to year basis, making it a good poaching ground for other retailers. Last year 140 junior structure in such a flexible way that an employee could earn twice their average monthly salary, given some initiative in retaining customers. The company's stores were so arranged that each customer care executive (CCE) monitored counters with some common items. They were given training to educate customers about products and why they should buy it. Every CCE got a bonus point for repeat customer purchases. At the end of the year, based on the accumulated bonus points, these employees also got surprise incentives.

Hemant's friend Kushal worked for a big multinational company. Kushal advised Hemant to closely study the organization's work culture and design a compensation package while considering the career development initiatives of employees. The core advice was to opt for an organizational work culture survey and ensure that employees' morale was high. For example, Maruti Suzuki reduced the rate of attrition by identifying and grooming potential achievers. Maruti provided regular training to employees to help them to achieve personalized career graphs.

Case Study
Case studies at the end of each chapter elaborate on various organizational problems and give a reader a chance to use the learning from the chapter to solve them.

Preface to the Second Edition

Compensation refers to all forms of financial return and tangible services and benefits received by employees as part of their employment contract. It is an extremely important aspect for both employees and employers. Given the importance of compensation in the organizational context, compensation management has become one of the most important human resource (HR) functions in any organization.

Compensation management, as a subject of study, has evolved considerably in recent years. Volumes of literature have been published on theories and strategies of compensation management. Academia has largely accepted its importance and therefore, compensation management has been made a core human resource management subject for students specializing in HR. The subject is covered at a very elementary level in courses on sales and distribution management with emphasis on sales-force compensation. Also, practitioners keep referring to compensation management literature to gain knowledge for their prudent participation in compensation design programmes. With globalization, organizational presence across the globe has now increased with constant mobility of people from one country to another. As a result of this mobility, issues pertaining to international compensation management, cross-cultural issues, performance-related pay (PRP), 'say on pay', etc. have been introduced. With changing business dynamics, compensation management is now a strategic issue, as compensation is the major cost factor for organizations across the world.

The second edition of this book is designed keeping in mind all the previously mentioned points. This edition not only has updated data and current legal provisions, but also provides additional content, new chapters, and new case studies to enable students to keep pace with the latest industry trends.

Key Features

- Provides a thorough understanding of the major concepts of compensation management
- Covers advance topics and focuses on quantitative aspects of compensation management
- Includes pedagogical features such as exhibits, chapter-end questions and problems, project assignments, key terms, and a recapitulation of the topics covered

New to this Edition

- New chapter on reward management
- New sections on topics such as factors influencing compensation, wage boards, wage policy, cost to company (CTC), 'say on pay' issues, economic value-added (EVA),

performance-related pay (PRP) in public sector enterprises (PSEs), compa-ratios, and more
- Improved explanations and coverage
- New online resources that include multiple choice questions and weblinks

Online Resources

The online resource centre provides resources for both lecturers and students. The following resources are available to support the faculty using the text:
- Instructor's manual
- PowerPoint slides

The students can use the following resources to further their understanding:
- Multiple choice questions
- Weblinks to seminal articles on the Internet

Structure of the Book

With its expanded coverage, the book now contains 17 chapters. *Chapter 1* introduces readers to the concept of compensation management. It includes sections on objectives of compensation, principles of compensation formulation, theories of wage determination, types of wages, significance of employee compensation, and ethical issues. New sections in this chapter include difference between compensation and payroll management, compensation and talent management, factors influencing compensation, CTC, compensation practices and base pay, and pay grades and pay bands.

Chapter 2 discusses compensation management in the Indian context. Topics such as determinants of compensation decisions, valence instrumentality expectancy (VIE) theory, compensation benchmarking, broad band pay plan, compensation trends in India, and employee reward system in India form this chapter.

Chapter 3 deals the employee compensation relating to the labour market. Macroeconomics of labour markets, neoclassical microeconomics of labour markets, criticism of labour economics, labour market changes, and trade unions are some of the topics discussed in detail in this chapter. A new section on labour welfare administration has been included in this edition.

Chapter 4 describes the economic theories relating to compensation management. Concepts such as economic theories and employee compensation, trade-offs and employee compensation, valuation of employee compensation, labour markets and employee benefits, econometric application in compensation decisions, and productivity-linked employee benefits have been explained in detail.

Chapter 5 explains the concepts of employee benefits. Topics discussed include non-monetary benefits, tax obligations on employee benefits, types of employee benefits, deferred compensation plans, and alternatives to employee benefits.

Chapter 6 introduces the concepts of employee motivation and compensation. New sections on motivating generation Y and compensation practices for talented employees have been added in this edition.

Chapter 7 discusses compensation management and job design. This chapter gives readers an overview of job design and its strategies, techniques, and components. It also explains job analysis and job description. A new section on compensation design through compensable factor has been included in this edition.

Chapter 8 on compensation management and job evaluation explains concepts such as job assessment, work measurement, ergonomics, and competency-based approach. A new section on Hay's method has been added in this edition.

Chapter 9 describes the concepts of performance-related compensation. It introduces readers to concepts such as compensation management and performance management system (PMS), selection of performance indicators, developing performance standards, effective performance modelling, various dimensions of performance, and compensation design through skill-based programmes. New sections on performance-related pay (PRP) in public sector enterprises (PSEs), sample key result areas (KRAs) and key performance indicators (KPIs), and economic value-added (EVA) have been included in this edition.

Chapter 10 delves deep into the various concepts of team-based compensation. A section on recent trends in team-based compensation has been included in this edition.

Chapter 11 explains the concepts of executive compensation with reference to topics such as executive compensation theories, relationship between fixed and variable pay, performance measurement in executive incentive programmes, and recent studies on executive compensation. A new section on 'say on pay' issues has been added in this edition.

Chapter 12 describes the concepts of sales compensation plan. Sales compensation design and administration, sales incentives and motivation, and contribution-based sales compensation are some of the topics included in this chapter. New section on designing an effective sales compensation plan and product and organizational lifecycle and sales compensation plan have been included in this edition.

Chapter 13, a new chapter, discusses the concepts of reward management. The difference between compensation and rewards, total rewards—concepts and strategies, rewards and recognition policy, and ethical issues in rewards and recognition have been discussed in this chapter at length.

Chapter 14 explains the legal and taxation issues on employee compensation. Concepts such as tax implications on compensation, perquisites, pay-at-risk, and wage fixation through collective bargaining have been elaborated upon in this chapter.

Chapter 15 discusses the concepts of strategic compensation. Some of the topics discussed include compensation design and strategy, aligning strategies to transform people, and strategic compensation policies. A new section on strategic compensation and talent issues in global hiring has been added in this edition.

Chapter 16 elucidates the quantitative tools and innovation in compensation. Topics such as variable compensation, retirement plans, quantitative analysis, incentive determination, overtime wages, and merit matrices find mention in the chapter. Newly introduced topics such as metrics and compa-ratios have also been included.

Chapter 17 describes the international compensation management within which topics such as concept of variation and international compensation design are explained. New topics added to this chapter include cultural issues, expatriate and repatriate compensation, foreigners working in India and related statutory compliances, and international compensation strategies facilitating talent engagement.

Suggestions and feedback for further improvement are welcome. These can be sent to dkbhattacharyya@yahoo.co.in.

Acknowledgements

This second edition has been updated with inputs from various individuals. First, I would like to thank my faculty colleagues and students of Xavier Institute of Management, Bhubaneswar (XIMB) who have shared inputs for further improvement of the book. Some feedback acquired from various social media has also been considered in this second edition, therefore, my special thanks to those who provided the same.

I am grateful to the editors of Oxford University Press for helping me in identifying the important points for value addition and editing the book so meticulously. Last but not the least, I would like to thank my family members for their support.

Dipak Kumar Bhattacharyya

Preface to the First Edition

Human resource management (HRM) is a source of sustainable competitive advantage to an organization. Motivation and retention of talent are important aspects of HRM. Compensation management is the key driver of motivation and retention. An effective compensation management system is a strategic need of an organization. The word 'compensation' refers to the strategic management of wages and salaries. It may be defined as all forms of financial returns as well as tangible services and benefits, which employees receive during the tenure of their employment. It is viewed as a system of rewards to motivate employees, which in turn, can help organizations to achieve intended goals and objectives. The modern definition of compensation considers both intrinsic (intangible) and extrinsic (tangible) components of compensation. While extrinsic compensation covers both the monetary and non-monetary rewards, intrinsic compensation reflects employees' emotional satisfaction through job accomplishment.

Compensation management is taught as a subject in the human resource (HR) specialization in the MBA programme in most business schools and universities in India and abroad. This subject is also important for HR professionals as it is one of the most critical areas both for optimizing cost and increasing employee motivation (to ensure their retention) in any organization.

About the Book

The book, designed primarily for management students, is an attempt to introduce them to the subject of compensation and its management. It discusses compensation management in the Indian context, as per the present day industry requirements. The book discusses the legal aspects of compensation management, and also focuses on strategic inputs to effectively design compensation for overall organizational effectiveness. The new generation of HR professionals need to master all these areas to render meaningful support to organizations, reducing their dependency on outside consultants. This text aims to greatly alleviate this problem and add value to HR students and professionals, making them independent on compensation-related decisions. The book, in addition to covering the course requirements of Indian business schools and universities, also addresses some new-age economic issues, preparing the students and professionals to master those knowledge and skill-sets, which will make them managers with vision, innovation, and strategic focus.

The book introduces the concept of compensation and its management and goes on to discuss labour market and impact of labour market on compensation issues, and economic theories and their implications on compensation management. It discusses the concepts relating to job design, elaborating the process, methods and techniques, and performance-linked compensation. It elucidates team-based compensation and executive compensation. The book covers topics such as non-monetary employee benefits, alternative employee benefits programme, motivation and compensation design, as well as concepts and issues in sales compensation. The text elaborates on legal and taxation issues in compensation management and the process of wage fixation through collective bargaining. It explicates strategic compensation design and policies, and quantitative tools in compensation management. The book ends with an elaborate coverage of international compensation management practices.

The detailed coverage of theory from multiple perspectives—economic, psychological, political, and sociological—well-balanced with practice assignments and real-life examples, is the main strength of the book.

The book is written in a lucid style, to make students and professionals understand the strategic importance of compensation management. The chapters of this book have theory and discussion on basic and strategic issues, research aspects, industry application, and end with a case study. The case studies are designed by the author, based on compensation management practices of Indian and global organizations.

Pedagogical Features

The various pedagogical features of the text are:
- Learning objectives before each chapter highlight major learning insights.
- Diagrams, charts, and illustrations have been used to explain theory.
- Each chapter ends with a summary followed by key terms.
- Concept review and critical thinking questions would help students reflect on various issues.
- Each chapter of the book starts with a corporate practice example of a major Indian or international organization and ends with a case study.
- The book includes case studies of Indian and international companies such as McDonald's, Dell Computers, Infosys Technologies, TCS, P&G, L&T, and ITC.

Acknowledgements

I gratefully acknowledge the contribution of my colleagues, friends, and students who encouraged and supported me in this endeavour. Dr Sudipti Banerjea of University of Calcutta deserves special mention for his constant encouragement. All my family members had to sacrifice a lot during the development phase of this manuscript. Finally, the editorial team of Oxford University Press deserves my sincere thanks for their untiring support and help in the painstaking task of reviewing and editing this manuscript.

Dipak Kumar Bhattacharyya

Brief Contents

Features of the Book   iv
Preface to the Second Edition   vii
Preface to the First Edition   xi
Detailed Contents   xv
List of Cases   xxiii

1. Introduction to Compensation Management	1
2. Compensation Management: The Indian Context	39
3. Employee Compensation and the Labour Market	57
4. Economic Theories and Compensation Management	77
5. Employee Benefits	105
6. Employee Motivation and Compensation	119
7. Compensation Management and Job Design	145
8. Compensation Management and Job Evaluation	171
9. Performance-related Compensation	207
10. Team-based Compensation	253
11. Executive Compensation	265
12. Sales Compensation Plan	291
13. Managing Rewards	309
14. Legal and Taxation Issues on Employee Compensation	323
15. Strategic Compensation Management	353
16. Quantitative Tools and Innovation in Compensation	373
17. International Compensation Management	425

Index   441
About the Author   447

Detailed Contents

Features of the Book iv
Preface to the Second Edition vii
Preface to the First Edition xi
Brief Contents xiii
List of Cases xxiii

1. Introduction to Compensation Management 1

Introduction *2*
   Wages and Compensation 3
   Wage Components 5
Objectives of Compensation *6*
   Other Objectives of Compensation 7
   Payroll and Compensation 8
   Compensation and Talent Management 9
   Factors Influencing Compensation 10
Principles of Compensation Formulation *13*
   Determinants of Wage Rates 13
Theories of Wage Determination *14*
   Traditional Theory of Wage Determination 14
   Theory of Negotiated Wages 14
   Principles of Compensation Determination 14
Types of Wages *16*
   Minimum Rate of Wages 16
   Need-based Minimum Wage 18
   Living Wage 19
   Fair Wage 20
Wage Boards *20*
Wage Policy *21*
   National Wage Policy in India 23
   Cost to Company 23
   Base Pay Calculation 25
   Compensation Philosophy 26

Significance of Employee Compensation 30
Ethical Issues 33
    Bases for Compensation Ethics 34

2. Compensation Management: The Indian Context 39

Compensation Decisions 40
Determinants of Compensation Decisions 42
    Principles for Compensation Decisions 42
VIE Theory and Compensation 43
Compensation Benchmarking 44
Broad Band Pay Plan 45
Components of Executive Compensation 45
Compensation Trends in India 45
Employee Reward System in India 47
    Elements of Employee Rewards in India 48
    Additions to Base Pay 48
    Employee Stock Options 49
Aims of Employee Rewards in India 49
Compensation Plan 50
    Compensation Practices in India 51
    Mistakes in Compensation Designing 51
Appendix 2A Best Practices—Functional Managers in HR/Finance 55
Appendix 2B Best Practices—Compensation in Call Centres 56

3. Employee Compensation and the Labour Market 57

Introduction 58
Macroeconomics of Labour Markets 59
Unemployment and its Impact on Labour Market 60
    Types of Unemployment 60
    Causes of Unemployment 61
    Costs of Unemployment 62
    Unemployment Rate 62
Neoclassical Microeconomics of Labour Markets 63
Internal Labour Market as an Institution 63
Neoclassical Microeconomic Model—Supply 64
Neoclassical Microeconomic Model—Demand 66
Implications of Economic Models of Labour Markets
    on Employee Compensation 68
Criticisms of Labour Economics 68
Labour Market Changes and Trade Unions 69
    Role of Trade Unions 69
    Trade Unions in India 69

Labour Market Policies in India 71
Labour Welfare Administration 72

4. Economic Theories and Compensation Management   77

Introduction 78
Economic Theories 78
Economic Theories and Employee Compensation 81
Trade-offs and Employee Compensation 82
Valuation of Employee Compensation 82
Pricing of Employee Stock Options 83
   Regulatory Framework 84
   Legal Perspective 84
   Black–Scholes Model 85
   Problem of Expensing 86
Labour Markets and Employee Benefits 87
Equity in Employment Benefits 88
Econometric Application in Compensation Decisions 88
Productivity-linked Employee Benefits 89
   Productivity 90
   Productivity Measurement 93
   Productivity Measurement for Knowledge Workers 95
   Productivity and Quality 95
   Employee Benefits and Productivity 95
   Organizational Level Data Support 97
   Productivity Bargaining—Impact on Remuneration 98

5. Employee Benefits   105

Introduction 106
Non-monetary Benefits 106
Tax Obligations on Employee Benefits 108
Types of Employee Benefits 109
Statutory Employee Benefits in India 110
Deferred Compensation Plans 111
   Fringe Benefits 112
Alternatives to Employee Benefits 114

6. Employee Motivation and Compensation   119

Introduction 120
   Related Concepts 121
Objectives of Motivation 124
   Mechanism of Motivation 124
   Relationship between Motivation and Compensation 126

Theories of Motivation *127*
  Related Theories 133
Motivation and Morale *136*
Motivational Research and Compensation Design *137*
Motivating Generation Y *138*
Compensation Practices for Talented Employees *139*

7. Compensation Management and Job Design — 145

Introduction *146*
Job Design *147*
  Characteristics of Job Design 149
Strategies and Techniques of Job Design *150*
Components of Job Design *152*
  Job Information 152
Job Analysis *153*
  Considerations 154
  Methods of Analysis 154
  Questionnaires 154
  Assessment Centres 158
Job Description *159*
Compensation Design Through Compensable Factor *162*
Appendix 7A Job Analysis Data Sheet *169*
Appendix 7B Job Description *170*

8. Compensation Management and Job Evaluation — 171

Job Evaluation *172*
  Job Evaluation Techniques 173
  Limitations of Job Evaluation 182
Job Assessment *182*
  Pricing Job Value 182
Alternate Methods of Job Assessment *183*
  Work Study 183
  Method Study 184
Work Measurement *188*
  Time Study 188
  Other Techniques 190
Ergonomics *191*
Ergonomics and Work Study *192*
Ergonomics and Management *193*

Working Areas 193
   Motion Economy 194
   Human Engineering 195
   Value Analysis 197
Competency-based Approach 198
Appendix 8A   Competency Framework Model 203

9. Performance-related Compensation   207

Introduction 208
Compensation Management and PMS 209
   Performance-related Pay 210
PRP in Indian Central Public Sector Enterprises (CPSEs) 213
   PRP Scenario in CPSEs 216
Economic Value-added (EVA)—Alternative Performance Measures 223
Selection of Performance Objectives 225
Selection of Performance Indicators 225
Developing Performance Standards 226
Developing a Performance Metric 228
Effective Performance Modelling 232
   Customer-focused Metrics 233
Effective PMS 234
PMS and Organizational Strategy 235
Various Dimensions of Performance 236
Compensation Design Through Skill-based Programmes 244
Competency-based Pay 246

10. Team-based Compensation   253

Introduction 254
Team-based Compensation 255
   Employee Evaluation System 256
   Group Incentive Plans 257
   Gainsharing Plan 258
   Problems in Rewarding Teams 258
Effective Design of Team-based Compensation 259
Recent Trends in Team-based Compensation 260

11. Executive Compensation   265

Introduction 266
Components of Executive Compensation 267
Calibration of Executive Compensation to Performance 268
Transparency in Executive Compensation 268
Executive Compensation Theories 269

Executive Compensation Design 272
  Use of Performance Criteria 274
  Context of Executive Compensation Design 274
Relationship between Fixed and Variable Pay 276
Performance Measurement in Executive Incentive Programmes 276
Executive Compensation and Organizational Strategy 278
  Organization Level Practices 279
Different Criteria of Executive Compensation 281
Recent Studies on Executive Compensation 283
  Say on Pay 284

12. Sales Compensation Plan   291

Introduction 292
Understanding the Sales Function 292
Sales Compensation Issues 293
  Sales Goals 293
Sales Compensation Plan 294
Sales Compensation Design and Administration 296
  Designing Effective Sales Compensation Plan 296
  Components of Sales Compensation 298
Sales Incentives and Motivation 299
Contribution-based Sales Compensation 300
Designing an Effective Sales Compensation Plan 300
  Top-down and Bottom-up Sales Quota 300
  Unique Sales Compensation Plan Model 301
  Industry Thumb Rules for Sales Compensation 301
Relating Sales Compensation Plans with Organizational Life Cycle 302
  Sales Compensation Constructs 302

13. Managing Rewards   309

Introduction 310
Definition and Concepts of Rewards 310
Differences between Compensation and Rewards 312
Benefits of Reward and Recognition Programme 313
Total Rewards—Concepts and Strategies 314
  Changing Views Toward Rewards 315
  Total Rewards Strategy—How it Benefits Organization 316
Rewards and Recognition Policy 317
Ethical Issues in Rewards and Recognition 318

14. Legal and Taxation Issues on Employee Compensation   323

Introduction 324
  Wage Determination in Organized and Unorganized Sector 326

Tax Implications of Compensation *327*
Compensation and the Income Tax Act *327*
Perquisites *328*
   Background 329
Cost to Company *337*
Pay-at-risk *338*
Legal Interpretation of Wage Fixation *338*
Wage Fixation Through Collective Bargaining *338*
Collective Bargaining in India *342*
Appendix 14A   Computation of Total Income (Structure) *348*
Appendix 14B   Valuation of Prerequisites *349*
Appendix 14C   CTC Computation *350*

15. Strategic Compensation Management   353

Introduction *354*
Strategy *354*
   Prescriptive Schools 355
   Descriptive Schools 355
Compensation Design and Strategy *357*
   Strategy Across Levels 358
   Tactics and Strategy 359
Aligning Strategies to Transform People *360*
Strategic Planning *361*
Strategic Compensation Design *362*
Strategic Compensation Policies *364*
Strategic Compensation and Talent Issues in Global Hiring *365*
Appendix 15A   Strategy and Action Plan *371*

16. Quantitative Tools and Innovation in Compensation   373

Introduction *374*
Theoretical Discussions on Compensation *374*
Variable Compensation *375*
   Variable Compensation Plans 375
Retirement Plans *378*
   Pension Plans 378
   401(k) Plans 380
   Health and Welfare Plans 380
Payroll Management *381*
Quantitative Analysis *382*
   Levels of Measurement 383
   Scaling Techniques 386
   Alternate Techniques 388

Employee Benefits *401*
   Gratuity Computation 401
   Provident Fund 404
   Dearness Allowance (DA) 405
Incentive Determination *407*
   Straight Piece Rate Method 408
   Differential Piece Rate Methods 409
Group Incentive Payment Practices in Organizations *417*
Overtime Wages *417*
Merit Matrices *418*
Economic Value-added (EVA) *418*

17. International Compensation Management   425

Introduction *426*
International Compensation *427*
Cultural Issues *428*
Concept of Variation *429*
Components of International Compensation *429*
Expatriate and Repatriate Compensation *430*
Issues Related to Repatriation *431*
Foreigners Working in India and Related Statutory Compliances *433*
International Compensation Design *433*
Approaches to International Compensation *434*
   Going-rate Approach 434
   Balance Sheet Approach 435
International Compensation Strategies for Talent Engagement *436*

Index 441
About the Author 447

List of Cases

Chapter 1
Opening Case	Compensation Redesign at DeriPharma	1
Case Study	New Delhi Shopping Point	36

Chapter 2
Opening Case	Duality in Compensation Management Practices—Case of CISCO	39
Case Study	Two Centurions Grow with a Difference in Compensation Strategy	52

Chapter 3
Opening Case	Infosys Technologies and TCS: A Comparison of Employee Costs	57
Case Study	Retention Problems at IndiaRetail	75

Chapter 4
Opening Case	ESOP as a Retention Tool	77
Case Study	Employee Empowerment at P&G	101

Chapter 5
Opening Case	Tata Consultancy Services	105
Case Study	Innovative Design of Employee Benefits at Narmada Ltd	117

Chapter 6
Opening Case	Motivating through Ownership	119
Case Study	Compensation Practices of a POL Major	142

Chapter 7
Opening Case	Effective Job Design and Recruitment Process at McDonald's	145
Case Study	Compensation Practices of DimondSoft	165

Chapter 8
Opening Case	Compa-ratio—Additional Tool Over Job Evaluation	171
Case Study	Where Job evaluation is Done Differently—Case of Apple	201

Chapter 9
Opening Case	Best Practices in Performance-related Pay	207
Case Study	Performance-related Pay at Auto India Ltd	249

xxiv List of Cases

Chapter 10
Opening Case	Team-based Compensation May Not Always Work	253
Case Study	Talent Management at Enlarge	262

Chapter 11
Opening Case	Why Do We Pay Our Executives More?	265
Case Study	Executive Compensation Strategy in Fortune Furnitech	288

Chapter 12
Opening Case	Quota-based Compensation System of Pharmaceutical Companies	291
Case Study	Itachi's Sales Compensation Plan Runs into Conflict	306

Chapter 13
Opening Case	Emphasis on Reward Practices in Indian Companies	309
Case Study	Strategically Managing Rewards for Business Gains	320

Chapter 14
Opening Case	All's Not Well at P&G	323
Case Study	Think Before You Leap: The Compensation Plan of a Chennai-based Two-wheeler Major	347

Chapter 15
Opening Case	Dell Strategy	353
Case Study	Strategic Compensation Initiative at NewAge Technologies	367

Chapter 16
Opening Case	Compensation Design at ITC	373
Case Study	Oxicom's Compensation Dilemma	421

Chapter 17
Opening Case	International Compensation Practices of the Lata Group	425
Case Study	Differential Pay Policy of Nita International	438

CHAPTER
ONE

Introduction to Compensation Management

Base

HRA

EPF

Gratuity

Variable

Bonus

LTA

Conveyance

Medical

Learning Objectives

After reading this chapter, you will be able to
- understand the term compensation from different perspectives
- analyse difference between wages and compensation
- study various principles of compensation/wage fixation
- examine theories of wage determination
- comprehend the basic dynamics of wage policy and objectives
- understand the various domains of compensation
- understand the concept of cost to company
- comprehend the terms pay grades and pay bands

OPENING CASE

Compensation Redesign at DeriPharma

Motivating and retaining good performers is an important priority for any organization. Companies cannot retain talent with high salaries alone. They also need to develop compensation packages that address the real and perceived needs of employees. It may include, among other things, making provisions for short- and long-term incentives, stock options, assistance in achieving financial goals, favourable tax incentives, and assistance with lifestyle requirements of employees. This requires strategic compensation design. Recently, DeriPharma, a global pharmaceutical major, noticed that its executives were leaving to join relatively lesser-known competitors. The company had always believed in stability and long-term incentives, focusing on secure post-retirement lives for all its employees. According to the company, the majority of executives leaving their jobs were in their mid-thirties. The average age of employees is 55, so the executives in their mid-thirties were the future torchbearers. An investigative study indicated that most of the employees left because of compensation issues. It was recommended that the compensation package be redesigned to increase the take-home pay and discount the deferred benefits[1] for this age group. This resulted in increased retention of employees.

INTRODUCTION

The term compensation as a substitute for wages or salaries is of recent origin. The literature on wages and salaries is enormous, but most of it approaches the subject from a legal perspective. The emphasis is on ensuring that the legal requirements for wages set by government are met. However, increased competition and specialized nature of jobs have transformed the job market from a seller's market to a buyer's market. Wages have now become very significant as a cost factor. Therefore, strategic management of wages has now become very important for organizations. With this shift in approach and focus, compensation has come to be viewed as the strategic management of wages and salaries. In India, literature on compensation is scarce. However, it has now become imperative for organizations to balance the cost of compensation and employee motivation to survive in a competitive world.

Pay or compensation represents an exchange between the employee and the organization. Each gives something in return for something else. What the employee provides the employer is a labour service, usually known as work. This labour service consists of many different kinds of employee behaviour such as showing up regularly and on time, carrying out tasks dependably, cooperating with others, and making useful suggestions. In the past, the compensation issue was often confidential and governed by the individual employer's preference and choices. However, in today's competitive world, compensation issues are more transparent and every employee can make an informed choice based on information available about compensation packages. Therefore, balancing the cost of compensation and retaining employees has now become the most important priority for today's organizations.

Different scholars in different countries have defined the word compensation from different perspectives. Before, we develop our own definition of the term compensation; let us briefly look at some of these perspectives. Globally, almost every country views compensation as a measure of justice. In addition, some countries (particularly the developed ones) consider compensation as a means of protection against potential job loss. Therefore, compensation should be fair, irrespective of economic considerations. Many scholars believe

---

[1]Deferred benefits are payable only after qualifying service or retirement. New-generation employees prefer take-home pay over deferred benefits.

that compensation is the outcome of productivity. The literal meaning of the term compensation is something that counterbalances the efforts of workers. In China, it was represented by the symbols for logs and water, that is, something which ensures the basic necessities of life. In Japan, it is viewed as providing something. In India, right from the Vedic age, the volume of work and the time required to perform the work were considered to decide compensation. In Europe, the church advocated the principles of just wage or compensation. Without further exploring the historical connotations of the term compensation and instead considering the modern organization, the word compensation may be defined as, 'all forms of financial returns, tangible services, and benefits that an employee receives in his/her tenure of employment'. It is viewed as a system of rewards to motivate employees, so that organizations can achieve their intended goals and objectives. The modern definition of compensation, however, considers both intrinsic (psychological) and extrinsic (tangible) components of compensation. While extrinsic compensation covers both monetary and non-monetary rewards, intrinsic compensation reflects the employees' mental satisfaction with their job accomplishments.

Wages and Compensation

A wage is a basic compensation for labour; and the compensation for labour per period of time is referred to as the wage rate. The two terms are sometimes used interchangeably. Other frequently used terms for wages are payment per unit of time (typically an hour) or earnings, which represent payment accrued over a time period (week, month, or year). Total compensation represents earnings and other benefits for labour. Wage income represents total compensation and unearned income. Wages are also referred to as economic rent, which is total compensation minus the opportunity cost. Opportunity cost represents cost of something in terms of an opportunity forgone (and the benefits which could have been received if that opportunity was utilized), or the most valuable forgone alternative (or highest-valued option forgone), that is, the cost of choosing the second best alternative. Etymologically, the term wage is derived from words that indicate making a promise in monetary form. The term emerged from the French word *wagier* or *gagier*, meaning to pledge or to make a promise.

Marxian economics suggests that the payment of wages to workers should be based on the optimal allocation of cooperative human labour. Optimization, here, does not indicate only a technical variable, because workers are not considered just a factor of production. Rather, workers' participation in the production process can be oppressive, irrational, and exploitative; it can also be beneficial, rational, or effective. Marxian economics believes that wages have a political dimension as the interests of workers and employers are different. Therefore, it believes that the most desirable form of labour organization in the workplace is one where workers manage themselves collectively and elect managers where necessary.

From a financial perspective, wage, in contrast with salary, is defined as cash paid for some specified quantity of labour. Wages are paid based on the wage rate (based on units of time), whereas salaries are paid periodically without reference to a specified number of hours worked. Given an established job description, wages can often be negotiated by workers through collective bargaining.

Economists define wages more broadly than just cash compensation and include any return on labour such as goods workers might create for themselves, returns in kind, or even the enjoyment that some derive from work. Even food hunted or gathered is considered wages and any return resulting from an investment in tools (e.g., an axe or a hoe) is deemed interest (a return on a capital investment).

Differences between wages and compensation

For a better understanding of the difference between wages and compensation, let us consider the International Labour Organization's (ILO) series of texts on labour costs.

The term labour cost is best understood from the definitions accepted in ILO's Eleventh International Conference of Labour Statisticians (Geneva 1966). Labour cost is the cost incurred by the employer in the employment of labour. The statistical concept of labour cost comprises remuneration for work performed. This also includes payments in respect of time paid for but not worked; bonuses and gratuities; the cost of food, drink, and other payments in kind; the cost of workers' housing borne by employers; employers' social security expenditures; the cost to the employer for vocational training, welfare services; and miscellaneous items such as the transport of workers, work clothes, and cost of recruitment, and taxes paid by the employers on employment. From the employers' perspective, therefore, the compensation of employees consists of all payments (in kind or in cash), and all contributions to employees' social security, pension, insurance, etc.

Labour cost and the compensation of employees are closely-related concepts with many common elements. The major part of labour cost comprises compensation of employees. However, definitions of labour cost and the compensation of employees differ from country to country. For example, some items of labour cost such as social security and vocational training are borne not by employers but by the respective governments. In India, the Central Board for Workers' Training and the Regional Labour Institutes provide either free or subsidized training for industrial workers. Similarly, the Regional Provident Fund Commission now marginally contributes to employees' pension along with the employers. The state's contributions to wage-related social security schemes are not included in the cost of compensation for employers. In some countries, payroll taxes or employment taxes are considered labour costs.

Operationally, there is no difference between the terms compensation and wages. Both are intended to price the efforts of employees. However, the word compensation is used more holistically to acknowledge the strategic importance of wages. Theoretically, compensation means something such as money given or received as payment for some damage. However, in human resource management literature, we consider the term from a broader perspective, that is, the strategic use of wages paid to employees. Some organizations prefer to use the term rewards instead of wages or compensation. In human resource management, we should not just use rewards to acknowledge good performances, instead, as a more strategic design of compensation. So that, when employees get paid at the end of the month, they feel they are not just getting their wages, but also being rewarded. In this chapter, however, the terms compensation, wages, and salary have been used interchangeably.

Compensation or wage structure in a given case should take into account industrial adjudication as well as considerations of right and wrong, and fairness and unfairness. Given social conscience and the welfare policy of the state, collective bargaining is now considered the most dynamic form of negotiation to decide wage structure in a particular organization. Wage issues are no longer purely mathematical issues. It was with this perspective that the framers of the Constitution drew up Article 43 (part of the Directive Principles of State Policy) which states that, 'The state shall endeavour to secure, by suitable legislation or economic organization or in any other way, to all workers—agriculture, industrial, or otherwise—work, a living wage, conditions of work ensuring a decent standard of life and full employment of leisure and social and cultural opportunities.' By this declaration, the state not only acknowledged its role in directly promoting social welfare, but also recognized the inadequacy of market forces in determining a wage level that is consistent with welfare standard of a living wage. The declaration, in effect, assured labour that where they were not able to secure a living wage for themselves, the government through legislation or other means will come to their aid. Two aspects of the state's role prevent employers from taking undue advantage of the workers'—strong bargaining strength and direct participation of the state in the economic life of the nation. The former gives the worker a fair share, and the latter enlarges this share.

Wage Components

Wage or compensation is any economic compensation paid by the employer to an employee for the services he renders. Although the term wages is all encompassing and includes any form of financial support and benefits, in a narrower sense wages are the price paid for the services of labour. Broadly, there are two wage components—the base or basic wages and other allowances. The basic wage is the remuneration by way of basic salary and allowances, that is, paid or payable to an employee per terms of the contract of employment for the work done. Allowances are paid in addition to the basic wage to ensure that the value of basic wages does not fall over a period of time. Some allowances are statutory, whereas others are voluntary. Most organizations pay allowances such as holiday pay, overtime pay, bonus, and social security benefits. Theoretically, these are not included in the definition of wages. In India, different Acts include different items under wages, though all the Acts include basic wage and dearness allowances. Under the Workmen's Compensation Act 1923 Section 2 (m), wages includes, 'Wages for leave period, holiday pay, overtime pay, bonus, attendance bonus, and good conduct bonus.' Under The Payment of Wages Act 1936 Section 2 (VI), 'Any award of settlement and production bonus, if paid, constitutes wages.' Further, under the Payment of Wages Act 1948, 'Retrenchment compensation, payment in lieu of notice and gratuity payable on discharge constitute wages.'

Without going into the theoretical debate on what constitutes wages and to summing up the provisions of different Acts, we can exclude the following types of remuneration from the purview of wages:

1. bonus or other payments under a profit-sharing scheme, which do not form a part of the contract of employment
2. value of any house or accommodation, supply of light, water, medical attendance, travelling allowance or payment in lieu thereof, or any other concession
3. any sum paid to defray special expenses entailed by the nature of the employment of a workman
4. any contribution to pension, provident fund, or a scheme of social security, and social insurance benefits
5. any other amenity or service excluded from the computation of wages by a general or special order of an appropriate governmental authority

A wage level is an average of the rates paid for the jobs of an organization, an establishment, a labour market, an industry, a region, or a nation. A wage structure is a hierarchy of jobs to which wage rates have been attached.

OBJECTIVES OF COMPENSATION

The objectives of compensation or wages can be classified under four broad categories—equity, efficiency, macro-economic stability, and optimum allocation of labour.

Equity

The first category is equity, which may take several forms. It includes income distribution through narrowing of inequalities, increasing the wages of the lowest paid employees, protecting real wages (purchasing power), and the concept of equal pay for work of equal value. Compensation management strives for internal and external equity. Internal equity requires that pay be related to the relative worth of a job so that similar jobs get similar pay. External equity means paying workers what other firms in the labour market pay comparable workers.

Compensation differentials, based on differences in skills or contribution, are all related to the concept of equity.

Efficiency

It is often closely related to equity, because the two concepts are not antithetical. The objectives of efficiency are reflected in attempts to link a part of wages to productivity or profit, group or individual performance, acquisition and application of skills, and so on. Arrangements to achieve efficiency may also be seen as being equitable (if they fairly reward performance) or inequitable (if the reward is viewed as unfair).

Macroeconomic stability

It can be achieved through high employment levels, and low inflation. For instance, an inordinately high minimum wage would have an adverse impact on levels of employment. Though the level at which it would occur is a matter of debate.

Although compensation and compensation policies are two of the many factors that influence macroeconomic stability, they do contribute to (or impede) balanced and sustainable economic development.

Efficient allocation of labour

The efficient allocation of labour in the labour market implies that employees will move to wherever they receive a net gain. Such movement may be from one geographical location to another, or from one job to another (within or outside an enterprise). The provision or availability of financial incentives causes such movement.

For example, workers may move from a labour surplus or low-wage area to a high-wage area. They may acquire new skills to benefit from the higher wages paid for skills. When an employer's wages are below market rates, employee turnover increases. When it is above market rates, the employer attracts job applicants. When employees move from declining to growth industries, an efficient allocation of labour due to structural changes takes place.

Other Objectives of Compensation

Apart from those listed common objectives, from human resource management perspective, a well-designed compensation package helps an organization to achieve additional objectives.

Acquire qualified personnel Compensation needs to be high enough to attract qualified applicants. Pay levels must respond to the supply and demand of workers in the labour market since employers compete for workers. Premium wages are sometimes needed to attract qualified applicants already working for others.

Retain current employees Employees may quit when compensation levels are not competitive, resulting in higher turnover.

Reward desired behaviour Pay should reinforce desired behaviours and act as an incentive for such behaviour to occur in the future. Effective compensation plans reward performance, loyalty, experience, responsibility, and other behaviours.

Control costs A rational compensation system helps the organization obtain and retain workers at a reasonable cost. Without effective compensation management, workers might be over-paid or under-paid.

Comply with legal regulations A sound wage and salary system considers the legal challenges imposed by the government and ensures the employer's compliance.

Facilitate understanding The compensation management system should be easily understood by human resource specialists, operating managers, and employees.

Promoting administrative efficiency Wage and salary programmes should be so designed that they can be managed efficiently, making optimal use of the human resource information systems (HRIS). However, this objective should be a secondary consideration compared with other objectives.

Payroll and Compensation

Payroll is an administrative function that integrates the functions of compensation management, or human resource management function, with accounting function of an organization. Payroll ensures employees of an organization regularly receive their paychecks, along with a statement, showing details of the net pay received by them. Depending on the size of the organization, there may be dedicated payroll manager to manage the payroll functions. However, in most of the cases, payroll management is left to the human resource management function. Payroll is often confused with compensation. However, these two are different operationally. Scope of payroll is limited to disbursement function of compensation, that is, it involves payment of regular salary and wages, and other monetary aspects of compensation such as bonus, commissions, and allowances. In one way, we can define payroll as detailed accounting of compensation, deductions from compensation—provident fund, service tax, income tax—and payment to employees at regular monthly cycle. Although, it is a part of compensation management function, in many organizations, payroll worksheets are prepared by the Accounts Division, based on the payroll data of human resource management department. Payroll preparation is now possible with standard payroll software. Some companies outsource the payroll function to achieve cost efficiency.

Compensation, therefore, is distinctly different from payroll, as it is more holistic in terms of all benefits and perquisites in addition to the regular wages and salaries of employees.

Compensation and Talent Management

Talent is rare and inimitable human resource value, for which organizations compete globally. A talent driven organizations can outperform their competitors (Barney and Wright 1998). Business dynamics, today, has changed the business landscape of the world. To sustain in this business environment, organizations globally compete for talent. It requires organizations to suitably craft their talent strategy to attract and retain talented people, and also to develop internal talent pipeline. Over the years, mobility of talented people, across organizations, has increased manifold. Cross-border hiring, cross-industry hiring, and even talent poaching, have now almost become a regular pursuit for organizations. Global companies such as CISCO, Apple, Microsoft, Yahoo, and Google often acquire companies just to get talented people in their payroll, rather than focusing on increasing their value chain of product portfolio through acquisition. For talent, organizations focus on strategic human resource management practices. First among such strategies is employer branding. Successful employer branding, creates a positive image of the employer in the minds of the people, and as a natural process attracts the potential talent for the organization. Therefore, employer branding is the result of proactive human resource management practice, which includes among other, compensating employees based on talent.

Talent is a people value, which contributes to the success of any organization. A talented person, through innovation, enhances the competitive strength of an organization. Competency-based human resource management practices, of late, have institutionalized talent management in organizations. Talent is now the key driver of organizational success and sustenance. A talent driven organization focuses on building the future leadership pipeline through various human resource development (HRD), and organizational development (OD) initiatives. However, institutionalized talent management practices, among others, require organizations to align their compensation policies and plans. Hence, in crafting talent management strategy, organizations, now, also emphasize on integration of their compensation policies and strategies. This ensures attraction and retention of talent, incubating talent, and ultimately making the organization talent driven. It is for this, we need to understand compensation management issues that encompass effective talent management in an organization. Determining compensation for integrated talent management encompasses job evaluation, market surveys for external benchmarking data, competencies, work measurement, identification of organizational key performance indicators (KPI) and corresponding key performance areas (KPA) of employees, internal benchmarking to assess internal equity, etc. All these, when considered, can ensure compensation design to attract and retain talent, and cascade to effective talent management. All these processes have been discussed in subsequent chapters. Here, however, we are more concerned about discussing compensation strategies and policy decisions that promote effective talent management in organizations.

Merit-based pay, performance related pay, innovative stock options, broad-based rewards and incentive plans, and provisions for deferred benefits and perquisites are all monetary compensation components used for effective talent management in organizations. Apart from these, organizations also make use of suitable non-monetary compensation components such as investing on learning and development opportunities, and vacation plans.

Some practices recommended for integrated talent management are listed below.

Incentivize and motivate high performing workers This can ensure attraction, development, and retention of talent in the organization. Some innovative incentivization policies are; performance based incentive plans, incentivization based on merit, decision on incentive-mix both monetary and non-monetary, etc. Incentives must be tuned with the expectations of employees. For this reason, many organizations adopt flexible reward policies which enable them to respond to the inputs received from talented employees. However, organizations must ensure that the overall spread of compensation is well within the policy limits.

Designing compensation to drive business results Compensation aimed at motivating and retaining talent may also create inequity in the organization. As long as such inequitable compensation outweighs revenue and profit growth of the organization, it can be sustained for talented employees. However, organizations may be required to consider the possible deteriorating effect on motivation and performance levels of other employees. It is for this reason; more emphasis is given on variables, contingent upon performance. This compensation strategy creates a sense of fair play by keeping the door of opportunity for greater compensation, open for all employees, whereas at the same time rewarding talented employees. This will not impair the overall compensation plan for the companies. While deciding on standard compensation, companies base their calculation on a number of factors, primary of which are their strategic and business goals, job roles, market data, internal pay ranges, and performance data for KPIs such as achievement of goal, performance ratings, and non-quantitative measures. Non-quantitative measures assess outcome of employees' performance, that is, the effect that the employees leave behind in achieving their performance results.

Factors influencing Compensation

There are a number of factors which influence the compensation design in any organization. In generic terms, such factors may be; productivity or performance trend of employees, organizational ability to pay, government regulations, collective bargaining powers of trade unions, cost of living, labour market trends, prevailing market rate, compensation philosophy of the organization, organizational culture, organizational strategies, organizational structure, etc. However, depending on the specific business goals and strategies, organizations assign different weight to different factors, while deciding on compensation.

However, based on the organizational compensation management practices, such factors can be classified, broadly, into two categories; internal factors and external factors. Internal factors are organization specific, whereas external factors are those which are outside the organization. Organizations respond to these factors to remain competitive in compensation they offer to their employees. Time to time calibration with internal and external factors helps organizations to remain competitive by acquiring and retaining talent, motivating employees, and by institutionalizing a performance-driven work culture.

To enhance our understanding of compensation design, let us now elaborate on such internal and external factors that influence it.

Internal factors

Internal factors being specific to the organization may widely vary even between two similar or peer group organizations. Further, some internal factors are attributable to organizations as a whole, whereas some others are specific to employees of the organization.

Internal factors attributable to organizations are as follows:

Ability to pay At organizational level, ability to pay is the most important determinant of compensation. Often organizations, despite their good intentions fail to pay competitive compensation to their employees, due to their financial handicap. Successive business failure challenges the sustainability of the organization, forcing them even to reduce the existing compensation level. Such organizations face the challenge of talent retention. In contrast, a financially viable organization can pay competitive compensation to their employees. Such organizations even at times pay more than their peer group companies. For example, Microsoft and Apple benchmark their executive compensation not only with their peer group companies, but also with other best paying world class organizations to attract and retain talent.

Organizational strategy Compensation programme of an organization is also influenced by their strategy and business goals. For accelerated pace of growth, some organizations (even in some cases, start-ups) offer higher compensation. Contrarily for stable growth, organizations may stick to reasonable compensation level, with more focus on fixed component. In the first case, organizations may deliberately encourage internal inequity so that average and poor performers become more productive to catch up with the compensation level of their peers. In the second case, organizations value more internal pay equity. For example, century old Murugappa Group values internal pay equity, while designing their compensation programmes; and surprisingly they are able to retain their talents and grow over the years.

Internal factors attributable to employees are as follows:

Competency level When employees' competency level matches with the organization's required competency level for the specific job positions, compensation would be higher. Contrarily, it would be less.

Performance of employees Performance related pay (PRP) is increasingly practised in compensation management across the world. Many Indian organizations, including public sector enterprises have already started using it as major determinant of compensation programme. Employees get more compensation when they meet and exceed the expected level of performance, and in the reverse case, they get less.

Seniority and job experience With experience and seniority, employees are expected to perform better due to their increased understanding of the job. Such employees are valued by the organization.

Employee potentiality For effective succession planning, firms assess the potentiality of their employees. Once they identify the potential employees for future leadership positions, differentiation in the compensation levels can be made by offering these employees higher pay.

Compensable factors for the job Through job evaluation, firms determine the compensable factors for a job. Jobs with higher compensable factors get higher compensation, whereas jobs with lower compensable factors get less compensation.

External factors

External factors have potential influence on the compensation design even though they are exogenous to an organization. Such factors are as follows:

Legal mandates Almost in all countries, including India, legal mandates influence the compensation design. For example, in India we have Minimum Wages Act, Factories Act, Payment of Wages Act, Payment of Bonus Act, Industrial Disputes Act, Equal Remuneration Act, etc. which have major influence on compensation design.

Labour market trends Labour market trends are not only limited to demand and supply of labour, it also encompass various other issues such as compensation trend, cost of living, and other organizational practices. All these have potential effect on compensation design.

Economic state of the country Economic ups and downs may have potential effect on compensation.

Inflation rate Fluctuation in the rate of inflation may affect the compensation levels.

Technological changes Technological changes bring compositional shift in skill requirements, resulting in increased pay for employees who acquire such skills.

All these internal and external factors have potential influence on compensation design of an organization.

PRINCIPLES OF COMPENSATION FORMULATION

The main factors affecting wage or compensation levels within an organization are external relativities, salary, and individual worth.

External relativities Market rates as affected by supply, demand, and general movements in pay levels.

Salary Salary relativities between jobs within the organization depending on the values attached to different jobs.

Individual worth The value of the individual's performance to the organization.

Determinants of Wage Rates

Depending on the structure and traditions of different economies around the world, wage rates are either the product of market forces (supply and demand), or they may be influenced by other factors such as tradition, social structure, and seniority. In the United States, market forces determine wage rates. In Japan, seniority is still the dominant factor for wage determination. Several countries, including India, have enacted a statutory minimum wage rate that fixes the price of certain kinds of labour. Though market forces determine the wage rate in most developed countries, workers often negotiate their wage rate through collective bargaining wherever unions are present.

Often, we use the term benefit to indicate wages. Theoretically, benefit refers to something which someone is entitled to receive. Workers' benefit component is the non-monetary part of the compensation.

Organizations often confuse unearned income with wages. Theoretically, unearned income includes interest, dividends, or realized capital gains from investments, rent from land, or property ownership, as well as any other income that is not derived from work. It means that even the interest earned on the provident funds of workers (in cases where the employers themselves are the trustee) cannot be construed as wages. Some parts of the unearned income are taxable, where as some other parts are not (e.g., interest on provident fund). Economists, however, have a differing point of view, as they consider unearned income as compensation for deferring consumption.

Economic rent is the difference between what a factor of production is paid and how much it would need to be paid to remain in its current use. There are multiple mechanisms that can create economic rent—political contrivance, network effect, monopoly power, etc. Neoclassical economists consider economic rent as the difference between the incomes from a factor of production in a particular use. However, this definition does not tell us whether the income is earned by virtue of a contribution to society, or simply created by natural occurrence or government sanction. Therefore, they are considered an unearned privilege.

The consideration of *opportunity costs* is one of the key differences between the concepts of economic cost and accounting cost. Assessing opportunity costs is fundamental to assessing the true cost of any course of action. In a case where there is no explicit accounting or monetary cost (price) attached to a course of action, ignoring opportunity costs may produce the illusion that its benefits cost nothing at all. The unseen opportunity costs then become the implicit hidden costs of that course of action.

THEORIES OF WAGE DETERMINATION

There are two key theories to determine wages—the traditional theory of wage determination and the theory of negotiated wages.

Traditional Theory of Wage Determination

Like all other factors of production, price of labour, that is, wages also depends on demand and supply of labour. This idea of classical economists is still found valid in wage determination, particularly in an open economy. In the United States, an electrician's job, due to higher demand, attract more wages than the wages of a manager of a retail store. This interplay between the demand and supply of labour depends on a number of factors such as availability of specific skill set, job location, and availability of jobs. When demand exceeds supply of workers, the wage rate rises; in the reverse case, the wage rate falls. At the intersection of supply and demand curve of workers, we get the equilibrium wage rate. However, this requires reaching the level of perfect competition, which for labour market, is elusive.

Theory of Negotiated Wages

Unionized employees can negotiate salaries. This is done through the *collective bargaining* process. Normally, in any unionized organization, unions periodically submit their memorandum to the management, asking for wage raises to keep pace with market standards and organizational profitability. Then, wages are negotiated in a collective bargaining meeting attended by the unions and the management nominees. For non-unionized employees, wages can be negotiated through *individual bargaining*. In some cases, there may even be regulatory intervention by wage boards. The wage boards are tripartite in nature and represent the workers, employers, and independent members. Wage boards help in finalizing wage recommendations. All wage boards, however, are not statutory. Wage boards are now less important because of the rising bargaining power of workers and employees.

Principles of Compensation Determination

Wage determination, apart from the statutory aspect, is influenced by different theories. These theories are elaborated in this section.

Subsistence theory David Ricardo (1772–1832) advocated the subsistence theory. In Ricardo's words, workers should be paid 'To enable them to subsist and perpetuate the race without increase or diminution'. The theory was based on the assumption that if the workers were paid more than subsistence wage, their numbers would increase as they would procreate more and this would bring down the rate of wages. If the wages fell below the subsistence level, the number of workers would decrease as many would die of hunger, malnutrition, disease, cold, etc. and many would not marry. If this happened, wages would increase. In economics, the subsistence theory of wages states that, in the long run, wages will be reduced to the minimum level needed to keep workers alive.

Wages fund theory This theory was developed by Adam Smith (1723–1790) on the assumption that wages are paid out of a predetermined fund of wealth, the surplus savings of the wealthy. This fund could be utilized for employing labourers for work. If the fund was large, wages would be high; if it was small, wages would be reduced to subsistence level. The demand for labour and the level of wages were determined by the size of the fund.

Surplus value theory The surplus value theory of wages owes its development to Karl Marx (1818–1883). According to this theory, labour is an article of commerce, which could be purchased on the payment of the 'subsistence price'. The price of any product is determined by the labour and the time needed for producing it. The theory proposes that labourer is not paid in proportion to the time spent on work, but is paid much less and the surplus is utilized for paying other expenses.

Residual claimant theory The residual claimant theory advocated by Francis Walker (1840–1897), assumes that there are four factors of production/business activity—land, labour, capital, and entrepreneurship. Wages represent the amount of value created in the production, which remains after payment has been made for all these factors of production. In other words, labour is the residual claimant.

Marginal productivity theory This theory assumes that wages are based upon an entrepreneur's estimate of the value that will probably be produced by the last or marginal worker. In other words, it assumes that wages depend upon the demand for and supply of labour. Consequently, workers are paid what they are economically worth.

Bargaining theory of wages This theory considers that wages are determined by the relative bargaining power of workers, trade unions, and employers. When a trade union is involved, basic wages, fringe benefits, job differentials, and individual differences tend to be determined by the relative strength of the organization and the trade union.

Behavioural theory of wages This theory was pioneered by several psychologists and sociologists such as Marsh and Simon, Robert Dubin, and Eliot Jacques. Based on their various research studies, we can identify the following areas of interest in behavioural theories on wages:

Employee's acceptance of a wage level Individuals believe in employment stability and prefer to stay on with the same organization, pacing with their salary level. There are, however, several other factors to be considered such as size and prestige of the company; trade unions' power in the organization; and their level of knowledge and competencies.

Internal wage structure Employees value internal pay equity. Moreover, some jobs also command social status (e.g., the job of a journalist). Organizations design wages for different cross sections of employees by also considering maximum and minimum wage differentials, norms of span or control, and demand for specialized skill sets. Balancing of wages with such internal equity enhances employee motivation.

TYPES OF WAGES

In this section, we have discussed various types of wages in India.

Minimum Rate of Wages

The minimum rate payable to a worker and basic terms of his work are prescribed in the Minimum Wages Act 1948. The Act not only defines what would constitute minimum wages, but also provides a base for different aspects of terms of employment. Following are the key features of the Act and what they prescribe for different aspects like wages and term of work.

The Act provides multiple ways to interpret minimum wages. Any minimum rate of wages fixed or revised may consist of a basic rate of wages and a special allowance; or, a basic rate of wages with or without a cost of living allowance, and the cash value of concessions in respect of supplies of essential commodities at concessional rates. It is also interpreted as an all-inclusive rate allowing for the basic rate, the cost of living allowance, and the cash value of concessions, if any.

Procedure for fixing and revising minimum wages The Central Government appoints a Central Advisory Board to advise the central and state governments on the fixing and revising of the minimum rates of wages, as well as to coordinate the work of advisory boards.

The Central Advisory Board consists of persons nominated by the Central Government representing employers and employees in the scheduled employments in equal number, and independent persons not exceeding one-third of its total number of members. One such independent person is appointed the Chairman of the Board by the Central Government.

Wages in kind Minimum wages payable under this Act are to be paid in cash. However, the payment of minimum wages can be made wholly or partly in kind, by a notification in the official Gazette, where it is customary to pay wages either wholly or partly in kind.

Payment of minimum rate of wages The employer is required to pay every employee wages at a rate not less than the minimum rate of wages notified for that class of employees. There cannot be any deduction except as may be authorized.

Fixing hours for a normal working day In regard to any scheduled employment, minimum rates of wages in respect of which have been fixed under this Act

1. the appropriate government may fix the number of hours of work which shall constitute a normal working day, inclusive of one or more specified intervals;
2. provide for a day of rest in every period of seven days which shall be allowed to all employees or to any specified class of employees and for the payment of remuneration in respect of such days of rest;
3. provide for payment for work on a day of rest at a rate not less than the overtime rate.

Overtime If any employee whose minimum rate of wages is fixed under the Act works on any day in excess of the number of hours constituting a normal working day, the employer is required to pay him/her for excess hours at the overtime rate fixed under this Act or under any law of the appropriate government for the time being in force, whichever is higher.

Wages for two or more classes of work If an employee does two or more classes of work, to each of which a different rate of wages is applicable, the employer is required to pay to such employee in respect of the time respectively occupied in each such class of work, wages at not less than the minimum rate in force in respect of each such class.

Maintenance of registers and records Every employer is required to maintain registers and records giving particulars of employees, the work performed by them, the wages paid to them, the receipts given by them, and any other required particulars.

Inspections The appropriate government may, by notification in the official Gazette, appoint inspectors for the purpose of this Act and define the local limits for their functions.

Claims The appropriate government may, by notification in the official Gazette, appoint the Labour Commissioner or Commissioner for Workmen's Compensation or any officer not below the rank of Labour Commissioner or any other officer with experience as a judge of a civil court or as a Stipendiary Magistrate, to hear and decide for any specified area, all claims arising out of the payment of less than the minimum rates of wages as well as payment for days of rest or for work done.

Penalties for offences Any employer who contravenes any provision of this Act shall be punishable with imprisonment for a term, which may extend to six months or with fine, which may extend to ₹500 or with both.

Statistics collected under the Minimum Wages Act 1948 All establishments covered under the Act are required to furnish to the concerned authority (Central or State) an annual return in prescribed form as per the rules framed under the Minimum Wages Act 1948. The centre/state governments in turn send a consolidated return to the Labour Bureau which compiles an all India report based on the data contained in these returns. Besides, quarterly returns sent by these agencies to the Bureau are also made use of in compiling information at all India level.

Addition of new employments The state governments and the union territories review the scheduled employments under their jurisdiction from time to time and add new employments in respect of which they are of the opinion that minimum rates of wages should be fixed statutorily in addition to the existing ones.

Need-based Minimum Wage

From normative perspectives, the Committee on Fair Wages indicated that the minimum wages provide 'not merely for the bare sustenance of life, but for the preservation of the efficiency of the worker by providing for some measure of education, medical requirements, and amenities'. This recommendation was further stretched to develop the concept of need-based minimum wages by the Indian Labour Conference (1957).

For the calculation of the minimum wage, the Conference accepted the following norms and recommended that they should guide all wage fixing authorities, including the Minimum Wage Committee, Wage Boards, and adjudicators:

1. the standard working-class family should be taken to consist of three consumption units for the earner—earnings of women, children, and adolescents should be disregarded
2. the minimum food requirements should be calculated on the basis of the net intake of 2,700 calories, as recommended by Dr Akroyd, for an average Indian adult of moderate activity
3. the clothing requirements should be estimated at a per capita consumption of 18 yards per annum, which means a total of 72 yards for an average worker's family of four
4. in respect of housing, the norms should be the minimum rent charged by the government in any area for houses provided under the subsidized housing scheme for low income groups
5. fuel, lighting, and other miscellaneous items of expenditure should constitute 20 per cent of the total minimum wage

A *subsistence wage* meets only the bare physical needs of a worker and his family. A *minimum wage* provides not only for bare physical needs, but also aims to preserve the efficiency of workers. It also provides for some measure of education, health, and other benefits. This is the legal minimum wage of the Minimum Wage Act (1948).

Summarizing the trend of minimum wages in India, Anant and Sundaram (1998) made the following interesting observations:
- inter-state variation exists in minimum wages for the same occupation
- significant variation in the minimum wage rates across the occupations or industries exists even within the state
- substantial gaps between revisions of minimum wages in the state
- no uniformity in computation of dearness allowance

One of the reasons for such a variation in inter-state minimum wages is that labour is listed in the concurrent list, as a subject on which both the state and the centre can pass laws.

Living Wage

Living wage is defined by the Committee on fair wages as, 'one which should enable the earner to provide for himself/herself, and his/her family not only the bare essentials of food, clothing and shelter, but also a measure of frugal comfort, including education for his children, protection against ill-health, requirements of essential social needs, and a measure of insurance against the more important misfortunes, including old age'. In other words, a living wage was to provide for a standard of living that would ensure good health for workers and their family, a measure of decency, comfort, education for their children, and protection against misfortunes. This obviously implies a high level of living.

Such a wage is determined keeping in view the national income and industry's capacity to pay. The Committee was of the opinion that although the provision of a living wage should be the ultimate goal, the present level of national income did not permit the payment of a living wage on the basis of standards prevalent in more advanced countries. The goal of a living wage was to be achieved in three stages. In the first stage, the wage to be paid to the entire working class was to be established and stabilized. In the second stage, fair wages were to be established in the community-cum-industry. In the third stage, the working class was to be paid the living wage. The living wage may be somewhere between the lowest level of the minimum wage and the highest limit of the fair wage. It would depend on the bargaining power of labour, the capacity of the industry to pay, the level of the national income, the general effect of the wage rise on neighbouring industries, the productivity of labour, the place of industry in the economy of the country, and the prevailing rates of wages in the same or similar occupations in neighbouring localities.

Therefore, a living wage should maintain a worker's health and decency, a measure of comfort, and some insurance against the misfortunes of life. In this context, Supreme Court has also laid down following principles for wage fixation.

1. There is a minimum wage, which must be paid in any event, irrespective of the extent of profits, the financial condition of the establishment, or the availability of workers at lower wages.
2. The wages must be fair, which should be sufficiently high to provide a standard family with food, shelter, clothing, medical care, and education of children appropriate to the workers.
3. A fair wage lies between minimum wage and the living wage, which is the eventual goal.
4. Wages must be paid taking into account ground realities of the industry and the region, while also showing due regard to the financial capacity of the unit.

The Bombay High Court has held in two cases that while fixing wages, a broad and overall view of the financial position of the employer must be taken into account.

Fair Wage

According to the Committee on Fair Wages, fair wage represents the wage above the minimum wage, but below the living wage. The lower limit of the fair wage is obviously the minimum wage; the upper limit is set by the capacity of the industry to pay. Between these two limits, the actual wages depends on following considerations:
- productivity of labour
- prevailing rates of wages in the same or neighbouring localities
- level of the national income and its distribution
- place of industry in the economy of the country

Therefore, fair wages are adjustable. They may increase according to the capacity of the industry to pay and the prevailing rates of wages in the area or industry.

WAGE BOARDS

In the 1950s and 1960s, the organized labour sector was at a nascent stage of its development. Trade unions had inadequate bargaining power. The government, aware of the problems which arise in the arena of wage fixation due to the absence of bargaining power, constituted various wage boards. The wage boards are tripartite in character, that is, representatives of workers, employers, and independent members participate and finalize the recommendations. The utility of such boards in the present context are debatable. The wage boards for journalists, non-journalist newspaper and news-agency employees are statutory wage boards; all other wage boards are non-statutory in nature. Therefore, recommendations made by these wage boards are not enforceable under the law.

The importance of non-statutory wage boards has consequently declined over a period of time. Therefore, no non-statutory wage board has been set up after 1966, except for the sugar industry, where such a wage board was constituted in 1985. The trade unions, having grown in strength, are now capable of negotiating their wages with the management. This trend is likely to continue in the future.

In a recent land mark judgement, Supreme Court upheld the recommendations of wage boards for journalists. The newspaper associations, companies, and news agencies challenged the recommendations of a wage board on the ground that newspaper industry although in private sector, still suffer from the brunt of government interference (wage board) in deciding on the compensation of their employees. Against their appeal, the Supreme Court Bench ordered, 'We hold the recommendations of the wage board are valid, based on genuine and acceptable considerations and there is no valid ground for interference.' This recent development once again renewed the role of wage board for adjudicating compensation in select industries.

WAGE POLICY

With increasing international competition, subsequent to globalization, wage policy issues have now become more important in India. Market globalization and competition has now increased the heterogeneity of organizations, in terms of size, business practices, and culture. This has lead to a wide variation in wage or compensation design practices. Concern for international competition now forces organizations to focus on cost and profitability. Currently, employee compensation in India constitutes 36 per cent of the net domestic product; whereas in the organized sector it is 61 per cent. In the organized manufacturing sector in India, wages constitute 9 per cent of the total input costs. Another reason for the study of wage policy has been appropriately identified by Solow (1990) with the observation that, 'Wage rates and jobs are not exactly like other prices and quantities. They are much more deeply involved in the way people see themselves, think about their social status, and evaluate whether they are getting a fair share out of society.'

In India, the government used to play a crucial role in wage determination. This is primarily because of the Articles 39 and 43 of the Constitution of India and the report of the Committee on Fair Wages. As per Article 39, 'The State shall, in particular, direct its policy towards securing that—(1) the citizens, men and women equally, shall have the right to an adequate livelihood, and (2) there is equal pay for equal work for both men and women.' Article 43 states, 'The State shall endeavour, by suitable legislation or economic organization or in any other way, to give to all workers, agricultural, industrial, or otherwise, work, a living wage, conditions of work ensuring a decent standard of life and full enjoyment of leisure and social and cultural opportunities.' In line with the constitutional convention, the Committee on Fair Wages (1948) provided guidelines for wage structures in the country. It is based on these guidelines that the concepts of living wage, minimum wage, and fair wages have emerged in India.

At the micro-level, a *wage policy* guides organizations in taking decisions on wage related matters. At the organizational level wage policies are framed keeping in mind the various regulatory requirements, and the organization's own strategies. Whatever wage policies are framed, the organization should consider the recommendations of the Committee on Fair Wages. These recommendations provide the basic approach for tribunals, wage boards, and others stakeholders to fix wages of workers. The importance of the Committee has been accepted by the Supreme Court in the case of Express Newspapers (Pvt.) Ltd and others versus The Union of India 1938.

Within the boundaries of the fair wage concept, every organization must strive to ensure fair growth in workers' remuneration. Firstly, the current purchasing power of workers should be maintained against any price rise by providing for adequate neutralization of the rise in cost of living. Therefore, there should be no erosion in total emoluments in terms of their purchasing power.

Secondly, the organization should aim for a reasonable growth in the real earnings of workers and an improvement in their living standards commensurate with their level of productivity, firms' profitability, and other factors.

An ideal wage and salary policy should
- establish good labour relations
- decide on appropriate wages
- decide wages based on the individual's capability
- develop a predetermined scheme for payment of wages
- establish linkages of wage payment with performances
- maintain parity of wages with other organizations
- provide for incentive payment
- guarantee minimum wages
- provide for neutralization of price rise
- develop wage structures that can attract talent

A sound wage policy also should adopt a job evaluation programme in order to establish fair differentials in wages based upon differences in job content. Besides the basic factors provided by a job description and job evaluation, following are usually taken into consideration for wage and salary administration:
- organization's ability to pay
- supply of and demand for labour
- prevailing market rate
- cost of living
- living wage

- productivity
- trade union's bargaining power
- job requirements
- managerial attitudes
- psychological and sociological factors
- levels of skills available in the market

National Wage Policy in India

International Labour Organization (ILO) has laid down certain guidelines for wage policy. The guidelines emphasize on abolition of malpractices and abuses in wage payment; recommend setting minimum wages even for unorganized workers; suggest for just share to workers, in the form of wages, in the fruits of economic development; and finally, also seek efficient utilization of manpower through desired wage differentials, even recommending introduction of systems of payment by results.

National Wage Policy of India was framed to realize similar objectives. Following are the objectives of National Wage Policy:

1. elimination of malpractices in the payment of wages
2. setting minimum wages to reduce wage differential between organized and unorganized sectors
3. reduce disparities between wages of public and private sector
4. compensate workers for cost of living adjustment
5. reduce the gap between highest and lowest paid workers
6. support trade unions and collective bargaining
7. ensure just share to the workers in the fruits of economic development
8. avoid substitution of capital for labour
9. restrain high profit making units to discriminate wages with high compensation offer
10. institutionalize collective bargaining within national framework
11. encourage incentive payment for increase of productivity and real wages
12. ensure efficient allocation and utilization of manpower through appropriate wage differentials

Cost to Company

Cost to company (CTC) is defined as the total cost of employment for an individual employee. While issuing the letter of appointment to a new hire, companies detail the CTC, which apart from the gross compensation payable also factors for several benefits, both monetary and non-monetary. Although, rationally CTC is supposed to consider the compensation and benefits related costs, organizational practices vary widely. Internationally, organizations also factor the rent value of office space allotted to an employee as CTC. Even support services enjoyed by executives, say secretarial support are also factored in CTC.

Many multinational companies operating in India even go beyond in factoring such costs—for benefits which are poorly linked to compensation—that is to the CTC. This widens the gap between the CTC and net payable compensation of an employee. Hence, increased CTC may not indicate incremental change in the net salary of an employee. All these are due to absence of some legal mandate in CTC calculation. For example, even a Friday get-together cost during office hours with coffee, though it provides benefit to the company through increased level of employee engagement and helps in developing a performance driven work culture, is factored by some organizations in calculating the CTC. In absence of a legal mandate, industry practices on CTC calculation require some clear guidelines. One possible way is to exclude all overhead costs from CTC. Similarly, costs incurred by the companies to develop employees, say costs of training and development, knowledge management practices, etc., should be excluded from the purview of CTC.

Example of CTC calculation

In absence of any structured guideline and legal connotation, CTC calculation varies from company to company. In many organizations, particularly IT and ITeS, difference between CTC and net pay may be as high as 50 per cent, which often leads to the confusion. Many multinational organizations operating in India take the advantage of showing high CTC to attract the talent. Such compensation package factors most of the variables, which are performance aligned and conditional deferred compensation, which requires employees to continue in the employment for a long period. Based on Indian organizations practices, a standard CTC can be illustrated as under:

Structured compensation Structured compensation forms the basis of gross pay. Following are the components of gross pay:
- Basic salary
- Dearness allowance
- House rent allowance
- Food coupons
- Entertainment allowance
- Transport/conveyance allowance
- Medical allowance
- Leave travel allowance (paid with monthly pay)
- Overtime allowance

Benefits Structured compensation provides a number of benefits to the employees. These benefits are as follows:
- Provident fund
- Retirement benefit fund
- Insurance
- Gratuity

- Leave encashment
- Club membership

Amongst these benefits, gratuity and leave encashment components are apportioned on monthly basis.

CTC in this case would be the structured compensation/gross pay + the benefits. For example, ICICI Bank for their campus hire (law graduates) provides for CTC of ₹9.05 lakh per year. The bank includes loans, assistance for housing, pensions, and various other benefits in calculating CTC.

Base Pay Calculation

Base pay is the core component of compensation packages. It is the pay for standard job duties, roles, and skills. Other top-ups on compensation vary with respect to the base pay. For employees, perspective base pay is important, as it is the fixed component of compensation. Most of the top-ups on base pay are known as variables, and are often aligned with the performance of employees and of the organization. Some are statutory in nature, say provident fund, gratuity, etc.; whereas others are voluntary. Similar to CTC, base pay design and calculation also vary across the organizations. It involves several contributing factors and strategic choices. Internationally, we find base pay is deliberately kept low by the companies, and more emphasis is given on variables. In India also, base pay varies across the organizations, and it hovers around 50 per cent of the total compensation or gross pay.

Some of the important objectives of base pay are; internal and external equity, compliance with legal provisions, individual and process equity, and efficient utilization of the compensation budget. Base pay designing requires job analysis and evaluation, labour market data analysis, and decision on pay ranges.

Based on the industry practices, factors contributing to the base pay calculation are

Strategic or competitive positioning of the organizations The degree of need for talent acquisition and retention also plays a role in companies decision on the base pay level. A talent driven organization provides for more base pay, as employees look for those employers who are more transparent with long term commitment in institutional employment. Such companies with a broad band pay structure can differentiate the base pay across the employees, depending on their knowledge and skill, and performance level.

Industry practices Companies can decide on the base pay levels based on the industry benchmarks. For this purpose, they also make use of compa-ratio or comparative ratio. We have discussed compa-ratio separately in this chapter.

Legal mandates Although we do not have specific legal mandates on base pay calculation, companies, particularly in India, cannot decide on base pay below the level of statutory minimum wages.

Organizational life cycle Depending on the life cycle stage, that is, start-up, growth, maturity, decline, and decision on base pay varies across the organizations.

For example, sales compensation for the start-up may offer less base pay and more variables, based on the contribution margin. The same organization, however, to stabilize growth may offer more base pay for retention of high performers.

Competency-based base pay Depending on the level of competency, companies may decide on the base pay. With wide competency gap between the required set of competencies for the employees and available competencies of employees, base pay may be reduced.

Labour market dynamics When demand for a particular profession or occupation group is higher than the supply of available workforce, companies may raise the base pay. In the reverse cases, base pay may get reduced.

Hence, it is evident that decision on base pay for any organization depends on multiple factors.

Compensation Philosophy

Effective management of compensation function requires a structured plan. Many organizations develop and document such compensation plans, partly to meet the requirements of legal compliance, and partly to achieve the strategic intents such as employee satisfaction, motivation, and retention. Compensation plan encompasses clarity on compensation philosophy, approaches to base pay design, decision on pay rates for various categories of jobs, job evaluation, performance management systems (PMS), process of reviewing compensation from time to time, etc.

Compensation philosophy consists of a bunch of guiding principles that form the basis of compensation design. It helps in developing a compensation plan that the organization intends to achieve through compensation. When such goals are to attract and retain the talent, create a performance driven work culture, motivate employees, and elicit desired behaviour from employees, a compensation philosophy is developed, which caters to all these aspects. To the contrary, when goals are to gain incremental change in performance and productivity, the approach to compensation philosophy is more opportunistic and oriented towards short-term gains. However, there are some organizations which have a system of communicating the compensation philosophy and plans to their employees, and even go to the extent of involving employees in framing the compensation plans. For example, TCS ensures employees' compensation and benefits are aligned with the global demographic diversity, and allow employees to have their say in defining their compensation and benefits programme. Compensation philosophy may also outline the modalities in framing decisions on compensation design. For example, companies may decide on their relative market position in compensation, choosing market level pay, below market level pay, or above market level pay. Again such decisions are aligned with their strategic and business goals. Compensation philosophy of a company may also incorporate their choice of mix between cash and benefits component of compensation, mix between fixed and variable pay, process of performance evaluation system, legal mandates, etc.

Using a sample compensation philosophy of a hypothetical company, we can describe a compensation philosophy of XYZ company from operational perspective.

Our compensation philosophy/plan rests on following principles:
- attracting and retaining talent
- pay at market rate for 80 per cent of employees who meet expectations
- pay 20 per cent above market rate for 20 per cent of employees who exceed expectations
- highly competitive compensation, and benefits among peer group companies
- internal equity in compensation plans
- provision for employee rewards
- cognizance to internal financial strength
- focus on competency and performance-based compensation
- strict adherence to legal provisions

The above compensation philosophy helps us to achieve high performance growth, acquisition and retention of talent, high employee motivation, and adherence to legal provisions.

Compensation planning

Compensation planning is deciding on employees' compensation for acquiring, maintaining, and retaining the human resources of an organization, so that they can feel motivated and become productive for organizational sustenance and growth. Effective compensation planning ensures individual, internal, and external equity. Individual equity establishes equal pay for equal job. Internal equity maintains balance in compensation structure within the organization. External equity on the other hand calibrates compensation with the labour market. Following are some important objectives of compensation planning:
1. Attracting talent
2. Retaining talent
3. Maintaining pay equities
4. Encouraging innovation through rewards
5. Compiling with legal provisions
6. Ensuring compensation cost optimization

We operate in a globally competitive market. Our compensation objectives are to attract and retain talented employees. We design our employees' compensation packages integrating the organizational and individual performance, respecting equity, law of the land, and our business goals. Broadly, our compensation objectives help us to design our compensation policies and practices encompassing the following areas:
1. attracting, retaining, and motivating talented employees, who drive our business results with competitive compensation

2. provisioning for more variable pay based on performance
3. validating compensation in alignment with measurable performance results
4. customizing compensation packages based on employees' needs, without exceeding the overall compensation amount
5. calibrating compensation with shareholders' value creation
6. ensuring total cost of compensation is in accordance with the company's affordability
7. using compensation policy as an important tool to communicate to employees our performance standard

Pay grades and pay bands

Most of the structured organizations follow some well defined pay grades, depending on the job responsibilities and job descriptions of employees. Each employee on his employment in the organization is placed in a specific pay grade, which indicates the amount of salary that he will receive within a pay band. Pay bands are broader than pay grades, as it incorporates several pay grades. It means two or three pay grades in an organization may be incorporated in a pay band. An employee is put in a pay grade of a pay band depending on his work experience, knowledge, and skill level at time of recruitment. Therefore, a pay band distinguishes compensation amount between several ranges of jobs, whereas a pay grade differentiates compensation within a job range. This we can illustrate using Table 1.1.

Interpreting Table 1.1, we can understand that within the same pay band, that is, PB–2, we have several grades. The compensation between such grades within the same pay band is differentiated in terms of grade pay. Grade pay is considered along with the base or basic pay for calculation of dearness allowances, when payable. Although, such differences are minimum for government organizations; they can be more for private organizations. For example, Walmart puts interns and store associates in the same pay band. Their compensation is fixed at the given pay band, but their pay varies widely depending on the grades.

TABLE 1.1 Pay band and pay grades

Grade	Pay band (PB)	Scale (in ₹ per month)	Grade pay (in ₹ per month)
Assistant executive engineer	PB–2	9,300–34,800	4,800
Private secretary	PB–2	9,300–34,800	4,600
Junior works manager	PB–2	9,300–34,800	4,600
Assistant staff officer	PB–2	9,300–34,800	4,200
Personal assistant	PB–2	9,300–34,800	4,200
Chargeman–Non technical	PB–2	9,300–34,800	4,200
Chargeman–Technical	PB–2	9,300–34,800	4,200
Junior hindi translator	PB–2	9,300–34,800	4,200

Source: Compiled from various reports of Central Government 6th Pay Commission

Nowadays, many organizations go for a flat structure to reduce hierarchical levels. Such an arrangement reduces the levels and thus the promotional opportunities. On the other hand, with flat organizational structure, organizations can implement shared decision-making on a larger scale. From the compensation management point of view, such structure require consolidation of various pay bands and pay grades into broader pay ranges, this is referred as broad banding of pay. Such wide pay band facilitates systematic pay increases, even though employees get limited promotional opportunities. Particularly in large hierarchically structured organizations, it becomes often necessary to reduce the levels, merging several levels into one, without impairing the compensation systems. In a broad band pay structure, employees can be put at a suitable pay level, which would have been their eligibility in a narrow band pay structure depending on the knowledge, skill, and performance levels of employees.

Using the two charts shown in Figs 1.1 and 1.2, we can explain the broadbanding. Y-axis here indicates the pay band, and x-axis indicates compensable factors. In traditional pay structure, we find multiple pay bands, whereas broad band pay structures have fewer pay bands.

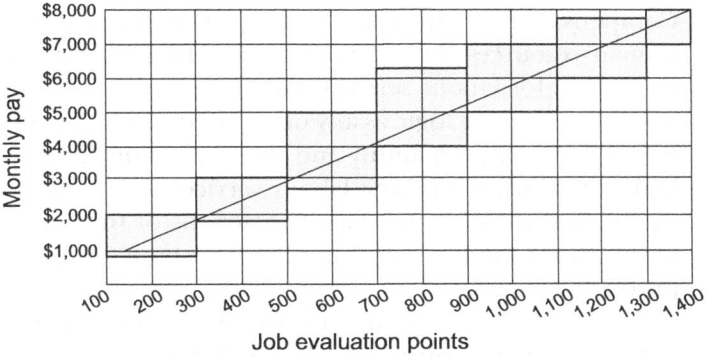

FIG. 1.1 Traditional pay structure

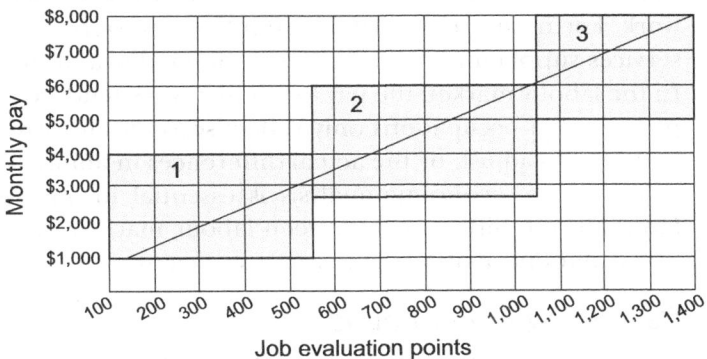

FIG. 1.2 Broad band pay structure

SIGNIFICANCE OF EMPLOYEE COMPENSATION

Compensation basically represents an employment contract. It is important to employees, organizations, and the economy. To an employee, pay is a primary reason for working. For some individuals, it may be the only reason. For most of us, it is the means by which we provide for our own and our family's needs.

Compensation is also important for organizations. It represents a large proportion of expenditure of an organization. In manufacturing firms, it is seldom lower than 20 per cent; in service enterprises, it can be as high as 80 per cent. Even more importantly, organizations try to accomplish many goals through compensation. These goals include attracting and retaining people, and motivating them to perform more effectively. Compensation is also significant in the operation of the economy as salaries and wages are the largest contributing factors to the national income of many countries in the world, including India. Hence, it is important for us to understand different theories applicable to compensation.

Economic concept

Compensation is a price for a factor of production. It serves to allocate scarce human resources for productive uses. To the employer, compensation is the price paid for labour services. As an economic concept, compensation is governed by the same logic as any other purchase by a firm. An organization strives to get the greatest quantity and the highest quality for its money. By the same logic, the worker is selling labour services to obtain income and holds out for the highest price obtainable. The actions of these buyers and sellers are supposed to set the price and to allocate labour (employee services) to its most productive use.

The market for labour services differs in many ways from the market for commodities. Labour service is perishable. If today's labour is not purchased today, it may have no value tomorrow. Besides, labour service may vary from hour to hour and day to day because it varies with the ability of a person to work. Furthermore, the labour supplier cannot be separated from the labour services supplied as he can change the quality and quantity of those services. In the labour market, the pay for similar work tends to be equal. Differences in pay between occupations only reflect scarcities for which the market had not had time to adjust, or the actual differences in ability.

Therefore, economic analysis is essential in any study of compensation. However, the differences between labour markets and other markets suggest that economic analysis alone is not sufficient.

Psychological concept

Compensation or pay represents the psychological contract between an individual and the organization. An organization's reward practices can only have consequences through this contract. Therefore, pay as a psychological concept is pay viewed from an individual's standpoint.

The factors that go in determining an individual's behaviour are situation, needs, perception, and attitude. However, the situation and the individual are not independent as the situation depends on the individual's perception of it. Needs that are felt states that they influence as well as are influenced by perceptions. The means for satisfying needs are those perceived by individuals and interpreted through attitudes. One need may be satisfied by a number of means and one mean may satisfy a number of needs. Relating compensation to the psychological concept complements the economic perspective by taking into account the perceptions of individuals.

Compensation and behavioural issues

Compensation management is an application of motivation theory. For this reason, motivation theory can be considered as a form of compensation theory. Here, our focus is just to establish the link between motivation and compensation administration.

Psychologists have focused on two psychological processes of motivation—arousal and choice. Arousal is the reason why people do anything and choice refers to the choices that people make. Similarly, we can distinguish between content and process theories of motivation. *Content theories* focus on the factors that motivate behaviour. It centers on needs or drives. Therefore, it is linked with arousal process of motivation through compensation designing. *Process or choice theories* explain the operation of motivation, or the factors that influence an individual to choose one action over another. *Process theories* can be subdivided into cognitive and non-cognitive approaches. Cognitive theories see behaviour as involving some mental process. Non-cognitive theories see behaviour as caused by environmental contingencies. The major cognitive theories are equity theory, goal-setting theory, and expectancy theory. All these theories focus on perceptions of the outcomes that flow from behaviour. Non-cognitive theories do not focus on what goes on inside the person's brain. Instead, they claim that it is the environment that determines the behaviour of the person. Therefore, to control behaviour, one must control the person's environment.

Compensation designing acts as operant conditioning, as employees show two types of behaviour—respondent and operant—while their behaviour gets reinforced. *Respondent behaviours* are controlled by instincts and direct stimulation. *Operant behaviours* are displayed in the absence of any apparent external stimulation.

Sociological concept

Pay can be a status symbol within organizations and society. In less complex societies, the status of individuals is a product of many standards of judgement. For example, their families, friends, occupations, education levels, and religious and political affiliations. In large, mobile societies, many of these standards are harder to measure and become less significant. Income, as a symbol of status, does not present this problem. Organizations create status structures of jobs. Status differences are measured by both organizations and individuals in terms of pay and pay differences. In fact, employees learn to place associates in the status structure of the organization according to how much they are paid.

Viewing compensation as a sociological concept focuses neither on the organization nor on individuals, but on the relationship between them. The mutual influence of individuals, organizations, and of groups within and without constitutes another dimension of compensation decision-making.

Political concept

Compensation as a political concept involves the use of power and influence. Organizations, unions, groups, and individual employees all use their power to influence pay. Unions exert influence at the time the contract is entered into, and during the life of the contract, through the grievance procedure. Similarly, compensation in unionized organizations influences that of non-union organizations. A political perspective stresses on accommodating the influence of all parties.

Equity concept

Few discussions of compensation are conducted without repeated appeals to fairness. Phrases such as *a fair day's pay* or *the just wage* are common. In both cases, the equity sought is distributive justice. The foundation concept is that returns should be proportionate to contributions. Viewing compensation as an equity concept means analysing pay from the separate viewpoints of the parties. Ideally, compensation should be adjudged fair by all of them.

Communication concept

Compensation is drastically affected by communication, particularly in this electronic age. Employees now have easy access to the competitive rates commonly paid for their positions within any given geographic area. Worldwide, employers now face a future where employees know more than their employers about the value of their positions in the competitive marketplace.

Multi-disciplinary concept

Economists have focused on the price (wage) of a factor of production and, considered employee behaviour in terms of labour units employed (typically in terms of working hours). Psychologists have focused on the needs of individuals and the means by which they may be met by organizations, with less emphasis on the needs of the organization. Sociologists, political scientists, and philosophers have often not studied compensation per se, but concepts

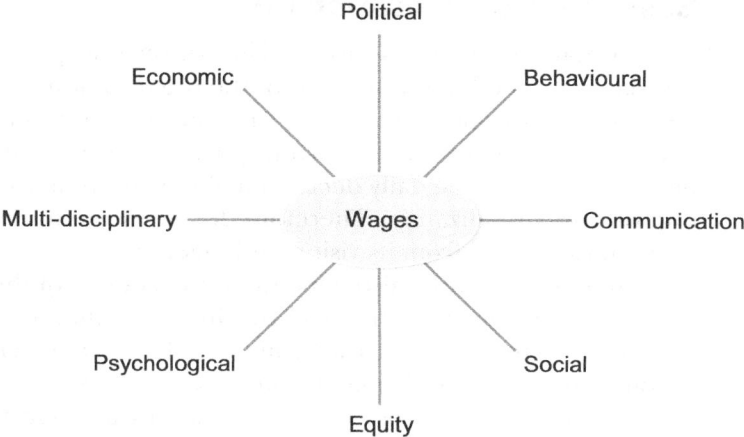

FIG. 1.3 Integrated Model of Compensation

they have developed for other purposes may be usefully applied to the study of pay. Management researchers and teachers have focused on the more esoteric aspects of compensation; few have focused on the ability to control costs. Those in separate disciplines have thus studied compensation selectively (see Fig. 1.3).

ETHICAL ISSUES

Ethics is the science (study) of morality. Ethical behaviour is about deciding what is right or good. It is often called moral philosophy. It emanates from value theory, that is, axiology. Other branches of ethics are aesthetics, metaphysics, epistemology, and logic.

Compensation management practices in any organization need to be ethical. Since many organizations align their incentives and variable pay components with performances, both at the individual and organizational level, it is often seen that organizations try to manipulate their performance metrics, without considering ethical issues. It may be imperative for organizations to optimize compensation cost to remain competitive in the market, but resorting to such practices is considered unethical. Even world-class organizations such as Wal-Mart often face this dilemma. To deal with this problem, organizations are now adopting separate codes of conduct for compensation management practices. Building a value-based organizational culture at the outset is the foundation of compensation ethics. Organizational values permeate workplace practices, letting people share such values in their day-to-day performances. Ethical organizations care about their people and even go beyond statutory limits when paying compensation and benefits. For example, Tata Steel in India pays compensation and benefits beyond the statutory limits.

Bases for Compensation Ethics

Every organization has a vision. This vision encapsulates its values, which translate into the long-term goals of the organization. It essentially guides the behaviour of the people working with the organization. Its vision also translates into the organization's current purpose, or mission. Both the vision and mission influence the daily decision-making and practices of the people working with the organization. Therefore, for every organization, core compensation ethics emerge from its vision and mission.

Compensation ethics also depend on the choices of the organization. Organizations may choose to be proactive in their human resource management practices, or reactive and traditional. With proactive choices, organizations become ethical in people management issues, as well as compensation. On the contrary, reactive practices focus on individuals acting in a self-defined vacuum, so ethical issues are often violated.

Compensation ethics also need to be aligned with the strategic choices of the organization. Strategic choices may differ from employee to employee, primarily on hierarchical level, performance criteria, the nature of the job, and the type of skill sets. Many Indian organizations, particularly in the IT sector, indulge in discriminatory compensation practices.

If the organization embraces compensation ethics, in the form of a structured code of conduct, it will inevitably ensure the following changes in the behaviour of its employees:
- work-related behaviour, decision-making styles, and interpersonal interactions will reflect ethical values
- organizational decisions based on values and ethics will help make people more cooperative
- compensation and rewards will become more structured
- organizational goals will be aligned with ethical practices
- regular performance feedback to people will help in continuous development
- human resources practices will become more congruent with values

In the case of employment matters, compensation ethics help in ensuring that the work environment is free from all forms of harassment, intimidation, or coercion. Recently, serious charges were levelled against global companies such as Citigroup and Merrill Lynch for unethical compensation practices. The CEOs of both these companies had to quit because of a drop in business, but both received huge accumulated benefits (even without their severance pay). Therefore, unethical compensation payouts, especially disproportionately large payouts to senior executives, have now become common in many organizations.

Many organizations set up their own ethics committees to monitor whether prescribed ethics are being strictly followed in the day-to-day activities of the organization. They systematically conduct ethics audits, ethics training, and even set up ethics hotlines to ensure that employees follow the ethics and values of the organization.

SUMMARY

Wages and salary administration is major human resource management function today. Apart from compliance with procedures and regulations, aspects such as cost to the organization and employee motivation also need to be considered. Human resource managers need to consider the trade-off between these considerations. Administration professionals, on the other hand, have to take care of payroll.

In percentage terms, salary, wages, and bonus taken together are still the major causes of industrial disputes in India. Hence, determining wages based on certain defined methodologies should receive priority. Linking wages to performance is again a major issue. Suitable incentive schemes need to be identified to reward good performers. Fringe benefits are another major instrument to motivate employees. With increased competition, the organizations need to become innovative in designing employee compensation. This has led to compensation becoming more and more interlinked with talent management.

Compensation is a methodical approach to assigning a monetary value to employees in return for work performed. Various factors—both external and internal—influence compensation. The term compensation is used to describe not only employees' salaries, but also all other benefits they receive. It is also referred to as remuneration. However, compensation is a more holistic term than remuneration. Traditional wages and salary administration has now started losing ground. Just complying with statutory norms and expecting employees to deliver results does not hold good in today's competitive scenario. Hence, organizations have to design compensation in such a manner that it should acts as a reward rather than just a monthly salary for the job done. They also have to come up with comprehensive compensation planning that includes considerations such as pay grades and pay bands and cost to company (CTC) for individual employees. Though organizations vary widely in their approach to compensation planning, their compensation management practices should be ethical and guided by the organizational vision.

Key Terms

Assessment centres One of the modern methods of performance appraisal. This method tests candidates in a social situation by a number of assessors, using a variety of criteria. This method is useful in measuring inter-personal skills, organizing and planning ability, creativity, resistance to stress, work motivation, decision-making power, etc.

Dearness allowance These allowances are paid to protect the real wages of employees from falling in value, by keeping pace with the price rise.

Employee stock options (ESOP) A type of employee benefit plan which is intended to encourage employees to acquire stocks or ownership in the company. ESOPs are often used as a corporate finance strategy and are also used to align the interests of a company's employees with those of the company's shareholders. These are offered as incentives by the organization to ensure increased level of motivation and retention of employees.

Fair wage It is the wage, which is above the minimum wage, but below the living wage. The lower limit of the fair wage is the minimum wage and the upper limit is set by the 'capacity of the industry to pay'.

Job evaluation Process of measuring the relative worth of a job to decide the wage rate.

Key result areas (KRA) These indicate the performance target of individual employees of an organization. These are aligned with business goals.
Living wages It is a wage rate which not only provides the bare essentials of food, clothing, and shelter, but also a measure of frugal comfort for the worker. It also provides for his children education, protection against ill-health, requirements of essential social needs, old age, and a measure of insurance against the misfortunes.
Minimum wages They are need-based and statutorily decided both by the central and the state government. Payment of minimum wages is obligatory for an organization.
Performance management systems System of integrating individual employee performance with the performance of the organization.
SMART Specific, measurable, attainable, realistic, and time-bound goals.
Time study It is carried out to decide the standard time required to perform a job and then base the wage and incentives on the same standards.

Exercises

Concept Review Questions

1. Explain the concept of employee compensation management. What is its significance?
2. What are the important compensation domains? Which domain do you feel influences compensation design in India?
3. Explain a compensation decision model and its determinants.
4. Identify the possible factors to justify an increment in your organization.
5. Discuss the important elements of employee rewards.
6. Write short notes on:
   (a) Broad band pay
   (b) Compensation benchmarking
   (c) ESOPs

Critical Thinking Questions

1. A particular organization, engaged in the business of pharmaceutical drugs, offers the best salaries in the industry to its employees. The company has started losing talented employees due to increase in inter-industry job mobility. Initially, the company did not pay any attention to this issue, as it can get skilled manpower from its relatively small competitors, because of its competitive compensation package.
   However, its talent flight has now become so acute that the company has decided to opt for an industry benchmark of their compensation packages. As a team leader of this project, chalk out your action plans detailing the types of industries that you may like to benchmark.
2. Prepare a wage policy for payment of wages to industrial workers.

CASE STUDY

New Delhi Shopping Point

New Delhi Shopping Point has about 300 employees, 200 of whom are on the permanent rolls, whereas the rest are outsourced. About 50 per cent of the employees were females. Since it was a new entrant in the business, the retail chain has adopted the ongoing practice of job evaluation rather than framing its own job evaluation and classification system. As a result, the chain failed to establish a mutually agreed compensation design plan and was accused of deliberate pay inequity, without valuing diversity issues. This institutional

(Contd)

CASE STUDY *(Contd)*

failure to establish pay equity ultimately led to successive strikes by dissatisfied employees. Eventually, these employees formed unions with strong opposing political affiliations.

The company then formed a task force with cross-functional team managers to educate employees on the methods of job correlation and job pricing. The idea behind the force was to receive the support of employees to develop a mutually accepted job evaluation scheme and rationalize the company's pay differentiation strategies. Although this scheme might have reduced the employees' dissatisfaction on pay parity, it failed to eliminate inequity, resulting in dissension amidst a small section of employees.

In a retail store, customers notice dissatisfied employees immediately, especially when their queries go unheard, when they are left to guess the price of an item whose price tag is missing, or when they are not properly informed about product features. The business of a retail chain suffers when it fails to captivate customers. The New Delhi Shopping Point faced all these predicaments, resulting in a substantial loss of business and significant reduction in customers.

Facing successive business losses, the company ultimately decided to discuss the pay parity issue and to arrive at a solution. It also agreed to develop a suitable job evaluation scheme, aligned with the compensation design plan. All the unions agreed to this proposition of the company and promised to come out with a win-win solution on the pay parity issue. Some of the issues suggested by unions for discussion in the joint meeting were—correctly capture some key features of work done by female employees, differentiate between the quality of customer relations offered by a male and female employee, understand the success rate (in terms of percentage of customers) of male and female employees, etc. A section of female employees complained that though their success rate was better than their male colleagues, they were still paid less than their male counterparts. They threatened to refer the matter to the Human Rights Commission, if conciliation failed.

Discussion question

As a team member, representing the management, suggest a way for the company to achieve pay parity through mutual consensus.

References

A System of National Accounts (1967), Studies in Methods, Series F, no. 2, rev. 3, United Nations, New York.

Anant, T.C.A. and K. Sundaram (1998), 'Wage policy in India: A review', *The Indian Journal of Labour Economics*, vol. 41, pp. 815–34, October–December.

Barney, J.B. and P. M. Wright (1998), 'On becoming a strategic partner: The role of human resources in gaining competitive advantage', *Human Resource Management*, vol. 37, pp. 31–46.

Bhattacharyya, D.K. (2006), *Human Resource Management*, 2nd edn, Excel Books, New Delhi.

Current international recommendations on labour statistics, International Labour Organization, Geneva, (1988).

Dasgupta, A.K. (1976), *A Theory of Wage Policy*, Oxford University Press, New Delhi.

Porter, L.W. and E.E. Lawler (1968), *Managerial Attitudes and Performance*, Irwin-Dorsey, Holmewood.

Solow, R.M. (1990), *The Labour Market as a Social Institution*, Basil Blackwell, Cambridge.

Subramanian, K.N. (1987), *Wages in India*, Tata McGraw-Hill, New Delhi.

The Cost of Social Security (1995), Fourteenth International Inquiry, 1987–89, International Labour Organization, Geneva, 1995.

Verma, P. (1987), *Labour Economics and Industrial Relations*, Tata McGraw-Hill, New Delhi.

Vroom, Victor (1964), *Work and Motivation*, Wiley, New York.

CHAPTER TWO

Compensation Management: The Indian Context

Learning Objectives

After reading this chapter, you will be able to
- learn in detail about compensation decisions
- understand the concept of VIE theory and compensation
- learn about compensation benchmarking
- assess various components of employee reward systems in India
- understand executive compensation issues

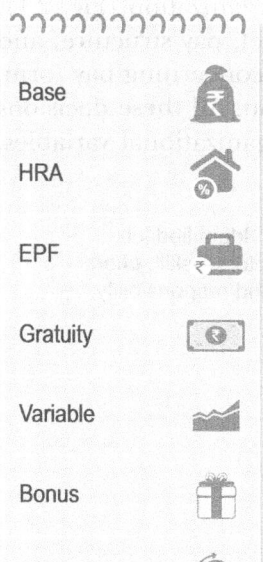

Duality in Compensation Management Practices—Case of CISCO

Cisco Systems, a global networking company, has been reducing its manpower for successive years. The company has made use of a mix of job cuts and early retirement packages to trim the workforce. In July 2012, Cisco announced its plan to further reduce its manpower by 1,300 jobs. With this round of job cuts, Cisco estimated its saving, from reduction in workforce, to cross the $1 billion mark. The year before, that is, in July 2011, Cisco had phased out 6,500 jobs. Cisco has been phasing out jobs to adjust its position to changing economic and competitive positions. Cisco is able to sustain such job cuts as with every move, they simplify their operations.

Cisco's example is a unique lesson for manpower analysts across the globe. The cuts in manpower helped Cisco maintain and improve profitability. However, many analysts do not agree with its strategy of making its workers the first casualty. Cisco's Chief Executive Officer, John Chambers, attributed frequent job slashing to exit less profitable businesses due to increase in number of competitors, who are able to offer price efficient products.

Although cutting manpower to save on the cost of compensation has become almost a regular feature for Cisco, the company is also known for compensation design for their executives, even above the market average. The 1984 company with current headcount of 65,223 is now operating from 420 locations in 93 countries. Their employees are broadly categorized in Engineering, Sales, and other business functions. Engineering represents 33.8 per cent of Cisco's workforce, followed by Sales (25.5 per cent), and other business functions (40.7 per cent). The benefits package for employees of Cisco is quite elaborate, and most of these benefits are also offered to their Indian employees. Cisco is a perfect company to practice duality in compensation management for its best strategic use for the growth and sustainability.

COMPENSATION DECISIONS

Compensating executives requires a series of decisions. The end result of these decisions is a pay rate for each executive in the organization (Fig. 2.1). There are three core decisions: those involving pay level, pay structure, and pay system. Supporting these are three other decisions concerning pay form, pay treatment for special groups, and pay administration. All these decisions are influenced by a number of environmental and organizational variables.

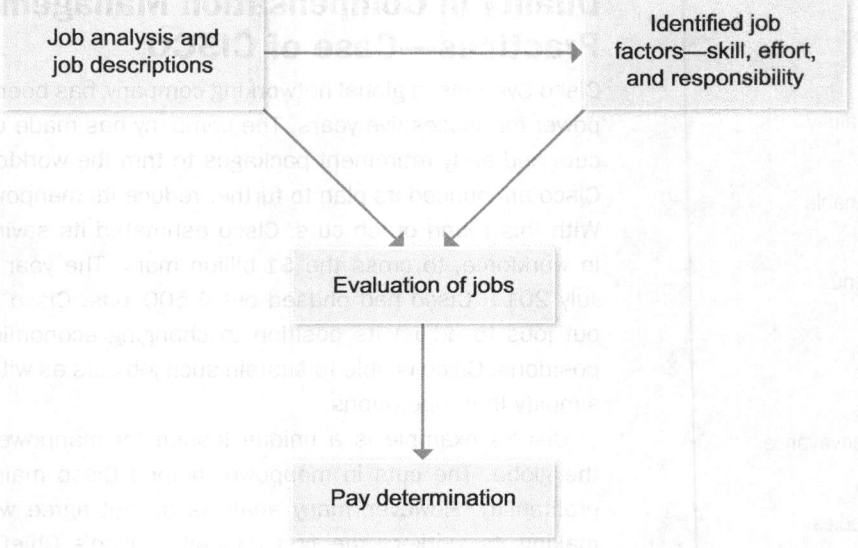

FIG. 2.1 Pay determination stages

Examples of these variables are the economic, social/cultural, and legal environments; as well as the organization's structure and workforce.

The broadest of the core decisions is the *pay level* decision. This decision determines how much the organization will pay for labour services, or what its average pay will be. Pay level refers to the average pay for jobs, for departments, or for the entire enterprise. An average pay must be set that will secure and keep workforce productive. The major considerations in pay level decisions are—public policy, pay for comparable work in the community or industry (usually called the 'going rate'), and the company's response to economic, political, and social issues. These considerations may be weighed unilaterally or together with the union(s) representing employees. Some of these decisions end with personal interactions (salaries) whereas some are provided on a group basis (medical insurance).

The second core decision is the *pay structure* decision, which focuses on the relationship between jobs within the organization. Pay structure decisions usually involve arraying jobs in a hierarchy and setting pay for these jobs relative to their status within the hierarchy. It also involves decisions by the organization regarding the amount and type of benefits to provide.

Together, the pay level and pay structure decisions determine the pay. In addition, they ensure conformity and compliance with external and internal standards. Presumably, pay level decisions ensure that the organization is in line with the requirements of the external environment; and pay structure decisions ensure that the pay for jobs is internally consistent.

The third core decision involves determining *individual pay* of employees, doing the same job. Of course, it is possible for all employees on the same job to get the same pay, in which case no decision is needed. However, once a decision is made to differentiate the pay of employees on the same job, two further decisions are required—(1) how to differentiate among employees and (2) whether to pay for time or for output. We can label the first of these decisions as individual pay determination and the second as the pay method decision. Adopting the designation of pay system for both decisions makes sense.

The first supporting decision is pay form, that is, the composition of the pay an employee receives. A major part of it is in the form of money, or take-home pay; however a significant proportion of it is in the form of benefits of several kinds. The second supporting decision involves the pay treatment of some special employee groups. Although the organization wants similar behaviour from all employee groups, compensation policies and practices may differ somewhat for Marketing, HR, Finance, Operations, etc. The final supporting decision involves ensuring that pay not only achieves organizational and individual objectives, but also meets public policy goals. Those responsible for compensation planning and control seek answers to questions of efficiency, effectiveness, and legality. Discrimination in pay is an important issue today.

DETERMINANTS OF COMPENSATION DECISIONS

Compensation decisions are not made in a vacuum; one must consider a number of environmental and organizational variables. As indicated earlier, compensation is, at least partly, an economic concept. Economic conditions are a major influence upon what an employee is paid. Tied to this economic environment is the impact of unions on the wages, both industry-wide and in each organization.

In a similar manner, social environment, also, has an impact on compensation decisions. Members of a society have ideas about the worth of different jobs, and these ideas need to be taken into account. The social environment has been changing dramatically, following entry of women into the workforce. Hence, while taking compensation decisions, valuing diversity is very important.

Compensation decisions are also affected by the dynamics of a particular organization. Employee pay must be consistent, within the organization's structure. The organization's culture helps in determining the priority to be given to various compensation goals. The organization's workforce characteristics influence the success of different compensation programmes.

Finally, compensation decisions are affected by the worldwide information highway. After all, compensation and benefits is data perfectly suited to the Internet. The impact will be significant. One can expect severe communication conflicts relating to competitive practices. E-mail, chat boards, and dotcom companies who attract visitors to their site by providing employees compensation data are now having an effect. Larger organizations are now administering their stock, salary, and incentive plans on a worldwide basis, via the Internet. In time, smaller organizations too will gain this capability. The Internet is about to give benefit and compensation administration a new identity.

Principles for Compensation Decisions

Industry practices on compensation decisions vary widely. Many organizations prefer to keep their compensation decisions secret from their employees. Similarly, organizations also make their compensation decisions discretionary, instead of backing them by logic and data analysis. Similarly disregard for market factors, competitors' compensation strategies, legal provisions, and suitable compensation mix, often vitiates compensation decisions. We have already discussed that compensation decisions must be strategic and aligned with the organizational business goals. When the companies are financially viable, we must design compensation in a way that it meets both ends, that is, employees' and organizational perspectives. Giving employees' the opportunity to have their say on compensation decisions also benefits the organization. Keeping in mind the strategic significance of compensation decisions, following principles can be adhered to by the organizations, while designing compensation.

Make your compensation decisions participative Let employees have their say. It does not mean that companies need to forget their economics. Within the overall constraints of the compensation budget, companies can accommodate employees' views in designing their compensation.

Guard against prevalent law and social norms A random testing of various organizational compensation designs would show how they hardly reflect the recommendations of National Wage Policy. Discriminatory compensation practices are quite common within the same organization, and even within the same job category, skill, and knowledge group. Compliance with legal provisions is seen more as compulsion than necessity. All these must be avoided.

Make your compensation decisions objective Let employees understand the science behind your compensation decisions. Subjectivity gets questioned, even when organizations are not biased in their compensation decisions. Compensable factors, compa-ratio, contribution margin, competencies, internal and external equity, benchmarked data, etc. are some of the parameters that could be used for making objective compensation decisions.

Make your compensation decisions performance linked While provisioning for variables and payment of incentives, it is always better to have a structured approach, and this must be pre-announced to employees. Unless employees understand how their compensation correlates with their performance, they are not convinced about the objectiveness of the calculations. The lack of transparency, ultimately, gives rise to employees' dissatisfaction and demotivation.

Value principles of equity It is important to not only value internal equity, but also to strive for external equity. A combination of internal and external equity makes employees feel motivated and they tend to remain longer with the organization. With internal and external equity in compensation, organizations can also get tremendous brand value.

VIE THEORY AND COMPENSATION

The valence instrumentality expectancy (VIE) theory was formulated by Victor Vroom (1964). Valence stands for value, instrumentality is the belief that if we do one thing it will lead to another, and expectancy is the probability that action or effort will lead to an outcome. An incentive or bonus scheme works only if the link between effort and reward is clear, and the value of the reward is worth the effort. Porter and Lawler (1968) developed a model in line with the VIE concept, which suggests that the following two factors determine the effort people put into their jobs:
- the value of the rewards to individuals, in so far as it satisfies their needs for security, social esteem, autonomy, and self-actualization

- the probability that rewards depend on effort, as perceived by individuals. In other words, their expectations about the relationships between effort and reward

Motivation and performance are influenced by—(1) the perceived link between effort and performance, (2) the perceived link between performance and outcome, and (3) the significance (valence) of the outcome to the person.

Effort depends on the likelihood that rewards will follow the effort and that such rewards would be worthwhile. The key emphasis of the theory is that there must be a link between effort and reward (line or sight). The reward should be achievable, and it should also be worthwhile.

COMPENSATION BENCHMARKING

In order to retain key employees, good organizations always practise compensation benchmarking. Unnecessary attrition enhances human resource costs due to the cost of replacing manpower. It also badly affects organizational brand image. If attrition is attributable to pay not being competitive, it shows the organization's failure to properly benchmark compensation. For successful compensation benchmarking, an organization can emulate the experience of Xerox Corporation (United States). The company adopted a compensation benchmarking process with four phases—planning, analysis, integration, and action. In each of these phases, following action items need to be accomplished.

Planning phase
- What will be benchmarked?
- Who will be the benchmark companies?
- How will the data be collected?

Analysis phase
- Are the benchmarked companies better?
- If so, how much?
- Why are they better?
- How can we apply what we have learned to our business?

Integration phase
- Have the results been accepted by management?
- Do goals have to be changed or modified based on the results?
- Have these new goals been communicated to all affected parties?

Action phase
- Have the steps, required to achieve the desired goals, been identified?
- Is progress being tracked?
- Is there a plan for recalibration of the benchmarks?

The Xerox experience showed that if the first two phases—the most important in the benchmarking process—are carried out effectively, the benchmarking efforts will have a greater chance of success in the next two implementation phases.

BROAD BAND PAY PLAN

Broad banding is a pay structure form that leads to the consolidation of existing pay grades and pay ranges into fewer, but wider pay grades. Therefore, it is a pay structure that consolidates a large number of pay grades and salary ranges into much fewer but broader bands with relatively wide salary ranges. These ranges typically have 100 per cent or more differences between minimum and maximum.

The plan simplifies the classification of positions, increases the emphasis on market-based pay, and promotes competency-based human resource systems including compensation. It also provides flexibility for the adoption of other job and employee-based pay components. The plan is drawn for combining different grades of pay and employees are fitted to a particular level based on their performance criteria.

COMPONENTS OF EXECUTIVE COMPENSATION

Executive compensation packages typically comprise of the following components:
- base salary
- annual incentives
- long-term capital accumulation
- deferred compensation arrangements
- supplemental benefits and perquisites
- special severance and retirement arrangements
- employment and change of control agreements

However, the weightage for each component depends on organization-specific strategies. For example, Microsoft's executive compensation gives 15 per cent of total compensation weightage on base salary. Other components are carefully designed, pacing with the strategic needs time to time. Apple keeps substantial portion of executive compensation for deferral benefits, more in the form of stock options. Both the companies put substantial portion of their executive compensation at risk, that is, requiring executives to strive for their best performance to earn the compensation amount.

COMPENSATION TRENDS IN INDIA

Utilizing information on practices and trends in the corporate world, we can highlight the following salient features of employee compensation in India:
- There is a substantial difference in gross compensation for managers and their immediate subordinates.

- There is difference in gross compensation, and sometimes also in compensation structure, offered to the project and support functions.
- Companies design personalized salaries, out of a basket of options, for individuals at senior levels.
- There has been a significant increase in basic salary, and hence in deferred benefits.
- Companies have restricted non-tax perks, in the form of reimbursement under various heads, to certain top levels of management.
- Companies provide higher annual increments, average increments varying from 50 to 100 per cent (especially for the private sector organizations) to different levels of management.
- There has been a shift in incentives to group/team incentives from individual based incentives. Different kinds of incentives such as performance incentive, commission, performance payment, and performance bonus are not always individual specific. They are usually team-based. Individual-based cash incentives are on the decrease except at very senior levels.
- A soft furnishing allowance is provided towards the purchase of curtains, carpets, cutlery, and crockery. This is usually paid as an annual, non-taxable allowance.
- Most companies have abolished components such as servants' wages and utilities allowances, as they are not non-taxable any longer. Conveyance is an area which provides a lot of scope for variation. Practices with regard to provision of car, driver, and reimbursement of expenses on car, parking, cleaning, petrol, and maintenance are covered under this category.
- The practice of providing company-owned cars to employees is on a decline. Instead the company encourages employees to buy the cars themselves through hire-purchase schemes, and the instalments are then paid by the company. This is to combat the problem of accumulation of used cars by companies with a high employee turnover.
- Loan to buy two- and four-wheelers is a common practice. Interest rates may vary with the repayment period varying from three to five years.
- Medical benefits are common, with tie-ups with insurance companies and hospitals in many cases. Companies organize annual medical check-ups for all employees. In some companies, though rare, hospital expenses are also entirely reimbursed by the company, based on grade or age-level slabs.
- Some companies assist employees in their higher education by sponsoring evening classes or providing sabbaticals at company cost.
- Special interest-free loans up to ₹3 lakh are sometimes extended to employees.
- Companies reimburse cost of books, periodicals, newspapers, journals, etc. against a predetermined limit. Subscriptions to professional bodies are also reimbursed.
- Club memberships in the form of reimbursement of one-time joining fee for a club, plus the monthly/annual subscription to one or more clubs,

is an attractive perk for senior management. Companies also go for bulk corporate club memberships.
- Soft loans for purchase of furniture, appliances, and computers are also extended to employees by some organizations.
- Housing loan or interest subsidy is also provided.
- Companies reimburse travel expenses for holidays including accommodation in guest houses and transit flats. Increasingly, this is being extended to cover holidays abroad for senior employees and their families. In most cases, this is used as a discretionary reward for exemplary performances rather than as a perk.
- There is a trend of providing pre-employment benefits for attracting talent, including coverage of all relocation expenses for the family, transport of personal goods, assistance in locating housing, schooling, etc.
- Some components such as long-term paternity or maternity leave, as well as part and flexi-time employment options, are also available.
- The trend has shifted to making components direct and taxable. There is a distinct shift towards schemes for asset creation.
- Under profit-sharing schemes, senior executives sometimes share accrued profits if the company earns profits beyond a certain fixed level. The average share is 20 to 25 per cent of the excess profit.
- Companies also provide employees with stock options (ESOP).

EMPLOYEE REWARD SYSTEM IN INDIA

The components of the system are—processes, practices, structure, schemes, and procedures.

Processes These are used to measure the value of jobs, the worth of individuals in those jobs, and the range and level of employee benefits to be provided. These processes consist of job evaluation, market rate analysis, and performance management.

Practices These are used to motivate people by the use of financial and non-financial rewards. The financial rewards consist of base and variable pay, employee benefits, and allowances. Non-financial rewards are provided generally by the culture and values of the organization and more specifically by the quality of management and leadership, the work itself, and the opportunities given to employees to develop their skills and careers.

Structure These are used to link pay and benefit levels to the value of positions in the organization and to provide scope for rewarding people according to their performances, competence, skills, or experiences.

Schemes These provide financial rewards and incentives to people according to individual, group, or organizational performance.

Procedures These are used for maintaining the system and to ensure that it operates efficiently and flexibly, and provides value for money.

Elements of Employee Rewards in India

Base pay or (basic) pay is the level of pay (the fixed salary or wage) that constitutes the rate for the job. It may act as a platform for determining additional payments related to performance, competence, or skills. It may also govern pension and life insurance coverage entitlement. Base pay may be expressed as an annual, weekly, or hourly rate. It may be adjusted to reflect increases in the cost of living or market rates by the organization unilaterally, or by agreement with a trade union.

Additions to Base Pay

Additional financial rewards may be provided that are related to performance, skill, competence, or experience. Special allowances may also be paid. The main types of additional pay are—individual performance-related pay, bonus, incentives, commissions, etc.

Individual performance-related pay Increases in base pay or cash bonuses are determined by performance assessment and ratings (also known as merit pay).

Bonus It refers to reward, which is paid in cash, for successful performance, and is related to the results obtained by individuals, teams, or the organization.

Incentives It refers to payments linked with the achievement of previously set targets. These are designed to motivate people to achieve higher levels of performance. The targets are usually quantified in such terms as output or sales.

Commissions A special form of incentive in which sales representatives are paid on the basis of a percentage of the sales value they generate.

Service-related pay It increases by fixed increments on a scale or pay spine depending on the length of service. There may sometimes be scope for varying the rate of progress up the scale according to performance.

Skill-based pay Also known as knowledge-based pay, it varies according to the level of skill the individual achieves.

Competence-related pay It varies according to the level of competence achieved by the individual.

Career development pay It rewards people for taking on additional responsibilities as their career develops laterally within a broad grade (a broad-banded pay structure).

Allowances Elements of pay in the form of a separate sum of money for such aspects of employment as overtime, shift work, or call-outs.

Employee benefits These benefits are also known as indirect pay. These include pensions, sick pay, insurance cover, and company cars. Benefits comprise elements of remuneration in addition to the various forms of cash pay and also include provisions that are not strictly remuneration, like annual holidays.

Total remuneration It is the value of all cash payments (total earnings) and benefits received by employees.

Non-financial reward It includes any reward that focuses on the need people have in varying degrees, for achievement, recognition, responsibility, influence, and personal growth.

Employee Stock Options

Stock options are common in executive compensation. In some organizations, it even represents over half of the total compensation, particularly for senior managerial level employees. By offering stock options to employees, companies dilute their ownership; however, it helps them in retaining talent and in moving ahead of competition. Due to its significance as a component of compensation component, we have discussed employee stock options in detail in a separate chapter.

AIMS OF EMPLOYEE REWARDS IN INDIA

Aim of employee rewards in India varies from organization to organization. It depends primarily on their business priorities. However, in this chapter, we have presented such aims from different perspectives. Keeping in view organizational requirements, the overall aims of employee compensation are as follows:
- contribution to added value
- contribution to competitive advantage
- management of compensation and reward
- integration of individual employees' aims with the compensation and reward systems in the organization
- optimization of employee costs

The primary aim of employee rewards in India is to help in attaining organizational, strategic, and short-term objectives. This helps in ensuring the availability of skilled, competent, committed, and motivated people. Scientifically-designed employee reward systems focus on the improvement of individual employees and also help in developing a team. In the process, organizational performance improves, and organizations are better-equipped to add value, thus achieving a competitive advantage. Added value is the difference between the incomes arising out of sales (output) and the amount spent on materials and other inputs. Only employees (human resources) can ensure sustainable value addition because of its inimitable character.

It is the people at various hierarchical levels, who create vision and values, translate them into missions, set goals and objectives, develop strategies, and draw action plans, all of which add value to organizations. Therefore, efforts to enhance added value through effectively designed employee rewards, benefit the organization by promoting a culture of high performance.

Innovation, quality, and cost effectiveness are the three essential prerequisites of added value. All three depend on the people who are employed in the organization. The employees ensure added value through their performances, only when organizational reward strategies truly track performance results and integrate with overall goals and objectives through effective performance management systems. Effective employee rewards motivate people and keep them satisfied, which ultimately improves performances.

In India, most organizations consider employee rewards as the only way to reinforce performance improvement. However, this is not always true. We have many such examples of corporate failure, despite the higher level of employee rewards. This is more prevalent in organizations, which have a long history of existence.

We can cite the examples of Bata India and Phillips. Bata India, despite offering employee rewards that were much higher than the industry average, failed to improve its performance, and was ultimately forced to scale down its manufacturing facilities and start outsourcing to ensure cost efficiency. Phillips had to hive off CTV manufacturing, with the entry of Samsung and LG into India, despite its high expenses on employee rewards. Therefore, employee rewards alone cannot make a marked difference in performance, unless it is integrated with the culture, values, and style of management.

COMPENSATION PLAN

A compensation plan is a detailed component-wise break up of employees' compensation structure with information such as provisions of pay increase, payment of incentives, etc. For organizations, it may be often be necessary to have a formal or documented compensation plan, primarily for legal compliances. Also a documented compensation plan helps the organization to attract and retain talent. Each component of a compensation plan has different connotation when viewed from statutory and strategic perspective. A suitably designed compensation plan, mixing both strategic and statutory perspectives, optimizes the cost of compensation and simultaneously helps the organization achieve its strategic intent. The definition of the word compensation also extends to the amount of benefits accrued in a deferred benefit plan or the amount of contributions allocated to accounts for a deferred contribution plan. A well-designed compensation plan helps ensure equity within the organization. Any compensation plan has two important statutory connotations, qualified compensation plans and non-qualified compensation plans. *Qualified compensation plans* are tax-exempt and *non-qualified* compensation plans attract tax burdens. Hence, even while designing deferrals, the organization has to look into these aspects. Similarly from a strategic perspective, a compensation plan should emphasize employee retention, cost efficiency, and a performance-driven culture. The best way to set up compensation plans is to tie them directly to the costs of running the company.

Compensation Practices in India

Findings of salary surveys in India, carried over the years, confirm that employee compensation is still not considered a major strategic issue, despite its cost and added value aspects. This will be clearer once we refer to such surveys released from time to time by Mercer or Hewitt Associates. Some of the parameters considered by the organizations, while designing compensation are—internal equity, industry trend, retention, organizational performance (usually in terms of profits), market conditions, employees' performance, and market positioning.

Appendices 2A and 2B illustrate the trend in employee compensation practices in India using some sample employment contracts (restricted only to the compensation part).

Both the examples are drawn from corporate practices. However, in reality it may vary. While calculating cost to company (CTC), we find wide variation in corporate practices. The elements of the salary which are normally included in the CTC are basic pay, HRA, city compensatory allowances (CCA), other allowances (mobile reimbursement, medical reimbursement, provident fund contribution, and Employee State Insurance contribution), any fixed portion of compensation (usually paid as ex-gratia), food coupons, holiday package, furnishing items, etc. Therefore, CTC in reality can be defined as the annual total cost of compensation to the company. This is in contrast to the net pay or take-home pay. The net pay is the fixed amount that an employee gets in cash every month.

Mistakes in Compensation Designing

There are three mistakes that are commonly made while designing compensation packages. Firstly, organizations often find it difficult to distinguish between a bonus and an incentive. An incentive is linked with some measurable outcomes, whereas bonus is not. In compensation management literature, we treat bonus as a price for best efforts, which contributes to organizational efficiency. It is more productivity-linked and performance-driven. Hence, including bonus as compensation component (when it is not measurable) encourages employees to expect it as a right.

The second mistake in compensation design is the propensity of organizations to solve compensation claims on an ad hoc basis. Often, organizations tend to compromise with their talent by overpaying, thus creating an imbalance in internal pay equity. Therefore, it is better for the organization to adopt a strategic approach, while designing compensation for their employees.

The third mistake in compensation design occurs when organizations devise equity participation plans that are too complicated. A number of times organizations are confused about the nature of these plans. For example, they are unable to decide whether it should be an expensing option, sweat option, phantom stock, etc. This ultimately drains organizational resources.

SUMMARY

Organizations need to emulate best practices, continuously benchmark their compensation designs, and understand what works for them. Decisions on fixed and variable components of compensation need to be taken after considering numerous factors such as the nature of the job, company's business goals, product life cycle, performance management systems, etc. Choosing the right incentive plans is another important area of compensation design. There are various short-term and long-term incentive schemes that an organization can choose from. Taking into account its human resource strategy, the organization should choose an alternative which meet the cost–benefit test.

Key Term

Compensation benchmarking It is an exercise to study the degree of competitiveness of an organization's compensation rate and policies with reference to industry standards.

Exercises

Concept Review Questions

1. Define the term 'executive compensation'. What are the important components of executive compensation?
2. Discuss different theories of executive compensation.
3. Discuss the salient features of employee compensation in India.
4. Write short notes on:
   (a) Employee rewards
   (b) VIE theory and compensation management

Critical Thinking Question

A manufacturing organization has to recruit a large number of both skilled and unskilled workers. These workers are easily available given the present economic conditions. Your company believes there is no need to pay the workers above the minimum wage set by the state government. However, you personally feel that since the company is capable of paying more (due to high profit margins and a sound financial position), fair wages should be paid to the workers. Provide your arguments accordingly.

CASE STUDY: Two Centurions Grow with a Difference in Compensation Strategy

Murugappa Group and ITC follow compensation strategies that are characteristically different. Murugappa Group is a family managed business entity with business turnover of ₹22,314 Crores. ITC on the other hand is a corporatized business entity with a business turnover of ₹36,000 cores. Both the companies are in business for more than 100 years. ITC started in 1910 and has present employee strength of 24,027; whereas the Murugappa Group, which started in 1900 has an employee strength of 32,000. One thing

(Contd)

CASE STUDY (*Contd*)

common in case of both the companies is their diversified business portfolio and impressive track record of growth.

Murugappa Group's compensation strategies are based on the performance of the individual. Individual performances are classified through quantifiable/objective measures. The company makes performance rating as under

- Exceptional contribution
- Significant contribution
- Good contribution
- Not meeting the requirements
- Not suitable

The incentives, a part of the compensation and linked to individual balanced scorecard, helped the company to initiate the process of

- Rewarding stretch, effort, and risk-taking
- Encouraging inter-functional and organizational perspective
- Providing thrust to sustainable processes
- Giving impetus to innovation and learning

Also certain incentives are paid based on the company's and SBU's results interpreted from organizational and SBU level balanced scorecards.

The compensation strategy of the group is further powered by rewards and recognition schemes such as Kaizen scheme, suggestion scheme, Q-Man award, Best Sales Engineer award, and Muthiah Memorial Best Performance award.

The Kaizen scheme encourages and recognizes management staff for their participation and contribution in work/method/productivity improvement and cost reduction exercises, which benefit the organization. This is aligned to individual contribution. The suggestion scheme encourages and recognizes employees for their participation and contribution in work/method/ productivity improvement and cost reduction exercises. This scheme again is aligned to individual contribution of all operators. The Q-Man award scheme is again designed for the staff members for their individual contribution to work/method/productivity improvement and cost reduction exercises. The Best Sales Engineer award recognizes the contribution of supervisory staff and management staff for their exceptional work. Muthiah Memorial Best Performance Award recognizes the breakthrough activities of all managerial and non-managerial employees that have benefited the organization.

The compensation of the managing director comprises of a fixed component and a performance incentive based on certain pre-agreed parameters. The compensation is determined based on level of responsibility and scales prevailing in the industry. The managing director is not paid sitting fees for any Board/Committee meetings attended by him.

The compensation of the non-executive directors takes the form of commission on profits. Though the shareholders have approved payment of commission up to 1 per cent of net profits of the Company for each year calculated as per the provisions of the Companies Act 1956, the actual commission paid to the directors is restricted to a fixed sum. This sum is reviewed periodically taking into consideration various factors such as performance of the Company, time spent by the directors for attending to the affairs and business of the company, extent of responsibilities cast on directors under general law and other relevant factors. Further, the aggregate commission paid to all non-executive directors is within the limit of 1 per cent of the net profits as approved by the shareholders. The non-executive directors are also paid

(*Contd*)

CASE STUDY *(Contd)*

sitting fees within the limits set by government regulations for every Board/Committee meeting attended by them. Employee Stock Options, as part of compensation, is restricted for those managerial employees whose job roles are critical for the company.

ITC's compensation strategy is anchored in three basic principles: market-led, performance leveraged, and the capacity to pay. Compensation is benchmarked with identified comparator organizations and reviewed periodically. Apart from the monetary component which comprises consolidated salary and supplementary allowance, managers are provided with quality accommodation, medical assistance for self and family, leave travel assistance, etc. At middle and senior levels, managers are provided with company maintained cars and the facility of a club membership for business purposes. All managers are members of ITC's retirement funds, the pension scheme being one of the most attractive in the country. Other benefits include the facility of holiday homes, assistance for further education/self development, etc.

The cornerstone of the performance management system is the appraisal system. The individual agrees to performance objectives at the beginning of the year with his superior(s). These objectives naturally flow from the objectives of the unit/business. At the end of the year, the individual's performance is assessed against the objectives set. The appraisal attaches as much importance to 'how' results were achieved, as to the results themselves. The rating is determined by the manager's boss and endorsed by his boss. Therefore, two individuals are involved in assessing a manager's performance. The appraisal process also gives the individual an opportunity to share, in a formal manner, his own career aspirations and what the individual needs from the organization to enhance his own development. Based on an assessment of development needs, a development plan is drawn up for each manager. Remuneration changes are made once every year based on the performance rating of the individual. The entire process is transparent and objective.

Some of the specific elements of ITC's compensation strategies are based on following principles:
- Domain expertise
- Proven capabilities
- Best of breed talent
- Small enough to care and big enough to dare
- Commitment beyond market

Domain expertise is measured based on the job position analysis. Proven capabilities account for global delivery capabilities, world class technical strengths, infrastructure, and solutions that address customers' pain areas. Best of breed talent considers agility and adaptability, leadership qualities, and capability to embrace the empowered job roles. 'Small enough to care and big enough to dare' is measured on relationship flexibility beyond strategic relationship, ability to invest in building long-term and fast-scaling strategic partnerships, stability, strength, and strong corporate governance. Commitment beyond market counts on triple bottom line reporting on economic, ecological, and social dimensions, and green partnership. Selective employee stock options as compensation top-up are also an important part of ITC's compensation strategy.

Discussion question

List the differences in the compensation strategies of these two centurion companies.

References

Porter, L.W. and E. E. Lawler (1968), *Managerial Attitudes and Performance*, Irwin-Dosey, Holmewood.

Vroom, Victor (1964), *Work and Motivation*, Wiley, New York.

APPENDIX 2A Best Practices—Functional Managers in HR/Finance

HR head	Finance head
Qualification: Post-graduates, preferably MBAs *Experience*: More than five years *Responsibilities*: • Manage the HR function of the SBU/division/region/zone • Frame strategies on sourcing • Develop and retain people • Play a crucial role in business strategy formulation and implementation • Support change management	*Qualification*: CA/MBA(Finance) *Experience*: Seven to eight years *Responsibilities*: • Manage the finance of SBU/division/region/zone • Contribute to sourcing funds • Mobilization of resources • Financial management, working capital management, planning, and control
Benefits: HRA (50 to 60 per cent of basic), house lease of ₹10,000–15,000 per month, or leased accommodation.	Same
Conveyance: Company buys a car within the sanctioned limit, with compulsory buy back after five years. In this case, the company maintains the car. However, when the cost of care is above the sanctioned limit, the company will fund the difference and charge interest on such amount.	Same
Medical: Group medical for self, wife, and two children not exceeding ₹2 lakh.	Same
LTA: One to two months' basic pay	Same
ESOPS: Share save scheme for more than one-year service. Company deposits the ESOP equivalent amount in bank to earn interest and pays a sizable amount at the end of three years	Same
Incentive schemes *Performance incentive*: Six–twelve months' salary on a four-scale rating *Annual performance incentive*: 40–50 per cent of basic salary *Bonus*: 20 per cent basic as bonus *Travel*: Free two-way airline ticket, to anywhere in the world	Same
Co-curricular activities • Cultural programmes, sports, etc. • In-house magazines • Picnic with family • Open chat with MD • Annual ball	Same
Other benefits Credit cards, club membership, and telephones are not part of the CTC	Same
Loans *General loan*: After six months with an interest subsidy of 2–4 per cent *Housing loan*: ₹3–5 lakh with 6 per cent interest *Car loan*: Up to 2 lakh at 6 per cent interest *Furniture*: Up to ₹90,000 *White goods*: AC and other amenities and only 10 per cent value charged *Soft furnishing*: Provided *Deferrals*: Provident fund (12 per cent of basic + DA), gratuity (4.8 per cent), and superannuation (15 per cent).	Same

APPENDIX 2B Best Practices—Compensation in Call Centres

Level	Asst manager and section manager
Entry procedures	Graduate/Post-graduate. (Technical back-ground in IT essential)
Requirements	• Three to five years of experience • Team player • Excellent managerial and supervisory capabilities • Analytical • Excellent communication skills
Responsibilities	• Handle a team of ten to fifteen people • Coordinate their activities and schedule project implementation • Plan
Work timing	Two to three shifts five days a week
Training	*Induction*: Three to seven days *Periodic training*: Three to four days per year per person
HRA	50–60 per cent of basic pay
Conveyance	₹800 per month
Medical	Group medical insurance for parents, spouse, and two children up to ₹2 lakh; ₹15,000 per annum
Deferrals	PF: 12 per cent; Gratuity: 4.8 per cent; Superannuation: 13 per cent
LTA	One month' basic pay
Loans	• General loan after six months with an interest subsidy of 2–4 per cent • ₹10,000 per year interest free
Rewards	• Cash award for consistent performer • Cash award, certificate, and medal once a month for the best team • Yearly best team award
ESOPS	• Share save scheme for more than one-year service • Company deposits the ESOP equivalent amount in the bank to earn interest and pays sizable amounts at the end of three years
Incentive Schemes	• Annual performance incentive 10–15 per cent of basic salary • Free two-way airline ticket, to anywhere in the world • Birthday dinner coupons • Shift allowance for night shift • 7 per cent basic as bonus per annum • Mobile phones
Utilities	• Tea, coffee, and free cool drinks throughout the day • Free transport door-to-door • Subsidized canteen or Sodexo lunch coupons worth ₹850 per month
Co-curricular activities	• Cultural programmes • Sports • In-house magazines • Picnic with family • Team outing • Open chat with MD • Annual ball • Event tickets once a month • Adoption of a village

CHAPTER THREE

Employee Compensation and the Labour Market

Learning Objectives

After reading this chapter, you will be able to
- understand the macro and micro perspectives of the labour market
- discuss the concept and implications of labour market flexibility
- analyse unemployment, its impact on the labour market, and compensation issues
- understand the supply and demand side of labour market
- learn about labour market changes and role of trade unions
- evaluate labour market policies in India

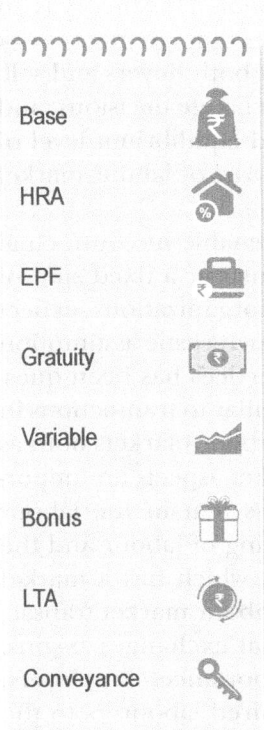

OPENING CASE

Infosys Technologies and TCS: A Comparison of Employee Costs

Infosys and TCS are two Indian software majors, both operating at the highest competitive level. Optimizing employee costs has been a major strategic challenge for both organizations. Even though N.R. Narayana Murthy, Chief Mentor of Infosys, and S. Ramadorai, CEO and Managing Director of TCS, may not have concurred on the exact approach to employee retention, they, for certain, would have agreed that designing compensation that optimized employee costs, and at the same time enhanced employee retention was a core issue. An employee's decision to switch from one organization to another depends upon a number of factors including the nature of their job and line of business. A major factor in their decision is the financial gains that they would accrue from such a move.

In the financial year 2006, the annual compensation of Infosys employees went up by 34.7 per cent against TCS's 32 per cent. The increase in employee costs for Infosys (34.7 per cent) was higher than the increase in compensation for Murthy and Nadan Nilekani, CEO of

Infosys (30 per cent). The increase in the compensation of Ramadorai for the same period was 100 per cent. The average annual cost per employee was ₹8.14 lakh for TCS and ₹7.24 lakh for Infosys. In both cases, the salary increase in real terms was around 5–15 per cent, depending on hierarchical and functional levels. The rest of the cost could be attributed to increase in other HR costs such as benefits, employment taxes, and recruiting expenses; cost of operating space; and cost of buying/maintaining equipment and services such as computer, telephone, and transport.

Source: Adapted from *The Financial Express*, 7 June 2006

INTRODUCTION

From the neoclassical perspective of labour economics, we have a demand for and supply of labour services in the labour market. Labour services are traded in this market, like any other product or service. The price for labour services is wages or compensation, the determination of which is done by the market forces, that is, the demand for and supply of labour. This theory is an extension of the rational workers concept, which assumes that labourers work solely for money. The rational concept also assumes that both buyers and sellers of labour services compete in a market for mutual exchange decisions, and such decisions determine the equilibrium wage rate and equilibrium level of employment. Therefore, these concepts are an integral part of labour market analysis and concept.

However, in theory, such precepts are usually more tenable in contractual employment relations, especially tenure-track assignments for a fixed sum of money. In institutional employment relations, where organizations expect their people to stay on and partner the growth process, such rustic assumption of market-mediated exchange for the price of labour services has been questioned. Labour market transactions may not always be similar to transactions in commodity markets. This is because workers appear in labour markets both as subjects and objects, and both the market and non-market aspects are important in employment relations. Pencavel (1991) suggests that in the labour market, exchange takes place in two distinct stages—hiring of labour and the actual exchange. Immediately after the hiring process, which has a market dimension, the non-market and non-wage attributes of labour market transactions, that is, the conversion of hired raw labour (actual exchange) begins. In this conversion stage, market dimension loses importance. Employers, that is, the buyers of labour services, now must adjust hired labourers to the production process, employing their efforts, quality workmanship, skills, and knowledge. Stiglitz (2000) thus appropriately said, 'Labour is not like other factors. Workers have to be motivated to perform.' Hence, we cannot ignore social values in the labour market. Social values have overriding priority over individual decisions.

Labour markets (in the context of labour economics) can be analysed from both the microeconomic and macroeconomic perspectives. Microeconomic perspectives study the role of individuals in the labour market, whereas macroeconomic perspectives study labour market interrelations with other markets, primarily to assess how such interrelations can influence macro variables such as employment, participation, aggregate income, and gross domestic product.

MACROECONOMICS OF LABOUR MARKETS

In any labour market, the available labour force includes both the employed and those who are unemployed but economically active. Economically active labour constitutes those individuals who are capable of offering their labour services. International Labour Organization (ILO) defines them as those who are in the 15–65 age group. In India, however, the definition of economically active labour only has a lower limit. People who have reached the age of 18 are considered as economically active; there is no such official upper age limit, as retirement ages vary from 58–70 years. The labour participation rate is the number of people in the labour force divided by the total economically active population. Non-labour forces are those individuals who do not participate in the labour market, for one reason or the other. For example, an economically active person may prefer to stay away from the labour market, in order to look after their children. The rate of employment is defined as those who are employed, divided by the population in the working age group. We also consider self-employed persons as employed.

Employment level, unemployment level, labour force, and unfilled vacancies are stock variables, as they indicate the quantity of labour available at a given point of time. These may be contrasted with the flow variables, that is, the natural population growth, net immigration, new entrants, and retirees from the labour force.

Ageing population

Ageing employees is a phenomenon common in countries with low birth rate and high life expectancy. At the macro-level, it causes many economic, social, and, political challenges. At the organizational level, it results in renewed attention to manpower replacement, compensation restructuring, succession planning, etc.

Labour market flexibility

Another important macroeconomic characteristic is the evidence of flexible labour markets. Economic flexibility is basically the ability to respond to economic change efficiently and quickly while safeguarding a degree of fairness. In a flexible labour market, the degree of occupational or functional flexibility increases, as workers become multi-skilled. With such transferable skills, workers can move from one job to another. In this era of technological advancement, the transfer of skills is further made easier by the similarities of computer-aided technologies. Individuals are now able to adapt more quickly to changing job requirements. Labour market flexibility also provides contractual flexibility. Organizations can hire people for a specific time frame and can get rid of them after the contract expires. It provides wage flexibility, introducing performance-related pay. Finally, geographical flexibility also increases, as workers move from one place to another. Some of the advantages of a flexible labour market are as follows:

- flexible wages and employment, which helps the organization remain lean
- increased occupational mobility, helping to reduce structural unemployment
- increased employment generation
- increased inflow of investment
- higher rate of growth in the long run
- better trade-off between inflation and unemployment

There are also some disadvantages of the flexible labour market enumerated as follows:

- lack of training for workers (this happens when companies engage labour for a short time frame), leading to increase in skill gaps
- increase in job insecurity for short-term employment contracts

UNEMPLOYMENT AND ITS IMPACT ON LABOUR MARKET

Before we initiate a discussion on unemployment and its impact on labour market, it is important for us to understand the various types of unemployment.

Types of Unemployment

A very common form of unemployment is seasonal unemployment. It is a situation where a person is employed only a part of the year. Some industries such as hotel and catering, tourism, and agro-based processing units are more prone to seasonal unemployment. The seasonal pattern of these industries can be attributed to fluctuations in the weather or demand patterns. Frictional or search unemployment occurs in transition phase, when people move from one job to another. Due to the lack of information about jobs, it often requires time to search for a new job. The longer the time duration, the higher will be the rate of frictional unemployment. A good illustration of frictional unemployment is the entry of redundant manpower in the job market. Imperfect labour market information increases the rate of frictional unemployment as the jobless remain unaware of a number of job opportunities available in the market.

Technological advancements aiding the flow of information can help substantially reduce frictional unemployment.

One other major form of unemployment is structural unemployment. It occurs when there is a change in the structure of the industry. For example, the Indian economy has experienced a structural shift, moving from manufacturing to service industries. This has caused large-scale unemployment in the manufacturing sector. Structural shifts may also lead to a decrease in demand for some products due to the availability of substitutes, or because of technological changes, both of which render available skill set(s) of existing workforce redundant. Historically, the primary reason for structural unemployment has been capital–labour substitution. This also leads to occupational immobility. In our country, unemployment in heavy industries can be attributed to this type of unemployment. Immobility of labour, pace of change in the economy, regional structure of the economy, etc. are all the effects of structural unemployment.

Apart from these, cyclical and natural unemployment are also common. Cyclical unemployment mostly results due to business recessions. According to Keynesian economics, an insufficient demand in the economy leads to cyclical unemployment. During recession, a deficiency in aggregate expenditure leads to the under-utilization of inputs (including labour). In simple economic logic, aggregate expenditure (AE) can be increased by increasing the consumption expenditure (C), investment spending (I), government spending (G), or the net of exports minus imports (X – M). This can be represented by using the formula

$$AE = C + I + G + (X - M)$$

Natural unemployment, which prevails in the long run, is the summation of frictional and structural unemployment.

Often, we witness the phenomenon of real wage or *classical unemployment* in the economy. This type of unemployment occurs due to disequilibrium between the real wages and jobs, sometimes prompted by trade unions or other labour institutions. In India, since the mid-1980s, we have experienced this type of phenomenon. Even today, in some industries, the demand of workers for payment of real wages above the market-clearing level requires firms to practise lean management, scaling down their labour requirements.

Causes of Unemployment

An economic interpretation of the causes of unemployment can be divided into two types—demand side and supply side. Demand side unemployment is simply the result of a lack of aggregate demand. Supply side unemployment is due to imperfections in the labour market. In a perfect labour market, all those who are looking for work will be working, and hence labour supply will match labour demand. In an imperfect labour market, unemployment will prevail, as wages will not scale down to market requirements. Firms will refrain from hiring.

The supply-side unemployment may also be because of occupational or geographical immobility.

The Phillips curve, propounded by A.W. Phillips, correctly drew the relationship between inflation and unemployment. His observations were based on the changes in the wage level between 1861 and 1957. He observed a trade-off between unemployment and inflation, and accordingly concluded that if the government wanted to reduce unemployment, it would lead to increased inflation. Hence, any attempt by governments to reduce unemployment is likely to lead to increased inflation. The economic stagflation (when unemployment and inflation both rise together) in the 1970s, however negated this theory, and resulted in the development of the expectations-augmented Phillips curve by Milton Friedman.

Costs of Unemployment

Those who remain unemployed are the first to face the brunt of the cost of unemployment. The collective suffering of unemployed people affects the economy as a whole. Prolonged unemployment makes people unemployable, as they lose their self-esteem and confidence, while their skills and knowledge become outdated. The macroeconomic effects of unemployment have been listed in this section.

Corresponding loss of output to the economy Increased unemployment lowers the gross domestic product (GDP).

Corresponding loss of tax revenue Government loses tax revenue when people remain unemployed.

Corresponding increase in government expenditure Along with the loss of tax revenue, government also has to spend more on support expenditure. Currently, unemployment allowances support the unemployed.

Corresponding loss of profits With increased employment, companies can scale up their activities, which leads to increased profits. Hence, companies also suffer from the increased rate of unemployment.

Therefore, unemployment not only affects labour market issues, but it also affects the economy as a whole.

Unemployment Rate

Unemployment rate (UR) is the per cent of the labour force that remains unemployed, and it can be computed using the following formula:

$$UR = \frac{\text{Number of unemployed}}{\text{Number in labour force}} \times 100$$

Labour force participation rate (LFPR) is the percentage of economically active population in the labour force, and can be estimated by using the following formula:

$$\text{LFPR} = \frac{\text{Number in labour force}}{\text{Number in population (economically active)}} \times 100$$

Along with the problem of unemployment, we also have the problem of underemployment, which occurs because of the mismatch of jobs and skill sets (either over or under) of individuals.

NEOCLASSICAL MICROECONOMICS OF LABOUR MARKETS

We have already understood the differences about the labour markets in the views of economists and others. Although economists view the labour market like any other market, where demand and supply jointly determine the price (wage rate) and the quantity of labour; the labour market per se is different from other markets in several ways. In commodity markets, when the price is high, firms usually increase their production until the demand is fully satisfied. In the labour market, however, the overall supply of labour cannot be significantly altered. This is because of the limited availability of time, in terms of man days, as the number of people cannot be increased. Similarly, with the increase in the price of labour (wages), the supply of labour need not necessarily rise, as workers may like to take more time off if wages are increased.

Another assumption about the labour market (in absence of laws and labour unions) is that it can be perfectly competitive when both workers and employers make an informed decision to sell or buy the labour, and there will not be any transaction costs. Just as in a perfectly competitive market, firms can only make marginal profit, so in a perfectly competitive labour market, workers can only earn their marginal wages.

INTERNAL LABOUR MARKET AS AN INSTITUTION

Large organizations develop an internal labour market. The internal labour market determines the pricing and allocation of labour, using a set of rules and procedures, rather than allowing determination by market forces. Within organizations, we find a structure, which explains hierarchies, jobs, tasks, skills, and the job ladder. All these are governed by certain rules and processes, independent of the labour markets' influence. The internal labour market institutionalizes work practices, reaching an agreement with unions, governments, and employers. This reduces the role of market forces as determinants of wages and employment. The efficiency of internal labour markets can be better understood in the context of human capital theory. In organizations, we sometimes observe even a 50 per cent or more variation in the employee compensation structure, which can be sustained without considering the effect of market forces.

NEOCLASSICAL MICROECONOMIC MODEL—SUPPLY

In microeconomics, it is assumed that people are rational and always seek to multiply their utility function. In the labour market framework, utility is determined by the choice between income and leisure, and constrained by available working hours. We can denote it as under:

$$\max U(wL + \Pi, A) \text{ such that } L + A \leq k$$

where, w = hourly wage; k = total waking hours; L = working hours; Π = other incomes or benefits; A = leisure hours

The utility function and budget constraint can be expressed using Fig. 3.1. The curve indicates the combinations of leisure and work that provide an individual a defined level of utility. The point where the highest indifference curve is just tangential to the constraint line (point A) illustrates the short-run equilibrium for this supplier of labour services.

The slope of the budget constraint represents the wage rate. The optimization point (A) shows the equivalency between the wage rate and the marginal rate of substitution of leisure for income (the slope of the indifference curve). As the marginal rate of substitution, leisure for income also represents the ratio of the marginal utility of leisure (MUL) to the marginal utility of income (MUY). It can be represented as:

$$\frac{MU^L}{MU^Y} = \frac{dY}{dL}$$

Accordingly, we can draw the curve as in Fig. 3.2 to represent its effect on wage increase.

When the wage increases, so does the constraint line of individuals. If wages increase, this individual's constraint line moves up from X,Y_1 to X,Y_2. Individuals

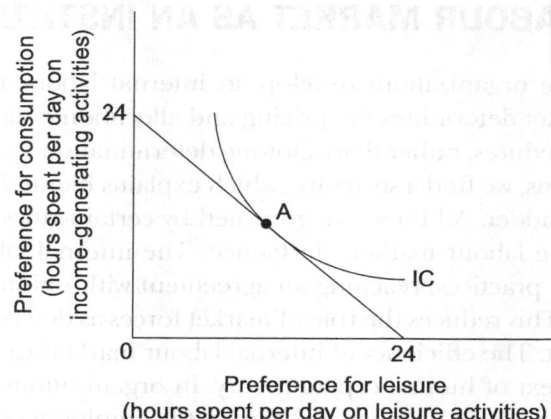

FIG. 3.1 Income/leisure trade-off in the short run

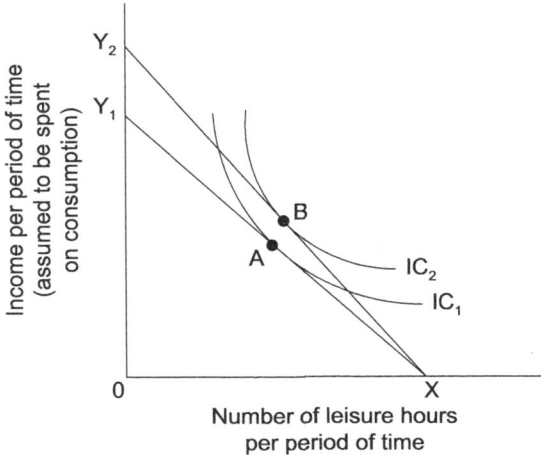

FIG. 3.2 Marginal utility of income/leisure and its effects on wages

can now purchase more goods and services, and his utility increases from point A on IC_1 to point B on IC_2. Hence, to measure the effect of individuals' decision on hours of work, we need to look at the income effect and substitution effect.

The wage increase can be divided into two separate effects, as per Fig. 3.3. The pure income effect is shown as the movement from point A to point C in Fig. 3.3. Consumption increases from Y_A to Y_C and—assuming leisure is a normal good—leisure time increases from X_A to X_C, and so does the employment time. Therefore, with the increase in wages, workers will prefer to substitute work hours for leisure hours to take advantage of higher wage rates. This is because of an increase in opportunity costs. This effect of substitution is represented by the shift from point C to point B, and the net effect is a shift from point

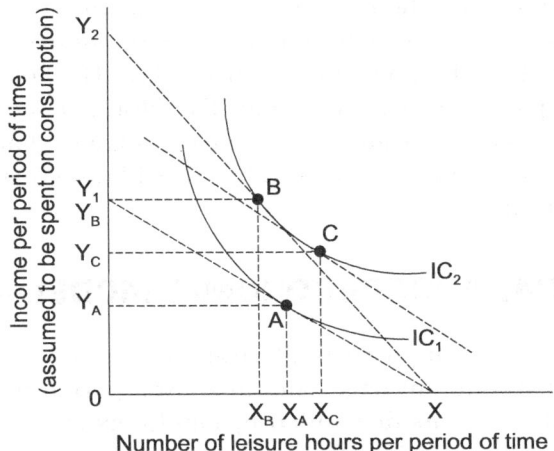

FIG. 3.3 Income and substitution effects of a wage increase

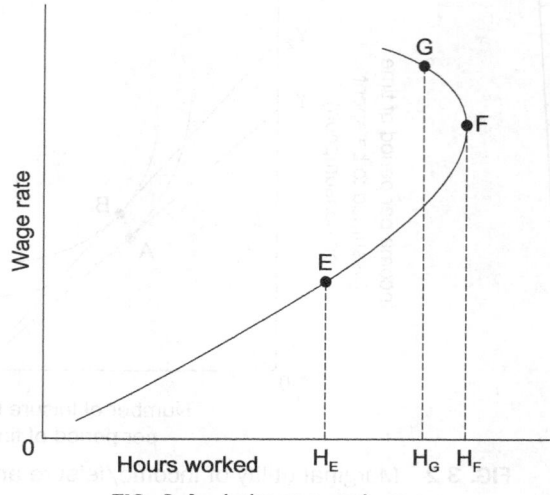

FIG. 3.4 Labour supply curve

A to point B. Therefore, this diagram represents two effects: the first, when substitution effect is greater than the income effect (in which case more time is allocated to working), and the second, when the income effect is greater than the substitution effect (in which case less time is allocated to working). In the second situation, the workers' marginal utility of leisure outweighs the marginal utility of income. In simplistic terms, when workers do not have time to spend, they cannot have time to earn more money. Figure 3.4 represents labour supply curve, within the framework of substitution effect and income effect.

When the substitution effect is greater than the income effect, the labour supply curve slopes upwards to the right as shown at point E in Fig. 3.4. This will continue to increase. That is, the supply of labour services will continue to increase, with the increase of the wage rate up to point F. Beyond this point, workers will reduce the amount of labour hours; for example, at point G, workers reduce the hours worked from H_F to H_G. For this reason, the supply curve is sloping upwards to the right. Therefore, we see the positive wage elasticity of labour supply, as substitution effect is greater than the income effect. Workers can also be influenced by other variables such as taxation, welfare, and work environment.

NEOCLASSICAL MICROECONOMIC MODEL—DEMAND

The labour supply curve illustrates the workers' willingness to put in hours of work at different wage rates in a given period of time. However, the quantity of labour hours demanded by employers at a given wage rate per period of time will depend on the product function. This is because labour demand is a derived demand, and depends on output levels in the market. Employers'

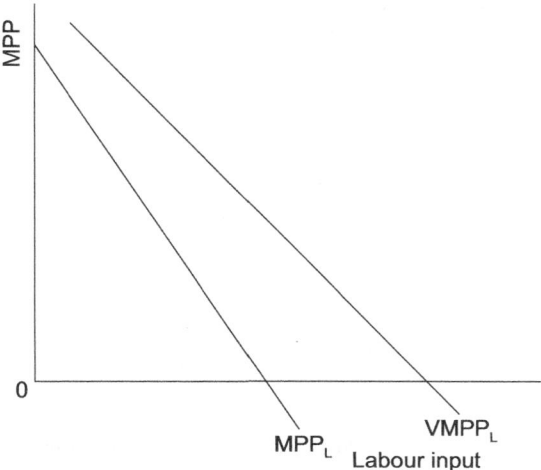

FIG. 3.5 Marginal physical product of labour

labour demand depends on the marginal physical product of labour (MPP_L), that is, the additional output that results from the increase in one unit of labour. We can illustrate this using Fig. 3.5.

With the increase in the range of outputs, the marginal physical product of labour declines. This means that with the engagement of more and more labour units, the additional output begins to decline. The slope of the MPP_L curve to the right indicates this. When the marginal physical product of labour is multiplied by the value of the output, we get the value of the marginal physical product of labour ($VMPP_L$).

$$MPP_L \times P_Q = VMPP_L$$

Therefore, $VMPP_L$ represents the value of the additional output produced by an additional unit of labour. In perfect competition, $VMPP_L$ equals the marginal revenue product of labour (MRP_L). The logic behind this is that in competitive markets, price equals the marginal revenue ($MRP = MPP \times MR$). Let us further discuss this issue in Fig. 3.6.

In a perfectly competitive market, the marginal revenue product of labour is used as the demand for labour in the short run. The elasticity of the supply of labour corresponds to the wage rate and the marginal resource cost of labour.

$$W = S_L = MFC_L$$

In imperfect markets, however, the variables in the Fig. 3.6 require adjustment as MFCL would be equal to the wage rate divided by the marginal costs. So, the firm will demand L units of labour for adopting an optimum resource allocation strategy, which requires marginal factor cost to be equal to marginal revenue product.

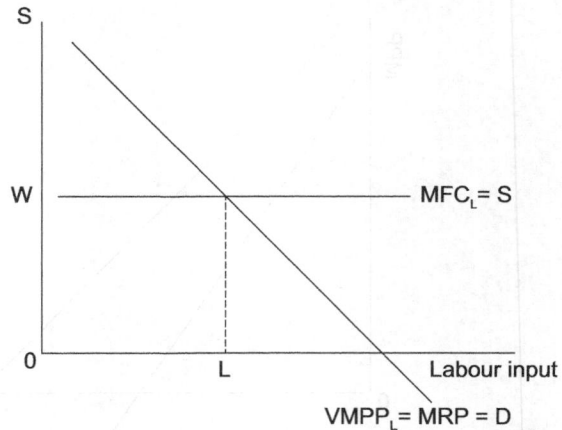

FIG. 3.6 Labour demand in the short run

Therefore, the neoclassical microeconomic model of labour market reaches equilibrium, summing up the demand for labour of all firms in the economy. This represents the aggregate demand for labour. Similarly, using the aggregate supply of labour, we can determine the equilibrium level of wages and employment level.

IMPLICATIONS OF ECONOMIC MODELS OF LABOUR MARKETS ON EMPLOYEE COMPENSATION

Although an economic interpretation of equilibrium of wages and employment level can be arrived at using our foregoing discussions, operationally organizations must consider various other aspects when making compensation decisions. A simple example of this would be the need to differentiate between hard-working and slow-working workers. At the entry level, both are recruited with a common compensation level. However, the productivity rates of these two types of workers are different. Although firms can vary the compensation between these two types of workers using various incentives and stock options, this may not always help the firm protect its interests. Employees who have accumulated stock options can over-inflate share values to further their personal gain. So, an imperfect knowledge about workers' ability may cost the organization dearly.

CRITICISMS OF LABOUR ECONOMICS

A major criticism of the economic analysis of labour markets is that it does not consider social issues. Individual employment decision of workers involves several social and emotional factors. Firms also take recruitment decisions based on various non-economic issues apart from the economic ones. Similarly, labour economics ignores the contribution of unpaid labour. Technically, future labour supply largely depends on the efforts of unpaid labour in our families, especially child bearing and rearing. Hence labour economics, *per se*, does not address all labour related issues, or compensation designing decisions.

LABOUR MARKET CHANGES AND TRADE UNIONS

The presence and activities of trade unions affects the labour market function. In this section, we have highlighted the labour market changes with respect to trade unions' response.

Role of Trade Unions

The traditional role of trade unions was to protect jobs and real earnings. Trade unions secure better work and living conditions for workers, while fighting against possible exploitation. Their core purpose is to ensure fairness and equity in employment. However, in recent times, this protective role of trade unions has changed. Currently, the protective role of trade unions is under debate, as now trade unions are increasingly expected to work as moral institutions. Globally, opinion on trade unions is hostile not because people are opposed to trade unions in principle, but because of the way today's trade unions and trade union leaders function. The membership of trade unions is decreasing sharply in India and abroad. In France, the density of union membership is only 10 per cent. In Holland, such density is around 25 per cent. In England, it is 44 per cent. In the United States, density is 16 per cent. In Japan, it is 25 per cent. In India, trade union density is as low as 10 per cent. Membership of the trade unions is dwindling globally except in countries such as Sweden (91 per cent), Denmark (82 per cent), and Norway (63 per cent). Trade unions are socially respected in Norway, Denmark, and Sweden; and they participate in state decision-making.

Trade Unions in India

The trade union movement in India is over a century old. The following statistical information will provide a basic idea about the state of Indian trade unions. The Indian workforce of ₹31.479 crore (₹314.79 million) constitutes 37.3 per cent of the total population. Of the total workforce, 91.5 per cent is accounted for by the unorganized sector, whereas the organized sector accounts for a mere 8.5 per cent. Further, only about ₹3 crore (30 million), or 9.5 per cent of the workforce, are employed on a permanent basis, implying that 90.5 per cent are being employed on a casual basis. It has also been reported that in December 1991, the claimed membership of the Indian trade union movement was ₹3.05 crore (₹30.5 million), or 9.68 per cent of the workforce.

With 82.24 per cent of the trade union membership being accounted for by the organized sector whereas, the unorganized sector is poorly represented in trade unions.

The World Labour Report (1992) summarizes the trade union situation in India, 'Indian unions are very fragmented. In many work places several trade unions compete for the loyalty of the same body of workers and their rivalry is usually bitter and sometimes violent. It is difficult to say how many trade unions operate at the national level since many are not affiliated to any all-India federation. The early splits in Indian trade unionism tended to be on ideological grounds, each linked to a particular political party. Much of the recent fragmentation, however, has centered around personalities and occasionally on caste or regional considerations.'

Apart from low coverage and fragmentation of trade unions, several studies point to a decline in membership and growing alienation between trade unions and members. These are particularly due to changing characteristics of the new workforce, who are more influenced by enterprise level unions than unions with national affiliations. Several studies indicate a shift in employment from the organized to the unorganized sector through subcontracting. Another employment practice that has emerged is that contractual relationships are more typical than institutional relationships.

Unfortunately, trade unionism in India suffers from a variety of problems, such as politicization of unions, multiplicity of unions, inter-union rivalry, uneconomic size, financial weakness, and dependence on outside leadership.

In the post-globalization phase, there has been a sea change in organization and work procedures. There are three major drivers of such change—technology (more particularly information technology), structural changes in the economy, and the competitive pressure. Technological changes have altered the demand for products and work processes, bringing about a significant shift in the size and the composition of the workforce. With the advancement of information technology, jobs in organizations have come to be divided into core and non-core, facilitating the outsourcing of many non-core jobs. With more and more IT applications and various other technological changes in the work process, jobs have become unstable in the organized sector. All this has lead to the increase in casual, part-time, contract, non-standard, and other forms of insecure work.

Secondly, structural changes in the economy facilitate free flow of goods and services among countries. In the process, some industries emerge as winners, whereas others as losers. In both cases, workers become the first casualty as organizations initiate internal structural changes through mergers and acquisitions, consolidation, changing the product lines, changing business focus, etc. Thompson TV's withdrawal from CTV production, hiving their activities off to Videocon India, is an example of a change in business focus. Even after selling its stake, Thompson continues to focus on plasma and LCDs. With these restructuring and consolidations, organizations are getting bigger and bigger, but they are also reducing their regular work force, increasing subcontracting, and hiring more casual labour.

Thirdly, with the increase in competitive pressure, organizations are required to constantly adjust to survive, be it the domestic or the global market. Such adjustment prompts organizations to relocate their manufacturing to countries like China where labour costs are relatively cheaper. This leads to the scaling down of workforce to the bare minimum. Despite protective labour laws, flexible or casual labour is now widespread in India.

Hence in the post-reforms period, the labour market in India has significantly changed. This has not only altered employment relations (which have shifted from institutional to contractual), but also weakened bargaining power available to labour through the trade unions, as the organizations can scale down their dependence on labour cost through job outsourcing.

Labour Market Policies in India

India has strong labour laws and stringent provisions to ensure compliance with those laws. In principle, the fundamental rights of workers are well accepted and protected. The report of the Second National Commission is more vocal on this issue. The Fundamental Rights enshrined in the Constitution of India include: Right to Equality (Article 14–18); Right to Freedom (Article 19–22); and Right against Exploitation (Article 23–24). In addition, we have the Directive Principles of State Policy (DPSP) enshrined in the Constitution, which mandate state action to secure a social order for the promotion of welfare of people (Article 28). Apart from these, the ILO declaration on *Fundamental Principles and Rights at Work*, adopted by the ILO Conference in June 1998, has also been ratified by India; thus, committing to comply with the following labour standards:

- freedom of association and the effective recognition of the right to collective bargaining
- elimination of all forms of forced or compulsory labour
- effective abolition of child labour
- elimination of discrimination in respect of employment and occupation

In theory, these comprehensive standards protect the rights and privileges of workers in India, however in practice, they are rarely achieved. Some of the distinctive features of the Indian labour market are—domination of the informal sector, dualism in the labour market, 90 per cent of the workforce are from the unorganized sector, high level of unemployment among the educated population, poor gainful employment, presence of child and bonded labour (although banned), gender bias, and large scale migration of labour from rural to urban areas.

Statistical data on Indian labour illustrates the high annual growth of labour force, which at present is 2.5 per cent, against the annual employment growth rate of 2.3 per cent. This means that for the Indian labour market, the challenge is not only to generate new employment, but also to augment the labour absorption rate to clear the backlog. Self-employed, casual workers, and the unorganized sector are highly represented in the labour market, making it imperfect. This also means that compensation decisions for large sections of people have to be made at sub-optimal levels, even at the cost of violating the Minimum Wages Act 1948 provisions.

A sector-wise analysis of Indian labour indicates that agriculture absorbs 62 per cent, followed by manufacturing and construction at 16 per cent, service sector absorbs 10 per cent of the labour force, whereas the miscellaneous sector absorbs 12 per cent. The maximum workers (59.41 per cent) are from the age group 15–59.

LABOUR WELFARE ADMINISTRATION

Labour welfare comprises of activities which are undertaken for economic, social, intellectual, and moral benefit of workers. Compensation management issues encompass different labour welfare issues, which cater to standard of living and social security aspects of labour. We can raise the standard of living of labour through continuous focus on skill renewal and improvement in quality of work life. Increase in standards of living of the workforce has a positive influence on the overall socio-economic development. This becomes possible, as with renewed skills and knowledge, workers become more productive, thus benefitting the firms. This improves workers earnings, as firms share part of their incremental gain with them in form of incentives. Hence, labour welfare measures hold potentiality of mutual benefits both for the workers and the organizations.

In India, a couple of labour welfare administration issues are legally mandated, primarily for good employment practices and governance. Some of the labour welfare administration issues are, however, voluntary. For example, good organizations, as part of their welfare measures, provide continuous training and skill development opportunities to workers, focus on more employment generation, ensure safety and security to workers, etc.

Ministry of Labour, Government of India, recommended the following initiatives for labour welfare:
- Skill development training
- Assistance and services to job seekers
- Labour welfare
- Administration and compliance with labour regulations

At the government level also, various initiatives have been taken to promote the culture of labour welfare, across the country and the organizations. For example, National Council of Vocational Training (NCVT), formed by the central government, is a tripartite body with representations from employers, workers, and the central/state government. Likewise at the state level too, we have State Councils for Vocational Training. Both the national and state councils of vocational training centres try to ensure steady flow of skilled workers, raise the quality and quantity of industrial workers, and also focus on reducing the unemployment of educated youth through skill development.

Similarly, to improve labour welfare and to increase productivity, along with social security measures, Government of India and the state governments are extending support through planned allocation. Such resource support is helping in skill formation and development, monitoring of working conditions, promoting harmony in industrial relations through development of health infrastructure with provisions for medical insurance and benefits, compensating for accidents, unemployment allowances, etc. All these welfare measures in one way or other reduce the adversity in employment conditions.

Some of the Acts for labour welfare and social security measures are as follows:
- The Workmen's Compensation Act 1923
- The Employees State Insurance Act 1948
- The Employees Provident Funds and Miscellaneous Provisions Act 1953
- The Maternity Benefit Act 1961
- The Payment of Gratuity Act 1972

Organizations in their employment practices are statutorily bound to comply with these Acts. To defray the expenses for such welfare measures, organizations have to allocate their resources in the compensation budget. Many organizations show such welfare costs while calculating the compensation cost, or cost to company (CTC). However, in addition to such statutory welfare provisions, many organizations provide some voluntary welfare measures, cost of which are also added to the compensation cost or the CTC.

SUMMARY

A neoclassical analysis of labour economics, or labour market, can be done both from macro and micro perspectives. Traditionally, we define a labour market as one where both suppliers of labour services (workers) and buyers of labour services (employers) exist. Hence, the price of labour, that is, the wages and the quantity of labour, that is, the level of employment, are determined by the interrelation between demand and supply. Such assumptions of labour market assume that workers are a rational, economic entity. An equilibrium wage rate and equilibrium employment level in a competitive market is possible when both workers and employers take mutual exchange decisions.

However, it has been argued that employment relations cannot always be termed as market-mediated exchange. Hence, labour market transactions are different from transactions in commodity markets. Both market and non-market forces are important in employment relations.

This chapter, within the framework of labour economics, first tried to explain the extent of the labour market's influence on compensation decisions. While examining this issue, it has been made clear that only in a perfectly competitive labour market, it can be partially possible. However, in India, where the labour market itself is imperfect, other variables also influence the compensation decision.

Key Terms

Frictional unemployment It occurs in the transition phase, when people move from one job to another, or when manpower redundancy occurs. Imperfect labour market information increases frictional unemployment. Technological changes can substantially reduce this type of unemployment.

Labour force participation rate (LFPR) It is the percentage of the economically active population in the labour force.

Labour market flexibility A labour market becomes flexible when the degree of occupational or functional flexibility increases. Workers with multi-skills can move from one job to another. It can provide contractual flexibility, wage flexibility, and geographical flexibility.

Marginal physical product of labour (MPPL) It is the additional output that results from an increase in one unit of labour. Labour demand is a derived demand and depends on the output levels in the market. Hence, the employers' labour demand depends on MPPL.

Phillips curve It shows the relationship between inflation and unemployment. Phillips's observation is based on the changes in the wage level between 1861 and 1957. He observed a trade-off between unemployment and inflation, and accordingly concluded that if the government works on reducing unemployment, it will lead to increased inflation.

Exercises

Concept Review Questions

1. Explain the concept of labour market flexibility. How does labour market flexibility influence compensation decisions at organizational level?
2. What are the different types of unemployment? Take example of an organization and explain how their employees can experience structural unemployment.
3. Explain in what ways unemployment costs society. How can we compute the rate of unemployment?
4. What is an internal labour market? How can an individual organization benefit from an internal labour market from the compensation point of view?
5. What are the labour market policies in India? How do labour market policies influence compensation designing decisions in organizations?
6. Prepare short notes on the following:
   (a) Classical unemployment
   (b) Role of trade unions' in determining employee compensation
   (c) Manpower redundancy
   (d) Multi-skilling
   (e) Cost of unemployment

Critical Thinking Question

Identify and visit an organization, which uses high-end machinery to manufacture ductile casting materials. Preferably, choose a firm whose manufacturing facilities are located in a remote village. Explain how labour market variables can affect its compensation decisions. While answering this question, first specify the variables in the context of the firm's operating premise and then relate your identified variables to the compensation decisions.

CASE STUDY: Retention Problems at IndiaRetail

Large organizations often face the challenges thrown by high attrition within a short span of time. It is not just limited to information technology enabled services (ITES). Sectors such as retail, banking, and automobiles also witness large scale movement of people. It is a challenge for the human resource (HR) managers of these sectors to retain employees using innovative compensation design. Considerations such as internal pay equity, loyalty, and commitment to the organization are often ignored by young executives. They prefer jobs that offer high compensation packages. So, high salaries are now considered the only way to retain talent.

With the entry of multinational companies (MNCs) and a positive economic growth, the problem of employee retention is of utmost concern to businesses in India.

Hemant Shukla was troubled while preparing the annual salary budget for his retail chain, IndiaRetail. The company had a presence in all the major metros. It had a 100 per cent growth on year to year basis, making it a good poaching ground for other retailers. Last year, 140 junior marketing executives had left to join rival companies. The company has been at a loss to understand what went wrong as it offers competitive salaries and deferrals. The fixed versus variable ratio of salary was 50:50. In addition, earning the variables did not require an employee to stretch, as the company had already achieved a brand identity. IndiaRetail made the shopping experience so compelling that customers enjoyed visiting their stores again and again.

Hemant was a very innovative compensation administrator, and he designed compensation structure in such a flexible way that an employee could earn twice their average monthly salary, given some initiative in retaining customers. The company's stores were so arranged that each customer care executive (CCE) monitored counters with some common items. They were given training to educate customers about products and why they should buy it. Every CCE got a bonus point for repeat customer purchases. At the end of the year, based on the accumulated bonus points, these employees also got surprise incentives.

Hemant's friend Kushal worked for a big multinational company. Kushal advised Hemant to closely study the organization's work culture and design a compensation package while considering the career development initiatives of employees. The core advice was to opt for an organizational work culture survey and ensure that employees' morale was high. For example, Maruti Suzuki reduced the rate of attrition by identifying and grooming potential achievers. Maruti provided regular training to employees to help them to achieve personalized career graphs.

Another friend of Hemant, Ravi Kant, had a different story to tell. He advised Hemant not to bow down to employees' pressure for a pay rise. He suggested that employees who wanted to leave should be allowed to do so. Ravi Kant believed in deferrals. He advised Hemant to make deferrals attractive, and employees by default would continue. Ravi cited the case of Air India, which had a retention reward of thirteen months' salary at the completion of five years of service. Hemant was advised to focus on long-term strategies.

(Contd)

CASE STUDY (Contd)

Apart from this, Hemant also learnt about signing non-competing clauses with other companies to prevent employees from joining rivals. He learnt about Microsoft and GE, which rewarded top performers with increased compensation packages. He also thought of providing opportunities to employees intrepreneurs, that is, managers or employees with entrepreneurial qualities.

Discussion question

Design an effective compensation package to enable the retention of customer care executives at IndiaRetail.

References

Adams, J.S. (1963), 'Wage Inequities, Productivity, and Work Quality', *Industrial Relations*, vol. 3, no. 1, pp. 9–16.

Bhattacharyya, D.K. (2006), *Human Resource Management*, 2nd edn, Excel Books, New Delhi.

Doeringer, P.B. and M.J. Piore (1991), *Internal Labour Markets and Manpower Analysis*, ME Sharpe, Lexington, Mass., Heath.

Marsden, D. (1986), *The End of Economic Man? Custom and Competition in Labour Markets*, St. Martin's Press, New York.

Papola, T.S. and G. Rodgers (eds) (1992), Labour Institutions and Economic Development in India, International Institute for Labour Studies, Geneva.

Pencavel, J. (1991), *Labour Market under Trade Unionism*, Blackwell, Cambridge.

Stiglitz, J. (2000), 'Capital Market Liberalization, Economic Growth and Instability', *World Development*, vol. 28, no. 6, pp. 1075–86.

World Labour Report (1992), International Labour Organization, Geneva.

CHAPTER
FOUR

Economic Theories and Compensation Management

Learning Objectives

After reading this chapter, you will be able to
- understand various economic theories and their implications for compensation management
- analyse the trade-off between economic theories and employee compensation
- assess employee stock options and the principle of equity in employee benefits
- learn about econometric application of compensation decisions
- evaluate productivity-linked employee benefits

OPENING CASE

ESOP as a Retention Tool

Tata Consultancy Services (TCS) has changed its salary structure. It has linked its variable compensation component to business performance. Most software organizations offer a compensation structure that includes employee stock options (ESOP) to help retain talent. Offering differential (variable) pay at the same hierarchical levels and linking it directly to business performance is undoubtedly a risky proposition. If there is no ceiling on the bonus, it may even equal the fixed salary component. All that TCS requires is growth in economic value-added (EVA). A good performer can earn more than his colleagues in the same position. The company now has to link individual appraisals with the overall performance of the organization. This is one of the best models of revenue sharing, to retain talent, in the absence of stock options. By introducing EVA to track corporate performance, benchmarking with competitors, and then cascading it to the individual cell level, TCS has

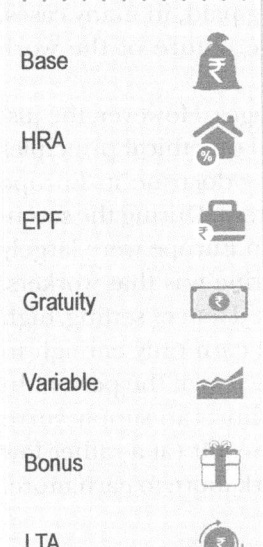

Base

HRA

EPF

Gratuity

Variable

Bonus

LTA

Conveyance

Medical

redefined compensation management practices, for all of us to emulate. 'We want each employee to feel as if they are running their business. They have to think like entrepreneurs and know the cost attached to their business and how they will add value to the investment,' according to S. Ramadorai, the Chief Executive Officer (CEO) of TCS.

INTRODUCTION

The economic consideration of wages dates back to the Vedic period of Indian civilization. In Vedic literature, payment of wages to workers was determined primarily in three ways—volume of work, time required to perform the work, and consideration of both the time and volume. Therefore, sculptors, builders, and carpenters used to earn more wages than those who used to perform relatively simpler work. In ancient India, social stratification was based on the skill of workers and the payment of bonuses to the workers as incentives was recommended. However, ancient Indian wage payment principles were diluted with the accession of the Moghuls; these were further diluted with the rise of the British Empire in India. The dilution led to workers being paid, in many cases, according to the whims of their masters rather than the nature of the work and/or time spent on the work.

In Europe, the church advocated the principle of just wages. However, the just wage concept during the Middle Ages in Europe was based on ethical principles rather than economic consideration. The utility of poverty doctrine in Europe was, however, based on economic consideration to some extent. During the seventeenth, eighteenth, and nineteenth centuries wage issues in Europe were largely governed by this doctrine. The basic premise of this doctrine was that workers, by nature, are lazy and satisfied with low living standards. Hence, setting high wages right at the beginning will not work, as workers will earn only enough to satisfy their minimum needs, and will remain absent for the rest of the period. In the language of economics, this doctrine proposes that a short-run supply curve of labour, expressed in terms of man-hours, will curve to the left (at a rather low wage rate). Hence, given low wages, workers will tend to work more to earn more.

ECONOMIC THEORIES

Adam Smith in his book *The Wealth of Nations* advocated many wage ideas. However, his ideas are contrary to the doctrine of utility of poverty. He recommended 'liberal reward of labour as it encourages propagation so it encourages the industry of the common people'. This age-old doctrine is known as the *economy of high wages*. It proposes that if high wages are paid, people by default will be active and diligent. This doctrine also subscribes to the view that employers will be bound to pay higher wages because of legislative control and pressure from trade unions. Today, however, the market compels an employer to pay higher wages to retain talent and better performance. Organizations paying higher wages to workers enhance purchasing power and, thus, help the economy to develop.

The *subsistence theory of wages* is considered to be the most prominent among the classical schools of thought. It advocates that wages should be equal to the means of subsistence. David Ricardo named it as the 'natural price of labour'. Ricardo opined that the wages should enable workers to purchase food, necessities, and conveniences.

Subsequently, Mill proposed the concept of *wage fund theory*. This theory advocates the supply-and-demand explanation of wages. The supply element is made up of workers, whereas the demand element is the wage fund (principally the part of circulating capital, which is used for purchase of labour). Average wage for the workers, therefore, is the amount resulting from dividing the wage fund by the number of workers. However, this theory loses its importance in complex business situations. Workers with more bargaining power can force employers to pay more, thereby defeating the basic premise of the wage fund concept.

The *marginal productivity theory of wages*, based on the *theory of income distribution*, advocates that wages tend to be equal to the marginal productivity of labour. By using the term 'tend to equal', the theory asserts that wages are not determined by marginal productivity. Rather, it asserts that changes in marginal productivity may lead to changes in wages. The primary reason for such an assumption lies in the fact that when the marginal productivity curve shows an increase in output, it may not always be due to the deployment of more workers. Instead, it may be due to the quality of performance of workers. Hence, the curve will characteristically be different for skilled workers and for unskilled workers. However, due to operational and other economic reasons, this theory of wages was not generally accepted.

A more practical approach to wage theories during the classical regime can be traced to the concept of *range theories*, which advocate that wages may have upper and lower limits, and a particular wage level may be decided within that limit, based on different circumstances. This theory is the extension of the *bargain theory of wages*, advocated by Davidson.

Some of the other economic theories of wages are the residual claimant theory, surplus value theory, bargaining theory of wages, employment theory, and competitive theory. The *residual claimant theory*, advocated by Walker, represents wage as the function of value creation in the production, after payment is made to other factors of production such as land, capital, and organization (entrepreneurship). Hence, labour becomes a residual claimant. The *surplus value theory*, advocated by Marx, views labour as an article of commerce, as the owner of the capital can buy it at a subsistence price. Hence, according to Marx, labour wages cannot be in proportion to the time spent. Workers can only earn subsistence level wages, as the surplus generated by the workers is used to pay off other factors of production. The *bargaining theory of wages*, advocated by Davidson, considers that wages are determined by the relative bargaining power of workers, the trade unions, and employers. *Employment theory* advocates that wages are determined depending on the employment situation. *Competition theory of wages* stresses on demand and supply.

The *neoclassical economic theory* argues that employees are better off if they can make their own choices among alternatives. Further, if the employees are adequately compensated, the economic welfare of society as a whole is increased. The basic premise for this argument is that the employees can decide what is best for them. However, in matters of employees' benefits, wages, or compensation, there are certain ground rules (such as laws, social norms, and exceptions), which define the range of choices.

Therefore, it is evident that we have a wide variety of economic theories relating to wages, which have evolved over time. We can discern at least six primary approaches to wages or employee compensation from economic perspectives—classical Marxian, neoclassical or marginalist, Keynesian, and post-Keynesian thoughts in the form of the Philips curve. There is no uniformity of approach within these schools. In each school, sub-variants exist. However, there exist some dominant common features within each school of thought. In Table 4.1 the consolidated thoughts of each school are presented.

TABLE 4.1 Various schools of thought and major focus areas

Schools of thought	Major focus areas
Classical school	Pioneered by Smith and Ricardo, it focuses on the concept of subsistence level of wages in the long run. Commonly termed as the natural price for labour, subsistence level is not limited to the expenses incurred for food alone. It also considers expenses, which are essential for minimum consumption, such as certain basic comforts. Both the pioneers agreed that in the short run, even though there may be a temporary variation in the wage rate, in the long run, it reduces to the subsistence level.
Marxian school	Within the ambit of classical thought, this school considers labour as the basic source of all value. Labour produces more than that needed for subsistence. The excess is what in Marxian terminology is known as 'surplus value', which contributes to capital accumulation. Depriving workers from above subsistence level wages is thus exploitation.
Neoclassical school of thought	Considers wages as a price like any other factor of production, which is determined by the market forces, that is, demand and supply. Labour supply depends on the disutility; hence it needs to be overcome by wages as an incentive. On the contrary, demand for labour depends on the marginal productivity of labour, which declines with the application of every unit of additional labour. Market wage rate, therefore, is the outcome of the interaction of demand and supply.

(Contd)

TABLE 4.1 (*Contd*)

Schools of thought	Major focus areas
Marginalist school	It is an extension of neoclassical thought, which advocates the law of diminishing marginal productivity. At the equilibrium wage rate, aggregate supply of labour gets fully absorbed, that is, the stage of full employment. Hence wage rate gets adjusted implicitly to the full employment level.
Keynesian school	This school, based on Say's law, subscribes to the view that supply creates its own demand. Hence, contrary to the belief that whatever is saved is automatically invested, the Keynesian school suggests that level of employment is dependent upon aggregate demand. At full employment, therefore, the level of income and consumption gets adjusted with the investment. Full employment through wage adjustment is possible only when demand for labour is considered as given. Thus, wage rates remain constant up to the level of full employment, as at this level labour market becomes tighter.
Philips curve or Post-Keynesian formulations	Phillips (1958), based on the empirical study of British economy, concluded that wage rate starts rising once the level of employment is increased. He observed a inverse relationship between the level of unemployment and the rate of increase of the wage level.

ECONOMIC THEORIES AND EMPLOYEE COMPENSATION

In this backdrop, therefore, it is important for us to understand the relationships between economic theory and employee benefits. Here, we use the term employee benefits in a more generic sense. In general, employees are not given the freedom to choose. Theoretically, rational choice (making decisions, which maximize employees' welfare) implies perfect knowledge and foresight. Therefore, there is a direct conflict between theory and the real world. In our country, as the labour market information is not scientific, employees obviously have imperfect information. This may compel them to make bad decisions. In contrast, however, due to the system of benchmarking of salaries, employers may have better information and, therefore, can make better decisions for employees. Employers, therefore, would like to negotiate salaries with employees, while considering a proper trade-off between benefits and costs. Another important aspect of the economics of employees' benefits is that many employers in India do not provide adequate information to their employees. They are not allowed to decide or even bargain. In fact, this may be one reason for the high rate of attrition among knowledge workers in India, along with increased job mobility.

We can cite the example of retirement benefits. From an economic point of view, organizations design the retirement benefits packages on an actuarial basis. This means that the benefits will be equal if the employees decide to take a cash lump sum payment instead of opting for a monthly payout (in terms of pension annuity). The choice between the two options is also completely discretionary. However, most employers in India still decide to take a paternalistic philosophy, on the grounds that the retirees might opt for a lump sum payment instead of a monthly annuity, then waste it and become destitute for the rest of their lives. Many organizations, however, decide to allow retirees to take a portion of their annuity payments in a lump sum. The monthly pension payment in such cases is proportionately reduced.

A review of all the economic theories on wages is not sufficient to determine wages. Hence, wage and compensation issues need to be studied from multi-disciplinary precepts, as already pointed out in Chapter 1 on Introduction to compensation management.

TRADE-OFFS AND EMPLOYEE COMPENSATION

Economic theories primarily illustrate underlying principles involved in trade-offs by considering only two choices. These choices are either from the employer's or from the employee's perspective. From the employer's perspective, the trade-off might be different mixes of direct compensation and benefit levels, while maintaining the same profit level. This is strategically more important because rising employee costs may reduce an organization's competitive advantage.

Here, however, we are more concerned about the trade-offs from the employee's perspective. Assuming that the employee has a choice, let us consider the trade-off between direct compensation and benefits levels. Economists express this concept in terms of budget-line/indifference curve analysis. While the budget line expresses the financial constraint, the indifference curve demonstrates the level of employee satisfaction. Theoretically, indifference curves are continuous, perfectly divisible, convex, and non-intersecting functions, which show that to get more benefits you have to give up more and more direct pay (and vice versa). This illustrates the law of diminishing marginal returns.

Retirement benefits are another form of trade-off. We also call it deferred benefits or non-wage labour cost (NWLC). Application of time-value analysis is crucial to understand the psychology and mathematics of this trade-off. Essentially, we introduce discount rates and the preference for current versus future consumption in this context. Employees make such trade-offs by choosing between their present and future consumption. Economic theory answers this question by pointing out that we may not live until tomorrow and hence prefer the certain satisfaction (utility) of consuming today versus the risk of never enjoying the consumption. The postponement of consumption is part of the underlying theory of saving.

VALUATION OF EMPLOYEE COMPENSATION

Another important dimension of the economics of employee benefits is the determination of value. The value may be for the employer, the employee, or

even their dependents or survivors, who are also by default successors to the organization (employer). Value can be determined by answering the following questions:
- Does the cost to the employer equal the value to the employee?
- What if the employee had to purchase the same benefit in the market (replacement value)?
- What if the employer wants to compare the cost of the benefits package of its employees to another employer, or an industry norm?
- How does the value of benefits compute into total compensation?

Unfortunately, we cannot answer these questions using theoretical abstractions. In practice, they are complicated. Many companies decide to focus on present benefits either by reducing their deferred benefits obligations or by removing them entirely to attract and retain talent. Employees in different age groups may have different priorities. Those in the exploratory age group (relatively young) may opt for present benefits. People in the establishment and maintenance age group, on the contrary, may prefer benefits in the future to sustain the family. Therefore, while designing the benefits for employees, employers need to consider all these aspects for a better trade-off.

PRICING OF EMPLOYEE STOCK OPTIONS

Employee compensation through stock options is a cost to the organization and needs to be expensed in financial reports to reflect the true value of the firm. However, it is also argued that expensing stock options is an improper accounting procedure as it inaccurately attributes costs to the firm that are actually born by shareholders through dilution of their shares. Even then, it is important as a series of studies worldwide, more particularly in the United States, indicate that executives who possess stock options earn 531 times the wages of an average employee.

A stock option gives an employee the ability to purchase specific numbers of shares of his company on a future date at a predetermined price known as strike price or grant price. This price is usually decided based on the market price of the stock on the day the option is issued.

Every stock option has four to five years of vesting period. As a practice, companies during this vesting period proportionately transfer stock or shares to the employees' credit, which he can sell. If an employee leaves his job within the period of vesting, the stock option gets forfeited. Only after vesting of these options, employees can be treated as shareholders and participate in voting.

From an employees' point of view, stock options are better as compensation when the market price of stock booms. In the reverse case, however, it generally acts as a deterrent. In such cases, restricted stock is better. Restricted stock allows an employee to retain some value, till the stock price reduces to zero. Unlike stock options, in the case of restricted stock employees actually own the shares, maybe as an incentive to join the company (a part of sign-off bonus). However, companies mostly use restricted stock as a compensation choice to retain talent. Another advantage of restricted stock from an organizational perspective is that it can effectively motivate employees to think like owners and become more focused on meeting goals. Stock options, on the other hand, cannot instil the sense of ownership. Internationally, companies such as Microsoft, Amazon.com, Altria Group, Dell Computer, Cendant Corp, and Daimler Chrysler AG have chosen restricted stock in lieu of stock options. In India, companies such as ITC, Grasim, Hindalco, and Infosys have made extensive use of stock option as part of their compensation package.

Therefore, there are three different types of stock options—incentive stock options (based on the performance track record), non-qualified stock options, and restricted stock options. In the case of incentive stock options, employees pay taxes only when they sell such options. In the case of non-qualified stock options, employees pay higher taxes (on the difference between the market value and the grant price). In the case of restricted stock, employees get a certain number of shares, which they can sell once the company meets certain goals or even after the expiry of a certain period.

Regulatory Framework

The regulatory framework applicable for listed companies is based on the principles of disclosure and shareholder approval. Any stock option scheme has to be approved by the shareholders through a special resolution. It is the prerogative of companies to decide the issue price of stock options. However, when the options price is below the market price on the date of grant, the difference needs to be expensed in the profit and loss account as part of employees' compensation package. In all stock options, the minimum vesting period is one year. Companies can, however, decide on vesting period above that mandatory vesting period, depending on their retention strategy. After the expiry of the vesting period, there is no lock-in period for employees who may exercise their options. Stock options can be granted to employees and directors of a company, its subsidiaries, or its holding company (whether in India or abroad). However, they cannot be granted to the promoters or large shareholders.

Legal Perspective

The Companies (Employee Stock Option Scheme and Employee Stock Purchase Scheme) Rules 2002 apply to any company, which grants employees stock options either under a scheme or otherwise as defined in subsection (15A) to Section 2 of the Companies Act 1956. As per the rules, employee stock option scheme (ESOS) refers to a scheme under which a company grants options to employees to purchase its shares and stocks. Employee stock purchase scheme (ESPS), as per this rule, refers to a scheme under which the company offers shares/stocks to employees. Certain other common terms such as exercise, exercise period, exercise price, grant, option, etc. have also been defined by these rules. *Exercise* means the employee can make an application for the issue of shares after the vesting period. *Exercise period* refers to the period after vesting, during which the employee should exercise his right. *Exercise price* refers to the price payable by the employee to exercise the option. *Grant* refers to the issue of options to employees. *Option* is a right, but not an obligation granted to an employee to apply for shares of the company at a pre-determined price.

Other basic principles such as the eligibility to participate in ESOS and terms and conditions of ESOS have already been discussed earlier. As per these rules, the shareholders' approval in exercising stock option is essential.

Black–Scholes Model

There are no clear standards for valuation of options. However, the two most common methods of option valuation are the Black–Scholes option pricing model (BSOPM) and the binomial option pricing model (BOPM). The Black–Scholes model is used extensively worldwide. This model uses derivative methods for ascertaining the ESOP valuation. It considers that discount rate of a warrant varies with time and stock price. This is now also used in the option pricing model. The equation of the model is as under

$C = SN(d_1) - Ke^{(-rt)}N(d_2)$ C = Theoretical call premium
S = Current stock price   t = Time until option expiration
K = Option striking price   r = Risk-free interest rate
N = Cumulative standard norm distribution   e = Exponential term (2.7183)

$$d_1 = \frac{\ln(S/K) + (r + s^2/2)t}{s\sqrt{t}}$$ $d_2 = d_1 - s\sqrt{t}$

S = Standard deviation of stock returns   ln = Natural logarithm

The model has two parts—the first part, $SN(d_1)$, derives the expected benefit from ESOP outright, which is found by multiplying stock price S with respect to the change in the call premium in the underlying stock price $N(d_1)$. The second part $Ke^{(-rt)}N(d_2)$ gives the present value of ESOP price on the expiration day. Expiration day may be considered in terms of employees' period of holding the stock, or may be specific to the organization's enforced lock-in period. The fair market value of the call option is then calculated by taking the difference between these two parts. The model has the following assumptions:
- no dividend payout during the option's life
- the option can only be exercised on the expiration date

- markets are efficient
- no commissions are charged
- interest rates remain constant and known
- and finally, returns are log normally distributed

Problem of Expensing

In India, there has been minimal research on the problem of expensing employee stock options. This may be due to poor corporate governance systems and absence of tough regulatory norms. Such loopholes are identifiable, when we find compensation differences between the top officials and other less senior executives. However, in economically advanced countries like the United States, such research has been carried out extensively. As a result, thought provoking studies on employee stock options have been released.

In the United States, equity holding of executives in public traded companies has increased from 3–4 per cent to 10–12 per cent between the 1980s and the year 2000. Francisco (2002) conducted a study and reported that in the 1960s, US managers earned about twelve times the wages of the average employee; but in 2000, they earned an estimated 531 times the wages of the average employee. A typical illustration is GE's stock options payout to its erstwhile CEO, Jack Welch. GE's financial reports showed these options as costless to the organization and its shareholders. Using an eighteen month maturity yield as the basis, it transpired that the market value of Jack Welch's stock options, at the time when they were awarded, was $20 million. Yet, there was no recording of equivalent expenses on the income statement. The reason is that $20 million was considered as an opportunity cost and not a cash expense. If GE had sold these stock options in the open market, it would have received $20 million, which would have been recorded as cash value. However when they were issued to Jack Welch, they were treated as compensation and were, hence, not considered as having any value. Therefore, they could not be expensed.

From an economic perspective, the market value of options should be shown as expenses. Such expensing of options can turn a solid accounting profit into a loss. To illustrate, eBay's accounting profit in the year 2001 was shown as $90.4 million. After including the value of compensation options, this profit turned into a loss of $14.5 million. In the year 2002, an estimate of high-tech companies revealed that the options expense was equivalent to 51 per cent of operating earnings in 1999.

While options certainly need to be expensed, we have some inherent problems in pricing. First of all, it is difficult to estimate accurate pricing, as all stocks may not have market liquidity. Hence, while pricing options, companies may exaggerate the true cost of options. Further, option expensing would require a company to continuously recalculate the value assigned to the options, due to a fluctuation in the company's financial performance and consequent variation in the market price of stock. In expensing options, senior managers and officials of the company may manipulate earnings. Hence, pricing may not be accurate. We have the example of Jeff Skilling, the former CEO of Enron, who used stock options to reduce the cost of compensation, but increased the gains (in terms of increased stock price).

LABOUR MARKETS AND EMPLOYEE BENEFITS

From the labour market perspective, the total wage concept is analysed in the demand–supply framework. Conventionally, the compensation management practices of Indian organizations have focused on attracting, retaining, developing, and compensating employees ignoring labour market perspectives. Here, labour policies of the government still play a major role. However, with the increase of economic activity and subsequent increase in the competition for organizations, employee retention has now become the most critical issue. Globalization has increased the mobility of labour. Talented employees now change jobs frequently, moving across the globe. All these factors are now compelling organizations to focus on labour market issues. Gradually, designing compensation, which keeps pace with the demand and supply of labour is now becoming a corporate practice.

National level data analysis reveals that even on date only 45.8 per cent of the total workers in India (other than those engaged in agriculture) are covered under some social security schemes, which are statutory in nature. What is more surprising that even in government sector, all workers are not fully covered under social security schemes. In fact, the trend is so alarming in the government sector that, over the years, concerns for social security for workers has declined from previous 87.23 per cent to 86.03 per cent (during the year 2009–2010). Similar declining concern for social security measures is also evident in public sector companies, where the decline is from previous 61.22 per cent to 58.05 per cent in 2009–2010. Although this phenomenon is attributable to large-scale casualization of the workforce, the scenario illustrates our lackadaisical national level concern for labour welfare.

There are other ways, too, to analyze the labour market discrimination in India. Indian labour market, by nature, is highly segmented. We can assess the labour market discrimination syndromes based on the data of National Sample Survey Organization (NSSO). Some of the discriminatory practices on compensation and employees' benefits issues, observed by the labour economists, can be grouped as follows:

Compensation and benefits are not diversity neutral Against the declared policies of the Government of India regarding diversity neutral compensation and benefits practices, data analysis indicates wage differentials by gender, caste, and religion. Although over the years such trend is decreasing.

Compensation and benefits differentials across educational groups This syndrome is also evident in segmented labour market in India. In many organizations (both in private and public sector, and even in departmental undertakings), workers with higher level of education are more covered under employee benefits than workers with lower education levels.

Industry-wise compensation and benefits differentials This phenomena is evident across industries and even within the same industry. For example, we can find the gap in employees' benefits programmes between manufacturing, mining, and public utility services industries. Similarly, we can find such differences within these industries too.

Compensation and benefits differentials by occupations Indian labour market also discriminates compensation and benefits in terms of occupation groups. Even within the same occupation groups, we find the differentials in terms of caste.

These discriminatory compensation and benefits practices in India can be primarily attributed to segmented labour market.

EQUITY IN EMPLOYMENT BENEFITS

Economic theories on employee compensation and benefits frequently conflict. Neoclassical economists argue that market competition is the best premise on which to base employee compensation. On the other hand, the approaches such as institutional, game theory, or Marxist argue that markets may not always be competitive. Therefore, the concept of equity in employee compensation may often get diluted. To reduce the problem of inequity, there is a need to ensure fair rules of pricing with government intervention. From the perspective of economic theory, we have two concepts of equity—vertical equity and horizontal equity (i.e., between-group versus within-group equity). Unequal compensation between different groups is tenable, but inequity among employees within the same group is not desirable. Regulations try to satisfy the principles of equity. Complying with such regulatory norms also facilitates principles of equity in compensation design.

ECONOMETRIC APPLICATION IN COMPENSATION DECISIONS

In economics, *x-efficiency* is the effective use of inputs to produce outputs. A company may be considered x-efficient, when it maximizes output with given inputs by making use of the best technology. When companies are not x-efficient, they become x-inefficient. The concept of x-efficiency was introduced by Leibenstein (1966). In a perfectly competitive market, x-efficiency will cause the company to withdraw from business, as the company will fail to make enough profit to survive in the future. In other types of markets, however, x-efficiency is possible; it will make one company more efficient than the other.

As human resources are the most sustainable and inimitable inputs for any organization, an x-efficient firm should try to sustain its position by suitably designing employee compensation. Hicks (1939) introduced the concept of compensating variation (CV) to measure utility change. By calculating CV, we can determine the amount of additional money an employee would require to reach the initial utility, after price changes, variation in product quality, or introduction of new products.

$$CV = e(p_1, u_1) - e(p_1, u_0)$$
$$= w - e(p_1, u_0)$$
$$= e(p_0, u_0) - e(p_1, u_0)$$

where w = wealth level; p_0 = old price; p_1 = new price; u_0 = old utility level; u_1 = new utility level.

Once the price changes, the new CV of the consumer, using the value function $v(p,w)$, would be as under:

$$v(p_1, w - CV) = u_0$$
$$e(p_1, v(p_1, w - CV)) = e(p_1, u_0)$$
$$w - CV = e(p_1, u_0)$$
$$CV = w - e(p_1, u_0)$$

Even though compensating variation metric is used in consumer behaviour research, we can make use of this equation to design employee compensation. We can also track the changing expectations of employees, price changes, product quality changes, and introduction of new products.

PRODUCTIVITY-LINKED EMPLOYEE BENEFITS

Technological advances, structural changes in the economy, and competitive pressures are the three major drivers of changing labour market scenario in India and other developing countries. Developed countries could relate wages to productivity better and thus, rationalize the economics of organizations. They are able to isolate labour cost from the total cost of production using better and more efficient scientific methods. This helps them in keeping control to remain competitive globally. In labour intensive production processes, pricing of labour based on productivity and performance is not easy. The concept of productivity has received international attention with the declaration of the International Year of Productivity in 1982. Although the concept originated in classical economic thought, it came into focus after 1982.

Traditionally, productivity was considered as an input–output relational measurement. Orthodox views attribute productivity to labour efficiency as output quantification can immediately be related to labour efficiency. However, this hypothesis suffers from a major lacuna. Many organizations, despite achieving high labour efficiency (measured in terms of value added in manufacturing) suffer from overall dysfunction and become sick.

Organizations operate on team efforts, by allocating different functional areas to different departments. Hence, ultimate success depends on the effective joint efforts of different teams. A lapse in a single functional area can offset the efficiency of other functional area, which may ultimately affect corporate efficiency.

Within the ambit of input–output relationship, the concept of input has widely changed under the present circumstances. Inputs are no longer confined to the direct materials used for production, but also include supportive functions in a more abstract form. Therefore, knowledge and ideas are also considered part of inputs. In an organization, the production section actually transforms physical inputs to outputs. Other functional departments, though not engaged in direct material transformation, provide supportive inputs to production departments for efficient functioning.

With the declaration of the International Year of Productivity in 1982, productivity consciousness has gained worldwide momentum. Classical economists such as Smith, Ricardo, and Mill enunciated the concept of productivity in the form of the law of diminishing returns of all resources. However in nineteenth century, Taylor's thesis *Task Study* came up with a more reasonable slogan, which says, human worth can be made infinitely more productive not by working harder, but by working smarter. In India, the productivity movement and consciousness gained momentum with the establishment of the National Productivity Council (NPC) in 1958.

Historically, the productivity concept originally emerged during the post-war period. After the Second World War, the war-ravaged economies of most countries needed to be urgently reconstructed, renovated, and rationalized. Growth was then everybody's concern. In such a milieu, economists advocated the growth theory. The focus on political, economic, social, cultural, anthropological, psychological, institutional, legal, managerial, administrative, and other related aspects have been instrumental in furthering economic growth. The following basic economic factors have been unanimously recognized as crucial factors in economic growth:

- capital formation for the present and to combat uncertainties in the future
- high productivity of all factors of production and inputs including time and knowledge

Productivity

From an economic point of view, productivity refers to the yield from the following:

- each factor of production (land, labour, capital, and organization)
- each input (raw materials, fuel, time, and knowledge)

- overall yield of the joint factors and resources enumerated previously in combination

From the management perspective, productivity in its broadest sense is the quantitative relationship between what we produce and resources that we use. There is a distinct difference between production and productivity. In simple terms, production refers to a process of transforming raw materials and other inputs into finished goods or services. However, productivity denotes a generation of surplus. In terms of input–output relationship, while production is transforming inputs into output by adding values, productivity is aimed at getting higher output for a given input. The excess output, therefore, is tantamount to generation of surplus. Interchanging the input ratios can increase productivity, whereas in such a changing process the outputs will proportionately increase more than the changes in input ratio.

Conventionally, productivity was understood as an inevitable outcome of labour efficiency, that is, only efficient functioning of workmen could contribute to productivity improvement. In a complex corporate system, this emphasis on a single factor gradually lost its importance, as productivity cannot be improved or corporate success achieved simply by having efficient workers.

Therefore, functional efficiency of all the factors of production is now considered the ultimate goal for overall corporate efficiency. Productivity is now considered as depending on the efficiency of all the factors of production, instead of being solely dependent on the efficiency of labour (single factor approach).

$$\text{Production} = \text{Value addition to new materials}$$
$$\text{Productivity} = \text{Efficiency of production}$$
$$= f(\text{Surplus efficiency of all points})$$
$$= f(\text{Men, materials, and management})$$

Factors to improve productivity

Six important factors, which affect productivity in an organization, have been identified. These factors are as follows:

Nature and quality of raw materials This factor demands better methods to eliminate waste and provide for efficient handling of natural resources.

Basic nature of process employed This factor demands that technologies should be used to the best advantage to constantly improve processes. Scientific research should continuously try to improve processes and procedures.

Plants and equipment employed In India, the physical effort of a workman is considerably more than many other countries of the world. Technically, it is highly uneconomical from a productivity point of view for an individual to do work manually, which could reasonably be done by mechanical equipment. Further, it is also counter-productive when a country's plant, equipments, and buildings are obsolete and ill designed. This is due to the failure to plough back enough capital into modern equipment. In India, this is particularly evident.

Technological obsolescence is one of the most important causes of industrial inefficiency. Many industries are very sluggish in growth and development, and are getting worse every day. This virtually forces them to finally close down their operations. Therefore, it is necessary to ensure that capital resources are used to the best advantage for productive efficiency. The amount of capital that should be invested in plant and equipment, including the periodic updating of existing technologies, varies from unit to unit.

Efficiency of plant and equipment This factor partly depends on the adequate supply of technology, but it also demands eagerness and action at all levels of the organization to obtain the best from existing resources. Information on production, performance, and cost must be made available to all concerned for maximum efficiency.

Volume continuity and uniformity of production The standardization of a product, resulting in longer and more economical production, depends upon manufacturing and marketing practices of an organization. Some customer education may be necessary, but this should not be difficult if good quality, low-priced products are available.

Productivity does not mean retrenchment or redundancy. Rather, productivity potentially increases employment.

The national conference on the role of trade unions in productivity improvement was organized during February 1990 by the National Productivity Council (NPC) in collaboration with the Ministry of Labour, Government of India, and the International Labour Organization at New Delhi. It deliberated on certain important issues of productivity. For the first time, the significance of total factor productivity was recognized at a national level conference. It was agreed that productivity increases will improve the quality of working life of employees. It was suggested that a national level productivity policy should be evolved to improve all aspects of production such as improving skills, educating workers, training to introduce attitudinal changes, creating a participative culture, and sharing gains of productivity. The conference emphasized the urgent need for attitudinal changes amongst managers towards workers and unions so that mistrust and misconceptions could be cleared. Finally, the conference also stressed the necessity of getting active cooperation from trade unions to spread the message of productivity, to successfully achieve productivity in all organizations, and contribute to the economic growth and development of the country.

Utilization of manpower Manpower is a fundamental resource. There is a real need to see that both general planning and detailed methods of work are not wasteful, and that fatigue and frustration are avoided. Finally, to understand the spirit of productivity from its true perspective, it is essential to clear some misconceptions. These misconceptions revolve around the aim, scope, and purpose of productivity. Some of the misconceptions are as follows:

- productivity is not concerned with any group of people, but with every member of the organization

- it does not signify just more production, but stands for functional optimization
- it does not mean making the worker work harder
- it does not mean working longer hours or more number of days in the week
- it is not confined to manufacturing organizations. It pervades all spheres of economic activities wherever human endeavour is involved

The labour force should be involved at the planning stage for technological changes and productivity improvements. Small group activities, such as quality circles and other consultative mechanisms, are increasingly likely to be used as tools to improve productivity in the future. While production improvements are important, equally important is an equitable distribution of productivity gains among different partners—labourers, shareholders, consumers, the organizations themselves, and the state.

The message of productivity should percolate to the shop floor level through necessary training sessions under the active guidance of local productivity councils.

Productivity Measurement

Conventionally, productivity measurement is left to ratio analysis. Let us illustrate this with an example.

Example

A company manufactures 50,000 desktops in a year. Each desktop sells at ₹25,000. The company spends ₹5,000 per desktop in material inputs and 2,00,000 man-hours to manufacture the desktops. Compute the following productivity ratios:
- Output/Labour ratio
- Output value/Labour ratio
- Value added/Labour ratio

Solution
- Output/Labour ratio (in terms of man-hours)
  = 50,000 desktops/2,00,000 man-hours
  = 0.25 desktop per man-hour
- Output value/Labour ratio
  (50,000 desktops × ₹25,000 per desktop)/2,00,000 man-hours
  = ₹6,250 per man-hour
- Value added/Labour ratio is computed by first computing the value added, which is Output value − Material cost
  = (50,000 × ₹25,000) − (50,000 × ₹5,000) = 10,00,000

Therefore, Value added/Labour (in man-hours) = 10,00,000/2,00,000
= ₹5 per man-hour.

This approach to productivity measurement—by linking it straight to wages—will neither benefit organizations nor workers in the long run, as discussed earlier.

In today's complex production system, where overall productivity is more important than labour productivity, the following two models of rational pricing of labour (i.e., linking wages), can yield better results.

Omni factor model

This model gives a composite productivity index for all input and output costs of all products. While input costs are taken for all, output costs are determined on average marginal costs (AMC) method. Input costs are as follow:
- raw material costs
- manpower costs
- capital costs, that is, depreciation, interest, stock investment, etc.
- indirect production costs
- cost of utilities

Assuming we have three products, A, B, and C, the output costs using AMC method are:

$$\text{Aggregate output} = \text{Output A} + \text{Output B} \times \frac{\text{AMC of B}}{\text{AMC of A}}$$

$$+ \text{Output C} \times \frac{\text{AMC of C}}{\text{AMC of A}}$$

$$\text{where AMC percentage of A} = \frac{\text{Total input costs of A}}{\text{Total output costs of A}} \times 100$$

$$\text{Productivity} = \text{Aggregate output}/\text{Input costs}$$

Surrogate model

This model primarily considers some qualitative factors to measure productivity. Factors such as the satisfaction of investors, employees, customers, and suppliers are considered in qualitative terms. The quantification of these qualitative terms is done as follows:

Investors' satisfaction (S_i) = Net profit/Total investment

Employees' satisfaction (S_e) = Total value added/Total number of man-hours

Customers' satisfaction (S_c) = Total sales revenue/Total number of customers

Suppliers' satisfaction (S_s) = Total purchases/Total number of suppliers

The composite productivity index, therefore, is:

$$A.S_i + B.S_e + C.S_c + D.S_s$$

where A, B, C, and D are constants, which indicate the relative weightage of the four parameters.

Linking wages to productivity, based on these two models, yields better results as organizations can objectively price labour. The labour can also get its legitimate share of productivity gain.

Productivity Measurement for Knowledge Workers

Measuring the number of units produced by a worker using a machine is not difficult as it can be quantified. However, the productivity of a knowledge worker is difficult to measure. This is primarily because of the difficulty involved in measuring the investment vis-à-vis the output. Other difficulties can be attributed to the following factors.

- Effects of a strategic decision, both positive and negative, may not be immediately evident. Such a time lag is, therefore, difficult to relate to a particular time period. Moreover, we cannot directly relate every strategic decision to the individual's efficiency and inefficiency. The outcome of some strategic decisions may depend on various external factors, which may be beyond the control of managers.
- Knowledge workers often extend services to other units of an organization. This may have some effects on final output, however it is difficult to quantify. For example, an advertising manager's efforts in increasing sales are difficult to measure.
- Knowledge workers often contribute indirectly to the achievement of the end result, which is difficult to measure. For example, a knowledge worker's contribution towards design and development is not directly attributable to final output. Yet, his efforts are all the more important.

Given such difficulties, the total factor productivity (TFP) study is a better approach, as it considers the functional efficiency/performance of all departments of an organization at aggregate level, without bothering to focus on individual productivity.

Productivity and Quality

When quality increases, productivity also improves. This is because wastes and rework are reduced, and inputs are optimally utilized. Higher productivity enables an organization to reduce price and gain a competitive advantage, both in terms of price and quality. Customers also feel happy as they get value for their money. As the organization's bottom line improves, it raises the satisfaction level of all stakeholders, including employees. Productivity should not be misconstrued as labour performance alone. It is the sum of total efficiency and therefore linking productivity to wages should be objectively done to create a win-win situation.

Employee Benefits and Productivity

The normal belief is that there exists a link between wages and organizational productivity. However, this is not a global trend. It has not been proved that linking labour productivity to wages helps an organization to derive cost savings, simultaneously increase labour motivation, and consequently increase performance and productivity.

To understand this, it is necessary to measure labour productivity, determine wages across organization, and then appreciate the relationship between the rate of growth of productivity and the rate of growth of wages at the national and international level.

Statistically, the real level of output in each organization is measured by dividing the total revenues received by the unit prices. Labour productivity, on the other hand, is measured by dividing the real level of output by the number of hours worked (man-hours) by employees in the organization. Hence, revenue per worker and output per worker can be different. This is because they are not linked. It is, therefore, possible for an organization to get increased revenues per worker due to increased price whereas the output per worker may fall. The reverse can also be true.

Let us further clarify this, before we look for data support for our critical observations. The common assumption is that if the labour output/productivity increases, the organization's revenue will increase because the workers' enhanced contribution to output will generate additional revenues for the firm. Hence logically, the workers should also get increased wages as productivity is linked to wages. However, this assumption is wrong. This is because we are already convinced that no connection exists between the output per worker and revenue per worker. Even if the output per worker rises, revenue per worker may fall. This is because when the output or productivity of workers increases, the organization has to increase its supply. By simple economic logic, we know that increased supply will reduce the price, which in turn would decrease the revenue per worker and the total revenue for the organization. This phenomenon is supported by data.

At the macro or national level, such a relationship is even more strong. When productivity gains drive up wages in one organization or occupation, it is anticipated that workers would be drawn from other organizations and occupations, thereby returning relative wages to its initial level. However if productivity increases at the national level, the equivalent effect will require that workers be drawn from other countries. If output increases in an organization, while everything else remaining the same, the organization may have to lower prices in order to sell that increase. However, when output increases in the nation as a whole, all workers will have higher incomes and those incomes may be used to purchase the increased output. In a sense, the increased output 'creates' the increased demand to purchase that output. Prices need not fall. And if prices do fall, the 'real' incomes of all workers will increase, that is, even if observed (or nominal) wages do not change, workers will be able to buy more goods and services with the same income. They will be better off in the 'real' sense. Therefore, an economy-wide increase in productivity could cause an increase in the welfare of workers, not through an increase in observed money wages, but through a decrease in average prices.

Therefore, there are sound theoretical reasons to propose that there is very little correlation between an organization's productivity growth and its wage growth. Empirical evidence provides strong support for this theory.

Organizational Level Data Support

Tables 4.2 and 4.3 illustrate the concept of employment costs and labour productivity. Table 4.2 shows labour cost (wages and other benefits) as a percentage of total cost in Steel Authority of India Ltd (SAIL). Labour cost as a percentage of total cost remained stable between 1988–89 and 1991–92 at 14.8 per cent, even though the wage bill alone had gone up by 63 per cent. Table 4.3 shows labour productivity of steel manufacturers. In the early 1990s, the average annual remuneration of public sector steel workers in India was ₹57,600 as compared to ₹54,500 in commercial banks, ₹49,000 in central government undertakings, and, ₹32,000 in railways, however, it was less than that

TABLE 4.2 Employment costs at SAIL

Particulars	1988–89	1989–90	1990–91	1991–92
Wages and salaries {₹ in million (%)}	4,276.2 (47)	5,540.5 (54)	6,180.4 (56)	6,952.5 (52)
Incentives and rewards {₹ in million (%)}	627.2 (7)	641.0 (6)	742.8 (6)	1,139.5 (9)
Other allowances {₹ in million (%)}	1,871.5 (21)	1,274.0 (12)	991.5 (9)	1,404.2 (11)
Fringe benefits {₹ in million (%)}	2,318.0 (25)	2,908.8 (28)	2,242.6 (29)	3806.4 (28)
Total	9,092.9	10,364.3	11,157.3	13,302.6
Average wages (salaries/employee/year) (₹)	31,671.0	34,833.0	37,204.0	45,665.0
Average benefit (cost/employee/year) (₹)	13,883.0	17,950.0	20,415.0	23,747.0
Average employment (cost/employee/year) (₹)	45,554.0	52,783.0	57,619.0	69,412.0
Labour as % of total cost	14.8	15.1	14.8	14.8

Source: SAIL annual report (1992)

TABLE 4.3 Labour productivity index (per tonne per employee)

Particulars	1981–82	1986–87	1987–88	1990–91	1992
BSL	71	61	66	98	108
DSP	38	39	41	45	45
RSP	47	44	47	56	56
IISCO	34	29	31	24	29
SAIL	55	51	56	70	78
TISCO	64	74	74	72	72

Source: SAIL annual report (1992)

TABLE 4.4 Turnover per Employee for BHEL and ONGC

Year	BHEL (₹ in crore)	ONGC (₹ in crore)
2007–08	0.49	1.860
2008–09	0.61	1.960
2009–10	0.74	1.880
2010–11	0.93	2.060
2011–12	1.00	2.336

of the oil and gas industries. In 1990–94, the average emoluments per employee in SAIL increased by 78 per cent (more than the three other leading public sector companies in the oil and energy sectors) whereas the value added per employee increased by 60 per cent. In each case, wage increases outstripped productivity gains. Other input costs rose much higher than wage costs.

The data in Tables 4.2 and 4.3 does not support the conventional theory of linking productivity to wages. Again, macro level data analysis on labour cost trends in India shows that, while average labour cost has significantly increased over the years, labour cost as percentage of total cost either remains stable or has even decreased over the period. It indicates that the cost of other inputs has surpassed labour costs in India. Table 4.5 provides macro-level data on the labour costs in India.

Although we do not have national level data on productivity trend of Indian labours, atleast looking at the data in Table 4.4, we can approximate that both in BHEL and ONGC turnover per employee has increased over the years.

However, wages and salaries as percentage of turnover, when studied for some public sector enterprises, show a reversal trend, indicating decline in compensation and benefits programme in real terms.

Productivity Bargaining—Impact on Remuneration

Productivity is a critical issue in designing compensation design. In most collective bargaining agreements, a rise in productivity is a precondition for a wage rise. This trend in organizations often contradicts our earlier discussion on wage productivity linkage. Most conventional manufacturing units like jute mills, believe that productivity rise is attributable solely to labour efficiency. However, factors such as investment, research and development (R&D), innovation, total quality management (TQM) practices, skill upgradation, work processes, organizational culture, structure, and finally compensation also affect productivity improvement. Therefore, focusing only on compensation or any one of the factors, taken singly, is not going to help in enhancing productivity of the organization. Increase in productivity requires attention to all the factors that affect it one way or another.

TABLE 4.5 Macro-level data on labour costs in India (1992–2000)

Description	1992-93 Census	1992-93 Sample	1993-94 Census	1993-94 Sample	1994-95 Census	1994-95 Sample	1995-96 Census	1995-96 Sample
Average labour cost per man-day worked (₹)	138.08	72.76	146.01	82.92	166.23	90.10	191.14	103.29
Percentage of total labour cost of								
(i) Salaries/Wages	80.70	81.20	81.40	81.80	79.50	81.00	79.20	81.00
(ii) Bonus	4.80	6.30	5.00	6.00	4.90	6.30	5.60	6.40
(iii) Contribution to provident funds, etc.	8.20	7.10	8.00	6.70	8.90	7.00	8.20	6.80
(iv) Workman and staff welfare expenses	6.30	5.40	5.60	5.50	6.70	5.70	7.00	5.80

Description	1996-97 Census	1996-97 Sample	1997-98 Census	1997-98 Sample	1998-99 Census	1998-99 Sample	1999-2000 Census	1999-2000 Sample
Average labour cost per man-day worked (₹)	210.76	115.89	258.43	130.88	240.21	125.96	235.25	137.38
Percentage of total labour cost of								
(i) Salaries/Wages	77.90	80.30	77.80	79.70	66.90	72.00	74.10	73.30
(ii) Bonus	4.70	6.50	4.70	6.20	4.40	5.90	5.10	5.60
(iii) Contribution to provident funds, etc.	10.00	6.90	9.70	8.20	14.20	12.90	12.00	14.00
(iv) Workman and staff welfare expenses	7.40	6.30	7.70	5.90	14.40	9.20	8.80	7.00

Source: Various issues of Indian Labour Journal, Labour Bureau, Shimla

However, because of the industry practice of relating productivity to wages, often initiatives to increase productivity are interpreted as a cut in wages or a move to minimize facilities at the work place. Such negative connotations of the meaning of productivity, therefore, have defeated productivity improvement initiatives. Whenever trade unions are urged to deliberate on productivity-linked wages, they oppose the move. In India, therefore, linking productivity to compensation for working class people has been unsuccessful. However, organizations often follow the principles of performance-related pay for executives. It is often argued that India ranks lowest in labour productivity, as well as in the overall productivity. In a globalized market, unless we respond to the need of the hour, our companies may be forced to close down. Wages constitute an important cost component of products/services. Hence, an increase in wages without any linkage to productivity would make the product uncompetitive.

SUMMARY

From an economic perspective, the cost of employee compensation is recognized as an expense. Historically, we find a trace of the economic dimension of wages in various societies across the globe. In the Vedic era, payment of wages to workers was determined primarily in three ways—volume of work, time required to perform the work, and consideration of both the time and volume. However, these scientific wage payment principles of India were diluted with the accession of Moghuls and the rise of the British Empire. Deviating from the heritage of scientific principles of wage payment, wages to workers were left to the whims of their masters or employers. In Europe, historically, principles of just wage were followed.

Employee compensation concepts, from an economic perspective, are divided into several theoretical clusters such as subsistence theory, wage fund theory, marginal productivity theory, range theories, residual claimant theory, surplus value theory, bargaining theory, etc. All these theories, in one way or the other, try to achieve a trade-off between the employers' and the employees' choices. There are also different contradictory views on the pricing of various compensation components. For example, in the expensing of employee stock options, there are many conflicting theories. A similar contradiction is also present in productivity-linked wage concept. Despite such divergence in the economic interpretation of employee compensation, it is now well recognized that firms' compensation design plans should be aligned with market forces such as supply and demand. However, market forces alone should not be the only consideration in compensation decisions. Several other forces such as the work, skill requirements, time spent, etc. also merit consideration.

Key Terms

Economic theory of employee compensation This theory primarily illustrates the underlying principles involved in trade-offs by considering only two choices. These choices are either from the employer's or the employee's viewpoint.

Marginal productivity theory of wages It is based on the theory of income distribution. This theory advocates that wages 'tend to equal' the marginal productivity of labour. By using the term 'tend to equal', the theory asserts that wages are not determined by marginal productivity; rather the changes in marginal productivity lead to changes in wages.

Omni factor model This model gives a composite productivity index for the input and output costs of all the products. While input costs are considered for all products, output costs are determined on average marginal costs (AMC) method.

Productivity-linked employee benefits Productivity is considered as an input–output relational measurement. Orthodox views attribute productivity to labour efficiency as output quantification can immediately be related to labour efficiency, and hence relate to employee benefits.

Stock option Employee compensation through stock options is a cost to the organization and needs to be expensed in the financial reports to reflect the true value of the firm.

Surrogate model This model considers qualitative factors to measure productivity. Factors such as the satisfaction of investors, employees, customers, and suppliers are considered in qualitative terms.

Exercises

Concept Review Questions

1. How does economic theory relate to employee benefits? Illustrate your answer with some examples.
2. In what way can an organization try to achieve a trade-off between employee benefits and costs? Can economic theories help in this regard?
3. How can employee benefits be valued? Provide some examples.
4. Does the labour market influence employee benefits? Explain.
5. Explain the concept of productivity-linked employee benefits.
6. Write short notes on the following:
   (a) Equity in employment benefits
   (b) Productivity measurement
   (c) Surrogate model
   (d) Omni factor model
   (e) Total factor productivity

Critical Thinking Question

Rupee appreciation, in recent times, has made Indian IT and ITES organizations prune compensation. Companies such as TCS even had to reduce incentive variables. One way for a company is to attribute such reduction in variables to performance, the other way is to consider this as economic phenomenon. Examine the effect on the compensation design of manufacturing organizations in the era of rupee depreciation.

Employee Empowerment at P&G[1]

Employee empowerment is, perhaps, the most important non-monetary employee retention tool for any organization. Given the present market conditions, organizations are finding it difficult to cope with increased compensation costs. Hence, recognizing and realizing the value of talented employees, and motivating them by creating a culture of empowerment, is now considered the best alternative approach to a raise in compensation, when such a raise is impossible.

Procter & Gamble (P&G), the global fast moving consumer goods (FMCG) major in detergents, bleaches, and fabric softeners provides an example. The company replaced its traditional hierarchy and introduced three layers—plant manager, managers, and technicians. This restructuring was done to introduce the culture of team organization.

Commonly known as 'Lima organizational premises' (the company is headquartered at Lima, Ohio), the approach highlights teamwork, responsibility, the essential link between individual needs and satisfaction, and the business's requirements and success. To promote teamwork, managers and technicians formulate a set of values, which are honestly shared and mutually supported. The Lima Plant has a set of checklists in the form of standard operating procedures (SOP) for continuous supervision of work processes and safety. However, it is unlike McDonald's SOP, which makes every activity protocol-bound. The SOP is not made of a fixed set of values. Rather, they are beliefs which can be discussed, re-examined,

---
[1]Adapted from Waterman (1994)

(Contd)

CASE STUDY (*Contd*)

and revisited. These are not straitjackets, but guidelines or boundaries within which autonomous teams or individuals can perform their work with confidence and competence.

This also means that the manager has a new role. With a flat organization and with principles and checklists as guidelines, management boils down to three main activities: firstly, building and supporting relationships; secondly, giving advice and coaching; and thirdly, development and communication strategies. The manager's responsibility is to decide what needs to be done and why. The technician and his team are free to decide how to do it.

Top management defines the game and sets the direction, and then leaves a well-matched and properly-trained team to do things its own way.

The P&G structure is flexible. When someone has reached the top qualification level as a technician, he can work both 'online', that is, anything directly connected to production, or 'offline', which means everything else. That way, employees from the line can be responsible for typical staff activities such as product development, training, staffing, and so on. Such assignments are always temporary. The whole idea is to move back and forth between line and staff activities. The company makes good use of direct online experience. Those who get the assignments are highly motivated and no permanent staff is needed.

The teams are empowered to decide on daily work and staff different projects. Qualifications and pay are also a team responsibility. Hiring is the responsibility of a special committee, not the personnel department. The selection of applicants is an intensive team job performed by the members of the committee. P&G uses a skill-based system with several qualification and pay levels. People are paid for their knowledge and accomplishments, not for seniority or position in the hierarchy. Everyone is on a salary and there is no bonus system. The company pays competitive salaries and each employee gets an annual stake in a profit-sharing programme. As with everything else in the system, teams decide who is qualified to move to the next level.

P&G's cultural values and working structures encourage employees and teams to take responsibility, take on new challenges, and develop individual and team competence.

Discussion question

Study the case and discuss how P&G's initiatives benefit compensation management practices.

References

Francisco, B. (2002), *Can justice be served? When execs disgorge or share the wealth*, CBS. MarketWatch.com, 15 October.

Bhattacharyya, D.K. (2007), *Human Resource Research Methods*, Oxford University Press, New Delhi.

Fox, Justin (2002), 'The amazing stock option sleight of hand: Justin Fox exposed corporate America's grandest illusion', *Fortune Magazine*, 25 June.

Harrison, Joan (2002), Challenges for companies valuing options', *Mergers & Acquisitions*, November.

Hicks, John (1939), 'The foundations of welfare economics', *Economic Journal*, vol. 49, pp. 696–712, December.

Jatras, Todd (2002), 'Expensing options', Forbes, 24 July.

Leibenstein, Harvey (1966), 'Allocative efficiency versus x-efficiency', *American Economic Review*, vol. 56, pp. 392–415.

Mullaney, Timothy J. (2002), 'Options: Clearing the fog for investors', *Business Week*, 23 September.

Phillips, A.W. (1958), 'The relation between unemployment and the rate of change of money wage rates in the United Kingdom, 1861–1957', *Economica*, vol. 25, pp. 283–9.

Waterman, Robert (1994), *The Frontiers of Excellence: Learning from Companies that Put People First*, Nicholas Brealey, London.

CHAPTER FIVE

Employee Benefits

Learning Objectives

After reading this chapter, you will be able to
- understand the meaning and context of employee benefits
- define non-monetary employee benefits
- evaluate employee benefits and tax issues
- discuss different types of employee benefits
- appreciate the statutory employee benefits in India
- evaluate deferred employee benefits plans
- discuss alternative employee benefits programmes

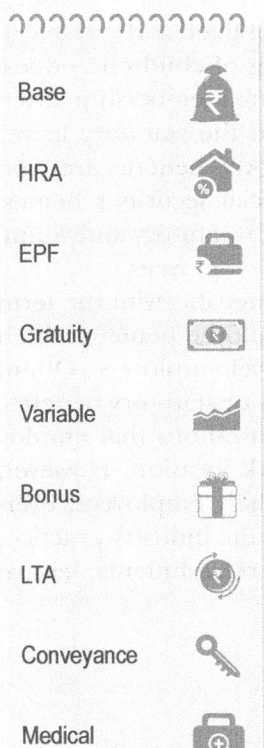

OPENING CASE

Tata Consultancy Services

Tata Consultancy Services (TCS), India's largest software exporter, introduced an across-the-board compensation cut for employees, in line with the decline in the company's performance. The rise of rupee against dollar had already signaled the increasing pressure on margins of software companies. Any remaining doubts were removed by cut in variables. The company's compensation structure gave some weightage to corporate performance for variables. A cut in variables, obviously, signaled that the company was unable to raise the compensation levels for employees for the coming year. The effective cut in compensation, as envisaged by the company, was about 1.5 per cent. Although the company did not foresee any change in the employees' loyalty and productivity, the cut was likely to demotivate them as it indicated that all was not well with the sector. The impact of the announcement was not limited to TCS. It sent ripples across the software industry and the stock market. Any negative change in the compensation policy of a company such as TCS adversely affects the stock market and industry sentiment. That was exactly what happened. Subsequent to the company's announcement, the stock market went down several points. For the employees of the other software companies, this indicated a future cut in their compensation package. Although Infosys, another major player in the software industry, did not immediately envisage any cut in employees' pay, it is widely believed that there will be a cut. Industry sources reported that TCS has ploughed back ₹ 83 crore from employees' pay into the company's coffers to maintain the expectations of shareholders.

Source: Adapted from *The Economic Times*, 30 January 2008

INTRODUCTION

Employee compensation comprises of both wage and non-wage components of the total labour costs. Non-wage components are given in the form of benefits in kind. Employee benefits are also known as fringe benefits, perquisites, or perks. The wage component of employee compensation is paid in cash, hence, it is more like normal wage or salary. When employee benefits are given in kind, they are referred to as a salary sacrifice, as employees avail of such benefits in exchange of their cash salaries. Both wage and non-wage components of employee compensation are taxable, barring a few. Drawing a comprehensive list of employee benefits, both with wage and non-wage components, is difficult. However, going by industry practice, we can categorize them into housing, group insurance, income protection (with optimization of fixed and variables), retirement benefits, tuition fees reimbursement, funding of children's education, contribution to different social security schemes, club membership, international tours, and different types of leave (other than the statutory leave) such as vacation leave, sabbatical leave, etc. Most employee benefits are paid by employers, whereas in case of some benefits like social security schemes, employees may also be required to contribute partly. Both statutory and voluntary employee benefits increase the economic security of employees.

In some organizations, the term *perks* is used interchangeably with the term *employee benefits*. Conventionally, perks denote those employee benefits which are discretionary in nature and usually paid to senior-level employees. Often, companies use the term perks even for non-discretionary or statutory benefits. For example, canteen facilities are mandatory for organizations that employ more than a certain number of employees at one work location. However, some facilities may be extended by organizations to their employees, even when they are not statutorily required to do so. Going by the industry practice, such common perks are company cars, hotel stays, free refreshments, leisure activities, lunch allowances, etc.

NON-MONETARY BENEFITS

Non-monetary benefits are used either when the organization feels that any additional monetary compensation will reduce the firm's cost competitiveness or when organizations strategically use them for motivation and retention. For organizations, achieving success is the first priority. Hence any reward or incentive that does not strain organizational financial health is always desirable. The aim is to motivate employees and turn them into good performers. Although monetary compensation is the prime mover, in this respect, carefully chosen non-monetary compensation can also do wonders. Non-monetary benefits can be provided—in various forms such as stock or fixtures—for no charge either instead of or in addition to money. Both monetary and non-monetary benefits are made available to an employee in accordance with the employment contract or agreement.

A Watson Wyatt (2000) study indicates that, globally, non-monetary compensation and benefits are gaining importance. Three common non-monetary incentives are—career advancement opportunities, flexible working hours, and opportunities to acquire new skills and knowledge. Non-monetary compensation and benefits are very important, particularly, for exploratory age group employees. This young age group values recognition and career advancement. Payment of cash compensation involves money, but all employees may not be motivated by money alone. Motivational theories teach us that many people are motivated through intrinsic reinforcers. Rewarding employees by creating opportunities is considered the best bet. Drawing a tentative list of non-monetary incentives is difficult. It depends solely on the firm's strategic selection of various alternatives to achieve intended goals and objectives. Functional autonomy, personal recognition, pleasant work environment, flexible work hours, training, and new and challenging opportunities help attract and retain employees. Many research studies have recognized the importance of non-monetary rewards over monetary rewards. Four possible advantages of non-monetary compensation, as identified by McAdams (1995), are as follows:

- recall value, which is more long lasting than cash payouts
- flexibility, because of ease of design, depending on organizational goals and budgetary constraints
- trophy value, because of the obvious display advantage to co-workers and colleagues
- less expensive, as employers have to pay less compared to cash awards

The effect of both non-monetary and monetary rewards on employees' productivity and performance is now recognized worldwide. Rewards imply recognition and payment of incentives to employees, individually and/or as members of teams. In this process, rewards recognize commendable performances and acknowledge employee contributions to the organization's mission. Rewards can improve employees' productivity to the tune of 20–30 per cent (Allen and Helms 2002). Therefore, organizations try to align rewards and compensation with their strategies, because of its positive effect on employee productivity.

However, organizations are not always capable of understanding the impact of non-monetary rewards on employee performance. This is because financial measures are easy to align with their business objectives. Non-financial measures such as quality of products and services, reliability in delivery, etc. are not so easily aligned with business objectives. Yet, such measures can significantly affect organizational performances. Employees may prefer to leave organizations if good performances are not recognized and there are no opportunities for career advancement. High employee turnover can prove costly. Therefore, rewarding employees with monetary or tangible as well as non-monetary or intangible compensation to limit their attrition will, in fact, benefit the organization as employee replacement may not be cost effective.

TAX OBLIGATIONS ON EMPLOYEE BENEFITS

As per tax laws, in most countries, including India, employee compensation, both monetary and non-monetary, are subject to tax liabilities. Provisions of the Indian Companies Act 1956 restrain companies from paying tax-free salaries to employees. In India, the Income Tax Act exempts employees from the tax burden if an employer pays tax on behalf of employees for the non-monetary perquisites. In a recent ruling by the Uttarakhand High Court, the word *perquisite* has been defined widely, to include any obligation of the employees met by the employer. Such ruling of the High Court is despite the contrary provisions of the Indian Companies Act 1956. However, such practices often lead to multiple tax gross-ups, that is, both the employers and the employees may claim tax benefits. Gross-up may be reimbursement of taxes paid by an employee, by his employer, or it may be a gift to an employee in the form of sharing his tax liability.

A detailed discussion on types of fringe benefits and tax obligations in India has been presented in Chapter 14 on Legal and taxation issues on employment compensation. Here, however, we will just spell out the tax obligations in different countries. For example, in the United States as per the terms of the Internal Revenue Code, employee benefits are in the form of a cafeteria plan, which allows employees to choose between different types of alternatives. Health benefits offered under a cafeteria plan may be health insurance, group-term life insurance, or reimbursement of actual medical expenses. Subject to a limit, any medical allowance paid to an employee in India is taxable. Hence, organizations provide health insurance cover, where employee's contribution is exempted from tax liability.

Employee benefits in the form of profit sharing are often used by organizations as incentive plans. Profit sharing depends on organizational profitability, and therefore, it is not a predictable or regular income for employees. These are payable in addition to the regular compensation. Whenever paid, they attract tax liability for employees. To avoid immediate tax obligations, many listed companies typically allot shares to employees in lieu of cash payouts on profit shares.

Organizations also offer *golden parachute* clauses as employee benefits, particularly to protect executives from possible termination in the event of their company acquisition. Such benefits may include severance pay, cash bonuses, stock options, or a combination of these.

Golden parachute clauses often worry investors, as these are silent about performance issues. It is more like a promise to perform, rather than a commitment to perform. According to a 2006 study by the Hay Group, the golden parachutes given to French executives are the highest in Europe, and equivalent to the funds received by 50 per cent of American executives. In contrast, French standard revenues for executives located in European countries are average. French executives receive roughly twice their salary and bonus as part of golden parachutes.

Similarly, a *golden handshake* clause entitles employees to receive huge benefits as a severance package. Organizations, because of restructuring, may hive off employees by giving them the option of premature retirement. With a golden handshake clause, such employees become entitled to receive benefits in the form of cash and equity. Such benefits attract tax liabilities, subject to some relief for voluntary retirees who invest the cash in some designated investment schemes announced from time to time by the government. For example, in India, voluntary retirees availing golden handshakes can invest their receipts in post offices up to a ceiling of ₹15 lakh, to get a relatively higher interest yield of nine per cent per annum. However, interest receipts from such investments in post offices are taxable.

TYPES OF EMPLOYEE BENEFITS

Organizational practices regarding employee benefits vary widely. However, some common employee benefits can be classified on the basis of employment security, health care, and retirement.

Employment security Unemployment allowances or insurance, pay for employees' adjustment to technological changes, leave pay, overtime pay, pay for holidays, pay for adjustment to the increased cost of living, lay-off compensation, retrenchment compensation, provisions for retiring rooms, jobs to children of the employees, etc. fall under this category.

Medical and health care Accident insurance, disability insurance, health insurance, hospitalization, life insurance, medical care, sick benefits, and sick leave are classified under this benefit category.

Old age and retirement Benefits classified under deferred income plans, pension, gratuity, provident fund, old-age medical benefits for retired employees, travelling concession to retired employees, jobs to dependants of the deceased employees, etc. fall under this category.

Miscellaneous benefits Organizations may offer benefits to recognize employees or to give them a social identity. Birthday gifts, marriage anniversary gifts, attendance bonus, canteens, cooperative credit societies, educational facilities, beauty parlour services, counselling support, recreational programmes, stress counselling, safety measures, etc. are classified under the miscellaneous category.

We can also classify employee benefits in other ways such as payment for time not worked, extra payment for extra work, etc. It is difficult to develop a detailed list of such benefits. Again, going by organizational practice, benefits can be in the form of premium pay, incentive bonus, shift allowance, old-age insurance, profit sharing, festival bonus, food subsidy, housing loan interest subsidy, housing rent subsidy, recreation facilities, etc.

STATUTORY EMPLOYEE BENEFITS IN INDIA

Indian labour laws require organizations to provide some statutory employee benefits. These are both monetary and non-monetary in nature. Here, we explain some of the statutory employee benefits that most organizations provide.

Bonus Literally, bonus is the payment of an extra amount to workers over and above the normal wages. Often, it is construed by employees as deferred wages as, in India, payment of bonus is both a convention and a statutory requirement. Bonus is the worker's share of organizational surplus. Operationally, it helps to bridge the gap between the actual wage and the need-based wage. Every organization classified as an industrial undertaking as per the legal provisions, is liable to pay 8.33 per cent of pay as minimum bonus irrespective of the profit or loss. Organizations that are not legally obliged to pay bonus to their employees make provision for payment of ex gratia.

Employee security Assuring physical and job security to employees promotes the security of both the employees and their family members. Organizations provide job security by confirming the employees on their regular payroll after they have completed the probationary period. Such confirmation creates a sense of job security in the minds of employees. Ensuring regular payment of wages, in compliance with the relevant labour laws, further strengthens this. Adopting adequate safety measures, on the other hand, ensures physical security. This includes accident prevention steps, pollution-free workplace, etc.

Retrenchment compensation The Industrial Disputes Act 1947 provides for the payment of compensation in case of lay-off and retrenchment. Non-seasonal industrial establishments employing 50 or more workers have to give one month's notice or one month's wages to all the workers who are retrenched after one year of continuous service. Compensation is paid at the rate of fifteen days wages for every completed year of service, with a maximum of 45 days' wages in a year. Workers are eligible for this compensation even in the case of closure of undertakings.

Lay-off compensation In case of lay-off, employees are entitled to lay-off compensation at the rate of 50 per cent of the total of the basic wage and dearness allowance, for the period of their lay-off except for weekly holidays. Lay-off compensation can normally be paid up to 45 days in a year.

Safety and health provisions Employee safety and health should be taken care of in order to protect them against workplace accidents and unhealthy working conditions. In India, the Factories Act 1948 stipulated certain requirements regarding working conditions with a view to provide a safe working environment. These provisions relate to cleanliness; disposal of waste and effluents; ventilation and temperature; dust and fume; artificial humidification; over-crowding; lighting; drinking water; and latrine, urinals, and spittoons. Provisions relating to safety measures include fencing of machinery; work on or near machinery in motion; employment of young persons on dangerous machines; casing of new machinery; probation of employment of women and children near cotton openers; precautions regarding striking gear, devices for cutting off power, self-acting machines, hoists and lifts, revolving machinery, pressure plants, floors, excessive weights, lifting machines, chains, ropes, and tackles; protection of eyes; precautions against dangerous fumes, explosives, or inflammables, gas, etc.; precautions in case of fire; power to require specifications of defective parts; tests of stability; safety of buildings and machinery; etc.

In India, employees drawing these compensation benefits are not covered under the Payment of Bonus Act 1965. However, the employer pays them a suitable lump sum known as ex gratia, which varies depending upon their level in the organization. This is not compulsory on the part of the employer, but acts as an incentive to the employee.

DEFERRED COMPENSATION PLANS

Many employee benefits are covered by the organization under deferred compensation plans. A *deferred compensation plan* is an arrangement whereby an employee or owner defers some portion of the employee's current income until a specified future date. Wages earned in one period are actually paid at a later date.

Life insurance can be used to fund a deferred compensation plan. The deferred amounts can be used to pay life insurance premiums. The cash value can then be available at retirement to supplement other income or, if the insured dies before retirement, the insured's designated beneficiary would receive the insurance policy's death benefit.

There are both qualified and non-qualified deferred compensation plans. A qualified deferred compensation plan receives certain tax preferences under the Income Tax Act. Employers are also entitled to make deductions for contribution to such plans. However, a qualified deferred compensation plan cannot discriminate among employees by adopting a differential rate based on hierarchical levels. In the United States, the Tax Equity and Fiscal Responsibilities Act (TEFRA) 1982, was enacted to curb such discriminatory practices. Employers' contributions to qualified deferred compensation plans being statutorily regulated, it is essential for organizations to file regular reports and returns with appropriate authorities.

A non-qualified deferred compensation plan does not receive favourable tax treatment. Employers cannot avail of tax benefits for such contributions until the time these are actually paid to employees. This is also known as the doctrine of constructive receipt. For employees, however, under the doctrine of constructive receipt, such non-qualified compensation benefits are taxable, irrespective of whether the benefits are actually paid or not. Such benefits are apportioned to the extent of annual values for tax purposes. For organizations, deferred non-qualified compensation provides many opportunities. Employers can adopt a strategic approach to award such benefits disproportionately to talented executives, in order to increase their retention and to motivate them to become good performers.

Fringe Benefits

The term fringe benefits refers to various extra benefits provided to employees, in addition to the compensation paid in the form of wages or salary. These benefits can be defined as any wage cost not directly connected with the employees' productive effort, performance, service, or sacrifice. It is also defined as those benefits, which are provided by an employer for the benefit of an employee, and which are not in the form of wages, salaries, and time-related payments.

Different terms such as welfare measures, social charges, social security measures, supplements, sub-wages, employee benefits, etc. are used to denote fringe benefits. According to International Labour Organization (ILO), fringe benefits can be defined as, 'Wages that are often augmented by special cash benefits, by the provision of medical and other services or by payments in kind, that forms part of the wage for expenditure on goods and services. In addition, workers commonly receive such benefits as holiday with pay, low cost meals, low-rent housing, etc. Such additions to the wage proper are sometimes referred to as fringe benefits. Benefits that have no relation to employment or wages should not be regarded as fringe benefits, even though they may constitute a significant part of the worker's total income.'

Therefore, fringe benefits are those monetary and non-monetary benefits given to the employees, during and after their employment, which are connected to their employment, but not to their contributions to the organization.

Coverage of fringe benefits

Fringe benefits cover bonus, social security measures, retirement benefits such as provident fund, gratuity, pension, worker's compensation, housing, medical facilities, canteens, co-operative credit, consumer stores, educational facilities, recreational facilities, and financial advice. Therefore, fringe benefits cover a number of employee services and facilities provided by employers to their employees, and in some cases to their family members too. The welfare of employees and their family members is an effective advertisement, and also a method of buying the gratitude and loyalty of employees. Some employers provide services over and above the legal requirements to make effective use of their workforce, whereas, some restrict themselves to those benefits which are legally required.

Need for extending fringe benefits

During World War II, certain non-monetary benefits were extended to employees as a means of neutralizing the effect of inflationary conditions. These benefits, which include housing, health, education, recreation, credit, canteen, etc., have been increased from time to time as a result of demands and pressures from trade unions. It has been recognized that these benefits help employees in meeting some of their contingencies and social obligations.

Most organizations have been extending fringe benefits to their employees, year after year, due to reasons such as employee demands, employer's preference, social security, etc.

Employee demands Employees demand more and varied types of fringe benefits rather than pay hikes because they want a reduction in tax burden. Other reasons for such a demand are the rising price index and cost of living.

Trade union demands Trade unions compete with each other to get more benefits, such as life insurance, health clubs, etc. If one union succeeds in getting a benefit, the other union persuades the management to provide a similar or new benefit. Therefore, the competition among trade unions within an organization results in more and varied benefits.

Employer's preference Employers prefer fringe benefits to pay hikes as fringe benefits motivate employees to contribute to the organization. They improve morale and also work as an effective advertisement.

Social security It is a security that society furnishes through appropriate organizations to protect members against certain risks. These risks may include contingencies of life, accidents, and occupational diseases. The employer has to provide various benefits such as safety measures, compensation in case of involvement of workers in accidents, medical facilities, etc. with a view to providing security to employees against various contingencies.

Human relations Human relations are maintained when employees are satisfied economically, socially, and psychologically.

Fringe benefits satisfy a worker's economic, social, and psychological needs. Consumer stores, credit facilities, canteens, recreational facilities, etc. satisfy a worker's social needs, whereas retirement benefits help during post-retirement life. However, most benefits are aimed at minimizing the economic problems of the employee.

Objectives of fringe benefits

From the employers' point of view, fringe benefits form an important part of employee incentives, because they help retain employees, and obtain their loyalty. The important objectives of fringe benefits are as follows:
- create and improve sound industrial relations
- boost employee morale
- motivate employees by identifying and satisfying their needs
- provide a good work environment and work life
- provide security to employees against social risks, through benefits such as old-age and maternity benefits
- protect the health of employees and provide safety to employees against accidents
- promote employee welfare by providing welfare measures such as recreation facilities
- create a sense of belonging among employees and to retain them
- meet the requirements of various legislations relating to fringe benefits

Need for extending benefits to employees

Employee benefit programmes are necessary as they help in the following ways:
- enable employees to guard against rising prices and cost of living
- avail of the most cost-effective compensation plan (from employers' point of view)
- attract and retain employees
- encash the tax saving opportunities (wherever possible)
- demonstrate employers' concern for employees
- meet the legal requirements of compensation and welfare of employees

Employee benefits, therefore, are given for the mutual benefit of employers and the employees. If organizations select an appropriate employee benefits plan, they can achieve their intended goals and objectives.

ALTERNATIVES TO EMPLOYEE BENEFITS

Many organizations adopt some alternative approaches to employee benefits programmes. One such alternative is moon lighting, which could range from *blue moon lighting* to *full moon lighting*. Despite provisions for benefits, some employees may feel that these are not adequate. Hence, such employees may opt for part-time jobs or businesses to meet the difference between wages or salaries and requirements. This is known as double jobbing or moonlighting. Organizations often indulge employees in this, considering moonlighting as a form of alternative benefits. Blue moon lighting refers to those cases where the employees fail to get a second job or income source, and, therefore, present a problem for the organization. Full moon lighting refers to those cases where the employees consider that their compensation from employment is negligible, and hence, they spend most of their time trying to find an alternative, keeping their job as a buffer. Whatever may be the form of moon lighting, it is not desirable for the organization. Tolerating such activities may ultimately lead to organizational failure.

Flexible employee benefits allow employees to pick benefits from a bundle of alternatives. Many organizations deliberately tailor-make such benefits for employees to address their needs. Internationally, fringe benefits comprise almost 40 per cent of the employees' salaries. Flexible benefits may be modular, core-plus, or flexible in nature. Modular plans are pre-designed packages of benefits. Core-plus plans consist of a core of essential benefits and some extra benefits options. Flexible spending plans enable employees to set aside benefits for some particular services in future.

Payment of flexible benefits is vogue in the developed world. However, in India, we restrict payment of such benefits to only very senior-level executives. This is because of opposition from trade unions, who consider it a violation of principles of equity.

SUMMARY

Employee benefits, as part of employee compensation programmes, have significant impact both on employees and organizations. For employees, it helps meet their financial needs; for organizations, it exerts significant financial and administrative influence, which can be both, positive or negative. Payment of employee benefits is made by the organization either to meet statutory requirements or voluntarily to motivate and retain employees.

Employee benefits need not always be in monetary terms; they may be non-monetary too. Organizations strategically balance monetary and non-monetary benefits in order to optimize benefits and costs, and simultaneously motivate and retain employees. By designing flexible employee benefit plans, organizations can customize total compensation as per employees' needs. The most commonly used employee benefits include health insurance, retirement plans, vacation, and sick leave. Designing the appropriate benefit plan requires the organization to consider issues such as taxation, legal aspects, and financial health.

Key Terms

Alternative employee benefits Moon lighting is considered the most prominent alternative to employee benefits. Some organizations, as they cannot pay adequate compensation, allow employees to indulge in part-time jobs or businesses.

Flexible employee benefits It allows employees to pick benefits from a bundle of alternatives. Many organizations deliberately tailor-make benefits for their employees to address their needs. Payment of flexible benefits is in vogue in the developed world. However in India, we restrict payment of such benefits to only senior-level executives. This is because of opposition from trade unions, as they consider it as a violation of principles of equity.

Golden parachute clause It is an employee benefits plan for executives. It is meant to protect them from possible termination of employment, in the event of a company being acquired. Benefits may include severance pay, cash bonuses, stock options, or a combination of these.

Trophy value These benefits help employees improve their standing among co-workers and colleagues. This type of employee benefits programme is highly sought after by some employees as they can be displayed to co-workers and colleagues.

Exercises

Concept Review Questions

1. Discuss the role of employee benefits programme in motivating employees. To what extent does statutory employee benefits programme help an organization motivate and retain employees?
2. What are non-monetary benefits? What type of non-monetary benefits do you recommend for marketing executives?
3. Explain the details of tax obligations in employee benefits programmes.
4. Explain how deferred compensation plans can be a part of an employee benefits programme.
5. What is a fringe benefit? Can it be made a part of an employee benefits plan?

Critical Thinking Question

Compare and study the employee benefits programmes of two award-winning organizations—National Express Limited and the Royal Bank of Scotland. Discuss how an innovative employee benefits programme can influence the existing employee benefits plan of any hypothetical Indian organization.

National Express Limited was selected for Watson Wyatt Worldwide sponsored *Employee Benefits Awards 2007*, along with McDonald's and Siemens for its innovative employee benefits programme. National Express Limited, a scheduled coach operator, started its employee benefits programme in 2004. To start with, it offered its employees coach travel passes. However, it extended the programme to a whole range of perks such as bus stations services throughout the UK, long-service awards, employee assistance programme for staff and their families, online discount scheme, interest-free loans to provide financial support, boxes of goodies for new parents, increased maternity provisions, flexible working hours, and the option of buying childcare vouchers through salary sacrifice. Other perks offered through salary sacrifice included a bikes-for-work scheme, and buying and selling holidays. Long service awards were divided into two types—five-year duration and twenty-five year duration. Employees with five years of service got a bottle of champagne, whereas, employees with twenty-five years' experience got a trip to Egypt.

This *lost cost but high value* employee benefits programme helped the company to reduce staff turnover from 50 per cent in July 2005 to 27 per cent in November 2006. Employees' level of satisfaction also increased significantly. Since the benefits initiative began, the company has experienced increases in turnover (from £192.4 million in 2004 to £200.5 million in 2006) and profit (from £18.8 million in 2004 to £21.5 million in 2006).

The Royal Bank of Scotland (RBS) Group, another winner in this category, designed an innovative employee benefits programme by launching a new flexible pension scheme, emphasizing group communications, group legal and compliance, and group logistics. This flexible pension scheme complied with all the legal requirements and also successfully met employees' expectations. Seventy seven per cent of exploratory age group employees (aged less than 35 years) opted for the scheme. Thus, it addressed the key issue of retaining young employees.

Innovative Design of Employee Benefits at Narmada Ltd

Narmada Ltd is a Gujarat-based oil refinery, having a capacity to produce nearly one-third of the country's petroleum, oil, and lubricant (POL) requirement. The company sources its crude oil requirement both through its captive wells and through import from Sudan. One of the biggest challenges for the company is to design a low-cost innovative employee benefits scheme, so as to remain competitive in the market. Sustaining a POL business without adequate cost control is difficult for any organization. With liberalization, the POL business has now become very competitive. Branding wars have made POL a more value-added product and customer expectations are higher. Attracting the customers on highways, rather than small retail buyers in cities, is crucial to earnings. Employees need to be on their toes at selling points and in refineries. Every stage counts; every wrong step adds to costs and affects quality.

Narmada Ltd has designed its compensation keeping in view the market rate, for fear of losing its employees. In the petroleum and oil industry, employees acquire industry-specific skills after hands-on exposure of at least five years. Competitors always look for ready-to-use manpower, both in the domestic market and abroad. Nurturing a motivating and high-performance culture through compensation and benefits programmes is a great challenge.

For the HR Director, Augasti Tendulkar, it is a challenge to devise the best compensation and benefits plan, without changing the total compensation cost to the company's disadvantage. Being educated abroad, Tendulkar observed how Western companies devise innovative compensation and benefits design plans. To start with, Tendulkar designed a voluntary benefits discounts scheme. With corporate tie-ups, the company built a mutual network on a reciprocal basis with retail malls, travel agents, hotels, airlines, health clubs, insurance companies, hospitals, and household appliance manufacturers. All the employees have been informed that any purchase of items or services from the designated outlets will make them eligible for a discount. However, such benefits are voluntary. While formally announcing such voluntary benefit schemes, Tendulkar said, 'We at Narmada want to offer our employees the most credible benefit schemes, to meet their varied needs at the best possible discounts. The company's HR will periodically make announcements of discount offers.'

Narmada offers its employees pensions after they have served 20 years. Pension is offered as a second benefit, that is, in addition to a contributory provident fund. While the provident fund is managed by the state-owned Provident Fund Commission, the company manages its own pension fund to ensure employee retention. Employees need to contribute a meagre percentage of salary to the pension fund, while the company contributes almost 12 per cent of the gross pay of each employee. For many employees, the pension is a great motivator.

To increase the pension entitlement, Tendulkar came out with another voluntary benefit scheme, a few months later, which gives employees the option of sacrificing a very small percentage of their salaries to the pension scheme. Tendulkar

(Contd)

CASE STUDY (Contd)

observed that subsequent to these announcements employees' loyalty towards Narmada increased, attrition rate dropped significantly, and new talent was attracted. Tendulkar's cost–benefit analysis showed that all these voluntary benefits, in fact, reduced the annual HR costs by two per cent.

Discussion question

Do you believe Tendulkar is right in his analysis? Support your answer with arguments. If no, offer an alternative model of voluntary benefits, which you feel is better than Tendulkar's.

References

Allen, R.S. and M.M. Helms (2002), 'Employee perceptions of the relationship between strategy rewards and organisational performance', *Journal of Business Strategies*, vol. 19, no. 2, pp. 115–140.

Bhattacharyya, D.K. (2006), *Human Resource Management*, 2nd edn, Excel Books, New Delhi.

Falicia, Nathan (1987), 'Analysing employers' costs for wages, salaries and benefits', *Monthly Labour Review*, October, pp. 3–10.

Hay Group (2006), 'Assessment of city's major employee benefits programme', October, www.haygroup.com, last accessed on 24 May 2007.

Henderson, R.I. (2003), *Compensation Management in a Knowledge based World*, 9th edn, Pearson Education, New Delhi.

McAdams, Jery (1995), 'Benefits of using non-monetary awards', Workforce Performance Newsletter, June.

Milkovich, G.T. and J.M. Newman (2005), *Compensation*, 8th edn, Tata McGraw-Hill Publishing Company Limited, New Delhi.

Motiwal, O.P. and H.K. Awasthi (1983), *Wage Settlements in Indian Industries*, Documentation Centre for Corporate and Business Policy Research, New Delhi.

Watson Wyatt (2000), 'Multinational pooling revisited', www.watson.wyatt.com/multinational/editions/2000/2000_10_01.asp, last accessed on 24 August 2007.

CHAPTER SIX

Employee Motivation and Compensation

Learning Objectives

After completing this chapter, the students would be able to
- understand employee motivation
- learn about various theories on employee motivation in India and abroad
- examine the relationship between motivation and compensation
- understand motivational needs of employees and translate them into a new compensation design
- learn the basics of motivational research
- analyse motivation and morale issues

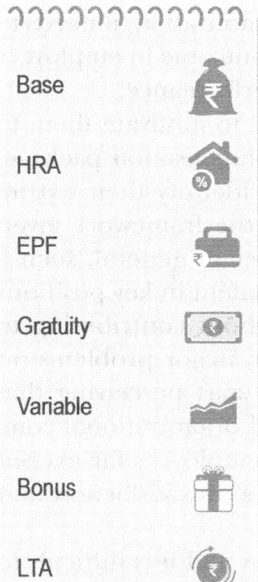

OPENING CASE

Motivating through Ownership

Sharing ownership through an employee stock ownership plan (ESOP) has been instrumental in establishing a successful ownership culture in Grasim Industries. The company's retail division is now in top gear. This year, it plans to open at least 30 new exclusive brand stores across the country. Such an ambitious growth programme requires the company to motivate its employees. Realizing the importance of ESOP in motivating employees, Grasim's Compensation Committee approved the grant of 2,22,670 stock options to the employees under the employee stock option scheme in 2007. Upon vesting, each stock option is convertible to one equity share of the company priced at ₹1,928.

However, employee ownership by itself cannot increase employee motivation and performance. It should be combined with employee participation to derive incremental organizational performance. Realizing this, Grasim made its employees responsible, as well as integrated its business with human resources and technology.

INTRODUCTION

Organizations design compensation as an additional motivation for employees. Motivated employees deliver their best and significantly contribute to organizational growth and prosperity. Motivated employees also tend to stay longer with the organization, thereby reducing the rate of attrition. However, designing compensation with employee motivation as the basis is not easy. It requires an understanding of factors that motivate them and the perceived reinforcers that can be included in the compensation structure. A well-designed compensation structure can motivate employees. In this chapter, we first discuss the basics of employee motivation and then outline how compensation can be designed based on the identified motivational needs of employees. A motivating compensation design not only motivates the employees to become good performers and continue with it, but also attracts others to join the organization. Jones (1955) defined motivation '….how behaviour gets started, is energized, is directed, is stopped and what kind of subjective reaction is present in the organisms while all these are going on.' Although many such definitions of the term motivation are available, all of them converge to what energizes human behaviour, what directs such behaviour, and how such behaviour can be maintained or sustained. For compensation design to derive the benefit of motivation, it needs to focus on all these aspects so that the desired behavioural outcome in employees could lead to significant changes in the organizational performance.

After employees are hired and trained, it is important to motivate them to get the desired results from them. While designing a compensation package, it is necessary that employee expectations that suitably identify their extrinsic and intrinsic needs are perceived to be met within the framework given by policies and procedures of the organization. However in general, such a compensation package is restricted to attract and retain talent in key positions where organizations can afford to become flexible, without contributing to the general dissatisfaction of other employees. However, major problems on employee motivation become evident when employees start perceiving that there is a wide mismatch between their expectations and organizational commitments. At times, such perceived expectations of the employees far exceed the organizational commitments, resulting in employees' dissatisfaction and demotivation.

Motivation is a dynamic human resource (HR) process and it is difficult to specify an organization-specific motivation tool. The topic of motivation has, perhaps, received the greatest attention from management thinkers worldwide. Even then, the problem has not been effectively addressed as employee demotivation continues to be a perennial issue from the days of industrial revolution. Before industrial revolution, this problem was non-existent as owners of labour services and owners of means of capital had the same identity. In such a home-centred production system, motivation for work was spontaneous.

Related Concepts

At the core of motivational factors lie the real and perceived needs of the employees. If these needs are satisfied, it contributes to an increase in performance and productivity of the employees. However, motivation can be better defined as a process, which governs choices. This process may be internal or external to the individual that arouse enthusiasm and persistence to pursue a certain course of action. Motivation process starts with a physiological or psychological deficiency or need that activates behaviour or a drive that is aimed at a goal or incentive (Luthans 1998). All the definitions, therefore, imply that motivation is a behavioural syndrome, which arises when there is a perceived mismatch in employee needs and expectations. With the widening of such a perceived gap, employees feel demotivated and reduce their level of performance and productivity. Contrarily, if the gap gets reduced, employees feel motivated and contribute their best to help achieve organizational objectives. From the organizational point of view, the motivation process follows certain defined steps, which as a continuum need to be periodically reviewed and strategized to ensure its proper renewal. This process helps to maintain employee motivation, which is evident from congruence between their displayed behaviour and behaviour required by the organizational objectives.

In the first stage, it is important to identify the need deficiency of the employees, if any. Need deficiency centres on extrinsic and intrinsic needs. Extrinsic needs are related to material and tangible gains. Increased pay, incentives, bonus, better medical facilities, better retirement benefits, and better canteen facilities are some examples of extrinsic needs. Intrinsic needs, on the other hand, are abstract in nature and related to mental satisfaction. Increased status, challenge, a sense of belonging, scope for growth, creativity, recognition, sense of achievement, etc. are examples of such needs. Identification of need deficiency is possible through direct observation of employees' behaviour and through a survey using response to a structured questionnaire. However, employees, by and large, feel sensitized about giving responses to a survey questionnaire fearing that they might be harassed for giving any response critical of the organizational policy. Confidentiality in survey responses can be ensured through a secret opinion poll, in which the questionnaire does not require disclosure of the employee identity. However, for better results, it is always desirable to integrate survey findings with personal interview, which can be in the form of an open discussion with employees by their respective supervisors. Some organizations document such information in a 360-degree performance appraisal, incorporating certain items in the appraisal form itself. Need deficiency can also be understood from the trend of employee performance by developing a performance index or productivity index.

In the second phase of motivational process, organizations identify the appropriate strategy to close the perceived need gap of the employees. There are many innovative ways to close such a need gap without increasing the compensation budget. For example, the need for increased pay can be met by reducing deferred benefits such as non-wage labour cost (NWLC) and including such reduced amount to the current pay of the employees. This is particularly important for organizations that employ mostly young people in the exploratory age group (less than 35 years). Similarly, linking pay to performance also facilitates developing of proper compensation structure to reward and motivate good performers. Similarly, intrinsic need gap can be reduced by adopting an enabling organization structure, which fosters creativity and growth among others.

To understand the importance of extrinsic and intrinsic needs, we have illustrated the industrial disputes scenario in India at a macro level. Table 6.1 shows

TABLE 6.1 Industrial dispute scenario in India

Cause group	1994 No. of disputes	1994 Percentage to total	1995 No. of disputes	1995 Percentage to total	1997 No. of disputes	1997 Percentage to total	1998 No. of disputes	1998 Percentage to total
Wages and allowances	354	29.4	320	30	305	23.4	233	21.2
Personnel	194	16.2	195	18.3	261	20.0	175	16.0
Retrenchment	19	1.6	10	0.9	7	0.5	8	0.7
Lay-off	3	0.2	4	0.4	7	0.5	6	0.6
Indiscipline	185	15.2	145	13.6	246	18.9	225	18.9
Violence	20	1.7	14	1.3	13	1.0	7	0.6
Leave and Hours of work/shift working	17	1.4	21	2.0	31	2.4	14	1.3
Bonus	92	7.8	79	7.4	112	86	123	11.2
Gherao	1	0.1	1	0.1	–	–	–	–
Non-implementation of Agreements, awards, etc.	37	3.1	43	4.0	43	3.3	32	2.9
Charter of demands	55	4.6	61	5.7	68	5.2	97	8.8
Workload	10	0.8	10	0.9	9	0.7	6	0.6
Surplus labour	1	0.1	–	–	1	0.1	–	–
Betterment of amenities	16	1.3	18	1.7	34	2.6	12	1.1

(Contd)

TABLE 6.1 (Contd)

	Years							
	1994		1995		1997		1998	
Cause group	No. of disputes	Percentage to total	No. of disputes	Percentage to total	No. of disputes	Percentage to total	No. of disputes	Percentage to total
Suspension/Change of Manufacturing Process	1	0.1	–	–	–	–	1	0.1
Standing orders/Rules/Service/conditions/safely Measures	50	4.2	52	4.9		2.6	13	1.2
Others	118	9.8	57	5.4	85	6.5	89	8.1
Not Known	21	1.7	29	2.7	37	2.8	49	4.5
Total	201	100	1066	100	1305	100	109	100

Source: Various yearbooks on Indian labour

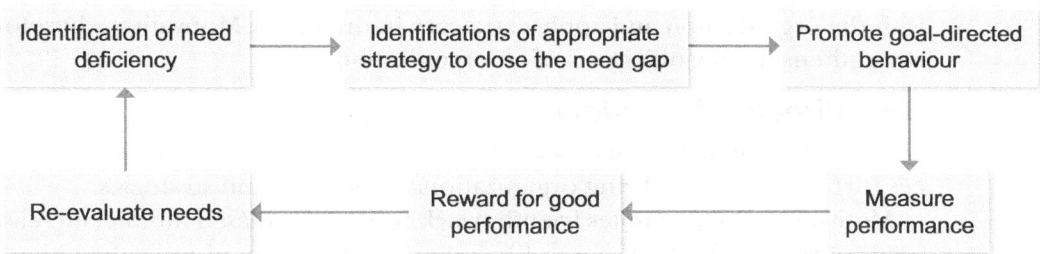

FIG. 6.1 Motivational model

that in terms of percentage share, intrinsic factors are also very significant. However, the severity of extrinsic and intrinsic factors in terms of *man-days loss* cannot be measured because of an inherent problem in the data collection of Labour Bureau, Shimla. The identification of appropriate strategy to close need gaps helps an organization achieve organizational objectives by inducing goal-directed behaviour among employees. Therefore, in the third phase of motivational process, organizations enforce goal-directed behaviour. Goal-directed behaviour enhances performance and productivity of employees, which in turn influences compensation strategy and other motivational reinforcers.

The cycle continues as an ongoing process in an organization and at the end of the continuum, needs are again re-evaluated to understand emerging need deficiency, if any. In Fig. 6.1, the model as a continuum is illustrated.

OBJECTIVES OF MOTIVATION

Motivation enhances performance and improves productivity. Therefore, motivation fulfils important objectives of an organization.

Productive use of resources

Physical, financial, and human resources are important resource constructs for an organization. Proper utilization of these resources is only possible when individuals in the organization feel motivated. Motivation leads to goal-directed behaviour, which in turn facilitates productive utilization of all available resources. Productive use of resources can be best understood from total factor productivity indices and labour productivity indices.

Increased efficiency

The second important objective of motivation is increased efficiency of the employees. The efficiency of motivated employees increases as increased motivation augments their willingness to work. Increased efficiency contributes to cost reduction.

Quality consciousness

Motivated employees also become quality conscious as they identify themselves with the organization and apply extra care in their jobs. Motivation, therefore, strengthens quality objectives of an organization.

Goal-directed behaviour

By promoting goal-directed behaviour among co-workers, motivated employees further help in realizing organizational objectives and strategies.

Motivation also promotes friendly work culture, increased morale, increased sense of responsibility, a sense of belonging, integration of individual identity with organizational identity, teamwork, participative decision-making, etc. All these factors together create an environment conducive for creativity and growth, leading to the transformation of the organization into an enabling organization. Finally, motivation ensures organizational stability by reducing employee turnover and absenteeism.

Mechanism of Motivation

The word *motivation* is used to describe the drive that impels an employee to work even when he can avoid it. The process starts with physiological (extrinsic) or psychological (intrinsic) needs of an employee. The satisfaction of extrinsic or intrinsic needs activates the drive of the employee to achieve a goal. This process is explained using Fig. 6.2.

At this stage, it is important to understand the basic differences between motive, motivation, and motivating. *Motive* is the inner state that activates and

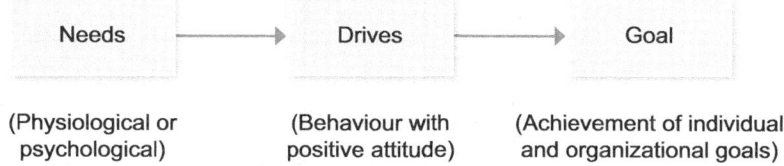

FIG. 6.2 Mechanism of motivation

directs the behaviour of individuals towards certain goals. Inner state of an individual is created out of perceived need imbalance. The degree of imbalance decides the need for a strong motive or a weak motive, and accordingly an individual propels himself into action. Therefore, motives create a drive that energizes individuals into action. While motive energizes action, *motivation* is the actual action or work behaviour. The degree of work behaviour decides the level of motivation. If employees perform well, putting in their best efforts, their motivation is considered to be high; whereas in the reverse case, their motivation is considered to be low. *Motivating* implies inducements to energize work behaviour. Motivating is part of a managerial task, as it satisfies both individual and organizational needs. Managers always endeavour to sustain the motivating environment to get the work done in an effective and efficient manner. For this purpose, a manager needs to understand the degree of motive strength of employees. The process of identification of need deficiency has already been explained. Since needs or motives are the enablers of work behaviour, managers need to plot the motives against their degree of importance to be able to make effective decisions. This can be done as shown in Fig. 6.3.

In Fig. 6.3, A, B, C, D, E, and F denote different motives, which may be compensation, promotional opportunities, functional autonomy, creativity, challenge, and flexibility in policies. Using the Pareto diagram, a manager can optimize the motive strength as the Pareto principle suggests that every

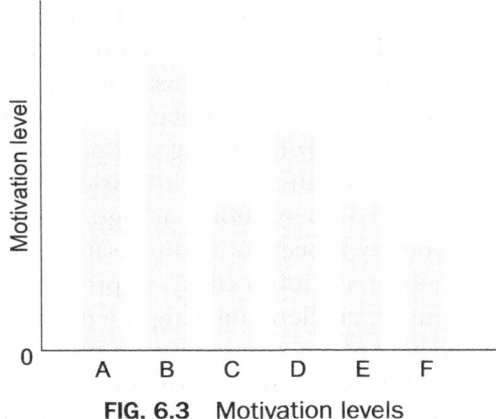

FIG. 6.3 Motivation levels

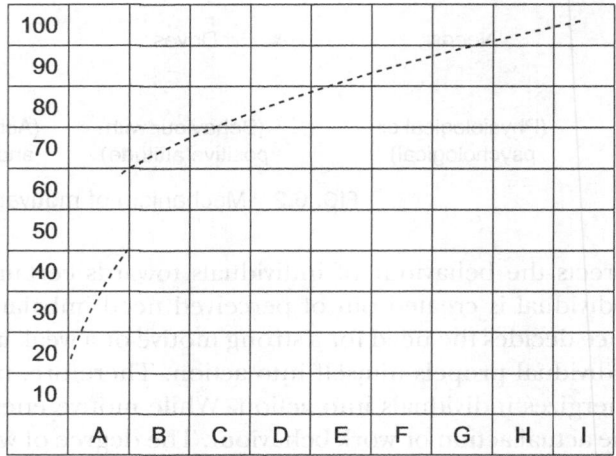

FIG. 6.4 Pareto graph

problem (in our case the motive strength) is the result of few causes (a vital few) and all causes (trivial many) are not equally important. This means by taking care of 10–15 per cent of motive strengths, managers can reduce the need gaps in 70–80 per cent of the motives because motives have interdependence and are interrelated. A typical Pareto diagram is shown in Fig. 6.4.

Relationship between Motivation and Compensation

Employee compensation is linked to both intrinsic and extrinsic factors of motivation of an individual. Among others, any compensation system needs to be motivating in order to
- attract individuals with knowledge, ability, and talent as demanded by specific organizational tasks
- retain effective, valued, and productive employees
- to get the desired level of performance
- promote high degree of job involvement and job satisfaction, and an attitude conducive to loyalty and commitment to the organization

Similar to motivation, compensation also has two important components, that is, monetary and non-monetary. Organizations fulfil the extrinsic motivational requirements by designing compensation that emphasizes on the cash component. On the other hand, intrinsic motivational elements are taken care of by a suitable compensation package, which among others emphasizes on the non-monetary aspects of compensation. Some of the intrinsic compensation components are job security, improved work conditions, status, sense of accomplishment, challenging assignments, increased job responsibilities, etc. For effectiveness of any compensation system, an organization needs to establish a correlation between performance and rewards. Intrinsic rewards can be achieved through job enrichment and job redesign.

THEORIES OF MOTIVATION

We have already discussed the theories of motivation in brief. In this section, we will discuss the major theories of motivation with some critical notes. Before we proceed further, let us examine the process of development of work motivation theory as given in Fig. 6.5.

Frederick Taylor (1911), the father of *scientific management*, observed that prosperity of management and workforce are inter-dependent. Individuals are inherently capable of working hard, but they show such qualities irregularly. To harness this feature of individual behaviour, pay and rewards (incentives) must be linked to achievement of optimum goals. So, good performers get rewards and better pay, whereas bad performers lose on this count.

Elton Mayo (1945) and his associates, through a series of experiments known as *Hawthorne Experiments*, established that work satisfaction and, hence,

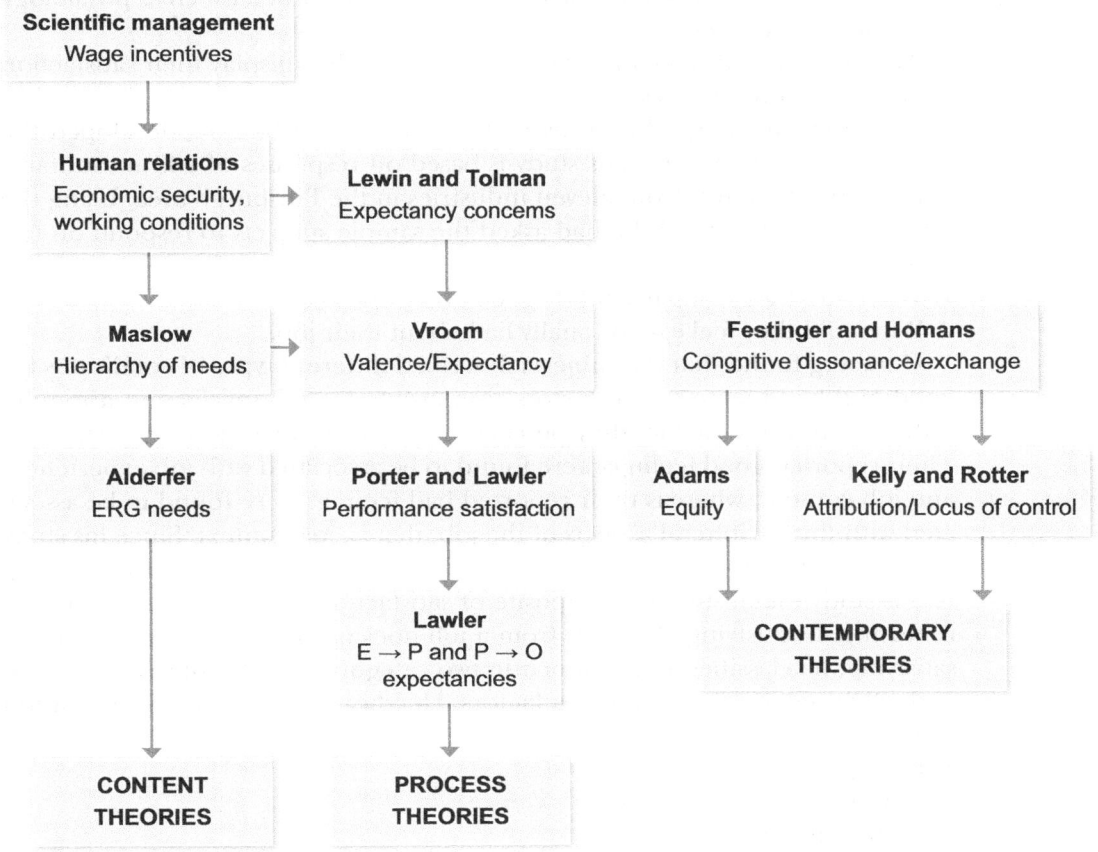

FIG. 6.5 Motivational theories

performance are not related in terms of monetary compensation. They depend more on working conditions and attitudes, communications, positive management response and encouragement, working environment, etc.

Maslow (1954), through his *need hierarchy theory*, established that motivation of individuals arises from a hierarchy of needs. This concept was briefly introduced earlier in this chapter. Now, we would elaborate Maslow's concepts by first examining essence of his theory and then by critically examining the theory. The essence of his theory can be summarized as follows.

- Wants and desires of human beings influence their behaviour. Already satisfied wants and desires do not act as motivators. Individuals show their motive or behaviour to fulfil their unsatisfied wants and desires.
- Needs of an individual are arranged in order of their perceived priority or hierarchy. Perceived need factors of individuals vary.
- Individuals can advance from one level of need hierarchy to another, only when their preceding need factors are satisfied. For example, an individual cannot advance to the satisfaction of a higher order need such as belonging or social needs without satisfaction of a lower order need such as physiological needs and safety.
- As individuals advance to higher order needs, they display their satisfaction and motivation to work.

Frederick Herzberg (1966), extending the work of Maslow, developed the *content theory of motivation*. His study is based on responses of 200 accountants and engineers, drawn from eleven industries in the Pittsburgh area. Using the critical incident method, he had asked the sample subjects to respond on two aspects.

1. When did they feel particularly good about their job?
2. When did they feel exceptionally bad about their job?

Herzberg found that the subjects described different types of conditions for good and bad feelings. The factors responsible for job satisfaction are quite different from the factors they perceive as contributors to job dissatisfaction. Their reported good feelings were found to be associated with job experiences and job content, whereas their reported bad feelings were found to be associated with the peripheral aspects of the job, that is, job context. Since his study was based on a two-factor hypothesis, his theory is known as the *two-factor theory*. As his study established that opposite of satisfaction is not dissatisfaction and removing dissatisfying elements from a job does not necessarily make the job satisfying, he classified the factors into two categories—(1) motivation factors, and (2) hygiene or maintenance factors. Herzberg mentioned six motivation factors.

- Recognition
- Advancement
- Responsibility
- Achievement

- Possibility of growth
- Job content or the work itself

Presence of these factors in the job creates a motivating environment, but its absence does not cause dissatisfaction. Similarly, Herzberg mentioned ten hygiene or maintenance factors.

- Company policy and administration
- Technical supervision
- Interpersonal relations with subordinates
- Salary
- Job security
- Personal life
- Working conditions
- Status
- Interpersonal relations with supervisors
- Interpersonal relations with peers

These factors are context factors. Their existence just creates an environment for executing work. However, these factors by themselves cannot motivate an individual to work. In Herzberg's words, 'their absence can dissatisfy employees but their presence per se cannot satisfy employees.' The crux of the two-factor theory of motivation, therefore, is that managers should address both satisfying factors and dissatisfying factors. A mere improvement of hygiene factors cannot guarantee a motivating environment.

Hackman and Oldham (1974) developed a job characteristic model, based on Herzberg's two-factor theory, showing how a good job design can lead to the internal motivation of the employees and contribute to better job performance. The theory postulates that five job characteristics lead to three psychological states, which affect the motivation and satisfaction of the employees. The five job characteristics are skill variety, task identity, task significance, autonomy, and feedback.

Skill variety is the extent or range of skills, abilities, and talent of the employees. The more they are able to utilize their skills in the job, the greater is their level of satisfaction. Hence, jobs are to be designed in a way that ensures utilization of the wide skill variety of the individuals. *Task identity* signifies the extent of employees' involvement in the total job. This enables individuals to identify their place in the total execution of the job, which gives them a sense of pride and satisfaction. *Task significance*, on the other hand, denotes significance of a job on the life of others, both within and outside the organization. Positive significance of a job gives psychological satisfaction to the individual who performs the job. *Autonomy* is the extent of freedom given for a job. The degree of autonomy depends on the extent of independence given to an employee in deciding job scheduling, formulating of procedures, and decision-making. The greater the job autonomy, the greater is the job satisfaction and also the motivation. *Feedback* provides the opportunity to assess the right way of executing a job.

Skill variety, task identity, and task significance provide *experienced meaningfulness*. Autonomy provides *experienced responsibility*, while feedback ensures *experienced knowledge of results*. Once an employee experiences arousal of these three psychological states, they feel intrinsically rewarded, which results in intrinsic motivation.

Hackman and Oldham developed a motivating potential score (MPS), based on their study, which measures the propensity of a job to become motivating. Their formula is presented below:

$$MPs = \frac{\text{Skill variety} + \text{Task identity} + \text{Task significance}}{3} \times \text{Autonomy} \times \text{Feedback}$$

Vroom's theory (1964) is based on the belief that employee effort will lead to performance, which will lead to rewards. Rewards may be either positive or negative. The more positive the reward, the more likely it is that the employee will be highly motivated. Conversely, the more negative the reward, the less likely it is that the employee will be motivated. Adams's theory states that employees strive for equity between themselves and other employees. Equity is achieved when the ratio of employee outcomes over inputs is equal to other employee's outcomes over inputs (Adams 1965).

Skinner's theory simply states that the behaviour that leads to positive outcomes will be repeated and behaviours that lead to negative outcomes will not be repeated (Skinner 1953). Managers should positively reinforce employee behaviour that lead to positive outcomes whereas they should refrain from employee behaviour that leads to negative outcomes.

Apart from these, there are classic research studies, which have some bearing on employee motivation. Most important of these is the pioneering work of Taylor. He developed the theory of *scientific management*. This theory assumes employees to be a rational economic entity concerned with maximizing economic gain. Taylor advocated that the main form of motivation is high wages, linked to output.

McClelland (1977) documented differences in needs of the employees in three important areas namely achievement need (nAch), affiliation need (nAff), and power need (nPow). Employees in achievement need category feel motivated with a sense of accomplishment and achievement. With affiliation need, employees desire to maintain satisfying relationships with the organization, peer groups, work groups, etc. Employees with power need feel motivated by controlling others. McClelland highlighted the importance of matching the individual and the job. Individuals with high achievement need always prefer challenging job assignments, whereas individuals with low achievement need prefer a job situation that ensures stability, security, and predictability. Organizations, by manipulating the achievement need, can get the complex jobs accomplished by high achievers. However, McClelland's work is criticized on many important counts as it does not address questions such as how a sense of achievement or other associated motives can be inculcated in an adult employee. Firstly, McClelland contends that such behaviour can be taught and thus motives related to achievement, etc. can be developed in an adult. This contention is not tenable in the psychological framework. Secondly, McClelland argues that needs can be changed through education and training. But psychologists put forth their view that needs are permanently acquired. Thirdly, thematic appreciation test (TAT) used for the study by McClelland is also subject to criticism as interpretation of responses using TAT is subject to the researcher's bias.

Expectancy theory, equity theory, and performance satisfaction model are other important approaches to understand the cognitive or process theories of motivation. The basic premise of *expectancy theory* lies in the fact that employees increasingly feel motivated if they perceive that their effort will result in successful performance and the successful performance will ensure desired results. Expectancy theory has other different names such as instrumentality theory, path–goal theory, and valence–instrumentality–expectancy (VIE) theory. It has its roots in the cognitive concepts of Lewin (1951) and Tolman (1951) and in the choice behaviour and utility concepts from classical economic theory. This theory often creates problems as it is not easy for a manager to understand its context in the right spirit. Vroom (1964) formulated an expectancy theory as an alternative to content models for work motivation. The theory identified relationships among variables which affect individual behaviour in a dynamic environment. It was an attempt to capture how individuals determine their extent of effort for a job and how their perceived expectation influences such effort. The strength of a tendency to act in a certain way depends on the strength of an expectation of an outcome, which is likely to accrue upon accomplishment of the job. So, motivation (M) is the product of strength of one's desire (valence) and perceived probability of a good outcome (expectancy). We can show such relationship as:

$$V \times L = M$$

Valence is the degree of desirability of certain outcomes. Therefore, it may be the strength of an individual's preference for a particular outcome such as a promotion, pay hike, recognition, etc. Since individuals may have a positive or a negative preference for an outcome, valence may be negative or positive. Hence, valence may vary from −1 to +1. *Expectancy* is the perceived possibility of a particular outcome that would follow after an action. Therefore, it is the strength of belief that an act will be followed by a particular outcome. The strength of expectations is based on past experience. Individuals expect things to happen in the future based on what has occurred in the past. As expectancy is an action–outcome association, it may range from 0 to 1. If employees perceive no possibility of an outcome from certain acts, its expectancy would be 0, whereas the value of expectancy would be 1 when they feel (from their experience of action–outcome relationship) that they are likely to achieve an outcome with certainty. Vroom has used one more term in between expectancy and valence, namely *usefulness* or *instrumentality*. It is the belief that the first level outcome would lead to the second level outcome. For example, an individual may be motivated for superior performance in a desire to get promoted. In this case, the first level outcome (superior performance) is seen as being instrumental for the second level outcome (promotion). Therefore, the strength of motivation to perform a certain act will depend on the sum of the products of the valences (including instrumentality) and the expectancies. It can be represented as

$$\text{Motivation strength} = V \times I \times E$$

Equity theory owes its origin to several contributors such as Festinger, Heider, Homans, Jacques, Patchen, Weick, etc. Adam's (1965) theory proposes that in a work environment, motivation is influenced by an individual's perception of how equitably they are treated compared to others. The theory is also known as '*social comparison theory*' or '*inequity theory*'. Perceptively, employees reduce their inequity through such comparison or by establishing a hypothetical exchange relationship. An individual evaluates the amount of work put in and corresponding rewards obtained for himself or herself, and then the individual compares it to the efforts and rewards of a similarly placed individual in the organization. If equity exists, the individual feels good. However, inequity propels the individual into action to create a condition of equity. Since inequity propels action, it is the motivator. The greater the perceived inequity, the greater would be the motivation to reduce it. While doing so, individuals can make any of the following choices:

- change or alter inputs
- change or alter outcomes
- distort inputs and outcomes
- distort inputs and outcomes of others (whom they compare with)
- select a different referent (to compare)
- withdraw from the field

Performance satisfaction theory advocated by Porter and Lawler (1968), based on Vroom's expectancy model, postulates that performance leads to satisfaction. This is contrary to our belief that satisfaction leads to performance. Other interesting observations made by them are that motivation (efforts), performance (accomplishment), and satisfaction are separate variables. This again is contrary to our belief that motivation leads to performance, which in turn leads to satisfaction. Efforts (force or motivation) do not directly lead to performance. Efforts are mediated by abilities, traits, and role perceptions. Performance is followed by rewards. The way rewards are perceived determine satisfaction.

The concepts of attribution and locus of control, advocated by Kelley, mainly address the cognitive process by which an individual interprets behaviour attributed to certain parts of the relevant environment. An individual interprets such causal relationships or attributes for the behaviour of the self or for others' behaviour. Heider (1958) contended that both perceived internal forces (ability, efforts, and fatigue) and external forces (others' supervision, machines, methods, climate, rules, and procedures) together determine the behaviour of an individual. Since the perceived causes are the determinants of work behaviour and the perception differs, individuals behave differently in a given situation. The concept of locus of control is different from the concept of attribution. While *attribution theory* is concerned with identifying the causes of individual's own as well as other's behaviour; *locus of control theory* is applicable only to the individual. Employees may perceive their own behaviour to be internally or externally controlled. Since external control factors (which influence their behaviour) are beyond their own control, employees believe that their rewards and punishments are dependent on factors such as fate, luck, or chance. For internal control factors, they feel they can influence their outcomes through their own ability, skills, or effort. Rotter (1967) developed a 23-item scale for measurement of locus of control known as the internal–external (I–E) scale.

In goal setting theory, Locke (1968) considered two cognitive determinants of behaviour—values and intentions (goals). Emotions and desires represent the form of values and value judgements. Intentions are goals to satisfy desires or emotions (values). This results in consequences, feedback, and reinforcement. The study suggests that individuals are willing to work hard when they know what is required from them. Setting specific attainable goals is related to high-level performance.

Related Theories

Murray (1938) discussed about manifest needs theory, which is basically a multivariate approach to the structure of needs. The basic difference between Murrary's formulation and Maslow's and Alderfer's formulations is that Murray does not suggest a hierarchical order of various types of needs. Based on several years of clinical observations at the Harvard psychological clinic, Murray argued that intensities of various personality-related needs, when taken together represent a central motivating force.

White's *competence motive theory* (White 1954) (somewhat similar to the power motive theory of Adler) relates motivation to the desire of employees for mastery over physical and social environs (Cornell Study). Schachter's *affiliation motivation theory* (Schachter 1959) relates motivation to the strong need for affiliation. Argyris's *maturity–immaturity theory* (Argyris 1957) relates motivation to an environment, which serves both the needs of the organization and the needs of the members of the organization. Whyte's *money motivation theory* (Whyte 1955) suggests that individuals are motivated primarily by the desire to earn money. However, Whyte contends that monetary incentives should not be considered in isolation from other non-monetary incentives.

Likert and Katz's Michigan studies (1948) emphasized a vital point that a productivity-motivated work team is really a function of a particular type of supervisory style. Since productivity has its roots in employee motivation, it can be harnessed by carefully designing an organization that enables an individual to develop a feeling of being important in the organization. Megginson (1977), for the sake of our convenience, classified the leading theories of motivation into three groups:

Perspective theories Taylor's scientific management approach, various human relations theories, McGregor's theory Y, etc., which, in reality, stress upon the management to motivate employees.

Content theories Maslow's hierarchy of needs theory, Herzberg's two-factor theory, McClelland's achievement need theory, etc., which try to identify the causes of behaviour.

Process theories Various behavioural theories, which believe in stimulus–response relationship vis-à-vis motivation (e.g. Skinner's behaviour modification theory) and cognitive theories (e.g., Vroom's expectancy theory and Porter–Lawler's future-oriented expectancy theory), which deal with the genesis of behaviour.

In India, not much empirical research has been carried out on motivation and its related aspects. There are some studies on industrial workers and some on technical personnel, supervisors, and managers. Most of the studies in India have attempted to ascertain the job satisfaction variables, which have been construed as motivational variables.

The first such study in India was done by Bose (1951) on industrial workers. This paved the way for other researchers to investigate the perceived importance of job factors to workers. Most of the studies relating to the industrial workers during the period 1951–1971 have rated adequate earnings, job security, boss, and personal life as main factors determining their behaviour. Ganguli's study (1964) on first-line supervisors (number of samples (N) = 44) ranked incentive, adequate income, promotional opportunities, job security, and sympathetic treatment from superiors as the important job factors related to motivation. Lahiri and Srivastava's study (1967) on middle-management personnel (N = 93) ranked good organizational policies and administration, better scope for promotion, good salary, good superior–subordinate relationship, and opportunity for growth as the major determinants of satisfaction.

The study by Sawalapurkar et al. (1968) on middle-level managers (N = 30) ranked nine job factors in the following order of importance—job content, opportunity for advancement, job security, boss, company, working conditions, facilities, working hours, and grievance redressal.

Padaki and Dolke's study (1970) on job attitudes of supervisors (N = 15), which was based on Herzberg's two-factor theory, found lack of recognition, unfavorable superior–subordinate relationship, lack of technically competent supervision, unfavourable organizational policies and administration, and inadequate salary as the major dissatisfiers. Another study conducted by them also found more or less the same factors as perceived dissatisfiers.

Rao's study (1970) on bank managers (N = 60), with a view to test the Herzberg's two-factor theory, found promotion, company policies, and salary on the dissatisfaction scale. Narain's study (1971) on public sector managers (N = 1213) ranked eight factors in the following order of importance—feeling of worthwhile accomplishments, recognition, decision-making authority, opportunity for personal growth and development, promotional opportunity, prestige of the organization in the community, pay and fringe benefits, and job security. As far as need deficiencies are concerned, Narain found that promotion, recognition, and personal growth and development, respectively, show very high degrees of dissatisfaction in that order.

Bhattacharyya's study (1972) on managers (N = 210) found lack of participation in goal setting, inadequacy of pay, inadequate job authority, and lack of opportunity given to help people on the dissatisfaction scale. Pestonjee and Basu's study (1972) on executives (N = 80) showed that promotion and growth, recognition, prestige, organizational policies and administration, and autonomy are the major determinants of satisfaction.

Singhal and Upadhyay's study (1972) on supervisors (N = 22) also found opportunities for promotion, job security, working conditions, work group, opportunities for training, competent and sympathetic supervisors, adequate income, and other facilitates, etc., as major motivational factors. Agarwal (1977) sharply criticized the Indian studies on work motivation, alleging that such studies suffer from a number of inconsistencies mainly because they were carried out practically as a part of the job done for the employers to help them reduce production costs. Therefore, the measures, suggested by such researchers, have always proved to be short-term remedies. The much-spoken-about theories on motivation act more like fads or fashion instead of contributing something substantial and lasting. Thinking in line with Pareek (1974), he developed a stratification model of work motivation with variables such as social system, self-status, and role. Pareek (1974) assumed the societal system as a very important variable in the field of motivation that causes or determines the behaviour of an individual in an organization.

Sharma's study (1986) on administrators in Delhi (N = 67) found power motive as the main guiding force of motivation. His study, in the same year, on supervisors (N = 3,378) drawing samples from 50 manufacturing organizations both in the public and the private sectors obtained score values for different factors that influence motivation. The values are presented in Table 6.2.

TABLE 6.2 Score values

Factors	Score values (%)
Superintendent–management relations	63.21
Monetary benefits	60.30
Objectivity and rationality	56.00
Recognition and appreciation	51.32
Welfare facilities	48.39
Scope for advancement	47.32
Grievance handling	45.83
Training and education	43.46
Participative management	39.68

The study was carried out on 3-point scale—low, medium, and high frequencies.

Neelamegham and Vaid's study (1986) on motivation of the sales force (N = 116) found highest need deficiencies with respect to prospects of promotion and recognition for good work.

It is important to note that the major Indian studies are on supervisory and managerial personnel. Another important feature of the Indian studies is that most of the studies have been carried out with a small sample using only conventional methods such as ranking, percentage calculation, etc. Some studies have been carried out simply to authenticate Herzberg's two-factor theory, whereas some others are highly opinionated studies without much adherence to the norms of sampling and survey methods. In most cases, even a suitable structured close-ended questionnaire was not administered. Therefore, the conclusions are simple inferences drawn after informal discussions with the samples elements which are mostly chosen without following the proper sampling procedure. Another feature is that most of the studies are based on experiences of single industrial units. Representative results are difficult to obtain from a survey based on a small sample drawn from a single unit.

MOTIVATION AND MORALE

Edwin Flippo (1989) defined morale as 'A mental condition or attitude of individual and groups which determines their willingness to cooperate.' Yoder Dale (1970), on the other hand, explained morale as 'The overall tone, climate, or atmosphere of work perhaps regularly sensed by the members. If workers appear to feel enthusiastic and optimistic about group activities, if they have a sense of mission about their job, if they are friendly with each other, they are described as having a good or high morale. If they seem to be dissatisfied, irritated, cranky, critical, restless, and pessimistic, they are described as having poor or low morale.' Mayo defined it as 'the maintenance of cooperative living', which means a sense of belongingness. There are several other definitions of the term morale. These define morale as a pursuit of a common purpose, attitude; individual and group job satisfaction; participative attitudes; team spirit, etc. Irrespective of the definitions, it is evident that morale is a cognitive concept that encompasses feelings, attitudes, and sentiments, which together contribute to a general feeling of satisfaction in the workplace.

Like morale, motivation is also a cognitive concept. However, the two differ on certain important aspects. Motivation stimulates individuals into action to achieve the desired goals. It is, therefore, a function of need and drives. It mobilizes energy, which enhances the potential for morale. Morale, on the other hand, is an individual's or a group's attitude towards a particular subject. It contributes to a general feeling of satisfaction at the workplace. It is, therefore, a function of freedom or restraint towards a goal. It mobilizes sentiments, which form an important part of organizational climate. Attitudes and sentiments, that is, morale per se affects productivity. High morale is an index of good human relations, which reduces labour turnover, absenteeism, indiscipline, grievances, etc.

Factors that primarily affect morale are attitude and job satisfaction level of individual employees. From an organizational point of view, such factors can be delineated into organizational goals, leadership style, co-workers' attitude, nature of work, work environment, and the employees themselves.

High morale is conventionally considered as a contributor to high productivity. However, such correlation may not be always true. This is because high productivity may be the outcome of many other organizational initiatives, which may be independent of employee morale. Hence, even with low employee morale, high productivity is achievable.

MOTIVATIONAL RESEARCH AND COMPENSATION DESIGN

To be able to design an appropriate compensation that motivates employees, it is important to understand the motivational research process. Understanding of effective motivational research process can help in identifying the appropriate compensation components. There are numerous studies on employee motivation in the literature. Most of the works utilize survey-based investigation, using scaled closed-ended questionnaire. The primary goal of the these research works is to identify correct reinforcers for employee motivation. The ranked order of motivating factors, as identified in most of research work are— (a) interesting work, (b) good wages, (c) full appreciation of work done, (d) job security, (e) good working conditions, (f) promotions and growth in the organization, (g) feeling of being, (h) personal loyalty to employees, (i) tactful discipline, and (j) sympathetic help with personal problems. The different

Organizations may use surveys to determine employees' motivation levels

motivational theories help clarify the concept of motivation. However for effective compensation design, we need a deeper understanding as the perceived need factors of employees differ from one organization to another. Motivational surveys are used in organizations to understand whether employees are motivated and are contributing their best.

Three models used primarily to understand motivation are traditional model, human relations model, and human resource model. These models are distinctly different from each other. The simple difference between these three approaches can be better understood by citing examples of some concepts forwarded by these models. For example, work as per the traditional model is perceived as inherently distasteful; as per the human relations model, work is perceived as something while doing which individuals want to feel useful and important; whereas, the human resource model suggests that employees want to contribute to meaningful work. With this model as context, organizations need to make work more meaningful and challenging to motivate employees. As employees are considered to be creative, responsible, and generally believe in self-direction, it becomes important to design jobs that make use of these skills. It is, therefore, important to draft the motivational questionnaire items in a way that considers the employees as human resources of the organization.

MOTIVATING GENERATION Y

Millennial or Generation Y employees are those who were born between 1976 and 1996. These employees are considered to be attitudinally different from Generation X (born between 1965 and 1975) and Baby Boomers (born between 1945 and 1964). Although, we do not have any empirical studies to authenticate this claim, it is widely believed that organizations, globally, decide on new motivational reinforcements for Generation Y.

Generation Y employees show more interest for career options, that can meet their job expectations. They are more demanding from their employers, and expect their workplaces should have the state-of-the art technology, with access to the Internet. They do not expect the workplaces to believe in all work and no play. Their preferred organizations should not differentiate between their work and non-work pursuits, should value their social life, etc. However, such beliefs are contested by many scholars. Often companies crave some different motivational reinforcers over the existing one to motivate the millennial employees. This often leads to the dissatisfaction of older employees. For such reasons, many scholars suggest that it is inappropriate to crave different motivational reinforcements for Generation Y. Generation neutral and all inclusive motivational strategies work better. Difference in age cannot merit different compensation strategies to motivate Generation Y. Also, more empirical studies are required to substantiate that differences in the age groups make employees different in their attitude, approach to work, and motivation.

COMPENSATION PRACTICES FOR TALENTED EMPLOYEES

Attracting and retaining talent in organizations require designing compensation plan that matches with the expectations of talented employees. We briefly discussed the relationships between compensation design and talent management practices in Chapter 1 on Introduction to Compensation Management. Here, we are more focused on compensation elements that can ensure effective management of talent in the organizations. Employee stock option plan (ESOP) is considered as the more important compensation element, which can be used by organizations to motivate talented employees. Most of the companies, in India and abroad, have now embraced ESOP as a compensation element to attract and retain talent in their organizations. In India, ESOP can significantly reduce the employee turnover along with retention of talent. Employees are given the option to acquire shares (stock options) of the company, as incentive for their higher performance. It is more in the form of deferred compensation. In our country, the Securities and Exchange Board of India (SEBI) Guidelines 1999 regulate the ESOP issues. As per these guidelines, employees must be permanent in order to become eligible for ESOP. ESOP also helps organizations, as it can give opportunity to the organizations to save on cash compensations. Also because of the vesting period, employees to gain from ESOP through exercise of stock options need to stay with the organizations over a considerably long period, which benefit the organization by captivating talent. ESOP being given to employees, as an additional benefit for performance, can motivate them to perform better. Therefore, ESOP can institutionalize the culture of performance in the organizations.

However, before we use ESOP as a possible compensation element, we must understand the tax implications. For example, an employee may be issued stock as rewards for his performance with a vesting period of three years. It means the employee can exercise his stock option only after three years. The difference between today's price and the price after three years would be the benefit to the employees, which is taxable.

ESOP is a taxable perquisite. At present, however, tax is levied on sale of stocks, as capital gains. If the shares are held for less than 12 months period, from the date of issue, we call it short-term capital gains tax, which is levied at the rate of 15 per cent. In case the shares are sold after one year, it attracts long-term capital gains tax (which for the present is zero).

SUMMARY

Motivation is a dynamic HR process and there cannot be any organization-specific motivational tool. The content and process theories on motivation suggested various methods of enhancing employee motivation. Many empirical studies carried out in India and abroad validated such tools, either partially or in their entirety. Motivation, either through intrinsic or extrinsic reinforcers, contributes to employee satisfaction, thus enhancing performance and productivity. At an organization level, systematic research on employee motivation is one of the most critical HR functions. Many HR-related problems are deep rooted in motivational issues. The biggest challenge faced by today's organizations is the retention of employees. High cost of labour turnover ultimately defeats the strategic intent of the company. Even though there are many well-researched theories on employee motivation, at an organization level the issue has to be considered keeping in view the specific requirements. Truly speaking, there is no universal model of employee motivation.

An HR researcher has to understand not only the theoretical implications of various motivational tools, but also needs to emulate the best practices from other organizations. A systematic review of employee motivation level is assessed by designing an innovative questionnaire. Simply administering the questionnaire alone will not serve the purpose. Translating the observed responses into a meaningful action plan requires the researcher to design appropriate motivational tools, which are sustainable in terms of cost–benefit analysis. In Chapter 1, we have discussed these aspects in detail. The consolidation of such collected information also needs to be done by the researcher through an understanding of the nature of data analysis and usage of various statistical tools.

Many organizations worldwide are even mapping employee motivation levels with customer satisfaction and are accordingly framing their strategies to get the benefit of customer retention. In this chapter, these aspects have been discussed in the critical review questions. The most important area of motivation research, therefore, is understanding the existing level of employee motivation, perceived gap between employee expectations and existing organizational resources, and then designing suitable sustainable motivational reinforcers.

Key Terms

Attribution theory The concept was advocated by Harold Kelley. It is mainly concerned with the cognitive process by which an individual interprets behaviour attributed to certain parts of the relevant environment.

Equity theory The theory proposes that in a work environment, motivation is influenced by an individual's perception of how equitably they are treated as compared to others. The theory is also known as 'social comparison theory' or 'inequity theory'.

Expectancy theory The basic premise of expectancy theory lies in the fact that employees increasingly feel motivated if they perceive that their effort will result in successful performance, and successful performance will ensure desired results.

Extrinsic motivation Motivational reinforcers that meet the tangible needs of the employees such as pay.

Intrinsic motivation This type of motivational reinforcers are primarily psychological. They are not intended to satisfy tangible needs.

Performance satisfaction theory It is based on Vroom's expectancy model and postulates that performance leads to satisfaction contrary to our belief that satisfaction leads to performance. Other interesting observations made by them are that motivation (efforts), performance (accomplishment), and satisfaction are separate variables.

Perspective theories Taylor's scientific management approach, various human relations theories, McGregor's Theory Y, and other theories, which, in reality, stress upon the management to motivate employees.

Process theories Various behavioural theories which believe in stimulus–response relationship vis-à-vis motivation (e.g., Skinner's behaviour modification theory) and cognitive theories (e.g., Vroom's expectancy theory and Porter–Lawler's future-oriented expectancy theory), which deal with the genesis of behaviour.

Exercises

Concept Review Questions

1. Define the term motivation. Why is it so important for HR managers?
2. Which motivational tool would you use for knowledge workers? Would your approach be different for operators in a shop floor?
3. Critically review the contribution of Maslow and Herzberg to motivational theories. Do you think they have any relevance for new-generation workers?
4. What is the distinction between process theories and content theories of motivation?

Critical Thinking Question

1. Can motivation be defined as perception? What are the circumstances in which perception can influence the motive strength of an employee?
2. The ABT Banking Co. has decided to computerize as many of its operations as possible in order to increase efficiency and customer convenience. One of their first steps was to place automatic teller machines (ATMs) in different locations in the city. The bank also started a programme that expands on telephone banking by allowing the owners of personal computers to conduct virtually all of their banking business from their homes. These successes have caused the bank to consider use of microcomputers or terminals in the homes of their employees so that they may work at home. It is believed that this will

allow greater flexibility for employees and reduces the need for office and floor space at the main and branch offices. It is clear that technology will stimulate many changes in the bank's current personnel practices as the relationship between work and the individual employee changes. The personnel manager has been asked to develop a report outlining the changes that will be necessary in the bank's personnel policies. Since the contact with immediate supervisors would be eliminated for many employees under this new work arrangement, what type of motivational theory would you suggest and why?

3. Can employee motivation be a strategic issue in an organization? Elaborate your answer with specific examples from organizations.

Compensation Practices of a POL Major

CASE STUDY

Oil exploration and production firms today are facing critical skill shortage to the extent of 40 per cent. Classified under the energy and power sector, this is a general phenomenon with regard to skill sets worldwide. A national petroleum, oil, and lubricant (POL) major in India reaped the advantage of globalization by acquiring oil fields in countries like Sudan. The company, however, was losing key personnel such as geologists and geophysicists, oil exploration engineers, pipeline engineers, etc. The company has recently entered into POL distribution, with their first presence in Bengaluru. Even in marketing and distribution, the company has started losing talent. Being an erstwhile departmental undertaking, the company follows a protected compensation structure, balancing between the present pay and deferrals. More employee benefits are offered when compared with the normal market trend, making it possible for the employees to feel a sense of pride because of their affiliation with the organization.

After liberalization many new players have entered into the market. In no time, the company experienced an unprecedented rate of attrition, surpassing all industry standards. In a single month, 234 professionals left the job, foregoing their protected benefits in deferrals such as provident fund, gratuity, pension, etc. The company now wonders if it should look into its compensation structure.

The company then retained the services of an organizational development (OD) consultant to make a diagnostic study to map the employee expectations. While analysing the results of the study, the company observed, to its surprise, that retention is primarily attributable to lack of career growth opportunities, followed by learning opportunities, compensation package, job satisfaction, job fit, etc. The company then formed a committee to look into the age-old seniority-based promotion systems, restructured its training activities, making it compulsory for each employee to undergo six man days of training in a year. Other trivial issues such as job fit and job satisfaction were ensured through minor restructuring and redeployment programmes.

On the compensation issue, the company adopted the model of performance-linked retention strategy in line with global practices. The company undertook this exercise, by apportioning some deferrals. LG Electronics gives additional incentives on completion of three years of service. So does DLF, a global major in infrastructure. The amount of incentive increases

(Contd)

CASE STUDY (Contd)

proportionately with the increase in the period of stay in the organization. The idea behind such adoption of performance-linked 'employee retention' incentive plan is to inculcate a feeling in the mindset of employees that their immediate gain is substantial in the event they continue with the company. Many professionals do not bother about long-term incentives (LTIs) in the form of deferrals. They prefer cash incentives or other forms of rewards to deferred benefits.

After disinvestments, the company was also considering the alternative stock options for increasing employee retention. However, employees of the company did not show interest because of uncertainty of returns.

Discussion question

Critically examine this case and suggest how the company can design its compensation structure in addition to other initiatives listed in the case study.

References

Adams, J.S. (1965), 'Inequity in Social Exchange' in L. Berkowitz (ed.), *Advances in Experimental Social Psychology*, Academic Press, New York.

Agarwal, K.G. (1977), 'Self, role, status and motivation: Towards stratification theory of work motivation', *Indian Journal of Industrial Relations*, vol. 10, no. 3, pp. 379–86.

Argyris, C. (1957), *Personality and Organization*, Harper and Row, New York.

Atkinson, John W. (1966), *An Introduction to Motivation*, Affiliated East-West Press, New Delhi.

Bhattacharyya, D.K. (2006), *Human Resource Management*, 2nd edn, Excel Books, New Delhi.

Bhattacharyya, D.K. (2007), *Human Resource Research Methods*, Oxford University Press, New Delhi.

Bhattacharyya, S.K. (1972), 'Perception of organizational characteristics in relation to need gratification among Indian managers', *Indian Management*, November, pp. 29–34.

Bose, S.K. (1951), 'Man and his work', *Indian Journal of Psychology*, vol. 26, pp. 1–20.

Flippo, E.B. (1989), *Principles of Personnel Management*, McGraw-Hill, Tokyo.

Fred, Luthans (1998), *Organisational Behaviour*, 8th edn, Irwin McGraw-Hill, p. 169.

Ganguli, H.C. (1964), *Structure and Process of Organisation*, Asia Publishing House, Bombay.

Hackman, J.R. and G.R. Oldham (1974), 'Motivation through design of work: Test of theory', *Organizational Behaviour and Human Performance*, vol. 16, no. 2, pp. 250–79.

Heider, Fritz (1958), *The Psychology of Interpersonal Relations*, John Wiley and Sons, New York.

Herzberg, F., B. Manser, and Synderman (1967), *The Motivation to Work*, John Wiley and Sons, New York.

Herzberg, Frederick (1966), *Work and Nature of the Man*, World Press, Cleveland.

Jones, M.R. (ed.) (1955), *Deficiency motivation and growth motivation*, Nebraska Symposium on Motivation, University of Nebraska Press, Lincoln.

Keith, Davis (1982), *Human Behaviour at Work: Human Relations and Organizational Behaviour*, Tata McGraw-Hill, New Delhi.

Lahiri, D.K. and S. Srivastava (1967), 'Determinants of satisfaction in middle management personnel', *Journal of Applied Psychology*, vol. 3, pp. 251–65.

Lewin, K. (1936), *Principles of Topological Psychology*, McGraw-Hill, New York.

Lewin, Kurt (1951), *Field Theory in Social Science*, Harper and Row, New York.

Likert, R. and D. Katz (1948), 'Supervisory practices and organizational structure as they affect employee productivity and morale', *American Management Association*, Personnel Series, vol. 120, pp. 14–24.

Locke, E.A. (1968), 'Towards a theory of task motivation and incentives, *Organizational Behaviour and Human Performance*, vol. 3, no. 2, pp. 157–89.

Maslow, Abraham (1954), *Motivation and Personality*, 1st edn, Harper and Row, New York.

Mayo, Elton (1945), *The Social Problems of an Industrial Civilization*, Harvard University, Boston.

McClelland, D.C. (1977), *Human Behaviour at Work*, Tata McGraw-Hill, New Delhi.

Megginson, L.C. (1977), *Personnel and Human Resource Administration*, 3rd edn, Richard, W., Irwin, Homewood, Illinois.

Murray, H.A. (1938), *Explorations in Personality*, Oxford University Press, New York.

Narain, L. (1971), 'Managerial motivation in public enterprises', *Lok Udyog*, vol. 9, pp. 861–75 and p. 883.

Neelamegham, S. and D.K. Vaid (1986), 'Sales force motivation: Challenging task', *Indian Management*, vol. 25, no. 12, pp. 21–5.

Padaki, O. and A.M. Dolke (1970), 'A study of job attitudes', ATIRA Research Monograph, Ahmedabad.

Pareek, U. (1974), 'A conceptual model of work motivation', *Indian Journal of Industrial Relations*, vol. 10, no. 1, pp. 15–23.

Pestonjee, D.M. and G. Basu (1972), 'A study of job satisfaction of Indian executives', *Indian Journal of Industrial Relations*, vol. 8, pp. 3–16.

Porter, L.W. and E.E. Lawler III (1968), *Managerial Attitude and Performance*, Richard D. Irwin, Inc., and The Dorsey Press, Homewood.

Porter, L.W., E.E. Lawler, and J.R. Hackman (1975), *Behaviour in Organizations*, McGraw-Hill, New York.

Rao, G.V.S. (1970), 'Determinants of job satisfaction in managerial personnel', *Indian Manager*, vol. 1, pp. 55–62.

Rotter, J.B. (1967), 'A new scale for the measurement of interpersonal trust', *Journal of Personality*, vol. 35, pp. 651–65.

Sawalapurkar, M.P., C.P. Dusad, and D.V. Khare (1968), 'Job motivation of middle managers', *Indian Journal of Applied Psychology*, vol. 5, pp. 7–10.

Schachter, S. (1959), *The Psychology of Affiliation*, Stanford University Press, Stanford, California.

Sharma, B.R. (1986), 'Motivational crisis in Indian administration: A case of existential sickness', Indian Institute of Public Administration, New Delhi.

Singhal, S. and H.S. Upadhyay (1972), 'Psychology of men at work: Employees perception of job incentives', *Indian Journal of Industrial Relations*, vol. 8, pp. 17–30.

Skinner, B.F. (1953), *Science and Human Behavior*, Free Press, New York.

Steers R. and L.W. Porter (1983), *Motivation and Work Behaviour*, 2nd edn, McGraw-Hill, New York.

Taylor, F.W. (1911), *The Principles of Scientific Management*, Harper & Brothers, Published in 1967 by W.W. Norrton and Company, New York.

Tolman, E.C. (1945), *Behaviour and Psychological Man*, University of California Press, Berkley.

Tolman, Edward (1951), 'A psychological model' in: Talcott Parsons and Edward, A. Shils (eds), *Toward a General Theory of Action*, Harper Torchbooks, New York.

Vroom, V.H. (1964), *Work and Motivation*, Wiley, New York.

White, R.W. (1959), 'Motivation reconsidered: The concept of competence', *Psychological Review*, vol. LXVI, no.5, pp. 297–330.

Whyte, W. F. (1955), *Money and Motivation*, Harper and Row, New York.

Yoder, Dale (1970), *Personnel Management and Industrial Relations*, Prentice Hall Inc., New York.

CHAPTER SEVEN

Compensation Management and Job Design

Learning Objectives

After reading this chapter, you will be able to
- understand the need for job design in the context of compensation management decisions
- define the process, methods, and techniques of job design
- define assessment centres and the approach for job analysis
- appreciate details of job descriptions and job analysis

Base

HRA

EPF

Gratuity

Variable

Bonus

LTA

Conveyance

Medical

OPENING CASE

Effective Job Design and Recruitment Process at McDonald's

McDonald's is among Time magazine's Top 100 employers. Its recruitment process is continuous. A candidate can apply at any time and join the company after successfully going through the recruitment process. All candidates have to fill up an online application form. The online application form consists of some essay type questions, mostly related to job requirements, and is quite easy to complete. After initial screening of the application, the company contacts promising applicants within two days, asking them to complete an online personality questionnaire. It is like a psychometric test and designed to gauge the applicant's personality. If the candidate clears the test and is considered suitable for their organizational requirement, they invite the applicant, within the next few days, to go through the assessment centre. McDonald's refers this part of the selection process as on-job-experience (OJE). OJE is store-based and takes the applicant through a typical day in a McDonald's restaurant, exposing the candidate to everything from health and safety; interviews and group work; to experiencing the kitchen, dining, and front counter areas. It is an ideal opportunity for candidates to assess whether McDonald's is the right place for them to work. After passing the test, a candidate is invited to a final interview with an operations manager. It is more of a chat than a formal interview. Within a week of the interview, an offer of employment is issued to successful candidates. In the intervening period, all candidates are given periodic feedback about their progress.

McDonald's can do all this effectively because of its well-documented job design, perfect alignment of jobs to their core values, and a standard level of services and quality worldwide.

INTRODUCTION

For compensation design and management, the important pre-requisites are effective job design, information and documentation of job analysis, job descriptions, and job evaluations. All these processes help in identifying job requirements. They also help in describing the job, job-families, skill-sets, and skill mapping apart from helping develop skill inventories in the organization. Traditionally, these critical inputs are used to decide about manpower requirements to meet present and future needs. However, specific job attributes are important for the effective design of compensation and its management.

Work systems encompass macro level organizational variables such as the personnel sub-system, the technological sub-system, and the external environment. Therefore, the analysis of work systems is essentially an effort to understand the allocation of functions between the worker and the technical outfit, and the division of labour between people in a socio-technical environment. Such an analysis can assist in making informed decisions to enhance systems safety, efficiency in work, technological development, and the mental and physical well-being of workers.

Researchers examine work systems according to divergent approaches such as mechanistic, biological, perceptual/motor, and motivational with corresponding individual and organizational outcomes (Campion and Thayer 1985). The selection of methods in work systems analysis is dictated by the specific approaches taken, the particular objective in view, organizational context, the job and human characteristics, and the technological complexity of the system under study (Drury 1987). Checklists and questionnaires are common means of assembling databases for organizational planners, when prioritizing action plans in areas of personnel selection and placement, performance appraisal, safety and health management, worker-machine design, and work design or redesign. Inventory methods of checklists such as the *position analysis questionnaire* or PAQ (McCormick 1979), the *job components inventory* (Banks and Miller 1984), the *job diagnostic survey* (Hackman and Oldham 1974), and the *multi-method job design questionnaire* (Campion 1988) are more popular tools and help achieve a variety of objectives.

Job design helps in organizing job tasks. It has a direct impact on the mental and physical health of employees and thus on their performance levels. The physical aspects of jobs require organizations to consider ergonomic issues such as reducing physical strain, fatigue, and even boredom, which occurs when doing repetitive tasks. Mental aspects require organizations to address behavioural issues such as developing work systems and a culture, which enables employees to get relief from the dehumanizing effects of long work hours. Compatible physical and mental aspects lead to employee satisfaction, which in turn helps develop a high performing organization.

To properly address ergonomic and behavioural issues, job design relates to the organization's structure and style of management. Management styles and structures may vary from autocratic to democratic decision-making, delegation, and formation of autonomous work groups. The management may also reduce the number and levels of managers, increase the span of control, or increase the productivity levels and the motivation of employees, etc.

Therefore, the job design principle focuses on motivating employees by making jobs more interesting and challenging. In the scientific management era, we have seen that jobs are broken into small independent elements, so the workers perform the same task repeatedly. The argument was that this process made jobs more scientific and workers' performance could be easily measured, enabling the system of financial incentives. However, this argument was negated with the emergence of the human relations school. The behavioural issues in job design have now started gaining acceptance, and organizations are trying to synergize productivity and employee satisfaction. The principles of job design incorporate the elements of variety, responsibility, and control. Job design should ensure that all jobs contain variety, some responsibility for decision-making, and some control over the way the jobs are done. Therefore, this chapter discusses the microeconomic aspects of compensation design.

JOB DESIGN

Every work undergoes constant modification because of implementation on new mechanization and automation techniques. Some jobs become redundant, while others are created, and still others are altered in content. This necessitates different types of education, experience, and other attributes. While designing a job, management must be concerned with the practical considerations of quantity and quality of available personnel, both within the organization and in the labour market. Personality conflicts and friction, boredom, and obsessive thinking also need to be taken care of. The organization also needs to respect the view of unions, who otherwise may stall the move on one ground or the other. Therefore, the factors which are likely to affect job design can be enumerated as follows:

- job specialization and repetitive operations
- changing technology
- labour-union policies
- abilities of existing personnel
- adequate availability of potential personnel
- interaction between jobs and the system, and
- psychological and social needs that can be met by the job

Breaking down the tasks associated with each component in the system has led to the concept of job design. Job design started gaining in importance with rapid technological advancements at the turn of the twentieth century, when mass production and assembly line operations emerged. As jobs continue to become more sophisticated and specialized, the need for an educated and motivated workforce has become indispensable.

The main purpose of job design (or redesign) is to increase both employee motivation and productivity (Rush 1971). The focus on increasing productivity can manifest itself in various forms. For example, the focus can be on improving the quality and quantity of goods and services; reducing operation costs; and/or reducing employee turnover and training costs.

On the other hand, increase in employee motivation can be achieved by increasing job satisfaction. The two-factor model of Herzberg (1966) describes two sets of factors, *satisfying and dissatisfying*, that affect an employee's self-esteem and his opportunity for self-actualization in the workplace (Table 7.1).

Herzberg (1966) made a critical distinction between these two factors, in the sense that a person does not move in a continuum from being dissatisfied to becoming satisfied or vice versa. Rush (1971) tried to explain Herzberg's point by stating that, 'The opposite of satisfaction is not dissatisfaction, but no

TABLE 7.1 Job content factors

Dissatisfying factors	Satisfying factors
1. Administrative policies	1. Achievement
2. Supervision	2. Recognition
3. Working conditions	3. Work itself
4. Interpersonal relations	4. Responsibility
5. Salary	5. Advancement
6. Status	6. Growth
7. Job security	
8. Personal life	

satisfaction; and that the opposite of dissatisfaction is not satisfaction but no dissatisfaction'. In a practical sense, this means that addressing dissatisfying factors helps in supporting and maintaining the structure of the job; while addressing the satisfying factors not only increases the motivation to continue with the job, but also helps the employees achieve self-actualization.

Characteristics of Job Design

Jobs where employees experience a high level of job satisfaction generally have at least one or more of the following characteristics:

Task variety It enables an employee to move from one job to another within the organization. Such variation in job provides a change in mental activity as well as physical well being. Change in mental activity takes place through movement from one job to another and changes in the physical well being takes place through different body posture requirement for different types of jobs.

Task identity Wherever possible, tasks should be fit together to make a complete job as this gives the employees a sense of doing the whole job from the beginning to the end, with a visible output. Task identity can help a worker trace his performance to the overall goals and target achievements of the organization. Workers develop a sense of belonging and start feeling that they are partner in the organization's progress.

Task significance By establishing task significance, organizations can make workers feel that they have achieved something meaningful in the course of their working. This establishes their importance and enhances their self-esteem. Workers can autonomously contribute to organizational growth and prosperity, after they have understood their task significance. This requires the organization to value each task by inculcating a culture of mutual respect.

Autonomy To ensure autonomy in job design, employees should be provided inputs such as how their jobs are done, the order of tasks, the speed of work, etc. Later, these employees should be given a free hand by reducing the extent of supervision and control, so that they realize that they are doing their own jobs and that they are the job owners. However, this process is not simple. Inculcating a sense of autonomy in workers requires the organization to allow them to commit mistakes. They have to be first allowed to take decisions independently, knowing that they may not succeed. In the process, the workers learn through mistakes and slowly become independent in their jobs.

Feedback The last characteristic of job design is the provision for feedback. Feedback provides an opportunity to workers to understand their strengths, weaknesses, and areas of opportunity. This helps them mature and do better in their job assignments. Many organizations provide for automated feedback systems so that workers can assess their performance.

STRATEGIES AND TECHNIQUES OF JOB DESIGN

Robertson and Smith (1985) have recommended following strategies for analysing jobs:
- review literature and other existing data such as prevailing job descriptions, training manuals, and assess job designs from manuals of technology providers or vendors.
- interview immediate managers to understand the responsibilities of a job and tasks required to perform the job well
- interview employees who are in the same type of job to assess job requirements
- observe employees while they do the job
- try to do the job wherever possible to rationalize the job requirements
- write job descriptions detailing all findings and observations

These apart, one must also refer to policies, incentives, and feedback systems of an organization while designing jobs as they affect the efficiency and motivation of employees. Some of the important techniques of job design are elaborated in this section.

Job rotation

Job rotation involves periodic vertical and horizontal movement of employees within a set of jobs or tasks. It provides some relief from the boredom and monotony of the repetitive jobs or tasks. However, implementing it requires organizations to initiate multi-skilling of employees through continuous training and learning activities. In some organizations, there may naturally be opportunities for interchanging skills due to the common features of tasks or jobs; however in some other organizations, the scope of interchanging skills may be limited due to the specialized nature of jobs. Even in the second case, multi-skilling initiatives can provide results. Apart from mental satisfaction, job rotation relieves employees from physical strain due to changes in working postures. It helps employees reduce their tiredness and muscle strain. Whatever be the objectives of job rotation, it should not be imposed. Instead, employees should be made a party to the process so that they can control job rotation systems and decide how and when jobs are to be rotated. This would also help develop their capability to make decisions.

Job enlargement

Job enlargement is essentially horizontal expansion of jobs. It involves grouping of a variety of jobs within bands rather than between bands. For example, a particular employee may be required to perform tasks or jobs of several employees in an assembly line. To some extent, it may increase the job load. However, the employee may feel satisfied by the variety of tasks and develop a sense of responsibility as he realizes his importance to the organization. Since jobs are horizontally integrated, keeping in view skill compatibility, organizations can also derive the benefits of cost optimization.

Job enrichment

Job enrichment is another important process of job design or redesign. It reverses the effects of repetitive tasks. Employees develop fatigue by doing the same repetitive tasks again and again. Boredom and lack of flexibility in jobs make them feel dissatisfied (Leach and Wall 2004). Through vertical expansion of jobs, job enrichment expands the scope of jobs. This makes employees feel more motivated and self-sufficient. Given the wide exposure to various jobs or tasks, employees can also prepare themselves for future higher positions. Organizations focus on job enrichment for effective succession planning. They do this by making employees understand the dynamism of various jobs. Through job enrichment, employees are provided exposure to all skill varieties, that is, conceptual, technical, human, and business. They can also derive satisfaction from the opportunities for future growth and development.

Herzberg developed the basis for job enrichment practices. Hackman and Oldham further refined this by using the job characteristics model. This model assumes that if five core job characteristics are present and three psychological states critical to motivation are produced, it results in a positive outcome (Kotila 2001). Table 7.2 illustrates this model.

Cunningham and Eberle (1990) suggested the use of following questions to ensure positive results from job enrichment. This can result in proper alignment between workers' needs and organizational needs.

- Do employees need jobs that involve responsibility, variety, feedback, challenge, accountability, significance, and opportunities to learn?
- What techniques can be implemented without changing the job classification plan?
- What techniques would require changes in the job classification plan?

Autonomous work groups

Job design or redesign through formation of autonomous work groups requires organizations to provide employees functional autonomy for their assigned tasks or jobs. This process makes workers self-managing. The group decides

TABLE 7.2 Job characteristics model

Job characteristics	Critical psychological state	Job outcome or internal work motivation
Skill variety		
Task identity	Experiences meaningfulness of work	Job satisfaction
Task significance	Growth satisfaction	
Autonomy	Responsibility for outcome	Low absenteeism
Feedback	Knowledge of results	High quality performance

independently who has to do what and when. The employees then select a leader to guide the group. In the corporate world, this approach was first used by Volvo in Sweden. The company allowed the work groups to decide the hourly output rate and the level of pay; it also allowed them to organize their activities to achieve the results. In such organizations, the management plays a supportive and facilitative role. Organizations become 'bottom up' to support the work group. However, this process still holds the management responsible for the results. When organizations truly invest in the learning and development of workers as a long-term strategy, the workers develop a sense of responsibility and take ownership of results.

Sub-contracting

It is another form of autonomous work group. The difference is that, in this process workers no longer remain on the payroll of organizations. They form their own organizations and become self-employed. Here, workers are responsible for the results. Such an arrangement helps to make work design more specific and measurable, price jobs more accurately, and fix responsibility properly.

COMPONENTS OF JOB DESIGN

This section illustrates the various components of job design.

Job Information

Job information is an essential input for effective job analysis. It not only facilitates job evaluation for compensation designing, but also helps with disseminating information to employees about their duties and responsibilities. Imperfect knowledge about duties and responsibilities due to inadequate job information affects employees' performance and the organization's productivity. Disseminating job information in the letter of appointment may not be adequate. Proper documentation and communication in induction training is the right approach.

Objectives of job information

The first objective of job information is to communicate duties and responsibilities attached to a job to employees for their clear understanding. This also helps employees understand organizational expectations.

Another objective of job information is organizational analysis. It helps in workflow analysis with respect to a job. It also helps in identification of redundant work elements in a job, thus facilitating job restructuring.

In addition, job information helps in analysing the individual employees' behavioural requirements so that appropriate behavioural improvement actions can be taken by the organization to enhance the competencies of people and to remain competitive. Job information also enables an organization to determine the scope of internal hiring and the requirements of external hiring for staffing various positions in the organization.

In setting performance standards and establishing job objectives, job information is essential both in qualitative and quantitative terms. It helps in appraising the performance of an employee against such set standards more scientifically. It also provides critical inputs for other human resource management related decisions such as promotion, transfer, relocation, redundancy, and compensation designing.

JOB ANALYSIS

Job analysis is the process of gathering information about the job and evaluating such information in terms of what is necessary and relevant. Essentially, job analysis involves three questions: What is a job? What should be analysed? What methods of analysis should be used?

A job is a group of essentially similar activities or tasks performed by a person or a group of persons. These activities or tasks together become a job. Tasks or activities need not be identical. They may be performed in different places, with different equipment, in a different sequence. In addition, some employees may perform certain activities in addition to the main job. Or some employees may perform a job occasionally or temporarily in order to fill in for persons who are absent or on vacation. This definition of a job is typically used in compensation designing and other management practices. However, a more generic description uses the term position instead of the term job. A position is a family of jobs in which specific duties may vary, but some interchangeability of work is possible and the functional nature of the work is similar. Examples include assemblers, clerks-cum-typists, and bookkeepers. A broader definition of a job facilitates development of accurate job information and this accurately reflects the work of each employee. On the other hand, the more precise the job definition, the more difficult it is to identify the job differences, which complicates management of employees.

Another basic issue for job analysis is, whether the organization should measure works assigned or work actually performed. Some compensation-designing experts argue that unless job analysis considers work performed, the organization may not give employees credit for what they are actually doing. On the other hand, analysing assigned work may imply that employees have been given the latitude to assign work to themselves. Whereas, in reality, it is a manager's responsibility to assign the job. The role of an analyst is essentially to gather job information and not to evaluate the logic of work assignments. He is primarily responsible for recording responsibilities that a manager has assigned to an employee. Appendix 7A illustrates the concept further by using a job analysis data sheet.

Considerations

The nature of job information for job analysis depends upon a number of considerations such as whether the analysis is required for evaluation purposes or for other purposes as well; what job level is to be analysed; what type of evaluation plan is to be used; and what job knowledge is held by the analysts who would conduct the evaluation. Certain basic areas of information may include the following:
- fundamental purpose of the job
- work elements in the job. It requires the study of specific tasks, areas of responsibility, and examples of work
- general importance of each job element, its relationship to the total operation, and how it is integrated with the total job
- approximate time spent on each task or specific area of responsibility
- scope of the job and its impact on the operation
- inherent authority (not only formal delegation but also latitude of action) and formal or informal audits of work
- working relationships (including supervision)
- specific methods, equipment, or techniques that are required for the job
- job climate, including objectives and work environment
- job conditions such as physical effort, hazards, discomfort, chasing of deadlines, travel requirements, creativity, and innovations required

Methods of Analysis

Job information can be obtained in various ways either by a staff analyst or by the individual line manager. Because of functional proximity, it is always better to involve line managers in compiling job information. One relatively simple and inexpensive method to conduct job analysis is through questionnaires. Direct observation of work performed is another important method of job analysis. Observation of work is essential to understand the job role. However, it is more costly and time consuming.

Valuable job information can also be obtained from organization manuals, time-study reports, former job descriptions, and method studies.

Questionnaires

A job questionnaire is a special tool for collecting job information. It is a printed form, in which essential information about the job may be listed either by the employee or by his supervisors. The major advantage of the job questionnaire is that it uses the knowledge of those who are proximate to the job. In addition, it gives each employee an opportunity to participate and contribute by giving responses to the questionnaire.

Another important advantage of the job questionnaire is that compiled information can be used as a job description. This eliminates the requirement of writing the job descriptions. Moreover, use of a job questionnaire helps organizations get the benefit of communicating up-to-date job information to the employees.

However, the major disadvantage associated with job questionnaires is that their success depends on comprehension skill and writing ability of individual employees and supervisors. Due to perceptual incongruence, inconsistencies in the response pattern may arise. Such inconsistencies in the response pattern may further multiply, if a large cross section of people participate in the questionnaire response/survey. In addition, job information compiled from the questionnaires may be exaggerated. These are the inherent issues affecting the quality of information collected through job questionnaires.

To eliminate such inherent problems, it is always better to compile the information through a combination of direct observation and job questionnaires. This approach may be time consuming and involve a huge cost, but it is more scientific as it eliminates the chance of error by taking account of the differences between what employees perceive and what they do.

Recently, there has been increasing concern about the quantification of the process of job analysis. A structured *position analysis questionnaire* (PAQ) can help the process. PAQ was developed in the early 1970s through the efforts of McCormick et al. It consists of 194 job elements of a 'worker oriented' nature, which are divided into six major categories. The analyst normally rates the job elements on a scale of 0 to 5. However, administering PAQ is not simple. The PAQ has six major divisions, comprising 189 behavioural items required for the assessment of job performance and seven supplementary items related to monetary compensation. The six major divisions of PAQ are as follows:

Information input   Where and how does one get information on the jobs to perform (35 items)

Mental process   Information processing and decision-making in performing the job (14 items)

Work output   Physical work done, tools and devices used (50 items)

Interpersonal relationships   Connection between two or more people (36 items)

Work situation and job context   Physical/social contexts (18 items)

Other job characteristics   Work schedules, job demands (36 items)

Standard job components inventory is a structured job analysis technique for performing a job. It contains seven sections. The introductory section deals with the details of the organization, job descriptions, and biographical details of the job holder. Other sections are as follows:

Tools and equipment uses of over 200 tools and equipment (26 items)
Physical and perceptual requirements strength, coordination, selective attention (23 items)
Mathematical requirements uses of numbers, trigonometry, practical applications, work with plans and drawings (127 items)
Communication requirements the preparation of letters, use of coding systems, and interviewing people (19 items)
Decision-making and responsibility decisions about methods, order of work, standards, and related issues (10 items)
Job conditions and perceived job characteristics mix of the work environment and the personal characteristics together with job

Another approach is *profile matching method*, which has some common elements—(1) a comprehensive set of job factors used to select the range of work; (2) a rating scale that permits the evaluation of job demands; and (3) the weighing of job characteristics based on organizational structure and sociotechnical requirements. *Les profils des postes*, another task profile instrument, developed in the French multinational company Renault (RNUR 1976). It contains a table with entries of variables representing working conditions and provides respondents with a 5-point scale, ranging from very satisfactory to very poor. The respondents can select the value of a variable by way of registering standardized responses. The variables cover—(1) the design of the workstation; (2) the physical environment; (3) the physical load factors; (4) nervous tension; (5) job autonomy; (6) relations; (7) repetitiveness; and (8) contents of work.

The concept of *advanced ergonomic technologies* (AET) developed by Rohmert and Landau (1985) is based on the stress–strain concept. Each of the 216 items of the AET are coded—one code defines the stressors, indicating whether a work element does or does not qualify as a stressor; other codes define the degree of stress associated with a job; and still others describe the duration and frequency of stress during the work shift. The AET consists of the following three parts:

Part A The man-at-work system (143 items) includes the work objects, tools, equipment, and work environment constituting the physical, organizational, social, and economic conditions of work.
Part B The task analysis (31 items) is classified according to the different kinds of work objects such as material and abstract objects, and worker-related tasks.
Part C The work demand analysis (42 items) comprises elements of perception, decision, and response/activity. (H-AET, an AET supplement, covers body postures and movements in industrial assembling activities).

Broadly speaking, the checklists adopt one of two approaches: (1) the job-oriented approach (e.g., the AET, *Les profils des postes*); and (2) the worker-oriented approach (e.g., the PAQ). The task inventories and profiles offer a subtle comparison of complex tasks and occupational profiling of jobs. They also determine the aspects of work which are considered a priori in improving working conditions. The emphasis of the PAQ is on the following: classifying job families or clusters (Fleishman and Quaintence 1984; Mossholder and Arvey 1984; Carter and Biersner 1987); inferring job component validity; and job stress (Jeanneret 1980; Shaw and Riskind 1983). From the medical point of view, both the AET and profile methods allow comparisons of constraints and aptitudes when required (Wagner 1985). The Nordic questionnaire is an illustrative presentation of ergonomic workplace analysis (Ahonen et al. 1989), which covers the following aspects:

- work space
- general physical activity
- lifting activity
- work postures and movements
- accident risk
- job content
- job restrictiveness
- worker's communication and personal contacts
- decision-making
- repetitiveness of the work
- attentiveness
- lighting conditions
- thermal environment
- noise

Following are the shortcomings of the general-purpose checklist format employed in ergonomic job analysis.

- With some exceptions (e.g., the AET and the Nordic questionnaire), there is a general lack of ergonomics norms and protocols of evaluation with respect to the different aspects of work and environment.
- There are dissimilarities in the overall construction of checklists as regards the means of determining the characteristics of working conditions, the quotation form, criteria, and methods of testing.
- The evaluation of physical workload, work postures, and work methods is limited on account of a lack of precision in the analysis of work operations, with reference to the scale of relative levels of stress.
- The principal criteria of assessment of the worker's mental load are the degree of complexity of the task, the attention required by the task, and the execution of mental skills. The existing checklists refer less to the underuse of abstract thought mechanisms than to the overuse of concrete thought mechanisms.
- In most checklists, methods of analysis attach major importance to the job as a position as opposed to the analysis of work, worker–machine compatibility,

and so forth. The psycho-sociological determinants, which are fundamentally subjective and contingent, are less emphasized in the ergonomics checklists.

A systematically constructed checklist helps us investigate the factors of work conditions which are visible or easy to modify. It permits us to engage in a social dialogue among employers, job holders, and others concerned. One should be cautious about believing in the simplicity and efficiency of checklists, or in their quantifying and technical approaches. Versatility in a checklist or questionnaire can be achieved by including specific modules to suit specific objectives. Therefore, the choice of variables is very much linked to the purpose for which the work systems are to be analysed. This, in turn, determines the general approach for construction of a user-friendly checklist.

The suggested *ergonomics checklist* may be used for various applications. Data collection and computerized processing of the checklist data are relatively straightforward.

Assessment Centres

Chartered Institute of Personnel and Development (CIPD) carried out a survey in 2006, which indicated that almost 50 per cent of employers are now using the assessment centres approach in selecting prospective candidates for the job. Apart from the selection process, assessment centres also help in job analysis. An effective recruitment process in an organization follows the sequence as shown in Fig. 7.1.

Assessment centres assist the whole process by giving candidates experience of a microcosm of the job, while testing them on work-related activities as individuals and in groups. Interviewers can assess existing performances and predict future job performances.

The design of an assessment centre should reflect the following:
- ethos of the organization
- actual skills required to carry out the job
- potential sources of recruits
- extent to which recruitment is devolved to line managers
- human resource strategy

Organizations in transition should assess learning ability in candidates, whereas *steady state* organizations should assess existing skills and abilities that can be used immediately. The assessment centre should reflect the reality of the job and the organization. New recruits have high expectations from their job. If the assessment centre encourages them to believe that the job or the organization fits their values when it does not, the disappointment caused

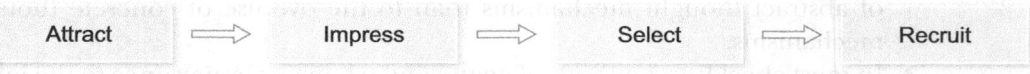

FIG. 7.1 Effective recruitment process

can be destructive. The cost of an assessment centre needs to be compared with the potential cost of recruitment error. To predict job performance, it is important to determine present and future skill requirements. In addition to the exercises, interviews should be used. Assessment centre tests would be valid only if the candidates for the job match the group norm. However, stand-alone assessment centre tests may not be adequate. They have to be used in conjunction with a variety of tasks. However, they have a high predictive validity in assessing future performances, and hence can be effectively used in compensation designing decisions.

Research has also shown that candidates who attend assessment centres feel impressed even if they are rejected as their attendance helps them to assess their job and the working condition of the organization. The essential job design criteria should include the following:

- duration of the centre (one day might be insufficient for more senior posts)
- location (ideal surroundings and accessibility for candidates with disabilities)
- number of candidates brought together (five may be too few for comfort under observation and more than eight gives problems in sharing the assessed time)
- candidate's background and comparability of past experience
- number, mix, and experience of assessors

Tasks involved in assessment centres

The essential skills or competencies of the candidates should be matched to the techniques and tasks which can test them. Depending on the nature of the job, the tasks might include individual or group work, written and/or oral input, in-tray, analytical work, individual problem-solving, group discussions, group problem solving, tasks that match business activities, personal role-play, and functional role-play.

Group exercises should be as real as possible. The group should set goals, create a climate for information sharing, and urge members to reach decisions. To the extent possible, participants should be able to appreciate the outcome of decisions. Assessors should make extensive use of role play, train the participants in problem-solving, group decision-making, and interpersonal skills. It is also desirable for the assessors to allow reasonable preparation time before the exercises start.

Attributes that can be verified through assessment centres are—understanding competitiveness, cooperation, creativity, idea-generation, aptitude for valuing diversity, etc.

JOB DESCRIPTION

The compiled job information is translated into job descriptions. These are written records of job duties and responsibilities, which provide a factual basis for job evaluation. Job descriptions are recorded on a standard form in a uniform manner.

As the preparation of job descriptions need writing skills, many organizations assign this task to trained and professional job analysts. However, this by itself cannot guarantee a flawless job description as a professional job analyst may not have specific job knowledge. Therefore, it is always better to involve employees in the scientific description of jobs in spite of the engagement of an analyst.

In terms of format, the job description should first name the job, using a title which accurately summarizes duties assigned. While naming a job, it is always better to consider the job family. To illustrate, if a HR job is named knowledge manager instead of HR manager, it would give a contemporary or trendy touch to the job title. However, for others including members within the organization, it may be a misnomer. Secondly, job description should then document in a single form, frequently with short sentences or phrases, a list of duties assigned. What is to be included in the listing of job duties and how those are to be written, would depend on the level of the position and the purpose to be served by the description. For top management, a job description may be the description of business goals and objectives. While at the operations level, job descriptions may be limited to listing of specific duties to be performed, equipments to be used, and procedures to be followed. The broader the use of the job description information and the higher the functional level, the longer is the job description. For operational positions, job description may be about one page; whereas for top management, it may run to several pages. Appendix 7B illustrates the concept further.

Objectives

Job descriptions help in getting things done. It helps management to accomplish the following objectives:
1. efficiently organizing of jobs
2. recruiting for the organization
3. assigning jobs to people by communicating their duties and responsibilities, and by setting job standards
4. reviewing performances of people
5. improving performances through appraisal and training
6. rewarding employees

Therefore, job descriptions play a very crucial role in key management activities. However, it is very important for the manager to ensure that job descriptions are correct and whatever jobs have been assigned are essential. He must ensure that only essential tasks have been grouped into jobs. Since job descriptions are interconnected, he has to align it to recruitment, performance appraisal, training needs, promotion, transfer, and relocation decisions.

From the employees' point of view, it should also show employees, what is expected of them and how to do the work assigned.

By listing the assigned duties in a job description, a manager can determine reasonable performance standards. Identification of such performance standards helps in benchmarking the performance of an employee against the best performer.

Job descriptions also facilitate proper manpower utilization. By periodically reviewing the listed duties, a manager can identify the jobs which are time consuming but require lower skill sets. He can reassign such jobs to lower-paid employees. In addition, the manager can also study jobs in terms of workload and determine man-hours required. For low-technology and low-skill jobs, he can consider offloading the job to subcontractors. Therefore, job descriptions have tremendous implications for effective human resource planning (HRP) in an organization. We may also call them an instrument for proper rightsizing of employees in an organization.

Finally, they can also be used as a basic management tool. In this role, they influence operating procedures by identifying the duplication of work, indicating a scientific work flow, suggesting better allocation of jobs, and by pointing out possible job bottlenecks.

Job specifications

In addition to providing information about duties associated with job assignments, job descriptions also outline the basic specifications of the job. Such specifications include the education or experience required to do the job; and the special knowledge and skills necessary to carry out the job. In addition, specifications also identify soft skills such as interpersonal skills, analytical ability, problem-solving skills, or decision-making skills required to perform the assigned duties. Figure 7.2 illustrates the concept further.

This exercise of processing job information is known as developing job specifications. It helps in the evaluation of jobs and at the same time defines the attributes required for a job position. Therefore, job specifications list attributes such as education, experience, age, and physical fitness along with the other soft skills required for performing a job. This exercise requires special skills of the analyst as any mistake in judgement may defeat the purpose. Any mistake would not only lead to selection of the wrong person for the job, but also lead to incorrect evaluation of the job. Evaluation of a job is directly associated with job pricing.

Transparency

These days, organizations are dynamic and require restructuring every now and then. This also necessitates the redesigning of jobs. Therefore, it is widely believed that showing a job description to employees may cause controversy and they may resist doing work which is not specifically listed in their original

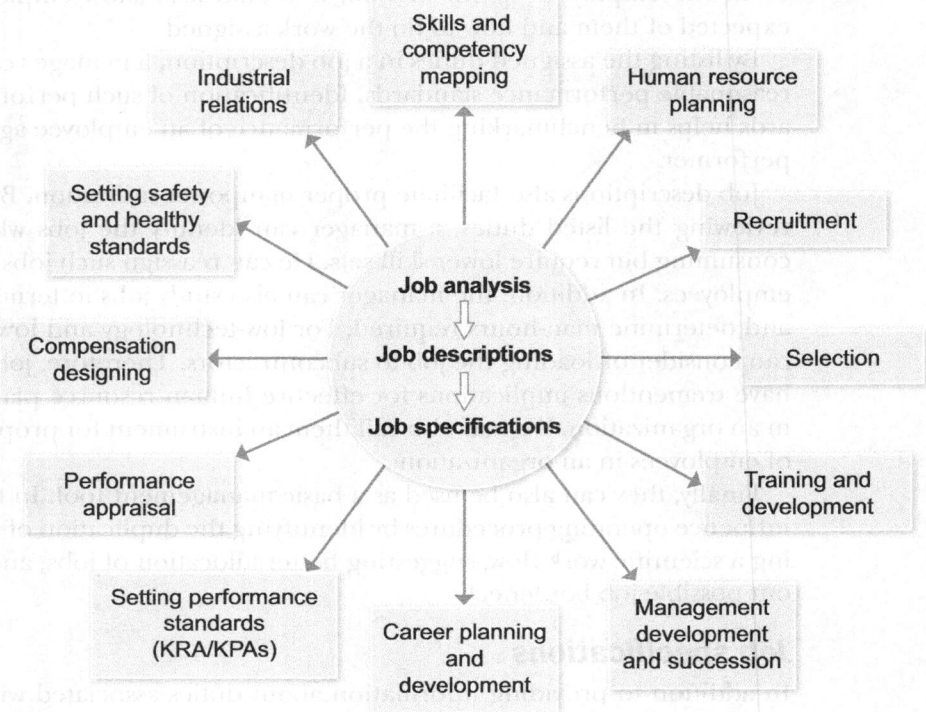

FIG. 7.2 A central peripheral relational model of job analysis

job description. However, if job descriptions are well developed, there is nothing wrong in sharing them with the employees as they spell out the list of duties employees are expected to perform. To eliminate the possibility of any controversy or conflict, an all-inclusive statement such as 'in addition to the listed duties and responsibilities, your superior may ask you to perform other tasks from time to time' could be included in the job description and contract.

By sharing job descriptions with employees, organizations can make their job-evaluation process participative and avoid any dissonance on job evaluation results. This is important as it helps organizations address employee dissatisfaction about job pricing. Communication of job descriptions enhances acceptance as employees are not left with any doubt about their duties and responsibilities. Such communication with employees should be an ongoing exercise it helps employees understand their changed job duties and responsibilities, if any.

COMPENSATION DESIGN THROUGH COMPENSABLE FACTOR

After successful job designing, it is important for organizations to list compensable factors for different job categories. Compensable factors are characteristics of a job on which organizations assign weights. These characteristics are identified as the ones that would help the organizations achieve its goals and strategies. Hence, compensable factors are used as job evaluation criteria. From organizational point of view, some 5–6 compensable factors are identified. Their degree of importance may differ in accordance with nature and level the job. Degree of importance is tested in a 5-point *Likert type scale* and the result is multiplied with the pre-assigned weight to get the total score. Aggregated scores are ranked and the job with highest rank gets higher compensation in comparison to other jobs.

As already mentioned, weights on compensable factors are pre-assigned depending on the goals and strategies of the organization. Total weights assigned for compensable factors adds to 100. For example, weight for consequence to errors for a quality control job may be 90 (out of 100); while for a computer operator, it may be only nine. Organizations design compensation based on the total ratings of the job position within the job family.

The process requires grouping of all jobs into separate job families. For example, all administrative jobs can be grouped into 'Administrative Job Family' and accordingly ranking of compensable factor can be done for each job family. This has been illustrated by an example in Table 7.3.

For Administrative Executive, individual job ranking is done based on total compensable factors, as illustrated below. This has been illustrated by an example in Table 7.4.

TABLE 7.3 Ranking of compensable factors

Administrative job family	Ranking of compensable factor
Administrative assistant	125
Administrative executive	131
Manager administration	164
General manager administration	222

TABLE 7.4 Calculation of aggregate compensable factor score for an administrative executive's position

Compensable factor	Degree	Weight	Total
Education and work experience	1	14	14
Communication skills	3	11	33
Job complexity and decision-making	1	22	22
Supervisory training and advisory role	2	9	18
Responsibility	1	24	24
Technical skills	1	20	20
		Total	131

In this example, with aggregate compensable factor of 131 for the job of Administrative Executive, the organization may decide compensation of ₹25,000 per month. As could be seen from the table, the company assigns weight on their pre-determined compensable factor depending on the job family and its importance. Thereafter, score of each compensable factor is evaluated by multiplying the assigned degree with the assigned weight. Although weight may be common across the job families, degree of importance may vary.

SUMMARY

Job design helps in organizing job tasks. It has a direct impact on the mental and physical health of employees as well as their performance levels. The physical aspects of jobs require organizations to consider ergonomic issues. Ergonomics helps in reducing physical strain, fatigue, and monotony, which occurs when doing repetitive tasks. Mental aspects require organizations to address behavioural issues such as developing work systems and culture, which enable employees to get relief from dehumanizing effects. Compatible physical and mental aspects help keep employees satisfied and lead to development of a high-performing organization.

For addressing ergonomic and behavioural issues at the workplace, job design must relate to the organization's structure and style of management. Management styles and structures may vary from an autocratic to democratic decision-making, delegation and formation of autonomous work groups, delayering the structure by reducing the number and levels of managers, increasing the span of control, increasing the productivity levels of motivation of employees, etc.

The job design principle focuses on the motivational aspects of jobs to make them more interesting and challenging to employees. With advent of scientific management, jobs were broken into small independent elements, which required the workers to perform the same task repetitively. The argument was that, by this process the jobs would become more scientific and workers' performance would be measured easily. However, this argument was negated with the emergence of the human relations school, and addressing the behavioural issues in job designs started gaining acceptance. Human aspects of job design now receive more importance in organizations, leading to a synergy between productivity and employee satisfaction.

Key Terms

Job rotation It involves periodic vertical and horizontal movement of employees between a set of jobs or tasks. Job rotation provides employees some relief from the monotony of the same repetitive jobs or tasks. However, this requires organizations to initiate multi-skilling of employees through continuous training and learning activities. The scope of job rotation depends on the nature of job and its similarity with other jobs in the organization. In some organizations, the opportunity for skill interchangeability is greater due to commonality of tasks or jobs. Whereas in other organizations, the scope of skill interchangeability may be very less due to the specialized nature of jobs. However, multiskilling initiatives can provide results even in the second case.

Task identity Tasks should be fit together to make a complete job since this gives the employee a sense of doing a whole job from the beginning to the end, with a visible output. Important benefits can be derived from task identity. It can help a worker trace his performance to the overall goals and target achievement of the organization. In addition, workers develop a sense of belonging and start realizing that they are partners in the organizational progress.

Task variety It varies the tasks to be performed so that an employee can move from one job to another within the organisation. Such variation provides a change in the employee's mental activity as well as physical well-being.

Exercises

Concept Review Questions

1. In what ways is job analysis different from job assessment? Select any job and analyse its individual content.
2. Write short notes on
   (a) Job characteristics model
   (b) Assessment centre approach in job design

Critical Thinking Question

Pulkit Shah is the HR manager of your organization. He does not understand the need for job descriptions. The company periodically restructures its operation and activities, including frequent changes in product lines. The company recruits multi-skilled professionals. Critically comment on the Shah's argument from the perspective of compensation management.

CASE STUDY: Compensation Practices of DimondSoft

DimondSoft is a US-based software major, which is in the business of executing turnkey projects in ERP software development. The company has an account of more than 100 large conglomerates, spread across the world. Team leader manages client accounts with support from software developers, who are stationed at client site till successful development and implementation. Team leaders are managed by regional vice presidents, who are stationed in the respective regions. Most of the deliberations, which include reporting and clarifications, between the team leaders and the regional vice presidents take place through videoconferences. Due to their exposure to different areas of business, software developers can quickly acquire knowledge in multiple business domains and become a target for poaching by other competing organizations.

Software development is not an entry-level job at DimondSoft. The company deliberately recruits people who are engineers with management degrees from leading business schools as management trainees. These trainees get a year-long induction training, which among other things includes three months of on campus full-time training in SAP from Siemens and Six-Sigma training from Motorola. Cost to the company per employee for induction training and their compensation comes to an astronomical figure of ₹25 lakh in the first year alone. The company puts each trainee under

(Contd)

CASE STUDY *(Contd)*

a mentor team leader, who helps the trainees get exposure to functional areas through on-the-job assignments. As a policy, the company restricts lateral entry and grooms management trainees to climb the ladder through structured succession plans.

For any competitor, DimondSoft's software developers are a prized possession. Hence, employee retention is the biggest challenge. Apart from nurturing a proactive work environment and giving self-respect to employees, DimondSoft offers a pay package designed, balancing the fixed variables, long-term incentives (LTI) and short-term incentives (STI) components, with strategic focus on employee retention. The company recognizes that compensation and benefits are critical factors in attracting and retaining good talent. In a recent review of employee compensation, the company observed the following features of its compensation management practices:

- substantial differentials in gross compensation of the team leader with that of the software developer
- differentials in gross compensation and sometimes compensation structure between the projects and support functions
- personalized salaries out of a basket of options for individuals at senior levels
- significant increase in basic salary and hence in deferred benefits (both statutory and voluntary)
- restriction of non-tax perks in the form of reimbursement under various heads to only certain top levels of management
- discrimination in increment percentages across levels, projects, and functions
- group and team incentives at lower levels, with individual based incentives at higher levels, resulting in less pay-outs of performance incentives, commissions, performance payments, and performance bonuses to outstanding software developers.
- provision of non-taxable allowances like soft furnishing allowance (curtains, carpets, cutlery, and crockery, etc.) for team leaders onwards, but not for software developers
- wide variation in conveyance allowance across levels, projects, and functions
- medical benefits are liberal across levels
- restriction of sabbaticals for higher studies to only those who are with the company for more than five years
- special interest free loans are extended to the tune of ₹3 lakh for various purposes
- reimbursement of books, periodicals, newspapers, journals, etc. against a pre-determined limit is common. Membership subscription to professional bodies is also reimbursed
- corporate club membership for all
- soft loans for purchase of furniture, appliances, and computers for all
- housing loans or interest subsidy is also provided for all
- discretionary rewards such as reimbursement for travel for a holiday including accommodation in guest houses, transit flats, etc. This is practised mostly for senior managerial employees. From team leaders onwards, the company has a system of offering fixed annual leave travel allowances
- sign-off bonuses and reimbursement of relocation expenses for top level managers
- expensing stock options to all
- annual profit sharing across levels
- compensation deferrals include provident fund, gratuity, pension, and loyalty bonus with separate time cap as vesting period

CASE STUDY (*Contd*)

The company systematically benchmarks compensation in order to remain in the top slot, attract talent, and increase retention. Recently, the company observed that the attrition rate for software developers has increased from 2 per cent to 5 per cent. Most of these left after gaining at least three years of experience with the company. Human resource accounting has enabled the company to assess the cost of such attrition. It comes to an estimated sum of ₹1.5 crore. Exit interviews and human resource audits, through a diagnostic questionnaire about employees' satisfaction, indicate that most of those who left the company (software developers) were not comfortable with the company's compensation structure.

Discussion question

Identify the areas of deficiency in the existing compensation structure for the software developers. Develop a suitable compensation structure, which you feel can increase the their retention.

References

Ahonen, M., M. Launis, and T. Kuorinka (1989), *Ergonomic Workplace Analysis*, Finnish Institute of Occupational Health, Helsinki.

Banks, M.H., and R.L. Miller (1984), 'Reliability and convergent validity of the job component inventory', *Journal of Occupational Psychology*, vol. 57, pp. 181–184.

Bhattacharyya, D.K. (2006), *Human Resource Planning*, 2nd edition, Excel Books, New Delhi. Bhattacharyya, D.K. (2007), *Human Resource Research Methods*, Oxford University Press, New Delhi.

Brown, R. (2004), *Design jobs that motivate and develop people*, http://www.media-associates.co.nz/fjobdesign.html, last accessed on 14 February 2004.

Campion, M.A. (1988), 'Interdisciplinary approaches to job design: A constructive replication with extension', *Journal of Applied Psychology*, vol. 73, pp. 467–81.

Campion, M.A. and P.W. Thayer (1985), 'Development and field evaluation of an indisciplinary measure of job design', *Journal of Applied Psychology*, vol. 70, pp. 29–43.

Carter, R.C. and R.J. Biersner (1987), 'Job requirements derived from the position analysis: Questionnaire and validity using military aptitude test scores', *Journal of Occupational Psychology*, vol. 60, pp. 311–21.

Cunningham, J.B. and T. Eberle (1990), 'A guide to job enrichment redesign', *Personnel*, February, vol. 67, no. 2, pp. 56–60.

Drury, C.G. (1987), 'A biomechanical evaluation of the repetitive motion injury potential of industrial jobs', *Seminars in Occupational Medicine*, vol. 2, pp. 41–9.

Fleishman, E.A. and M.K. Quaintance (1984), *Taxanomics of human performance: The description of human tasks*, Academic Press, Orlando.

Hackman, J.R. and G.R. Oldham (1974), 'Motivation through design of work: Test of a theory', *Organisational Behaviour and Human Performance*, vol. 16, no. 2, pp. 250–79.

Hay, E. (1981), 'The guide chart profile method of job evaluation', Hay Associates, New York.

Henderson, Richard (2005), *Compensation Management in a Knowledge-based World*, 10th edn, Pearson Education, London.

Herzberg, F. (1966), *Work and the Nature of Man*, World Publishing Co., Cleveland.

Jeanneret, P.R. (1980), 'Equitable job evaluation and classification with the position analysis questionnaire', *Compensation Review*, vol. 1, pp. 32–42.

Kotila, O. (2001), *Job enrichment*, www.academic.empuria.edu/smithwil/001, last accessed on 15 February 2007.

Leach, D. and T. Wall (2004), *What is job design*, http://www.shef.ac.uk/~iwp/publications/whatis/job_design.pdf, last accessed on 15 February 2007.

McCormick, E.J. (1979), *Job Analysis: Methods and applications*, AMACON, New York.

Mossholder, K.W. and R.D. Arvey (1984), 'Synthetic validity: A conceptual and comparative review', *Journal of Applied Psychology*, vol. 69, pp. 322–33.

Robertson, I. and M. Smith (1985), *Motivation and Job Design: Theory, Research, and Practice*, West Publishing Co., St. Paul.

Rohmert, W. and K. Landau (1985), *Analysis*, Taylor and Francis, Londres.

Rush, H. (1971), *Job Design for Motivation: Experiments in Job Enlargement and Job Enrichment*, The Conference Board, New York.

Shaw, James, B. and John H. Riskind (1983), 'Predicting job stress using data from the position analysis questionnaire', *Journal of Applied Psychology*, vol. 68, pp. 253–61.

Smyth, Richard and Murphy Matthew (1948), *Bargaining with Organized Labor*, Funk and Wagnalls, New York.

Wagner, R. (1985), 'Job analysis at ARBED', *Ergonomics*, vol. 28, no. 1, pp. 255–73.

Wood, Robert and Tim Payne (1998), *Competency-based Recruitment and Selection*, John Wiley & Sons, New York.

APPENDIX 7A Job Analysis Data Sheet

JOB ANALYSIS DATA SHEET

Job title   Code:
Other titles
Suggested title
Department   Dept. No.   Dept. head
No. on job _____   Rank _____   Supervised by _____
Persons interviewed
Analysis   Date   Location of Job
Other identification

Job summary (Key phrases that cover job):

Relation to other jobs:
    Promotion from:
    Promotion to:
    Transfer to and from:

Work performed: What–How–Why (Use additional sheets if required)

    Major duties:
    Other tasks:
    Equipment, machines:

Skills involved/physical demands:
    Experience (Type and amount):
    Education and training (Specific skills required):
    Responsibility for product and material:
    Responsibility for equipment and machinery:
    Responsibility for work of others:
    Other jobs directly affected:
    Resourcefulness:
    Monetary:
    Visual efforts:
    Physical efforts:
    Surroundings:
    Hazards:

APPENDIX 7B Job Description

Form No. 2

Job identification data   :
 Present job title   :
 Department/Section   :
 Suggested job title   :   Date:
 Job code   :
 Employees interviewed   :
 Job summary
     1. Regular tasks:
         (a)
         (b)
         (c)
         (d)
     2. Casual tasks:
         (a)
         (b)
         (c)
     3. Equipment or machine used:
     4. Working conditions and hazards:

Form No. 3

Job specifications
     Job title (Existing):   Job code no.:
     Job title (Suggested):
 Department/Section   Total points classification
     1. Education   Points
     2. Experience   Points
     3. Responsibility for product or materials   Points
     4. Responsibility for machinery and equipment   Points
     5. Responsibility for works of others   Points
     6. Responsibility for safety of others   Points
     7. Manual skill   Points
     8. Physical effort   Points
     9. Working condition including hazards   Points

CHAPTER EIGHT

Compensation Management and Job Evaluation

Learning Objectives

After reading this chapter, you will be able to
- understand job evaluation and its relation to compensation design
- evaluate various methods of job assessment
- discuss competency-based approaches to compensation design
- understand Hay's method of job evaluation

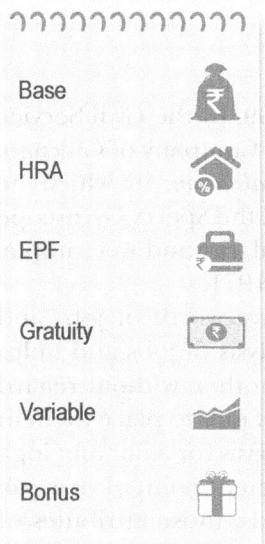

Compa-ratio—Additional Tool Over Job Evaluation

Salary range midpoints and market reference points (MRPs) represent the market average pay for positions. An employee's salary compa-ratio, the ratio of pay to the market rate for the job, indicates how his salary compares to the average market rate. Salary compa-ratios should reflect employee work experience, skills, and performance. Compa-ratios are used to measure an employee's pay relative to the market average pay for his position and to facilitate salary equity among groups of employees.

There are three common uses for compa-ratio calculations:
- to extend a salary offer to a new hire
- to budget the total amount of a merit pay programme
- to determine an appropriate pay raise for an individual

The amount of increase awarded to an employee is usually dependent on the employee's performance and compa-ratio. Let us consider the example in Table 8.1.

TABLE 8.1 Compa-ratio and pay increment

Employee	Salary (₹)	Mid-point	Compa-ratio	Performance
X	42,500	50,000	0.85	Excellent
Y	56,000	50,000	1.12	Excellent

An employee who is an excellent performer with a compa-ratio of 0.85 should receive a larger raise than an excellent performer with a compa-ratio of 1.12. Calculating compa-ratios is a simple process that provides complex information to compensation specialists. If your compa-ratio significantly exceeds 1, your employer is extremely generous, or your job is in great demand, or you are ready for a promotion.

Most organizations provide for a recommended course of action to take if the compa-ratio falls within a certain percentile range. For example, an organization may provide that if the ratio percentage falls between 0 to 33 per cent, the result is a grade demotion. If the ratio falls between 34 and 66 per cent, the result is a lateral movement, and if it falls between 67 and 100 per cent, the action is a promotion.

JOB EVALUATION

Study in the field of job evaluation was pioneered in 1909, by the Civil Service Commission in Chicago and the Commonwealth Edison Company of Chicago. In 1926, Merill Lott authored *Wage Scales and Job Evaluation*, in which he described job evaluation techniques used in his company, the Sperry Gyroscope Company Inc. Job evaluation techniques gained in popularity and were implemented by several organizations in the United States in 1971.

Job evaluation systematically differentiates the relative worth of jobs and helps establish pay differential. It requires detailed analysis of jobs and helps determine the worth of one job in relation to that of another, without regard to the personalities. It analyses and assesses the content of jobs to place them in some standard rank order. The end result is used as the basis for a fair and logical remuneration system. From a compensation management point of view, job evaluation helps identify the compensable factors, that is, those attributes of a job which are capable of being priced to determine pay level. Some of the commonly agreed compensable factors are skills, efforts, responsibility, and working conditions.

A properly devised job evaluation scheme provides the management with definite systematic and reliable data for determining wage and salary scales. The data is used for logical wage negotiation which reduces wage grievances, dissatisfaction with wage differentials, and ensures fair treatment for each employee. It also provides a logical basis for promotion. A survey carried out by

the British Institute of Management indicated that it is used for the following purposes:
- reduce layout turnover
- increase output
- improve morale
- reduce loss of time due to wage negotiation and disputes
- reduce complaints regarding wages
- reduce wage and salary anomalies

Several types of job evaluation processes can be used, while designing compensation. If jobs for evaluation are of a similar nature, a single commonly applicable job evaluation technique may serve the purpose. However in most organizations, employees are differentiated by function and hierarchy. A marketing manager's job has hardly anything in common with an HR manager's job. Similarly, a field sales person's job may have less strategic requirements than a marketing manager. Hence, most of the organizations require multiple job evaluation techniques. Some organizations set up a job evaluation committee to address job evaluation issues. The various steps in job evaluation are as follows:

1. detailed examination of the job (job assessment)
2. preparation of job description (recording its characteristics to determine assessment method)
3. analyzing the job to set out the requirements of the job under various factor headings
4. comparison of one job with another
5. arrangement of jobs in a progression
6. relating the progression of jobs to a financial scale

Compensation designing using only the job evaluation method cannot always be foolproof. So, organizations try to minimize the risk of wrong job evaluation by following certain common features as outlined in this section.

Relative comparison Job evaluation results cannot be absolute; they can only provide a relative comparison.

Analytical approach Even though the raters follow certain systematic guidelines to perform job evaluation, it often becomes highly subjective because of their judgemental discretion. However, some raters follow an analytical approach to make an informed judgement and in the process try to make the exercise more scientific.

Systematic and structured approach Organizations follow a definite structure while evaluating jobs. This structured framework lays down details of tasks to be performed and thus tries to make the process scientific.

Job Evaluation Techniques

There are following four basic types of job evaluation techniques.

Ranking

This is a simple system to judge each job as a whole and understand its relative worth by ranking one whole job against another job. To start with, a job description is prepared, in a narrative form, stating the duties, responsibilities, and qualifications required for the job. This is followed by ranking of jobs in order of their relative difficulty or value to the company, defining of grade levels, and finalization of wage levels.

The disadvantage of this method is that the degree of difference between jobs cannot be indicated. Therefore, the rankings may be incorrect and unduly influenced. In fact, it may be the ranking of the relative value of the employees currently occupying the jobs, instead of the jobs themselves. This method may be adequate for the easily defined jobs of a small number of workers, but is regarded as impractical for complicated jobs and a large number of workers.

Classification

This is different from ranking as in this case grade and wage levels are predetermined before jobs are ranked and descriptions are written defining the type of job which should fall into each group. Under this method, usually a committee allocates jobs to each group using the job description. The system is simple but suffers from limitations similar to those of the ranking system.

Points rating

Under this system, each job is broken down into its component factors or characteristics to achieve a higher level of accuracy. The components are then evaluated separately rather than evaluating the job as a whole. A narrative job description is prepared and supplemented by a statement of the various requirements. Characteristics such as experience, training, and mental and physical effort common to the jobs are selected, and a point value for each characteristic or factor is determined. Factors are defined objectively and points are given to each factor based on its estimated importance. Consolidated point values are finally converted into financial terms. For this purpose, compensable factors are selected on the basis of benchmarked jobs. Compensable factors are measurable qualities, features or characteristics of jobs such as skills, mental requirements, physical characteristics, and the working conditions. Benchmarked jobs outside organizations provide important reference points for evaluation of in-house jobs. While deciding compensable factors for the benchmarked jobs, organizations should ensure that they represent the scope of their jobs and are capable of defining skill, effort, responsibility, and working conditions. Such compensable factors are then categorized into specific related factors or sub-factors. To illustrate, competency as a job factor can be broken down into several sub-factors such as skill, knowledge, ability, and attitude. Job responsibility as a factor can be broken down into sub-factors such as administrative, functional, and strategic. Compensable factors depend on the key features of a job. The concept of critical success factors (CSF) could be used for a job to identify the areas of evaluation.

After identifying the compensable factors, the degree of factors is defined. For example, the degree of knowledge (as a sub-factor) for a routine and mundane clerical job is less as compared to the requirement for an accountant's job. Based on the degree of requirement, weights are assigned to each factor to assess the relative worth of a job. Accordingly, point values for the compensable factors of each job are evaluated to design a suitable compensation package. Table 8.2 illustrates the method for giving weight to compensable factors for the job of an HR manager.

Number of points assigned to each factor indicates the weight of the factor. Degrees are assigned to profile the factor. Similarly, assigning degrees to the above compensable factors and breaking it into sub-factors can be done as illustrated in Table 8.3.

Remember, degrees here have been assigned only for the sub-factors of identified compensable factors. As in the case of domain knowledge, sub-factors can be developed for other compensable factors and degrees can be assigned depending on the specific job requirements. After identifying compensable factors and sub-factors for all jobs and assigning weights and degrees to them, the job evaluation can be started by preparing a job evaluation sheet for each individual job, as per Table 8.4.

In the justification column, the rater documents his observations and finally evaluates the job to decide a suitable compensation package.

TABLE 8.2 Compensable factors and weights

Compensable factors	Percentage of high-rated factor	Factor weight
Domain knowledge	100	35.7 (100/280)
Strategic focus	80	28.6 (80/280)
Problem-solving ability	50	17.9 (50/280)
Interpersonal relations	50	17.8 (50/280)
Total	280	100.0

TABLE 8.3 Compensable factor domain knowledge

Compensable factor-domain knowledge	Degree	Points
General bachelor degree	1st	10
Bachelor degree with B-school diploma	2nd	15
Bachelor degree with B-school diploma and membership of professional association	3rd	20
Postgraduate management degree	4th	25
Postgraduate management degree with membership of professional associations	5th	30

TABLE 8.4 Compensable factors analysis format

Compensable factors	Degree	Point	Justification

Traditionally, a wage curve shows the relationship between wage rate and unemployment, representing graphically the average wage rate on vertical axis and unemployment on horizontal axis. The downward slope of a wage curve indicates that unemployment reduces with high wage rates. Such negative relationship between the levels of unemployment and wages arises region-wise. The explanation given is that with higher wage rates, people volunteer to work. A typical wage curve is developed based on the job evaluation points and individuals falling within the same curve are paid accordingly. Figure 8.1 illustrates a wage curve from a compensation management perspective.

The following rating scales are used in weighting and rating of compensation factors:

Lott's point method It recognizes 15 compensable factors, not of equal importance or value, to measure job differences.

Benge's factor comparison method It develops a wage rate scale for each universal factor.

Hay's profile method This method, developed by Edward Hay (1981), focuses on three factors—know-how (KH), problem-solving (PS), and accountability (AC).

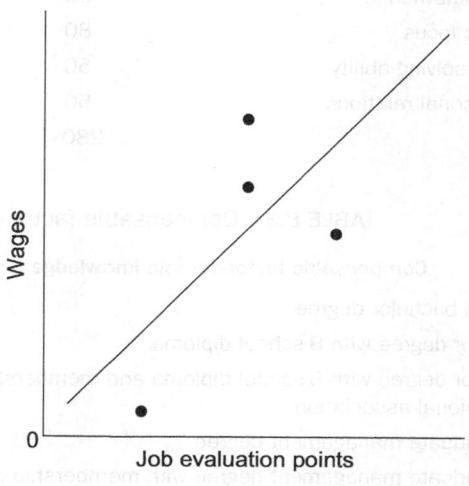

FIG. 8.1 Wage curve

NEMA method It identifies sub-factors for five universal compensable factors and then measures it with a rating scale to arrive at a suitable compensation design.

Hay's method of job evaluation Hay's method of job evaluation is the most widely accepted process of evaluating jobs. It helps in designing effective organizations; clarifying interdependencies and accountabilities; managing succession and talent; and setting competitive, value-based pay policies. Pay-related costs have become an important issue, given the battle for talent in a globalized world. Many organizations need to become flexible in designing their pay structures, sacrificing their set standards and norms. To ensure a reasonable balance between flexibility and control, the Hay Group revamped the processes of valuing work by aligning pay with value creation. Hay's method of job evaluation also helps in defining appropriate pay levels, providing organizations a common framework and language for designing jobs, defining career progressions, analysing organization structures, and strategically managing human resources.

Hay Group pioneered the 'factor comparison' job evaluation method and modified it in its guide charts in the early 1950s. Organizations use the Hay methodology to evaluate jobs against a set of common factors that measure inputs (required knowledge, skills, and capabilities), throughput (processing of inputs to achieve results), and outputs (end results from applying inputs constructively). During the evaluation process, each job's content is analysed relative to each factor and represented by a numerical value. These factor values are then added to determine the overall job 'size'. The various job size relationships, as well as the factor proportions associated with each job, can be useful in a number of organizational and HRP applications.

A clear understanding of impact and its relation to overall accountability is critical when designing and evaluating jobs. Every job exists to add value to the organization by delivering some set of results. The *input–throughput–output model* is reflected in the Hay method as *know-how, problem-solving,* and *accountability*. Each grouping can be further broken down into eight elements for the work-value assessment. The output factor accountability is covered first, since every job is designed to achieve predetermined results. This factor typically receives the least attention and weight in many other evaluation methodologies.

Know-how In Hay's terminology, know-how is the aggregation of all capabilities or skills required for successful job performance. Therefore, know-how or its inputs are technical/specialized skills, managerial skills, human relations skills, etc.

Problem-solving The value of know-how is assessed through its application to achieve results. Problem-solving refers to the use of know-how to identify, delineate, and resolve problems. Utilization of know-how through problem solving has two dimensions—thinking environment and thinking challenge. Thinking environment is assessed in the job context; while thinking challenge is assessed through the measurement of addressable problems and the difficulty in identifying value-added solutions.

Although the definitions of these job criteria evolved several decades earlier, they are still accepted as the most scientific way for valuing work. Hay's method, however, continuously refers to the current organizational value systems and compensation system to ensure improvement in the market pricing and increasing confidence in job evaluation results.

Based on the Hay's job evaluation criteria, Table 8.5 illustrates the compensable factors for a clerical employee and a driver. Characteristically these two jobs are different; the job of a clerical employee requires more education and knowledge. Therefore, the clerical job should be considered for more pay. However, in this hypothetical example, we find the aggregate compensable factors for a driver's job are more, resulting in more pay for a driver than a clerical employee.

Working conditions such as the physical environment, hazards, manual effort, and mental concentration can also be included in job-context factors. However, many of these factors—unlike the three Hay factors identified earlier—can be potentially discriminatory. Therefore, there is a need for a complimentary process to design and utilize supplementary factors alongside the guide charts.

Accountability Accountability measures the type and level of value a job can add. In this sense, it is the job's measured effect on an organization's value chain. It has three dimensions:

Freedom to act The degree of empowerment to take action and the guidance provided to focus decision-making.

Scope The business measure(s) the job is designed to positively impact.

Impact The nature of the job's influence on business results.

Impact can be contributory, shared, and primary. Contributory impact is appropriate when jobs are advisory or counselling in nature. This type of impact is more visible in staff advisory services. Shared impact is visible in a participative (both with in-house members and outsiders) decision-making situation. In this case, attempt is made to measure the relationship between

TABLE 8.5 Compensable factors

Hay's constructs	Clerk	Driver
Know-how	100	89
Problem-solving	19	16
Accountability	25	22
Working conditions:		
Physical effort	2	9
Physical environment	1	7
Sensory attention	6	9
Mental stress	2	8
Total compensable factor	155	160

the jobs and functions, degree of partnership, joint accountability, etc. Primary impact is assessed through the analysis of end results, assuming contributing inputs are secondary. Hence it makes use of key result areas (KRA).

Factor comparison

This method is also similar to the points rating system as here too each job is broken into factors. The only difference here is that five factors are used, that is mental requirements, skill requirements, physical requirements, responsibility, and working conditions. After job descriptions, key jobs are judged and related to one another. The jobs are considered one by one and reviewed to understand how much of the current wage rate for the job is paid for each factor. Key jobs are arranged in a scale in order of their value for each factor.

The remaining jobs are compared with the key job factors and a comparative money value is determined for each factor of each individual job. The total of the factor values so determined for each job represents its rate. This is a complex system, but a higher degree of accuracy can be attained through this.

Other methods

Depending on the organizational capabilities, we can also use the *market pricing method* of job evaluation. Market pricing method accounts for the realities of the market. Henderson (2005) recommended two types of market pricing approach—pure and guideline method. *Pure market pricing method* uses labour market trends to understand the worth of a job. For this purpose, organizations need to collect market information based on their own job narratives, which they have already developed on the basis of job analysis, and then arrive at the pay rate for their comparable jobs. However, market pricing by itself cannot be used as an independent job evaluation method because of the difficulty of matching the job with families; differing compensation practices across organizations; inadequate information sharing by comparing organizations, etc.

Smyth and Murphy (1948) and Henderson (2005) developed the *market pricing guideline method* to eliminate the weaknesses of the pure market pricing approach. They developed a guideline scale, job description scope data, market pricing, and the horizontal guideline display. The guideline scale provides a standard scale of salary ranges. Job description scope data realistically identifies benchmarked information of key jobs. Market pricing collects back-up information through a compensation survey; and horizontal guideline displays relate jobs department-wise to ensure equity within the pay structure for the same jobs across departments.

Another method of job evaluation is the *maturity curve method*, developed by Bell Laboratories (now taken over by Lucent Technologies) in the 1950s. It is basically intended for deciding the rates of pay for scientists and engineers. The method requires the development of a series of curves to map differing levels of worth or value for individuals with similar periods of post-qualification experience. It resembles a learning curve, which rises very fast in the initial years, then plateaus and even drops. A downward trend in the curve indicates knowledge and skill obsolescence, which is more valid for scientific and engineering disciplines. Therefore, the analogy is that scientists and engineers with twenty to twenty-five years of experience should get less pay. However, organizational practices indicate that things are the other way round. Skills and knowledge are both renewable, and so are competencies. Hence, even if they are older, experienced scientists and engineers can perform much better than those who are in the establishment and maintenance age groups.

The traditional methods of job evaluation described earlier are more commonly used in organizations for convenience and easy interpretation. However, it is recommended that no single method of job evaluation be used. Instead, organizations should use two or more methods in combination for better compensation design. The following criteria are recommended for consideration before selecting a particular job evaluation technique:

Validity The selected method should be technically sound and should be able to consistently evaluate jobs. Consistency ensures uniformity of results across the jobs being evaluated.

Usability The selected job evaluation method should be the right fit for the organization and the nature of jobs. For example, in a research and development organization, scientists' job evaluation methods cannot hold good for manual workers of the same organization and for similar workers in other organizations.

Acceptability Since job evaluation is used for designing compensation structure, the selected method should be acceptable to members of the organizations, so that they can be free from apprehension about any possible manipulation by raters. In fact, helping employees to understand the selected methods can ensure better acceptability.

Sustainability Once job evaluation methods are selected by an organization in consultation with workers or unions, it is desirable to sustain it unless the organization faces a major change in its job content.

A tentative point-rating plan to evaluate the job of a marketing executive is presented in Exhibit 8.1.

Graded pay structure

A graded pay structure is designed by organizations based on the job evaluation reports. Some organizations develop a series of pay grades even for the same position to differentiate the intrinsic worth of the individual job. One HR manager may be entrusted with the compensation design function, while another may be entrusted with industrial functions, even though both may be in the same pay band. However, the functional differences and intrinsic worth

EXHIBIT 8.1 Point rating plan

Job title:
Department
Section:

Factor	Rating	Basis of rating
(1) General knowledge	1 (5)	Ability to understand instructions and recognize signs and symbols to carry out the job.
(2) Experience	4 (48)	
(3) Judgement	3 (21)	
(4) Initiative and integrity	2 (14)	
(5) Manual dexterity	4 (24)	
(6) Accuracy	2 (16)	
(7) Physical activity	4 (28)	
(8) Strength	5 (25)	

may be different for organizations, depending on their functional importance. A graded pay structure within the same pay band may be developed. In addition, a graded pay structure may be applicable for different hierarchical levels within the same job family. For example, an HR job family starting with the HR executive may elevate to senior executive (HR), deputy manager (HR), manager (HR), etc. For each hierarchical level, pay grades are different. The graded pay structure has been illustrated in Fig. 8.2 by plotting level of wages on the y-axis and nature of jobs classified on the x-axis. As is evident from the illustration, a rise in wage level is accompanied by a change in the nature of jobs with an increase in hierarchical level.

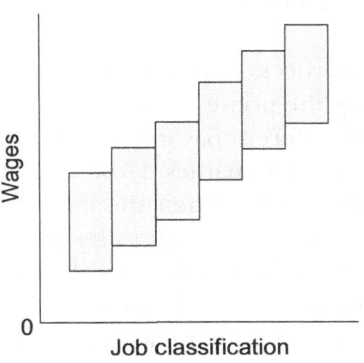

FIG. 8.2 Graded pay structure

Limitations of Job Evaluation

Job evaluation alone cannot establish a wage scale. For wage fixation, we need to take into cognizance statutory requirements like the Minimum Wages Act, 1948. Similarly, other factors of wage fixation such as the capacity to pay, inter-industry wage variation, inter-regional wage variation, and collective bargaining agreements, if any, also need to be given importance. Job evaluation is highly subjective due to it being based on judgemental estimates. Similarly, it cannot take into account the cyclical effect of market value of occupations. For example, finance jobs were highly priced in the market at one point of time; now, IT and marketing jobs are preferred. With failure of non-banking financial companies (NBFC), finance jobs are not valued very highly in the market, even though no material change in the job profile of finance professionals has taken place. Despite such limitations, the job evaluation technique is considered very useful for reasons explained earlier.

JOB ASSESSMENT

At this stage, information about each job is made available to the assessors. Every job, whether manual or not, is closely observed and inspected in actual operation by the assessors. If required, the assessors question the operators and their supervisors to collect details about the job to clear any doubts they may have. To keep pace with the changing job content, brought primarily by technological changes, it is necessary to periodically assess the job keeping in mind the old job description.

Pricing Job Value

The purpose of job evaluation is to establish the relative job value, in terms of points/rankings and pay levels, within the organisation. The next step is to translate this data into a pay structure through job correlation. This involves first deciding the pay grades and then developing pay ranges for each grade.

The initial process of pricing jobs and fitting them into a pay structure calls for translating the points into different job grades. Thereafter, jobs have to be grouped into different pay grades and the result has to be related to comparable jobs in other companies. However, this may not be possible for jobs which are unique in nature. When the jobs are properly grouped, it is not difficult to price each such job group. After pricing each job group, pay structure can be developed on the mathematical principle that 'things which are equal to the same things are equal to each other'. From the survey report of other companies, base salary for each pay grade is established after considering the average paid by the companies surveyed.

The next step in job pricing is to develop pay ranges around base salaries. Once this is developed, individual compensation based on performance and other considerations can be calculated. Different pay ranges enable the organization to adopt a flexible approach in hiring new employees, taking into cognizance labour market flexibility. To illustrate, in a manufacturing organization, a fitter may have a pay grade ranging between ₹5,000–10,000 per month. This pay grade can be broken into different ranges, such as Fitter grade-I (₹8,000–10,000 per month), Fitter grade-II (₹6,000–8,000 per month), and Fitter grade-III (₹5,000–6,000 per month).

ALTERNATE METHODS OF JOB ASSESSMENT

There are various other methods of job assessment for pricing a job value, which is an essential factor in compensation design. At the same time, such methods ensure the simplification and humanization of jobs. Even though some of these methods do not directly contribute to job pricing, these are still useful for achieving productivity and efficiency. In a subsequent part of this chapter, these methods have been discussed briefly.

Work Study

Work study literally implies study of human work. The British Standards Institute defines work study as, 'A management service based on those techniques, particularly method study and work measurement, which are used in the examination of human work in all its contexts and which lead to the systematic investigation of all the resources and factors which affect the efficiency and economy of the situation being reviewed, in order to effect improvement'.

Therefore, it is a generic term for two interdependent techniques—method study and work measurement. The British Standards Institute defines *method study* as 'The systematic recording and critical examination of the factors and resources involved in existing and proposed ways of doing work, as means of developing and applying easier and more effective methods and reducing costs'. *Work measurement*, on the other hand, is defined by the British standards as 'the application of techniques designed to establish the time for a qualified worker to carry out a specified job at the defined level of performance'.

Contextual analysis of the agreed definition of work study given by the British Standards Institute enables us to define the subject as a procedure for understanding and determining the truth about activities of people, plant, and machinery. It also helps identify the factors which affect their efficiency and optimum utilization. Most productivity improvement techniques involve major capital expenditure on plant or equipment. Work study, on the other hand, ensures productivity by using existing resources. In work study, the human element is emphasized and importance is given to operation rather than to the

technical process. This assists management in meeting following three major objectives:
- effective use of plant and equipment
- effective use of human effort
- evaluation of human work

Work study and trade unions

If work study techniques are not properly applied, they are likely to encounter resistance at all levels. Therefore, it is important to understand human reactions before designing and implementing programmes. Most unions are aware of the fact that work study provides benefits to workers by eliminating monotony, frustration, and an unhealthy working environment. It also gives an opportunity to workers to increase their earnings on micro level and the nation as a whole at macro level. However, the following need to be considered to satisfy the unions:

1. Workers should be consulted before the introduction of any scheme, which is likely to affect their interest, in one way or the other.
2. There should be a definite policy for those workers who will become redundant after implementing the recommendations of the work study team.
3. The procedure to deal with changes in methods of work and for the measurement of work should be specified and communicated to the workers.

In 1952, International Labour Organization (ILO) emphasized the importance of such sharing of information with workers in a resolution concerning consultation and cooperation between employers and workers in its 35th session at Geneva.

Method Study

Method study is a productivity improvement step, which helps produce the same output using less resources or produce more with a proportionately smaller increase in the inputs. Therefore, it reduces waste, even if it does not eliminate it. Method study ensures creativity, innovativeness, optimal decision-making power, good organizational practices, and better communication. It is essential to keep the following factors in mind while carrying out a method study:
- economic considerations
- technical considerations
- human reactions

From the above discussions, we can summarize that the method study helps do the following:
- appraise the purpose and objectives of the organization
- assess the tasks of the organization
- evaluate the communication and control structure of the organization
- optimize the use of resources of the organization

- improve the procedures, methods, and processes of the organization
- ensure individual and group effectiveness, and at the same time satisfaction of workers in the organization

The objective of method study is to find better ways of doing things and to improve efficiency by eliminating unnecessary work, avoidable delays, and other forms of waste. It achieves the aforesaid objectives through systematic recording, analysis, and critical examination of methods and movements involved in the performance of existing or proposed ways of doing work. The importance or objectives of method study will be clearer, if we review its contributions. The contributions of method study include the following:

- reorientation of corporate objectives and mission
- review of plans and programmes
- evaluation of tasks, targets, and available resources
- balancing the structure of the organization
- introduction of a good communication system in the organization
- better design of plants and equipment
- simplification of processes and methods
- standardization of products and procedures
- improvement of workflow
- planning and control of work
- managing resources, inventory control, and replacement of plants and machinery
- quality and cost control
- improving the layout of the shop floor
- betterment of working environment and working conditions
- optimum utilization of resources
- higher standards of safety, security, and health
- performance satisfaction

Basic procedures and steps

The method study technique is flexible enough to accommodate different situations. The steps for its application in any given circumstances are as follows:
- Select the work to be studied
- Record all the relevant facts of the present (or proposed) method
- Examine facts critically and in sequence
- Develop the most practical, economic, and effective method with due regard to all contingent circumstances
- Install that method as standard practice
- Maintain that standard practice by regular routine checks

Select the job Once the method study idea is conceived, the first step is orientation and determination of objectives. The problem must be defined. The method study investigators usually face the following types of challenges:
- bottlenecks which disrupt the smooth flow of materials or processes

- products which need to be produced economically by application of cost-reducing techniques
- economic utilization of space, including land and buildings
- economic utilization of labour, material, and plant
- elimination of idle items or time which add no value

While selecting the subjects for study, it is essential to keep in mind that the ultimate objective of the method study is to improve achievements by raising productivity and increasing satisfaction at work. Secondly, the term 'select' should not be taken in a narrow sense, that is, to choose from restricted subjects. Instead, it must include a preliminary survey which enables the investigator to decide on the continuity of the study. Similarly, select does not necessarily mean just selection of the job but also selection of the appropriate techniques to achieve the end result.

Record the facts Before discarding the existing method or procedure, adequate facts about the present system must be collected. This is required to prepare an objective record of the way the job is carried out. To eliminate the charge of bias, this record is not compiled from second-hand accounts or from the manager's or operator's version of how the job is done, but based on direct observation by the concerned investigator.

Critically examine the facts It is also an important stage of method study. Information collected is scrutinized and each part of the job critically examined to determine whether any part may be:

- eliminated altogether
- combined with any other part of the job
- changed in sequence
- simplified to reduce the content of the work involved

For effective examination of the facts, the following questions are generally asked:

- what is done and why?
- what it does and what that person does?
- where is it done and why there?
- when is it done and why then?
- how is it done and why this way?

By rearranging, simplifying, combining, eliminating, or modifying the facts or records, a basis is obtained for an improved method.

Develop the new method Alternatives selected are used to reshape and develop the new method, layout, or procedure. These may require test runs to determine their feasibility. Tests of this nature should preferably be carried, if possible, out at a place away from the work site. To ease the problem of acceptance for new methods in the department, it is good to involve the department. The end result must be an improved method and must be acceptable to departmental staff and workers. It must meet all their practical requirements and technical specifications.

Install the method To install the method, decisions must be taken with regard to the ordering of new plants or material (if any), phasing in changes in production process, deciding the extent of redeployment, training, introducing new documentation procedures, setting new quality standards, and testing procedures. It is good to have a detailed time table for effecting such changes. The outcome of the installation stage should be that when the new method is in operation at the work site, the line management should be in complete control and all members of the department should be fully conversant with the method.

Maintain the method When a method has been installed, it tends to change slowly because of small alterations made by operators or supervisors. A reference standard (job instruction sheet) is needed against which the job can be compared to detect any alteration. Similarly, a corresponding document for an incentive scheme—which also contains details of the standard time for each job—called a job specification is prepared. Changes in methods can be detected using data in these documents. If changes are considered to be useful, the instruction sheet can be amended to incorporate them; but if they are thought undesirable, they can be removed through line management.

However, in a real situation the study may not necessarily follow the sequence or pattern. Selection of the subject of study may be preceded by the study of possibility of data collection. Similarly, a preliminary critical examination, pilot study, may be needed in order to identify the problem area. During a pilot study, there may be need for more detailed data. Or, it may be revealed during preliminary critical examination that the real problem is something other than the selected one. Therefore, sticking to a rigid procedure of analysis may often mar the prospect of getting a productive solution. In method study, there should not be any secrecy. Discussion, exchange of views, and efforts at mutual understanding are part of every basic step of method study. There are several undefined stages. Before implementation, the final plan should be discussed with all concerned. Similarly, installing the new system should be preceded by a plan to familiarize all concerned through reorientation programmes. After installation, the system has to be maintained to ensure that this becomes an accepted standard. The processes of method study may be enumerated as follows:

1. initial data collection
2. preliminary/pilot survey and assessment
3. identification of problem areas
4. collection and assembly of data concerning the factors
5. determining their inter-connection
6. finalizing the subjects for study
7. defining the problems/subject for study
8. assessment of their impact/reaction
9. evolving alternatives

10. deciding optimal solutions
11. testing the solutions
12. preparation of the report
13. presentation of recommendations
14. decision on implementation
15. preparation for implementation
16. installation of the newly evolved system
17. maintenance of the newly installed system
18. evaluation of improvements achieved

WORK MEASUREMENT

ILO has defined work measurement as 'The application of techniques designed to establish the work content of a specified task by determining the time required for carrying it out at a defined standard of performance by a qualified worker'. Conventionally, it is known as time study. It is primarily carried out to determine the standard time to perform a specific task. Such time standard is used for—planning and scheduling work, cost estimation, labour cost control, or a wage incentive plan.

There are different techniques of work measurement. However, the following are the principal techniques:
1. Time study
2. Ratio-delay study (statistical sampling technique)
3. Synthesis from standard data
4. Pre-determined motion-time standard
5. Analytic estimating

Out of all these, only time study technique is widely used, the others being complicated in nature. Here, we will discuss in detail the time study only, while simply defining the other techniques.

Time Study

ILO defined *time study* as 'a technique for determining as accurately as possible from a limited number of observations the time necessary to carry out a given activity at a defined standard of performance'. For carrying out a time study, equipment such as stopwatches, study boards, pencils, and slide rule are required. The stopwatches may be of following types:
- Stopwatches which record one minute per revolution by intervals of one-fifth of a second with a small hand recording 30 minutes
- Stopwatches which record one minute per revolution, calibrated in 1/100th of a minute with a small hand recording 30 minutes
- Decimal-hour stopwatches recording 1/100th of an hour and a small hand records up to one hour in 100 divisions

The following steps are necessary to carry out a time study for the measurement of work.
1. Collect and complete all available information about the job, which should also include the surrounding conditions and the attributes of the operators, which are likely to affect the work.
2. Record the details of the method and also break down different operations into elements.
3. Record the time taken by the operators to perform different elements of the operation, preferably measuring with a timing device like a stopwatch.
4. Assess the working speed of operators and compare it with a predetermined normal speed.
5. Convert the observed time to normal time.
6. Decide the rate of allowance that may be given over and above the normal time of the operation.
7. Determine the time allowed for operation.

Time study is a work measurement technique, which is widely used in industry to decide the standard time to do a work. Though it basically helps in pricing a job, it is also used for other purposes such as deciding training requirements, payment of incentives, and rewards. Let us try the following problem to understand its computational details.

Example

Swapna Sinha has been asked to set the standard time for manufacturing ball-point pens per activity details in Table 8.6. Sinha has observed the ongoing job for 100 hours and has seen that within this period 1,000 ball-point pens have been manufactured. Assume that during work, workmen get personal time allowance at the rate of 10 per cent. Compute the standard time for manufacturing a single ball point pen.

Solution

To solve this problem, it is necessary to compute the average cycle time, dividing observed period by number of ball point pens produced

Average cycle time = 100 Hours/1,000 ball point pens
= 1/10 of an hour = 6 minutes

TABLE 8.6 Activity details

Activity	Rate (%)	No. of times jobs observed
A	120	200
B	90	300
C	80	500
D	70	100
Idle time		200
		Total = 1,300

Therefore, it takes an average of 6 minutes to manufacture a ball point pen. Now we have to compute the activity-wise distribution of time using this formula

Average cycle time × (Observed time/Total time) × Rating

Average cycle time has already been computed, which is 6 minutes

Observed time is the activity-specific time, already shown in the problem

Total time is total observed time. Rating is the perceived rate of efficiency of the rater given in the problem.

(i) Time taken for activity 'A'

$$6 \times (200/1{,}300) \times (120/100) = 1.1$$

(ii) Time taken for activity 'B'

$$6 \times (300/1{,}300) \times (90/100) = 1.2$$

(iii) Time taken for activity 'C'

$$6 \times (500/1{,}300) \times (80/100) = 1.8$$

(iv) Time Taken for activity 'D'

$$6 \times (100/1{,}300) \times (70/100) = 0.3$$

Total normal time = 4.4

Now, let us compute standard time using this formula:

$$\frac{\text{Total activity-wise time or normal time}}{\{1 - \text{Personal fraction time}\}}$$

$$4.4/(1 - 0.1) = 4.4/0.9 = 4.8 \text{ minutes}$$

Other Techniques

Since carrying out time-study for each job is a time consuming task, statistical technique like ratio-delay study is often carried out. Ratio-delay is a sampling technique, which instead of carrying out a complete job study uses a sufficiently large number of readings that are taken at random intervals. Like all other sampling techniques, there are bound to be some errors under this method. However, with the cost of such a study being far less, many organizations prefer this method. Moreover, this method encounters no resistance from workers as ratings are not done under this method, only the time is recorded directly using a stopwatch.

Standard data method synthesizes time standard that are built up from data elements previously obtained from direct time study. Organizations that do not have independent work study departments build a table synthesizing common elements. Some units also use time records of other organizations as standard data. However, this type of synthesis may not always be correct due to the obvious non-commonality of technology, skill, process, and working environments.

Pre-determined motion-time standards have been developed for different job elements based on elementary movements. Usually, time measurement takes in account work factor and basic motion times. Work study analysts use such time standards as the basis for comparing the observed times of the current workers. This enables the managers to quickly decide the efficiency or otherwise of the workers and take decisions accordingly.

Analytical estimation is normally used in plant maintenance and repair work. This is a compromise between straight rate fixing and time study. Since maintenance and repair jobs require adequate planning and may also require creativity and innovation, it is difficult to enforce straight rate fixing. In these cases, analytical estimating is difficult in nature and is also not always foolproof because of the inexperience of the work-study managers.

ERGONOMICS

Ergonomics is derived from two Greek words; *ergon*, meaning work and *enomos*, meaning laws. It is the study of the effects of a work system on workers and aims at fitting the work to the mean to increase their efficiency, comfort, and satisfaction. ILO defined ergonomics as, 'The application of human biological sciences in conjunction with engineering sciences to the worker and his working environment, so as to obtain maximum satisfaction for the work which, at the same time, enhances productivity.'

An analysis of the ILO definition provides a meaningful basis to understand ergonomics. An ergonomist tries to integrate the work system, which broadly includes the tasks, working equipment, working conditions, and working space, with the capabilities and requirements of work in order to make work more effective. By this, he also tries to ensure job satisfaction for the workers.

Ergonomics can be applied in all schemes of human activity, be it in offices, factories, shops, ships, or airlines. Some of the areas where ergonomics has been successfully applied are as follows:
- design of equipment, power, and hand tools
- design of displays and warning systems
- design of furniture, seats, rests, and steps for operators
- design of tools, jigs, and fixtures
- plant layout
- improvement in working conditions and environments
- computation of relaxation allowances for workers
- selection, training, and placement of personnel
- motivation of workers

Detailed application areas of ergonomics can be understood from the discussions below:

Human characteristics Health, physique, anthropometric data, personal background, education, training, experience, age, sex, intelligence, aptitude, reaction time, interest, personality characteristics, temperament, attitude towards work, motivation, etc.

Work Physical load, perceptual load, mental load, displays and warning systems, controls, and compatibility of inputs and outputs.

Working conditions Workplace layout, postures, motion and movements, fatigue, monotony and relaxation allowances, comfort, safety and health, working hours, and shift work conditions.

Environment Illumination, ventilation, temperature and humidity, colour dynamics, fumes, dust, odour and smoke, landscape, scenery and garden, cleanliness and sanitation. Many alternative terms such as human engineering, human factors in engineering, engineering psychology, applied experimental psychology, applied and human engineering research, and man-machine system analysis are used to designate the discipline. It was developed during World War II with the coordinated efforts of physiologists, psychologists, and design engineers. Its earliest application can be traced to Taylor. His experiments were mainly to arrive at the optimum design of equipment for specific types of work and also to train the workers to use the right equipment for each type of task. Frank and Lillian Gilberth recommended the principles of motion economy and introduced rest breaks and spacing of work to reduce fatigue and eliminate stress. Since then, the understanding of the effects of working conditions and environment on the human body and mind has been greatly enhanced due to advancements in the fields of experimental physiology, psychology, and method study.

ERGONOMICS AND WORK STUDY

Work study, which aims at scientific analysis of a work system to increase productivity and satisfaction at work, is dependent on ergonomics for research data on human reactions to a given work situation. Such input makes the task of a work study practitioner more scientific and result-oriented. These inputs mostly relate to the following areas:

1. limits of sustained physical endurance, normal speeds of movement, and optimum method of handling controls
2. receptivity to sensory inputs and time required for perception of deviations
3. reaction time for motion output and time required for evaluation and decision-making
4. anthropometric data to guide the design and layout of equipment, work place, and furniture
5. effects of different types of environmental conditions in order to generate improvements
6. effects of working conditions so as to raise the standards of comfort, safety, and health
7. qualitative and quantitative analysis of factors contributing to industrial fatigue for computation of 'relaxation allowances'

ERGONOMICS AND MANAGEMENT

Ergonomics is a discipline that helps the management in the planning and design stage of a work system. To be able to control and direct human efforts towards a specific end, the management needs to have an appreciation of the human factors involved in a work system.

The findings of ergonomic research, particularly in the field of perceptual and mental loads, have a special bearing on the work situation influencing managerial performance in an organization. The aim here should be to eliminate all perceptual and mental burdens that may arise from the perusal and evaluation of reports on the normal activities of the organization, thereby highlighting only deviations from the equilibrium state. This will permit more effective application of the managerial talent to really important problems over a wide span. In other words, ergonomics can help in increasing the productivity of managerial brain power. This single improvement by itself, without any changes in the methods on the shop floor, can lead to a spectacular increase in the overall productivity of organizations.

Working Areas

The working area of an operator may be categorized into three groups— normal, immediate, and maximum working area. The *normal working area* can be reached by the operator using any movement up to and inclusive of class three movements. Two arcs made by the fingers using the elbow as the pivot bound this area. The *immediate working area* is the surface immediately in front of the operator, where the two arcs of the normal working area overlap. The maximum working area is the one that can be reached by the operator using arcs made by the fingers with the shoulders as the pivot.

The space between the normal and the maximum working areas is accessible through a class four movement, which require entire arm and twisting of the body to do the job. Anything beyond the maximum working area may be reached only through a class five movement, including body bending or stretching.

The immediate working area is most suitable for bi-manual operation. If the equipment, materials, and tools are replaced within the normal working area, they can be reached without using the upper arm and shoulder muscles. It is not desirable to place anything outside the maximum working area.

The field of vision should also be taken into account while considering working areas. The normal cone of vision, without head movement, is restricted. Covering the whole perimeter of the normal working area will impose undue eyestrain and sometimes involves excessive head movements. Therefore, due care must be taken to position all the materials well within a workers cone of vision. In inspection work, most of the work must take place directly in front

TABLE 8.7 Class of movements

Class	Pivot	Body member movement
(i)	Knuckle (finger joint)	Finger(s)
(ii)	Wrist	Hand and fingers
(iii)	Elbow	Forearm, hand, and fingers
(iv)	Shoulder	Upper arm, forearm, hand, and fingers
(v)	Trunk (body apart from limbs)	Torso, upper arm, forearm, hand, and fingers

of the operator. For better understanding, class of movements can be grouped under five categories, based on the pivots around which the body part moves (Table 8.7).

A similar classification is available of the movements of corresponding parts of the leg. For economy of motion, the movement should be of the lowest classification possible and compatible with the normal capacity of the body part affected.

Motion Economy

Motion economy is the process of minimizing the physical and perceptual loads imposed on people engaged in any type of work; whether be it in the office, the shop floor, the kitchen, or at the driving wheel. It leads to better design of equipment, jigs and fixtures, hand tools, furniture, and labour-saving devices. In addition, it facilitates better layout of offices, warehouses, plants, and operating areas such as office desk, work bench, aircraft, cockpit, and crew compartments of armoured fighting vehicles. Application of the principles of motion economy eliminates or minimizes wasteful and fatiguing movements, and increases the productivity of workers. It aims to minimize movements as follows:

- number of movements
- length of movements
- classification
- number of parts of body used
- necessity for control
- muscular force
- complexity of movements
- distance between eye fixation
- time required for eye fixation

For achieving motion economy, the following principles have been evolved by different specialists:

- minimum movement
- natural movement
- simultaneous movement

- rhythmic movement
- habitual movement
- continuous movement

Simultaneous movements reduce fatigue and increase the rate of output. More fatigue is caused when only one hand is working, while the other is idle. Simultaneous movement include the movements of the feet, while both hands are operating as in driving a car. Application of this principle leads to the better design of jigs, fixtures, and duplication of tools so that both hands work at similar tasks simultaneously.

The principle of symmetrical movements should be applied in conjunction with simultaneous movements. Proper balance is achieved only when the movement of one hand is the 'mirror image' of the other so that fumbling is eliminated. When movements of the hands are asymmetrical, there is a tendency on the part of the operators to interpolate additional non-productive movements in order to achieve balance.

Rhythm is the regular repetition of a movement pattern. It often incorporates the accentuation of a specific part of a cycle. Rhythm contributes to speed, elimination of fumbling, and reduction in fatigue. Examples of rhythmic movements are boat rowing, hammering as a blacksmith, and drawing water from a well using a see-saw lift.

The pattern of movement should be designed to facilitate habituation. When a cycle of activities are performed habitually, the movements are executed almost as a reflex action. Habitual movements eliminate hesitation and increase speed of performance. Rhythm helps in speed habit formation. Tools, materials, displays, and controls must always be located in the same position. The pattern must be standardized for similar types of panels, work places, and equipment. Continuous movements, which are smooth and curved, are superior to jerky or straight line movements, which involve sudden changes of direction and loss of momentum. Materials, tools, and jigs must be positioned to incorporate smooth, curved, continuous movements and eliminate undue changes of direction.

The above principles should be treated merely as guides and not rigid rules. Quite often, one principle will be in conflict with another and a proper evaluation of the principles in their totality would be needed for optimization. Conditions differ from job to job. It may sometimes be necessary to give priority to load over the various muscles or give more weightage to the principle of continuous movement. It is essential that the principles are applied with flexibility.

Human Engineering

Method study seeks to determine the most effective combination of man, machine, and the working environment. In doing so, it is necessary to determine which functions are performed better by man and which by machine. Both man and machine can surpass each other in certain ways. The question of economy again influences man–machine combination. The term human engineering is used to refer to the field of study aimed at resolving man–machine problems in design, operation, and maintenance of plants and machineries. In a broad sense, it comes under the purview of ergonomics. Therefore, it is not appropriate to designate human engineering as an independent discipline, separating it from ergonomics. However, to understand the context and meaning of human engineering, it is considered necessary to define it. McCormick defined it as the mechanism for adaptation of human tasks and working environment to sensory, perceptual, mental, physical, and other attributes of people. This adaptation for human use applies to functions such as the design of equipment, instruments, man–machine systems, consumer products; as well as to the development of optimum work methods and work environment.

Human engineering and machine design

The designer of a machine should know the way individuals function, their body dimensions, physical limitations, and the conditions under which they perform efficiently. For performing a task, an individual normally does the following things:
1. receiving information through different sense organs
2. making decisions using the perceived information
3. taking action that is implementing the decision

Therefore, the basic control cycle for human beings consists of these parts—sense, decide, and act. The powers to reason inductively, exercise judgement, develop concepts, and make decisions and create methods are unique to human beings. The quick performance of repetitive routine tasks, power to perform rapid computations, apply great force, and simultaneous performance of many different functions are characteristic features of a machine.

The designer of the machine is required to consider all the above details before developing a better designed machine for productive use. Most of the computer numerically controlled (CNC) machine centres developed by large industrial organizations in India are not performing well as they have been designed without considering the human factor. In fact, many sophisticated machine centres have caused a perpetual industrial relations problem as they were designed without properly considering the human factor, and thus affected workers adversely. This is because the cycle time printed in the machine literature is considerably less than the actual time taken by the workers. This complicates the correlation of the job with the workers' payment, as technically they are supposed to be paid as per the printed cycle time.

Since a badly designed machine can be cause for poor performance of the workers, application of ergonomics/human engineering techniques is necessary to design the machine. Modern machines are ergonomically designed to prevent stress and fatigue of the workers, to make them work in ease, and at the same time, to increase productivity. We find application of human engineering/ergonomic techniques even in the designing of consumer products such as kitchen gadgets and furniture. Recently, Blow Plast Ltd, under technical collaboration with Klober of Germany, launched ergonomically designed office chairs.

Value Analysis

In 1947, Henry Erlicher of General Electric, drawing lessons from World War II, observed that substitution of materials—manufacturers were forced to substitute materials due to shortage of original materials—often led to cost reduction and better functionality. This prompted further research in the field of alternative materials and processes. Miles, another top executive of the company, introduced the concept of value analysis. By 1949, this approach, in a more institutionalized form, was used by General Electric and then by the US department of Defence. By 1970, the concept of value engineering gradually received international attention.

Value engineering is an organized creative technique to analyse functions of a product, service, or a system to accomplish the required functions at the lowest cost while ensuring their performance, reliability, and maintainability. It is also known as value analysis or value management. Literally, value is the worth of an article/product/service. Value is determined in terms of cost and function. The value of a product can be improved in the following manner:
- improving function, while keeping cost constant
- by reducing cost, while keeping function constant
- both by improving function as well as by reducing cost

There are different types of values of an industrial product. These may be classified in the following manner:

Use value The properties and qualities which are useful and which enable individuals to accomplish work.

Esteem value Aesthetic features or properties which attract customers.

Cost value The cost required to manufacture the product.

Exchange value The properties which enable the owner to exchange it, if he desires to do so in the future.

For all practical purposes, in an industrial situation, we are primarily concerned with the use value and esteem value.

Therefore, value analysis can be defined as, 'a method of search, a systematic procedure resulting in the orderly utilization of alternative materials and processes. It focuses on engineering, manufacturing, and purchasing with the

> **EXHIBIT 8.2** Value analysis
>
> The following steps are followed for value analysis:
> 1. collection of full facts and information about the product
> 2. get the details of the cost break-up
> 3. determine the function
> 4. think creatively
> 5. compare and evaluate alternatives
>
> To succeed in each step, it is necessary to take the following lines of action:
> 1. eliminate the redundant parts
> 2. initiate action of cheaper substitutes without impairing the use value
> 3. standardize the parts
> 4. develop alternative methods
> 5. redesign, if necessary

objective of obtaining an equivalent or even better performance for lower cost.' Exhibit 8.2 illustrates the concept further.

Advantages   Following advantages can be derived from value analysis:
- lowering of cost
- better quality of product
- increased efficiency
- high level of morale and team spirit
- increased customer's satisfaction
- optimum resource utilization
- improved methods of production
- increased job satisfaction and motivation of workers through use of their creative ability

The term value analysis has now been replaced by value engineering in corporate circles. In most organizations, implementation of value engineering practices includes forming a value engineering team consisting of workers. This provides an opportunity to workers to derive creative satisfaction and also to fulfil their intrinsic needs. At the same time, the organization also gets active service from the workers.

COMPETENCY-BASED APPROACH

The competency approach has two initial stages—identifying or analysing competencies and assessing competencies. The first is concerned with what competencies are used in the job; while the second is concerned with measuring the extent to which existing employees, or would-be recruits, possess them. This information can be used in making better judgements in selection and

recruitment, career development, promotion, and pay. According to Wood and Payne (1998), the most commonly adopted competencies are as follows:
- communication
- achievement/results orientation
- customer focus
- teamwork
- leadership
- planning and organizing
- commercial/business awareness
- flexibility/adaptability
- developing subordinates
- problem-solving
- analytical thinking
- building relationships

While designing jobs, competency mapping is done by collecting inputs from the following activities:
- workforce skills analysis
- jobs analysis
- supply and demand analysis
- gap analysis
- solution analysis

Workforce skills analysis describes skills required to carry out a function. *Job analysis* focuses on tasks, responsibilities, knowledge, and skill requirements which are required for successful job performance. *Supply analysis* is done considering workforce demographics in terms of occupation, structure, race, origin, gender, age, service experience, education, training, health status, retirement time, and similar other information; trends; and present workforce competencies. This helps understand the existing workforce status. *Demand analysis*, on the other hand, helps identify the workforce for the future in line with the vision, mission, objectives, goals, and strategies of an organization. Critical inputs from demand analysis contribute to development of a competency model for the workforce of the future. With these inputs, organizations undertake a gap analysis to understand the differences between the workforce of today and the workforce of the future. After identification of differences, organizations need to plan to address these gaps.

Addressing such gaps is done through solution analysis, taking into account both ongoing and unplanned changes in the workforce. Solution analysis also weighs different options available, such as institutional or contractual employment, to get the work done. In this phase, activities such as recruitment, restructuring, training, retraining, redeployment, and rightsizing are done while considering the new competency model.

Job design using the competency framework is illustrated in Appendix 8A. This model has been developed for some common categories of employees in a textile manufacturing company, using the aforementioned approach.

SUMMARY

For effective compensation management, critical inputs related to a job are necessary. Although job analysis and job evaluation are considered important techniques for such a purpose, we have discussed other important issues that help in developing a holistic understanding of a job. Job design serves to improve performance and motivation. Job design analysis starts by looking at a job with a broad perspective and then swiftly moves toward identifying specific activities required to do the job. This is done for the purpose of identifying and correcting any deficiency that may affect performance and motivation.

Key Terms

Factor comparison It is a method used in job evaluation by using five factors—mental requirements, skill requirements, physical requirements, responsibility, and working conditions. After the job descriptions are finalized, key jobs are judged and related to one another. The jobs are considered one by one and reviewed to understand how much of the current wage rate for the job is paid for each factor. Key jobs are arranged in a scale in order of their value for each factor.

Motion economy It is the process of minimizing the physical and perceptual loads imposed on people engaged in any type of work, whether it is in an office, shop floor, kitchen, or at a driving wheel. It leads to better design of equipment, jigs and fixtures, hand tools, furniture, and labour-saving devices. In addition, it facilitates better layout of offices, warehouses, plants, and work areas.

Position analysis questionnaire (PAQ) It was developed in the early 1970s through the efforts of McCormick and others. It consists of 194 job elements of a 'worker oriented' nature. These job elements are divided into six major categories. The analyst normally rates job elements on a scale of 0–5.

Value engineering It is an organized creative technique to analyse functions of a product or service, or a system to accomplish required functions at the lowest cost while ensuring their performance, reliability, and maintainability. It is also known as value analysis or value management.

Exercises

Concept Review Questions

1. What are the purposes of job evaluation? Discuss the steps involved in job evaluation.
2. Discuss different types of job evaluation techniques. Which type do you consider more suitable and why?
3. How is compensation structure linked with job evaluation?
4. What are the important roles of method study? Identify the important contributions of method study and discuss at least five such contributions in detail.
5. Discuss in detail the steps involved in a method study programme.
6. Define work measurement. What are its different techniques? Discuss at least three techniques elaborately.
7. What are the steps involved in a time study programme? How does it help a work measurement programme in an industrial unit?
8. Define ergonomics. How does it help to increase productivity? Discuss with examples.
9. What are the basic principles of motion economy? Discuss these principles in relation to a work area you are familiar with.

10. Explain how human engineering techniques influence machine design. Select an advertisement of a furniture item and discuss its ergonomic features.
11. What are the steps involved in value analysis? What course of action can you suggest for a successful value analysis study?
12. Write short notes on:
    (a) Job assessment methods
    (b) Competency-based approach in job design

Critical Thinking Question

A company engaged in the manufacture of lifestyle drugs and cosmetics gives 80 per cent weightage to the competencies of marketing managers. You have been entrusted to help the company design a competency-based job description for marketing managers. Prepare the report and explain your reasons.

Where Job evaluation is Done Differently—Case of Apple

Apple has a 'walled garden' corporate strategy to restrict customers from modifying its devices using competing products and services. This is what IBM did during its initial years to force customers to use their software and hardware for their devices, a strategy they could not sustain in the long run. 'Walled garden' strategy is different from 'open-plan' strategy or 'open-architecture' strategy. This strategy does allow the customers to extend their offerings using others' products and services. Many corporate analysts feel that this is the calculated gamble by Apple to delight customers captivating them.

Apple's goal for its executive compensation programme is to attract and retain a talented, entrepreneurial, and creative team of executives, who will provide leadership for its success in dynamic, competitive markets.

Apple seeks to accomplish this goal in a way that is aligned with the long-term interests of its shareholders. The Compensation Committee oversees the executive compensation programme and determines the compensation for Apple's executive officers. Apple believes that the compensation programme for the top executive officers was instrumental in helping it achieve strong financial performance in challenging macroeconomic environment.

Apple's executive teams are expected to contribute as a member of the executive team to its overall success rather than merely achieve specific objectives within that officer's area of responsibility. Each top level executive officer has been an employee of Apple for at least 10 years, and none has an employment agreement or severance arrangement.

The executive compensation programme for the executive officers consists of three elements, namely long-term equity awards in the form of restricted stock units (RSUs), annual performance-based cash bonus awards, and base salaries.

Apple continues to rely primarily on long-term equity awards in the form of RSUs to attract and retain an outstanding executive team and to ensure a strong connection between the executive compensation programme and the long-term interests of its shareholders.

In general, Apple's RSU awards to the executive officers have been made every two

(Contd)

CASE STUDY (Contd)

years and no shares vest prior to the end of an approximate four-year vesting period.

Exceptions are made for executives who are promoted to the executive team or are recent hires, and in special cases as determined by the Compensation Committee.

Apple places less emphasis on total cash compensation than on long-term equity awards. Accordingly, the design of Apple's annual performance-based cash bonus programme for the named executive officers remained the same over years with target bonuses set at 50 per cent of base salary and maximum bonuses set at 100 per cent of base salary. As noted below, these target and maximum bonus opportunities are substantially lower than the range commonly provided by peer companies.

Of late, however, Apple changed the performance criteria used in its bonus programme from revenue and operating income prepared to adjusted sales and adjusted operating income. Adjusted sales and adjusted operating income differ as they exclude the effects of subscription accounting related to sales of iPhones and AppleTV.

As Apple believes these measurements help evaluate the underlying performance of the business, it uses such measurements to evaluate management performance and determine appropriate levels of compensation.

However, Apple's Retail Store Staff Compensation plan is criticized. These employees are responsible for fueling the booming sales in the division. Apple is not paying its retail staff enough given the success of the stores, and is instead relying on its employees' devotion to the company and a strong fan base providing a massive pool of job applicants to keep its retail stores staffed.

Roughly 70 per cent of Apple's 43,000 US workers are retail store employees, with many of them earning in the neighbourhood of $25,000 per year. Apple's pay rates are above average for the retail sector. Each retail store employee brings in an average of $500,000 in sales per year. They are on hourly pay.

Apple was formed by Steve Jobs and Steve Wozniak in 1976. As of 24 September 2011, Apple had 60,400 permanent full-time employees and 2,900 temporary full-time employees worldwide. Its worldwide annual revenue in 2010 totalled $65 billion, growing to $108 billion in 2011. After Steve Jobs, the company is now managed by Tim Cook as Chairman.

Discussion question

How does Apple evaluate the job? Do you think Apple's way of job evaluation and subsequent compensation design is scientific? Develop your arguments.

References

Hay, E. (1981), 'The guide chart profile method of job evaluation', Hay Associates, New York.

Henderson, Richard (2005), *Compensation Management in a Knowledge-based World*, 10th edn, Pearson Education, London.

Smyth, Richard and Murphy Matthew (1948), *Bargaining with Organized Labor*, Funk and Wagnalls, New York.

Wood, Robert and Tim Payne (1998), *Competency-based Recruitment and Selection*, John Wiley & Sons, New York.

APPENDIX 8A Competency Framework Model

S. no.	Designation	Business management competencies	Professional competencies	Technical competencies
1.	Assistant manager (SQC)	1. Quality assurance 2. Outcome measures and evaluation 3. Planning and scheduling 4. Time management and prioritization 5. Getting unbiased information	1. Communication 2. Thinking clearly/ analytically 3. Identifying and solving problems 4. Giving clear information 5. Teamwork	1. Disciplining and counselling 2. Quality testing at lab and shop floor 3. Statistical calculations 4. Computer skills 5. Knowledge of ISO 9000, ISO 14000, SA 8000, OHSAS 18000
2.	Assistant manager (PM & HR)	1. Organizational awareness 2. Negotiating skills 3. Planning and scheduling 4. Time management and prioritization 5. Getting unbiased information	1. Communication 2. Conflict management 3. Interpersonal skills 4. Listening and organizing 5. Teamwork	1. Pay administration 2. Human resource fundamentals 3. Labour-management relations 4. Discipline and adverse action 5. Knowledge of ISO 9000, ISO 14000, SA 8000, OHSAS 18000
3.	Assistant manager (Production) weaving, wool combing, flax RSM, worsted fabric	1. Product knowledge 2. Cost–benefit analysis 3. Planning and scheduling 4. Time management and prioritization 5. Getting unbiased information	1. Communication 2. Interpersonal skills 3. Identifying and solving problems 4. Listening and organizing 5. Teamwork	1. Disciplining and counselling 2. Knowledge of machines and production process 3. Knowledge of computers 4. Knowledge of ISO 9000, ISO 14000, SA 8000, OHSAS 18000
4.	Assistant manager (MIS/ Accounts/ Purchase and Stores)	1. Business awareness 2. Customer relations 3. Financial management 4. Planning and scheduling 5. Time management and prioritization 6. Getting unbiased information	1. Communication 2. Interpersonal skills 3. Thinking clearly/ analytically 4. Giving clear information 5. Teamwork	1. Disciplining and counselling 2. Knowledge of accounting/ export import/taxes 3. Knowledge of computers 4. Knowledge of ISO 9000, ISO 14000, SA 8000, OHSAS 18000
5.	Assistant manager (Engineering) flax SPG, Engineering department, RSM, maintenance	1. Outcome measures and evaluation 2. Organizational awareness 3. Planning and scheduling 4. Time management and prioritization 5. Getting unbiased information	1. Thinking clearly and analytically 2. Communication 3. Teamwork 4. Technology application 5. Identifying and solving problems	1. Detailed technical knowledge regarding machines and process knowledge 2. Computer skills 3. Disciplining and counselling 4. Knowledge of ETP/ERP/ Energy conservation as required 5. Knowledge of ISO 9000, ISO 14000, SA 8000, OHSAS 18000

(Contd)

APPENDIX 8A (Contd)

S. no.	Designation	Business management competencies	Professional competencies	Technical competencies
6.	Assistant manager (Sales and marketing) RSM, worsted fabric	1. Customer relations 2. Negotiating skills 3. Planning and scheduling 4. Time management and prioritization 5. Getting unbiased information	1. Communication 2. Interpersonal skills 3. Cross-cultural sensitivity/ creativity 4. Giving clear information 5. Teamwork	1. Product/market knowledge 2. Knowledge of taxes, duties, etc. 3. Computer skills 4. Disciplining and counselling 5. Knowledge of ISO 9000, ISO 14000, SA 8000, OHSAS 18000
7.	Officer (SQC)	1. Quality assurance 2. Planning and scheduling 3. Time management and prioritization 4. Getting unbiased information	1. Communication 2. Thinking clearly/ analytically 3. Giving clear information 4. Teamwork	1. Quality testing at lab and shop floor 2. Statistical calculations 3. Computer skills 4. Knowledge of ISO 9000, ISO 14000, SA 8000, OHSAS 18000
8.	Assistant officer (SQC)	1. Quality assurance 2. Planning and scheduling 3. Time management and prioritization	1. Communication 2. Analytical thinking 3. Teamwork	1. Quality testing 2. Statistical calculations 3. Computer skills
9.	Officer (PM & HR), assistant administrative officer (Fabric)	1. Negotiating 2. Time management and prioritization 3. Planning and scheduling 4. Getting unbiased information	1. Conflict management 2. Communication 3. Interpersonal skills 4. Giving clear information 5. Teamwork	1. Human resource management fundamentals 2. Labour-management relations 3. Pay administration 4. Knowledge of ISO 9000, ISO 14000, SA 8000, OHSAS 18000
10.	Officer/ senior officer (Production) weaving, wool combing, flax, RSM, worsted fabric	1. Product knowledge 2. Planning and scheduling 3. Time management and prioritization 4. Getting unbiased information	1. Communication 2. Interpersonal skills 3. Identifying and solving problems 4. Teamwork	1. Knowledge of machines and production process 2. Computer skills 3. Knowledge of ISO 9000, ISO 14000, SA 8000, OHSAS 18000
11.	Assistant officer (Production) weaving, wool combing, flax, RSM, worsted fabric	1. Product knowledge 2. Planning and scheduling 3. Time management and prioritization	1. Communication 2. Interpersonal skills 3. Teamwork	1. Knowledge of machines in production process 2. Knowledge of computers

(Contd)

APPENDIX 8A *(Contd)*

S. no.	Designation	Business management competencies	Professional competencies	Technical competencies
12.	Officer/Senior officer (MIS, Accounts, Purchase, Stores)	1. Business awareness 2. Customer relations 3. Planning and scheduling 4. Time management and prioritization 5. Getting unbiased information	1. Communication 2. Thinking clearly/analytically 3. Giving clear information 4. Teamwork	1. Accounting knowledge 2. Knowledge of computers and their application in accounting 3. Knowledge of ISO 9000, ISO 14000, SA 8000, OHSAS 18000
13.	Assistant officer (MIS, Accounts, Purchase, Stores, MS)	1. Customer relations 2. Planning and scheduling 3. Time management and prioritization	1. Communication 2. Thinking clearly/analytically 3. Teamwork	1. Accounting knowledge 2. Computer skills
14.	Officer/Assistant officer (Computers)	1. Planning and scheduling 2. Time management and prioritization 3. Getting unbiased information	1. Thinking clearly/analytically 2. Identifying and solving problems 3. Communication 4. Giving clear information 5. Teamwork	1. Technical knowledge as required 2. Knowledge of production and commercial system 3. Knowledge of ISO 0000, ISO 14000, SA 8000, OHSAS 18000
15.	Officer/senior officer (Engineering) flax SPG, engineering department, RSM, maintenance	1. Quality assurance of machines 2. Planning and scheduling 3. Time management and prioritization 4. Getting unbiased information	1. Thinking clearly/analytically 2. Communication 3. Teamwork 4. Technology application 5. Listening and organizing	1. Technical knowledge of machines 2. Computer skills as required 3. Knowledge of ISO 9000, ISO 14000, SA 8000, OHSAS 18000
16.	Assistant officer (Engineering) flax SPG, engineering department, RSM, maintenance	1. Planning and scheduling 2. Time management and prioritization	1. Thinking clearly/analytically 2. Teamwork 3. Communication	1. Technical knowledge of machines 2. Computer skills
17.	Assistant officer (Guest Relations)	1. Organizational awareness 2. Negotiating 3. Planning and scheduling 4. Time management and prioritization	1. Communication 2. Interpersonal relations 3. Pleasing personality/courteous 4. Thinking clearly	1. Computer skills 2. Experience in the field (if any)

(Contd)

APPENDIX 8A (Contd)

S. no.	Designation	Business management competencies	Professional competencies	Technical competencies
18.	Officer (Excise)	1. Business awareness 2. Negotiating skills 3. Customer relations 4. Planning and scheduling 5. Getting unbiased information	1. Communication 2. Interpersonal skills 3. Decision-making 4. Thinking clearly	1. Thorough knowledge of excise rules and regulations 2. Knowledge of export and import
19.	Officer/Senior officer (Sales and Marketing)	1. Business needs awareness 2. Customer relations 3. Negotiating skills 4. Planning and scheduling 5. Time management and prioritization 6. Getting unbiased information	1. Communication 2. Networking 3. Interpersonal skills 4. Creativity 5. Teamwork	1. Knowledge of market and product 2. Computer skills 3. Knowledge of ISO 9000, ISO 14000, SA 8000, OHSAS 18000
20.	Assistant officer (Sales and Marketing) RSM, worsted fabric	1. Customer relations 2. Negotiating skills 3. Planning and scheduling 4. Time management and prioritization	1. Communication 2. Cross cultural sensitivity 3. Teamwork 4. Interpersonal skills	1. Knowledge of market and product 2. Computer skills
21.	Development officer (RSM)	1. Planning and scheduling 2. Time management and prioritization 3. Getting unbiased information	1. Communication 2. Thinking clearly/ analytically 3. Giving clear information 4. Decision-making	1. Knowledge of old products and new products to be developed 2. Market demand for various products 3. Knowledge of yarns, shades etc. 4. Computer skills 5. Knowledge of ISO 9000, ISO 14000, SA 8000, OHSAS 18000
22.	Commercial officer (Warehouse)	1. Business awareness 2. Planning and scheduling 3. Time management and prioritization 4. Getting unbiased information	1. Communication 2. Analytical thinking 3. Interpersonal skills 4. Giving clear information	1. Knowledge of products 2. Accounting knowledge 3. Knowledge of ISO 9000, ISO 14000, SA 8000, OHSAS 18000

CHAPTER NINE

Performance-related Compensation

Learning Objectives

After reading the chapter, you will be able to
- appreciate the difference between performance appraisal and performance management system
- select appropriate performance objectives and performance indicators
- develop performance standards
- develop performance metrics and matrix
- design performance models
- build performance management systems
- align performance management systems with organizational strategy
- conceptualize balanced scorecard and its relation with compensation design
- appreciate competency and skill-based compensation design
- design compensation using performance parameters as criteria

Base

HRA

EPF

Gratuity

Variable

Bonus

LTA

Conveyance

Medical

OPENING CASE

Best Practices in Performance-related Pay

Best practices in performance-related pay followed by some leading organizations have been illustrated here:

Larsen & Toubro Engineering major Larsen & Toubro (L&T) has developed a competency matrix, which lists 73 competencies. These competencies vary widely across managerial levels. The competency matrix enables the management to assess the developmental needs of employees as well as their compensation level. Each listed competency set is associated with a combination of knowledge, skills, and attributes. L&T appraises each employee on the listed competencies to identify functional, managerial, and behavioural skill gaps. This helps the company provide customized training to bridge the identified skill gaps. As the competency matrix is linked with business strategy, L&T can design suitable competency-based pay to meet organization needs, while reaping the benefit of improved employee motivation and performance at the same time.

National Panasonic The Japanese major has developed a performance assessment system driven by key result areas (KRAs). The KRAs describe performance goals for business, functional, and behavioural domains with defined time frames. These are decided upon jointly by individual employees and their manager at the beginning of the financial year. Identification of KRAs is a structured exercise executed in a written format. It is then used to map the employee progress. Results from the performance evaluation are used to plug performance gaps with the help of relevant training inputs. National Panasonic places a great deal of emphasis on this process for re-skilling employees as it believes in growing talent within the organization instead of opting for expensive mid-career hires from outside the organization.

Hughes Escorts This company is a subsidiary of the US-based telecom company Hughes. It uses a competency-based performance enhancement model. Each position in the organization is defined in terms of 23 key competencies categorized into four groups—attitude-based, knowledge-driven, skill-centred, and value-based. The company uses these competencies to measure deficiency of employees in each of the four groups and accordingly provides relevant training inputs. This exercise is undertaken by Hughes Escorts to maximize productivity as well as create awareness among employees about their professional standing.

These examples show that performance management systems can help organizations realize their strategic intent including compensation design.

INTRODUCTION

Employees form the core strength of any organization. An effective performance management system (PMS) ensures good quality of this core resource. The performance system links the ability and contributions of employees, individually and as a team, to the overall performance of the organization. The increasing cost of employee compensation acts as a catalyst for adoption of PMS. An effective design of employee compensation should focus on PMS. Performance-linked pay or compensation has a strategic significance. It helps organizations optimize the cost of compensation and at the same time rewards good performers. Reward for good performance motivates employees and helps the organization become an employer of choice. This chapter discusses the basics of PMS and then links PMS with the employee compensation design.

A performance appraisal system is used to formally analyse, review, and evaluate employee performance. Though useful, performance appraisal is being gradually replaced by performance management. Performance appraisal

is an important human resource management activity, whereas performance management is an integrated process. It involves setting objectives, appraising employees, translating objectives into individual key performance areas (KPAs), and compensation design. It also involves a number of things such as thinking through various facets of performance; identifying critical dimensions of performance; and planning, reviewing, developing, and enhancing performance-related competencies. Performance management can be called a development tool as it facilitates performance improvement, career development, and training. It is an ongoing communication process that requires both the managers and the employees to accomplish the following:
- identify and describe essential job functions, and relate them to the mission and goals of the organization
- develop realistic and appropriate performance standards
- give and receive feedback about performance; write and communicate constructive performance appraisals
- plan education and development opportunities to sustain improvement in employee work performance

To sustain competitive advantage, an organization should recruit the best talent that fits the organization culture, and then systematically train and develop them. It should also monitor the performance of employees and focus on performance improvement through various human resource interventions. It has now been well established, through a series of empirical research, that performance management is an important area of focus and is gradually evolving into top priority of organizations.

COMPENSATION MANAGEMENT AND PMS

From compensation management point of view, PMS helps in achieving the following critical goals.
- It helps in recognizing the efforts and contributions of employees objectively, and thus facilitates effective job pricing through cost optimization and rewarding of talented performers.
- It facilitates suitable compensation design by providing for rewarding employees based on performance metrics.
- It helps intrinsically improve employee motivation by helping employees understand their strengths and weaknesses as part of feedback on performance; employees develop themselves through self-introspection and thereby feel intrinsically motivated.
- It also helps the employees getting extrinsically motivated through provision of performance-based pay; motivational constructs lead to improved performance.
- It helps employees develop their core competencies and achieve their goals.

- It helps retain good performers through competitive compensation design, and offer flexibility for increased income based on performance.
- It helps attracts good performers from competition.

Introduction of performance-related pay (PRP) is operationally difficult for many organizations that follow structured pay scales. In such organizations, a number of senior-level employees stagnate at the top slab of their pay scales. As a consequence, these employees get demotivated, decrease their performance levels, and wait for the opportune moment for job switch. Steel Authority of India (SAIL) experienced this problem when it lost many senior-level employees, who took premature retirement under the company's voluntary retirement scheme. It benefited many steel plants under private ownership as they could get quality talent for their projects. The State Bank of India (SBI) also experienced attrition of this kind. These problems are clearly attributable to the absence of performance-linked pay or compensation system. Another operational issue for these organizations is designing incentives and aligning them with performance without specifying any minimum performance requirement. Such a system makes every employee eligible for the incentives as individual contributions are not factored into designing the compensation. While 100 per cent factoring of individual performance is not desirable as it results in conflicts, total ignorance of individual performance is also not desirable. Effective performance-linked compensation in such cases provides for incentives if results exceed the stated individual, departmental, and organizational goals.

In order to reap the strategic benefits of pay for performance, many organizations limit the increase in the pay only to a statutory minimum while increasing the variable pay for good performers. In these cases, compensation decisions are based on realistic assessment of performance and organizations do not consider factors such as the cost of living and seniority for designing compensation. Such practices have both advantages and disadvantages. The advantages include rewards for merit, improvement in teamwork, increased job satisfaction, and achievement of the desired results. Disadvantages include issues such as difficulty in institutionalizing systems and their monitoring; difficulty in identifying appropriate performance evaluation tools; and dilution of loyalty of employees as it ignores the seniority factor.

Performance-related Pay

The term performance-related pay (PRP) encompasses several company-wide schemes such as employee participation and share ownership schemes awarded to the employees. Employee participation is measured in terms of commitment to teamwork and involvement of the employee in problem-solving. Performance-related pay schemes are designed and administered from a company's perspective. Even then, they fail to deliver if they are not aligned closely to business strategy. Contrary to popular belief, performance-driven compensation can support constant change and performance improvement, but they cannot deliver these by themselves. Line managers can also muddle the process, unless they get support from other divisions. Despite these difficulties in implementing PRP, organizations adopt this scheme due to the benefits it can offer. Some important areas which deserve attention from organizations while implementing PRP are listed in this section.

Competition and cost control Performance-related pay enhances corporate performance in a competitive environment. When performance and pay are linked together, it would be reflected in employee behaviour. For example, when organizations focus on customer satisfaction, employees also focus on this aspect ensuring quality of goods and services.

Individualization Collective relationships in the workplace are a common organizational pursuit to achieve teamwork. Workplace and employer relationship can be individualized through reward mechanisms. Performance-related pay can be used in a teamwork environment. However, when organizations focus on merit, only the pay increases, which is the extreme form of compensation individualization. Hence, effective PRP requires organizations to balance individualization and collectivization.

Mismatch with the strategy Organizations adopt various strategies depending on their business priorities. Different strategies have different implementation requirements. For instance, a common cost minimization strategy requires a different range of behaviours. In addition, there exist possibilities or coexistence of different compensation programmes for different functions and divisions in the same organization. The time dimension should also be given due consideration while adopting a strategy. Short-term focus, individual effort, and the other parameters need to be supported by a compensation policy, which is different from a long-term focus. An organization has to devise a PRP structure in tune with its strategies.

Monitoring and evaluation Monitoring and evaluation are important. However, organizations often lack focus in these areas. Introducing PRP systems alone is not sufficient. It is also important to understand how a PRP structure actually benefits the organization. Tracking changes after introduction of PRP through an effective monitoring and evaluation system can be used to achieve this objective.

Culture A PRP system often runs into conflict with the organizational culture. Organizations which support diversity and pursue principles of equity may not find it easy to implement it as PRP makes differentiation in pay packages on the basis of merit. There are several other examples where an organization would experience issues of this nature. Some organizations give priority to quantitative achievement of results. These would adopt a PRP system that is oriented towards achievement of quantitative results. However, some functions in these organizations may demand high quality of performance leading to mismatch between the PRP system and the requirement of these functions. The requirement of these functions cannot be ignored as quality translates into customer satisfaction. Again, the compensation culture of some organization may assign maximum weightage on the fixed component, reducing variables to a bare minimum. Incentives and other variables also may be at a fixed proportion depending on hierarchical levels and independent of functional domains. Introducing PRP in organization with this kind of culture would also pose challenges. Therefore, designing a PRP structure compatible with organizational culture may prove to be difficult.

Use of PRP

Many organizations use PRP as an instrument of management control, payroll control, or performance control. In a true sense, an effective PRP system can help in empowering employees. However, using PRP as a control mechanism defeats the purpose of empowering employees. Again, in teamwork systems, linkage between the base pay and team contribution hardly exist. Therefore, organizations must use PRP system for strategic benefits and not as a tool for control mechanism.

Problems in monitoring PRP

A PRP system provides role clarity to employees in terms of what they are expected to do in their jobs. Organizations embracing PRP jointly set clear goals which are stretching, challenging, and achievable. It is also important that a PRP system can be monitored. Performance-related pay initiatives often fail because they are too complicated and line managers do not know how to implement them. In addition, line managers often fail to relate PRP with areas they need to manage, that is, their business priorities. Therefore, organizations need to train the line managers to facilitate effective monitoring. This would ensure that they understand PRP's basics and job correlation. In many organizations, PRP becomes a perennial trade union issue too. Once PRP is understood properly, it can be monitored effectively.

Selection of performance appraisal tools Performance-related pay initiatives can also fail due to wrong selection of appraisal tools. Many organizations assign more weightage on factors beyond the control of the employees. For example, some organizational policies may limit the extent of customer services. Such deficiencies may have adverse effects on customer satisfaction. However, the onus of customer satisfaction would incorrectly be assigned to the individual employee by linking the PRP systems with the customer feedback.

Differences between managers and employees Employees often perceive compensation of senior managers to be disproportionately higher. PRP is perceived to deprive employees of their genuine share. It is also believed that PRP benefits the senior management more as the contributions of the senior management personnel are visible and can be tracked. To alleviate such an apprehension, the mechanism of design of PRP should be communicated to the employees so that they can also track their contribution and are rewarded a matching compensation.

Lack of employee participation In most organizations, PRP is designed by the top management and then implemented down the line. Since PRP system alters the existing compensation structure, participation and involvement of all cross sections of employees, line managers, and trade union leaders is essential. Their involvement makes employees feel that they are part of the organization so they cooperate in its implementation.

Often organizations emphasize on improved performance through financial rewards alone. However, this may not always be the right approach, as there are other types of rewards that may work better. Financial incentives are necessary but not sufficient for motivation enhancement and performance improvement. Hence, a stronger link must exist between reward strategy and business strategy.

PRP can be designed either based on individual performance criteria like piece rate wages or collective performance pay schemes like profit sharing. Empirical studies have shown that in general profit sharing arrangements have smaller productivity effects as compared to the piece rate schemes. It was also established that PRP increases productivity of any organization substantially.

PRP IN INDIAN CENTRAL PUBLIC SECTOR ENTERPRISES (CPSEs)

The root of PRP lies in the agency theory given by Jensen and Meckling (1976). This theory sets the ambit of relationships between the principals (owners) and agents (managers). In case of central public sector enterprises (CPSEs), government being the majority shareholder plays the dominant role of principals. Managers of the CPSEs, that is, the agents can be better aligned with the interests of the principals, if PRP-based compensation design is developed. Eisenhardt (1989) and Hart (1995) extended the discussions on agency theory to encompass compensation design issues. The inherent conflict between the principals and the agents, extending the arguments of agency theory, can be better resolved through PRP-based compensation design.

A performance-linked or performance-related pay (PLP or PRP) method may focus primarily on achievement of goals and objectives for the organization. From this perspective, it can be said that it is business aligned. However, a better approach is to link compensation elements with KRAs or KPAs (key performance areas) driven performance measures (Bhattacharyya 2011, 2013). In CPSEs of India, the culture of PRP has now been institutionalized. The Department of Public Enterprises (DPE) in India requires institutionalization of PRP in public sector companies in order to create an enabling culture of performance. The arguments for this rest on the premise that managers of PSEs work smarter if they expect that it would help them earn more. Even though, money as a motivating factor to create a performance driven culture in organizations have been contested by many scholars (Ambrose and

Kulik 1999; Milkovich and Newman 2002; Bhattacharyya 2013), PRP-based compensation design in CPSEs has been embraced globally and India is no exception. The rationale behind is to bring efficiency in managing PSEs using PRP as a driver. Several scholars have supported adoption of PRP. For example, Vroom's expectancy theory (1964) argues in its favour. In addition, the approach does not offend Adam's equity theory (1963). A well designed PRP provides opportunity to managers or agents to earn rewards, making them feel motivated to perform better. A well designed PRP also make it possible for managers to measure its efficacy in the context of equity or inequity through internal and external comparisons (Bender 2004).

The adoption of PRP is recommended by several scholars. However, there are a number of scholars who have argued against the adoption of PRP. Huber (2010) while studying the effect of PRP on CPSEs observed that it may not work primarily for reasons such as less potentiality to motivate employees because rewards are constrained by disbursable cash availability; subjective evaluation of individual performance; and lack of diversity neutrality.

While among private organizations PRP design varies, as they craft their own compensation strategies, factoring their own business interests, PSEs are constrained to follow the mandates of the government. For CPSEs, such mandates comes from DPE. Schuler and Rogovsky (1998) based their studies on 24 countries analysing the link between culture and compensation management practices. Their study reported that PRP works well when it is crafted within the cultural constructs of the company. In a culture of high uncertainty avoidance where employees are comfortable with stable compensation, PRP may not work. It is also not a right fit for organizations that are more attuned to culture of collectivism as PRP assigns more weight to individual contribution than group and team performance. Compensation culture nexus is the best fit in the institutional theory (DiMaggio and Powel 1983; Scott 1995) as firms' behaviour, managerial practices, and compensation management practices, as per this theory, are culture congruent. Gielen, Kerkhofs, and Ours (2010) in their studies on Dutch firms observed the positive effects of PRP on labour productivity (9 per cent) and employment growth (5 per cent). Similar improvement in productivity and profitability (6 per cent) was observed in Finnish firms by Piekkola (2005). Forest (2008) studied the effect of PRP on French Civil Service and observed negative effects on motivation. The study suggests participative management practices along with task enlargement and enrichment can work better in motivating French Civil Servants than PRP. Schmidt's (2011) study on the effect of PRP on German Civil Services corroborates Forest's findings on France. In Germany too, participative management with balanced focus on material interest and social recognition can ensure better effectiveness than PRP.

PRP is often seen as narrowly focused compensation strategy as it is more individual-based than collective (Lee et al. 2011). This study also reported its poor effect on collectivist work culture of Japan except its positive effect on young employees. In addition, researchers like Rubery (1995) observed that PRP distributes income more in favour of the highly paid executives and managers. Dahlstrom and Lapuente (2009) study indicated that PRP in public sectors is more intended to enforce control over employees. Perry, Engbers, and Jun (2009) observed that problems with PRP can typically be attributed to its insignificant impact on motivation, potential problems of designing job responsibilities, and problems in implementation. Kohn (1993) argued that PRP cannot ensure enduring change in performance behaviour. It often inhibits risk-taking. Bregn (2008) also warned individualization of pay through PRP in PSEs requires caution as it may run against the underlying philosophy behind PSEs. Hence, designing an objective PRP in PSEs is not easy as it requires balancing all its important constructs.

PRP as a tool to reward the performance in a cost effective manner was commended by Lewis (1998). As a moderating variable for behavioural modification, it acts efficiently, resulting in productivity enhancement (Belfield and Marsden 2003; Latham and Huber 1992). Despite criticisms, PRP can be factored with both individual performance and collective performance. Globally positive effects on PRP have been empirically tested. For example, Cahuc and Dormont (1997) observed two per cent increase in productivity in French organizations after PRP implementation. Lazear (2000) could observe PRP based incentives increase 20 per cent productivity in US firms. In Canadian organizations, Paarsch and Shearer (2000) observed 22 per cent rises in productivity after the introduction of PRP. Scholars such as Perry and Wise (1990), Perry et al. (2009), and Houston (2000) have recommended adoption of PRP in public services as an alternative to variable pay. Booth and Frank (1997) and Lazear (1986) recommended PRP to attract quality workers in the organizations. Brown (1990) observed that in addition to attraction and retention of competent employees, PRP can promote the culture of achievement and inculcate sense of responsibility among workers.

From the aforesaid discussions, we can discern that debates on PRP in PSEs can be grouped under two generic categories, agency theories and expectancy theories. In the context of PSEs, we need to understand its extended implications on worker performance. Implications of agency theory for the PSEs was studied by Dixit (1999) who attributed two major problems in principal–agent relationships in a PSE setting, moral hazard and adverse selection. *Moral hazard* problems arise as the actions of workers (i.e., agents) ultimately lead to the pay-offs of the organization (i.e., principal). To reduce the problems related to moral hazard, it is necessary to make workers' actions observable to enable the principal to suitably align them to outcomes. Hasnain et al. (2012) observed problems of performance measurability for coping or procedural jobs. They consider it as the most challenging task for the PSEs. However, such problems become manageable in case of craft jobs like production due to their easy measurability.

Adverse selection syndrome in PSEs is attributed to general propensity of low quality workers to prefer a job with fixed/guaranteed pay. This can be reversed when the pay system is more merit-based, that is, individualized.

Hence, selecting the appropriate performance measures in both the cases can significantly reduce the problems of ill-designed PRP in PSEs.

Expectancy theory though pioneered by Vroom (1964), its institutionalization is more credited to Porter and Lawler III (1968). Its psychological insights get extended to the reinforcement theory, pioneered by Skinner (1969) and Luthans (1973). To elicit consistent good performance and behaviour, PSEs need to make their PRP more specific and participative. In this context, reinforcement theory suggests the need to build a performance enabling culture, so that workers volunteer for performance. This again requires proper alignment of PRP cascading DPE mandated memorandum of understanding (MOU) to individual workers' level. Rischer (2012) in the draft report on PRP in OECD countries (Gov/PGC/PEM 2012–3) emphasized on the need for gaining acceptance of PRP from managers and employees. He also emphasized on organizational change to set the organizational premises before its implementation. Unfortunately most of the PSEs in India, including our sample PSEs, do not have balanced scorecard driven KRAs covering all cross sections of workers. The method used to factor individual performance is very often a discretionary mandate of PSE executives and managers.

PRP Scenario in CPSEs

Each CPSE signs a memorandum of understanding with the Government, which clearly specifies objectives and obligations, and becomes a basis for performance evaluation. MOU constitutes both financial and non-financial parameters to assign performance targets to each CPSE, which is measured using the 5-point scale. Based on the composite score the performance index of the CPSE is determined, which is known as MOU rating. The DPE recommended scale for MOU rating is presented in Table 9.1.

We have 202 MOU signing CPSEs as of 2011. A partial summary of the MOU rating of CPSEs in India, as provided by the DPE, is presented in Table 9.2.

In Table 9.2 showing MOU rated performance of CPSEs, the number of CPSEs in the poor category is only two during the year 2011. This indicates DPE has taken a liberal view presumably to make CPSEs eligible for PRP.

To attract and retain talent, Indian CPSEs ensured competitive compensation structure over their peer companies in the private sector, except for their Chairman and CEOs. Although it is said that such difference is attributable to the higher risks involved in private sectors' management and operations, CPSEs in India are now equally innovative to churn higher returns over their peer companies in private sectors. The degree of equity in PRP and the total compensation as a whole is much higher in CPSEs as compared to Indian private sectors companies.

TABLE 9.1 MOU rating scale of DPE

MOU composite score	Rating	Percentage score
1.00–1.50	Excellent	100
1.51–2.50	Very good	80
2.51–3.50	Good	60
3.51–4.50	Fair	40
4.51–5.00	Poor	0

Source: DPE

TABLE 9.2 Performance rating of MOU signing CPSEs

Rating	2007	%	2008	%	2009	%	2010	%	2011	%
Excellent	46	45.1	55	49.1	47	37.9	73	50.3	67	42.1
Very good	37	36.3	34	30.4	34	27.4	31	21.4	42	26.4
Good	13	12.7	15	13.4	25	20.2	20	13.8	24	15.1
Fair	6	5.9	8	7.1	17	13.7	20	13.8	24	15.1
Poor	0	0	0	0	1	0.8	1	0.7	2	1.3
Total	102	100	112	100	124	100	145	100	159	100

Source: DPE

PRP calculation in ONGC and SAIL

For SAIL Physical and financial performance weightage for PRP in SAIL has been assigned as in Table 9.3. Based on data in Table 9.3, SAIL's formula for PRP payment can be written in the following manner:

[0.60 × Annual Basic Pay × MOU Rating × 77.5 (performance factor for the company as a whole) + 2.5 × Plant's Saleable Steel% + 2.5 × Plant's specific energy consumption% + 2.5 × Plant's yield from crude steel to saleable steel% + 7.5 × Plant's Budgeted PBT% + 7.5 × Individual performance rating] × [Grade Incentive × ratio of available to required amount] − Adjustment of performance-related payments already made].

TABLE 9.3 Weightage for PRP in SAIL

Company performance (MOU rating)	77.5%
Unit's Performance	
• Linked to saleable steel production	02.5%
• Linked to specific energy consumption	02.5%
• Linked to yield from crude steel to saleable steel	02.5%
• Linked to actual PBT vs budgeted PBT	07.5%
• Individual performance	07.5%

TABLE 9.4 MOU Rating by DPE

Sample CPSEs	2002–2003	2003–2004	2004–2005	2005–2006	2006–2007	2007–2008	2008–2009	2009–2010	2010–2011	2011–2012
ONGC	1.29	1.70	1.77	1.43	1.44	1.81	1.70	1.53	1.791	1.222
SAIL	1.48	1.37	1.13	1.36	1.07	1.13	1.22	1.10	1.090	1.180

Source: DPE and Companies Financial Results

For ONGC In line with DPE guidelines, the PRP formula for ONGC is calculated in two components:

PRP-I = Pool proportion (60% of the component) × MOU rating × grade ceiling × annual basic pay × individual performance × pool availability factor (relevant for 60% component)

PRP-II = Pool proportion (40% component) × MOU rating × grade ceiling × annual basic pay × individual performance × pool availability factor (relevant for 40% component)

For calculating individual payout of PRP, PRP-I and PRP-II are added.

Pool proportion in both the cases and so also for all CPSEs is 5% of PBT. This 5% is arrived at considering 3% of PBT + 2% PBT from 10% incremental profit. Pool availability factor is derived by dividing amount available with amount required.

Table 9.4 shows decadal trend of MOU rating by DPE for these two CPSEs:

The MOU rating data in Table 9.4 shows that both the CPSEs consistently performed well over the decade.

Sample KRA and KPI

In this part, we would discuss sample KRA and KPI of Durgapur Steel Plant (DSP), under the aegis of SAIL. With the current manpower strength of 12,645 as on 31 March 2012, DSP is now achieving annual sales of ₹6983.49 crore (2011–12), exceeding its production capacity in all products segments by more than 100 per cent. With 5.8 million tons of steel production in hot metal, crude steel, and saleable steel combined with continuous improvement in labour productivity since 2007–2008 shows that DSP is continuously growing and operating successfully in a globally competitive steel market despite being a CPSE.

Like other CPSEs in India, SAIL mandates the annual performance standards to the Chief Executive Officer of DSP. DSP translates the same to their performance goals by aligning it with their balanced scorecard (BSC). DSP's BSC then cascades to departmental scorecards. A typical analysis of HR Department's scorecard presented in Table 9.5 indicates high focus on investment in human capital.

TABLE 9.5 Departmental scorecard

PERSONNEL AND ADMINISTRATION

S. no.	Strategic objective	Level-1 (ABP/ Benchmark)	Level-2 (MOU Level-1/Best achieved)	Level-3 (MOU Level-2/ Achieved during previous year)	Actual	Unit of measure	Weightage
			TARGET				
Financial perspective							
1.1	Improving labour productivity	242	235	232	0	TCS*/man/year	10
1.2	Keeping administration expenditure within budget	0	(+) 7.5	(+) 10	0	Deviation	5
							15
Customer perspective							
2.1	Enhancing employees satisfaction level	10	7	5	0	Satisfaction index	5
2.2	Maintaining conducive IR climate	15	10	5	0	%	7
2.3	Providing manpower for expansion units as per HRP	100	90	80	0	%	7
2.4	Providing manpower for other areas as per HRP	100	90	80	0	%	7
2.5	Quality of work life	3	2	1	0	Number	4
							30
Internal business process perspective							
3.1	Augmenting employee services through IT	3	2	1	0	Number	7
3.2	HR system improvements	3	2	1	0	Number	5
3.3	Compliance to SA-8000: Settlement of audit observation(s)	20	25	30	0	Days	5
3.4	Online PF remittance by contractors	October 2012	November 2012	December 2012	0	Date	5

(Contd)

TABLE 9.5 (Contd)

PERSONNEL AND ADMINISTRATION

S. no.	Strategic objective	Level-1 (ABP/Benchmark)	Level-2 (MOU Level-1/Best achieved)	Level-3 (MOU Level-2/Achieved during previous year)	Actual	Unit of measure	Weightage
3.5	Online gate pass system for contract labour	January 2013	February 2013	March 2013	0	Date	5
3.6	Facilitating online attendance of employees	5	25	2	0	Number	8
							35
Organization capability building perspective							
4.1	Identification and training for skill preservation w.r.t employees superannuating by 2014	100	90	80	0	%	5
4.2	Identified skill induction	30 September 2012	31 October 2012	30 November 2012	0	Date	5
4.3	Enhancing competencies of HR group	25	15	10	0	%	5
4.4	Enhancing employees' involvement through direct communication	4	2	1	0	Number	5
							20
	Total weightage for all the perspectives						100

*Tonnes of crude steel
Source: DSP

TABLE 9.6 Departmental scorecard and CHRD

S. no.	Strategic objective	CHRD Level 1 (ABP*/Benchmark)	TARGET Level 2 (MOU Level 1/Best achieved)	Level 3 (MOU Level 2/Achieved during previous year)	Actual	Unit of measure	Weightage
Financial perspective							
1.1	HRD expenditure as per allocated budget (As per MOU, i.e., 0.5% of Employee cost)	100	90	80	0	%	10
							10
Customer perspective							
2.1	Training of identified employees for skill preservation w.r.t employees separating by 2014	36	35	33	0	%	6
2.2	Actualisation as per annual training plan (7079 employees including 1-day training)	100	95	90	0	%	10
2.3	Achieving training-man days per employee per year	4.5	4.2	4	0	Man-days per employee per year	6
2.4	Average training rating 3.0 Out of 4.0 (For duration > 2 days) conducted at chrd	100	90	80	0	%	5
2.5	Conducting training impact survey (internal)	2	1	1	0	Number	3
							30
Internal business process perspective							
3.1	Development of new training modules	5	4	3	0	Number	5
3.2	Training for deployment in expansion areas	100	90	80	0	%	4

(Contd)

TABLE 9.6 (Contd)

CHRD

S. no.	Strategic objective	Level 1 (ABP*/ Benchmark)	TARGET Level 2 (MOU Level 1/Best Achieved)	Level 3 (MOU Level 2/ Achieved during previous year)	Actual	Unit of measure	Weightage
3.3	Developing critical mass of leaders through leadership programmes	50	45	40	0	Number	5
3.4	Organising stress management programme	6	5	4	0	Number	6
3.5	Facilitating organising of PIWs	10	8	7	0	Number	4
3.6	Developing executives as per EPMS training needs	30	25	20	0	%	4
3.7	Facilitating employee involvement through direct communication	5	4	3	0	Number	2
							30
Organization capability building perspective							
4.1	Developing trainers/faculties in new training modules	5	4	3	0	Number	6
4.2	Improving infrastructure at CHRD centre (renovating classrooms/conference hall/ MP hall)	4	3	2	0	Number	6
4.3	Developing new training facility	3	2	1	0	Number	5
4.4	Upgradation of MT Hostels	14	12	10	0	Number	4
4.5	Participation in HR Excellence Award	1	1	1	0	Number	3
4.6	New Initiative in HR (Organizing mentor development program)	1	0	0	0	Number	6
							30
Total weightage for all the perspectives							100

*Alliance Best Practice
Source: DSP

DSP understands how HR Department's scorecard cascades further to Corporate Human Resource Development (CHRD) functions. Table 9.6 shows the CHRD scorecard, which shows DSP's holistic concern for various aspects of human capital management (HCM).

The Tables 9.5 and 9.6 illustrate sample KRA and KPI. It is important to mention that by achieving KRAs and KPIs, organizations can achieve their business goal.

ECONOMIC VALUE-ADDED (EVA)—ALTERNATIVE PERFORMANCE MEASURES

Economic value-added (EVA) was pioneered by Stern Stewart and Co., a US-based management consultancy firm. It is defined as, 'return on invested capital (ROIC) minus an appropriate charge for the cost of capital invested in an enterprise as a financial performance measure that captures the economic value added of an enterprise'.

EVA forces people to think differently. It is all about change management and getting a much sharper focus. In a conventional profit and loss-based set-up, organizations juggle with revenues and costs; in an EVA set-up, they have to juggle with the balance sheet, available resources, and long and short-term considerations.

EVA is often compared with return on investment (ROI). However, contextually they are one and the same. EVA is criticized as EVA or ROI-based performance measures restricts growth. EVA tackles the criticism by focusing on incremental value creation. It is not a stock measure, rather a flow measure across the plan period. Value creation is not so much about being EVA-negative or EVA-positive. Companies need to chart out the EVA-improvement trajectory for the forecast period and rigorously follow the target. That is the key to sustainable value creation. Suppose, a company targets ₹100 crore of value increase every year and pursues it rigorously., At the end of five years, the absolute value of the company would increase by ₹500 crore. As long as the company orients itself to a right strategy and delivers incremental value on a year-on-year basis, the shareholders are most likely to be content with the company's performance in the long term.

EVA recognizes that in capital-intensive industries returns cannot be expected in a short time. Initial EVA-negative years are built into the EVA capital budgeting framework, as is the year in which the company is scheduled to go EVA-positive. If the company fails to achieve the desired level of performance as forecasted in the capital-approval process, it would be an accountability issue.

The analysis done for some Tata companies using EVA showed that the future growth value of the company would be positive, whereas the current operational value was not so high. This means that the capital markets place a premium on the company because they are confident that it will come up with strategies to propel itself to a higher value creation level.

One of the most contentious issues in EVA is the change in weighted-average cost of capital (WACC) due to changes in the financial markets. WACC indicates the expected average rate of return (ROI) of organizations to compensate all investors. It helps the company to estimate the expenses of funding future projects. With lower WACC, company can identify the cheaper source of funding new projects. WACC is calculated for each of the companies undertaking the project. WACC is reviewed after every two or three years unless there is a significant change in the underlying assumptions.

EVA module essentially comprises of three parts, namely value-based goal setting and investment management process. *Value-based goal setting* provides the framework to measure the gap between the fair value and projected value of a company. This framework helps the management evolve options to bridge the performance gap by increasing the net present value (NPV) of the company. Options to increase the value can range from cost reduction, improvement in operating efficiency, and rationalization of business portfolio to acquisition of businesses to grow inorganically. The framework is capable of panning out a year-by-year gap in NPV based on the business plan.

Investment management process in the EVA framework provides robustness to the capital allocation decision and foster accountability for capital invested in the business. Once these processes are rolled out, the senior management is able to improve their quality of decision-making by using these sophisticated analytical tools.

The third module is *measurement and management*, which is the core of the EVA framework. During this phase, the measurement framework and the EVA drivers' analyses is taken down to the business unit level of the company. The operating managers of the company get involved in cascading EVA consciousness across the organization. The company starts inculcating value creation as a 'way of life' across the decision-making process in the company.

The greatest benefit of EVA will be an improvement in the quality of decision-making. Once EVA becomes a way of life in the organization, there would be an improvement in the quality of decision-making within the company, which has to sooner or later translate into improved EVA.

The five-stage process for implementing EVA can be listed as follows:
- Sharing the vision that is creation of awareness among employees
- Value diagnostic that is identification of gaps and opportunities
- Value audit and goal setting
- Measurement and management
- Training and knowledge transfer from working groups to employees

SELECTION OF PERFORMANCE OBJECTIVES

Many organizations fail to identify their objectives. Objectives such as higher profits, shared values, and customer satisfaction are common. However, these alone cannot map the compensation design. Performance research also requires delving into the issues of identifying performance objectives both for the individual employee and also for the organization as a whole. The performance objectives must have the following attributes:
- focused on a result, not an activity
- consistent
- specific
- measurable
- related to time
- attainable

Emphasis should be placed on SMART, that is, specific, measurable, attainable, realistic, and time-bound objectives. It gives an opportunity to scientifically measure the performance targets; trace the possible loopholes in setting the targets; effectively map the future strategies, and align objectives of individual employees with that of the organization.

SELECTION OF PERFORMANCE INDICATORS

After selection of performance objectives, the HR manager needs to identify appropriate types of performance indicators. The selection of such indicators largely depends on organizational needs. However, a general list of performance indicators is illustrated in Table 9.7.

Organizations should select the indicators based on their specific requirements. A template for mapping performance indicators is presented in Table 9.8.

Human resource managers can use this template to scientifically define the performance indicators.

TABLE 9.7 Performance indicators

Cost	Amount spent to manufacture the goods or to provide services	Average amount actually spent by the organization for per unit of output
Input	Resources employed to manufacture the goods and to render the services	Amount of resources employed by the organization per employee
Output	Goods or services provided to the customers	Value of goods and services
Outcome	The actual impact and value of the goods and services delivery	Percentage of satisfied customers with the goods and services

TABLE 9.8 Template for performance indicators

Process	Product	Goal	Measure	Metric

DEVELOPING PERFORMANCE STANDARDS

For effective compensation design, developing performance standards is another important task. The approach an organization should adopt should be either a top-down or a bottom-up collaborative approach. Neither of the two approaches is foolproof. In fact, an organization has to arrive at an effective trade-off keeping in view its employee diversity. Simply benchmarking performance standards with competing organizations may not always be the right approach. Excessive expectation in setting performance standards and thereby requiring employees to overstretch is a common organizational syndrome, particularly with new start-ups which aim to grow disproportionately. Human resource managers must appreciate the need for back-up support so that employees can deliver results. Performance standards should be aligned with the job descriptions, mission, goals, and objectives that by default help in evolving the right performance appraisal model. Performance standards should be specific. A hypothetical performance standard for a CTV manufacturer is illustrated in Table 9.9.

Guidelines

Organizations must keep in mind the following guidelines while developing performance standards.

- Performance standards should be related to the employee's assigned work and job requirements
- Reporting systems should be adequate to measure and, therefore, should have more quantitative data
- Quantifiable measures may not apply to all functions; describe in clear and specific terms the characteristics of performance quality that are verifiable, and that would meet or exceed expectations
- Accomplishment of organizational objectives such as cost control, improved efficiency, productivity, project completion, process redesign, or customer service should be included where appropriate

Checklist

After developing performance standards, they should be checked using the following list of questions to ensure their appropriateness.

- Are the standards realistic? Standards should be attainable and consistent with job requirements. Performance standards which meet expectations

TABLE 9.9 Performance standards for a CTV manufacturer

Level	Description
Level 1	Simple description of a general expectation
	Example: *Task description*: Assemble CTVs.
	Standard: Put different subassembled CTVs in the assembly line
	Example: *Task description*: Write annual reports.
	Standard: Annual reports will be submitted by agreed upon date.
Level 2	Simple description of specific expectations.
	Example: *Task description*: Assemble CTVs.
	Standard: Complete assembly of 5 error-free CTVs per day.
	Example: *Task description*: Write annual reports.
	Standard: Prepare annual reports and submit the same to the business heads within 7 working days before March 31.
Level 3	Description of specific expectations and success indicators.
	Example: *Task description*: Assemble CTVs.
	Standard: Ensure simultaneous error-free assembly of 5 CTVs per operator in 10 lines.
	Example: *Task description*: Write annual reports.
	Standard: Produce annual reports as per departmental format and submit to the business heads within 5 working days before January 15.
Level 4	Description of specific expectations, success indicators, and conditions, if any.
	Example: *Task description*: Assemble CTVs.
	Standard: Ensure 5 correct assembly of CTVs per day per operator in 2 shop floors and also ensure that the necessary equipments are in working order.
	Example: *Task description*: Write annual reports.
	Standard: Produce annual reports as per departmental format and submit to the business heads within 5 working days before 15 January.

represent the minimum acceptable level of performance for all employees in a defined position.

- Are the standards specific? Standards should describe specific actions and results the employee is expected to accomplish.
- Are the standards based on measurable data, observation, or verifiable information? Information verification can be done through unobtrusive data. Performance can be measured in terms of timeliness, cost, quality, and quantity.
- Are the standards consistent with organizational goals? Standards should link individual and team performance to organizational goals, and should be consistent with these goals. Successful achievement of the organizational and departmental mission depends on this strategic connection.
- Are the standards challenging? Standards may describe performance that exceeds expectation. Recognizing performance that is above expectations or outstanding is crucial to motivating employees.

- Are the standards clear and understandable? Employees whose work is to be evaluated on the basis of the standards should understand them. Standards should use the language of the job.
- Are the standards dynamic? Standards should evolve in conjunction with organizational goals, technologies, operations, or change in experiences.

DEVELOPING A PERFORMANCE METRIC

A performance metric is a standard measure to assess performance in a particular area. Metrics are based on customer-focused processes, management systems, and any programme directed at continuous improvement. The focus on customers and performance standards is defined in the form of metrics that assess an individual's ability to meet customer needs and business objectives. Most organizations use traditional performance measures such as profit performance, return on investment, or earnings per share to determine their success. These measures provide reasonable estimates of whether a company achieved its ultimate goal of making profits, but do not reveal how the business achieved this position. Therefore, many organizations have created complete operating as well as process measures and ratios to track how well the business manages each process and use of resources. Many CEOs, particularly those who are required to make a quarterly business forecast, have become interested about performance models which integrate the measures to predict future performance. The balanced scorecard (BSC) is one of the most popular conceptual modelling tools.

The organization can develop a performance matrix by taking into account performance metrics. Developing a performance matrix and emulating examples of world-class performance excellence models help organizations to scientifically list the action plans for improving PMS.

Gilbert (1978) contributed immensely to the development of a performance matrix. Performance matrix is a construct of a performance system which sequentially illustrates decisions to be taken to improve PMS in an organization. A simple model of performance matrix deals at three levels—policy, strategy, and tactics. It is also referred to as the performance engineering model (PEM). Like three levels, this simplified performance matrix or PEM has three stages—stage A, stage B, and stage C. Stage A considers identification of accomplishments, decisions on important requirements together with decision on unit of measurement, and finally development of standards. In stage B, the measurement of opportunity is considered, duly identifying critical performance improvement plans as well as measuring and analysing it. In stage C, the methods of accomplishment are analysed using environmental methods, people programmes, and management action. Based on these three inputs and in line with Gilbert's recommendations, a sample PEM has been illustrated in Table 9.10.

Exemplary performance is the worth of the historically best instance of the performance. Potential for improving performance (PIP) is a conceptual tool

TABLE 9.10 Performance matrix

Stages Levels	A Accomplishment models	B Measures of opportunity	C Methods of improvement
I Policy (Institutional systems)	Organization models: 1. Cultural goal of the organization 2. Major missions 3. Requirements and units 4. Exemplary standards	Stakes analysis: 1. Performance analysis 2. Potential for Improving performance (PIP) 3. Stakes 4. Critical roles	Programmes and policies: 1. Environmental programmes (data/tools/incentives) 2. People programmes (knowledge, selection, recruiting) 3. Management programme (organization, resources, standards)
II Strategy (Job systems)	Job models: 1. Mission of job 2. Major responsibilities 3. Requirements and units 4. Exemplary standards	Job assessment: 1. Performance measures 2. Potential for improving performance (PIP) 3. Critical responsibilities	Job strategies: 1. Data systems 2. Training designs 3. Incentive schedules 4. Human factors 5. Selection systems 6. Recruitment systems
III Tactics (Task systems)	Task models: 1. Responsibilities of tasks 2. Major duties 3. Requirements and units 4. Exemplary standards	Task analysis: 1. Performance measure or observations 2. PIP 3. Specific deficiencies 4. Cost of programmes	Tactical instruments: 1. Feedback 2. Guidance 3. Training 4. Reinforcement 5. Others

which provides the basis for comparing potential opportunities to improve performance. Comparing two indices expresses exemplary (which is the standard) and exemplary worth index. Suppose the objective is to measure PIP for the outbound caller in a call centre. An average outbound caller makes 40 effective calls in a day and each call ensures business worth ₹80, whereas the total cost per day for the company is ₹2,000. The exemplary index is indicated as Wav, which is $(40 \times ₹80)/₹2,000 = 1.6$. Suppose an exceptional outbound caller makes 80 successful calls in a day with all other data remaining the same. In that case, the exemplary worth index is indicated as Wex = $(₹80 \times ₹80)/₹2,000 = 3.2$. In this case, the PIP of the average outbound caller is computed as Wex/Wav, that is $3.2/1.6 = 2$. This is an excellent guide for managers to keep a track of decisions they must make and the sequence of these decisions. Some other examples of performance matrix for the whole organization can be drawn from the models of EFQM, Malcolm Baldrige, and Shingo™.

Shingo Prize Model™

The Shingo Prize Model™ lists criteria, practices, techniques, and processes that can be incorporated by an organization to achieve world-class level of quality, cost, delivery, and business results. Such practices and techniques may not be applicable for every organization. The practices have to be strategically incorporated, aligning with organization-specific needs. The Shingo Prize Model™ was established in 1988 to promote the awareness of *lean manufacturing* concepts and the world-class philosophy of business performance. Adoption of this model in performance management practices enables an organization to focus on improvements in core manufacturing and business process to achieve world-class business performance. The model is illustrated in Fig. 9.1.

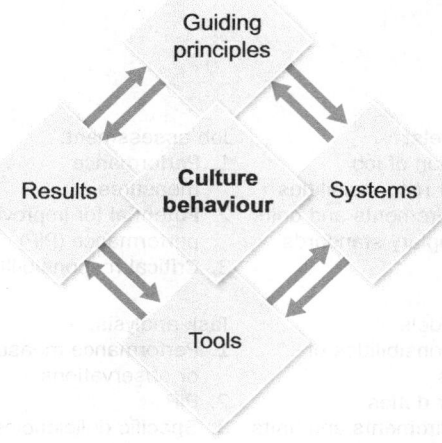

The guiding principles

Results
Create value
for the customer

Enterprise alignment
Create constancy of purpose
Think systemically

Continous improvement
Flow and pull value • Assure quality at the source
Focus on process single • Embrace scientific thinking
Seek perfection

Cultural enablers
Lead with humility
Respect every individual

FIG. 9.1 Shingo Prize Model™
© The Shingo Prize Model™
Used with permission

EFQM Excellence Model

The European Foundation for Quality Management (EFQM) business excellence model is another example of world-class PMS. This model is a nine-box business excellence model, intended to help an organization conduct self-assessment in measuring its performance results in terms of financial parameters, customer satisfaction, people satisfaction, and impact on society. Leadership, policy and strategy, people management, resources, and process management act as enablers to improve the performance results. This model is illustrated in Fig. 9.2.

Malcolm Baldrige criteria

ISO 9000-based documentation of quality management systems of an organization can be extended to Baldrige criteria for performance excellence framework. This model enables an organization to integrate its quality management system with the PMS. This framework is explained in Fig. 9.3.

The business management system (BMS) or performance excellence framework using Baldrige criteria requires the same documentation like quality documentation system of ISO 9000 except for some additional practices. Such additional practices in Baldrige criteria are as follows:

- strategic planning process
- customer-focused operating system
- operating system
- teamwork structure and guidelines
- administration of compensation and recognition systems
- advanced quality planning process for bringing new products to market

The existing corrective and preventive action system (ISO 9000) by default evolves into a continuous improvement system.

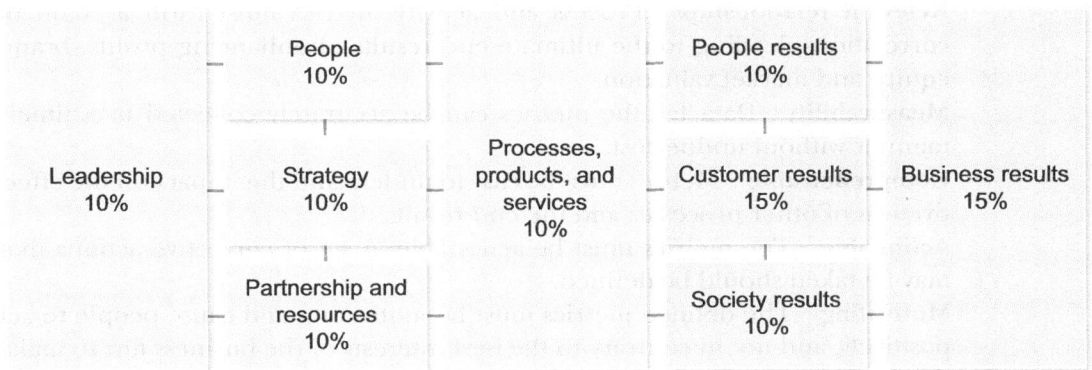

FIG. 9.2 EFQM Excellence Model
© EFQM 2012
Used with permission

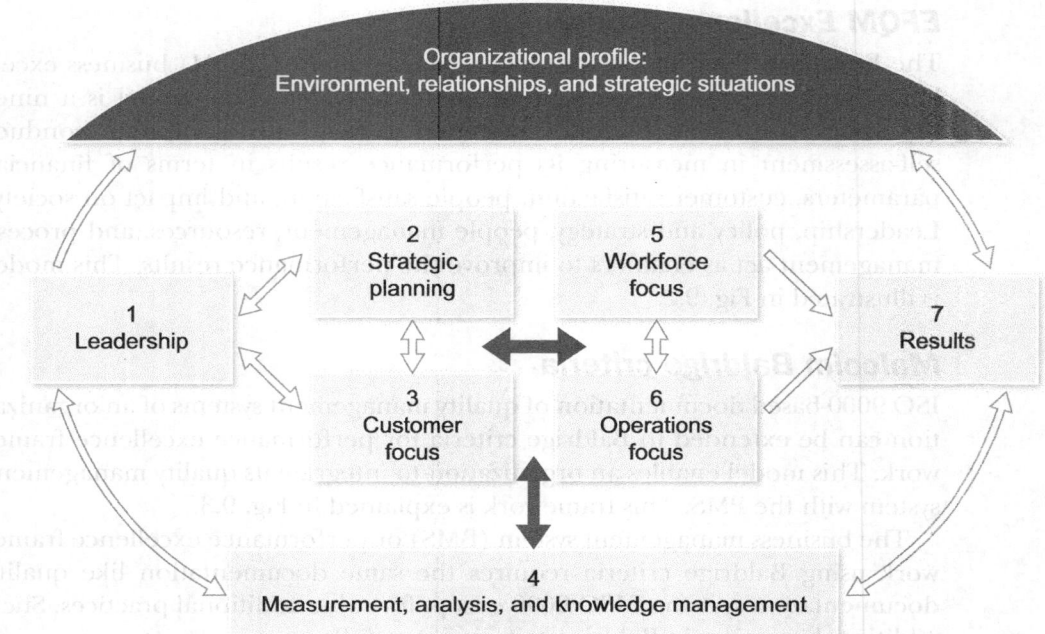

FIG. 9.3 Malcolm Baldrige criteria for world-class performance
Source: Baldrige Performance Excellence Program, 2013, *2013–2014 Criteria for Performance Excellence* (Gaithersburg, MD: U.S. Department of Commerce, National Institute of Standards and Technology, http://www.nist.gov/baldrige/publications/business_nonprofit_criteria.cfm).

EFFECTIVE PERFORMANCE MODELLING

An effective performance model enables the management to be specific that the end results are not arbitrary, but a summation of all the different activities and processes. The requirements of such a model are discussed in this section.

Relevant relationships Process and activity metrics must form a chain of correlations, leading to the ultimate end results of enhancing profits, brand equity, and market valuation.

Measurability Data for the metrics can be accurately collected in a timely manner without undue cost.

Comprehensible Metrics must be easy to understand the impact on the effectiveness of other processes and the end results.

Actionable The metrics must be actionable. A set of corrective actions that may be taken should be defined.

Motivating The defined metrics must be motivating and cause people to act positively, and not in contrary to the best interests of the business just to make their numbers.

Automation Data collection and analysis should be automated so that employees do not have to be diverted from their main activity into these activities.

For a performance model to work, employee performance appraisal criteria must be aligned with the performance metrics, that is, if an employee performs well, such performance is directly linked to process performance and to department/division performance as well as the ultimate goals of the company.

Enthusiastic acceptance, not mere passive understanding, is required from managers and employees at all levels of the organization. Successful metrics must be capable of being cascaded down the line and to reinforce the desired behaviour.

Customer-focused Metrics

For most businesses, achievement of the end objective of profits, brand equity, and market valuation are dependent largely on how well the organization meets and exceeds customer expectations. Metrics must be developed to assist internal organizations to meet external expectations. The following process is important to develop a customer-focused metrics:
- Identify customers and the outputs they require, and the processes through which such outputs are created. Process block diagrams or flowcharts may help at this point.
- Determine customer needs/requirements in terms of quality and service standards; determine the existing gaps in organizational delivery system.
- Determine the direct metrics that will help in meeting customer expectations.
- Cascade these metrics horizontally and vertically through other processes that may impact their performance to develop measures to ensure customer satisfaction.
- Establish current performance levels, short-term objectives, long-term objectives, and competitive benchmarks.

Designing metrics

The development of a proper portfolio of organizational performance metrics has proven to be the most difficult aspect of the BSC approach. It requires deep and perhaps unprecedented re-examination of the vision, mission, and strategy of an organization. The relationship between customers and the organization's own survival needs have to be considered. One way to address this issue is to select appropriate metric instruments, which can help managers assess future strategic decisions. Any metric instrument should incorporate the following important features:
- facilitate measuring of lead indicators such as forecast future trends inside and outside the organization
- be objective and unbiased
- have the essence of normalization, that is, the capability of benchmarking against other organizations

- be statistically reliable
- essentially be unobtrusive and not disruptive of work or trust
- provide inexpensive way to collect data from even small-size samples
- be balanced—qualitative/quantitative and multiple perspectives
- facilitate appropriate measurements of the right parameters
- have quantitative features for ease of aggregation, calculation, and comparison
- be efficient enough to draw many conclusions out of data set
- be comprehensive enough to accommodate all the features of organization
- have the discriminating feature even to track small meaningful changes

Even though designing the performance metrics of an organization is a difficult task, complying with these required features indisputably helps an organization in efficient performance management. Based on the above inputs, performance metrics can be developed for most of the critical performance areas of any organization.

EFFECTIVE PMS

Performance management system (PMS) is a set of techniques and procedures for improving organizational performance. To sustain competitive advantage, an organization not only has to recruit the best people, but also focus on their continuous development through an effective PMS. While development of people is possible through ongoing training and development, it must precede PMS, as PMS establishes the basis for identifying training and development needs. According to Bevan and Thompson (1992), the main features of PMS can be outlined as follows.

Objective setting Objectives are the targets, which are set for its employees by the organization. It is in the form of an action statement. The overall organizational objectives are defined at the strategic or corporate level. PMS helps percolate organizational objectives to employees, translating organizational objectives to individual targets.

Review of objectives Through the process of periodic performance review, PMS helps to keep a track on achievement of objectives. Such a review system largely depends on the type of PMS techniques used by an organization. It may be a management by objectives (MBO) system, a 360-degree PMS (multidimensional), or a tracking technique like BSC. A review of objectives helps in performance control and initiates steps to correct deviation in performance or to revise the targets.

Personal improvement plans Since PMS helps in individual performance monitoring, it ensures developing of personal improvement plans for the employees. A particular employee may lack in performance or may exceed the targets given. In both the cases, it is important to design the personal improvement plan. While in the first case, it may be important to provide performance counselling as well as training and development reinforcement; in the second case, the employee may be motivated further through proper reward system. Therefore, PMS helps in developing personal improvement plans in both the cases.

Alignment with training and development   Since the focus of PMS is to manage and develop employee performances as well as sustain competitive advantage of an organization through proper alignment, it helps in identifying training and development needs. This helps in developing need-based training and measuring the return on investment (ROI).

Formal appraisal with feedback   By introducing a formal appraisal system, PMS delivers performance feedback to employees. Both negative and positive feedback sensitizes employees to the real situation and helps them objectively analyse their shortfalls and positive attributes. While shortfalls can be met by learning reinforcement and setting the right direction; positive attributes can be leveraged by the employees to set higher targets.

Pay review   Performance-based pay is the modern concept. It aids in objective designing of a compensation package for employees, which facilitates rewarding performers and reducing variable pay of non-performers. This helps the organization remain competitive by optimizing the cost of compensation.

Competence-based organizational capability   It helps in making appropriate organizational change to keep pace with competition. It also helps in human resource planning. Through qualitative and quantitative appraisal, PMS can assess the prevailing competency level of employees and thus help in the review of organizational capability.

PMS AND ORGANIZATIONAL STRATEGY

Strategy is the direction and scope of an organization over the long term matching its resources to the changing environment and in particular its markets, customers, and clients, so as to meet the expectations of all the stakeholders.

Strategic human resource management (SHRM) is a competency-based approach to management. SHRM focuses on developing HR for sustainable competitive advantage. SHRM requires formulation of HR objectives, strategies, and policies. These enable the provision of skills and abilities needed to meet the requirements of an organization's overall objectives. In other words, they provide the framework which ensures that the people needs of the organization are met.

PMS is one of the most important HR strategy factors. HR strategy factors largely encompass six areas: recruitment and selection, career development, performance appraisal, training and development, compensation designing, and human resource planning. Career development and performance

TABLE 9.11 Performance goals and strategies

Goals: business unit, work group, or key process	Individual goals and/or tasks	Measures and targets
Contribute to the company's manufacturing of CTVs	Manage employees in execution of assigned task	• Completion on time • Quality standards met • Interim and final reports, complete and on time
	Complete own assigned tasks and present reports	• Completion, on time • Quality standards met • Interim and final reports, complete and on time
Achieve effective and efficient technical effectiveness	Contribution to the production team on quality systems improvement	• Meeting attendance requirement • Full contribution from all • Team report, complete and on time
Operational effectiveness	Carry out administrative roles and tasks	• Timeliness, accuracy, and service, meet agreed standards

appraisal are directly linked to PMS. While career development considers career mapping and succession planning, management development integrates career development with organization development (OD) initiatives. Performance appraisal designs appropriate tools and aligns such appraisal with compensation, training needs, promotion, transfer, and relocation. Performance management is a strategic function to manage business and increase organizational effectiveness which adds value by enhancing existing capabilities and building new ones. Performance management focuses on continuous development of an organization's broad strategic capabilities as well as specific capabilities of individuals and teams. Performance management is strategic from the following perspectives:

- the broader issues that the business has to face in its changing environment
- the general direction in which the business intends to go to achieve long-term goals

PMS involves thinking through various facets of performance, identifying critical dimensions of performance, planning, reviewing, developing, and enhancing performance-related competencies.

Table 9.11 illustrates the alignment of PMS and organizational strategy. It captures the performance goals for the organization and also details the various measures.

VARIOUS DIMENSIONS OF PERFORMANCE

Performance is defined as the expected deliverables by an individual or a set of individuals within a time frame. The deliverables could be stated in terms of

results or effort, tasks, and quality along with specification of conditions for the delivery of work. Many dimensions of performance are as follows:
- output or result dimension
- input dimension
- time dimension
- focus dimension
- quality dimension
- cost dimension

Output or result dimension The most acceptable, visible, and measurable dimension of performance is the result or the output. An output or a result describes the consequence of inputs in a summary, product, or service form. The product or services may be in final or semi-final form. The result describes the standard, which is easily measurable. Salary figures, customer numbers, financial targets, production targets, completion of tasks to meet some deadlines, etc. are all stated in results/output form. Sometimes, these are also referred to as KRAs.

Input dimension The input dimension deals with the activities or tasks to be accomplished by the individual. The nature of activities to be undertaken by the individual, the time frame, the quality of inputs to be given, etc., constitute the input dimension. Performance can be managed better if the nature of inputs can be envisaged without mistake.

Time dimension Another dimension of performance is time. Performance can be defined for a task, for a day, for a week, for a month, for a year, or for life. The time period for performance is important. The time frame for information technology organizations is limited to a quarter or a three-month period. In some cases, they may also be defined by tasks or project, and not time.

Focus dimension Performance also has a focus dimension. The focus can be on one of the performance parameters. For example, a marketing executive's focus of, performance can be on market share, profits, new areas covered, some of these, or all of these.

The focus of performance can be on many other dimensions. It could be on quality, cost, or financial dimensions. Quality dimension focuses on quality standards of performance, below which it is assumed as bad workmanship. Similarly cost or financial dimensions of performance are some mandated ratio or percentage, like cost of sales ratio.

PMS through management by objectives

Management by objectives (MBO) is a comprehensive management approach adopted for performance appraisal and organizational development. PMS utilizing MBO requires strategies to set mutually agreed upon, observable, and measurable objectives for the employees and their superiors. Each level of the organization sets goals that complement those set at the next highest level. In many cases, individual monetary rewards like bonuses are tied to MBO goals (Wright 1994). When MBO is used only for performance appraisal, its primary focus is on developing objective criteria for evaluating the performance of individuals. The superior and subordinate managers of an organization jointly identify common goals. After identification of goals, each individual's major area of responsibilities is defined. The defined responsibility becomes the basis for evaluating the performance of the individual employee.

Most of the organizations emphasize on developing key result areas (KRA) through MBO exercise as this approach necessitates joint meeting of the supervisor and the employee to define, establish, and set objectives, which the individual employees would achieve within a prescribed time limit. Such an exercise also establishes ways and methods to measure performance. Goals are mostly work-related or career-oriented, and are integrated with the overall organizational objectives. Periodic evaluation of employee performances is done in terms of goals. If required, the goals may be revised. Management by objectives also calls for superior–subordinate interaction and supportive role of the supervisor which includes counselling and coaching.

MBO system lays more stress on tangible goals. Hence, intangible goals such as morale, good interpersonal relations, and commitment to the job are often ignored. Moreover, the MBO exercise involves investment in terms of time and money.

PMS and assessment centre method

This method is to test employees in a social situation by a number of assessors using a variety of criteria. It may be a written test, interviews, in-basket exercise, business game, role playing incident, or a leaderless discussion. The assessors or evaluators are drawn from experienced executives working at different levels of the management. Under this method, the performance of employees is evaluated both individually and collectively. This method is useful in measuring interpersonal skills, organizing and planning ability, creativity, resistance to stress, work motivation, decision-making capacity, etc.

PMS and human asset accounting method

This method estimates the manpower of an organization in terms of monetary value. The process is somewhat like estimating the goodwill value and can be appraised by developing a procedure to undertake periodic measurement of certain variables. Such variables are either categorized as key variables or intervening variables. *Key variables* refer to the policies of an organization, its leadership strategies, skills, and behaviour of an employee, etc. *Intervening variables* refer to loyalties, attitudes, motivations, interpersonal relations, communication, and decision-making skills. Measuring such variables over several years and the quantification of human assets is difficult because of the obvious problem in developing an accounting procedure. It is not a very popular method of performance appraisal. However, this system is more appropriately used for evaluating the collective performance of an organization, rather than individual appraisal of employees.

This method is useful for organizational development, as it helps in identifying the changed areas more scientifically than any other method.

PMS and BARS

Behaviourally anchored rating scales (BARS) are descriptions provided on appraisal forms and surveys, which describe a precise level of performance. This scale is similar to graphic rating scales, but uses specific behaviours to anchor the scale. These are designed to reduce the rating errors of conventional scales. The scale includes a number of performance dimensions such as leadership, teamwork, communication, initiative, and adaptability. For each performance area, some standard statements are provided. These are then put on the scales in BARS. It was developed with the hope of improving rater accuracy by providing job-related behavioural anchors and altering the format of rating scales. It anchors each rating interval with descriptions of a behavioural incident. Normally, BARS are presented vertically with scale points ranging from 5 to 9. BARS eliminate the confusion and common error caused by open-ended rating scales. Another advantage provided by BARS is that they focus the appraisal on behaviour rather than personality characteristics (Brown 1985). Unfortunately, while behavioural anchors offer specificity in setting performance levels, research has indicated that BARS offer no performance measurement superiority over conventional systems. They are also time-consuming and difficult to develop, especially if there are many dissimilar job slots. To develop BARS for just one job, the job must be separately and carefully analysed, and performance levels must be described in detail for several of the job's areas (Edwards et al. 1985).

PMS and the mixed-standard scale

The mixed-standard scale (MSS) is considered superior to BARS in reducing halo and leniency errors. MSS disguises dimensions and ordinal relationships among items so that the rater cannot detect an order of merit in the items. In the MSS, all items are presented in random order and raters must respond without knowing whether a low, medium, or high rating for a particular item has a positive, neutral, or negative correlation to performance. Raters are required to choose one of the following three responses for each item: the ratee's performance is lower (or poorer) than the item description (−); the ratee's performance fits the item description (0); or the ratee's performance is higher (better) than the item description (+). This format provides for error counts that can be used to identify rater errors, systematic rating tendencies, and ambiguous dimensions, thereby providing the opportunity for rater feedback. MSS can be used with multiple raters. Despite its advantages, many raters experience frustration with this system and it has little industry support (Edwards and Sproull 1983).

PMS and behavioural observation scales

Latham and Wexley (1981) developed behavioural observation scales (BOS), combining both conventional graphic rating scales and BARS. It requires supervisors to make vague judgements. BOS is a list of 'critical' behaviours, which the supervisor has to rate in terms of frequency. Items indicate either desired or undesirable aspects of work performance:
- worker never needs her/his work to be double checked _____
- worker misses workdays _____

PMS and 360-degree appraisals

This appraisal method is now widely used throughout the world. It requires performance feedback from all important stakeholders of the organization such as the ratee and his superiors, peers, customers, and suppliers. Apart from its effectiveness in reporting performance, this method ensures total employee involvement (TEI) and employee empowerment. This method also reduces subjective evaluation system in an organization.

For example the following two cases show how people are affected by 360-degree feedback. N.K. Sahay, General Manager (Operations) in a BPO outfit knew he was a demanding boss. During a 360-degree feedback from his subordinates, he was in for a shock. The subordinates did not stop at saying he was a hard taskmaster; they also called him a 'cold and uncaring individual'. Sahay was dumbfounded when he could realized that not appreciating people and not tempering his criticism were having a rundown effect on his subordinates. Today, he says, 'When people are doing well, I take care to tell them about it. I am more open in my discussions. The results have been amazing. Teamwork is up and lead times are down.'

Chitra, Head of Human Resources at a call centre, was surprised to know that colleagues thought she had no sense of humour. She would be one of the first people to laugh at herself in college. Her rueful reaction to this feedback was, 'I do have a sense of humour but, evidently, I've become very good at hiding it. I guess that needs to change.'

360-degree feedback is also known as multi-rater feedback, full-circle appraisal, or group performance review. This feedback system has today become a very popular tool for employee appraisal worldwide. It involves collecting feedback on an individual's behaviour and the impact of that behaviour from superiors, colleagues, and fellow members of project teams as well as internal and external customers. However, 360-degree appraisal can be considered only when the following are true for an organization.
- The organization is not able to meet challenges that come its way because of increased competition or global expansion.

- Employees in the organization feel the need to change their behaviour to combat increasing competition and to progress in their careers but are unsure about what and how to change.
- There is no formal system in place through which employees receive information on what others think about their behaviour.

360-degree feedback is not a package, which can be delivered by a given date; it is a process that needs to be implemented in steps. Before implementation of 360-degree feedback, it should be designed to support a corporate strategy or goal. The essential prerequisites for implementation of 360-degree feedback are as follows.

- Every employee should understand 360-degree feedback and how it works.
- Employee development should be high on the organization's agenda and employees should believe that the organization and manager would support feedback processes.
- Sufficient resources should be available to ensure that the integrity level of the process is high.
- The staff should be trained in the process.
- Employees must trust that the information would be used for developmental purposes and should be willing to receive and give feedback.

Most companies implement 360-degree feedback in stages. It is a good idea to start with small groups using them as tools to gain maximum value from the total experience. Some of the areas of implementation of 360-degree feedback are discussed in this section.

Performance appraisal Even though 360-degree feedback is primarily used for performance appraisal, it is not desirable to make use of such feedback as the basis for appraisals at least for the first few cycles. Linking 360-degree feedback to appraisal is a complex process and employees are likely to be less honest in the beginning if they feel that their compensation is going to be affected by this process. An atmosphere of trust develops after one or two rounds and employees would not resist it being used for appraisal.

Cultural change Many organizations bring this process to effect cultural change and develop a more open atmosphere in the organization. 360-degree feedback does add to openness in the atmosphere and also increases employee empowerment provided a top-down approach is taken while implementing it.

Organizational development Aggregating 360-degree feedback can help identify skill gaps in the organization and provide direction vis-à-vis competition. Therefore, it can help realistically assess training needs of the organization as a whole.

PMS and the balanced scorecard

A new approach to strategic management was developed in the early 1990s by Robert Kaplan and David Norton. They named this system as *balanced scorecard* (BSC). This system provides a clear prescription as to what companies should measure in order to balance the financial perspective.

BSC is a management system. It is more than just a measurement system. It enables organizations to clarify their vision and strategy and translate them into action. It provides feedback around both the internal business processes and external outcomes in order to continuously improve strategic performance and results. When fully deployed, BSC transforms strategic planning from an academic exercise into the nerve centre of an enterprise. Kaplan and Norton (1992) describe the innovation of the BSC as follows:

'The balanced scorecard retains traditional financial measures. However financial measures tell the story of past events, an adequate story for industrial age companies for which investments in long-term capabilities and customer relationships were not critical for success. These financial measures are inadequate, however, for guiding and evaluating the journey that information age companies must make to create future value through investment in customers, suppliers, employees, processes, technology, and innovation.'

BSC suggests that organizations be viewed from the following four perspectives:

- learning and growth perspective
- business process perspective
- customer perspective
- financial perspective

They should then develop metrics, collect data, and analyse the collected data relative to each of these perspectives.

Learning and growth perspective This perspective includes employee training and corporate cultural attitudes related to both individual and corporate self-improvement. In a knowledge-worker organization, people—the only repository of knowledge—are the main resource. In the current climate of rapid technological change, it is becoming necessary for knowledge workers to be in a continuous learning mode. These metrics guide managers in focusing on training employees. Kaplan and Norton emphasize that 'learning' is more than 'training'; it also includes things such as mentors and tutors within the organization, as well as that ease of communication among workers that allows them to readily get help on a problem when it is needed. It also includes technological tools, what the Baldrige criteria calls *high performance work systems*.

Business process perspective This perspective refers to internal business processes. Metrics based on this perspective allow the managers to know the health of business operations and whether the organization's products and services conform to customer requirements, that is, the mission. These metrics have to be carefully designed by people possessing intimate knowledge of these processes.

In addition to the strategic management process, two kinds of business processes may be identified—(1) mission-oriented processes and (2) support processes. Mission-oriented processes are special functions of an organization. Many unique problems are encountered in these processes. The support processes are more repetitive in nature. Hence, they are easier to measure and benchmark using generic metrics.

Customer perspective Modern management philosophy has shown an increasing realization of the importance of customer focus and customer satisfaction. These are leading indicators. If customers are not satisfied, they will eventually find other competitors who will meet their needs. Poor performance from this perspective is thus a leading indicator of future decline, even though the current financial picture may look good. In developing metrics for satisfaction, customers should be analysed in terms of kinds of customers and the kinds of processes for which the organizations provide a product or service to these customer groups.

Financial perspective Kaplan and Norton do not disregard the traditional need for financial data. Timely and accurate funding data will always be a priority and managers should ensure that necessary data is provided. In fact, often there is more than enough handling and processing of financial data. With the implementation of a corporate database, it is hoped that more of the processing can be centralized and automated. However, the point is that the current emphasis on financials leads to an unbalanced situation with regard to other perspectives. There is perhaps a need to include additional financial-related data such as risk assessment and cost–benefit data in this category.

Balanced scorecard is a concept to help organizations translate strategy into action. It starts from company vision and strategies, based on which critical success factors are defined. Measures are constructed that aid target-setting and performance measurement in areas critical to the strategies. Hence, BSC is a performance measurement system, derived from vision and strategy, reflecting the most important aspects of the business. The BSC concept supports strategic planning and implementation by federating the actions of all parts of an organization around a common understanding of its goals, and by facilitating the assessment and upgrade of strategy.

Compensation broad banding using PMS results

Broad banding is a type of salary programme that replaces multiple grades and ranges with a limited number of wide ranges. Employees move through salary ranges without traditional promotions or job delineation based on individual skill attainment and expansion of duties rather than on any prescribed time pattern. Broad banding reduces grade levels and job titles by combining multiple jobs levels into a single range. It increases pay ranges by recognizing dual career tracks. It accommodates a flat organizational hierarchy; emphasizes on skill development rather than vertical promotions; eliminates unnecessary job titles and hierarchy; and overall simplifies compensation administration process. However, it may confront with the organizational culture, creating a large pool of overpaid employees. Collectively, it may limit promotional opportunities because of fewer job titles and levels.

COMPENSATION DESIGN THROUGH SKILL-BASED PROGRAMMES

Compensation design through a skill-based programme rewards employees for attainment of additional skills and knowledge. A skill-based pay system enables employees to enjoy addition payment for new learning, which enhances their level of performance. Learned skills and knowledge of employees significantly improve their competencies. To introduce skill-based compensation programmes, organizations at the outset break the jobs or group of jobs into different components. Initial placement of employees is done at the base level jobs, assuming employees can autonomously be able to develop individual proficiency in executing their job assignments. Organizations then encourage such employees to acquire additional skills. Wherever required, organizations extend training support. This way the employees can acquire new set of competencies and raise their base pay level. This process can help develop multi-skilled employees competent to execute jobs in different cross functions. Often skill-based pay is deliberately introduced by the organization to urge employees develop new skills. It is different from PRP as enhanced compensation become payable to employees on attaining new skill, knowledge, and competencies recognized by the organizations. For example, bank employees become eligible for additional increments after completion of CAIIB examination. Similarly, college lecturers become eligible for additional increments after completing a PhD. Every organization likewise adopts certain predetermined standards. Some important aspects of skill-based pay are more focused on individualized skill, thus eliminating unnecessary competition. It focuses on individual skill development and helps the organization accomplish its goals.

Problems

Although skill-based pay provides multiple benefits, organizations encounter serious problems in introducing this performance metric. Some of the major obstacles in introducing skill-based pay can be listed as follows:

Defining skill sets Documenting skill sets of a job is difficult. Even though organizations can at the outset document skill sets for a well-defined job, it becomes obsolete quickly. Jobs get restructured often with changing technologies and product designs, rendering earlier documented skills redundant. Another problem encountered by the organization is to narrow down skill sets as jobs are highly interrelated. Job-specific competency differences can be identified.

Pricing skill sets This is another major obstacle to introducing skill-based pay. Effective pricing of skill sets is difficult for organizations. Often jobs are benchmarked with market pricing, but many organizations may require some unique skill sets for their typical nature of job. In such a case, price rationalization becomes difficult, as subjective assessment has to be relied upon. Some of the skill price rationalization criteria could be—competitive value of the skill; amount and degree of effort required for acquiring the skills; amount and degree of effort required to implement the learned skills in tasks and jobs; etc.

Validation of skills Validation of some skill sets is also difficult. For some jobs, job trial or performance tests to validate the skills and competencies of employees can be used. However for many others, subjective assessment has to be relied upon. Hence, to achieve success in implementation of skill-based pay, it is necessary to introduce a credible skill validation process.

Skill recertification tests For some skill sets, it is necessary to ensure that concerned employees are able to sustain their skills through a periodic skill recertification programme.

Skill obsolescence Technological changes often require upgradation of skill sets. This makes earlier learned skills obsolete, requiring organizations to renew the existing skills through sustained training and development initiatives.

High cost of training To introduce skill-based pay, organizations need to focus on learning of new activities by employees. Any training and learning initiative enhances downtime by keeping employees away from productive work, apart from usual cost of training. Often, the benefits accrued fail to recover the expenses resulting in a failure of the organizational initiatives. Such possible threats outweigh the benefit of skill-based pay.

Increased payroll costs Often skill-based pay increases the overall payroll cost. However, this depends on the nature of the job. If the jobs are simple, employees can quickly learn the skill sets required to perform the job and maximize their income by stepping up production. This would be done even if the organization requires curtailing of the production. This problem would be more acute for organizations whose production planning is market-dependent. It would be difficult for such organizations to practise lean management or lean manufacturing.

Regulatory bottlenecks Skill-based pay programmes require organizations to increase variables which put the pay at risk. Therefore, reduced fixed or base pay may lead to problems for average or below-average performers, who would fail to earn the variables due to their inability to acquire new skill sets.

Application of skill-based pay

Despite of the major obstacles in introducing skill-based pay, many organizations can make good use of it for all cross sections of employees, including managerial levels. To successfully apply skill-based pay, organizations need to design this initiative with considerations to technological advancements so that identified skills do not get quickly redundant. Identified skill elements should be relevant and accepted both by the employees and the management. In addition, skill elements should be consistent and implemented with integrity. A participative task force should be formed to look into various aspects, right from development to implementation of skill-based pay. The task force considers all the issues pointed out in the list of obstacles and then determines the relative value of skills. The task force implements the skill-based pay in a phased manner.

COMPETENCY-BASED PAY

In modern organizations, the term competency is used more widely than skill. Competency is more holistic as it aggregates knowledge, skill, and abilities of employees along with the behavioural requirements. Instead of compensating for the position and the job title, competency-based pay emphasizes job accomplishments, which is much wider than job efficiency that is outcome of skill only. Competency-based pay directly measures knowledge and skills in terms of the depth of the job content and the breadth of skills.

Obstacles

A major goal of any compensation programme is to motivate employees to deliver their best performance. Merit-based pay mainly focuses on employee performance. The traditional merit pay can also be termed as performance-linked pay. It is important to remember that performance-linked pay or compensation is not the absolute criterion for compensation design. It is one among the various criteria. We have discussed all through this book the various dimensions of compensation determination. Relating compensation directly to performance is not so easy. In fact, in some types of organizations, it may not be even desirable. Both the management and the employees need to agree to relate compensation to performance.

Performance guide charts

Organizations develop performance guide charts to introduce a performance-linked pay programme. Such a chart is prepared after performance evaluation. It tentatively covers degree of performance, which includes the performance rating and the recommended rate of increase in different quarters. Table 9.12 shows it for an organization that carries quarterly review of performance.

The employees, shown as an example in Table 9.12, have been ranked on a 5-point scale. Each employee's present performance ranking has been mapped using this scale and the recommended quarterly raise in the compensation has been indicated. Notice that employees do not get any raise in pay when they fail to meet the expectations.

TABLE 9.12 Performance guide charts

Name of the employees	Performance rating	First quarter	Second quarter	Third quarter	Fourth quarter
A	Outstanding (1)	15%	13%	11%	9%
B	Exceeds expectations (2)	13%	11%	9%	No increase
C	Meets expectations (3)	11%	9%	No increase	No increase
D	Meets minimum expectations (4)	Token raise to boost morale	No increase	No increase	No increase
E	Does not meet expectations (5)	No increase	No increase	No increase	No increase

SUMMARY

The purpose of PRP is to reward employees for factors other than the value of the job. This chapter discusses the methods of designing PRP beyond the traditional paradigm of compensation design, which considers cost of living and other statutory wage provisions. This chapter also focuses on the possible dangers of designing compensation based solely on performance criteria, as it may often ignore other vital issues of people management aspects. It may not be always possible or even desirable to introduce PRP in organizations. Many organizations embrace the system for cost control as well as to derive strategic benefits such as employee motivation and retention. Introduction of PRP requires organizations to understand the basics of PMS and its relation to other facets of human resource management issues.

Rewarding employees on the basis of performance requires correlating the position of employees on a performance scale and effect changes in the wage structure accordingly. An effective performance evaluation system stresses performance achievement. The chapter has also discussed many performance evaluation tools too. Their selection depends highly on the nature of organization and its activities. Developing a performance standard for all types of jobs may be difficult, despite having advanced mechanisms such as balanced scorecard and competency-based assessment. Though setting of performance standards is an effective tool, it requires adequate groundwork and feasibility study before introduction.

Key Terms

360-degree feedback An appraisal method that requires performance feedback from all important stakeholders of the organization.

Assessment centres Test measures for evaluating employees in a social situation.

Balanced scorecard Measurement criteria balancing the financial perspective of business performance.

BARS A scale that anchors each rating interval with the descriptions of a behavioural incident.

Behavioural observation scale A scale that lists frequency of critical behaviours in an employee.

Competency mapping A map to illustrate knowledge, skill, abilities, and behavioural parameters required for competent performance.

EFQM Excellence Model World-class business excellence model pioneered by the European Foundation for Quality Management.

HR scorecard Measurement criteria that ensures strategic alignment between HR and the enterprise at all levels.

Key result areas Mutually decided targets and goals assigned to employees, aligned with organizational objectives.

Malcolm Baldrige model Performance excellence framework, which enables an organization to integrate its quality management systems with the performance management systems.

Management by objectives (MBO) A comprehensive management approach used for performance appraisal and organizational development.

Mixed standard scale A scale that disguises dimensions and ordinal relationships among items, to reduce leniency errors.

Performance appraisal A process of periodic evaluation of employees' performance.

Performance indicators Specific performance objectives based on specific needs of the organization.

Performance management system Systems which integrate employees' performance with organizational performance.

Performance matrix A construct of performance systems.

Performance metric A standard measure to assess performance in a particular area.

Performance standards Quantifiable level of performance, which an employee has to achieve.

Shingo Model™ The model lists criteria, practices, techniques, and processes, which can be incorporated by an organization to achieve world-class level of quality, cost, delivery, and business results.

SMART objectives Specific, measurable, attainable, realistic, and time-bound approach adopted while developing objectives both for the individual employee and for the organization.

Exercises

Concept Review Questions

1. Design a PMS for software programmers, marketing executives, finance executives, and human resource executives of a large IT company having global presence.
2. How can we integrate individual performance with the performance management system of an organization? Do we require performance appraisal systems? Justify your answer.
3. Traditional performance appraisal system emphasizes on assessing the individual performance as an isolated factor. Briefly discuss the newer techniques of performance appraisal, mentioning how they can benefit an organization in designing a suitable compensation structure.
4. Discuss effectiveness of MBO and BARS in designing performance-related pay. Develop KRA for an HR Manager of an organization and identify five important performance criteria for assessing the performance and its relation to your compensation design.
5. What is a balanced scorecard? What are its different perspectives? How are such perspectives related to compensation design?
6. Explain the concept of competency. How does competency development help in compensation design?
7. Write short notes on:
   (a) Performance-related pay
   (b) Assessment centre method
   (c) Performance guide charts
   (d) 360-degree performance feedback
   (e) Key performance areas

Critical Thinking Question

Develop some performance indicators for operation managers of a steel manufacturing unit. In addition, suggest possible tools which you may like to use for measurement of such performance indicators. Relate your identified performance indicators with a hypothetical compensation design, assigning weightage to each identified area.

(Hint: First understand the steel manufacturing process, identify a particular operation department, and then decide on the indicators and their relative weightage.)

Performance-related Pay at Auto India Ltd

Performance-related compensation schemes are commonly used by organizations to reward improved productivity through increased salary or benefits. Often, this scheme is misconstrued as an indirect management control system. Auto India, a leading manufacturer of automobile spares, recently adopted a bonus scheme with the basic intention of reaping benefits of increased productivity. This called for significant alteration of existing compensation systems, including making employees more accountable or responsible for results.

In the months succeeding the introduction of the new bonus scheme, the high achievers of the company significantly increased their compensation level, whereas a large number of employees faced significant reduction in their compensation package. The company had explained to all stakeholders the genesis and operational procedures before introduction of the new bonus scheme. All the line managers were trained individually to help them understand how the bonus scheme works and help in achieving business goals.

All the employees of the company are members of one of the two major registered and recognized unions. One of the union leaders collected payroll information for six months following the introduction of the new bonus schemes. Its analysis indicated that actual compensation costs have decreased over the period. Both the union leaders jointly issued a notice to the management explaining their understanding of the systems, an extract of which is reproduced here:

'Performance-related pay is defined as an approach of linking pay to performance. It is based on the assumption that organizations are able to measure output at the individual as well as team level as it contributes to organizational performance. In addition, performance-related pay should be administered in a way that organizations can capitalize the expected value from employees. Any performance-related pay initiative should match the organizational performance budgeting, duly considering the economic constraints of the organization. Therefore, performance-related pay should attempt to trade-off between various options, taking into account the background and culture of the organization.

While designing new performance-related pay schemes, organizations should ensure its acceptability to all cross sections of employees. The right fit performance appraisal tools form the basis for performance-related pay scheme. It should balance individual and team performance, bring changes in the human resource management practices, understand the impact on employees' motivation, and develop a culture of mutual trust. Organizations, after introduction of the bonus scheme, should also ensure periodic evaluation to understand its success or otherwise.

We feel that our organization has failed to account for all these issues, leading employees

(Contd)

CASE STUDY (Contd)

to survive in uncertainty and suffer from extreme financial hardships. Hence, we oppose the newly introduced performance-related pay and appeal to the management to revert to the old compensation system, which followed the principles of equity and assigned weightage to seniority without harming the collective interests of the employees.'

While explaining the genesis of the new bonus scheme, the company did make it clear to both the unions that the company wanted to reward high achievers and differentiate them from others who failed to achieve. This would enable the company to relate the compensation to market rates and at the same time motivate employees to deliver their best performance.

Discussion question

As a compensation expert, critically analyse the case and suggest what was lacking in Auto India's introduction of performance-related pay.

References

Adams, J.S. (1963), 'Towards an Understanding of Inequity', *Journal of Abnormal and Social Psychology*, 67(5), pp. 422–36.

Ambrose, M.L. and C. T. Kulik (1999), 'Old Friends, New Faces: Motivation Research' in the 1990s, *Journal of Management*, vol. 23, issue 3, pp. 231–92.

Arthur, J.B. (1994), 'Effects of human resource systems on manufacturing performance and turnover', *Academy of Management Journal*, vol. 37, pp. 670–87.

Becker, B. and B. Gerhart (1996), 'The impact of human resource management on organizational performance: Progress and prospects', *Academy of Management Journal*, vol. 39, no. 4, pp. 779–801.

Belfield, R. and D. Marsden (2003), 'Performance Pay, Monitoring Environments, and Establishment Performance', *International Journal of Manpower*, vol. 24, issue 4, pp. 452–71.

Bender, R. (2004), 'Why Do Companies use Performance Relate Pay for Their Executive Directors?', *Corporate Governance*, vol. 12, issue 4, pp. 521–33.

Bevan, S. and M. Thompson (1992), 'An overview of policy and practice' in Bevan and Thomson (eds), *Performance Management in the UK: An Analysis of the Issue*, Part One, IPM (now IPD), London.

Bhattacharyya, D.K. (2006), *Human Resource Management*, 2nd edn, Excel Books, New Delhi.

Bhattacharyya, D.K. (2007), *Human Resource Research Methods*, Oxford University Press, New Delhi.

Bhattacharyya, D.K. (2011), *Performance Management Systems and Strategies*, Pearson, New Delhi.

Bhattacharyya, D.K. (2013), 'Performance-Related Pay: Evidence Based Studies in Indian Central Public Sector Enterprises', *Compensation & Benefits Review*, vol. 45, issue 4, pp. 215–22.

Booth, A.L. and J. Frank (1997), Performance Related Pay, CEPR Discussion Papers 364, Centre for Economic Policy Research, Research School of Economics, Australian National University.

Boselie, P. (2002), 'Human resource management, work systems and performance: A theoretical–empirical approach', Tinbergen Institute Research Series 274, Thela Thesis, Amsterdam.

Bregn, K. (2008), 'Management of the new pay systems in the public sector – some implications of insights gained from experiments', *International*

Review of Administrative Sciences, vol. 74, issue 1, pp. 79–93.

Brown, B.A. (1985), 'Performance appraisals: How to make them work?', *Employment Relations Today*, Spring, pp. 39–42.

Brown, C. (1990), 'Firms' Choice of Method of Pay', *Industrial Labour Relations Review*, vol. 43, issue 3, pp. 165–82.

Cahuc, P. and B. Dormont (1997), 'Profit-sharing: Does it increase productivity and employment? A theoretical model and empirical evidence on French micro data', *Labour Economics*, vol. 4, issue 3, pp. 293–319.

Dahlstrom, C. and V. Lapuente (2009), 'Explaining Cross-country Differences in Performance-Related Pay in the Public Sector', *Journal of Public Administration Research and Theory*, vol. 20, issue 3, pp. 577–600.

DiMaggio, P.L. and W.W. Powel (1983), 'The Iron Cage Revisited: Institutional Isomorphism and Collective Rationality in Organizational Fields', *American Sociological Review*, vol. 48, issue 2, pp. 147–60.

Dixit, A.(1999), 'Incentives and Organization in the Public Sector: An Interpretative Review', *Journal of Human Resources*, vol. 34, issue 4, pp. 696–727.

Edwards, M.R. and J.R. Sproull (1983), 'Rating the raters improves performance appraisals', *Personnel Administrator*, August, pp. 77–82.

Edwards, M.R., W.C. Borman, and J.R. Sproull (1985), 'Solving the double bind in performance appraisal: A saga of wolves, sloths, and eagles,' *Business Horizons*, May–June, pp. 59–67.

Eisenhardt, K.M. (1989), 'Agency Theory: An Assessment and Review', *Academy of Management Review*, vol. 14, issue 1, pp. 57–74.

Evans, W.A. (1970), 'Pay for performance: Fact or fable', *Personnel Journal*, pp. 726–29.

Forest, V. (2008), 'Performance-related pay and work motivation: theoretical and empirical perspectives for the French Civil Service', *International Review of Administrative Sciences*, vol. 74, issue 2, pp. 325–39.

Gielen, A.C., M.J.M. Kerkhofs, and J.C.v. Ours (2010), 'How Performance related pay affects productivity and employment', *Journal of Population Economics*, vol. 23, issue 1, pp. 291–301.

Gilbert, T.F. (1978), *Human Competence: Engineering Worthy Performance*, McGraw-Hill, New York.

Guest, D.E. (1997), 'Human resource management and performance: A review and research agenda', *The International Journal of Human Resource Management*, vol. 8, no. 3, pp. 263–75.

Hart, O. (1995), 'Corporate Governance: Some Theory and Implications', *The Economic Journal*, vol. 105, issue 430, pp. 678–89.

Hasnain, Z., N. Manning, and J.H. Pierskalla (2012), 'Performance-related Pay in the Public Sector – A Review of theory and Evidence', *Policy Research Working Paper 6043*, The World Bank.

Houston, D. J. (2000), 'Public-service motivation: A multivariate test', *Journal of Public Administration Research and Theory*, vol. 10, issue 4, pp. 713–27.

Huber, N. (2010), 'Analysis: Calls for Performance-related Pay in the Public Sector Splits HR and employment experts', Personnel Today, downloaded from www.personneltoday.com/articles/17/06/2010/55989 on 12th February 2012.

Huber, N. (2010), 'Performance-related Pay Should be Increased In the Public Sector to Drive Reforms', CIPD, Personnel Today, downloaded from http://www.personneltoday.com/articles2010/06/16/55960/performance-related-pay-should-be-increased-in-the-public-sector-to-drive-reforms-says-the-cipd.html/, last accessed on 12 February 2012.

Huselid, M.A. and N.L. Rau (1997), 'The determinants of high performance work systems: Cross sectional and longitudinal analyses', Academy of Management Annual Meetings, Human Resources Management Division, Boston, Massachusetts.

Jensen, M. and W. Meckling (1976), 'Theory of the firm: Managerial behavior, agency costs, and capital structure', vol. 3, issue 4, pp. 305–60.

Kaplan, R.S. and D.P. Norton (1992), 'The Balanced Scorecard: Measures that drive performance', *Harvard Business Review*, Jan–Feb, pp. 80–91.

Kohn, A. (1993), 'Why Incentive Plans Cannot Work', *Harvard Business Review*, vol. 71, issue 5, pp. 54–63.

Latham, G.P. and K.N. Wexley (1981), Increasing Productivity through Performance Appraisal, Addis on Wesley, London.

Latham, G.P. and V.L. Huber (1992), 'Pay for Performance Research: Lessons From the Past, Issues for the Future', *Journal of Organizational Behavior Management*, vol. 12, pp. 121–49.

Lazear, E. (1986), 'Salaries and Piece Rates', *Journal of Business*, vol. 59, issue 3, pp. 405–31.

Lazear, E. P. (2000), 'Performance Pay And Productivity', *American Economic Review*, vol. 90, pp. 1346–61.

Lee, H-J., Y. Iijima, and C. Reade (2011), 'Employee preference for performance-related pay: predictors and consequences for organizational citizenship behaviour in a Japanese firm', *International Journal of Human Resource Management*, vol. 22, issue 10, pp. 2086–109.

Lewis, P. (1998), 'Managing Performance Related Pay Based on Evidence from the Financial Services Sector', *Human Resource Management Journal*, vol. 8, issue 2, pp. 66–77.

Luthans, F. (1973), *Organizational Behaviour*, New York, NY, McGraw-Hill.

Milkovich, G.T. and J.M. Newman (2002), *Compensation*, New York, McGraw-Hill.

Paarsch, H.J. and Bruce Shearer (2000), 'Piece rates, Fixed rates and Incentive Effects: Statistical Evidence from Payroll Records', *International Economic Review*, vol. 41, issue 1, pp. 59–92.

Perry, J. L. and L.R. Wise (1990), 'The Motivational Bases of Public Service', *Public Administration Review*, vol. 50, issue 3, pp. 367–73.

Perry, J.L., T.A. Engbers, and S.Y. Jun (2009), 'Back to the Future? Performance-Related Pay, Empirical Research, and the Perils of Persistence', *Public Administration Review*, vol. 69, issue 1, pp. 39–61.

Pfeffer, J. (1994), Competitive Advantage through People, Harvard Business School Press, Boston, Massachusetts.

Piekkola, H. (2005), 'Performance-related pay and firm performance in Finland', *International Journal of Manpower*, vol. 26, issue 7/8, pp. 619–35.

Porter, L.W. and E.E. Lawler III (1968), *Managerial Attitudes and Performance*, Homewood, IL, Dorsey Press.

Rischer, H. (2012), Draft report on PRP in OECD Countries, OECD, Report No. Gov/PGC/PEM (2012–3), OECD, Paris, France.

Rubery, J. (1995), 'Performance-related Pay and the Prospects of Gender Pay Equity', *Journal of Management Studies*, vol. 32, issue 5, pp. 637–54.

Schmidt, Werner (2011), 'Performance-related Pay in German Public Services: The example of local authorities in North Rhine-Westphalia', *Employee Relations*, vol. 33, issue 2, pp. 140–58.

Schuler, R.S. and N. Rogovsky (1998), 'Understanding Compensation Practice Variations across Firms: The Impact of National Culture', *Journal of International Business Studies*, vol. 29, issue 1, pp. 159–77.

Scott, W.R. (1995), Institutions and Organizations, London, Sage.

Skinner, B.F. (1969), *Contingencies of Reinforcement*, New York, Appleton-Century-Crofts.

Vroom, V.H. (1964), *Work and Motivation*, New York, Wiley.

Wright, S. (1994), *Anthropology of Organisations*, Routledge, London.

CHAPTER TEN

Team-based Compensation

Learning Objectives

After reading this chapter, you will be able to
- understand the definition and concept of a team
- appreciate concepts of team-based compensation
- evaluate team-based compensation and employee evaluation systems
- understand team-based compensation and gainsharing plans
- discuss problems in team-based compensation
- understand the process of designing effective team-based compensation

Team-based Compensation May Not Always Work

Superpower, an FMCG major, introduced team-based incentive system for its employees. The employees of the company worked in cross-functional teams that were driven by a common goal. Team-based compensation was determined using criteria such as customer satisfaction, profitability against budgeted goals, and retail sales. Managers and executives stood to lose 10 per cent of their salaries if they did not satisfy these criteria. On the upside, the new incentive system gave them an opportunity to earn 12.5–25 per cent more than what they would have normally earned under the straight compensation system. For three consecutive years, 90 per cent of the managers and executives lost 10 per cent of their salaries on account of poor customer satisfaction. The employees attributed this to the faulty system used to analyse customer satisfaction. Customers were dissatisfied because the company did not have adequate manpower to address their complaints. Complaints were attended to only after repeated requests from customers, which resulted in accumulation of complaints and loss of business. The lone customer care executive in the customer care department found it difficult to help

Base

HRA

EPF

Gratuity

Variable

Bonus

LTA

Conveyance

Medical

customers on her own. The company, after some research, blamed the marketing team for low customer satisfaction claiming that they did not adequately educate customers on product handling. All the problems were attributed to uninformed customers and the failure of the marketing team. The marketing team urged the company to redesign the team-based incentive plan and link it with sales targets.

INTRODUCTION

The team-based compensation system rewards employees who work in a team. This means that individual employees are compensated based on the team performance. Mohman et al. (1995) defined team as, 'groups of individuals who work together to develop products or deliver services for which they are mutually accountable.' It has been proved that employees working in a team deliver better results than those who work individually. Teamwork requires effective design of the organizational structure. It also requires the adoption of a collective performance evaluation method instead of individual assessment based on the key result areas (KRAs) and key performance areas (KPAs). A team-based compensation system emphasizes on team performance. Team-based compensation system rewards the behaviour of people working in a team who can sustain team performance. Designing a compensation structure based on individual performances will conflict with the team set-up. To avoid clerical hassles associated with computing team-based compensation, organizations usually prefer a team performance linked compensation plan where the variables are distributed among the team members following the principles of equity although individual employees may receive base pay different from each other.

Organizations adopted the idea of teamwork during the late eighties, when teamwork was found more effective and competitive operationally. Collective effort of people in a team setting increases overall performance and productivity. In addition, it enables team members to take quality decisions as they can pool cross-functional knowledge and skills of their team members. The term *team* is used interchangeably to describe a group of people as a whole or working together. Teamwork helps organizations benefit from synergy, cooperation, and the unity of command. It is driven by one goal, provides flexibility, and ensures better customer service. However, teamwork can only be efficient if the team is composed of 'like-minded' intelligent people and not just intelligent people. It is not easy to build a team as it very often requires bringing together people from different backgrounds. For instance, a strategy group may include people from marketing, finance, HR, and systems. In this, the expertise of the sales team represented by sales people lay in selling products and services to customers, whereas that of marketing team lay in designing customer-centric products and services. The finance team controls costs to make products and services competitive, whereas the human resource team provides quality manpower to achieve sales goals. Expertise of systems people lay in providing information which aids decision-making. Bringing people from these disparate groups and make them function as one is, at the least, a tough task. To be able to build a successful team, it is important to first understand the common goal of the team and then decide who can help achieve this common goal. Developing a cross-functional team to pursue common goals depends on the corporate culture. Unless the organizational culture and value systems in principle endorse and promote team building, it is impossible to implement a team-based compensation system. The stages of team building followed by organizations are as follows:

- clarifying team goals
- identifying issues that deter team goals
- addressing these issues

TEAM-BASED COMPENSATION

Designing team-based compensation in an organization is not always feasible. This may be because absolute teamwork is often more of a myth than a reality. In general, while calculating team-based compensation, organizations consider a portion of the individual's base pay, and some other forms of financial and non-financial rewards. Gainsharing considers rewards for employees' performance as well as involvement. It is done through monthly or quarterly rewards to employees based on the degree of improvement in their performance. Honeywell et al. (1997) developed a team-based compensation structure by integrating both group and individual incentive systems. The exact mix of the two compensation systems is a matter of organizational practice. Usually, about 5–10 per cent of base pay is provided as an incentive to reward individual performance. While determining team-based compensation, apart from the team performance several other criteria such as team members' contribution to productivity, cost savings, and quality are also considered. Different organizations choose the components of team-based compensation differently. However, lump sum rewards, irrespective of base pay or discretionary bonuses, are commonly used by organizations to reward team members. The reward can be both financial as well as non-financial. Gifts and international holidays are common examples of non-financial team-based compensation.

Organizational strategy and culture are important areas of consideration in designing of team-based compensation. Compensation plans should be in sync with the organization's culture and strategy. For example, task-centric organizations, which put undue emphasis on target achievement, often suppress employee-centric issues. The strategy and culture of an organization indicates, what it wants to emphasize and how the employees are expected to behave. A team-based compensation that fails to take into account the prevailing strategy and culture of the organization becomes useless. However, compatibility between strategy, culture, and team-based compensation may not be easily achieved. Organizations need to practise it and draw lessons from their past mistakes to achieve the right fit. Hence, customizing an effective team-based compensation requires constant review and evaluation to achieve compatibility.

Ideally, the aim of any team-based compensation plan is to urge team members or employees to volunteer for the achievement of assigned goals. Using *tournament competition approach* to design team-based compensation can help increase voluntary participation of team members. As per this theory, compensation is viewed as the prize in a series of tournaments or contests.

Team-based compensation encourages members to cooperate, as they are rewarded based on the performance of the team as a whole. Moreover, the best outcome can only be achieved when team members work as partners. However, organizations provide for individual rewards to the best performers in a team in the form of enhanced rate of bonus, promotions, etc. Such relative rewards systems are often considered against the principles of collectivism. However in reality, they benefit team members who appreciate that their talent is being recognized. Relative rewards naturally induce competition and a moderate rate of competition in teamwork is always desirable.

Employee Evaluation System

The design of team-based compensation needs to be supported by an employee evaluation system. The most important aspect of teamwork is group dynamics. It brings team members together to support each other, so that all members of the team become effective. The absence of group dynamics in a team isolates team members. They tend to drift away from the team and forget the need to pursue a common goal. Supervisors can play a big role in the development of group dynamics.

It is important for team members to clearly understand the goal and performance standards. Each team member needs to be properly informed and educated about the criteria used by the organization to measure performance, levels of motivation, experience, skills, and personality. Employees can understand the system better when these elements and their relation to the compensation is clear. This information should be supplemented by information about tools that can help the team member meet organisation's expectations and requirements.

The performance evaluation system needs to be fair and comprehensive. It must be able to track individual and team performances differently. Giving too much weightage to external criteria, over which the employees have hardly any control, may not always be correct, as has been observed in the opening case. In a team-based compensation system, the performance of both individuals and teams needs to be in sync. Therefore, it is necessary for organizations to draw up a performance evaluation system that can segregate individual's contribution from team's contribution and compensate employees both individually and for their team effort. Let us illustrate this with a hypothetical example. An individual team member in a marketing team is responsible for achieving a target of two new product designs in a year. The company may assign 50 per cent weightage to achievement of this target, attributing it to individual efforts, whereas the other 50 per cent is assigned to team efforts. Here, team effort gets a 50 per cent weightage because designing a new product requires support from several departments such as the research and development wing to develop the prototype; the tool room to develop tools for bulk manufacturing; and the shop floor for pilot testing in the manufacturing line. In the same manner, every performance area needs to be understood in the context of individual and team performance measures. The different performance measurement criteria that an organization can adopt to design a compensation plan has already been discussed in detail in Chapter 5 on Employee benefits.

To align individual and team performance to the compensation plan, an organization has to follow certain steps.

1. Identify performance criteria and behaviour expected of employees. The organization has to adequately define this and then communicate it to all the team members so that each member of the team understands this. This is the most difficult phase of designing team compensation.
2. Clarify management's expectations and goals. Team members should understand what role they are expected to fulfil. They should also understand how their contribution would help the organization achieve its goals and objectives.
3. Create a performance evaluation process. The process includes a periodic evaluation of an individual's performance, and communication between management and the employee. It should include the following:
    - assess an individual's performance behaviour
    - evaluate performance clearly and objectively
    - create a forum for dialogue between the management and the employees
    - create a forum for employee coaching to help them set goals to maximize their performance
    - link performance and compensation

Group Incentive Plans

In team-based compensation design, providing group incentive to team members is quite common. A group incentive is also known as team-based alternative reward as it differs from other common incentive plans. The entire team shares the rewards based on performance gains, which are linked with the overall profitability of the organization. To design an effective group incentive plan, an organization should first identify performance targets and the standards of performance required to achieve the performance targets. It then needs to document these standards so that it can properly guide team members. In the documentation, the organization also needs to specify how rewards will be allocated. The group incentive plan thus helps the team members focus on specific performance targets. Employees can self-assess their accomplishments and therefore, stay highly motivated. However, some organizations find it difficult to administer group incentive plans because of its obvious de-emphasis on individual performance. In addition, if performance targets are not selected properly, the whole exercise may prove costly.

Gainsharing Plan

Like group incentives, gainsharing is also a type of team-based alternative reward system. Gainsharing plans can be better implemented in situations where the team represents a homogeneous group such as a department or a division. Here, the compensation is linked to the achievement of departmental or divisional targets. Here too, the documentation of performance targets, performance standards, and the allocation of compensation amongst group members is necessary. The advantages and disadvantages of gainsharing plans are similar to group-incentive plans.

Whichever team-based compensation plan is used, its effectiveness depends largely on clearly informing team members about its nature and specific conditions. Team members also need to participate in designing the compensation plan and should perceive it as fair. However, only forming a work team and designing effective team-based compensation may not always ensure success. Organizations need to adopt clear team objectives, decide criteria to measure team performance, and ensure that team members share the same attitude and goals.

Problems in Rewarding Teams

Organizations often find it difficult to reward teams as it is difficult for them to map the knowledge, skills, attitudes, and the competencies of the employees. As a result, organizations fail to effectively rate their talent through team-based rewards. This leads to a situation where talented team members feel perturbed and demotivated when they see that their rating is same as that of the poor performers. Further, awarding compensation based on individual performance criteria is deep-rooted in organizational practices globally, particularly in the Western world. This dissuades organizations from adopting team-based rewards. Besides, its operation may be very costly due to an increased level of clerical work.

EFFECTIVE DESIGN OF TEAM-BASED COMPENSATION

Designing an effective team-based compensation system is a challenging task for any organization. To effectively design team-based compensation, organizations need to do the following:
- link the proposed compensation design with the strategy and culture of the organisation
- understand the nature and types of teams and job categories
- evaluate performance properly
- design a base pay system

Organizations can have different types of teams such as parallel teams, process teams, full-time or project teams, and hybrid teams (a mixture of all three). In a *parallel team*, team members are temporarily assigned some tasks to accomplish. They are selected from different functional areas. On the completion of the assigned tasks, they are sent back to their mother department. Since this type of team is only temporary, the design of team-based compensation for a short time frame becomes difficult. Hence, the organization prefers to continue with existing compensation systems. A *process team* is formed primarily on the test of homogeneity. Such team members collectively carry out a process, which is part of the total system. Incentive plans cannot be indiscriminately applied to this type of team. Gainsharing, which rewards employees based on departmental or divisional performance, is usually considered the right choice. Members work full-time in a *project team*, so the reward or compensation system largely follows the principles of equity. In case of a *hybrid team*, it is difficult for the organization to employ a specific compensation plan. Hence, managers try to continue with the prevailing compensation systems, against which the employees are already covered.

An understanding of job categories helps in the broad banding of team compensation. It helps organizations put more jobs into fewer bands, and accordingly determine the pay grades. Narrow pay-bands help organizations to achieve pay equity. Another aspect of team-based compensation is the design of a performance evaluation system, that is, the selection of performance criteria based on which the rewards are given. As explained already, these are done in keeping with the organizational culture and strategy. The most commonly used criteria for team-based compensation design are—appropriate behavioural competencies; demonstration of skill and knowledge acquisition; achievement of specific time-bound objectives; and quantitative and qualitative results. These criteria may differ depending on the nature of the team. For example, it is better to use the management by objectives (MBO) approach to track behavioural competencies of a parallel team. For a process team, behavioural competencies are better understood through the acquisition of skills, knowledge, and results. For a project team, results are the most important criteria, followed by demonstration of behavioural competencies and the achievement of specific objectives in a specified period of time.

RECENT TRENDS IN TEAM-BASED COMPENSATION

In team-based compensation, team trust is considered to be the most important ingredient. Hence, it is the primary role of HR manager to ensure that the team trust level is high before implementing team-based compensation plan. Ferrin and Dirks (2003) defined trust, more specifically interpersonal trust or the team trust, as the belief of one individual on another individual, that is, the faith that the other individual will be honest enough to uphold commitments and will not take any advantage of the opportunity. Therefore, interdependence and risk are two important conditions in team-trust (Rousseau, Sitkin, Burt, and Camerer 1998). With team trust, organizations can benefit from the synergy and excel in performance. Team-based compensation plan can also encapsulate incentive pay, recognition, profit sharing. However, this compensation plan should be sensitive enough as often team overrides the good individual efforts. To balance the situation, organizations strategically give differential weights on team and individual performance. Baring the disadvantage of undermining individual spirit, team-based compensation can promote collaboration, and facilitate integration of team goals with the organizational goals and objectives (Haines and Taggar 2006). There are three important preconditions for the success of team-based compensation: high degree of team trust; high degree of task interdependence; and positive attitude towards team rewards. It is important for organizations to design a team-based compensation plan that is objective, fair, and based on certain observable and measurable criteria.

Some of the recommended principles for designing an effective team-based compensation plan for an organization can be listed as under.

- ensure team-based compensation plan meet both the ends, creating a win-win situation. This requires participation of team members in compensation design, followed by their acceptance of the plan.
- factor success of both the team and business
- make provision for rewarding individual performances that contribute to team success
- factor skills and competencies for compensation design
- communicate team-based compensation plan
- review the team-based compensation plan based on changing business needs of the organizations

All the aforesaid principles are based on organizational experiences.

SUMMARY

A team represents a group of people working together to achieve common organizational goals. Teamwork leads to enhanced performance as the organization tries to achieve its goal by optimizing its resources. Globally, organizations are now shifting towards teamwork. This requires organizations to change their old practices of compensating employees individually. In a teamwork culture, individual performance alone cannot contribute to organizational success as it depends on the collective performance of the team. A well-designed team compensation plan assigns importance to the individual performance and also to the performance of the team as a whole. In this chapter, we have discussed how to integrate both individual and collective compensation systems in a teamwork culture. Whatever may be the team compensation plan, the organization has to consider the principles of equity and fairness, and make such a plan transparent. The plan should be aligned with the strategies and culture of the organization; if not, it may fail to get results. In order to make the compensation plan effective, the organization must also consider and select the appropriate performance measurement tools. It is also very important to ensure that information about how they are being evaluated and compensated should be disseminated to the team members. Individual performances in a team also need to be recognized in order to promote competition. In addition, organizations need to frame a compensation plan based on the nature of the team.

Key Terms

Cross-functional team This type of team is represented by employees who perform different functions, but try to achieve a common goal.

Hybrid team This type of team is a mixture of process, parallel, and project or full-time team. It is difficult for the organization to implement a team-based compensation plan for this type of team. Hence, the organization prefers to continue with the existing compensation plan.

Parallel team In this type of team, team members are temporarily assigned some tasks to accomplish. They are selected from different functional areas. On completion of the assigned tasks, they are sent back to their mother department. Since this type of team is only temporary, the design of team-based compensation for a shorter time frame becomes difficult.

Process team This type of team is formed mainly on the test of homogeneity. Such team members collectively carry out a process, which is a part of the total system.

Exercises

Concept Review Questions

1. Explain the concept of teamwork. Do we need to form a cross-functional team? Justify your answer.
2. What is team-based compensation? Why a team-based compensation plan needs to be different from other compensation plans? Justify your answer.
3. How do employee evaluation systems influence a team-based compensation plan? What type of employee evaluation system do you recommend for a software development

project team? Substantiate your answer with reasons.
4. How do group incentives and gainsharing plans influence a team-based compensation plan?
5. What types of problems may arise when introducing a team-based compensation plan?
6. What precautions do you recommend when designing an effective team-based compensation plan in an organization?

Critical Thinking Question

Your company is seriously considering switching to a team-based compensation plan from the existing individualistic approach to compensation design. It develops prototypes of machines, based on clients' requirements. Most of the employees are scientists and specialists in their respective areas. Draw up a suitable switch-over plan clarifying the necessary steps.

Talent Management at Enlarge

CASE STUDY

Employees are the biggest source of competitive advantage. This is now accepted in organizations across the world. However, organizations still do not make use of the right compensation mix to attract, motivate, and retain talent. McKinsey's study (1997) indicated the acute shortage of talent worldwide. In developed countries, such shortage has now reached an alarming level. The problem in developed countries is largely attributable to the demographic trend. In the era of emerging markets, developing countries, including India, are now facing a talent crisis. Multinational and transnational companies now attract talent from the developing world causing a huge shortage of capable executives and managers in developing countries.

Concern for the shortage of talent is also evident in the McKinsey's recent study (2007). World-wide, organizations have concentrated on streamlining their human resource management. Talent management has not been a priority. However, the absence of talented human resources can ultimately ruin organizational plans and programmes. It weakens the competitive edge of organizations and may even force them to liquidate.

To introduce effective talent management systems in organizations, it is important to first adopt talent strategies, extending the focus from good performers to a wide cross-section of diverse manpower. Systematic knowledge management initiatives can mitigate this problem, but cannot act as stand-alone solutions. Cost-effective compensation strategies must be adopted; first to pull and attract the talents; then to motivate and retain them.

Innovative compensation design has always been a concern for global cement major Enlarge. The company is now on an acquisition spree and is trying to extend its reach to new emerging markets including India. In the restricted market era, cement industry in India grew very slowly. In the post-liberalization era, the industry revived due to price de-control and booming economic activity. Its current rapid growth has attracted many foreign players, a number of whom are buying and developing new cement manufacturing units in the country. Enlarge is one such organization, which is trying to find a foothold in the Indian market.

Most large cement manufacturing companies in India are owned by big business houses and managed professionally. Grasim, the Aditya

(Contd)

CASE STUDY (*Contd*)

Vikram Birla Group Company, has now acquired L&T in an effort to consolidate its market share. ACC, Gujarat Ambuja, India Cement, and Madras Cement now manage their units more efficiently. Apart from these, we also have many medium and small cement manufacturing companies who cater to local market needs by efficiently using their logistics and supply chain management. All this is possible because they have learnt from past mistakes. In the initial stage of India's economic liberalization, many Indian companies could not survive due to competition from global majors. Soft-drink manufacturers who had to submit to global majors and even became their franchisees to survive in the market are a good example.

Enlarge's initial compensation strategy was to pay salaries above the market rate to executives and managers, while outsourcing low-key operation jobs. High compensation packages immediately attracted executives and managers across levels from local cement companies. However, Enlarge could not attract operations-level workers and employees because of their unfriendly employment terms. Enlarge believed that it would be able to attract workers from cement units that had been shut down. It also believed that it would get the privilege of ready-to-use expertise at the operations level. However, it did not materialize. The failure to attract operations-level workers reduced Enlarge's cost competitiveness, forcing it to scale down its activities and restructure the organization. The problem escalated to such an extent that executives and managers started leaving the organization. Many of them were rehired by their past employers, whereas some had to shift to other industries.

The industry believes that Enlarge's predicament is attributable to its failure to recognize the need for an inclusive approach to talent issues. Organizations cannot sustain themselves with only a few talented executives and managers. Talent should be recognized across functions and at all levels.

We have many good examples from the corporate world, where organisations have been successful in adopting an inclusive approach to talent management. One of the best examples is the international oil major Schlumberger. The company motivates operations-level technical people by providing assured time-bound promotional opportunities, status, and compensation levels comparable to their senior executives. The company recognizes the life cycle needs of all cross-sections of employees.

Discussion question

Study the case of Enlarge and suggest how a suitable compensation plan can positively influence talent retention.

References

Bartol, K.M. and L.L. Hagmann (1992), 'Team-based pay plans: A key to effective teamwork', *Compensation and Benefits Review*, vol. 24, no. 6, pp. 24–49.

Bhattacharyya, D.K. (2009), *Organizational Behaviour*, Oxford University Press, New Delhi.

Cohen, S.J. and D.E. Bailey (1997), 'What makes teams work: Group effectiveness research from the shop floor to the executive suite', *Journal of Management*, vol. 23, pp. 239–90.

DeMatteo J.S., L.T. Eby, and E. Sundstorm (1998), 'Team-based rewards: Current empirical and directions for future research', *Research in Organizational Behavior*, vol. 20, pp. 141–83.

Ferrin, D.L. and K.T. Dirks (2003), 'The Use of Rewards to Increase and Decrease Trust: Mediating Processes and Differential Effects', *Organization Science*, vol. 14, issue 1, pp. 18–31.

Gomez-Mejia, L. and B. Balkin (1998), 'Effectiveness of individual and aggregate compensation strategies', *Industrial Relations*, vol. 28, no. 3, pp. 431–45.

Gross, S.E. (1995), 'Compensation for teams: How to design and implement team-based reward systems', American Management Association, New York.

Haines, V. and S. Taggar (2006), 'Antecedents of Team Reward Attitude', *Group Dynamics: Theory, Research, and Practice*, vol. 10, no. 3, pp. 194–205.

Honeywell, J.A., A.M. Dickinson, and A. Poling (1997), 'Individual performance as a function of individual and group pay contingencies', *Psychological Record*, vol. 47, no. 2, pp. 261–74.

McAdams, J. (2000), 'The essential role of rewarding teams and teamwork', *Compensation and Benefits Management*, vol. 16, no. 4, pp. 15–27.

Mohman, S.A., S.G. Cohen, and A.M. Mohman (1995), *Designing Team-based Organisation*, Jossey-Bass Inc., San Francisco.

Rousseau, D.M., S.B. Sitkin, R.S. Burt, and C. Camerer (1998), 'Not so different after all; A cross-discipline view of trust', *Academy of Management Review*, vol. 23, no. 3, pp. 393–404.

CHAPTER ELEVEN

Executive Compensation

Learning Objectives

After reading this chapter, you will be able to:
- understand the concept of executive compensation
- define various components of executive compensation
- discuss different theories of executive compensation
- evaluate different methods of designing executive compensation
- understand importance of performance as a criteria in executive compensation
- relate executive compensation to organizational strategy

Base

HRA

EPF

Gratuity

Variable

Bonus

LTA

Conveyance

Medical

OPENING CASE

Why Do We Pay Our Executives More?

N.R. Narayana Murthy, Chief Mentor of Infosys, strongly believes that organizations are now paying excessive salaries to managers, especially at senior levels. He has recommended three basic principles for determining managerial remuneration—fairness, transparency, and accountability. Fairness requires that executive compensation be considered with respect to other employees of the organization. Transparency requires sharing of information about executive compensation with other stakeholders, whereas accountability calls for linking executive compensation with corporate performance.

Based on Infosys' HR practices, Murthy has suggested that executive compensation should have a fixed component and a variable component. The variable component should be linked with the long-term objectives of the company. According to him, 'senior management should swim or sink with the fortunes of the company.' The compensation committee of the board should review executive compensation issues, which also need to be approved by the independent directors and the shareholders. On the subject of paying high compensation packages to promoter CEOs of organizations, Murthy has stated that a promoter CEO is different from a professional manager. A promoter CEO takes a huge risk and hence should be compensated accordingly. We should not confuse the issues of entrepreneurial compensation and professional executive compensation. He also emphatically stated that there should not be a huge difference between top executives and the bottom-rung employees of the organization. *The Financial Express* reported that the annual compensation of Murthy in 2006 was ₹41.60 lakh while that of CEO, President, and Managing Director, Nandan Nilekani was ₹41.17 lakh. Tata Consultancy Services (TCS) hiked the total compensation of its CEO and Managing Director, S. Ramadorai, by 100 per cent to ₹2.44 crore in 2006. Annual employee cost for TCS has gone up by 32 per cent to ₹5,113.96 crore, whereas it has gone up by 34.7 per cent to ₹3,818 crore for Infosys. The increase in employee costs for Infosys (34.7 per cent) was higher than the increase in compensation for Murthy and Nilekani (30 per cent). The average annual cost per employee works out to ₹8.14 lakh for TCS and ₹7.24 lakh for Infosys.

Infosys follows the predictability sustainability profitability de-risking (PSPD) model. The long term success of any organization depends on scaling up profitably. Therefore, every organization must have a good de-risking approach to recognize and mitigate risk in every dimension, including executive compensation.

INTRODUCTION

Executive compensation issues are now a crucial concern worldwide, as a series of studies indicate a correlation between executive compensation and organizational performance. The earliest study on this subject was conducted by Taussig and Baker (1925). This study found a very tenuous relationship between executive compensation and organizational performance. However, subsequent researches undertaken globally have established a strong relationship between the two. In fact, some studies even found that organizational performance dips due to the burden of executive compensation, that is, due to unresolved issues or dissatisfaction with the compensation. Debate on this issue still continues as new researches have thrown up new information about various dimensions of executive compensation. Gomez-Mejia (1994) conducted the most thought provoking research in this respect and offered new insight into several dimensions of executive compensation. Keeping in view the enormous researches conducted on executive compensation, which differ in dimensions and results, this chapter analyses various theoretical issues by utilizing information from corporate practices worldwide. There are three main areas of focus—understand the criteria (firm's performance, size, and individual characteristics of executives), consequences (implications in terms of pay level and pay risk), and the mechanism to determine executive compensation. In fact, other characteristics of executive compensation design can be subsumed within these three dimensions.

Executive compensation plays the most important role in motivating critical performances. Such critical performances help a company to achieve results. In this context, it is important to understand that base salary is not the only component of executive compensation. Organizations have to make available various short-term and long-term incentives. Such incentives need not be in form of cash. They may include stock options and various other innovative deferrals such as loyalty bonus with a time-cap and golden parachute schemes. An executive compensation package needs to be designed in such a way that it helps executives achieve financial goals. Although increased executive compensation package acts as a great motivator and helps in retention, organizations need to optimize it by adopting innovative approaches. Otherwise, it may adversely affect profitability. In addition, organizations need to design tax-efficient executive compensation.

COMPONENTS OF EXECUTIVE COMPENSATION

Components of executive compensation can be studied from three perspectives—variable pay such as bonuses, commissions, and profit sharing; base pay such as salary and perquisites; and employment status such as promotions and termination. The difference between these perspectives focuses on the uncertainty of present and future wealth and emanates from agency discussions of risk bearing. In particular, it is recognized that fixed pay and variable pay represent different aspects of executive wealth and carry different risks or threats to wealth. For example, employment consequences (in particular threat of termination) represent the most severe threat to wealth since they involve a complete loss of current income as well as a threat to prospects for future income by lowering the market value of an executive (Agarwal and Walking 1994; Fama 1980). Base pay consequences represent a more important, but less severe threat to wealth than employment consequences since uncertainty in base pay generally concerns an erosion of buying power resulting from loss of market adjustments, cost of living adjustments, merit raises, etc. In contrast, true variable pay consequences represent the least threat to current wealth since this form of pay is not counted as part of wealth until it is actually awarded. Failure to receive a performance award does not affect an individual's standard of living, as would failure to receive one's salary, or even failure to receive cost of living adjustments. It must be noted that some forms of pay generally counted as variable such as some forms of bonuses and stock options may not be truly variable, and would therefore not be included in the category of variable pay. In cases where bonuses are regularly awarded, they become more like an entitlement and, thus, are more like fixed pay. Effective executive compensation packages typically comprises of the following components:
- base salary
- annual incentives

- long-term capital accumulation
- deferred compensation arrangements
- supplemental benefits and perquisites
- special severance and retirement arrangements
- employment and change of control agreements

CALIBRATION OF EXECUTIVE COMPENSATION TO PERFORMANCE

The concept of calibrating pay to performance is a *market value measure* (Fig. 11.1). On the x-axis, we could include shareholder value, revenue growth, or other suitable metrics of business performance. On the y-axis, we can plot the total compensation percentile. The key to the model is ensuring that the parameters being selected are pertinent so that the right set of behaviour is being encouraged. To simply say that a particular executive is a high performer may not only be a sweeping generalization, it may also be in reference to measures that are not currently important to the organization.

It helps in fair and objective measures to evaluate performance and accordingly decide the market rate of executive compensation.

High pay/Low performance	High pay/High performance
Low pay/Low performance	Low pay/High performance

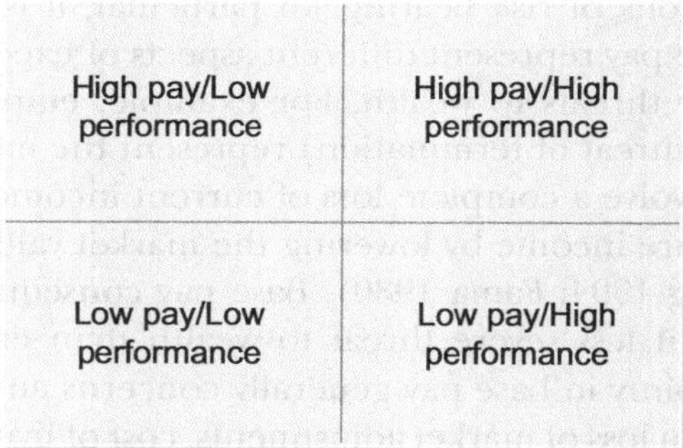

FIG. 11.1 Pay calibration

TRANSPARENCY IN EXECUTIVE COMPENSATION

Executive compensation issues have now become more complicated because of increased transparency and tough information disclosure norms. Due to emergence of international pay markets in a globalized economy, executive compensation is now being increasingly linked with performance. Following are some emerging trends in executive compensation.

- Increase in the number of corporate meltdowns is now dragging executive pay and corporate governance into the public domain.

- Business conditions are putting pressures on existing pay levels and structures.
- Corporate restraint and accountability make controlling executive compensation a major issue in tough economic times.
- Executive compensation movements at the median of the market are getting subdued over the years.

EXECUTIVE COMPENSATION THEORIES

To sustain competitive advantage, organizations always focus on retention of executives because of their inimitable skill and knowledge base. Neoclassical economists consider profit maximization, which in turn maximizes the gains of the owners or shareholders, as the core objective of an organization. In the era of corporatization, executives are preferred to manage organizations. Shareholders and owners trust executives with managing the show in the belief that their professional skills would help the organization succeed. However, executives may take undue advantage to pursue their own interests by overriding owners' or shareholders' interest. Since the goals of shareholders (principal) and executives (agents) are not congruent, executives may engage in opportunistic behaviour for maximizing their personal gains at the cost of the principal. Executives can be dissuaded from such pursuits if they get higher than market level compensation. However, organizations cannot ignore their core objective of profitability for the sake of increased level of executive compensation. Therefore, there is need to design executive compensation innovatively, primarily with three core components—cash (salary and bonus), perquisites and supplementary benefits, and long-term incentives.

Most executive compensation theories centre on the theories of firms. With profit maximization as the core objective, firms rely heavily on their executives. This syndrome encourages executives to expect above normal compensation. However, granting cash compensation without considering cost aspects adversely affects the interest of firms. Although firms can always benchmark their compensation packages with the market rate, they may not be able to make good performers out of executives even after payment of the benchmarked salary rate. They need to identify compensation options that help them derive benefits of performance satisfaction and increased executive retention.

Perquisites and supplementary benefits represent a very small fraction of executive compensation due to tax burden. Organizations need to design tax-efficient long-term incentive packages. However, the worth of long-term incentive packages is difficult to determine. For example, the future value of stock options is uncertain. Its value cannot be predicted with surety even by using different established models. Four classes of variables such as corporate size, firm performance, industry characteristics, and human capital attributes are considered primary determinants of stock value.

In general, a firm's size is ascertained based on its sales, assets, and number of employees. Executive jobs in a large organization are more complex than in a small one. Hence, large firms pay higher compensation to executives. Another reason for large firms to pay more to executives is the number of hierarchical levels. Organizations make pay differentials between hierarchical levels, resulting in more pay for executives.

Another analogy for a higher level of executive compensation is *sales maximization hypothesis*. Executives achieve better results by increasing sales, which makes them beneficiaries of higher compensation. With sales maximization, organizations achieve growth that leads to increase in the power of executives at the expense owners. This makes it possible for executives to pursue their own interests and accumulate wealth.

Another important economic determinant of executive compensation is the performance of the firm. Executives are accountable for the firm's performance. Hence, their compensation is linked to the results of organizational performance. Although, there is a lack of adequate empirical evidence in this respect, changes in executive compensation can be indexed or aligned to the performance of the organization. Following is a simple statistical model to explain the influence of organizational performance on the growth of executive salary:

$$\text{Base salary growth} = a + b_1 \text{ Revenue growth} + b_2 \text{ Profit growth} + e$$

where a = Intercept term; b_1 and b_2 = Coefficients of revenue growth and profit growth; e = Standard error

Executive compensation can also vary with the type of industry. For example, the compensation packages in the service sector are higher than those of the manufacturing sector. Again, within the service industry, IT and ITES organizations pay higher compensation than transport service providers. All these cannot be explained in terms of the quality of manpower required. Typical occupational hazards, security, and safety involved in a job could also be reasons for compensation differences. For example, the ground engineer of an airline may get less salary than in-flight personnel.

Another important economic variable is the difference in human capital. Variation in human capital makes significant differences in performance and productivity on the job, and may be due to education, work experience, and skill differences. The underlying rationale for increased level of executive compensation is that those who have invested more in enriching their value should be paid better than others.

Political and social factors also influence executive compensation. Due to their proximity with authority, executives can manipulate and get higher compensation. This is known as power politics. In the same manner, social norms can also make a significant difference in executive compensation. Based on the previous discussions, following are some theories of executive compensation:

Agency theory Shareholders are principles of the company because of their ownership rights. They delegate control to top executives who represent their ownership interests. Compensation for the top executives is designed keeping in mind the mutual interests. The compensation is designed in a way that serves the best mutual interests of shareholders as well as the virtual owners, that is, the top executives of the organizations.

Tournament theory According to this theory, compensation is viewed as the prize in a series of tournaments or contests among middle and top-level managers who aspire to become the CEO. Winners of the tournament at one level enter the next tournament. In other words, an executive's promotion to a higher rank signifies a win and more lucrative compensation represents the prize.

Social comparison theory This theory suggests designing compensation by comparing it with earned by similar individuals. The idea behind this theory is to ensure social justice by complying with the principles of equity. In organizations, this approach is enforced by not varying the pay levels in the same grade, despite the fact that new incumbents may possess more skills and knowledge.

Balance sheet approach This approach aims to provide expatriates compensation based on the standard of living they normally enjoy in their own country. When Indian companies depute their executives and employees abroad, they allow their current salary to accumulate and provide a separate salary to accommodate their cost of living in countries where they are posted.

Headquarters-based pay It refers to compensation to all according to the rate used at headquarters. Global organizations, like the UN, may follow this principle of compensation design. However, this approach may not work well in the era of globalized economy as organizations seek to expand their arms beyond national boundaries to enjoy cost competitiveness by varying their pay levels.

Golden handcuffs It refers to compensation components earned over a period of time that assist in retaining an employee. Many organizations practice this approach to control attrition. Some organizations deliberately provide newly recruited or relatively less experienced employees a salary or designation disproportionate to what they deserve. For example, an MBA with two years of experience may be given the designation of vice-president with a compensation package much higher than the market benchmark. This dissuades young executives from leaving the job as they know that they will not get a similar salary and status in other organizations. In India, such practices are evident in many new generation companies.

Another example of golden handcuffs may be giving loyalty bonus points or phantom stock for every year of completed service with a cap (qualifying services) at five or ten years of service. This means that to get the benefit, employees need to remain with the company.

Competency-based pay It refers to a pay directly related to the kinds and levels of competencies required in the performance of the work or job. This requires identifying the set of competencies required for the job and then assessing the employees individually to identify the level of available competencies and aligning the same with their compensation level.

Golden parachutes It refers to the practice of providing pay and benefits to executives after their termination resulting from a change in ownership or a corporate takeover. This is particularly true for very senior level executives, who may dictate this condition in their terms of employment to protect their interests in the event of a takeover. However in India, some recent judgments of Supreme Court questioned the sanctity of such practices leaving them to the discretion of the acquiring organization, which may or may not alter service conditions of employees of the organization being acquired. A Hay Group study in 2006 showed that French executives' golden parachutes are the highest. They receive double their salary and bonus.

An alternative to golden parachutes is the golden handshake plan. If a golden handshake is provided for in the terms of appointment of executives, they become eligible for a significant severance package if they are fired, retired, or required to quit due to organizational restructuring.

Cafeteria plan Executives may be given the option to choose different types of benefits, which is commonly known as the cafeteria plan. For example, health insurance, group-term life insurance, and flexible spending accounts all represent medical benefits. Executives may select either of these alternatives as compensation benefits. Cafeteria plan is also used in some Indian organizations, which give the employee the flexibility to choose between contributory provident funds and pensions.

Profit-sharing plan It provides direct or indirect payments based on the organization's profitability, apart from regular compensation. Although employee stock options are a good example, a more applicable fit is the Tata Group's economic value-added (EVA) plan.

EXECUTIVE COMPENSATION DESIGN

Executive compensation design process links compensation criteria such as organizational performance or size to compensation consequences such as pay at risk. Such process or mechanism is categorized into two forms—the process that centres on contract and the process that involves direct monitoring of the executive. Organizations that follow the contract process make it a time-bound employment offer, which becomes a legal arrangement. Contracts specify criteria for compensation, basis of compensation (in the form of schedules), and some predictable conditions for linking compensation consequences to criteria. Direct monitoring is a behavioural approach to monitor the performance of the executive. It is a subjective evaluation. The contractual process differs from direct supervision with respect to a number of characteristics such as objectivity, specificity, and precision. Each process can be studied further with respect to approach, level of analysis, and degree of consistency. In this section, critical differences between the contract and direct supervision mechanism are explained in detail.

Direct supervision or control process is based on the agency theory, which advocates the need to monitor agents (executives) by organizational board members, who are knowledgeable and capable of judging the quality of executive performance. For junior level executives, it may follow the system of mutual monitoring through senior level managers, or by peers or the subordinates in cases where the system of 360-degree performance evaluation is followed. In some cases, organizations can extend such monitoring to the alignment of incentives and bonus to the shareholders' (that is, the principal's) interests. The underlying reason for this is that shareholders or principals bear more risk if the agents (executives) fail to deliver. Therefore, contractual risk is always assessed under some criteria or the other. Agency theory focuses considerable attention on specification of the contract (Jensen and Meckling 1976). From an agency perspective, principals are always susceptible to opportunity costs as an ideal convergence of interests of principals and agents is highly improbable. Agents may be tempted to take advantage of their positions leading to an increase in cost for the principals.

Keeping in view such probable risk, Eisenhardt (1989) suggested two possible mechanisms—principal–agent and positivist. *Principal–agent perspective*, as already mentioned, always focuses on control of agency costs. Hence, it always tries to adopt an optimal employment contract to optimize the joint utility of both agents and principals. The underlying assumptions are that agents are risk averse and try to further their own self-interests, which are different from those of the principals. We cannot examine one form of pay without the other because of their differences in relative risk characteristics. From a principal's perspective, the award of fixed pay carries more risk and uncertainty than variable pay. Therefore, principals try to transfer more risk to agents by increasing the proportion of variable pay. When principals are unable to assess agents' behaviour in designing compensation, they tend to make a trade-off between the cost of measuring agents' behaviour and the cost of transferring risk to the agent, and in the process balance the compensation design. However, as observed by Jensen and Murphy (1990), there is little support in the agency theory for the notion that optimal contracting aligns executive and shareholder interests. Optimal contracting is the positivist approach to executive compensation design, and based on ethical and political considerations.

Of all the theories, only the principal–agent tradition within the agency theory explicitly examines the role of compensation consequences. The central argument of this tradition considers risk properties of each consequence to explain risk preferences. In general, executives' risks are tagged with the employment, which cannot be diversified. On the contrary, principals may diversify the risk by changing their investment options. Such difference between the agents and the principals produces agency cost by causing principals to prefer high return or high risk strategy and agents to prefer low risk or low return strategy (Hill and Snell 1988). Therefore, the amount of compensation risk incurred by the agent is expected to have a direct effect on managerial decisions such as capital investments, R&D expenditures, diversification, and industry choices (Boschen and Smith 1995).

Use of Performance Criteria

Use of performance criteria to design executive compensation depends on measurable performance targets, behaviour, job requirements, experience of the executives, job role, peer compensation, market considerations, and the size of the organization (Table 11.1).

These criteria are then studied in the context of time span such as long or short-term compensation, and the nature of measurement. The nature of measurement, on the other hand, accounts for profitability versus market-based measures, qualitative versus quantitative measures, etc. (Gomez-Mejia and Balkin 1992).

Context of Executive Compensation Design

Executive compensation design affects the firm's strategy and the culture in various ways. This requires us to examine executive compensation from different contexts. The decision context encompasses the individual choices of executives. The strategic context examines organizational goals and suggests

TABLE 11.1 Measurement of performance criteria

Criteria	Parameters
Performance targets	Key result areas (KRA), Key performance areas (KPA), Key sales objectives (KSO), or even some protocol bound performance specification
Behaviour	Performance impact
Job requirements	Quality of actions in terms of job requirements or fulfilment of a prescribed role
Experience of the executives	Experience, talent, and skills
Job role	Hierarchy and role requirements
Peer compensation	Pay differences between the executives
Market considerations	Benchmarked compensation information
Size of the organization	Large, medium, or small
Nature of the organization	Public limited, closely held, or family business

matching resources to goal achievement. Environmental and cultural factors examine industry characteristics, national and global, economic, cultural, and political factors. The influence of contextual factors on executive compensation decisions has now started gaining importance in a globalized world. Cultural factors examine the effect of compensation strategies across countries. This aspect is more important for multinationals and transnational organizations. At times, it may require organizations to vary compensation rates among their foreign subsidiaries, considering the local culture where they operate. Environmental contexts require that firms design compensation, keeping in view fluctuations in the environment. Therefore, compensation issues have multiple dimensions. Following are some important contexts of executive compensation.

Decision context

Compensation design in the decisional context considers a decision maker's problems and is part of behavioural economics. Executive compensation decisions, either negative or positive, affect the decision makers' perception of the problem as well as the preferences. According to utility or preference theory of decision making, in the case of small, trivial issues (trivial employment clauses) decisional preference may not show a risk aversive propensity. However, the same decision maker may be very risk averse when employment clauses are very tough with huge risk attached. Therefore, an individual employee may be risk averse at one point of time and a gambler at another point of time, while considering the same decision. In the compensation context, an individual employee may prefer opting for a job in a large organization with stringent targets over a more stable job with decent compensation in a smaller organization.

Culture and executive compensation

Organizations are distinguished by *the way they do things*. The values, beliefs, norms, and behaviour that employees internalize and use to fit in as well as to do their work and interact with each other and the marketplace represent the culture of an organization. The culture of an organization evolves over time and is influenced by several factors. It is moulded by unusual business conditions. Organizational culture influences managerial practices and compensation decisions. One example of the negative influence of organizational culture on compensation practices is that of legacy-bound Phillips. The company had to hive off its CTV and electric lamps divisions because of high legacy costs, that is, a disproportionately high rate of compensation paid to executives in the past. On the other hand, IBM, another legacy bound organization, has kept pace with the market trend and controlled its compensation costs to remain competitive in the market. Successful compensation design for an organization is possible only when it aligns business strategy, culture, and a vision for the future.

TABLE 11.2 Typical executive compensation component

Base pay	• Cash salary • Flexible benefits • Statutory benefits • May include expatriate payments
Annual incentives	• Linked to business plan • Delivered in cash and/or equity • May include deferral • May be linked to value-added measures
Long-term incentives	• 3- to 5-year timeframe • Cash • Equity shares and/or options • Shareholder value focus • Referenced against peer group

RELATIONSHIP BETWEEN FIXED AND VARIABLE PAY

Globally, fixed compensation still comprises 52 per cent of the total pay structure. The remaining 48 per cent is distributed into short-term incentives (17 per cent) and long-term incentives (31 per cent). However, change in the pay-mix in a volatile, globally competitive market is always possible. With these three—base pay, short-term incentives, and long-term incentives—as core elements, executive compensation in a dynamic marketplace may vary from organization to organization (Table 11.2). The fixed pay component remains more or less unchanged across the organization, whereas the variables such as short-term incentives and long-term incentives may increase or decrease. An evolving international model of executive compensation includes these typical components. However, such components may change from time to time to keep pace with the market.

PERFORMANCE MEASUREMENT IN EXECUTIVE INCENTIVE PROGRAMMES

In most organizations, executives are rewarded independent of company performance. Such practices lend weight to the argument that executives get rich at the expense of shareholders. Due to such negative perceptions, linking executive compensation to organizational performance and the creation of value for shareholders has become extremely important. Effective performance measures ensure that executive compensation is commensurate with performance. Regardless of the industry, the incentive performance measures should ideally meet. They should be the following:

- capable of being aligned with shareholders' interests
- definable
- measurable

- controllable
- easily communicated and understood

Assessing potential performance objectives against these criteria can help to ensure the appropriateness of the measure or measures being used. As an indication of how certain measurement categories stack up, Table 11.3 briefly evaluates shareholder return-based measures and company-specific measures against the criteria discussed previously. Total shareholder return (TSR) has become a popular performance measurement criterion, particularly for stock options plans. However, some organizations emphasize other internal financial performance criteria such as return on equity (ROE), earnings per share (EPS), and economic value-added (EVA). In the context of previous discussed criteria, there is merit in both shareholder return based measures and company-specific measures.

The important point that can be deduced from Table 11.3 is that in some cases company-specific measures may be more appropriate than shareholder return measures, particularly in circumstances where executives have very little influence over the market valuation of their companies. A thorough process, as laid out in the following section, can ensure that the most effective and appropriate measures are used.

Organizations need to consider various external and internal factors to identify the correct performance measures over time. Some of the external inputs for performance measures could be the following:

- follow industry standards for short, medium, and long-term incentives
- identify external value drivers to understand the state of the economy

TABLE 11.3 Shareholders' returns versus company-specific measures

Criteria	Shareholder return based measures (TSR, share price growth)	Company-specific financial measures (ROE, EPS, etc.)
Aligned with shareholder	Directly aligned	Indirectly aligned. Proper measures may reinforce interest performance that drives value creation over long term.
Definable	Yes	Typically definable, assuming adequate financial reporting standards.
Measurable	Easily measured. Relative TSR presents issues related to choosing appropriate peer groups.	Easily measured. Progress can be communicated quarterly. Harder to measure relative performance in timely manner.
Controllable	Somewhat, unless economic and/or market factors dominate price. Influence may be limited to top tier executive group.	Typically more controllable than those subject to market volatility.
Easily communicated and understood	Yes, if properly designed.	Yes, if properly designed.

TABLE 11.4 Short- to long-term performance objectives

Timeframe measurement criteria	Short-term (1 year)	Mid-term (3 to 5 years)	Long-term (5 to 10 years)
Measurement focus	Profit, efficiency, and operational objectives	Reinforce performance, which drives value in the long run	Assess market return
Measurement examples	Operating profit,	ROE, EVA, ROI, TSR, EBIT, and EBITDA	TSR or share price or share price
Measurement vehicle	Cash	Performance cycle plan, payable in cash or shares	Options and/or shares

- understand the relevance of any financial ratio, which is generally attributable to industry situation

Similarly, internal inputs for performance measures could be:
- understand internal value drivers
- focus on key strategic objectives
- link executive behaviour to business performance

Both internal and external value drivers significantly influence decisions on executive incentives. Another executive incentive determinant is the time frame of performance objectives. Short-term incentives are payable for short-term performance objectives as it is inappropriate to link them with the long-term incentives. The same is true for long-term performance objectives. Performance measurement criteria also change with the time frame of performance objectives. Some indicative measurement criteria are presented in Table 11.4.

Stock options as long-term incentives for executive compensation create problems for both the organization and executives. Therefore, performance-based incentive plans are now getting more attention. Following are important benefits of performance-based incentives plans:

- increased retention of key executives, allowing organization to focus on strategic goals
- feasibility of rewarding executives for meeting performance goals, even when stock prices are low
- better control over incentives to manipulate the performance of executives

Determining appropriate performance measures and relating the same to executive compensation in the short- and long-term is a difficult task for any organization.

EXECUTIVE COMPENSATION AND ORGANIZATIONAL STRATEGY

There is much debate over how executive compensation can be related to organizational strategy or organizational performance. Without going into the details of the debate, it is pertinent to mention that the alignment of work with business strategy takes priority. Hence, organizations need to design executive compensation to reward the work, which will then by default fulfill organizational strategy. Designing executive compensation in the era of economic uncertainty, while rationalizing expectations of the executives and fulfilling organizational strategy, is a very challenging task. Following are some action plans to meet this strategic intent, while retaining a trade-off between executive compensation and organizational objectives.

1. Optimize the cost of compensation for health and welfare benefits, while identifying vendors. An overall health care platform can be created in the organization, varying the coverage and contributions, keeping pace with hierarchical levels.
2. Rationalize the compensation budget by restructuring the deferral components of compensation. For example, a qualifying period for retention bonuses can be stretched to the future to dissuade executives from encashing their loyalty or retention bonus amount. This will persuade executives to continue with the company to enjoy the high rate of interest.
3. Optimize the cost of retirement benefits using funded pension assets through stock build-up. This will not only ensure cost optimization, but also help in realizing other HR-related costs such as cost of severance, disability, and bonuses.
4. Identify wasteful HR costs by reviewing and restructuring the terms of contracts. When executives are retained from HR outsourcing vendors, organizations can consolidate their decentralized activities and achieve economies of scale.

Based on these action plans, executive compensations are reframed, while considering contracts and monitoring mechanism. Some of the criteria, which are considered, are executives' performance, behaviour, size, market, etc. Apart from these, firms also consider peer performances, individual characteristics, and role or position criteria. These action plans can help organizations realize their objectives.

Organization Level Practices

Executive compensation policies adopted by organizations are very complex and differ from one organization to another. In addition, it is difficult to measure the output and effort of executives leading to difficulty in exerting control over factors in any earnings equation. Differences in organizational approaches can be classified into—human capital approach and organizational performance approach. In *organizational performance approach*, contributing factors are used as an explanatory variable as such factors actually contribute to the improvement of organizational performance. This approach is not usually followed by Indian organizations, who generally adopt a human capital approach. Indian organizations largely make use of performance data as criteria to determine efficiency. However, internationally several organizations use both criteria as determinants of executive function. Ang et al. (2002) developed an executive compensation model for the IT companies of Singapore using both human capital and institutional variables (organizational performance) as criteria. The results indicated that human capital variables such as education and experience were strong determinants of executive compensation. Their study further indicated that institutional variables such as the size of the organization moderated the relationship between compensation and human capital. The rationale is that large organizations pay more to executives with higher education, whereas small firms pay more to executives with lower education. A study of Indian IT companies by Parthasarathy (2007) using both human capital and organizational performance as determinants of executive compensation provided the following equation.

$$\text{Executive compensation} = f(\text{Level of hierarchy, Firm effects, Time effects, Education, and Work experience}) \tag{7.1}$$

This is similar to the tournament model of executive compensation. The spread in compensation between successive levels keeps on increasing as executives move up the hierarchy. In this equation level of hierarchy, firm effects, and time effects are institutional variables, whereas education and work experience are human capital variables. They found that a tournament structure existed because of differences in compensation between levels. Hence, prima facie hierarchy was the dominant determinant of executive compensation. However, the study failed to track any evidence of human capital variables acting as determinants of executive compensation.

The benefit plans employees like best are not always the most expensive. People value things other than money. Convenience is a huge benefit, whether it comes in the form of an on-site cafeteria or the ability to work from home on occasions. Lack of hassle also counts. Not many employees want to have to evaluate health care providers or car leasing companies. Anything that makes life easier is usually more than welcomed. This applies to the way benefits are administered as much as to the actual benefits themselves. However, benefits cost a lot—25–30 per cent on top of payroll—and organizations need to know they are getting value for money. Therefore, organizations need to be smart about benefit programme design and even smarter about implementation.

According to critics, it is not possible to align compensation with business results. Compensation can be aligned only with the work that executives perform. Such alignment through work of executives ensures the achievement of the strategic intent of the organization. Hence, some compensation management experts prefer to create compensation systems that reward the work of executives who help in realizing the strategy.

Organizations often face problems due to resistance from people during the introduction of a new compensation system. Some of the important guidelines for reducing such resistance are—making executives understand the system, listening to their feedback, convincing top management to appreciate that enhanced compensation can improve productivity and performance, etc. Implementation of new compensation systems would be more effective, if it is decided through a conversation rather than through an order.

DIFFERENT CRITERIA OF EXECUTIVE COMPENSATION

Some important perspectives of executive compensation are elaborated in this section.

Strategy criterion

Executive compensation issues are now much discussed because of their performance implication and strategic perspective. Although we all believe that strategic design of executive compensation may have significant bearing on the financial performance of companies, empirical evidence to prove this is lacking. It is also difficult to come out with an executive compensation model that truly integrates an organization's strategies and performance outcome. The strategic dimensions of executive compensation are much discussed due to the rising cost of compensation, which for many organizations is their second biggest expense. Hence, aligning executive compensation with organizational performance and overall strategy has some legitimacy. Some of the important steps taken by organizations to elevate executive compensation to a strategic level are—making incentive pay contingent upon the product life cycle, emphasizing on technology, relating compensation to organizational strategies, and finally following an organic compensation strategy rather than a mechanistic one. Organic strategies are adopted keeping in view contingency factors to ensure flexibility for organizations to review and change such strategies time to time in order to sustain themselves in a competitive environment. Mechanistic strategies are adopted by organizations on the assumption of market linearity and the absence of economic volatility.

Gerhart and Milkovich's (1990) study of managerial compensation found that variable pay design differs from organization to organization. It is not related to organizational characteristics such as size, type of industry, and performance. Based on such observations, they suggested that differences in compensation design match with differences in strategy. However, in this case also, we lack any conclusive evidence of a causal relationship. From corporate practice, it is evident that approaches towards strategic fits of compensation differ on the type of strategies to be adopted by organizations. A defender-oriented organization prefers annual bonus plans and cash incentives. Such organizations also prefer performance accounting. A prospector-oriented organization prefers stock-based incentive plans with market-based criteria. Therefore, a link between strategy, performance, and compensation, even though not empirically established is attempted by many organizations because they want to address both compensation cost aspects and the firm's profitability, and also achieve a trade-off between compensation and performance outcome. In this chapter, we began by explaining the difference in compensation practices between executives and other lower rung employees, stating that firms should always try to minimize the compensation differences between these hierarchical levels. In reality, it is observed that firms pay low salaries to workers who are available in abundance or for jobs which can be easily outsourced. Almost all the private sector banks in our country practice this to lower their cost of services and remain competitive in the market. Therefore, compensation designing from strategic perspectives is widely practised by organizations, even though it is not explainable by a cause–effect relationship.

Role or position criterion

Hierarchical positions or organizational roles also have a contributing effect on executive compensation design. Gomez-Mejia (1992), Simon (1957), and Lazear and Rosen (1981) focused on the importance of this aspect. They attributed the linking of compensation to position as a strategy to stimulate others to achieve the same results. In addition, executives act as figureheads and hence, they should be compensated more than others in the lower rungs. However, organizations are now experimenting with structures to respond to the changing environment. It may be essential at times to delay and sacrifice the traditional hierarchical structure. In such cases, executive compensation may not be aligned with their figurehead roles. This can be illustrated citing examples of higher pay for some professions such as airline pilots, SAP consultants, etc. They get high salaries, which do not depend on their hierarchies, because of their functional importance.

Individual characteristics criterion

Human capital theory (Agarwal 1981) argues that the individual holding the position, especially their accumulated knowledge and skills, explains compensation levels. This theory assumes that the amount of human capital possessed by executives influences their productivity and, thus, should influence their compensation. That is, 'an executive with a greater amount of human capital would be better able to perform his job and, thus, be paid more.'

Performance criterion

This perspective of executive compensation is widely applicable. It emanates from the agency theory approach, which suggests linkage of executive compensation to the firm's performance. Executives contribute to the firm's performance, which is measurable. Hence, their compensation should be based on their contribution to the organization.

Behaviour criterion

Actions and processes of executives, while performing the jobs, depict their behaviour. Behaviour criteria are associated with the monitoring mechanism, and executives take strategic initiatives while making a subjective analysis of business decisions. Therefore, executive compensation design based on behaviour criterion makes sense. However, executive behaviour is difficult to measure and all behavioural inputs cannot be linked with the specific outcome. Further, outcome of behaviour is contingent upon circumstances and difficult to interpret. Hence, in designing executive compensation, this aspect did not receive much attention from the corporate world, although it is practised by some in a limited way.

Size criterion

Size of organizations as a determinant of executive compensation is a much discussed issue. However, it is less important than the performance perspective. Within the same business group, large organizations often offer higher executive compensation than smaller ones in order to retain talent.

Market criterion

Market perspective of executive compensation emanates from the marginal productivity theory (Roberts 1956). It argues that market forces (supply and demand for executive talent) determine executive pay. As per this theory, the services of the executive to the firm should be treated as any other factor or input of production. The price or value of that input (i.e., compensation in the case of the executive) is determined by the intersection of supply and demand in the market for that input, (i.e., labour market for executives) which in equilibrium, is equal to its marginal revenue product.

Peer compensation criterion

The social comparison theory (O'Reilly et al. 1988) suggests that the compensation of selected peers may play a role in setting executive pay. Unlike market forces, social comparison theory is concerned with deliberate decisions. Often board members of an organization use themselves as a referral point in their executive pay recommendations.

RECENT STUDIES ON EXECUTIVE COMPENSATION

According to a new study by Watson Wyatt and the Human Resource Planning Society (HRPS), functions such as performance management, rewards, succession planning, recruiting, communications, HR technology, and the overall HR function can significantly contribute to shareholder value if companies design and implement their programmes in a formalized way. Watson and HRPS surveyed 50 companies, in the Fortune 1000 list, that averaged $3.5 billion in annual revenue and employed more than 6,000 people. In each area, the study identified practices that were linked to high employee engagement, financial performance, and effectiveness.

The most significant part of the study is the rewards programmes, which add the most to a company's market premium. It is targeted at high-potential employees. In addition, it is aligned with business goals and integrated with talent management. Value is added in performance management by avoiding a preset distribution of performance ratings. According to Ilene Gochman, national practice leader in organization effectiveness for Watson Wyatt and the study's author, the study highlights 'the need to be pretty deliberate about how you spend your time and money on programme design and implementation'.

Most organizations today try to set up a template—how you acquire it, value it, and add to it—for base salary or incentive compensation, profit sharing, goal setting, measurement, and equity sharing. They pay competitively by benchmarking with the local labour market and national trends within the industry. The base pay increases based on the merit. Profit sharing and equity plans are adopted to reward employees. In fact, organizations today try to link their compensation strategy with business strategy. If the two don't align, compensation design may give a different direction, which would not be in line with the visions of the organization.

Organizations may also design compensation for executives using a balanced scorecard approach. For example, the financial perspective measures financial ratios necessary to run the business. Executives can be rewarded based on how financially profitable the business is. Similarly from a customer perspective, customer satisfaction is considered the most important factor. Hence, executive compensation can be based on meeting customer satisfaction targets. From internal business process perspectives, parameters, such as response time, back-office efficiencies, assets under management per employee, etc., can be linked to executive compensation. Finally, from the learning and growth perspective, executive compensation can be designed based on who increase the value of the organization.

Although there are operational differences in executive compensation design, the most commonly used methodologies try to measure employees using a one-to-five scale on attributes such as client sensitivity, attitude, initiative, reliability, job knowledge, judgment, corporate/team impact, work quality, work quantity, and communication skills.

Say on Pay

Excessive executive compensation even at the cost of stakeholders' interest has now become a global issue. In India too, we find differential compensation management practices between executives and non-executives in the same organization. Due to increase in the focus on corporate governance, executive compensation issues in India are now required to be more transparent.

Globally some of the executive compensation issues have become important centre for discussion. For example in 2008, Robert A. Iger of Walt Disney was given 78 per cent more compensation, over the package of previous year offered to their earlier CEO. Similarly in 2001, CEO of Ford Motor Co. Jacques Nasser was offered very high executive compensation despite mounting loss suffered by the company. In India, we also have similar examples in companies such as Jindal Steel and Power, Hero Honda, and Bharti Airtel.

Increased compensation to those in the C-suite, even when the organization is struggling to survive is common across the world. *Say on pay* is a movement, which gives opportunity to company's shareholder to oppose or approve executive compensation by voting against or for it. Such shareholder endorsement on executive compensation has almost now become essential in public limited companies.

Executive compensation is now the top most corporate governance issues across the world. Disproportionate hike in executive compensation without aligning it with pay and performance can be attributed to the growth of the say on pay movement. Two shareholders' advisory firms, Institutional Shareholder Services (ISS) and Glass, Lewis & Co., come out with their recommendation either in favour or against the say on pay. They do so based on their select peer group comparison of pay and performance. These two advisory firms significantly influence company's decisions on executive compensation. For example, companies now consider inputs from the select peer groups, go for performance alignment, and also account for the negative influence of pledging of shares. Advisory firm like ISS annually conducts study on pay for performance and come out with their recommendations on peer group alignment, absolute alignment, etc. These recommendations have significant influence on shareholders' say on pay.

Robert Iger, the CEO of Walt Disney Co. over the years has become one of the centre of discussion on say on pay movement across the world. Iger's compensation was questioned by several critics, including some pension funds (institutional investors). Despite much negativity on Iger's compensation package, shareholders of Disney approved his pay plan with a wide margin. Therefore, advisory firms' recommendations may not necessarily influence the say on pay decisions of the shareholders.

In India, executive compensation issues are gradually becoming more transparent. Companies Act 2013 has a provision that puts maximum limit of managerial remuneration at 11 per cent of net profit. In addition, companies are now required to disclose the rationale behind the executive compensation increase in relation with the business performance and the median compensation of the employees. In spite of these, we still find disproportionate compensation packages in Indian organizations. Aon Hewitt study indicates average difference in compensation package between Indian CEOs and entry-level employees is highest in the world. Institutionalized approach to say on pay can help alleviate this age old malice in Indian companies.

SUMMARY

Executives, who make up only a small percentage of the workforce, are the most important group of employees for any organization. Executive compensation represents the highest percentage of cost to total compensation in organizations. Executive compensation design has direct relevance to the achievement of strategic and business objectives of the organization. Optimizing executive compensation cost and at the same time keeping executives satisfied so that they can continue with the organization is the most important challenge for organizations.

The usual components of executive compensation are base pay and variables (incentive pay). Base pay is fixed and usually remains more or less constant across organizations. Variables and incentive plans are performance aligned, which organizations design keeping in view the strategic fit. Hence, it differs from organization to organization. Benchmarking the best compensation management practices, HR managers design variables and incentive plans that relate it to the work performed by executives, the business results, or the overall strategy of the organization. In the process, such practices differ. Various short-term and long-term incentives are innovatively selected to ensure that executives continue with the organization and perform. Although stock option plans are often chosen as the best alternative, organizations in general and executives in particular do not like to link it to performance incentive plan due to difficulty in its valuation. Various other innovative deferral compensation plans such as loyalty bonuses (at the incremental rate of appreciation with the number of years served), pensions, and non-monetary benefits are chosen keeping in view cost efficiency, executives' satisfaction and performance. In a competitive industry, we also have examples of high executive compensation going up to as much as 500 times workers' pay. Globally, executive compensation is now part of corporate governance systems. Designing executive compensation requires knowledge about strategic and business issues, performance management aspects, market rate, and appropriate selection of criteria.

Key Terms

Agency theory This theory requires designing compensation in a way that it serves the best mutual interests of shareholders and the top executives of organizations.

Benchmarking The practice of comparing compensation with other competing organizations to offer a competitive pay package to employees. It is used to enhance employee retention.

Broadband pay It is a pay structure form that leads to the consolidation of existing pay grades and pay ranges into fewer but wider pay grades.

Cafeteria plan It offers a choice between different types of benefits. For example, health insurance, group-term life insurance, and flexible spending accounts, represent medical benefits. Executives may select any of these alternatives as a compensation benefit. Cafeteria plan is also evident in some Indian organizations, which give employees the flexibility to choose between the contributory provident fund and pension.

Decision context It considers the framing of problems of a decision maker, and is part of behavioural economics. Executive compensation decisions, either negative or positive, affect decision makers' perceptions of the problem, and also their preferences.

Earnings per share (EPS) It represents the organization's net income divided by the number of shares.

Golden handcuffs Compensation components earned over a period of time that assist in retaining an employee.

Golden parachutes This approach provides pay and benefits to executives after their termination resulting from a change in ownership or corporate takeover.

Return on equity (ROE) The organization's net income divided by the average of shareholders' equity.

Tournament theory As per this theory, compensation is the prize in a series of tournaments or contests among middle and top-level managers, who aspire to become CEOs.

Exercises

Concept Review Questions

1. What are the components of executive compensation? Which components do you feel are more important for retention of executives?
2. Examine different theories of executive compensation. Which theories do you consider are more applicable for a labour-intensive manufacturing organization?
3. Explain the importance of performance criteria in designing executive compensation.
4. How can you align executive compensation to organizational strategy? Answer using example of an organization.

Critical Thinking Question

Critically review the following pay package details of a human resource manager, who will be on probation for the first year (Table 11.5). Comment whether the company, keeping in view the need for retention of business school graduates, should consider any other executive compensation component.

TABLE 11.5 Pay package

	Component	Amount (₹) per annum	Remarks
A	Basic salary	1,23,750	
B	Cash emoluments	38,023	
	Leave travel allowance		Taxable cash out if not availed
	Out patient medical	7,500	No cash out allowed if not availed
	Special allowance	23,023	Balancing figure does not attract PF, superannuation, or gratuity
C = A + B	Total cash	1,61,773	
D	Conveyance	12,000	
	Conveyance allowance		
E	Retirement benefits	39,353	
	Provident fund	14,850	12% of Basic salary
	Superannuation	18,563	15% of Basic salary
	Gratuity	5,940	4.8% of Basic salary
F	Housing	61,875	
	Company leased housing/HRA	61,875	Maximum of 50% of basic salary in metros
G = C + D + E + F	Total fixed pay	2,75,000	Any tax liability shall be borne by the executive

CASE STUDY: Executive Compensation Strategy in Fortune Furnitech

Fortune Furnitech is a state-of-the-art modular furniture manufacturer, which was started with an initial ₹500 crore investment by raising a term loan from different financial institutions and about 65 per cent contribution from the traditional family business. The group has a traditional family history of woodcraft manufacturing. Leveraging the know-how, the present owner Asim Singh and his wife Ragini ventured into this business. Asim Singh has toured extensively all over the world, right from his childhood, with his father. According to Singh, India has top quality berg woods in its North-eastern states, which are imported by countries like the US. However, Indians use them as firewood due to lack of awareness. The company launched an ambitious plan to manufacture and sell hardwood furniture worldwide as their study indicated that the Indian market for furniture is still unorganized and that the affluent class uses imported furniture made out of concentrated wood dust or waste products.

To achieve this goal, the company recruited the best designers, business heads, and production people from around the world. Many designers were either Italian-born, or trained in Italy. The biggest challenge the company faced was in designing managerial compensation.

Management compensation received attention primarily because of its performance implications and strategic fit in Fortune Furnitech. The HR manager claimed that it had a positive effect on the company's financial performance and recommended the appropriateness of different compensation for specific strategic situations. However, he could not convince the top management of the need to formulate an executive compensation package accordingly.

Asim Singh only considered such alignment for executives on the board, arguing that their achievement was traceable. The HR manager argued that compensation cost in the company was the second largest expense category, the first being the cost of raw materials and other implements (except labour). Hence, it had to be managed strategically aligning with the performance of the organization and its fit with overall organizational strategy. He supplied extensive literature to sell his argument. He complained that the organization did not have a well-documented compensation philosophy, despite evidence that there should be one. In addition, some incentives were counterproductive. He argued that it is time to develop executive compensation, de-emphasizing the immediate financial gains and tagging it with long-range strategy of the organization. After listening to the HR head's argument, the CEO directed him to develop a model that may work in the organization.

Discussion question

Imagine you are the HR manager. Design the appropriate pay model for executives of the organization.

References

Agarwal, N.C. (1981), 'Determinants of executive compensation', *Industrial Relations*, vol. 20, pp. 36–46.

Agrawal, Anup and Ralph A. Walking (1994), 'Executive careers and compensation surrounding takeover bids', *Journal of Finance*, vol. 49, pp. 985–1014.

Ang, J., B. Lauterbach, and B.Z. Schreiber (2002), 'Pay at the executive suite: How do US banks compensate their top management teams?', *Journal of Banking & Finance*, vol. 26, pp. 11–43.

Balkin, D.B. and L.R. Gomez-Mejia (1987), 'Toward a contingency theory of compensation strategy', *Strategic Management Journal*, vol. 8, pp. 169–82.

Balkin, D.B. and L.R. Gomez-Mejia (1990), 'Matching compensation and organizational strategies', *Strategic Management Journal*, vol. 11, pp. 153–69.

Balkin, D.B., G.D. Markman, and L.R. Gomez-Mejia (2000), 'Is CEO Pay In High-Technology Firms Related to Innovation?', *Academy of Management Journal*, vol. 43, pp. 1118–29.

Bhattacharyya, D.K. (2007), *Human Resource Research Methods*, Oxford University Press, New Delhi.

Boschen, J. and K. Smith (1995), 'You can pay me now and you can pay me later: The dynamic response of executive compensation to firm performance, *Journal of Business*, vol. 68, no. 4, pp. 577–608.

Comp Flash (1995), Executive compensation, American Management Association, p. 3.

Conion, E.J. and J.M. Parks (1990), 'Effects of monitoring and tradition on compensation arrangements: An experiment with principal-agent dyads', *Academy of Management Journal*, vol. 33, no. 3, pp. 603–22.

Coughlan, A.T. and R.M. Schmidt (1985), 'Executive compensation management turnover and firm performance: An empirical investigation', *Journal of Accounting and Economics*, vol. 7, no. 1, pp. 43–66.

Eisenhardt, K. (1989), 'Agency theory: An assessment and review', *Academy of Management Review*, vol. 14, pp. 57–74.

Fama, E. (1980), 'Agency problems and the theory of the firm', *Journal of Political Economy*, vol. 88, no. 2, pp. 288–307.

Gerhart, B. and G.T. Milkovich (1990), 'Organizational differences in managerial compensation and financial performance', *Academy of Management Journal*, vol. 33, pp. 663–91.

Gomez-Mejia L.R. (1992), 'Structure and process of diversification, compensation strategy, and firm performance', *Strategic Management Journal*, vol. 13, pp. 381–97.

Gomez-Mejia, L.R. (1994), 'Executive compensation: A reassessment and future research agenda', in G.R. Ferris (ed.), *Research in Personnel and Human Resource Management*, vol. 12, pp. 161–222.

Gomez-Mejia, L.R. and D. Balkin (1992), *Compensation, Organizational Strategy, and Firm's Performance*, South Western College Publishing, Cincinnati.

Gomez-Mejia, L.R., H. Tosi, and T. Hinkin (1987), 'Managerial control, performance, and executive compensation', *Academy of Management Journal*, vol. 30, pp. 51–70.

Hill, C. and S. Snell (1988), 'External control, corporate strategy, and firm performance in research intensive industries', *Strategic Management Journal*, vol. 9, pp. 577–90.

Jensen, Michael and Kevin Murphy (1990), 'Performance pay and top-management incentives', *Journal of Political Economy*, vol. 98, pp. 225–64.

Jensen, Michael and William Meckling (1976), 'Theory of the firm: Managerial behavior, agency cost and ownership structure', *Journal of Financial Economics*, vol. 3, pp. 305–60.

Lazear, E.P. and S. Rosen (1981), 'Rank order tournaments as optimum labor contracts', *Journal of Political Economy*, vol. 8, no. 5, pp. 841–64.

O'Reilly, C., B. Main, and G. Crystal (1988), 'CEO compensation as tournament and social comparison: A tale of two theories', *Administrative Science Quarterly*, vol. 33, pp. 257–74.

Parthasarthy, A. (2007), 'Best practices: Off-shoring and outsourcing, summary of compensation and benefits survey', 29 May, www.sandhill.com/opinion/daily_blog.php?id=27&post=308, last accessed on 27 August 2007.

Roberts, D. (1956), 'A general theory of executive compensation based on statistically tested propositions', *Quarterly Journal of Economics*, vol. 70, no. 2, pp. 270–94.

Simon, H. (1957), 'The compensation of executives', *Sociometry*, vol. 20, pp. 32–5.

Steers, R. and G.R. Ungson (1987), 'Strategic issues in executive compensation decisions', in Balkin, D.B. and L.R. Gomez-Mejia (eds), *New perspectives on compensation*, Prentice Hall, Englewood Cliffs, New Jersey.

Taussig, F.W. and W.S. Baker (1925), 'American corporations and their executives: A statistical inquiry', *Quarterly Journal of Economics*, vol. 40, no. 1, pp. 1–51.

Watson Wyatt and Human Resource Planning Society (2006), 'How human capital practices link to shareholder value', April, www.watsonwyatt.com, last accessed on 15 February 2007.

CHAPTER TWELVE

Sales Compensation Plan

Learning Objectives

After reading this chapter you will be able to
- understand the concept of sales compensation plan and the issues involved
- analyse the process of sales compensation design and its administration
- examine different components of sales compensation
- assess the relationship between sales incentives and sales force motivation
- understand the concept of contribution-based sales compensation

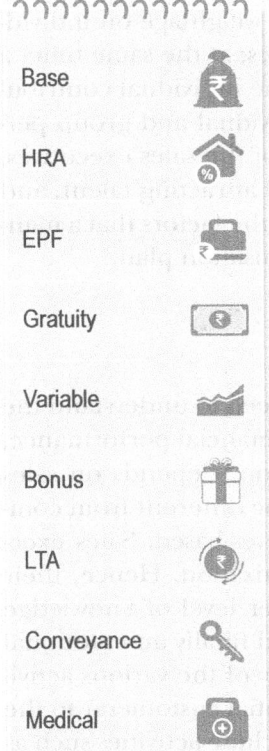

Base
HRA
EPF
Gratuity
Variable
Bonus
LTA
Conveyance
Medical

OPENING CASE

Quota-based Compensation System of Pharmaceutical Companies

Pharmaceutical companies are now increasingly replacing the conventional sales compensation model, based on territory quota, for their medical representatives. The new approach is to offer rewards based on relative performance of peers. The companies believe that this system provides a level playing field for all sales executives. The companies are of the opinion that through this reward system the best performers would win the largest share of the rewards, whereas the worst performers would relatively earn no rewards. The Hay Group survey of 1995 on the compensation trend in pharmaceutical companies indicated that 80 per cent of the pharma sales executives are covered under territorial sales quota-based compensation plan. Traditionally, territorial sales quotas are translated into sales goals for each territory. The major practical difficulties of a quota-based system include aligning new product launches with the quota system and neglect of individual contribution. Often organizations set unrealistically high sales quota for a territory. This, ultimately, frustrates the sales executives as they fail to achieve the targets. Many sales executives are forced to leave their jobs and even change the industry. The biggest operational problem with the quota-based compensation structure is that it encourages sales executives to stop selling after they have achieved the territorial quota, even when possibility for more sales exists, fearing that it would lead to increase in their next year's target.

INTRODUCTION

A sales compensation programme consists of a series of decisions to objectively reward the sales executives, based on individual and group achievement. A sales compensation design requires adequate focus on strategies and business objectives of the organization. While individual sales compensation plan is easy to design, a group sales compensation design requires considerable thought and planning. The most important aspect is to synergize the objectives of the organization to group and individual level performance standards based on the management by objectives (MBO) approach, and then decide on variables and incentives. Therefore, the sales compensation varies with respect to nature of the job and types of products and services. The decision on sales cycle is also another important part of the managerial job. A higher weightage on individual performance may lead to a conflict among colleagues; at the same time, a higher weightage on group performance may neglect the individual contribution. Hence, an appropriate trade-off between the individual and group performance is very important. Understanding behaviour of the sales executives, their expectations, market trend, need for retaining and attracting talent, and competitive pricing of the products/services are some of the factors that a manager needs to understand while designing a sales compensation plan.

UNDERSTANDING THE SALES FUNCTION

Before designing a sales compensation plan, managers need to understand the sales function as it differs from other job families. The financial performance, that is, the top line and bottom line of the organizations depends on sales executives' performance. Sales compensation needs to be different from compensation for other departments as it is largely incentives-based. Sales executives work with customers, who are outside the organization. Hence, their work requires persuasion and interaction skills; a higher level of knowledge of products and services offered by the organization; and finally an emotional balance. Understanding the sales function involves study of the various activities involved from the beginning (i.e., tapping the potential customers) to the end (i.e., concluding a sale deal). Most sales positions include activities such as order-taking, servicing customers, seeking out buyers, obtaining information, making cold calls, and product promotion. Some sales personnel also engage in information collection and analysis of credit, technical advice and assistance, product modification, and training of customer service personnel. Moreover, all sales positions require the sales executives to perform administrative work such as generating reports and maintaining records. The activities performed by the sales personnel and the relative importance of these activities depend upon the market, products, and organization. Further, although some of these activities are important and necessary, they may not be related to sales indicating that sales personnel do more than just sell.

SALES COMPENSATION ISSUES

Many organizations follow a common compensation plan, which is applicable even to the sales function. These organizations consider it necessary to ensure pay equity. The logic behind this practice is that sales results are ultimately an outcome of teamwork. Counter-logic to such practice is also proposed. It argues that organizations need to design a separate sales compensation plan for cost control; achievement of goals and objectives; and to face competition. Another important argument perhaps is that this is the only function in which results are clearly visible and so efforts of good sales executives can be suitably rewarded with variables and incentives. It is observed that sales compensation costs, for the organizations worldwide, are almost 25–35 per cent of their gross profit. They exceed the average compensation cost for the organization as a whole by the extent of 5–15 per cent. The difference can be attributed to the fact that the sales department is the lifeline of organizations. It directly helps in achieving the organizational goals and objectives. Hence, if an organization seeks to attain an accelerated pace of growth, a strategic design of sales compensation, without altering the overall compensation structure, can help achieve the objective. Further, successful sales executives are achievers. They need to be motivated to sustain their aggressiveness. This is not possible without a suitable sales compensation plan.

Sales Goals

Apart from understanding the sales activity, organizations need to understand the sales goals before designing the sales compensation plan. Sales goals vary depending on the nature of the organization. Some organizations assign more weightage to sales volume within a time frame; some may be more interested in new business development; some may value customer retention; some may emphasize on selling a product-mix; some may feel that customer awareness is more important; while some may be more interested in sales strategies of the competitors. Organizations may also have more than one sales goal. After determining the sales goals, organizations should determine their compensation plan.

SALES COMPENSATION PLAN

The sales compensation plan varies from one organization to another depending on their compensation practices and strategic intent. In a monopoly organization, salary is considered as the right option. During the price control regime of steel, Steel Authority of India (SAIL) used to emphasize on salary for their sales force. After economic liberalization and steel price decontrol, SAIL and other steel manufacturers adopted a variable sales compensation structure. A commission on sales is considered as the other alternative model of sales compensation. However, sales commission is not legally tenable for payroll employees. Insurance advisors or agents in most of the cases get only a commission for selling insurance policies. Such advisors or agents are not on the payroll of the companies. They are given assurance that subject to their performance over a period, they would be absorbed into the company. Another alternative is a combi-plan, that is, both salary and commission.

A straight salary plan is simple to administer. It also provides security to the sales executives as their pay is not at risk. It may be desirable in some of the cases. For example, salary is desirable if the product type itself is very complex; sales cycle is unduly long (as in case of industrial products); or the sales function is a teamwork (in case of software projects). Organizations also prefer this for newly inducted sales executives as they need time to understand the markets and the customer. However, sales executives may not always like the straight salary plan as it fixes their earnings and fails to reward good performance. This is the primary disadvantage of straight salary plan for sales executives. Another disadvantage is organizational commitment to compensation or salary payment, even when sales executives fail to deliver the results.

Due to the disadvantages of the straight salary plan, incentives for the sales executives apart from a fixed salary component are considered important. The sales function requires independent functioning. Sales cannot be directly supervised as it involves field work. Setting compensation based on the results achieved is always desirable for a job that requires independent functioning.

Incentives to sales executives in the form of a straight commission plan are simple to administer. The basic purpose of such a plan is to achieve results in the short term and to promote an aggressive sales force. Many organizations adopt a mix of straight salary and straight commission. Apart from a fixed salary, they may adopt a commission structure as illustrated in Table 12.1.

TABLE 12.1 Sales commission structure

Sales	Commission
Under ₹10 lakh per year	Nil
Between ₹10 lakh and ₹15 lakh	6% of sales
Above ₹15 lakh	8% of sales

Before deciding on a commission payout, it is important to account for the costs, prevailing compensation structure, and the compensation level required to motivate employees. If the organization decides the commission structure without considering these issues, it may adversely affect the overall compensation plan. A high commission level reduces the firm's competitiveness, whereas a low commission level demotivates and adversely affects the performance and retention of the sales executives.

A well designed combi-compensation plan reduces the burden of the organizations by preventing high compensation for non-performers and at the same time motivates good performers who remain committed to the organization. The worldwide trend is that the straight salary of an organization's sales force constitutes 60–70 per cent of its total compensation. However, this percentage may vary depending on the nature of the products and services, or in cases where the contribution of the sales force is low. Some organizations also assign weightage to non-sales activities such as market development, customer awareness, and brand recall. In such cases, the commission component of the incentive may not always be directly linked to the actual sales and may even be lower.

Combi-plan in sales compensation may be of various types such as commission-plus-draw, commission-plus-salary, and bonus-plus-salary. In the first case, sales executives receive a structured salary which is referred to as a 'draw'. Periodically, total commissions proportionate to the sales generated by the sales executives are calculated and subtracted from the draw to pay the residual amount to the employees. In the second case, the sales executives receive a base salary and a percentage of their sales as an incentive. The total payout in this case could be lower than the first case. In the third case, the employee receives a base salary and a bonus. The bonus is linked to the performance.

A straight commission or combination plan should be selected after arriving at a measurement criterion using the MBO philosophy to ensure control over the sales executive's performance. A sales executive's performance is easy to track and is directly related to the bottom line or profits of an organization. MBO helps in setting clearly defined goals, participation of all cross sections of employees in setting the goals, and feedback to the employees on their performance.

A carefully crafted sales compensation plan considers three levels of performance, that is, threshold, target achievement, and exceed-expectations level. *Threshold level* specifies minimum sales volume against which the sales executive is evaluated. *Target achievement level* performance considers the achievement of sales quota, whereas *exceed-expectation level* performance recognizes an outstanding performance. Compensation level of the sales personnel can be calibrated to all these three performance levels.

Similar focus on the nature of the sales function is also important. If the sales executive is a channel sales manager, bonus is paid on the basis of the volume of sales generated by distributors. In case of a sales representative, bonus points are given for signing a contract and its execution. Finally, for a sales account manager, commission is paid on the basis of volume of sales generated from selected accounts.

Sales cycles

A sales cycle is the time required to initiate and conclude a sale. Depending on the nature of the products and services, organizations select short-sale cycles or long-sale cycles. Short sales may extend up to a 12-month period with a provision for periodic payouts to motivate the employees. Long-sale cycles extend beyond the period of 12 months. Long-sale cycles apply when the organizations are unable to ascertain closure of a sales deal within a short time frame because of the nature of products and commodities. To ensure that the sales personnel do not suffer from demotivation due to longer sales cycles, organizations design a tier system for payment of incentives or commissions. In these cases, commissions are paid at periodic intervals in accordance with the various milestones in sales achieved by the sales personnel.

SALES COMPENSATION DESIGN AND ADMINISTRATION

The sales force of an organization plays the most important role in improving the financial performance, that is, the top line and bottom line of an organization. Sales personnel adopt an active approach in carrying the message about the company's products and services to the prospective customers. Effectiveness with which the sales team markets the company and, in turn, the success of the organization is directly related to the sales compensation programme. A sound sales compensation package enables the organization to focus on sales activities to achieve the desired results and rewards the outcomes with a compensation related directly to the level of achievement.

Although no model on sales compensation programme applies uniformly across all organizations, some common steps are adopted while designing sales compensation. Such steps can be broadly classifiable into the following points—(1) identification of realistic and challenging sales goals; (2) translating sales goals into measurable objectives; and (3) designing sales compensation, which is competitive and motivational for the employees. Operationally these steps are illustrated in more detail to help managers use them as guidelines.

Designing Effective Sales Compensation Plan

Organizational practices on sales compensation plan vary widely. Without going into the debate of the appropriateness of these practices, the following fundamental steps in effective designing of sales compensation can be recommended.

Basic understanding of the sales job descriptions

This is very important as the nature of the sales job cannot be uniform for all types of products and services. For example, a medical representative's sales perception, an outbound telecaller's sales perception, an insurance advisor's sales perception, or a fast-moving consumer goods (FMCG) product seller's sales perception is not the same. Again, such perception also varies with the company's philosophy. One organization may consider sale as a deal that is finalized, whereas another may consider sales as a relationship building exercise. Coupled with these perceptive differences in the approach, success or failure of sales personnel vary widely due to several factors such as nature of the customer, degree of competition, economic trends, market trends, and political situation. Effectively describing the role of a sales executive and then developing a suitable compensation structure requires organizations to first decide about the job description of the sales executives.

Understanding the objectives

Organizational objectives are all encompassing and all pervasive. For the sales function, the overall objectives of the organization based on the MBO approach should cascade to key result areas (KRA), key performance areas (KPA), and key sales objectives (KSO). These could be identified for an individual sales executive or for a sales team. The objectives should be clearly understood before an effective sales compensation design is planned.

Understanding of controllable and measurable elements of the sales function

Sales compensation plans are linked largely to performance. To understand the performance and the possible bottlenecks, and degree of performance achievement, emphasis should be placed on the controllable and measurable elements of the sales function. It requires adoption of a suitable performance management system as explained in Chapter 5 on Employee benefits.

Determine the level of compensation

At this stage, the organization designs a compensation matrix with the job role on one axis and salary, incentives, and the total compensation on the other axis. Along with this design, the organization also needs to determine industry's average compensation, fixed–variable mix for the salary, salary–incentive mix, and other determinants of compensation level.

Understanding the compensation method

Straight salary, straight commission, and the combination of both are considered while designing sales compensation. Only straight salary or straight commissions is not a suitable model for sales compensation. So the organization is required to adopt a combination approach requiring identification of a suitable mix of salary, incentives, benefits, and expenses.

Pilot testing of the designed compensation method

A newly designed sales compensation method should be tested for administrative feasibility, sales compensation expense optimization, and motivation enhancement of the sales force. A better understanding of all these factors would be possible by fitting the organization's last year's sales performance data into the new model and studying its impact.

Rollout of the plan

Finally, the newly designed compensation plan is rolled out in the organization. Organizations should study, as an ongoing process, the motivation level of sales force, keep a track on the performance changes, and incorporate possible changes, if required. To increase the acceptance of the plan by the employees, organizations also can create a dashboard showing regular updated individual and group performance of employees.

Components of Sales Compensation

Like any other employee compensation package, sales compensation packages consist of one or more of the following components:
- base salary
- short-term incentives linked with short-term goals
- long-term incentives, linked with annual target achievement. It can also extend to a longer sales cycle depending on the organizational policy
- perquisites to support sales initiatives

A corporate decision on sales compensation package is illustrated here with a hypothetical example for a better understanding of the concept. The hypothetical organization in our discussion is assumed to be a financial services company. The organization is confronted with the task of designing an effective sales compensation package. At the outset, the issues to be addressed through the sales compensation plan should be listed. The following issues are assumed in this hypothetical case:
- giving direction to sales team to focus on boosting sales of new products and services
- design competitive compensation, compatible with the market trend
- more emphasis on incentives and other variables
- development of a sales compensation package that is aligned with both the individual and team performance

After the issues are listed, the organization would search for suitable solutions. In this hypothetical case, the solutions could be as follows:
- benchmark base level salary and total compensation by utilizing market information or study of competitors' sales compensation plan

- design appropriate mix of fixed and variable salary
- assign weightage to different goals based on the degree of importance
- recognize team efforts
- differentiate sales compensation based on the job role
- develop guidelines for easy administration of the newly designed sales compensation plan

Non-cash incentives as sales compensation

When designing a sales compensation plan, it has to be kept in mind that cash is not the only reward that motivates sales personnel. Though, cash may constitute a major percentage of sales compensation, there are several non-cash incentives that are much sought after by sales personnel. Non-cash incentives may be plaques/awards, recognition dinners, leisure trips/travels, gifts, etc. It is important to involve sales personnel in the sales compensation design process. For sales executives who need to travel, organizations often make available a fixed amount of daily reimbursement to meet their expenses incurred on food, accommodation, and other incidental expenses. This is referred to as 'per diems'.

SALES INCENTIVES AND MOTIVATION

The ability to motivate sales personnel depends on an understanding of their needs. Managers can understand the needs of sales executives better through a day-to-day interaction with them. This understanding would help them design an incentive programme that can motivate and lead sales personnel to the desired level of performance. A sales incentive is defined as a reward for the sales personnel on achieving specified results. Depending upon the needs of sales executives, managers may select financial and non-financial sales incentives. Financial incentives may again be linked with the achievement of short-term results or long-term results. Non-financial incentives are mainly used in specific cases like when the sales people achieve results with a special extraordinary effort. Recognition of such efforts with special honours, awards, etc. constitutes non-financial incentives. The sales incentives, financial or non-financial, need to be aligned with the long-term goals of the organization. Financial incentives may be direct monetary payments in the form of wages and salaries, or may be in the form of indirect monetary rewards such as paid vacations and retirement plans.

Incentives in any form exert a significant influence upon the performance of the sales personnel. When the incentives increase the capability of the sales executives, organizations achieve the desired results. Hence, appropriate selection of sales incentives plan is very important. Apart from meeting the motivational needs of the sales personnel, a properly designed sales incentive plan can also increase the retention of the sales personnel, who are more prone to frequent job switch.

CONTRIBUTION-BASED SALES COMPENSATION

A contribution-based sales compensation strategy benefits the organization by relating the compensation to the operating costs of the organization. Sales personnel contribute to the expenditure and profitability of the organization. The design of compensation based on their contribution benefits the organization as this form of compensation plan is rational. A contribution-based sales compensation approach benefits the organization in the following ways:
- it gives an opportunity to the sales personnel to earn with no limits or a payment ceiling, without straining the organization's compensation budget
- it makes recruitment of sales executives more flexible as organizations can avoid payment to those who fail to perform
- it ensures long-term profitability as it enhances the performance of the organization and makes the organization financially stable

A contribution-based sales plan is designed on the following considerations:
- coverage of organizational expenses, fixed and variable, with allocation to individual sales executives
- provision for built-in profit into the allocation of expenses
- decision on commission levels
- design of contribution-based compensation plans
- optional for the sales personnel as all sales personnel may not like the plan

DESIGNING AN EFFECTIVE SALES COMPENSATION PLAN

Any sales compensation plan requires rewarding the top performers. This can be achieved by designing a tiered compensation plan differentiating the incentive rate with sales target figures, market segments, new customers' development, cross-selling, etc. In designing a tiered compensation plan, it is always better to use 4–5 sales metrics to ensure design of a simple and transparent sales compensation plan.

Top-down and Bottom-up Sales Quota

Top-down sales quota is based on the decision made by top management to increase the sales. Bottom-up quota is the quota fixation for the sales territory. The bottom-up quota is reconciled with the top-down goal for appropriate assignment of sales goals across the sales territory and then it is cascaded to the individual level sales people.

To understand the effectiveness of sales compensation plans, it is necessary to consider following aspects:

Reinforcement of strategy and desired behaviours It can be ensured by selecting the right performance measures with appropriate differential weights.

Reflection of the nature of the sales role in compensation This can be done by proper documentation of sales incentive eligibility, clarifying sales roles, and aligning pay-mix and eligibility with the sales job role.

Maximizing motivational impact of incentive earnings It can be ensured by pay distribution, pay differentiation, and pay and performance correlation.

Supporting talent attraction and retention It can be ensured by ensuring competitiveness of total compensation and maintaining appropriate internal pay equity.

Ensuring ease in governing, designing, and administering sales compensation plan It can be ensured by making it possible to track and manage compensation cost of sales (CCOS), identifying potential financial and behavioural risks, and creating a formal governing process.

Unique Sales Compensation Plan Model

Global HR consulting organization Towers Watson developed a sales talent management and reward model in alignment with the unique growth needs of an organization. The model facilitates effective rewarding of sales force with simultaneous benefit of high engagement and motivation. The model is explained in Table 12.2.

Industry Thumb Rules for Sales Compensation

Industry thumb rules are based on the organizational practices. In sales compensation, we find the general industry practices as in Table 12.3.

Apple emphasizes more on long-term equity than on cash compensation. Interestingly for this reason, annual cash bonus programme for Apple

TABLE 12.2 Towers Watson sales compensation model

Focus of the model	Market performance
Positive impact on customer experience	Higher customer satisfaction
Higher employee retention	Higher customer retention
Better employee engagement	Higher product utilization
Higher recurring revenue	Deeper relationships and resultant cross sales

TABLE 12.3 Commonly accepted sales compensation practices

Performance	Below threshold (%)	Target (100% of goal) (%)	Excellence (%)	Above excellence
Percentage of sales force	10–15	Above 55, below 45	10–15	Same fraction of excellence
Amount to pay	10–50	100	200–300	No cap (strategic decision)

executives has remained unchanged for several years. Bonus opportunities for their executives are substantially lower than their peer companies. Recently the company restructured its bonus programme using adjusted sales and adjusted operating income as performance criteria. This excludes the subscription-based sales thereby reducing the bonus opportunities for the executives by restricting their actual achievement. Apple's sales compensation plan in their retail stores is criticized because of the adjusted sales concept.

RELATING SALES COMPENSATION PLANS WITH ORGANIZATIONAL LIFE CYCLE

Organizational strategies change at different stages of organizational life cycle. Such changes in the strategies exert influence on sales compensation plan. We can explain this with a hypothetical product life cycle. Like organizational life cycle, product life cycle too moves through four distinct phases, that is, introduction or start-up phase (Phase 1), growth phase (Phase 2), maturity phase (Phase 3), and finally the optimization phase (Phase 4). In these different phases, organization's business priorities vary which necessitate change in the sales compensation plan.

In Phase 1, most of the companies expect their sales force to be more aggressive to achieve their sales target. More emphasize would be on variable pay in the form of incentives. Company may also vary the incentive percentages at different levels of sales to trigger more efforts from the sales force. In Phase 2, the emphasis on variable component of sales compensation would get reduced as the focus of the company would shift to volume growth due to a change in priorities. The company will come out with some innovative retention modifiers to boost performance. In Phase 3, that is, the maturity phase, companies reassess the different components of their product strategies such as price management, cost reduction, and effective price realization through discounting. Such strategies are intended to sustain the product in the long run. This change in strategy leads to corresponding changes in the sales compensation plan. In Phase 4, that is, the optimization phase, the companies again review their compensation metrics as strategies shift to new market development, new value addition to products, etc. Reasons for reviewing sales compensation metrics at different stages of the product life cycle can be primarily attributed to changing sales objectives of the organization.

Sales Compensation Constructs

Depending on organization specific strategies and sales objectives, organizations make use of accelerators to boost sales. Common accelerators are increased differential rate of sales commission for selling of product volumes. In sales compensation, accelerators are considered as those events which are valued more in compensating the sales forces of an organization. For example, a company may consider sale in an unrepresented market, as an important accelerator for the sales people, and accordingly may compensate him more. Based on the study of organizational practices, the following common sales compensation constructs can be identified.

Profit-based sales compensation As per this construct, sales commission rates increase with the increase in sales margin. This is the most commonly used sales compensation construct.

Revenue or quota-based sales compensation As per this construct, sales compensation varies with respect to the percentage change in the quota or revenue target. Previous sales cycle is considered as a reference point for calculating the percentage change.

Balanced sales compensation As per this construct, sales compensation is designed after factoring variables such as profit margin, revenue, and quota achievement. It is more rational as important sales compensation constructs are embedded in the sales compensation plan.

Use of quota-based sales compensation plan is criticized as this plan often ignores potentialities of territory, market, and sales people. Let us assume, a sales person has a target earning potential as in Table 12.4 (a).

The company earns a 30 per cent margin on the sales revenue.

Now, suppose we are offering differential commission rate on different level of sales margins. Table 12.4 (b) shows that variable compensation payouts, with tiered rate of commission, to the sales person impact margin variation.

However, such problem can be mitigated by lowering the commission rate. With improved variation to margin, company would be able meet its expenses before it pays its sales force.

TABLE 12.4 (a) Target earning potential

Salary	₹1,00,000
Variable	₹50,000
Margin (%)	30

TABLE 12.4 (b) Impact of variable compensation payouts on margin variation

Sales revenue (₹)	Margin (30%) = Net sales (₹)	Commission rate (%)	Payout (₹)	Variation to margin (difference between variable revenue and variable cost) (₹)
5,00,000	1,50,000	5.0	25,000	25,000
7,50,000	2,25,000	6.7	50,250	74,750
10,00,000	3,00,000	7.5	75,000	1,25,000
15,00,000	4,50,000	10.0	1,50,000	2,00,000

Example

A company's target incentive plan for sales manager is 30 per cent of his annual salary. Let us assume that the annual salary for the sales manager is ₹1 lakh and the performance cycle is six months, that is, twice in a year. At the end of each performance cycle proportionate target incentives are paid to the sales manager. The company assigns weighted goals to calculate the target incentives. A weighted goal is calibrated with accelerator adjustment to increase the incentives payout for a sales manager who achieves more than 100 per cent of target levels. Calculate the six-monthly figure of target incentive of sales manager based on the following information.

- Sales manager's overall performance score is 110 per cent.
- Accelerator adjustment for performance score of 110 per cent is 135 per cent.

Solution

110% × 135% × 15,000 (50% of Annual target incentive) = ₹22,275

Accelerator/multiplier/bump can also be explained using a sliding scale model. Sales commission percentage can be adjusted both upward and downward based on sliding scale movement. Let us assume, if the target gross margin percentage of a company is 30 per cent, the sales person earns sales commission at the rate of 10 per cent of gross margin. The commission rate would be higher if the gross margin percentage is more than 30 per cent and vice versa (Table 12.5). Some of the incentives offered in the sales compensation plan, in addition to fixed rate of commission are; new business development, team selling, cross-selling, sales of specific products, increases in customer satisfaction, etc.

TABLE 12.5 Sliding scale commission example

Margin (%)	Base commission (%)	Multiplier	Net commission (%)
40	10	1.50	15.0
35	10	1.25	12.5
30	10	1.00	10.0
25	10	0.75	7.5

SUMMARY

This chapter emphasizes on the need for a separate compensation plan for sales personnel. Sales executives contribute to the financial performance of an organization. Organizations cannot survive unless they achieve success in generating revenue and profits. Therefore, differentiating sales compensation from others is extremely important to ensure that the sales personnel remain motivated and committed to the organizational needs. Organizational practices on sales compensation varies widely. Straight salary or straight commission, as a stand-alone compensation package, is not desirable. Organizations need to draw a suitable combination of salary, commission, and incentives to arrive at the most effective sales compensation plan. Depending on the nature of products and services, every organization has to decide on the appropriate mix under the combination plan. Designing performance-linked commissions and incentives requires scientific measurement techniques and a decision on the sales cycles. Strategic focus on sales compensation design is very important to ensure that organizations are able to motivate and retain the sales force and at the same time optimize the cost of sales compensation.

Key Terms

Contribution-based sales compensation This approach considers compensation as part of the operational costs of an organization. Sales personnel contribute to the expenditure and profitability of the organization. Design of compensation based on their contribution benefits the organization as the compensation plan becomes more rational.

Management by objectives (MBO) The overall objectives of the organizations provide a sense of direction to all the employees of the organization. For the sales function, the overall objectives of the organization based on the MBO approach may cascade to key result areas (KRAs), key performance areas (KPAs), and key sales objectives (KSOs). These could be set for individual sales executives or for a sales team.

Sales cycle It is the time required to conclude a sale. Depending on the nature of the products and services, organizations select short-sale cycles or long-sale cycles.

Sales goals Sales goals are the goals assigned to the sales people in the form of targets. Organizations decide the sales goals before designing the sales compensation plan. Depending on the nature of the organization, sales goals may vary. Organizations may have more than one sales goal. After determining the sales goals, organizations draw their compensation plan.

Exercises

Concept Review Questions

1. Discuss how a sales compensation plan is different from other compensation plans? Is it necessary for an organization to design a separate sales compensation package for the sales personnel? Justify your answer.
2. Explain how a sales compensation package is designed and administered. Will this process be same for all types of sales jobs? Elucidate.
3. What are the components of a sales compensation plan? Which component or components would you want to emphasize more for a sales executive selling FMCG products of a newly established company?
4. What is a sales cycle? How is the sales cycle determined for industrial products?

Critical Thinking Questions

1. Design a contribution-based sales compensation plan, assuming hypothetical figures, for a company engaged in retail sales of tea.
2. You have been asked to mandate a suitable sales compensation plan for your company's newly launched product. Following sample plans (Tables 12.6(a) and 12.6(b)) have been developed by your company. Suggest which plan/scheme would be more effective in attracting talented sales force.

TABLE 12.6 (a)   Plan A: Different commission percentage

Plan A	Scheme 1	Scheme 2
Base salary (₹)	70,000–80,000	70,000–80,000
Annual sales quota (₹ in lakh)	15	15
Commission (%)	5	2.5

TABLE 12.6 (b)   Plan B: Different base salary

Plan B	Scheme 1	Scheme 2
Base salary (₹)	90,000–1,00,000	70,000–80,000
Annual sales quota (₹ in lakh)	12	12
Commission (%)	3	3

CASE STUDY: Itachi's Sales Compensation Plan Runs into Conflict

Organizations design sales compensation to meet their sales objectives, improve sales performance and productivity, and reward sales results. Successfully devising an effective sales incentive plan is a complex task. This was the task faced by Itachi, a Noida-based Indian subsidiary of Japanese origin global consumer electronics major by the same name. It was engaged in the design of a sales compensation plan aimed at raising its market share in India against the Korean and Indian majors, who have established strong business presence in the country over the past 10 years. The Indian market for consumer electronics is typically divided into two segments—low-price segment and premium-price segment. A high proportion of the Indian population cannot afford a television set. Earlier, it was believed that non-availability of electricity is a major impediment in the growth of the market for television sets. However, with the increased availability of electricity even in remote villages, the belief is now considered more of a myth than reality. Budget constraint is the main factor. A one-time spend of a few thousand rupees for an entertainment gadget in addition to increase in monthly electricity expenditure of the household is still considered as luxury by much of the rural household.

Itachi's success as a global brand in the US and UK markets is attributable to its technological leadership and quality. Introducing a low-priced television set in the Indian market by sacrificing quality and technological innovation is literally impossible for Itachi. With R&D backup, Itachi could design a maintenance-free television set in the price range starting from ₹6,500 for a 19-inch colour television set. Indian customers are yet to switch to frequent replacement of electronic goods to reap the advantage of technology. Buying one television set is a lifetime investment for many Indians.

To persuade an Indian customer to spend few hundred rupees more to buy an Itachi's television is not an easy task for the sales team. Itachi's

(Contd)

CASE STUDY *(Contd)*

HR team is struggling to come out with some innovative sales compensation plan, which can successfully help in positioning Itachi's products in the Indian market. Some of the issues under the HR team's consideration are—(1) possibility of introducing sales incentives based on long-sales cycles, (2) incentives based on unpredictable orders, (3) provisions for compensation on multi-year orders, and (4) emphasis on both absolute and relative performance benchmark.

Itachi's sales cycle is divided into two types—retail sales with a 12-month sales cycle and institutional sales with a 3-year sales cycle. Each sales executive has dual responsibility. To start with, Itachi has divided the sales executive's target into 80 per cent retail sales and 20 per cent institutional sales. Itachi believes that unless retail sales increase, institutional sales would not pick up. Hence, the sales team should place more emphasis on increasing the retail sales so that Itachi can become a household name in India. Institutional sales, however, cannot be altogether ignored. Hence, identifying dealers of other competitors and persuading them with attractive discount structure and extended credit facilities, and occupying their shelf space can make Itachi more visible. Itachi's retail sales strategy is through customer awareness by house-to-house visits, road shows, advertisements, and distribution of product literature through newspaper vendors. Sales executives earn their variables on achieving the retail sales target and enjoy incentives on exceeding the target, a portion of which is shared with the team leader.

Institutional sales cycle ends every three years, at the end of which Itachi plans to reward the sales executives both for individual contribution and for their contribution to the group. The rewards are based on both development of new dealerships and billing. However, Itachi did not make this part of the compensation plan transparent leaving employees to ponder over what they are going to get after 3 years. First long-term sales cycle for institutional sales concluded in December 2004. Employees, to their surprise, found that they got almost 10 per cent of their 3-year aggregate salary as rewards. They were joyous and it was the time for them to celebrate. Employees were feeling satisfied and motivated. For all of them, achieving the best was now the only pursuit. This led to good teamwork within the organization. However, the second 3-year institutional sales cycle in December 2007 surprised everyone. Employees got only 2 per cent of their 3-year aggregate salary as rewards. This is despite Itachi's successful market penetration and it becoming the number two leader in the market within a span of six years.

Employee unions were furious and issued notice to the management to explain on what basis the company has paid the employees 2 per cent rewards despite a 300 per cent increase in institutional sales. Itachi explained that within the three years from 2004 to 2007, the cost of other inputs increased multifold and the commission structure for dealers had to be upwardly revised to dissuade their association with the competing companies. Moreover, the first long-term sales cycle assigned more weightage on new dealer development than billing. The current one, however, assigned more weightage on billing than new dealer development. The management contended that rewards were

(Contd)

CASE STUDY (Contd)

dependent on the achievement of organizational goals. Unions did not find the management's explanation to be reasonable. They have given a call for an indefinite strike.

Discussion question

What went wrong in Itachi's sales compensation plan? How do you expect Itachi to respond to the strike call?

References

Barney, J. (1991), 'Firm resources and sustained competitive advantage', *Journal of Management*, vol. 17, pp. 99–120.

Barry, J.W. and P. Henry (1981), *Effective Sales Incentive Compensation*, McGraw-Hill, New York.

Belcher, D.W. (1955), *Compensation Administration*, Prentice Hall, Englewood Cliffs, New Jersey.

Bhattacharyya, D.K. (2007), *Human Resource Research Methods*, Oxford University Press, New Delhi.

Canning, Jr., G. and R. Berry (1982), 'Linking sales compensation to the product life cycle,' *Management Review*, pp. 43–6, July.

CHAPTER THIRTEEN

Managing Rewards

Learning Objectives

After reading this chapter, you will be able to
- understand the concepts of rewards and recognition
- appreciate the benefits of rewards and recognition
- understand the total rewards concepts and strategies
- examine the benefits of total rewards strategy to organization
- examine the importance of rewards and recognition policy
- assess ethical issues in rewards and recognition

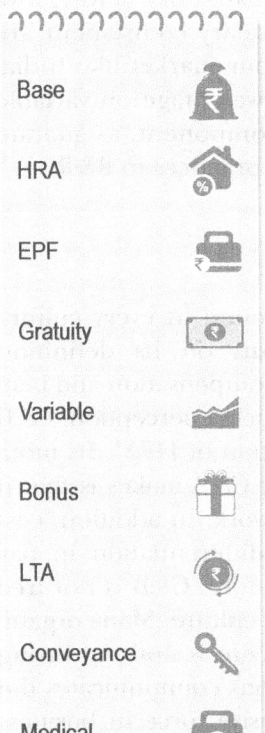

Base

HRA

EPF

Gratuity

Variable

Bonus

LTA

Conveyance

Medical

OPENING CASE

Emphasis on Reward Practices in Indian Companies

Since the global recession of 2008, organizations are struggling to come out with some reward strategies that can reduce the cost of compensation and at the same time retain talent. For example, Hay Group, based on their study of 230 companies in 20 countries in 2010, came come out with the 'changing face of reward'. Globally, organizations are now struggling to institutionalize performance-related pay (PRP) aligning rewards with the performance, differentiating reward for mission critical job roles, etc. In line with global practices, Indian organizations have also started emphasizing on employee rewards. Rewarding employees can gradually make organizations more productive and efficient. However, organizational practices on rewards widely vary. For example, Hexaware emphasizes on point-based rewards to employees who elicit some pre-decided desired performance behaviour. Employees can accumulate such reward points and later on can redeem it for merchandise from some designated stores. Siemens's Puraskar is a reward programme that combines both the monetary and non-monetary elements, with the unique concepts of e-cards. Tracking e-cards Siemens can assess which employee is recognized more and how such increased recognition can be matched with the performance level of the employee. Similar innovative rewards programme of Blue Dart, under the names Bravo Blue Darter, Super Darter, and True Blue Darter, make the company more performance driven.

INTRODUCTION

Rewards and recognition (R&R) has a rich history. R&R practices can be found in different civilizations including India (Bhattacharyya 2013). Examples showing that R&R can bring positive change in workers' behaviour can also be observed in history. Today, R&R is practiced in organizations along with our compensation and benefits (C&B) programme. Both the practices, R&R and C&B, run concurrently to get the best from the employees. Organizations craft their R&R programs innovatively by blending monetary and non-monetary packages. Increased motivation, enhanced employee engagement, and retention of talents are some of benefits organizations target to achieve through their R&R programs. Operationally, C&B and R&R programmes are considered as one and the same. In this era of performance-related pay (PRP), protective C&B practices, with more weightage on fixed salary component are slowly losing importance. Even in highly regulated labour market like India, we have embraced PRP, started giving more and more weightage on variable components, beyond the statutory minimum as fixed component, as guaranteed fixed wages. This, in reality, slowly transforms C&B practices to R&R.

DEFINITION AND CONCEPTS OF REWARDS

Although the term rewards has historical basis and is found in every culture and religion across the globe, there is no consensus on its definition (Bhattacharyya 2013). Often, it is considered as strategic compensation and benefits management practices. There are valid reasons for such a perception. C&B in its present form is looked more as maintenance function of HRM. Its motivational benefits are limited. The only difference higher C&B makes is that it makes the workers feel that they get paid well for their work. In addition, cost optimization pressure in organizations often requires differentiation in pay which creates both internal and external inequity. Therefore, C&B is not free from vices of master–slave relationship. It is a question of culture. Many organizations legitimately follow the no-work no-pay model. There is nothing wrong in it. However, managing C&B like any other cost functions communicates the impression to employees that they continue to be a passive force in business process. They get paid because they deliver. This is an economic rationality. No behavioural dynamics exists in it. Contrary to this, if C&B is managed as R&R,

people feel more engaged, motivated, and prefer to stay with the organization. Getting pay as reward excites employees more than getting it for the services they render.

Hay Group defines reward as everything—monetary and non-monetary, tangible and intangible—a person gets from going to work. Hay group does not differentiate literally between compensation and reward. However, the group concedes that reward is a term with broader connotation and C&B programme is a part of it. WorldatWork, a global association for human resources management professionals, instead of using the term reward recommends the term *total rewards*. It defines the term as everything the employee perceives to be of value resulting from the employment relationship. Some professional bodies consider rewards as a total of compensation, benefits, incentives, any other material thing, and non-material recognition. Irrespective of the debate and cross debate, the reward is now considered more inclusive than the traditional compensation and benefits components. Couple of reward components such as career opportunities, work-life-balancing, enabling work culture, and company social clubs are non-material in nature. Organizations consider these aspects while designing a total reward package. However, we cannot consider such components as part of compensation and benefits programme. Similar distinctiveness of the term reward can be understood from varying organizational practices. For example, in some organizations reward is considered as an award for performance, while compensation is the payment for work done. Therefore, reward is an add-on to compensation.

Reward is always an additional and discretionary type of compensation which can be cash or not, and generally under the exclusive control and definition of the organization. It is generally attached to a certain program or policy like performance appraisal/management. Many organizations use the term awards or incentives instead of rewards and recognition. Whatever may be the way of naming it, R&R is increasingly becoming strategically relevant for organizations to achieve results. Renaming C&B as R&R makes sense as it makes a more integrated effort to align people with the organization and offers better motivational benefits.

Forester is a membership-based global fraternal benefits organization. The company crafted its rewards and recognition programme for their employees, offering the following:
- competitive base and variable compensation programmes
- performance-based salaries and incentive programmes
- group benefits coverage
- pension plan to support your retirement savings
- competitive vacation
- on-site parking
- fitness and wellness programmes
- employee and family assistance programme

- discount programmes
- through employee recognition program, all employees are acknowledged for the following:
  - years of service
  - individual and team achievements, celebrated at our all-employee meetings
  - on-the-spot recognition with gift cards
- employee referral programme bonuses
- flexible work arrangements

The company's R&R programmes helped create a culture of performance which enabled the century old organization sustain and grow.

DIFFERENCES BETWEEN COMPENSATION AND REWARDS

It can be made out that it may be difficult to make any difference between compensation and rewards. Operationally too organizations across the globe make use of these two terms interchangeably to broadly indicate compensation and benefits management practices. However, we also have organizations which prefer the term rewards over compensation and use the term total rewards practices instead of compensation and benefits management. Total rewards design in organizations integrates compensation and benefits management aspects. Rewards are different from compensation and benefits on following counts.

1. Rewards are more inclusive in approach as it balances monetary and non-monetary needs of individual employees, while they keep pace with organizational culture and strategies. Compensation and benefits management practices cannot have an effective inclusive approach due to its perennial focus on payment for work.
2. Compensation and benefits alone cannot derive the desired motivational benefits and retain talent. Rewards being more holistic can balance employees' motivational need with focus on quality in work life, career development opportunities, etc.
3. Rewards being more holistic can attract and retain talent. Compensation and benefits management lacks this holistic focus.
4. Rewards can strike a balance between human resource strategies on one side and competitive strategies of organization with mediating role of culture on the other. Such a balancing act often becomes difficult for compensation and benefits management practices as cost minimization is its primary agenda.
5. Concept of rewards moves the focus from traditional cost to investment approach, whereas compensation and benefits focus only on traditional cost percepts.
6. Rewards can influence both the cognitive and behavioural dynamics of employees, whereas compensation and benefits can only influence the behavioural dynamics of employees.

Even though many organizations use rewards as part of compensation, the above differences can be found between their approach and the concept of rewards as recognized today.

BENEFITS OF REWARD AND RECOGNITION PROGRAMME

Researchers such as Lawler (1990) and Schuster and Zingheim (1992) argued that organizations can elicit desired behaviour from their employees through effective reward strategy. In framing the reward strategy, Lawler (1995) recommended consideration of reward elements such as values that strengthen the reward strategy, reward structures, and reward processes. In crafting a reward strategy aimed at eliciting desired behaviour from the employees, it is necessary for the organization to understand at the outset as to what they intend to change and what is the basis for such change. Once this is clear, organizations can chalk out the desired behavioural constructs from their employees.

Every organization frames its reward strategy by basing it on its business strategy. As with business strategy, reward strategy is also framed with due consideration to dynamics of internal and external environment. Extending this argument further, Lawler (1984) recommended that reward strategy of any organization should be in congruence with its HR strategy. Subsequently, Lawler recommended that reward elements such as core reward values, structural features and processes, when embedded in the rewards programme make it strategically more relevant for the organization.

Characteristics of rewards management

After understanding the differences between compensation and rewards, and the benefits of rewards, it is important to briefly introduce the characteristics of rewards management. Following are some of the characteristics of rewards.

Rewards are people oriented Rewards being intended to elicit desired behaviour from employees, organizations focus on people issues such as objective basis of rewarding, benchmarked standards of skills, and contribution in designing rewards programme.

Rewards factor stakeholders' interest Organizations design rewards for attraction and retention of talent, motivating employees for increased level of performance, etc. Both tangible and intangible forms of rewards require additional expenses. Hence, while managing rewards organizations need to balance the interests of different stakeholders. For example, say on pay is institutionalized now in most of developed countries to allow shareholders' to vote for or against the compensation of the CEO of a company. This has been already discussed in Chapter 11 on Executive compensation.

Rewards must be integrated In managing rewards, organizations need to integrate with the business and human resource management strategies, the culture of the organization, etc. Having a rewards policy without any concern for performance-related-pay system does not make any sense. Similarly, when organizations emphasize on competencies of individual employees as criteria for rewards, they must also provide competency development opportunities to employees.

Rewards must be strategic Having a rewards policy without focus on strategies does not make any sense. Strategic focus can ensure achieving of the goals of the organizations. It can also help understand the cost benefit implications of rewards.

Rewards must be more grounded to reality Reward policies and rewards management aspects need to be grounded in reality and not in unfounded assumptions. Some scholars use the term evidence-based reward management to convey this idea. While grounding their rewards management practices, many organizations emulate the best practices from world class organizations.

TOTAL REWARDS—CONCEPTS AND STRATEGIES

The term *total rewards* is now used instead of the term reward and recognition or R&R. Almost all the global HR consulting organizations have now come out with their own total rewards model. All these models recommend integration of total rewards strategy with human resource strategies, business strategies, and the organizational culture. This can ensure motivation of employees and their retention, ultimately leading to improved business performance and results. WorldatWork, based on their study in different organizations, identified the following elements of total rewards:
- compensation
- benefits
- work-life
- performance and recognition
- development and career opportunities

Towers Watson, another globally renowned HR consulting organization, sees total rewards as monetary and non-monetary mix of all programmes and policies that an organization uses to attract, retain, and engage employees. Hence, elements of total rewards are pay and benefits, training, career development, and work-life balancing.

Rewards can be divided into four types: transactional, relational, individual, and communal. Transactional rewards are tangible, whereas relational rewards are intangible. Individual rewards emphasize more on individual performance, whereas communal rewards are for the overall work and performance of the organization (Armstrong 2007).

Total reward strategy being aligned with business and human resource strategies of the organizations at the outset, it requires holistic understanding about several points, namely how the strategy can influence decisions related to human resources; how it can influence the performance of employees, both individually and in a team; what would be the possible impact on talent attraction and retention; how it is going to influence employer branding, etc.

Following are some of the recommended steps for designing a total reward strategy.

Understanding of context and issues A holistic understanding of the organization gives insights about the external and internal factors that influence the organizations and enable possible assessment of business and human resources strategy of the organization.

Understanding of business imperative As total rewards are business aligned, an understanding of how total reward strategy influences organization's competitive positioning, cost efficiency, performance, etc is necessary.

Accommodating flexibility in total rewards strategy So that time to time reward strategy can be changed depending on the business needs.

Drawing effective implementation plan Provide prior communication to the employees about the total rewards programme, ensure their acceptance, and then go for implementation. Draw inputs from implementation review to bring future changes in the rewards programmes.

Ensuring measurability Total rewards programme must be designed with easy measurability. Employees should be able to cross-check whether their reward matches their performance.

It is important for the organization to come out with a total rewards programme that is holistic, integrated, aligned, measurable, and understood by employees.

Changing Views Toward Rewards

As per Mercer, human resource and related financial services consulting firm, rewards programme goes beyond just attraction and retention of talent, it contributes to business success. Mercer suggests total rewards strategy is to ensure right rewards to the right people at the right time for the right reason. For employees, therefore, rewards are the overall value proposition that their employers offer. It includes the following:
- all remuneration (including base pay, short-term, and long-term incentives)
- benefits (including retiral, work-life balancing, statutory, and voluntary welfare benefits)
- careers (including career development opportunities)

According to Hay Group (2010), organizations globally are now struggling to strike a balance between cost control and performance improvement. With such a balance, organizations intend to retain and motivate talent. These organizations are now focusing more and more on intangible rewards, motivational leadership, challenging work assignment, increased career development opportunities, etc. All these intangible rewards can effectively promote employee engagement and retention.

Total Rewards Strategy—How it Benefits Organization

So far in this chapter, we have debated the importance of compensation and benefits management from rewards management perspectives. Even though we understand rewards and total rewards, designing a rewards or total rewards programme with strategic focus is not so easy. The basic problem is to embed all the rewards or total rewards elements in the rewards program and to successfully align them with the business and human resource strategies of the organizations. Following are some important benefits that an organization can derive from their total rewards strategy:

- frame a sustainable reward budget
- allows flexibility to invest in reward depending on the evolving needs of the organization
- strategic allocation for talent retention
- helps put in place a rewards program that is aligned with business strategy of the organization
- helps develop a performance driven culture
- helps maximize ROI (return on investment) from investments made in reward
- enables use of reward as a strategic tool for employer branding

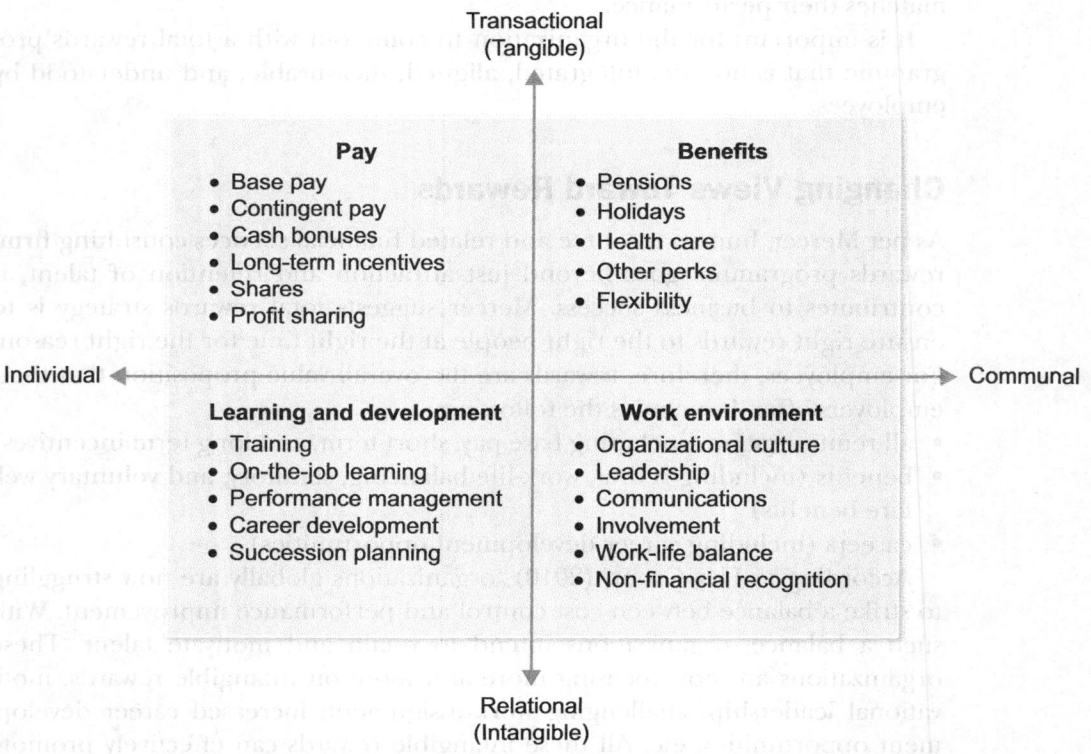

FIG. 13.1 Towers Perrin model of total rewards

Various global consulting organizations have come out with their version of total rewards model. These models try to incorporate almost all common aspects of tangible and intangible elements of compensation and benefits programmes. Of these models, the Towers Perrin model of total rewards stands out due to its simpler yet comprehensive approach (Fig. 13.1).

The model encapsulates different types of transactional (tangible) and relational (intangible) rewards in upper and lower quadrants. The upper quadrant divides the transactional rewards into pay and benefits categories, whereas the lower quadrant divides the relational rewards into learning and development, and work environment categories. The model also suggests balancing the weight between individual and communal performance.

Apart from the Towers Perrin model, we also have the total rewards model of WorldatWork. This model, at the outset, integrates organizational culture, business strategy and human resource strategy with total rewards. It views total rewards as aggregation of compensation, benefits, work-life, performance and recognition, and development and career opportunities.

REWARDS AND RECOGNITION POLICY

Rewards and recognition policy provides formal guidelines to successfully implement rewards and recognition programme in the organization. Most Indian organizations practice rewards and recognition programme as part of their compensation and benefits programme, hence elaborate stand-alone policy on rewards and recognition can hardly be expected in these organizations. Some organizations name their compensation and benefits policy as rewards and recognition policy. For example, Tata Teleservices Limited (TTSL), one of the Tata group companies, outlines its rewards and recognition policy as '.....to create a framework for recognising and rewarding the contributions of individuals and teams, and institutionalises a culture of openness, transparency and meritocracy.'[1] Some recognition programmes of the company are Spotlight (on-the-spot recognition), Star of the Month, Super Stars for achievers, Customer First Reward, and Valuable Reward.

Thermax India, a Pune based company with substantial global presence in energy and environment business verticals, has adopted the following well documented rewards and recognition policy[2]:
- *Innovator of the Year* award given to individuals or teams that introduce process improvement, develop product, or give an idea that makes sustained contribution to the bottom-line of the company

---

[1] http://www.tata.in/company/articlesinside/GAI3QG4hIfs=/TLYVr3YPkMU=

[2] http://www.thermaxindia.com/Careers/Rewards-Recognition.aspx

- reward and recognition policy to give instant appreciation and recognition for good work, accomplishments beyond normal duty, and for outstanding achievement for exceptional contribution towards the company
- long service award given to employees on completing 25 years of service at Thermax
- highlighting employee achievements in the Thermax House magazine, Fireside
- rewards to contract workmen for safe work practices

Therefore, a reward policy details the way employees are rewarded in the organizations. From this perspective, we can say a reward policy is a guideline for effective rewards management. A well documented reward policy considers both the financial and non-financial (transactional and relational) rewards components. It also considers how they are given, on what basis they are given, and at what frequency they are given. When R&R and C&B practices of any organization are merged, the result is elaborate policies on rewards and recognition covering all compensation and benefits components.

ETHICAL ISSUES IN REWARDS AND RECOGNITION

While designing rewards and recognition programme, it is also important to understand the ethical implication. In the absence of this consideration, the rewards and recognition programme may be unethical and counter-productive. Globally researchers like Heery (1996) argued that in designing rewards and recognition programme, organizations often neglect the mental and physical health issues of the employees. A significant portion of total rewards or compensation is deliberately kept at risk, signaling to the employees that these are contingent to your performance. Employees in their attempt to get the rewards at risk strive for more work often neglecting their health and general well-being issues. In addition, often organizations put disproportionately higher percentage of rewards or compensation in variables and make those payable only when employees are able to deliver the expected performance. Such misuse is a gross violation of the principles of performance-related pay (PRP) and is an unethical practice. Wood (1996) also identified similar propensities of the organization to put more and more pay or rewards at risk requiring employees to struggle to achieve the targets in order to earn the subsistence level income. While designing the rewards programme, the organizations should not neglect the ethical issues.

Following are some ethical issues developed based on industry practices:
1. Avoid any unfair rewards plan. Unfair rewards plan are those which persuade employees to violate ethical business practices to achieve performance goals.

2. Carefully choose casual incentives. Giving expensive gifts without any consideration to the performance results should be avoided.
3. Avoid giving stretched goals. Decide performance goals on basis of some rationale consideration and communicate the goal to employees.
4. Carefully assign weights to individual and team performances. While deciding on PRP constructs, ensure both individual and team performances are factored and distribute weights logically.
5. Refrain from using health and wellness as rewards. This gives a wrong signal to those who are non-recipient of such rewards as it embarrasses them and makes them feel vulnerable.
6. Ensure pay equity The organization should try and ensure pay equity to the extent possible as it helps develop a sense that rewards have been decided upon fairly.

Compliance with the above issues can substantially reduce the risk of non-compliance with ethical norms while designing a rewards programme.

SUMMARY

Globally, organizations are putting more and more emphasis on their rewards and recognition programmes. This chapter, at the outset, introduces the concepts of rewards and recognition. While explaining the concepts, it draws inputs from the world class HR consulting organizations as both conceptual and empirical studies on rewards and recognition are still inadequate. The chapter then goes on to explain the benefits of rewards and recognition, introduces the concept of total rewards and its strategies, and how total rewards strategies benefits the organizations. Finally, the chapter also highlights the need for developing rewards and recognition policy and the importance of compliance with the ethical issues.

Key Terms

Performance-related pay (PRP) Alignment of pay with performance.
Rewards Strategic compensation and benefits management practices.
Compensation Payment for work done.
Reward strategy Strategies framed after taking into account business and human resource management strategies of the organization and aimed at eliciting desired behaviour from employees.
Total rewards Inclusive concept that brings together compensation and benefits, work-life balancing, performance and recognition, and career development opportunities.

Exercises

Concept Review Questions

1. Explain the concept of rewards and recognition. How is it different from compensation and benefits programme?
2. What is total rewards? What are its strategies? In what ways total rewards strategies benefit an organization?
3. In designing policies on rewards and recognition, what are the factors an organization must consider and why?
4. Explain ethical issues in rewards and recognition programme.
5. Write short notes on the following

   (a) Work-life balancing
   (b) Total rewards
   (c) Rewards policy
   (d) Casual incentives
   (e) Non-monetary rewards

Critical Thinking Question

Visit websites of two organizations having diversified business portfolio. Study information about their rewards and recognition programmes. Make comparative analysis between these two organizations and adjudicate whose R&R programme is better and why?

CASE STUDY: Strategically Managing Rewards for Business Gains

The Royal Bank of Scotland Group (RBS), one of the largest financial institutions in the world, with 1,40,000 people on its payroll has a culture of recognizing employees for their good work. The company's reward programme addresses self actualization needs of its employees through structured rewards and recognition programme, including promotion opportunities with the prospect of life long career development with the group. The most important reward and recognition programmes benefit for the RBS employees is ample opportunities for work-life balancing. The company provides its employees opportunities to strike work-life balance thus helping them meet their work and non-work commitments. *Right to work flexibly* helps RBS employees to achieve better work-life balancing. Job sharing, part-time working, home working, variable working hours, compressed hours, etc. are some of the ways of work flexibalization practiced by RBS. Carefully crafted reward and recognition programme has helped RBS not only attract and retain talent, but also achieve enhanced performance due to increased motivation and performance of its employees.

3M, another global manufacturing giant also makes effective use of reward and recognition programme. The message of 3M's model rewards and recognition programme is *Engage employees and drives energy saving efforts*.

To make rewards and recognition programme more meaningful, companies across the globe are coming with strategic and innovative solutions. For example, early recognition scheme is preferred instead of waiting year long for recognition and reward. Companies are also trying to institutionalize the culture of recognition. In addition, companies are coming out with rewards programme that are easily understood and liked by their employees. A greater emphasis on intangibles is making rewards

(Contd)

CASE STUDY (Contd)

and recognition programme cost effective and result oriented.

Discussion question

It is now known that organizational rewards programme serve multiple purposes. List rewards and recognition programme of an organization and critically discuss how this organization achieves its business results by leveraging such programme.

References

Armstrong, M. (2007), *Employee Reward Management And Practice*, Great Britain: Bell & Bain.

Bhattacharyya, D.K. (2013), 'R&R Are More Holistic Than C&B: We Should Rename C&B to R&R', *Compensation & Benefits Review*, vol. 45, issue 5, pp. 286–8.

Heery, E. (1996), 'Risk, representation and the new pay', *Personnel Review*, vol. 25, issue 6, pp. 54–65.

Lawler, E.E. III. (1984), 'The Strategic Design of Reward Systems', in R.S. Schuler & S.A. Young-blood (Eds.), *Readings in Personnel and Human Resource Management*, 2nd edition, St. Paul, MN, West Publishing.

Lawler, E.E. III. (1990), *Strategic Pay: Aligning Organizational Strategies and Pay Systems*, San Francisco, CA: Jossey-Bass.

Lawler, E.E. III. (1995), The New Pay: A Strategic Approach, *Compensation & Benefits Review*, vol. 27, issue 4, pp. 14–22.

Schuster, J.R. and P.K. Zingheim (1992), *The New Pay: Linking Employee and Organizational Performance*, New York, Lexington Books.

Wood, S. (1996), 'High Commitment Management and Pay Systems', *Journal of Management Studies*, vol. 33, issue 1, pp. 53–77.

CHAPTER
FOURTEEN

Legal and Taxation Issues on Employee Compensation

Learning Objectives

After reading this chapter you will be able to
- understand the legal definition of compensation and wages
- analyse tax implications of wages and compensation
- study the legal definition of perquisites
- understand tax implication of perquisites
- assess the concept of cost to the company
- assess the process of wage fixation through collective bargaining

OPENING CASE

All's Not Well at P&G

Procter & Gamble (P&G) is not just a company—it is an economic powerhouse with annual sales of $76 billion and 1,38,000 people on its payroll, operating in more than 80 countries. With 300 brands under its fold, the company's HR is now in one of the most acute phases of its transformation. It aims to make use of the company's talent across the world to sustain and grow in a fiercely competitive FMCG sector. P&G's consolidation strategy started in 1992 and aimed to look into redundant capacity in manufacturing plants across the world, to frame optimum inventory-holding policies, and the development of the techniques to optimize the supply chain. With 30 managers and 1,000 employees in this consolidation process, P&G is now reformulating its business strategy. The company's new organizational design keeps a track of organizational structure and inflow of talent. P&G has developed a flow model taking into account variables such as hiring rates, attrition, retirement, movement between jobs, and promotion rates. This model shows the likely flow of people moving in and out of an organization and helps determine whether new hiring is required or not at a particular point of time. With the global mushrooming of FMCG companies, P&G has to offer competitive compensation packages, but with tough performance targets leading to frequent manpower redundancy in the form of employees who fail to perform to the company's expectation. Initial years of work, for the marketing executives, take them through different phases of ground level activities, to allow them to gain experience, and then mature and grow.

INTRODUCTION

The topic employee compensation and wages in India has been dealt with in several Indian labour laws. A number of these laws have been examined in this chapter. Since, legal interpretation cannot be altered or modified, literal presentation of legal definitions has been made.

Section 2 of Payment of Wages Act 1936 defines wages as any remuneration (whether by way of salary, allowances, or otherwise) expressed in terms of money or capable of being so expressed, which would, if the terms of employment express or implied were fulfilled, be capable to a person employed in respect of his employment or of work done in such employment and includes the following:

- any remuneration payable under any reward or settlement between the parties or order of a court
- any remuneration to which the person employed is entitled to in respect of overtime work or holidays or any leave period
- any additional remuneration payable under the terms of employment (whether called a bonus or by any other name)
- any sum by means of termination of employment of the person employed is payable under any law, contract or instrument, which provides for the payment of such sum, whether with or without deductions, but does not provide for the time within which the payment is to be made
- any sum to which the person employed is entitled under any scheme formed under any law for the time being in force

However, this definition of wages does not include the following:

- any bonus (whether under a scheme or profit sharing or otherwise), which does not form part of remuneration payable under the terms of employment, or which is not payable under any award or settlement between the parties or order of a court
- the value of any house accommodation, or of the supply of light, water, medical attendance, or other amenity or of any service excluded from the computation of wages by special order of the state government

- travelling allowances or the value of any travelling concession
- any contribution paid by the employer to any pension or provident fund, and the interest which may have accrued thereon
- any sum paid to employed persons to defray special expenses entailed on them by the nature of their employment
- any gratuity payable on the termination of employment in cases other than those specified in subclause (d)

The Payment of Wages Act 1936 regulates payment of wages to workers and ensures a speedy and effective remedy for them against illegal deductions and/or unjustified delay caused in paying wages. The wage ceiling under the Payment of Wages Act 1936 has now been raised to ₹10,000 per month with effect from 8 August 2007. It means henceforth employees drawing monthly wage/salary up to ₹10,000 can file their claim to recover dues from their employers for any illegal deductions from their pay.

Section 2 of the Industrial Disputes Act 1947 defines wage as any remuneration capable of being expressed in terms of money, which would, if the terms of employment, express or implied, were fulfilled be capable to a workman in respect of his employment or of work done in such employment and includes the following:

- such allowances (including dearness allowance) as the workman is for the time being entitled to
- the value of any house accommodation or of supply of light, water, medical attendance, or other amenity or of any service or of an concessional supply of food grains or other articles
- any travelling concession

However, the Industrial Disputes Act 1947 does not include the following:

- bonus
- any contribution paid or payable by the employer to any pension fund or provident fund or for the benefit of the workers under any law for the time being in force
- any gratuity payable on the termination of their service

Similarly, Section 2(b) of the Minimum Wages Act, 1948 has defined the word wages as all remuneration capable of being expressed in terms of money, which would, if the terms of the contract of employment, express or implied were fulfilled be payable to persons employed in respect of their employment or of work done in such employment and includes house rent allowance but does not include:

- the value of:
  - any house accommodation, supply of light, water, medical attendance, or
  - any other amenity or any service excluded by general or special order of the appropriate government
- any contribution paid by the employer to any travelling concession
- any travelling allowance or the value of any travelling concession

- any sum paid to the persons employed to defray special expenses entailed on them by the nature of employment
- any gratuity payable or discharge

Apart from these, the Payment of Bonus Act 1965, The Equal Remuneration Act 1976, and Regulation of Managerial Remuneration under Section 198 of the Companies Act 1956 also provide legal interpretation of the term wages or compensation.

The Payment of Bonus Act 1965 provides for payment of bonus to employees of factories and establishments employing 20 or more persons. Clause 13 of Section 2 of Payment of Bonus Act 1965 provides for payment of bonus to every employee, whose salary/wage does not exceed ₹10,000 per month in any industry provided he has worked not less than 30 working days in that year. For calculation of bonus, Section 12 of the Act, however considers wage/salary of ₹3,500 per month.

Wage Determination in Organized and Unorganized Sector

In India, a uniform and comprehensive wage policy covering all sectors of the economy is not available. However, wage determination both in the organized and unorganized sectors follows certain uniform norms. In organizations classified under the organized sector, wage determination is primarily based on negotiations and settlements. In the unorganized sector, the central and state governments intervene in the scheduled nature of employments through the enforcement of the Minimum Wages Act 1948.

The minimum rate of wages also includes special allowance, that is, variable dearness allowance (VDA) linked to consumer price index (CPI). VDA is revised twice a year, in April and October. Central government and twenty six states or union territories have adopted VDA as a component of minimum wage. The 28th Indian Labour Conference in 1985 recommended a national basic subsistence level wage below which no wages may be fixed regardless of the nature of work, nature of employment, and other considerations. In the absence of uniformity in minimum wages, the central government adopted the concept of national floor level minimum wage. The national floor level minimum wages as on 1 February 2004 determined by the central government is fixed as ₹66 per day.

In Chapter 1 on Introduction to compensation management, we have already discussed the definition and concepts of wages from different perspectives. However, the legal definition of wages, according to various labour laws, need not necessarily match with the concepts discussed earlier. In addition, payment of some of the allowances has been made mandatory under legal provisions. For example, payment of DA (dearness allowance) is considered as part of wages under Section 2(n) of the Industrial Disputes Act 1947. Similarly, we have many other allowances, which organizations need to pay depending on the type of industry, nature of job, level of employment, etc. The Income Tax

Act 1961 defines wages and compensation from a much broader perspectives for computing tax obligations of the employees.

TAX IMPLICATIONS OF COMPENSATION

Tax implications of compensation vary between countries. In India, the Income Tax Act stipulates the tax payable for income from salary. In this chapter, some of the salient features of the Act have been reviewed briefly and suggestion provided for designing compensation, which can reduce the tax burden both for the employees and the employers.

Salary The word salary generally means monetary compensation, which an employee gets from the employer. However, the definition of the term salary under the Income Tax Act is much wider than what is normally understood. The term salary for the purpose of Income Tax Act includes monetary as well as non-monetary payment in the form of facilities such as housing accommodation, interest-free loans, and certain reimbursements. However, for any income to be termed as salary, there should exist a relationship of an employer and an employee between payer and payee.

COMPENSATION AND THE INCOME TAX ACT

In the Income Tax Act, the term compensation is used as a synonym of the term salary. Hence, the definition of salary can also be applied to compensation. The term salary has been defined differently for different purposes in the Income Tax Act. Under Section 17(1), salary includes the following:

- wages
- any annuity or pension
- any fee, commission, perquisite, or profit in lieu of salary or in addition to any salary or wages
- any advance of salary
- any payment received in respect of any period of leave not availed by him
- the portion of the annual accretion in any previous year to the balance at the credit of an employee participating in a recognized provident fund (PF) to the extent it is taxable
- transferred balance in a recognized PF to the extent it is taxable

Since organizational compensation practices differ widely, Income Tax Act has further extended the term salary to include profit in lieu of salary, under Clause (iii). This clause extends the term salary to any amount of compensation due to or received by an assessee from his employer or former employer at or in connection with the termination of his employment. In addition, the amount of any compensation, due to or received by an assessee, from his employer or former employer, at or in connection with the modification of the terms and conditions of employment. The actual import of the principles of Income Tax Act is that the payment must be arising due to master–servant relationship between the payer and the payee. With the exceptions of gratuity, commuted pension, retrenchment compensation, house rent allowance, etc. all such payments are construed as part of compensation and taxable under the Income Tax Act.

PERQUISITES

Compensation in the form of perquisites is defined under Section 17(2) of the Income Tax Act. In general, perquisites are non-monetary benefits, apart from the salary, received by the employee. In other words, incidental benefits received in addition to regular wages or salary constitute perquisites. Since the perquisites are non-monetary benefits, they have to be valued and converted into monetary terms.

The term *salaries* under Section 17(1), includes perquisites, which are taxable. The underlying reason for considering perquisites as part of salaries is that perquisites are benefits received by the employee over and above the salary. In addition, perquisites are incidental to and in addition to regular wages. While designing compensation, it is important to understand what constitutes perquisites as per the Income Tax Act. Section 17(2) considers following components of compensation as perquisites:

- the value of rent-free accommodation provided to the employee by his employer
- the value of any concession in the matter of rent respecting any accommodation provided to the employee by his employer
- the value of any benefit or amenity granted or provided free of cost or at concessional rate in any of the following cases:
  - by a company to an employee who is a director thereof
  - by a company to an employee being a person who has a substantial interest in the company
  - by any employer (including a company) to an employee to whom the provisions of paragraphs (a) and (b) of this subclause do not apply and whose income under the head 'salaries' (whether due from, or paid or allowed by, one or more employers), exclusive of the value of all benefits or amenities not provided for by way of monetary payment, exceeds ₹50,000

Provided that nothing contained in this sub clause shall apply to the value of any benefit provided by a company free of cost or at a concessional rate to its employees by way of allotment of shares, debentures, or warrants directly or indirectly under any employee's stock option plan or scheme of the company offered to such employees in accordance with the guidelines issued in this behalf by the central government.

Also it has been made clear that any stock option plan of the company by way of free and concessional allotment of shares, debentures, etc. will be treated as taxable perquisites.

Background

The Finance Act 2001 inserted a subclause (vi) to bring fringe benefits or amenity as may be prescribed under the tax net and to be taxed at the cost of the employer. Therefore, the Central Board of Direct Taxes notified the final rules vide notification dated 25 September 2001 by substituting Rule 3 of the Income tax Rules 1962 relating to valuation of perquisites. The new rules are effective from 1 April 2001, that is, assessment year 2002–03. Under new Rule 3, perquisites of all employees are taxable. Some of the norms for item-wise valuation of perquisites are presented in the following sections.

Motor car

Where the employer provides the employee a motorcar exclusively for his private and personal purposes, the amount actually spent by the employer on the maintenance and running of the motor car including remuneration, if any, paid to the chauffeur plus 10 per cent of the actual cost of motor car representing the normal wear and tear of the motor car (i.e., depreciation on motor car if the car is owned by the employer) is considered as part of the employees compensation.

However, where the employer provides car to the employees exclusively in the performance of his official duties, such values shall be nil provided documents specified are maintained by the employer.

In cases where the employer makes available car partly in the performance of his duties and partly for his private and personal purposes, all the expenses on the maintenance and running the car are met or reimbursed to the employee by the employer. ₹1,200 per month plus ₹600 per month where the employer also provides the chauffeur in case where the cubic capacity of the engine of the car does not exceed 1.6 litre. ₹1,600 per month plus ₹600 per month where the employer also provides the chauffer in case where the cubic capacity of the engine of the car exceeds 1.6 litre. The employee meets all the expenses on the maintenance and running for its user for the employee's private or personal purposes. ₹400 per month plus ₹600 per month where the employer also provides the chauffer in case where the cubic capacity of the engine of the car does not exceed 1.6 litre. ₹600 per month plus ₹600 per month where the employer also provides the chauffeur in case where the cubic capacity of the engine of the car exceeds 1.6 litre. The figures would be added or deducted from employees' compensation.

In some cases, the employer also provides more than one motorcar to the senior management personnel. If more than one motor car is allowed to be used by the employee, the value of one of the motor cars should be calculated in the manner stated previously as the case may be and the second and subsequent motor cars shall be deemed to have been used wholly for private and personal use and hence it should be computed as if the car is wholly and exclusively used by the employee for his private purpose.

In cases, where the employee owns the motorcar and all the expenses are met by the employer for exclusive use in the performance of official duties, the value shall be nil provided documents specified are maintained by the employer. When it is used by the employee partly in the performance of his/her duties and partly for his private and personal purposes, provisions mentioned previously will be applicable.

For having other vehicles by the employee, if it is used exclusively for the performance of his official duties, the value shall be nil provided the employer maintains documents specified. For part use in the performance of official duties and partly for private and personal purposes, ₹600 is reduced from the actual expenditure incurred by the employer per month.

Rent-free residential accommodation

Such perquisites are valued differently for government employees, employees of statutory organizations, and for the employees of other organizations.

HRA calculation – Section 10 (13A) of the Income Tax Act Employees receiving HRA and also incurring expenditure on rent can claim can claim income tax exemption for the least amount of the following calculation.

(i) HRA amount actually received from the employer.
(ii) Rent actually paid less 10 per cent of salary.
(iii) 40 per cent of salary (50 per cent in case of Mumbai, Chennai, Kolkata, Delhi). Salary here means Basic + Dearness allowance (DA), if dearness allowance is provided per the terms of employment.

Income tax exemption amount can be calculated as follows. Say your Basic salary is ₹5,000, DA is ₹1,000, and HRA is ₹2,000 per month, and you actually pay ₹2,000 monthly rent. Let us put the information in following order:

Basic salary = (₹5,000 × 12) = ₹60,000
Dearness allowance (DA) = (₹1,000 × 12) = ₹12,000
House rent allowance (HRA) = (₹2,000 × 12) = ₹24,000
Actual rent paid = (₹2,000 × 12) = ₹24,000

Let us assume, you stay in a place where 40 per cent of the Basic + DA is considered to be slab for HRA. The calculation then would be:

Actual HRA received = (₹2,000 × 12) = ₹24,000
Rent paid in excess of 10 per cent of salary = (₹24,000 – ₹7,200) = ₹16,800
40 per cent of salary = ₹28,800

Therefore, ₹16,800 shall be exempt and the balance ₹7,200 shall be included in gross salary.

If one stays in his own house, the entire HRA received from the employer is taxable. Therefore, conditions such as inclusion of HRA in the salary component, staying in the rented house, and payment of actual rent more than 10 per cent of salaries are three important requirements of getting tax benefits for HRA. Staying with parents in a parental house and paying HRA to them can qualify for tax exemption. However, claiming exemption for payment of rent made to spouse is not allowed.

Section 80D: medical insurance premiums

Health insurance, popularly known as Mediclaim Policies, provides for a deduction of up to ₹35,000 (₹15,000 for premium payments towards policies on self, spouse, and children and read as in addition to ₹15,000 for premium payment towards non-senior citizen dependent parents or ₹20,000 for premium payment towards senior citizen dependent.

This deduction is in addition to ₹1,00,000 savings under IT deductions clause 80C. For consideration under a senior citizen category, the incumbent's age should be 60 years. This deduction is also applicable if Mediclaim premium cheques are paid by the company on behalf of the employees and such payment is shown as part of CTC of the employees.

Some clauses providing tax benefits to salaried persons Table 14.1 explains different clauses providing tax benefits to salaried persons. However, such provisions keep on changing with fiscal policies of the government.

Leave travel concession [Sec 10(5)]

Leave travel concession (LTC) is an important perquisite received by the employees from their employers. LTC is paid by the employer for the employee and his family for travel to any place in India. LTC is given either in a block of two years or in a block of four years. It is paid as a lump sum (in most cases one month basic plus dearness allowances). In government and public sector banks, LTC entitlement of employees varies with their ranks or hierarchical levels, and often it is limited to a certain distance. Whatever may be the LTC amount, income tax exemptions is limited to actual cost of journey, that is, the actual amount spent on transportation—either by air, rail, or road. Other travel expenses in the city of destination such as taxi/cab fare and auto fare cannot be claimed as exempt.

To claim the income tax exemptions, it is important to preserve the proof of travel, that is, the actual ticket receipts from the travel agency.

Some organizations have a system of payment of leave travel allowance, instead of LTC, along with the monthly salary. This is taxable with effect from 1 April 2012.

Home loan and tax planning

In case of home loan, income tax exemption is available both for the repayment of principal amount as well as for the payment of interest. For repayment of principal amount, maximum allowable deduction for tax exemption is ₹1,50,000, but it is covered under section 80C. Hence, in case your section 80C allowable benefits amount is already ₹1,50,000, you may not get the tax exemption benefit for repayment of principal loan amount. However under section 24(b), interest on housing loan can be claimed as tax exempt

TABLE 14.1 Tax benefits available for salaried employees

S. no.	Section	Details of deduction	Limit
1.	80C	General deduction for investment in PPF, PF, Life Insurance, ULIP, Stamp duty on house, Fixed deposits for 5 years, bonds, etc.	Maximum ₹1,50,000 is allowed. Investment need not be from taxable income.
2.	80CCC	Deduction in case of contribution to pension fund. However, it should be noted that surrender value or employer contribution is considered as income.	Maximum is ₹1,50,000. Run concurrently with section 80C.
3.	80CCD	Deduction in respect to contribution to new pension scheme. Employees of central and others are eligible.	Maximum is sum of employer's and employee's contribution to the maximum: 10% of salary. Run concurrently with sections 80C, 80CCC.
4.	80D	Medical insurance on self, spouse, children, or parents	₹15,000 for self, spouse, and children. Extra ₹15,000 for insurance on parents. If parents are above 65 years, extra sum should be read as ₹20,000. Therefore, maximum is ₹35,000 per annum. Additional ₹5,000 for preventive health check-up. Therefore, maximum is ₹40,000 per annum.
5.	80DD	For maintenance including treatment or insurance of the lives of physically disabled dependent relatives.	₹50,000. In case disability is severe, the amount is ₹75,000.
6.	80DDB	For medical treatment of self or relatives suffering from specified disease	Actual amount paid to the extent of ₹40,000. In case of patient being Senior Citizen, amount is ₹60,000. For physically disabled assessee, under section 80U deduction is up to ₹1 lakh.
7.	80E	For interest payment on loan taken for higher studies for self or education of spouse or children.	Actual amount paid as interest and starts from the financial year in which he starts paying interest and runs till the interest is paid in full.
8.	80G	Donation to charitable societies	100% or 50% depending on the nature of societies.
9.	80GG	For rent paid	This is only for people not getting any House Rent Allowance. Maximum is ₹2,000 per month. Rule 11B is method of computation.
10.	80GGA	For donation to entities in scientific research or rural development.	Only those tax payers who have no business income can claim this deduction. Maximum is equivalent to 100% of donation.
11.	80U	Deduction in respect of permanent physical disability including blindness to taxpayer.	₹50,000 which goes up to ₹75,000 in case the taxpayer is suffering from severe disability.
12.	80QQB, 80RRB	Royalty income from books (other than text books) and patents.	Royalty income or ₹3,00,000, whichever is less.

to the maximum extent of ₹2,00,000, provided it is self occupied. In case the house is given on rent, then the difference between rent for the let out has to be deducted from the actual interest paid for the housing load and only the difference amount can be claimed as tax exempt.

Payment of tax on non-monetary perquisites by employer

Income Tax Act provides for employer to pay tax on the value of non-monetary perquisites given to employees. Perquisites are given as an incentive to employees and employers do not deduct any TDS for them. This practice is known as *tax gross-up*, that is, a system of payment to an employee some compensation for which the tax is paid by the employer. Tax gross-up practices are more prevalent in case of executive compensation. This practice is restricted globally by the regulatory authorities as it is considered a process of hiding the actual income of the salaried person.

Perquisite includes the following:
1. the value of rent free accommodation
2. the value of any concession in the matter of rent in respect of any accommodation
3. the value of any benefit or amenity granted or provided free of cost or at concessional rate in any of the following cases:
   a) by a company to an employee who is a director of such company
   b) by a company to an employee who has a substantial interest in the company
   c) by an employer (including a company) to an employee, who is not covered by (i) or (ii) and whose income under the head Salaries (whether due from or paid or allowed by one or more employers), exclusive of the value of all benefits and amenities not provided by way of monetary payment, exceeds ₹50,000
4. any sum paid by the employer in respect of any obligation which would have been paid by the assessee
5. any sum payable by the employer, whether directly or through a fund, other than a recognized provident fund or an approved superannuation fund or other specified funds u/s 17, to effect an assurance on the life of an assessee or to effect a contract for an annuity
6. with effect from 01 April 2010 (AY 2010–11), it is further clarified that the value of any specified security or sweat equity shares allotted or transferred, directly or indirectly, by the employer, or former employer, free of cost or at concessional rate to the assessee, shall constitute a perquisite in the hand of employees

Following are the rules for valuation of perquisite:

Accommodation For purpose of valuation of the perquisite of unfurnished accommodation, salaried taxpayers' valuation of perquisite in respect of accommodation would be at the following prescribed rates.

1. Where the accommodation provided to the employee is owned by the employer, the rate is 15 per cent of salary in cities having population exceeding 25 lakh as per the 2001 census. The rate is 10 per cent of salary in cities having population exceeding 10 lakh but not exceeding 25 lakh as per 2001 Census. For other places, the perquisite value would be 7.5 per cent of the salary.
2. Where the accommodation provided is taken on lease/rent by the employer, the prescribed rate is 15 per cent of the salary or the actual amount of lease rental payable by the employer, whichever is lower, as reduced by any amount of rent paid by the employee.

For furnished accommodation, the value of perquisite as determined by the previous method shall be increased by:
(i) 10 per cent of the cost of furniture, appliances and equipments, or
(ii) where the furniture, appliances and equipments have been taken on hire, by the amount of actual hire charges payable as reduced by any charges paid by the employee himself

Accommodation includes a house, flat, farm house, hotel accommodation, motel, service apartment, guest house, a caravan, mobile home, ship etc. However, the value of any accommodation provided to an employee working at a mining site, or an on-shore oil exploration site, or a project execution site, or a dam site, or a power generation site, or an off-shore site will not be treated as a perquisite.

However, for not being treated as perquisite such accommodation should either be located in a remote area or where it is not located in a remote area, the accommodation should be of a temporary nature having plinth area of not more than 800 square feet and should not be located within 8 kilometers of the local limits of any municipality or cantonment board.

A project execution site for the purposes of this sub-rule means a site of project up to the stage of its commissioning. A remote area means an area located at least 40 kilometers away from a town having a population not exceeding 20,000 as per the latest published all-India census.

If an accommodation is provided by an employer in a hotel the value of the benefit in such a case shall be 24 per cent of the annual salary or the actual charges paid or payable to such hotel, whichever is lower, for the period during which such accommodation is provided as reduced by any rent actually paid or payable by the employee. However, where in cases the employee is provided such accommodation for a period not exceeding in aggregate fifteen days on transfer from one place to another, no perquisite value for such accommodation provided in a hotel shall be charged.

Personal attendants The value of free service of all personal attendants including a sweeper, gardener, and a watchman is to be taken at actual cost to the employer. Where the attendant is provided at the residence of the employee, full cost will be taxed as perquisite in the hands of the employee irrespective of the degree of personal service rendered to him. Any amount paid by the employee for such facilities or services shall be reduced from the amount mentioned previously.

Gas, electricity, and water For free supply of gas, electricity and water for household consumption, the rules provide that the amount paid by the employer to the agency supplying the amenity shall be the value of perquisite. Where the supply is made from the employer's own resources, the manufacturing cost per unit incurred by the employer would be taken for the valuation of perquisite. Any amount paid by the employee for such facilities or services shall be reduced from the amount mentioned previously.

Free or concessional education Perquisite on account of free or concessional education shall be valued in a manner assuming that such expenses are borne by the employee, and would cover cases where an employer is running, maintaining, or directly or indirectly financing the educational institution. Any amount paid by the employee for such facilities or services shall be reduced from the amount mentioned previously. However, where such educational institution itself is maintained and owned by the employer or where such free educational facilities are provided in any institution by reason of his being in employment of that employer, the value of the perquisite to the employee shall be determined with reference to the cost of such education in a similar institution in or near the locality if the cost of such education or such benefit per child exceeds ₹1,000 per month.

Interest free or concessional loans It is common practice, particularly in financial institutions, to provide interest free or concessional loans to employees or any member of his household. The value of perquisite arising from such loans would be the excess of interest payable at prescribed interest rate over interest, if any, actually paid by the employee or any member of his household. The prescribed interest rate would now be the rate charged per annum by the State Bank of India as on the 1st day of the relevant financial year in respect of loans of same type and for the same purpose advanced by it to the general public. Perquisite value would be calculated on the basis of the maximum outstanding monthly balance method. For valuing perquisites under this rule, any other method of calculation and adjustment otherwise adopted by the employer shall not be relevant.

However, small loans up to ₹20,000 in the aggregate are exempt. Loans for medical treatment specified in Rule 3A are also exempt, provided the amount of loan for medical reimbursement is not reimbursed under any medical insurance scheme. Where any medical insurance reimbursement is received, the perquisite value at the prescribed rate shall be charged from the date of reimbursement on the amount reimbursed, but not repaid against the outstanding loan taken specifically for this purpose.

Use of assets It is common practice for an asset owned by the employer to be used by the employee or any member of his household. This perquisite is to be charged at the rate of 10 per cent of the original cost of the asset as reduced by any charges recovered from the employee for such use. However, the use of computers and laptops would not give rise to any perquisite.

Transfer of assets Often an employee or member of his household benefits from the transfer of movable asset (not being shares or securities) at no cost or at a cost less than its market value from the employer. The difference between the original cost of the movable asset (not being shares or securities) and the sum, if any, paid by the employee, shall be taken as the value of perquisite. In case of a movable asset, which has already been put to use, the original cost shall be reduced by a sum of 10 per cent of such original cost for every completed year of use of the asset. Owing to a higher degree of obsolescence, in case of computers and electronic gadgets, however, the value of perquisite shall be worked out by reducing 50 per cent of the actual cost by the reducing balance method for each completed year of use. Electronic gadgets in this case mean data storage and handling devices such as computer, digital diaries, and printers. They do not include household appliance (i.e. white goods) such as washing machines, microwave ovens, mixers, hot plates, and ovens. Similarly, the value of perquisite in case of cars shall be worked out by reducing 20 per cent of its actual cost by the reducing balance method for each completed year of use.

Medical reimbursement Medical reimbursement by the employer exceeding ₹15,000 per annum u/s. 17(2)(v) is to be taken as perquisites.

It is further clarified that the rule position regarding valuation of perquisites are given at Section 17(2) of Income Tax Act 1961 and at Rule 3 of Income Tax Rules 1962. The employers may look into the previous provisions carefully before they determine the perquisite value for deduction purposes.

It is pertinent to mention that benefits specifically exempt u/s 10(13A), 10(5), 10(14), 17, etc. would continue to be exempt. These include benefits such as travel on tour and transfer; leave travel; daily allowance to meet tour expenses as prescribed; and medical facilities subject to conditions.

Income tax slabs for the financial year 2014–15/ assessment year 2015–16

For the Financial year 2014–15 and assessment year 2015–16, income tax slabs will be as given in Table 14.2. Educational cess at the rate of 3 per cent of income tax will continue.

TABLE 14.2 Income tax slabs for FY 2014–15

Income level	Male/female assessee (less than 60 years)	Senior citizen assessee (60–80 years)	Senior citizen assessee (more than 80 years)
Income up to ₹2.5 lakh	No tax	No tax (up to 3 lakh)	No tax (up to ₹5 lakh)
₹2.5–5 lakh	10%	10% (3–5 lakh)	No tax
₹5–10 lakh	20%	20%	20%
Above 10 lakh	30%	30%	30%

Treatment of special allowances to meet expenses

Section 10(14) of Income Tax Act allows payment of special allowance or benefit to meet expenses wholly, necessarily, and exclusively incurred in the performance of the duties of an office or employment of profit, to the extent to which such expenses are actually incurred for that purpose. Any such allowance granted to the assessees either to meet their personal expenses at the place where the duties of their office or employment of profit are ordinarily performed by them or at the place where they ordinarily resides, or to compensate them for the increased cost of living, provided such personal allowance granted to the assessee not to remunerate or compensate them for performing duties of a special nature relating to their office or employment unless such allowance is related to the place of their posting or residence. These are not in the nature of entertainment allowances. Appendix 14A provides a template for computing total income.

A tabular presentation on valuation of perquisites with the relevant provisions is presented in Appendix 14B. Students are advised to refer to the relevant sections of the Income Tax Act and the Rules for updates.

COST TO COMPANY

After a detailed discussion on the different definitions of wages, it is now important to understand the definition and context of cost to company (CTC) and the components that an organization should consider in computing the CTC. The concept of CTC originated in the US. Although there is no uniformity in practices, there are some common parameters, which are considered by all organizations while computing the CTC. A more generic definition of CTC is expenditure a company makes directly on employees excluding the cost of infrastructure such as space, desktop computers, air conditioning, and cost incurred for training. It includes the salary paid directly to the employees, the benefits directly attributable to the employees such as company's contribution to the Provident Fund, pension funds (varies between countries), medical insurance premium, life insurance premium, cost of loans offered to the employee (some companies even include the cost of the loan the employee is entitled to but not availed of), expenses for mobile phone connections, expenses for land-line connections, and benefits offered for visiting the home country or hometown.

Calculation of CTC The total compensation includes the value of all the perks and benefits an employee is offered by the company in addition to the employee's salary. Calculating annual CTC is important both from the organization and from the employee perspectives. Organization can ascertain the HR cost, whereas the employees can understand what they are being offered, as they can benchmark their CTC with the other comparable organizations. It also helps them to decide on job switch. However, as mentioned at the outset, it is apparently difficult to arrive at the CTC as many components of the CTC considered by the company may not be construed as a part of total compensation package. Therefore, organizations need to carefully add all the compensation components or their equivalent cash value to arrive at a comprehensive CTC value. Appendix 14C provides a template to compute the annual CTC using a typical organization's practices.

PAY-AT-RISK

Although not legally tenable, some organizations across the world require employees to set aside a portion of their base pay-at-risk until key sales or financial targets are met. For example, at the new Saturn plant of General Motors in Tennessee, employees have to set aside 10 per cent of their base pay-at-risk—5 per cent of the work year (92 hours) for compulsory attendance of training programmes arranged by the company and rest 5 per cent for the plant to meet certain quality and production targets for its cars. Likewise, any organization can consider introducing the concept of pay-at-risk by duly assigning some weightage to some critical areas of the company's performance. However, it is desirable to restrict pay-at-risk out of that component of base pay, which is paid by the company over and above the mandatory minimum wages.

LEGAL INTERPRETATION OF WAGE FIXATION

In a landmark judgement in the Express Newspapers Pvt. Ltd versus Union of India case (AIR 1958, SC 578), the Supreme Court adjudged that the main consideration which is to be borne in mind is that the industry should be able to maintain production with efficiency. Fixation of wages should not constrain the capacity to pay principles. However, the principles governing the capacity to pay have been suggested to be considered in the following perspectives:
- the selling price of the product
- the volume of the output
- profit and loss in the business
- the rate which have been agreed to by a large majority of the employers
- the amount of unemployment brought about or likely to be brought about by the imposition of the increased wages, etc.

WAGE FIXATION THROUGH COLLECTIVE BARGAINING

Collective bargaining basically determines the working conditions and the terms of employment through negotiations between the employer and the workers. Hence, broadly it also encompasses wage fixation. Once both the bargaining parties through a negotiation process agree on wages, the agreement is legally binding on both the employers and the workers. In a collective bargaining process, negotiation takes place between employer and one or more workers' organizations. The negotiation process helps to reach an agreement. Without going into different theoretical definitions, collective bargaining converges into three basic issues—(1) a means to contract for sale of labour, (2) a form of industrial government, and finally (3) a system of industrial relations.

International Labour Organization (ILO) defines collective bargaining as 'negotiations about working conditions and terms of employment between an employer, a group of employers or one or more employers' organizations, on the one hand and/or more representatives of workers organization on the other hand with a view to reach an agreement.'

In collective bargaining, the objective is to arrive at an agreement on wages and other conditions of employment about which the parties start with divergent viewpoints but ultimately attempt to make a compromise. As soon as the agreement is reached, the terms of agreement are put into operation. On the other hand, the major task of the bargaining process relates to sharing of information and suggestions with regard to issues of common interest including health, safety, welfare, and productive efficiency.

Role of government

The government may influence collective bargaining and employment conditions in ways which differ greatly among countries.

- It may determine employment conditions by law, for example, through setting minimum wages, legislating the length of holiday, or preventing ethnic discrimination.
- It may provide some benefits directly; for example, pensions.
- It may set the ground rules that govern the parties' conduct; for example, through the granting of the right to bargain to the trade unions, restricting the conditions under which labour strikes may occur, or determining the scope of bargaining.
- It may settle disputes which the parties are unable to settle within themselves often through mediation or arbitration. In Australia, conciliation and arbitration play a major role in determining the conditions of employment.
- Through its macroeconomic and social policies, the government has an influence on the terms of bargaining agreements.
- The government is a major employer itself and often bargains with unions representing its employees, frequently setting a pattern for the entire economy. In fact, union density is higher in the public sector than in the private sector in most countries today.

Furthermore, as the presumed representative of the public interest, the government is interested in industrial peace, price stability, increased productivity, and non-discriminatory employment patterns. To achieve these objectives, it can apply pressure on the negotiating parties (often through legislation). On the other hand, the parties can pressurize the government (often through political action). Therefore, the government is a third party in collective bargaining, combining the often conflicting roles of neutral observer and bargainer.

Characteristics

From the definitions of collective bargaining described earlier, some essential characteristics may be enumerated as follows.
- It is a group action as opposed to individual action and initiated through the representatives of workers and delegates of the management at the bargaining table.
- It is flexible and mobile and not fixed or static. It has flexibility and ample scope for compromise for a mutual give and take before the final agreement.
- It is a two-party process. It can succeed only when labour and management want to arrive at a healthy solution to all the problems. There must be a mutual eagerness to develop the collective bargaining procedure and the process should result in harmony and progress. It can flourish only in an atmosphere free from animosity and repraisal.
- It is a continuous process, which provides a mechanism for continuing and organized relationships between management and trade unions. The heart of collective bargaining lies in the process for continuing joint consideration and adjustment of plant and problems.
- The term is dynamic by itself because the concept is growing, expanding, and changing.
- It represents industrial democracy at work.
- It is not a competitive process but a complementary process, that is, each party needs something that the other party can offer, namely labour can make a greater productive effort and management has the capacity to pay.
- It is an art, an advanced form of human relations. To substantiate this, the bluffing, the oratory, dramatics, and coyness mixed in an inexplicable fashion, which may characterize a bargaining session, are an example.

Importance and need

It is evident from the foregoing discussion that to settle differences on the work-related issues, collective bargaining as a process is perceived as an important mechanism both by employers and the employees. We have adequately covered the general issues that are usually settled through collective bargaining.

The need for collective bargaining in India arose due to controversial issues the Indian industry had to face in the period after the Second World War. One of the most important aspects among these issues is that of modernization. The problems of modernization and productivity should be viewed in the context of industrial development. Indian industry cannot compete in global markets if it does not follow modern methods of production. Since, modernization causes displacement of workers, it naturally invites hostility, and the workers and management must, therefore, come together in their viewpoint through collective bargaining. The solution to common problems can be affected by legislative measures. Collective agreements provide the climate for smooth progress as there is ample scope for a synthesis between demands from one side and concessions from the other.

1. In individual bargaining, the workers may be tempted to accept undesirable conditions, which may thus bring down the general level of remuneration. Due to immobility of labour, all workers are not in a position to desert a wage-cutting employer. This immobility may be due to ignorance and illiteracy and industry-specific skill factors.
2. The workers who execute the work faster may accept a lower rate of payment, which may yield them a reasonable amount of wages, but such a low rate of wages would yield insufficient earnings to a great majority of workers.
3. Sometimes employers are in a position to control the bulk demands of the labourers and they may, through a concerted action, force the workers to accept low wages. Collective bargaining is the only mechanism that can avert such concerted action and prevent the creation of monopolistic tendencies.
4. The market apparatus consisting of the two forces of demand and supply can settle only the problem of determination of wages. Some of the non-wage issues such as the length of working day, health and safety of workers, operational speed, and introduction of rationalization measures of job security have to be settled by personal decisions and not by the forces of demand and supply.
5. Collective bargaining also provides a voice for the labour in the conduct and management of the industry. Workers have now a definite place in the exercise of a real influence in the determination of labour issues affecting them from time to time.
6. To ensure continuity of production, workers and employers must cooperate with each other and to achieve cooperation, collective bargaining inevitably becomes a regular feature of industrial life.
7. The problem of good human relations can be tackled successfully by the collective bargaining process.

Prerequisites

The success of a collective bargaining mechanism largely depends on the respective attitudes of workers in general and trade union in particular on one hand and the attitude of employer's management personnel on the other. However, the following factors are essential, if collective bargaining is to exist in a country successfully.

1. It is necessary for the management to recognize trade unions and to bargain in good faith. There is also pressure on the trade union to formulate plans and demands in a systematic manner.
2. There should be a change in the attitude of employers and employees. They must realize that collective bargaining approach does not imply litigation

under adjudication. It should be kept in mind of both parties that they are to resolve their differences on their respective claims quietly and calmly, within their own resources, reducing their dependence on the third party intervention.

3. For the purpose of collective bargaining, employers should be represented by the management and workers by their trade union representatives. Careful thought and selection of the negotiating team is very much essential. For management team, it is better to have a mixed composition, such as experts in production, finance, industrial relations, and headed by an expert in personnel management.
4. It is also appreciable to have open minds, listening to each others' concern and point of view and to have some flexibility in making adjustments to the demands.
5. To ensure collective bargaining, unfair labour practices should be avoided and abandoned by both parties; otherwise atmosphere and confidence will be vitiated by malpractice if either side takes advantage of the other by resorting to unfair practices.
6. Either side should avoid placing any irrational or unreasonable demand.
7. Negotiations can be successful only when the parties rely on facts and figures to support their points of view. That is why, trade union should be assisted by specialists, namely, economists, productivity experts, etc.
8. Trade unions should encourage the internal union democracy and periodic consultation with the general rank and file of the members of the union.
9. The outcome of negotiations and the terms of contract should be in writing and embodied in a document. If no agreement is reached, the parties should proceed to conciliation, mediation, or arbitration. If no settlement is arrived at even then, the workers should be free to go in for a labour strike and the employers on lockout. However, utmost care should be taken to resolve differences mutually.
10. Strikes and lockouts should be the last resort. Periodic discussions may be necessary between the management and trade unions to interpret the provisions of the contract and clarify doubts.
11. Trade unions should be equally concerned with quality of work, leading to a consistent concern for the viability of the organization and its products and services.
12. Once the agreement is reached, it must be honoured and fairly implemented.

COLLECTIVE BARGAINING IN INDIA

There are certain differences in the labour or trade union characteristics in developed and developing countries. In United Kingdom, workers form a union of their respective trades. Such a formation, which is more concerned for the group well-being, in reality provided the base for bargaining with the management on different employment issues.

The term collective bargaining in fact originated in Great Britain and was coined by Beatrice Potter in her book *The Co-operative Movement* in 1891.

In India collective bargaining is a late development. Its presence for the first time was visible in the year 1918 in Ahmedabad. Voluntary collective bargaining in industry and commerce has developed in India since independence. The textile industry in Ahmedabad, which has the longest history of settlement of disputes by mutual negotiation and voluntary arbitration, can claim to have paved the way towards modern collective bargaining although the experiment at Ahmedabad was not directly followed elsewhere. The inspiration for peaceful settlement of differences between the management and labour at Ahmedabad came from Gandhiji, who set out his philosophy of industrial relations in his autobiography.

In 1918, Gandhiji was leading the textile workers of Ahmedabad in their demand for better working conditions, but even though he had supported their strike, he was advocating the resolution of conflict by negotiation and mutual discussion between the accredited organizations of labourers and employers. When negotiation failed, the recommended conciliation, he suggested, is reference to an agreed arbitrator or board of arbitrators whose decision would be binding on both the conflicting parties. In 1918, when the wage disputes were eventually settled at Gandhiji's intervention by reference to an arbitration board representing both employers and workers, he declared that he did not see any reason why all future differences should not be settled in the same way.

Gandhiji was successful in bringing the Ahmedabad Mill Owners' Association to accept his point of view and in 1920, it was agreed that any dispute or difference of opinion, which could not be settled in the workplace, should be referred to Gandhiji and Seth Mangal Das, President of Ahmedabad Mill Owners' Association, as arbitrators. In case they could not reach an agreement, provision was made for reference to an arbitrator whose award would be final.

This system prevailed until 1939 in Ahmedabad. The system of voluntary arbitration could hardly be called collective bargaining. Usually, they were able to reach agreement, but on several occasions, they had to take recourse to an arbitrator on some unresolved points. In the first 16 months of its existence, the arbitration board delivered 23 judgments, but not all the questions that were referred to its attention were the subject of actual disputes.

Just before the Second World War, the system of arbitration in Ahmedabad seemed to be breaking down and in 1940, under war time conditions, a reference was made for compulsory adjudication under the Bombay Industrial Regulation Act, 1946.

In 1952, after a lapse of about 14 years, the Ahmedabad Mill Owners' Association and the Textile Labour Union signed two agreements, initially for

a period of two years, by which the machinery of voluntary arbitration was revived. This was proper collective bargaining between the two representative organizations, who agreed that in future, all disputes between the management of mills and their employees should be settled out of the court. Collective bargaining in textile industry in Ahmedabad is now carried on at two levels:
- between Mill Owners' Association and Textile Labour Association
- between individual mills and Textile Labour Association

In 1955, a general agreement on the subject of annual bonus was reached for the years 1953–1957, covering all the mills. In 1957, a joint productivity council was set up for textile mills in Ahmedabad. From the previous discussion, it is clear that a continuing collective bargaining process has evolved in the Ahmedabad textile industry.

There was, however, another early instance of an employers' association and an industrial union coming together to solve their problems. This was in the coir industry in Tranvancore (Kerala). However, both in Ahmedabad and Kerala, collective bargaining process was for a group of employers.

The earliest example of collective bargaining with individual concern was that of Joint Steamer Companies in Calcutta. Their first written agreement with Bengal Mariners Union was in the year 1946. Among the manufacturing enterprises, the earliest record of the post-War collective agreements was signed by Dunlop Rubber Company at Shagunge in West Bengal in 1947. The Bata Shoe Company in West Bengal signed its first agreement in 1948, Indian Aluminium Company in 1951, the Imperial Tobacco Company in 1952, the Mysore Iron and Steel Company in 1953, TISCO, Jamshedpur in 1955, National Newsprint and Paper Mills at Nepanagar (M.P.) in 1956 signed their collective agreements with their workmen.

From the previous discussions, it is clear that from 1950 onwards, collective bargaining attained prominence in India. The new industry groups, in sectors such as engineering and chemicals with a higher degree of professionalism in management have developed collective bargaining as an institution. In India, collective bargaining takes place at various levels, that is, plant level, industry level, and national level. We have illustrated a few plant level and industry level collective bargaining agreements in the past. The agreements at the national level are generally bipartite agreements and are finalized at conferences of labour and managements convened by the Government of India. The Delhi Agreement of 7 February 1951 and Bonus Agreement for Plantation workers of January 1956 are examples of such bipartite agreements in the past.

The issues of bargaining in India are generally related to wages, dearness allowance, retirement benefits, bonus, annual leave, casual leave, paid holiday, etc. A study of Employers' Federation of India shows that wages feature as a prominent issue among employers. Information about collective bargaining settlement, compiled by Labour Bureau, Shimla for the quarter

TABLE 14.3 Month-wise collective bargaining agreements in quarter ending 31 December 1994

S. no.	Subject	Number of agreements						Total	
		October	1994	November	1994	December	1994		
1.	Wages/DA	09	–	13	–	05	–	27	–
2.	Bonus	17	–	11	–	02	–	30	–
3.	Overtime	02	–	02	–	02	–	06	–
4.	House rent	04	–	04	–	–	–	08	–
5.	Health	01	–	02	–	01	–	04	–
6.	Welfare	01	–	04	–	02	–	07	–
7.	Hours of Work	02	–	–	–	–	–	02	–
8.	Conveyance	03	–	02	–	–	–	05	–
9.	Leave	04	–	03	–	02	–	09	–
10.	Liveries	04	–	06	–	–	–	10	–
11.	Service matter	32	01	20	–	19	–	71	01
12.	Others	07	–	09	–	01	–	17	–
	Total	86	01	76	–	34	–	196	01

Source: Various issues of *Indian Labour*, published by Labour Bureau, Shimla.

ending December 1994 shows that 115 agreements have been arrived at through collective bargaining during the quarter ending December 1994 in India. Out of these, only one settlement relates to the states whereas 114 fall in under the central government's purview. We have illustrated the position in Table 14.3.

Politicization of trade unions, failure of both parties to devote adequate time, third party intervention, etc. are some of the problems of collective bargaining in India. Mary Parker Follet criticized the collective bargaining process particularly for absence of workers' rights and privileges, which itself stand against their bargaining power. Workers, being weak bargainers, can never expect to gain from collective bargaining process.

SUMMARY

In this chapter, the legal interpretation of wages or compensation provided in various Indian labour laws is defined. Although there exists some finer distinction in the understanding and definition of the terms, wages and compensation in general are payouts from the employers to the employees for the services rendered.

The legal treatment of compensation under the provisions of Income Tax Act in India, in some cases, even provides independent definition. Due to wide coverage of the Income Tax Act, any tax-exempted incentives could hardly be offered to employees. Even perquisites and non-monetary incentives are covered under the provisions of the Act.

Apart from the legal interpretation and taxation aspects of compensation design, which organizations need to understand while designing the compensation structure, collective bargaining as a voluntary process of negotiation between employers and employees to determine compensation also need to be understood. The process of collective bargaining ensures organizational democracy. However, it often becomes as ineffective process for reaching an agreement. Over the years, the importance of collective bargaining is receding globally. Most organizations prefer to have enterprise-wide bargaining rather than industry-wide bargaining. Even industry-wide bargaining agreements are not implemented by many organizations within the same industry group. The example of banking industry is relevant in this context. In a collective bargaining situation, HR mangers need to play a crucial role to strike a win-win deal. To achieve this objective, they have to enrich their negotiation skills by practising on collective bargaining simulation games on a regular basis.

Key Terms

Cost to company (CTC) It is a company's expenditure spent directly on employees excluding the cost of infrastructure. It includes the salary directly paid to the employees, the benefits directly attributable to the employees, such as a company's contribution to the Provident Fund, pension funds (varies between countries), medical insurance premium, life insurance premium, cost of loans given to the employee (some companies even include the cost of the loan the employee is entitled to but not availed of), telephone expenses for mobile phone connections and land-line connections, and benefits offered for visiting the home country or hometown.

Enterprise-wide bargaining Collective bargaining, specific to an organization, is independent of the bargaining process in a similar industry.

Pay-at-risk It is a system of putting a portion of base pay-at-risk. Although not legally tenable, some organizations require employees to set aside a portion of base pay 'at-risk' until key sales or financial targets are met.

Perquisites These are additional benefits received by the employee, apart from the salary, in non-monetary terms. In other words, incidental benefits received and benefits in addition to regular wages, salary etc. constitute perquisites. Since the perquisites are non-monetary benefits, they have to be valued and converted in monetary terms.

Exercises

Concept Review Questions

1. Explain how the term wages has been used in various labour laws in India? List out some differences in a tabular form.
2. List out the various tax obligations for wages and salaries.
3. What are perquisites? How are perquisites valuations done according to tax laws? Can any organization offer perquisites that are tax-free? If so, how?
4. Explain the concept of collective bargaining. How does it influence the compensation design in a company?

Critical Thinking Question

Study any collective bargaining agreement of an organization. Analyse the clauses relating to wages. List out the points of agreement and then study how it is going to affect the compensation design of the organization.

Think Before you Leap: The Compensation Plan of a Chennai-based Two-wheeler Major

CASE STUDY

In 2001, a Chennai-based two-wheeler major introduced a bonus scheme for its employees. Employees covered under this bonus scheme are evaluated through a three-tier process—(1) meeting production schedules, (2) maintaining machines, and (3) reducing overtime, scrap, and shipping errors. In 2002, productivity surged and some employees even added as much as 15 per cent to their paychecks.

The two-wheeler company started facing competition from international players and also was riddled in patent issues. A court order forced them to stop production of many models requiring significant manpower restructuring and compulsory retirement for more than 20 per cent of its employees. With successive drop in sales, the company was forced to withdraw the bonus scheme and asked employees to be prepared for a financial structure, which would mean a reduction in their benefits and perks. This message had a highly demoralizing effect on the employees and many efficient designers and engineers left their jobs to join competitors. The trade unions also took up the matter as only the workers faced pay-cut whereas the senior management remuneration remained unchanged.

A portion of the employee compensation is paid as variable pay, of which bonus is a major part. Other variable incentives are based on allocated weightage on group target achievement. To rationalize the compensation cost, the company decided to switch over to individual performance track record. A formal announcement to this effect made the workers furious and led to workers' protest resulting in production loss on a regular basis. The company made it clear to the employees that their behaviour would lead to the closure of the company, which would put them in financial hardship. The workers did not respond to the company's statement and went on an indefinite strike.

A few months later, the company obtained clearance from the court and the production of all the premium high-selling brands, which was stopped earlier could be resumed as the patent issue was found to be untenable. The company feels that the whole issue was masterminded by competitors to poach valuable employees from the company.

Discussion question

Study the case and provide an alternative compensation design, which would redress the problem faced by the two-wheeler major in Chennai.

References

Belcher, D.W. (1955), Compensation Administration, Prentice Hall, Englewood Cliffs, New Jersey.

Bhattacharyya, D.K. (2006), *Human Resource Management*, 2nd edn, Excel Books, New Delhi.

Locke, R., T. Kochan, and M. Piore (1995), 'Reconceptualizing comparative industrial relations: Lessons from international research', *The International Labour Review*, vol. 134, pp. 39–161.

Various issues of Indian Labour, published by Labour Bureau, Shimla.

APPENDIX 14A Computation of Total Income (Structure)

Particulars	(₹)	(₹)	Amount (₹)
A. Income from salaries salary/bonus/commission etc.	XXXX		
Add: Taxable allowance	XXX		
Add: Value of taxable perquisites	XXX		
Gross salary		XXXX	
Less: Deductions u/s 16 (Net taxable income from salary)		XXX	
B. Income from house property			XXXX
Net annual value of house property			
Less: Deductions u/s 24(I) (Income from house property)		XXXX	
C. Profit and gains of business and profession	XXX		
Net profit as per P&L account			
Less/Add: Adjustments required to be made to the profit as per provisions of Income Tax Act.		XXXX	XXXX
D. Capital gains			
Capital gains as computed			XXXX
Short-term capital gain/Long-term capital gain			
Less: Exemptions u/s 54, 54(B), 54(D), etc.	XXX	XXXX	
E. Income from other sources		XXXX	
Other income		XXXX	
Less: Deductions		XXXX	
Net income from other sources		XXX	
Gross total income (A + B + C + D + E)			
Less: Deduction available under Chapter VIA (Sections 80CCC to 80U)		XXXX	XXXXX
Total income rounded off			XXXXX
Agriculture income			XXXX
Tax on total income		XXXX	
Less: Rebate u/s 88, 88B, 88C, 89		XXXX	
Net tax payable including surcharge			XXXX
Less: Pre-paid tax			
TDS		XXXX	
Advance tax paid		XXXX	
Net tax/refund			XX

APPENDIX 14B Valuation of Prerequisites

	Is it taxable if the employee is a		Section	Rule
	Specified employee	Non-specified employee		
Rent-free/concessional accommodation	Yes	Yes	17(2)(i)/(ii)	3(1)
Car/conveyance				
– If car/conveyance is owned by employee and bills are paid by employer	Yes	Yes	17(2)(iv)	3(2)
– Otherwise	Yes	No	17(2)(iii)	3(2)
Domestic servants (watchman, gardener, sweeper, personal attendant)				
– If domestic servant is engaged by employee and salary is paid by employer	Yes	Yes	17(2)(iv)	3(3)
– Otherwise	Yes	No	17(2)(iii)	3(3)
Supply of gas, electricity or water for household consumption				
– If connection is in the name of employee and bills are paid by employer	Yes	Yes	17(2)(iv)	3(4)
– Otherwise	Yes	No	17(2)(iii)	3(4)
Education facility				
– If bills are issued in the name of employee but paid by employer	Yes	Yes	17(2)(iv)	3(5)
– Otherwise	Yes	No	17(2)(iii)	3(5)
Transport facility allowed by transport undertakings (other than railways or airline)	Yes	No	17(2)(iii)	3(6)
Interest-free or concessional loans	Yes	Yes	17(2)(vi)	3(7)(i)
Holiday home facilities	Yes	Yes	17(2)(vi)	3(7)(ii)
Free meals during working hours	Yes	Yes	17(2)(vi)	3(7)(iii)
Gifts on ceremonial occasions or otherwise	Yes	Yes	17(2)(vi)	3(7)(iv)
Credit card facility (including add-on card)	Yes	Yes	17(2)(vi)	3(7)(v)
Club facility	Yes	Yes	17(2)(vi)	3(7)(vi)
Use of employer's compuler/laptop	No	No	17(2)(iii)	3(7)(vii)
Use of employer's other movable assets	Yes	Yes	17(2)(vi)	
Transfer of employer's movable assets	Yes	Yes	17(2)(vi)	3(7)(viii)
Telephone (including mobile phone)	No	No	–	–
Perodicals and journals for official use	No	No	–	–
Medical facility				
– If bills are issued in the name of employee but paid by employer	Yes	No	17(2)(iv)	–
– Otherwise	Yes	No	17(2)(iii)	–

(Contd)

APPENDIX 14B (Contd)

	Is it taxable if the employee is a		Section	Rule
	Specified employee	Non-specified employee		
Perquisite mentioned in para 14.2	No	No	–	3
Leave travel concession	No	No	10(5)	–
Stock option	No	No	17(2)(iii)	–
Any other perquisite				
– If bills are issued in the name of employee but paid by employer	Yes	Yes	17(2)(iv)	3(8)
– Otherwise	Yes	No	17(2)(iii)	3(8)

APPENDIX 14C   CTC Computation

	Components	Applicability	Amount
1.	Salary Details:		
	Basic salary	Yes/No	
	House rent allowance	Yes/No	
	Company leased accommodation	Yes/No	
	Daily allowance	Yes/No	
	City compensatory allowance	Yes/No	
	Special allowance	Yes/No	
	Conveyance allowance	Yes/No	
	Lunch allowance	Yes/No	
	Entertainment allowance	Yes/No	
	Books/Periodicals allowance	Yes/No	
	Education allowance	Yes/No	
	House maintenance allowance	Yes/No	
	Furnishing allowance	Yes/No	
	Dress/Uniform allowance	Yes/No	
	Other allowances	Yes/No	
2.	Benefits/Perks/Reimbursements		
	Value of company car	Yes/No	
	Car subsidy (or equivalent tax savings)	Yes/No	
	Driver's salary	Yes/No	
	Maintenance and petrol expenses	Yes/No	

(Contd)

APPENDIX 14C (Contd)

	Components	Applicability	Amount
	Leave travel allowance	Yes/No	
	Canteen subsidy	Yes/No	
	Telephone expenses	Yes/No	
	Mobile phone	Yes/No	
	Club membership	Yes/No	
	Electricity/Gas	Yes/No	
	Servant/Gardener	Yes/No	
	Credit cards	Yes/No	
	Furnishings/Durables	Yes/No	
	Holiday facilities	Yes/No	
	Medical reimbursements	Yes/No	
	Medical insurance	Yes/No	
	Personal accident scheme	Yes/No	
	Other benefits	Yes/No	
3.	Retirals		
	Provident fund	Yes/No	
	Superannuation fund	Yes/No	
	Gratuity	Yes/No	
4.	Bonus		
	Fixed bonus	Yes/No	
	Productivity-linked variable bonus	Yes/No	
	Any other performance oriented incentive	Yes/No	
	Including stock option plan		
5.	Soft Loans		
	Interest subsidy	Yes/No	
	Gross Compensation		

CHAPTER FIFTEEN

Strategic Compensation Management

Learning Objectives

After reading this chapter you will be able to
- understand the meaning and concept of strategy
- examine different schools of strategy
- assess strategy across various levels in the organization
- examine the difference between tactics and strategy
- analyse the alignment of strategies with the transformation of people
- understand the process of framing strategy
- analyse strategic compensation design
- understand strategic compensation policies

OPENING CASE

Dell Strategy

To ensure that HR objectives meet the requirements of both employees and the organization, Dell Computers actively seeks and cultivates a certain type of employee mindset. With the change in business focus from renting a computer to selling one, Dell required an HR department that could partner with the company's business units. To achieve this objective, Dell divided HR into two areas—operations and management. While the HR operations support Dell employees in general, HR management supports Dell's business. Dell's HR management team identifies personnel needs, determines lines of reporting, formulates organizational charts, and defines training needs. HR management consults with the business units on strategies. This ensures that there is no confusion about strategy. Accountability and roles of the people at Dell are very clear, which makes speedy execution of the plans possible. At Dell, strategy formulation starts with an executive team that develops key objectives, which are very quantitative and measurable, for the coming year. These objectives are articulated and

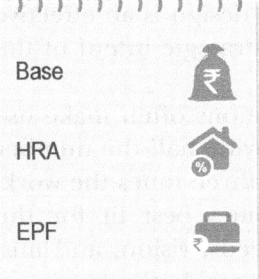

Base

HRA

EPF

Gratuity

Variable

Bonus

LTA

Conveyance

Medical

circulated globally. In this way, Dell creates a culture of ownership and develops shared visions, which give opportunity to mutually fulfill the objectives of organization and employees.

INTRODUCTION

Compensation is paid to employees for services they render to the organization. The term compensation itself is used strategically, replacing age-old terms of wages and salaries. Traditionally, organizations pay compensation to employees based on their expertise, nature of job, and hierarchical level. From the employer's point of view, compensation involved only a cost aspect. Hence, organizations indulged in rationalizing the compensation costs to maximize their return on investment (ROI). However in today's competitive business environment, organizations need to use compensation as a strategic tool. While cost rationalization and ROI maximization still continue to drive organizational compensation design, organizations also need to use compensation to motivate their workforce, retain talent, and drive employee performance and productivity. Hence, strategic compensation design is an effective trade-off between cost optimization and achieving the strategic intent of the organization.

While strategically designing compensation, organizations often make use of 1/2–2–3 principle. This principle recommends employing half the number of people, paying them double the salaries, and getting three times the work. A strategically designed compensation structure becomes best fit for the organizations, when it is aligned with their business needs, vision, and mission. However, such a compensation structure cannot override the legal and institutional requirements. This chapter first reviews the basics of strategy and then establishes linkage between compensation design and strategy.

STRATEGY

Strategy is a pattern of decisions concerning policies and practices associated with an organizational system. The organizational system encompasses all functional areas. Understanding organizational system helps in the formulation of organization-wide strategies. Strategies need to be formulated for each functional area of an organization and also at each level of an organization. For example, the HR function adopts a competency-based approach in framing strategies to develop people in order to sustain the organization's competitive advantage. In a similar manner, organizations adopt strategies for motivation, communication, design and structuring, etc. to manage compensation.

Mintzberg et al. (1998) identified ten schools of strategy, which are broadly classified under prescriptive and descriptive viewpoints. *Prescriptive schools* are again classified into design, planning, and positioning. *Descriptive schools* are classified into seven distinct schools of thought—entrepreneurial, cognitive, learning, power, cultural, environmental, and configuration. All these schools of thought directly or indirectly influence organizational behaviour studies.

Prescriptive Schools

All the three different schools under the prescriptive schools are discussed in this section.

Design school   It views strategy as a process of conception. Strategy formation under this school is a process of matching the task environment (internal to the organization) to the mega environment (external to the organization). It emphasizes on a fit between the strength and weakness (internal) and the opportunities and threats (external) of an organization. This school applies conscious thought. Conscious thought is not analytical (formal) or intuitive (informal). It is the culmination of collective inputs of members of an organization for informed decisions.

Planning school   It sees strategy formation as a formal sequence of steps. This school makes strategy formation a formal process, or rather a cerebral one, by breaking down strategy formation into some distinct and identifiable steps. This school emphasizes on making managerial decisions more formal and documented by using norms such as a standard operating procedure (SOP) to ensure consistency in a series of actions.

Positioning school   It views strategy formation as an analytical process. It places the business within the context of the industry, that the organization is in, and evaluates how the organization can improve its competitive positioning within that industry. This school leverages value chains, game theories, and other ideas within an analytical framework.

Descriptive Schools

The seven descriptive schools are discussed in this section.

Entrepreneurial school   It emphasizes the central role of the leader and considers strategy formation to be a visionary process. Like the design school, the entrepreneurial school centres around the strategy formation process at the chief executive level and relies on intuition and gut feeling. Hence, this school shifts the strategies from precise designs, plans, or positions to visions or perspectives, typically through metaphor.

Cognitive school   It considers strategy formation to be a mental process, and analyses how people perceive patterns and process information. The cognitive school looks inwards into the minds of strategists. This school subscribes to the view that strategies are developed in people's mind as frames, models, or maps.

An extension of this school of thought adopts a more subjective, interpretative or constructivist view of the strategy process, that is, cognition is used to construct strategies as creative interpretations rather than simply to map reality in some objective way.

Learning school It regards strategy formation as an emergent process, where the management of an organization pays close attention to what works and does not work over time and incorporates these lessons learned into their overall plan of action. Hence for this school, strategies emerge as people learn about a situation as well as their organization's capability to deal with it.

Power school It is a process of negotiation between power holders within the company, and/or between the company and the external stakeholders. The power school views strategy as emerging out of power games within the organization and outside it. This comparatively small, but quite different school has focused on strategy formulation as being rooted in power and gives two viewpoints—micro power and macro power. Micro power sees the development of strategies within the organization as essentially a political process involving bargaining, persuasion, and confrontation among inside actors. Macro power views, on the other hand, recommend use of collective strategies in the form of network and alliances.

Cultural school It views strategy formation as a collective process involving various groups and departments within the company. Therefore, the strategy developed is a reflection of the corporate culture of the organization. The cultural school views strategy formulation as a process rooted in the social force of culture. As opposed to the power school that focuses on self-interest and fragmentation, the cultural school focuses on common interest and integration. Strategy formation is viewed as a social process rooted in the organizational culture. The theory also concentrates on the influence of culture in discouraging significant strategic change.

Environmental school It sees strategy formation as a reactive process—a response to the challenges imposed by the external environment. The environmental school believes that an organization's strategy depends on events in the environment and the organization's reaction to them. This does not constitute strategic management per se in a strict sense, if one assumes that the term is concerned with how organizations use their degrees of freedom to create strategy. The environmental school nevertheless deserves attention for the light it throws on the demands of the environment. Among its most noticeable theories is the *contingency theory*, which considers the type of responses expected of organizations facing particular environmental conditions and *population ecology*, which claims severe limits to strategic choice.

Configuration school It mandates strategy formation as a process of transforming the organization from one type of decision-making structure into another. The configuration school views strategy as a process of transforming the organization. It describes the relative stability of strategy interrupted by occasional and dramatic leaps to new ones. This school currently enjoys the most extensive and integrative literature and practice. One side of this school, a more academic and descriptive one, sees organization as a configuration—coherent clusters of characteristics and behaviours—and performs a singular role of integrating the claims of the other schools.

COMPENSATION DESIGN AND STRATEGY

After studying the contribution of all these schools, it is clear that the process of strategy formulation is still a mystery. Even at this stage it is not clear, how an individual or group is able to leap from the collection and analysis of information to the conceptualization of alternative courses of action, although it is conceded that the cognitive school comes closest. Hence, it is for the organizations and for its leaders to decide which school of thought suits them most, especially in compensation designing. Organizational practices in strategically designing the compensation structure vary widely. In fact, compensation designing is generally influenced by more than one school of thought.

While framing compensation strategies, an organization should align its policies and practices with its strategy. This ensures fulfillment of role expectations for employees within the organization. According to Barney (1991) and Prahalad and Hamel (1990), only the employees of an organization can give sustainable competitive advantage as characteristically people are rare, inimitable (features cannot be found in any other resource of an organization), and non-substitutable sources for achieving competitive advantage. Human capital theory of Becker (1964) linked the strategic importance of people to other economic assets arguing that knowledge, skills, and abilities of the people also have economic values. This concept was later developed into the human resource accounting by Flamholtz (1981) and others. The transaction cost theory of Williamson (1981) suggests that organizations could ensure cost minimization by considering people as a strategic resource as this process would enhance periodic monitoring and governance. The agency theory of Eisenhardt (1989) suggests strategic alignment of interests of agents (employees) and principals (employers) in an organization, thus streamlining the employment relations and systems.

The common characteristic features of all the above theories justify alignment of employee roles with organization-wide strategy and are grouped under rational choice theories. Similarly, we have institutional (Meyer and Rowen 1977; Powell and DiMaggio 1991) and dependency theories (Pfeffer and Salancik 1978) on strategy. These theories focus on constituency-based interest as a strategic approach to people is not empirically proven as a contributor to organizational performance. Institutional theory argues the need for acceptance of strategy by stakeholders, whereas the dependency theory considers that such a strategy acceptance would unduly enhance the level of employees influence over the organizations and thereby would defeat the purpose.

Environmental, organizational, institutional, and technological factors are potential influencers of strategy. The potential influencers are factors that directly or indirectly affect organizational strategy formulation process. The relative importance of each factor depends on organizational characteristics. Each factor should be taken cognizance of, else the organization cannot sustain growth and profitability.

Based on the discussion so far, strategy can be defined as the direction and scope of an organization over the long term, matching its resources to its changing environment and in particular its markets, customers, or clients so as to meet the expectations of all the stakeholders. It is either the plans made or the actions taken to help an organization fulfill its intended purposes. A strategic plan for the future is referred to as the intended strategy and strategic actions are known as realized strategy. Strategic means are plans and policies, whereas strategic ends may be either broad vision and mission, or focused goals and objectives.

Mintzberg et al. provided five P's of strategy. Although essentially the five P's are used to describe the characteristics of strategic planning from different perspectives, these are also relevant in compensation designing. Following is a description of the characteristics of strategic planning from different perspectives.

1. Strategy as a plan guides an organization through different courses of action and provides a path from a current state to a desired future end state.
2. Strategy as a pattern ensures consistent behaviour over time.
3. Strategy as a position determines the location, namely positioning of particular products in particular markets or particular leadership style in a particular situation.
4. Strategy as a perspective represents a philosophy or value system, namely style of communication or interpersonal relations in an organization
5. Strategy as a ploy refers to gaining some advantages through specific maneuvering like motivating employees in an organization through participative leadership.

Strategy Across Levels

Strategy is all-encompassing and function specific. Organizational structure and design, whether hierarchical or non-hierarchical, has three levels—corporate, business, and operational. The *corporate level* is also known as the top level or strategic level. Corporate level is considered a strategic level as senior management at this level formulates the overall organizational strategies. Corporate level strategies focus on three areas—(1) overall scope of an organizational activities; (2) structural and financial aspects; and (3) resource allocation. Corporate level strategies emanate from organizational mission. The *business*

or *competitive level* is also known as the middle or tactical level. Strategies at the corporate level are translated into specific action plans at the middle level. Middle level managers frame intermediate strategies, specific to their functions or divisions. Strategies framed at this level deal with issues such as:
- market competition strategies
- match product or service development strategies with market requirements
- strategies for meeting and satisfying customer needs
- strategies for achievement of organizational objectives such as long-term profitability, sales growth, and efficiency

The *operation level* is also known as the first or execution level. Operation level managers frame strategies, which are necessary for routine day-to-day activities. Operation level strategies include strategies on inventory, quality, production planning, etc. Even though corporate level largely frames strategies for the overall organization, business and operational level managers are also required to frame their specific strategies and action plans within the ambit of corporate level strategies. Therefore, strategies are formed at every level, but their nature differs from one level to another.

Tactics and Strategy

An organization can have long-term strategies and short-term strategies. Continued focus on product development by investment in state-of-the-art research facilities is an example of long-term strategy. Strategy to increase the number of add-on customers in a particular quarter is an example of short-term strategy. Tactics deals with the *how* of strategy. It involves deploying means to accomplish the action plans set by strategies.

Implementation of strategies, at each operational level, requires identification of *critical success factors* (CSF). For example, marketing decisions need to focus on product, price, market, and promotion; whereas financing decisions may focus on capital acquisition, allocation, dividend, and working capital management. Research and development (R&D) decisions focus on basic research, commercial development, lead time, organizational fit, basic R&D posture (defensive, offensive, innovation, development, etc.); whereas organizational behaviour decisions have to focus on managing cross-cultural issues due to increasing cultural diversity at the workplace. This requires understanding of different cultural constructs and identification of the best fit for cultural synergy. CSF analysis was developed at MIT's Sloan School by John Rockart and C. Bullen (1981) to guide businesses in creating and measuring success. It is a top-down methodology that is especially suitable for designing systems, identifying the tasks and requirements needed for success, and a mean to prioritize requirements.

After strategy formulation and implementation, the process of strategy evaluation needs to be understood. Strategy evaluation ensures understanding of

the extent of strategic fit, that is, the match between the adopted strategies and organizational requirements. It requires the following, among others things:
- internal and external consistency
- availability of resources
- degree of risk
- lead time
- workability

ALIGNING STRATEGIES TO TRANSFORM PEOPLE

Organizations transform employees by first aligning strategies to processes, technology, systems and relationships, and then by cascading it to every employee. With a change in technology, the work process changes along with the required set of competencies of people working with the organization. Competency development and renewal requires thrust not only on knowledge and skill, but also on attitudes of people. Strategies give organizations a direction to achieve their intended objectives through well-charted action plans. All employees should have a clear understanding of the organization's strategies. One possible way to do this is to develop a strategy map and communicate it to all members of the organization. This ensures all of them can relate to critical business drivers and help in identifying gaps between plans and execution. Organizations translate corporate strategy into operating business units using some measurement criteria or matrices.

Actual strategy formulation, however, may not always be value driven, that is, tracing its roots only to the vision. Market competitiveness often requires adoption of dynamic portfolio approach, which among other things requires consideration of BCG matrix to map the current business position and SWOT analysis or even analysis of competitive forces in line with Michel Porter (1985). These steps help not only in strategy formulation, but also in strategy implementation and evaluation. They can also be used as measurement criteria to check effectiveness of organizational strategy. However at this stage, we will restrict our focus only to value-based strategy formulation to explain the basics.

BCG matrix pioneered by Boston Consulting Group (BCG) recommends organizations to take stock of their current position in terms of four different perspectives, star, cash cow, question mark, and dogs. Organizations in star indicate operating in high growth market, and have long-term future. Profit from the star may not be super normal, but for its long-term sustainability, organizations always try to invest more and more in star to consolidate their position in the market. Organizations in cash cow states can get the opportunity to generate extra cash, super normal profit, but the position gets eased out within a short time frame for limited market growth opportunities. Hence organizations dissuade from investing in cash cow ventures with a long-term perspective. Organizations in question mark may face the eventual problems either for some changes in the legislation, or customers' taste and preferences, etc. Organizations in dogs being incur losses for successive years, are recommended to withdraw from the venture.

STRATEGIC PLANNING

Strategic planning is the process of thinking through the current mission of the organization with due cognizance of current environmental conditions, both external and internal. Such plans set guidelines for future decisions and results. The following sections discuss the different stages of strategic planning that set the premise for strategy framing.

Vision

Vision refers to intentions that are broad, all inclusive, and forward thinking. The vision of an organization describes its aspirations for the future. It does not specify the means that would be used to achieve the desired ends. In addition, it must be inspirational and, though often unwritten, must be communicated. Vision can be communicated in two ways—(1) in the form of mission statement; and (2) through personal selling (e.g., behaviour of the visionary). Attitude towards quality or customer complaint handling are examples of vision or intentions of an organization.

Mission

Vision in tangible form is a mission statement. The mission statement articulates the vision. An organization's mission statement can change from time to time, depending on a change in its business focus. Organizations attempt to answer the following questions through a mission statement:
- basic purpose of existence
- unique or distinctiveness of an organization
- likely difference in the business 3 to 5 years in the future
- principal customers, clients, or key market segments
- principal goods and services, present, and future
- principal economic concerns
- basic beliefs, values, aspirations, and philosophical priorities of the firm

Key elements The key elements of the mission statement address the following:

View of the future Anticipated regulatory, competitive, and economic environment. Such perspective view influences the business focus of an organization.

Competitive arenas Business and geographic business arenas where the organization will compete.

Sources of competitive advantage The skills that the company will develop for gaining competitive advantage; a description of how the company intends to succeed.

Benefits An organization by developing a mission statement primarily sets the direction for employees working with it. A mission statement may also depict the company's concern for meeting different stakeholders' expectations. Some of the benefits of a mission statement can be categorized as follows:
- establish boundaries to guide strategy formulation
- acknowledge responsibilities to various stakeholders and establish standards for organizational performance
- suggest standards of individual behaviour

Goals A mission statement tries to make a vision more specific, while goals are attempts to make a mission statement more concrete. Goals have several features, which are as follows.
- They address both financial and non-financial issues.
- They facilitate reasonable trade-off (range of goals should be perfectly consistent with one another).
- They can be reached with a stretch.
- They cut across functional areas.

Objectives

Objectives are the operational definitions of goals. They describe what the organization hopes to accomplish in specific measurable terms within a specified time frame. The top management of an organization decides the overall objectives, which then cascade to divisional, departmental, and individual employee level objectives. Individual employee level objectives are known as key result areas (KRA), key performance areas (KPA), key performance indicators (KPI), key sales objectives (KSO), etc. Such individual level objectives then become the basis for performance evaluation. Therefore characteristically, objectives can be measured; they have a time dimension; and they reduce conflict (misunderstandings) by setting a common direction for all employees who work for the organization.

Strategy and action plan for human resource management (HRM) for a hypothetical organization has been discussed in Appendix 15A by listing the details in the light of vision, mission, goals, objectives, strategies, and action plan.

STRATEGIC COMPENSATION DESIGN

Strategic compensation is a systematic approach adopted by an organization to achieve several objectives to assist in recruitment, job performance, and job satisfaction. It is used as a tool in designing compensation, matching with the business needs, organizational goals, and organizational resource availability. Organizations align strategic compensation with vision, mission, values, objectives, strategy, leadership, and performance management systems to achieve

long-term success. Organizations design such compensation in a flexible, competitive, and performance-oriented manner by adopting the following processes:
- looking into the history and background of the organization to understand the principles and norms
- using various workgroups to understand the issues such as cost management, principles of equity, and collective bargaining systems of the organization
- focusing on performance management, structure setting and adjustment, job/work evaluation, pay progression strategies, variable pay, premium/special pay, paid time off, and other strategic rewards
- ensuring compliance with legislative and regulatory norms
- integrating the results of the entire processes to develop the desired compensation programme

While designing strategic compensation, organizations emphasize on matching it with the competitors' compensation plans and differentiate in the variable components such as bonuses, incentives, and stock options. Organizations ensure internal equity for the base compensation part, but for variables assign more weightage on external competitiveness. Market competition is a major driver of strategic compensation design. Some organizations, to derive the benefit of strategic intent, refrain from adopting a common compensation model. In these organizations, compensation is varied across functions and levels to meet specific business needs. Some important areas of strategic compensation design considers aspects such as job/work evaluation, structure setting and adjustment, pay progression, performance management, variable pay, premium/special pay, and paid-time off.

Job evaluation is a formal process to determine the relative worth of various jobs. Through job evaluation, organizations assign grade structure (commonly based on hierarchical index of job value). On the contrary, work evaluation assigns value to work and not to job. It primarily considers roles or competencies. A pay structure represents collection of pay rates or ranges. Organizations develop, adjust, and maintain a pay structure through the process of structure setting and adjustment. After job evaluation, organizations place jobs in suitable pay structures complying with the principles of internal equity. To make the compensation design competitive, organizations consider market pricing for job/work evaluation. Person-based approaches, position-based approaches, skill- or competency-based approaches, and hybrid approaches are also followed in job/work evaluation systems. Strategic compensation designs using job/work evaluations also consider issues such as equity, cost control, accountability, and feasibility. *Equity issues* consider the degree of compensation variation across the employees. *Cost control and accountability issues* consider affordability and defensibility of the compensation. *Feasibility issues* consider resource constraints to sustain a particular compensation plan.

Pay progression refers to changes in the base pay primarily based on career ladder promotion, competitive promotion, and performance-based promotional issues. It includes both the within-grade increases and the quality step increases. Pay progression is similar to merit-based pay progression. However, organizations often feel constrained to follow time-based pay progression under collective bargaining situation. System of allowing pay progression on attainment of specific skills or competencies is also common in many organizations.

Use of variable pay as a strategic compensation component is quite common across organizations. However, this requires adequate precaution as issues such as pay-at-risk often dissuade trade unions to accept such compensation plans. Other issues such as premium/special pay are considered by the organizations depending on the degree of hazards, which may be occupational or environmental. Vacation allowances may also be part of such a compensation plan.

STRATEGIC COMPENSATION POLICIES

To frame a strategic compensation programme, organizations emphasize at the outset on developing a compensation policy by duly forming a compensation committee to decide on issues such as the degree of differences in the pay structures across the hierarchical levels, functions, degree of market compatibility, and differences in the ratio of base pay and variables. The designated compensation committee, after going through all these aspects, adopts compensation policies which become the primary guidelines for compensation design. Job analysis, job evaluation, determination of pay grades, establishing pay ranges, developing compensation administration policy, obtaining the approval of top management, communicating the final compensation plan to all cross-sections of employees and, monitoring the compensation programmes are common to all compensation design programme.

However, compensation policies and philosophies should not ignore the organizational business and operations strategy to ensure that they are compatible with business needs. Some compensation strategy statements for a hypothetical organization can be listed as follows.

- To allow attraction and retention of high-quality professional employees.
- To reward employees based on their support of organization-specific mission, strategies, and operating plans.
- To reward employees based on their experience and performance.
- To achieve and maintain consistency, equity, and fairness in evaluating and compensating employees; also the efforts should be consistent with the organizational vision
- To promote communication with and participation by different departments of the organization in developing effective compensation programmes.

STRATEGIC COMPENSATION AND TALENT ISSUES IN GLOBAL HIRING

Due to an increased shortage of talent, organizations today scout for it not just domestically but also globally. Talent is increasingly becoming the major competitive differentiator and source of organizational success and sustenance. Organizations with long-term perspective navigate the world to hire talented people. Before hiring talent globally, organizations must try to understand the implication of their strategic compensation decisions. For example, the US based multinational companies that emphasize more on variables may not apparently find any difficulty in attracting and retaining talent in their home country. However, their strategic compensation design may not work for Indian talents. This is because of cultural incongruence. Indian employees still value the fixed compensation component. They make organizations that focus more on performance-related pay or variables as their second choice. These issues are commonly faced by the multinational organizations. For example, two European multinationals Solvay and Pentair underwent a change in their business focus. The change brought through acquisitions not only changed their business portfolio, but also their market reach. The biggest challenge these two organizations faced recently is in transferring talented managerial manpower to their international operations for a longer duration more or less due to issues related to compensation cost effectiveness. Both the companies then started incubating local managerial talents in their global business units (GBUs).

Employers around the world are focused on attracting, retaining, and motivating key talent. However according to experts, the complexities of varied cultures and global economies means many employers are struggling with the details.

Apart from the cultural issues that influence the strategic compensation design for global talent hiring, organizations also face the challenge of investing in training and career planning. The challenge being optimizing the cost of compensation, and yet achieve success in hiring global talent. Strategic compensation management focuses on following important points.

1. Reinforce performance-related pay (PRP) with logical distribution of weights, thus balancing individual and collective achievement of goals.
2. Engage people in deciding the elements of compensation as there may be every possibility that some compensation elements may not be the right fit in a particular country or culture. For example Cisco's employee benefits programme consists of multiple options. However, some of the benefits are not offered globally, they are restricted to some specific locations.
3. Communicate the compensation plan to the employees to avoid confusion; lack of transparency would lead to employees smelling something fishy in the plan. Communication ensures transparency and helps employees get clarifications, if required.

4. While designing compensation strategy, organizations may, wherever required, follow the segmented reward strategy. However, they need to be careful about too much inequity, which may frustrate the dormant talents.

SUMMARY

The process of framing compensation strategies is important for an organization. Traditionally, organizations perceived compensation to an employee as a cost factor and believed that minimizing it would increase their revenue. However, the modern approach to compensation negates this perception. In fact, it argues that ROI would be higher if compensation is strategically designed as it enhances performance and productivity. In addition, increased retention of good performers provides sustainable competitive advantage to the organization.

Various kinds of compensation schemes have already been discussed in previous chapters. These provide an insight into strategic compensation design. At the core, they require identification of suitable variable components of pay and aligning of those to the employees' performance so that organizations can refrain from unnecessary expenditure on non-performers. These help not only in motivating the employees, but also in encouraging them to perform and deliver better results. Even the concepts of team pay, competency-based pay, and contribution pay can be strategically determined for increased retention of employees and for nurturing a culture of high performance.

Key Terms

Corporate strategy Strategies that provide overall guidelines for the organization.
Functional strategies Strategies for specific functions.
HR strategy Strategies specific to HR functions like compensation strategies.
Operational strategy Strategies framed at the operation level. These are usually short-term (such as monthly or weekly production).

Strategic control Mechanism of periodic evaluation of strategies.
Vision The philosophies and value systems of the organization.

Exercises

Concept Review Questions

1. Discuss the importance of compensation strategies. Can HR strategies be independent of compensation strategies?
2. How can you align compensation strategies with corporate strategies? Give your answer with examples.
3. Design a strategic compensation policy for an organization. Highlight the important areas of consideration for managerial employees.
4. Write short notes on:
   (a) Vision and mission of a compensation plan
   (b) Strategic compensation design
   (c) Compensation strategy factors

Critical Thinking Question

Assume that a service organization, which largely employs management and engineering graduates, is experiencing an acute retention problem. Develop a strategic compensation plan showing each compensation component and justify its inclusion from the retention point of view.

CASE STUDY: Strategic Compensation Initiative at NewAge Technologies

NewAge Technologies is a new generation computer-aided manufacturing unit and a pioneer in the production of static electrical switches. In order to control compensation cost and at the same time to increase productivity and customer satisfaction, it decided to switch to strategic compensation plan. The company, which is based in Sweden, emphasizes on pay equity. However, in a competitive market, the company started losing clients due to high cost of manufacturing and consequential uncompetitive product pricing. Static electrical switches are procured in bulk by various State Electricity Boards and other private power-generating companies to be installed at users' premises. The international level benchmarked quality for static electrical switches is ±3 per cent variation. Any deviation from this value is considered as rejected. The company has recently experienced serious defects in their production batches, which led the company to reject a huge quantity of meters during their in-house inspection.

The HR manager of the company has been asked to develop new employee compensation strategies that emphasize on its alignment to business goals of the organization. To start with, the HR manager developed a performance management system emphasizing on 360-degree performance evaluation systems which encompass customer feedback analysis even for employees involved in operation. The company with the new performance management system expanded the roles for employees requiring them to accept more responsibility and accountability. Some of the other initiatives taken by the company are developing a flatter organization structure, 24 hours customer helpline, five hours response time to resolve customer complaints, designing of compensation matching with the capabilities, and reducing the fixed pay component from existing 90 per cent to 50 per cent, while increasing the variables from existing 10 per cent to 50 per cent.

An analysis of the proposed changes in the compensation plan, as prepared by the HR manager, indicates that with the current level of productivity, workers will continue to earn their wages as usual. However, they may face wage-cut for bad workmanship when they produce meters with more than ±3 per cent variation in quality. Since the company follows ISO standards, every worker can be traced to individual meters through their structured systems of product traceability.

The company has adopted a compensation philosophy, detailing the set of values and beliefs, emphasizing on customer satisfaction, highest quality achievement, and performance above the set standards as the core to compensation plan. The HR manager documented the compensation strategy and various measurement criteria for compensation

(Contd)

CASE STUDY (Contd)

TABLE 15.1 Changed compensation plan

Base pay	Job based vs individual based, number of levels, structure of levels, pricing strategies, adjustment method, and quantifying individual performance.
Organizational performance or variable pay	Role in total compensation strategy, structure, measures, targets, tolerance for pay-at-risk, risk–reward ratios, use of other monetary rewards, use of non-monetary rewards, and individual performance recognition.
Fringe benefits	Usually determined at corporate level; limited scope another levels, link with business and human resource objectives. Coverage, cost, and communications (purpose–coverage–value).
Compensation administration	Stakeholder role in compensation administration, performance management and evaluation, overtime policy (exempt and non-exempt categories), shift differentials, attendance policies, and role of seniority.
Employee inputs and preferences	Perceptions of external pay equity, perceptions of internal pay equity, pay delivery beliefs, form (cash, gain sharing, benefits), method (individual, small group, large group), risk tolerance, and trust in management.
Business and operating inputs	Operations and manufacturing strategy, sales development strategy, percentage of compensation costs to total product/service costs, percentage of compensation costs to controllable product/service cost, existing markets/products, potential markets/products, anticipated volume, reinforce/enhance work design, maintain cultural change processes, other operating issues.

billing by the operations managers. A tabular structure, prepared by the HR manager, explaining the areas of consideration for the changed compensation plan is reproduced in Table 15.1.

When the proposed strategic compensation plan was communicated to the unions, they refused to mandate its acceptance citing that the changes are against the principles of existing compensation philosophy of the organization and hence detrimental to the interest of the workers.

Discussion question

Assuming that you are the HR manager, explain how you are going to persuade the unions to accept such a strategically designed compensation plan.

References

Balkin, D.B. and L.R. Gomez-Mejia (1987), 'Towards a contingency theory of compensation strategy', *Strategic Management Journal*, vol. 8, no. 2, pp. 169–82.

Balkin, D.B. and L.R. Gomez-Mejia (1990), 'Matching compensation and organizational strategies', *Strategic Management Journal*, vol. 11, no. 2, pp. 153–69.

Barkema, H.G. and L.R. Gomez-Mejia (1998), 'Managerial compensation and firm performance: A general research framework', *The Academy of Management Journal*, vol. 41, no. 2, pp. 135–45.

Barney, J. (1991), 'Firm resources and sustained competitive advantage', *Journal of Management*, vol. 17, pp. 99–120.

Becker, Gary S. (1964), *Human Capital: A Theoretical and Empirical Analysis*, Columbia University Press, New York.

Bhattacharyya, D.K. (2006), *Human Resource Management*, Excel Books, New Delhi.

Eisenhardt, K.M. (1989), 'Agency theory: An assessment and review', *Academy of Management Review*, vol. 14, no. 4, pp. 57–74.

Ellig, B.R. (1982), *Executive Compensation—A Total Pay Perspective*, McGraw-Hill, New York.

Flamholtz, Eric (1981), *Personnel Management, Human Capital Theory and Human Resource Accounting*, Institute of Industrial Relations, University of California.

Galbraith, G.S. and G.B. Merrill (1991), 'The effect of compensation program and structure on SBU competitive strategy: A study of technology-intensive firms', *Strategic Management Journal*, vol. 12, no. 5, pp. 353–70.

Gomez-Mejia, L.R. (1992), 'Structure and process of diversification, compensation strategy, and firm performance', *Strategic Management Journal*, vol. 13, no. 5, pp. 381–97.

Gomez-Mejia, L.R. (1994), 'Executive compensation: A reassessment and future agenda', *Research in Personnel and Human Resources Management*, vol. 12, pp. 161–222.

Gomez-Mejia, L.R. and T.M. Welbourne (1988), 'Compensation strategy: An overview and future steps', *Human Resource Planning*, vol. 11, no. 3, pp. 173–89.

Haigh, T. (1989), 'Aligning executive total compensation with business strategy', *Human Resource Planning*, vol. 12, no. 3, pp. 221–27.

Hitt, M.A., R. Ireland, and R.E. Hoskisson (2001), *Strategic Management: Competitiveness and Globalization*, South-Western College Publishing, Cincinnati.

Kerr, J.L. (1985), 'Diversification strategies and managerial rewards: An empirical study', The Academy of Management Journal, vol. 28, no. 1, pp. 155–79.

Kotler, P. (2000), *Marketing Management*, Prentice Hall, Upper Saddle-River, New Jersey.

Lawler, E. (1981), *Pay and Organization Development*, Addison-Wesley, Reading, Massachusetts.

Meyer, John W. and Biran Rowen (1977), 'Institutionalised organizations: Formal structure as myth and ceremony', *American Journal of Sociology*, vol. 83, pp. 34–6.

Miles, R.E. and C.C. Snow (1978), *Organizational Strategy Structure and Process*, McGraw-Hill, New York.

Mintzberg, H., B. Ahlstrand, and J. Lampel (1998), *Strategy Safari: A Guided Tour Through the Wilds of Strategic Management*, The Free Press, New York.

Pfeffer, J. and G.R. Salancik, (1978), *The External Control of Organizations: A Resource Dependence Perspective*, Harper & Row, New York.

Porter, M. (1985), *Competitive Advantage: Creating and Sustaining Superior Performance*, Free Press, New York.

Powell, Walter W. and Paul J. DiMaggio (1991), *The New Institutionalism in Organisational Analysis*, University of Chicago Press, Chicago.

Prahalad, C.K. and G. Hamel (1990), 'The core competence of the corporation', *Harvard Business Review*, vol. 68, no. 3, pp. 79–91.

Rajagopalan, N. (1997), 'Strategic orientations, incentive plan adoptions, and firm performance: Evidence from electric utility firms', *Strategic Management Journal*, vol. 18, no. 10, pp. 761–85.

Rockart, J.F. and C. Bullen (1981), *A primer on critical success factors*, Center for Information Systems Research, Sloan School of Management, Massachusetts Institute of Technology.

Saura, M.D. and L.R. Gomez-Mejia (1997), *The linkage between business strategies and compensation* policies using Miles and Snow's framework, Working paper no. 9669, Universidad Carlos III, Madrid.

Singh, P. and N.C. Agarwal (2002), 'The effects of firm strategy on the level and structure of executive compensation', *Canadian Journal of Administrative Sciences*, vol. 19, no. 1, pp. 42–56.

Veliyath, R., S.P. Ferris, and K. Ramaswamy (1994), 'Business strategy and top management compensation: The mediating effects of employment risk, firm performance and size', *The Journal of Business Research*, vol. 30, no. 2, pp. 149–59.

Vittaniemi, J. (1997), *Top executive compensation and company performance in Finland*, Working paper no. 97/10, Centre for Labour Market and Social Research, Aarhus.

Williamson, Oliver E. (1981), 'The economics of organization: The transaction cost approach', *American Journal of Sociology*, vol. 87, pp. 548–77.

Wines, L. (1996), 'Compensation plans that support strategy', *The Journal of Business Strategy*, vol. 17, no. 4, pp. 17–20.

APPENDIX 15A Strategy and Action Plan

Vision

1. We are committed to provide an enjoyable work environment to our employees to promote teamwork, quality improvement, and excellence.
2. Our employees are our valued customers and most important stakeholders.
3. We are committed to achieve financial growth of our organization by encouraging organizational growth and fostering the creativity of our valued employees.

Mission

The company's mission is:
'To achieve excellence in human resource management by fostering growth and creativity.'

Goals

The goals of the organization are to:
- promote teamwork
- ensure quality improvement
- foster growth and creativity

Objectives

Goal 1
- Achieve group cohesiveness by inculcating participative management
- Reduce dissonance in managerial decisions
- Reduce conflict and grievances to achieve
- Zero man-days loss and increased productivity

Goal 2
- Achieve increased quality consciousness in the organization
- Reduce costs of quality to zero by next 5 years
- Provide error-free product and services to customers to increase their retention and to increase further market share

Goals 3
- Promote creativity in the organization
- Provide opportunities for growth of the employees
- Increase retention of employees so as to reduce current employee turnover by 80% in next 5 years

Strategies

Goal 1	Improve participative management
Goal 2	Initiate organization-wide quality improvement
Goal 3	Develop a culture that promotes growth and creativity

Action Plans

Strategy 1	Establish small group forums such as quality circles (QC), self-managed teams (SMT), value engineering teams, total quality management (TQM) clubs, etc. in the organization Shift focus from statutory participation to total participation Empower employees by involving them in decision-making process Implement transparent communication network
Strategy 2	Implement quality awareness programmes through regular training and development Develop TQM culture by increasing formal and informal interaction with all cross-section of employees Practise TQM philosophy through personal selling (reflected through behaviour of all)

(Contd)

APPENDIX 15A (Contd)

Action Plans

Strategy 3 — Encourage directed creativity culture and practices with clear documented policy
Emphasize on in-house talent rather than outsourcing
Implement reward system for focused and need-based creative ideas
Implement documented promotion policy to provide growth opportunities for employees

CHAPTER SIXTEEN

Quantitative Tools and Innovation in Compensation

Learning Objectives

After completing this chapter, you would be able to
- understand the contextual issues in employee compensation theories
- analyse various plans of compensation
- assess various components of compensation
- appreciate production-linked employee benefits
- use quantitative tools in compensation research
- understand various incentive schemes and their computation

OPENING CASE

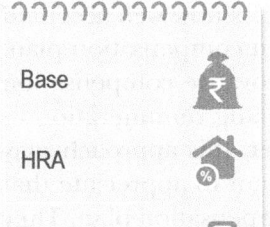

 Base

 HRA

EPF

Gratuity

Variable

Bonus

LTA

Conveyance

Medical

Compensation Design at ITC

ITC's approach towards its employees is summarized by 'We nurture excellence and keep alive the spirit of healthy competition by providing each of our employees equal opportunities to grow as well as numerous performance incentives.' It ensures that employees enjoy their work environment by devising multiple reward systems and incentives. ITC's reward and recognition programme is aligned with its performance management systems. The company's competitive compensation system compares with the best in the industry and provides for fair and equitable compensation opportunities for individual contribution to the organizational success. A dynamic year-round performance management system involves setting of objectives; managing performance; assessing performance as well as means employed; evaluating individual effectiveness as well as the contribution to corporate objectives; and recognition systems. This system ensures attraction, retention, and honing of the best talent available in the market. It also enables the company to offer its employees a promising future. Some features of ITC's compensation system such as instantaneous award, excellence/value award, and best achievement award require tracking of employees' achievement even beyond what is generally accomplished through formal performance management systems. These features make ITC's compensation management practices distinctive.

INTRODUCTION

In this chapter we will discuss the current trends in the literature of compensation management. We will also provide guidelines on how these inputs together with various compensation-related quantitative models and tools effectively augment the acumen of human resource researchers. From an employee perspective, compensation means value and not money. It is their primary area of concern. A good compensation programme is aligned with not only business goals but also people requirements. To achieve this, the compensation design makes a trade-off between the cost and benefit. Compensation managers have to strike a perfect balance by emulating the best practices. Organizations can identify best practices through compensation research. It is now well accepted that most human resource outcomes are results of a given compensation plan. Organizations across the world are aiming to adopt innovative compensation plans to remain competitive. Pay-for-performance or linking remuneration to results is often considered as a right approach. However, this approach may run into conflict with the teamwork culture. It is important to appreciate that employees do not always demand the most expensive compensation plan. They also value non-monetary aspects. Quite often organizations are unnecessarily obsessed with aligning compensation with business results. This approach does not yield results by default. In designing a scientific compensation plan, it is more important to align work with an organization's business strategy. Therefore, designing a compensation plan that rewards work is more important.

This chapter explains compensation analysis tools using various mathematical and statistical techniques. All these tools are elementary but very effective for scientific compensation designing. Many organizations still largely believe in qualitative analysis of compensation design, which may not always be correct. Using mathematical and statistical analysis techniques in compensation design can at least minimize the risk of a wrong compensation design.

THEORETICAL DISCUSSIONS ON COMPENSATION

Compensation is a methodical approach to assign monetary value to employees in return for work performed by them. Compensation may include any or all of base pay, overtime pay, commissions, stock option plans, merit pay, profit sharing, bonuses, housing allowance, vacations, and other benefits. Compensation is a term used to describe not only employee salaries but also all other benefits received. It is also referred to as remuneration. Human resource management makes compensation issues a prerogative of managers as they can make use of compensation as a tool to enhance the performance of employees at workplace to sustain competitive advantage. The strategic use of rewards to regulate behaviour and performance has led to the concept of *compensation management* or *reward systems*. Remuneration refers to monetary rewards, which are considered an arm of total compensation.

The way an organization designs a compensation plan plays an important role in motivating critical performance of employees, which is essential for the efficient operation of the organization. Base salary is not the only component of a typical compensation package. Short- and long-term incentives, which comprise of cash and often include stock, provide an organization with means to focus the employees' attention on the achievement of financial goals. Effective total compensation packages help in employee retention, which has now become almost essential for sustaining competitive advantage.

VARIABLE COMPENSATION

Variable pay is that part of the employee compensation, which varies with the organization's business performance. Variable compensation plans continue to gain popularity. A classic example of variable pay is sales commission in which a sales executive receives an award (usually expressed as a percentage of sales) for each sale closed. The more sales the sales executive closes, the higher is his total commission income and higher is the revenue and profits of the organization. On the other hand, if the sales executive fails to sell, the organization does not earn adequate revenue; but at the same time, it does not incur any expenditure on sales commission. Therefore with variable pay systems, the interests of the organization get closely linked to the interests of the individual employee. In contrast, the traditional base salary represents fixed compensation. It is paid to employees regardless of the organization's performance.

Variable Compensation Plans

The growing popularity of variable compensation plans is driven by three scenarios: variable pay is countercyclical; organizations incur extra cost of variable pay when performing well and are better placed to afford the extra cost on account of better revenue and profits; organizations incur less cost when the business is not doing well and are less able to afford variable pay. In the past, organizations could reduce employee compensation only by reducing the number of employees through layoffs. A variable pay system works well when the organization's business performance is equal to or better than the industry average. However, if the organization is performing poorly while the industry is doing well overall, then an employee's total compensation (variable plus fixed pay) would be less than that of those working in other companies in the industry leading to poor morale and/or increased attrition.

Employee goals and organizational goals

Variable pay links employee goals with organizational goals. If the organization performs well, then the employees earn more income based on their individual performance through variable pay. Therefore, the employees and the organization enjoy mutual benefits. In such a scenario, the design of the variable pay system assumes importance. For the variable pay plan to be optimally successful, the employees must understand how their individual performance affects their variable pay and the company performance. This is referred to as *line of sight*. Line of sight improves as organizations reduce layers of management.

Motivated employees

The most effective variable pay systems have been based on established team or business unit performance targets. Although the line of sight is better with individual goals than team goals, team goals have the advantage of peer influence, which can be a very strong motivator. On the other end of the continuum are company-wide goals (for a small organization, team goals and company goals are basically the same). These too can be effective; although the line of sight is less and therefore, the motivation to achieve the goals may be less.

Bonus or incentive plans

In a variable pay, bonus or incentive plans are common and popular. These plans are typically available for top management although participation in these plans is widening, especially as organizations tend to reduce layers of management. The formal bonus award is typically paid on an annual basis. The size of the award is usually based on a combination of the employee's individual job performance, the business performance of the employee's division or department, and/or the performance of the entire company. Typical performance criteria include profit before tax or operating profit, sales level or sales growth, and/or the achievement of specific company or division goals.

Profit-sharing plans

This type of variable pay is charged against the organizational profits based on a specific formula. The profit-sharing pool is then allocated to employees by some formula, usually a percentage of their base salary. Profit-sharing plans, like variable pay plans in general, are growing in popularity. A typical profit-sharing award is five per cent to six per cent of the employee's base salary.

Lump sum merit awards

Lump sum merit awards provide financial recognition for an individual's job performance. These are given in lieu of merit-based salary increases. It is an effective way to provide financial recognition, especially to those individuals whose base salary is already relatively high. The lump sum merit award must be re-earned each year and is usually paid during an annual salary review period.

Spot bonuses

Spot bonuses are also financial awards to recognize an individual's work accomplishments. Typically, these bonuses are paid immediately after a significant job performance event; unlike a lump sum merit award, which is paid as a part of the annual salary review process.

Gain-sharing plans

Gain-sharing plans allow employees to share productivity gains of an organization in accordance with a pre-determined formula. Typically, the plans are established with employee involvement and are designed for specific work groups; however, company-wide programmes also exist.

Alternative pay

Alternative pay refers to alternative ways of paying employees other than for their time, which is the most common method. Alternative pay plans generally include the schemes already listed under variable pay systems.

Skill-based pay or pay-for-knowledge is also considered as an alternative pay structure. Under this pay system, an employee's compensation is based on the number of specified skills or tasks the employee has acquired.

Stock plans

Stock plans are very popular. In a compensation system, stock plans are implemented by issuing stock options to employees. Under this scheme, an employee is offered a specific number of shares with option of selling them at some specified time in the future. The price at which the employee can buy the stock is equal to the market price at the time the stock option is granted (grant price). The employee's gain is equal to the market value of the stock at the time it is exercised less the grant price. If the market price of the stock remains the same or decreases relative to the grant price, then the stock option is worthless. It is used by the organization strategically as a long-term incentive and retention tool. Motivated employees help the company to perform well, which in turn, leads to an appreciation in its stock value.

Different stock incentive options Some stock option schemes are as follows:
- ESOP at a predetermined price, which attracts capital gains tax.
- Non-statutory ESOP at a discounted price, which attracts income tax.

- Restricted stock at a discounted rate with minimum lock-in period, which attracts capital gains tax. Before lock-in period, the price would remain the same (no appreciation).
- Phantom stock, which is a hypothetical stock with the option of conversion only after minimum vesting period. It attracts capital gains tax.

Due to its extensive usage, we have made a detailed discussion of ESOP models and issues in Chapter 3 on Employee compensation and the labour market. The valuation of ESOP is done using option pricing models, like the Black–Scholes model, after taking into account the following factors:
- price exercise
- expected life of the option
- current price of the given stock and its expected volatility with respect to market fluctuations
- expected dividends from the stock
- risk-free rate of interest rate for the expected term of the option

In India, the Securities and Exchange Board of India (SEBI) guidelines govern the corporate governance issues related to ESOP. Due to elaborate disclosures and compliance requirements provided in these guidelines, many organizations cannot make use of this tool for effective executive compensation. A typical disclosure norm with respect to SEBI guidelines requires an organization to provide pricing formula, options vested, options exercised, number of shares arising after exercising options, options lapsed, variation of option terms, money realized by exercise of options, employee-wise details of the options granted, and the diluted earnings per share. Such disclosures must be made in the Directors' Report.

RETIREMENT PLANS

Retirement plans typically cost organizations three per cent of payroll cost. The cost is substantially higher in organizations that offer a pension plan in addition to a defined contribution (generally in larger and older companies). For example, State Bank of India offers pension as a third benefit to its employees.

Pension Plans

Pension plans are also referred to as *defined benefit plans* as employees are aware of their pension entitlement. In most organizations, pension plans are self-funded and accumulate by systematic transfer to pension funds. However, such self-funded pension plans are difficult to administer due to regulatory restrictions. Therefore, organizations are increasingly shifting to professional pension fund managers to manage their pension plans.

In many organizations, pension is still paid instead of contributory provident fund. Some give lower rate of pensions as third benefit, even after providing for contributory provident fund. Exhibit 16.1 illustrates the pension computation template of companies, which give pension as a second benefit, the first being general provident fund (non-contributory).

EXHIBIT 16.1 Pension Calculation—Sample Sheet

1.	Name	Mira Singh
2.	Designation	Supervisor
3.	Department	Assembly
4.	Date of birth	20.09.1942
5.	Date of joining service	10.04.1965
6.	Date of superannuation/retirement	30.09.2000
7.	Qualifying service	(30.09.2000 – 10.04.1965) = 20(Y) 05(M) 35(D)
8.	Addition to qualifying service	Nil (conventionally 5 years weightage is given only after completion of 25 years of service).
9.	Period of service not qualifying for pension	Nil
10.	Last 10 months average emoluments	₹5,875
11.	Addition of special pay, personal pay, if any	₹100
12.	Average monthly pay eligible for pension computation	₹5,975
13.	Eligible monthly pension	₹1,901 (This has been arrived by using the following formula: 50% of the last drawn pay is payable as pension, however, 50% of pay as pension is paid subject to 33 years of service.) In this case, total service rendered by Mira Singh has been considered as 21 years (by approximation). Average monthly pay of ₹5,975 has been multiplied by the factor of (50/33) × 21 to arrive at the pension figure. It should be noted that giving 5 years service weightage is often followed in a discretionary manner. Some organizations also give this 5 years' service weightage even if in such cases, that is, where service exceeds 20 years or more.
14.	Commutation of pension	Some organizations allow pension commutation to the maximum extent of 40% of total pension, in which case eligible pension get reduced proportionately and the individual who commutes pension, gets cash compensation, value of which varies depending on the age of the retiree. However, admissible DA will be payable on total pension amount to the pensioner.

However, fixed pension annuity concepts are now getting outdated. Although pension schemes linked to stock market are still being opposed, they are likely to replace the present pension system. Fixed pension annuity can be purchased from various financial institutions. These offer this payment together with life risk coverage against a payment of premium. Some financial institutions have also started offering market-linked pension equity. To understand the present value of a fixed pension annuity, the present worth of any sum to be paid in n years can be computed using the following formula.

$$\text{Present value} = \frac{\text{Initial sum}}{(1+\text{Interest rate})^n}$$

A pension plan that promises to pay monthy ₹10,000 after 33 years of service with present rate of interest of 10% is equivalent to:

$$\text{Present value} = \frac{₹10,000}{(1+0.10)^{33}} = \frac{10,000}{23.22} = ₹430.66$$

401(k) Plans

These plans are very popular. Today, almost all companies in the US offer 401(k) plans. They have several advantages over pension plans. These plans are transparent. With periodic statement of accounts, employees can keep a track of their investments. They also enjoy the opportunity to invest in their chosen funds. Another advantage is that these plans are portable. Employee can carry their accumulated pension benefits even when they prematurely leave their job in an organization. Hence, a qualifying period of service as a mandatory requirement in a conventional pension plan is absent here. In addition, the operational cost is least for these plans as these are managed by professional fund managers. Employers share 50 per cent of the contribution of employees; which together aggregates to 6 to 8 per cent of the employees' salary. In India too, new pension plans are structured on the lines of the 401(k) plan.

Health and Welfare Plans

Health and welfare plans typically cost organizations 8 per cent to 10 per cent of payroll. To install health and insurance plans, organizations make use of various schemes provided by insurance companies. Insurance companies, in addition to helping install the plans, can also help negotiate contracts and administer plans. In countries like India, this cost component is not so high. However, such costs are ever increasing in economically developed countries due to increasing medical and health care expenses. In some countries, this cost is rising at the rate of 20 per cent per year. In some countries, different health care related costs are covered separately by different insurance plans such as medical insurance cost, prescription drugs plans, dental plans, vision plans, and orthodontic plans. However in India, comprehensive medical and health care benefits schemes, which do not require separate earmarking of the area of benefits is provided by each scheme. Comprehensive life insurance policies with separate riders for medical and health care, and accidental and death benefit are also offered by many Indian insurance companies.

In India, employers are statutorily required to provide for medical benefit schemes. They are also required to provide leave with pay and holidays on which employees are entitled to full payment of wages, as part of compensation benefits. It includes vacation pay, sick pay, personal time-off, sabbaticals, etc. Some of these benefits are government-mediated, whereas some organizations voluntarily make them available to their employees.

PAYROLL MANAGEMENT

Payroll is compensation record of each employee, which shows gross pay, deductions, and net pay. It also provides the details of cost to the company. With a detailed list of employees and their salaries, a scientifically structured payroll ensures that employees are paid correctly after deduction of taxes and other dues. Designing of a payroll system requires designing of workflow systems followed by development of a software program to track all payroll-related transactions. Some important guidelines followed in payroll preparation are segregation of duties for payroll preparation; establishment of written control systems; maintaining accurate payroll records; and complying with regulatory requirements and other employer obligations.

The term *payroll management* is used often in compensation management literature. It involves accounting and administration of payroll. In the accounting part, calculation of earnings of employees and various deductions, either for taxes or otherwise, is considered. It also keeps record of payrolls and helps in preparation of tax returns. Payroll accounting can be automated by using payroll software. It would help in preparing payroll reports with speed and accuracy. Payroll administration deals with the managerial aspects of maintaining a payroll such as managing employee information and compliance with various statutory provisions. All payroll management systems comply with some basic accounting standards and principles. These norms are country-specific. In addition to these norms, many organizations develop their own guidelines for payroll management. Such guidelines are more in the form of policy statements detailing scale of pay, allowances, deduction, etc. However, some organizations also make use of standard software. One such template of payroll module for Kurl-On Limited is illustrated in Exhibit 16.2.

EXHIBIT 16.2   Payroll Management

	KMIS		
Module	HRM	Form	Pay slip
Description	Pay slip sample		

```
Payslip - Microsoft Internet Explorer                                    _ □ ×
Kurl-on    KURLON LIMITED , III Floor, North Block, Manipal Center , 47   Date : 4/6/2002
           Dickenson Road , Bangalore - 560 042
              Pay Slip For The Month Of May  2002  ( HO - Bangalore )
  Employee Code | Name          | Grade | Designation      | Department
  1196          | ARUN RAO G    | R1    | BUSINESS OFFICER | MARKETING

  Father's Name | PF No     | ESI No | Pan No | Bank | Account No
  GOPAL RAO     | 3694/4900 | ----   | ----   | HDFC | 0761050035800
         Gross                  Earnings                  Deductions
  Basic       : 3175.00    Basic       : 3175.00    ESI            :  75.80
  HRA         :  555.63    HRA         :  555.63    EPF            : 318.00
  CONVEYANCE  :  600.00    CONVEYANCE  :  600.00    VPF            :   0.00
  Arrears     :    0.00    Arrears     :    0.00    P.Tax          :  25.00
  OverTime    :    0.00    OverTime    :    0.00    I.Tax          :   0.00
                                                    LIC            :   0.00
                                                    Fest. Adv      :   0.00
                                                    Salary Adv     :   0.00
                                                    Loan Ded       :   0.00
                                                    Other Deduction:   0.00
  Gross       : 4330.63    Total Earnings : 4330.63    Total Ded.  : 418.80
              Net Sal. ( Total Earnings - Total Deductions ) : 3912.00

        Leave Balance     | Loan / Advance Balance  |      Attendance
  Annual Leave   | 12.5   | Salary Adv.    |  0     | Days Worked  | 31
  Casual Leave   |   9    | Festival Adv.  |  0     | Loss Of Pay  |  0
  Sick Leave     |   3    | Loan Adv.      |  0     | ESI Leaves   |  0
  Employee Signature                                       Authorized Signature
```

QUANTITATIVE ANALYSIS

In compensation designing and management, intuition is often used rather than mathematical systems. This devoids organizations of the objectivity that these systems offer. Mathematical systems follow certain norms. For example, the observations must be independent, that is, one measurement should not bias the other; the measurements must be from a normally distributed population, that is, the traditional bell-shaped curve; the population must have the same variance; the measurement must be of at least an interval scale, and the effects must be additive.

Levels of Measurement

While performing research, it is often necessary to collect responses from samples. The nature of the responses depends largely on the type of scale used by the researcher. Respondents communicate their feelings, attitudes, opinions, and evaluations in some measurable form. Developing a proper scale helps measure the responses. Each scale has unique properties.

Some scales are limited in their mathematical properties to the extent that they can only establish an association between variables. Other scales have more extensive mathematical properties and help in establishing cause and effect relationships between variables. There are four basic kinds of measurements—nominal, ordinal, interval, and ratio.

Nominal measurements

Nominal measurements (or scales) are composed of numerical values that serve to identify discrete categories, that is, the numbers are labels for the categories and imply no quantitative (measurable) differences that can be handled meaningfully in numerical operations. The numbers on front doors, for instance, constitute such a scale; social security numbers are another example. In salary surveys, the numbering of positions or companies is just such a scale; the numbers are used merely as labels.

Table 16.1 illustrates only one single position, that is, software developer in hypothetical software companies. Software developers' position code differs from organization to organization and so do their salary levels.

Nominal measurements allow only the most limited application like counting classes. For example, the number of positions numbered '2', or count Yes–No where 0–1 correspond to Yes and No respectively. However, most human resource administrators would find that using nominal measurements in any kind of mathematical operation is bound to get error, as human resource management considers many qualitative and behavioural factors that cannot be measured in quantitative terms.

Ordinal measurements

Ordinal measurements, in addition to nominal properties, rank differences. That is, the numerical value of these scales indicates that there are not only differences between categories but that these are quantifiable differences. An ordinal scale ranks *observations* with regard to the extent to which they possess

TABLE 16.1 *Position-wise salary level across the organizations*

Company name	Company code	Position	Position code	Gross monthly salary (₹)
Mega Soft	001	Software developer	010	50,000
India Systems	002	Software developer	09	55,000
Innova Systems	003	Software developer	05	45,000

more or less of a given quality. However, the ranks do not indicate the degree of difference (how much more or less) of the property each observation has.

There are events with dimensions that cannot be readily quantified. It would be absurd to state that a painting is twice as beautiful as another, or that a particular restaurant serves food one-third as tasty as another. For this reason, ordinal scales are often applied to observed events that differ along qualitative rather than quantitative dimensions (especially when the qualitative dimension cannot be easily expressed quantitatively).

For example, the following job evaluation factors cannot be easily broken down into quantifiable units.
- problem complexity
- responsibility
- human/social challenges
- skill
- authority
- profit impact

Can one job have two times as much the problem complexity as another? However, each factor can be broken down in steps. For example, problem complexity might be broken down as shown in Table 16.2.

TABLE 16.2 Perceived differences in compensation

Degree of perceived differences in compensation	Perceived rank order, assigned by samples
Very significant differences	2
Significant differences	3
Moderate differences	4
No differences	1

This measurement is very important. Performance appraisals are usually done using ordinal scales, yet human resource practitioners often try to utilize mathematical tests and computations that require assumptions that are more stringent.

Interval measurements

Interval scales are equal unit scales, that is, the distance between adjacent units on an interval scale is the same irrespective of the magnitude of the adjacent scale units. For instance, the distance between ₹5,000 and ₹6,000 is the same as the distance between ₹61,000 and ₹62,000, since it reflects a measurable increase in terms of rupees.

Interval scales, however, are only relative. For example, if these amounts (₹5,000–₹6,000 and ₹61,000–₹62,000) were to represent sales compensation, the amount of actual sales required to produce the increase in sales compensation in the previous example may be different at ₹5,000 (to ₹6,000)

TABLE 16.3 Interval measurement scales

Annual first premium collection (in ₹)	Commission to development officers/team leader	Commission to advisers/agents
10,000	0	0
10,001–15,000	500	800
15,001–20,000	1,500	2,400
20,001–25,000	2,000	2,900

and ₹61,000 (to ₹62,000). Therefore, the scale reflects relative rather than absolute changes. An example is shown in Table 16.3.

Interval scales are the most frequently used measurement scales in human resource pay practices. However, many human resource measurements cannot satisfy the requirement that measurements be similar and equidistant in their measurement intervals. Their ordinal or nominal characteristics must be recognized in order to understand the explanations of tests.

Example

Let us explain interval scale in the context of salesman commission. A salesman sells a product for ₹90,000. His broker's commission is 5 per cent after the first ₹30,000. The salesman receives 60 per cent of the broker's commission. What is the salesman's commission?

Solution
Step 1: Calculate the commissionable revenue, that is, the difference between actual sales and commissionable sales, which in the example is ₹90,000 − ₹30,000 = ₹60,000.

Step 2: Calculate the total or the broker's commission, which is the product of commissionable revenue multiplied by salesman's percentage, which in the example is ₹60,000 × 0.05 = ₹3,000.

Step 3: Calculate the salesperson's commission, which is the product of total commission multiplied by salesperson's percentage, which in the example is ₹3,000 × 0.06 = ₹1,800.

These types of salesperson's commission plans are used by the organizations in variety of sales promotion schemes such as new client solicitation, new market, or product introduction.

Ratio measurements

The ratio scale has the properties of the nominal, ordinal, interval scales, and an absolute zero. The absolute zero represents a point below which no value

TABLE 16.4 Ratio measurement scales

First year premium collection (in ₹)	Head-wise allowable expenses (in ₹)	Expenses ratio (%)
10,00,000	Travelling allowances = 5,000	0.5
	Annual salaries = 5,00,000	50
	Loyalty bonus = 1,80,000	18

can be assigned. Zero represents no less than one of the properties being gauged by the scale. For example, in salary administration, rupees in value can be shown on the interval scale, whereas percentages can be shown on a ratio scale. Compensation amount can be a ratio (i.e., if no negative exists). However, a division by zero is not an acceptable mathematical operation. Hence, ratio measurements have certain computational limitations. Examples of ratio measurements are shown in Table 16.4.

Example

Company XYZ has three departments and has budgeted salary increases for the coming year as per the following schedule:

Department A: 7 per cent raise for 2 employees
Department B: 9 per cent raise for 3 employees
Department C: 11 per cent raise for 95 employees

Assume all the employees are receiving ₹10,000 as annual base salary. Estimate the budgeted salary increases for the coming year.

Solution

The calculation is shown in Table 16.5.

TABLE 16.5 Budgeted salary increase

Department	Number of employees	Percentage of salary increase	Total base salary (in ₹)	Total salary increase (in ₹)
A	2	7	20,000	1,400
B	3	9	30,000	2,700
C	95	11	9,50,000	1,04,500
Total	100	27	10,00,000	1,08,600

The overall increase in salary budget, that is, the real average salary increase is 10.86 per cent.

Scaling Techniques

Various types of scales used in research fall into two broad categories—comparative and non-comparative. In comparative scaling, the respondent is

Quantitative Tools and Innovation in Compensation

asked to compare one brand or product against another. In non-comparative scaling, respondents need only to evaluate a single product or a brand. Non-comparative scaling is frequently referred to as monadic scaling, and this is the more widely used type of scale in commercial marketing research studies. Some scaling techniques are described here.

Semantic scale

This type of scale makes extensive use of words rather than numbers. Respondents describe their feelings about products or brands on scales with semantic labels. When bipolar adjectives are used at end points of the scales, these are termed as semantic differential scales. Semantic scale and the semantic differential scale are illustrated in Fig. 16.1.

Likert scale

A Likert scale is termed as a summated instrument scale. This means that the items making up a Likert scale are summed to produce a total score. In fact, it is a composite of itemized scales. Typically, each scale item will have five categories, with scale values ranging from −2 to +2 with 0 as the neutral response (Table 16.6).

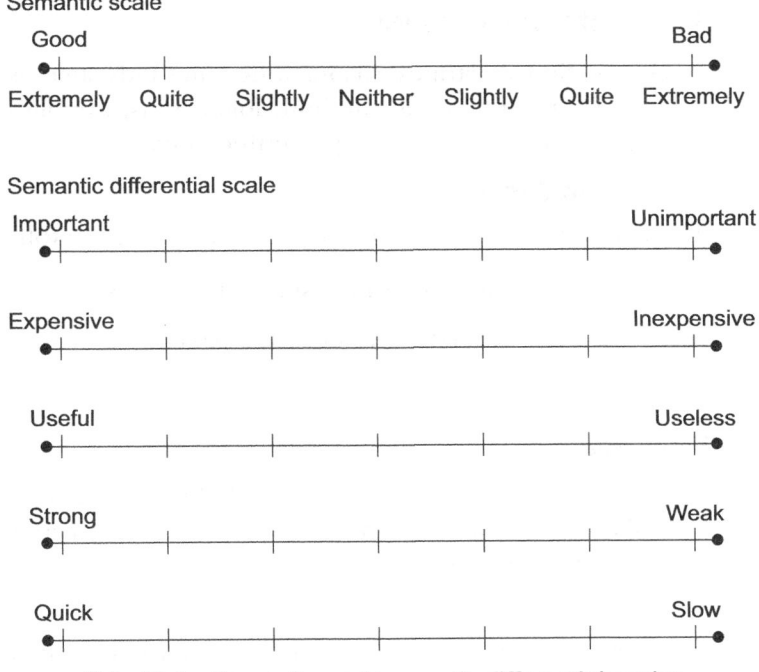

FIG. 16.1 Semantic and semantic differential scales

TABLE 16.6 Likert scale

	Strongly agree	Agree	Neither	Disagree	Strongly disagree
If the price of raw materials fell, firms would reduce the price of their food products.	1	2	3	4	5
Without government regulation, the firms would exploit the consumer.	1	2	3	4	5
Most food companies arc so concerned about making profits that they do not care about quality.	1	2	3	4	5
The food industry spends a great deal of money making sure that its manufacturing is hygienic.	1	2	3	4	5
Food companies should charge the same price for their products throughout the country.	1	2	3	4	5

A majority of management researchers treat Likert scales as yielding interval data. The scales, which have been described in this chapter, are among the most commonly used in marketing research. Whilst there are many more forms scales can take, if students are familiar with the scales described in this chapter, they would be well equipped to deal with most types of market research problems.

Alternate Techniques

This section illustrates various other methods such as compound interest, rule of 72, present value method, logarithms, averages, medians, weighted average, modes, percentages, percentiles, etc.

Compound interest

The compounding of interest is calculated using the following formula:

$$\text{Ending sum} = \text{Initial sum} \times (1 + \text{Interest rates})^{\text{Years}}$$

eg., $\qquad ₹10,816 = ₹10,000 \times (1 + 0.04)^{2*}$

Example

In the year 2007, an average MBA student starts with a salary of ₹30,000. Assume that salary will increase at the rate 9 per cent per year. Ascertain the starting salary for an MBA in the year 2023.

---

*It should be remembered that the exponent (power) means that the operation or number should be multiplied by itself that many times. In the example, therefore, the process is (1.0 + 0.04) × (1.0 + 0.04). Always perform the operation in parentheses first.

Solution

$$\text{Starting salary in the year 2023} = \left(\text{Initial amount} \times (1+\text{Interest rate})^{\text{Years}(2023-2007)}\right)$$
$$= ₹1,19,110$$

Rule of 72

Rule of 72 is a very useful tool in compensation calculation. According to this rule, when the number 72 is divided by an interest rate, the result indicates the number of years it would take to double the salary if the salary increases at that rate every year. Let us stretch the earlier example to estimate the year at which the salary of the entry level MBA will get doubled, that is, ₹60,000. Applying rule of 72, we can easily calculate it as year 8th, that is, by dividing 72 by the interest rate of 9 per cent.

Present value method

This method helps ascertain the current level of compensation, discounting the future compensation rate. Suppose a company has made an agreement with their unions that current value of salary of ₹1,000 will be increased to a sum of ₹2,000 in next 5 years' time, allowing annual increment at the rate ₹200. Using present value method, value of ₹2,000 can be approximated (receivable after 5 years) using this formula:

$$\text{Present value} = \frac{\text{Initial sum}}{(1+\text{Interest rate})}$$

Present value method is used extensively in retirement planning.

Logarithms

A logarithm is the exponent of the power to which a fixed number must be raised to produce a given value. For example, if the fixed number is 10 (the most common base), the logarithm of 1,000 is 3. You have to multiply 10 three times by itself ($10 \times 10 \times 10$) to produce the desired result (1,000). Logarithms are commonly used in human resource surveys, especially in graphs that show salaries versus some size dimension. The reason for their use is that they allow visual comparison of data that may be quite dissimilar in size.

Working with logarithms requires the exercise of manipulating the exponents (power of the numbers). Logarithms at a base of 10 are best illustrated as follows:

$$10 = 10^1 = 1$$
$$100 = 10^2 = 2$$

Dividing or multiplying with logarithms is like dividing or multiplying with other exponents. To multiply, the exponents are added. To divide, the exponents are subtracted. For example:

$$10^3 \times 10^4 = 10^7$$

or

$$10^8 \div 10^2 = 10^6$$

Averages

It is required for arriving at the average salary level of employees working in any organization. The mean or average of a distribution is defined as the sum of the values of the variables in the distribution divided by the number of observations in that distribution. When the distribution is a sample:

$$\text{Average} = \frac{\text{Sum of variables}}{\text{Number of observations in sample}}$$

An observation is a discrete event to which the value of a variable has been assigned. Several observations can have the same value. A variable is an aspect being observed to which a value has been assigned.

Medians

A median is the midpoint of a distribution. Half of the observations in a distribution are above the median, the other half are below the median. When the sample or population consists of an even number of observations, the true median may lie halfway between the two middle observations. It is used in pay banding.

Example

Let us assume a salary survey of ten HR managers' salaries in FMCG companies reveals the monthly pay of ₹14,000, ₹15,000, ₹15,000, ₹15,000, ₹16,000, ₹16,000, ₹18,000, ₹21,000, ₹28,000, and ₹42,000. Find out the median salary.

Solution
Count the number of salaries (n = 10)
Count up halfway or down halfway (5)
The median salary is halfway between ₹16,000 and ₹18,000, that is, ₹17,000.

Weighted average

In compensation management, weighted average represents the average of total population, and not just a subset. The following example will illustrate this. Assume Company A and Company B's hourly rate for production workers is as shown in Table 16.7.

The weighted average is calculated in Table 16.8.

TABLE 16.7 Hourly rates for production

| Company A | ₹7.60 | ₹8.40 | ₹9.90 | ₹10.30 | ₹10.70 | ₹13.10 |
| Company B | ₹7.30 | ₹9.70 | – | – | – | – |

TABLE 16.8 Calculation of weighted average

	Company A	Company B
Sample sum	₹60.00	₹17.00
Sample number	6	2
Average	₹10.00	₹8.50
Company sum	₹18.50	
Company number	2	
Company average	₹9.25	
Weighted product	₹60.00 + ₹17.00	
Weighted sum	₹77.00	
Sample number	8	
Weighted average	₹9.63	

Modes

The mode is that category of the distribution that contains observations that appear with the greatest frequency; that is, the most frequent set of measurements is the mode of the distribution. In grouped data, the mode is associated with the midpoint of the category that has the greatest frequency. The category with the greatest frequency concentration often tends to be located at or near the center of a distribution. However, this is not always the case; thus, as a measurement, the mode leaves much to be desired. Since it gives the most frequent level salary or compensation of some positions or posts across the organizations, it is possible for the company to compute the market trend of salaries for some positions to design competitive rate.

Example

A salary survey of marketing managers' salaries in consumer electronics industry finds the following monthly salary data: ₹15,000, ₹15,000, ₹15,000, ₹16,000, ₹16,000, ₹18,000, ₹21,000, ₹28,000, ₹42,000. Find out the mode salary.

Solution
The highest number of occurrences of any single event—in this case three times—is ₹15,000. Therefore, ₹15,000 is the mode.

Percentages

Percentages are the most commonly used form of fractions. Computed in 100ths, they allow a representation of a fraction in terms of 100s or 'cents',

Percentiles

Percentiles are arbitrarily selected units determined by dividing a whole into a distribution of 100 equal parts. A percentile distribution is based on the number of observations constituting a given percentage of the total number of observations in the distribution, irrespective of category; percentiles are frequently used to determine what proportion of the distribution falls below a given level.

Example

You have started a company and have hired an administrative assistant at ₹28,000. He is the tenth highest paid of 123 secretaries. His salary is at what percentile?

Solution
Table 16.9 shows the calculation.

TABLE 16.9 Salary percentile calculation

Rank	10th highest of 123
Standing	Maximum − Ranking = 123 − 10 = 113
Percentage	(Standing/Maximum) × 100 = (113/123) × 100 = 91.87
Percentile	91th percentile (In determining test scores, it is a common practice to drop the decimal place and round down.)

Pay structure formation

Each year most companies review adjustments to their salary structures. Many use survey data to aid in determining the necessity for changes in the structure. For example, a regression analysis of survey results might show average survey positions (as defined in a company's hierarchical level range approach) as earnings (Table 16.10).

TABLE 16.10 Comparative analysis of salary structure

Level	Present salary structure (in ₹/month)	Competitive levels salary structure (in ₹/month)
1	10,000	11,200
2	12,000	13,000
3	14,400	15,800
4	17,300	19,500

TABLE 16.11 Salary structure (recommended)

Grade	New structure (in ₹/month)
1	11,000
2	13,200
3	14,800
4	19,000

From the data, Table 16.11 can be derived.

Calculating new salary structures can also be done using the same calculation.

Based on a point factor job evaluation plan, a company has at the bottom of the structure 800 points and at the top 7,000 points. We assume the salaries to increase at the rate 7 per cent at the bottom and at the rate 10 per cent at the top. To frame the salary structure matching with these rates we calculate

$$11 \times 800 \text{ points} + ₹4,000$$

$$11 \times 7,000 \text{ points} + ₹4,000$$

Low ₹12,800 + 0.07 × 12,800 = ₹13,696

High ₹81,000 + 0.10 × 81,000 = ₹89,100

Therefore, Slope × 800 points + Intercept = ₹13,696

Slope × 7,000 points + Intercept = ₹89,100

Having determined the two new points on the line, a new structure can be developed.

Maturity curves

Maturity or career curves are descriptive techniques often used in professional or engineering environments. This curve plots salary on y-axis and years of work experience or years since degree on x-axis. The maturity curve is shown in Fig. 16.2.

As reporting devices for surveys, maturity curves allow a grouping similar to grading (or they can be used with grades) to define the average expected rate of pay. Their underlying importance in salary surveys is that *time on the job* has a great impact on pay. An average pay implies understanding of the average tenure in that position for all incumbents. (One would expect an inexperienced individual to be at the bottom of the salary range; more experienced employees would be at the top). Should one conduct a survey and sample only senior or only recently hired employees, the results are likely to be erroneous.

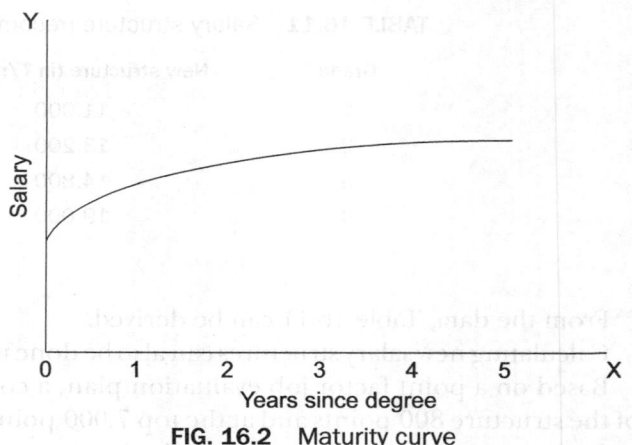

FIG. 16.2 Maturity curve

Example

Construct a maturity curve from the data given in Table 16.12.

TABLE 16.12 Data for constructing a maturity curve

Years of experience	Average salary (₹/month)
0	12,000
5	20,000
10	26,000
15	30,000
20	28,000
25	26,000

Are there any other concerns that might be shown with such a curve?

Solution

Yes, but constructing a downward sloping curve could very well result in discrimination against older workers who are now protected by government legislation.

Axes

The bottom line of a graph (the horizontal line) is known as the base line or the *horizontal axis*. By convention, it is called the x-axis. The line perpendicular to the x-axis (i.e., at the left) is known as the *vertical axis*, which is referred to as the y-axis. In equations, these axes are often defined in the following format.

Value of y = Value of x (another value) + a constant

That is, $y = mx + b$

where m = Slope of a line in relation to the x-axis; b = Intercept of the y-axis when x is equal to zero (x = 0).

The slope is the change in the value of y that corresponds directly to a change in the value of x. The equation is useful because it describes any value of y if any value of x is known.

Example

Suppose a survey of test scores of all programmers produces the following results: 120, 100, 90, 80, 70.

Correspondingly, the age of each programmer is found to be 55, 50, 45, 35, 30 years. What would be the x-axis if this data is plotted?

Solution
The data is shown in Table 16.13. See the plotting of the data in Fig. 16.3.

TABLE 16.13 Age and score data

Age	Score
55	120
50	100
45	90
35	80
30	70

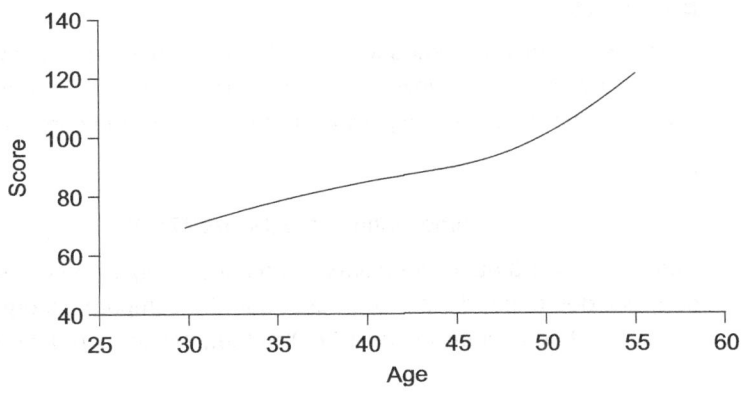

FIG. 16.3 Age and score graph

However, either age or score values can be plotted in x-axis.

Compa-ratios

Compa-ratios are a percentage representation of a company's pay levels as they compare either to the company's own structure or to competitive levels. This concept can be explained using a very simple example. Say a company pays

₹9,000 per month as compensation for a given position; whereas for the same position, the competitive level compensation per month is ₹10,000. Compa-ratio would then be 9/10 or 90 per cent. In other words, the market or compa-ratio is determined by dividing the company's level by the competitive structure:

$$\text{Compa-ratio} = \frac{\text{Company level}}{\text{Competitive structure}}$$

This term is used in compensation administration for employees. It can also be appropriately applied to departments, companies, and other comparative situations.

Example

A company pays salaries at average 90 per cent of competitive rates. Competitive rates are reflected through position standards, all of which form the comparison salary structure. Since competitive forecasts are for 10 per cent, both the structure and the annualized salary increase are 10 per cent. What will the company's compa-ratio be at the end of next year?

Solution
Next year's compa-ratio will be equal to (Present salaries/Competitive salary) × 100.

Example

Suppose a company wishes to utilize the benchmark ranking evaluations and chooses to pay 10 per cent below the market. The competitive average for a position is ₹30,000 and the company pays ₹23,000. Find out the compa-ratio.

Solution

Compa-ratio = ₹23,000/₹27,000 = 85 per cent

Note that even though the salary in competing organization is ₹30,000 as the company decides to pay 10 per cent less than the comparative organizations, competitive salary has been construed as ₹27,000 (i.e., 10 per cent less than ₹30,000).

Compa-ratio is also used for the internal benchmarking of the salaries in an organization. Take an employee's annual salary and divide it by the salary range midpoint associated with the grade level of the employee's position, or the MRP if the position has one. Then multiply the result by 100. This produces a salary compa-ratio, or the employee's salary as a percentage of the midpoint/MRP.

The lines of best fit (practice line) to an organization's base salary and total remuneration data are indicator of organizational pay policy. Up to 20 per cent variation in the total remuneration from the practice line is considered as normal. If the gap is more, the compensation design has to be re-evaluated.

Compa-ratio helps to measure the degree of displacement from the practice line. It is an index to illustrate the relationship between an individual employee's salary with that of the other employees. Hence, calculation of compa-ratio can also be done using the following formula:

$$\text{Compa-ratio} = \frac{\text{Actual salary}}{\text{Practice line salary}} \times 100\%$$

Therefore, compa-ratios should serve as a measure of relative performance of individuals within an organization. If the compa-ratio is greater than 100 per cent then the individual is being paid more than what a competent performer in the job would be paid normally. Conversely, if the compa-ratio is less than 100 per cent, the individual is being paid less than what the competent performer in the job would be paid on average. This analysis can be used to align an individual's pay with their performance and is a valuable tool in the implementation of reward for performance. Consider the following example.

Annual salary of ₹47,000 divided by a salary range midpoint of ₹54,900, multiplied by 100 results in a compa-ratio of 0.86 or 86 per cent. This means that the employee's salary is 86 per cent of the current Salary Range Midpoint, or average market pay.

A compa ratio of < 1 (or less than 100 per cent) means that the employee is being paid lower than his band's mid-point (average).

To calculate compa-ratio, the compensation specialist places the salary as the nominator and midpoint as the denominator. The answer is a decimal. The specialist usually converts the decimal to a percentage by multiplying it by 100.

Salary = ₹44,000
Midpoint = ₹50,000
Compa-ratio for this example is 0.88 or 88 per cent.
There are three common uses for compa-ratio calculations:
- to extend a salary offer to a new hire
- to budget the total amount of a merit pay programme
- to determine an appropriate pay raise for an individual

When the organization extends an offer to a fully competent applicant, the target compa-ratio may be 90 per cent. If the midpoint for the new hire's position is ₹50,000, the compensation specialist may recommend a salary offer of 90 per cent of ₹50,000 or ₹45,000. Standard compensation practice does not support extending salary offer to a new hire at a compa-ratio above 100 per cent.

To calculate compa-ratio for annual merit pay budgeting, the compensation specialist will add all salaries within the organization and divide it by the sum of all midpoints.

Total salaries = ₹57,04,000
Sum of midpoints = ₹62,00,000

TABLE 16.14 Compa-ratio

Employee	Salary (₹)	Midpoint (₹)	Compa–ratio (%)	Performance
X	42,500	50,000	85	Excellent
Y	56,000	50,000	112	Excellent

The organization's compa-ratio is 92 per cent. Because the competitive target compa-ratio is 100 per cent, the organization has room for salary growth and can justify a salary increase program.

The amount of increase awarded to an employee is usually dependent on the employee's performance and compa-ratio. Let us consider information provided for two employees in Table 16.14.

An employee who is an excellent performer with a compa-ratio of 85 per cent should receive a larger raise than an excellent performer with a compa-ratio of 112 per cent. Calculating compa-ratios is a simple process that provides complex information to compensation specialists. If your compa-ratio significantly exceeds 100 per cent, it indicates at one of the following three possibilities: your employer is extremely generous, your job is in great demand, or you are ready for a promotion.

Most organizations recommend a course of action if the compa-ratio falls within a certain percentile range. For example, if the ratio falls between 0 to 33 per cent, the result is a grade demotion. If the ratio falls between 34 and 66 per cent, the result is a lateral movement, and if it falls between 67 and 100 per cent, the action is a promotion.

Cost–benefit analysis

Organizations often resort to cost–benefit analysis, while designing the compensation structure. It produces a ratio that plots a company's cost against the real benefit received by an employee. To illustrate, a company may pay ₹2.00 as salary but the real cost may be ₹1.00 (if 50 per cent corporate tax level is considered). Differing cost–benefit ratios exist for different elements of compensation. This is particularly true in the case of perquisites. The real value can be determined by the nature of the benefit, the company's tax status, and the employee's own tax status.

Salary increases

By definition, a salary increase is the additional amount to be paid to an individual within a given time period. It is not, in itself, the extra amount; rather, it is a promise to pay additional amount. Quite often, mistakes are committed by disregarding the differences between annualized and budgeted salary increases. *Budgeted costs* relate to a definite plan of expending additional real amount, whereas *annual salary increases* refer to the total percentage actually granted. The only time when annualized and budgeted percentages are the same is when all increases are granted effective the first day of the year.

Example

Assume that a company has budgeted to grant 8 per cent increase on 1 April (April to March is considered to be the financial year) based on performance record and two per cent general salary increase on 1 October to offset the inflation factor. Against this budgeted salary increase plan, the company actually granted 7 per cent increase on 1 April and 2 per cent general salary increase on 1 October. Compute the annualized salary increase percentage in the year under consideration.

Solution

Budgeted salary increase = 8% merit + 2% (1/2 year) + 2% of 8% merit increase (1/2 year)
= 8% + 2% (1/2 year) + (0.02 × 8%) (1/2 year)
= 8% + (2% + 0.16%) (1/2 year)
= 8% + 1.08%
= 9.08%

Actual salary increase = 7% + 2% (1/2 year) + 2% of 7% merit increase (1/2 year)
= 7% + 2% (1/2 year) + (0.02 × 7%) (1/2 year)
= 7% + (2% + 0.14%) (1/2 year)
= 7% + 1.07
= 8.07%

In this example, the actual salary increase is less than the budgeted salary increase. Therefore, the company incurred under-budget expenditure in its salary increases for the year under consideration.

Cost of living

It refers to a measure of cost of goods and services purchased by consumers. All employees are consumers. Most often, cost of living information is expressed in terms of an index or a percentage compared against the cost of living at some previous period. The most common cost of living index provides this data, establishing a base period for comparison and using the rupee value of that time to establish present costs.

Demand and supply

No review of human resource statistics, particularly related to cost of living, would be complete without mention of the law of supply and demand.

A supply curve is defined as price (y-axis) versus quantity (x-axis), and it traditionally slopes upward. As the price of goods increases, the quantity available usually increases because suppliers (e.g., potential workers) more readily bring the goods into the market. Contrarily, the demand curve traditionally is explained by a decrease in quantity desired as price goes up. The intersection of demand and supply is, in economic terms, *the market price* of the item.

In a free market economy, it is the demand and supply curves of jobs and employees that create the wage and salary levels of a market. *Cost of living* may have no bearing on the price of labour (for example, in Dallas, the cost of living is low but wages are high because the laws of demand and supply are at work). An understanding of the mechanics of supply and demand is essential for effective compensation administration.

Compensation metrics

Compa-ratio is one of the major compensation metrics used by organizations in general. Apart from compa-ratio, organizations also make use of various other compensation metrics for effective compensation management as per their requirement. Using such compensation metrics, organizations try to assess the effectiveness of their compensation plan in terms of attracting, retaining, developing, and rewarding talent. Based on the trend of compensation metrics, organizations time to time calibrate their compensation plans. Some general compensation metrics, apart from the ones discussed earlier, are as follows:

Voluntary turnover of talented employees This metrics can be developed to check as to what extent talent turnover rate can be attributed to compensation and benefits programme of the organization. Voluntary separation may be due to other reasons such as poor work culture and lack of opportunity to grow. However using this metric, we can understand as to what extent such separation is attributable to compensation and benefits programme, based on information collected during exit interviews. The calculation for this metric would be as follows:

$$\text{Voluntary turnover of talented employees} = \frac{\text{Voluntary turnover of talented employees}}{\text{Total head count on payroll}}$$

Compensation to revenue This is an important metrics, which helps us to assess the trend of compensation in organizations in real terms. The calculation for this metrics would be as follows:

$$\text{Compensation to revenue} = \frac{\text{Total cost of compensation}}{\text{Revenue}}$$

Compensation to operating expenses Like the previous one, this metrics also helps in assessing the compensation trend. It helps determine whether the cost of compensation as a percentage to operating expenses increases or decreases over the years. The calculation for this metrics would be as follows:

$$\text{Compensation to operating expenses} = \frac{\text{Total cost of compensation}}{\text{Operating expense}}$$

Average per employee compensation cost This also gives us some meaningful insights on compensation trend in an organization. Such metrics can be used for comparing with other metrics of the organizations. For example, if we have labour productivity rate, we can compare it with the average per employee compensation cost to study, how labour productivity gets influenced with the increase or decrease of per employee compensation cost. The calculation for this metrics would be as follows:

$$\text{Average per employee compensation cost} = \frac{\text{Total cost of compensation}}{\text{Headcount on payroll}}$$

Performance-related pay (PRP) to total compensation This is helpful in understanding the effectiveness of the trend of PRP, which is now used globally including India, to slowly deviate from fixed pay concept. The calculation for this metrics would be as follows:

$$\text{PRP to total compensation} = \frac{\text{PRP}}{\text{Total compensation}}$$

Apart from these compensation metrics, organizations can design their own metrics to assess the trend in compensation and/or to strengthen their compensation related decision-making.

EMPLOYEE BENEFITS

This section discusses the various employee benefits provided to employees by their organizations.

Gratuity Computation

Payment of gratuity is a statutory obligation. Many organizations minimize their cost of gratuity payment by participating in group gratuity schemes of various financial institutions. Otherwise, they need to make provisions for gratuity payment by transferring a certain percentage of the total revenue to reserve fund to meet their future liability towards gratuity payment. Gratuity is one of the deferred benefits and is a load to wage costs. The minimum qualifying period of service to earn gratuity is five years. It is admissible at a uniform rate of ¼th of a month's assessable emoluments, that is, pay plus classification allowance and DA for each completed six-monthly period of qualifying service subject to maximum of 16½ months emoluments and is restricted to ₹10 lakh. It is important to mention that a firm's obligation for payment of gratuity is independent of status of employment. The only condition is continuous five-year service. Based on prevailing organizational practices, a sample of gratuity computation is illustrated in Exhibit 16.3.

EXHIBIT 16.3 Gratuity Computation Sheet for Shama Shah, Retiring Public Relations Officer of M/s ABC & Co., New Delhi

Date of birth	2.8.1957
Date of joining the service	2.8.1975
Date of voluntary retirement	31.8.1999
Qualifying service	24 years 1 month
Non qualifying service	Nil
Pay scale	₹3,900–100–6,200
Last pay drawn (per month)	₹4,200
Classification allowance (per month)	₹100
Gratuity payable	[(Last pay drawn + Classification allowance + DA) × (Six monthly period of qualifying service)/4] = [(4,200 + 100 + 1,376) × 58]/4 = ₹82,302

In actual computation of gratuity, often organizations give five years weightage to pension and gratuity payment, subject to maximum of 33 years service. In this case, the total qualifying service is 24 years. Therefore, even after giving five years weightage, the total service period considered for gratuity payment fall short of 33 years. Hence, Shama's computation of gratuity has been considered after giving five years' weightage, which makes 58 six-monthly periods for 29 years of service (24 + 5). Gratuity payment obligation is ¼th of a month's assessable emoluments. Therefore, to arrive at gratuity payment obligations the total has to be divided by four.

In case of payment of gratuity in the event of premature death, service periods considered for payment of gratuity may vary as per Table 16.15.

The gratuity may be wholly or partially forfeited by the employer if the termination of services of an employee is due to his riotous or disorderly conduct or any other act of violence or any offence, including moral turpitude

TABLE 16.15 Counting of reckonable service for payment of death gratuity

1.	For service less than 1 year	2 times of reckonable emoluments
2.	1 year or more but less than 5 year	6 times of reckonable emoluments
3.	5 years or more but less than 20 years	12 times of reckonable emoluments
4.	20 years or more	1/2 of reckonable emoluments for each completed six-monthly period of qualifying service subject to minimum of 12 times and maximum of 33 times of reckonable emoluments. The maximum amount of death gratuity is ₹3.5 lakh.

committed in the course of his employment. Another important provision of the Payment of Gratuity Act 1972 provides consideration of period of maternity leave towards reckoning of qualifying service.

Income tax issues in payment of gratuity

As per Section 10 (10) of the Income Tax Act, gratuity is paid to an employee when he completes minimum 5 years of service with an employer. Minimum 240 days of service in a year is considered as eligibility for gratuity computation. If an employee completes five years and seven months service, his gratuity computation will be based on six years of completed service. However, if it is five years and five months, the eligible service for gratuity computation would be five years. Suppose, an employee has completed five years and seven months service with a company and now he intends to leave the job, the gratuity calculation in this case would be based on the following formula:

$$\text{Gratuity} = \frac{15}{16} \times \text{Last salary drawn} \times 6$$

Last salary drawn is calculated based on Basic + DA. One month is considered as 26 days, instead of 30 days.

Gratuity is taxable as it is considered under the head *income from salary*. However, tax treatment varies depending on the organization with which the assessee is employed. If the assessee is a government employee, then the gratuity received is fully exempt from income tax. Non-government employees are categorized into two types, namely: employees covered under the Payment of Gratuity Act 1972 and employees who are not covered under the Payment of Gratuity Act 1972. In case, the assessee is a non-government employee and is covered under the Payment of Gratuity Act 1972, income tax exemption for the gratuity amount received would be the least of the following:

- actual gratuity received
- ₹10,00,000
- fifteen days' salary for each completed year of service or part thereof

Here, Salary = Basic + DA + any other salary equivalent fixed amount, say fixed commission, etc.

Completed year of service means full time service. Full-time service of more than six months is considered as one year, whereas less than six months is ignored. Similarly, number of days in a month is considered as 26 days. Hence, 15 days salary is calculated as, Salary × (15/26).

In case of the employee is not covered under the Payment of Gratuity Act 1972, maximum exemption from tax would be the least of the following:

- actual gratuity received
- ₹10,00,000
- half-month's average salary for every completed year, without considering the part thereof, that is, if the full time service is 1 year seven months, it would be considered as 1 year and not 2 years as was done in the previous case

The tax implications on gratuity amount can be understood using the following example.

Example

Let us assume, an assessee is working with an organization, covered under the Payment of Gratuity Act for last five years and eight months. The company has a policy of paying a minimum gratuity amount of ₹2,00,000 to all after completion of five years service. The assessee is drawing a monthly salary of ₹30,000, DA of ₹10,000, and fixed commission of ₹5,000. The assessee is resigning from his present job. Assume the gratuity paid to the assessee is a sum of ₹92,00,000. Assess the tax implications for the same. In addition, assess the tax implications for the assessee, considering his organization is not covered under the Payment of Gratuity Act.

Solution

The tax obligation in both the cases would be as given in Table 16.16.

TABLE 16.16 Tax obligation for gratuity payment

When covered under the Payment of Gratuity Act 1972	When not covered under the Payment of Gratuity Act 1972
Exempted gratuity will be the least of the following amounts: 1. Actual gratuity received = ₹2,00,000 2. ₹10,00,000 3. 15 days salary for each completed year of service or part = ₹45,000 × 15/26 × 6 = ₹1,55,769 Gratuity exempted from tax = ₹1,55,769 Taxable gratuity = ₹2,00,000 − ₹1,55,769 = ₹44,231	Exempted gratuity will be the least of following amount: 1. Actual gratuity received = ₹2,00,000 2. ₹10,00,000 3. Half month's average salary for each completed years' of service (no part thereof) = ₹45,000/2 × 5 = ₹1,12,500 Gratuity exempted from tax = ₹1,12,500 Taxable Gratuity = ₹2,00,000 − ₹1,12,500 = ₹87,500

Provident Fund

The Employees' Provident Funds and Miscellaneous Provisions Act 1952, provides for compulsory contributory fund for social security of the employees and their dependents (in case of death of the employee). It extends to every factory or an establishment employing 20 or more persons. However, the central government, by notification, can bring any establishment under the purview of the Act even in cases where such establishments employ less than 20 persons. Cooperative Society employing less than 50 persons and working without the aid of government, newly set up establishments (for initial 3 years), and state or central government establishments (where they have their own schemes) are immune from the provisions of this Act.

The central government has framed three schemes under the Act: Employees' Provident Fund Scheme 1952 for provident funds; Employees' Family Pension Scheme 1971 for providing family pension and life assurance benefit, which has since been merged with Employees' Pension Schemes 1995; and the employees' Deposit Linked Insurance Scheme 1976. The Act requires employers to contribute amount equivalent to 12 per cent of the wages, DA etc. (10 per cent in case of Board of Industrial and Financial Reconstruction (BIFR) referred establishments; or establishments employing less than 20 persons; or any establishment in the jute, *beedi*, brick, coir, or gaur gum industry), ensure similar deduction from employees, and deposit the same together with administrative charges and required returns/attachments to the regional provident fund office or to their own private provident fund scheme approved by the provident fund commissioner.

Dearness Allowance (DA)

Dearness allowance (DA) is an allowance paid to employees to compensate erosion of real income/wage due to inflation, with respect to a specified benchmark date. This benchmark date is generally the date from which a pay structure/a set of pay scales are implemented. An increase in the cost of living and the consequent erosion of income is measured in terms of a consumer price index (CPI) number. The DA to be sanctioned to the employees is calculated on the basis of percentage increase in that index or the point-factor system.

The concept of DA is a post Second World War phenomenon. Initially, the frequency and quantum of DA given was more or less on an adhoc basis, mostly in response to demand of the employees for wage increase to mitigate their financial hardship. Later on, the payment of DA was linked to the CPI number.

Consequently, a formula was evolved with reference to the following:
- basis for computation of increase in cost of living
- frequency of DA revision, and
- extent to which neutralization of such increase would be given

After certain percentage of DA rise, it is neutralized with the basic pay, thus raising the real wage level. However, such neutralization varies from one organization to another depending on their specific policy. In case of government organizations, the designated committee of the Government makes DA neutralization announcements from time to time.

DA calculation

The payment of DA is a measure that examines the weighted average of prices of a basket of consumer goods and services such as transportation, food, and medical care. Price change for each item in the predetermined basket of goods is calculated and averaged to arrive at the CPI. The goods are weighted according to their importance. Changes in CPI are used to assess price changes associated with the cost of living, referred to as *headline inflation*. There is a common allegation from Indian economists that wrong methodologies are followed to compute inflation. In India, inflation is calculated on the basis of changes in the wholesale price index (WPI), which is then used to determine the quantum of DA enhancement. Data on the price levels of a total of 435 commodities data is tracked through WPI, which is used as an indicator of change in the prices of commodities in all trade and transactions. It is also the price index, which is available on a weekly basis with the shortest possible time lag of only two weeks. The Indian government utilizes WPI as an indicator of the rate of inflation in the economy.

CPI is a statistical time-series measure of a weighted average of prices of a specified set of goods and services purchased by consumers. It is a price index that tracks the prices of a specified basket of consumer goods and services, thus, providing a measure of inflation. It is a fixed quantity price index and considered as a cost of living index. For determining CPI, the index is scaled so that it is equal to 100 at a base year. However, in the first bi-monthly monetary policy statement, the Reserve Bank of India adopted the consumer price index on 1 April 2014. Till date, the RBI was using Wholesale price index to measure indicative inflation projections. Most countries use CPI as a measure of inflation, as this actually measures the increase in prices that a consumer incurs for goods and services.

Table 16.17 shows a sample indicator of CPI for industrial workers, agricultural labourers, and rural labourers.

DA can be computed using several methods. Some of which are as follows:
1. DA not linked to CPI:
    – flat DA
    – graduated scale of DA
2. DA linked to CPI:
    – DA computed according to changes in CPI
    – DA linked to pay scales and to CPI

TABLE 16.17 Sample CPI indicator for industrial workers, agricultural labourers, and rural labourers

Index number	Base year	All India consumer price index (AICPI)	
		August 2007	September 2007
Consumer price index numbers for industrial workers (CPI(IW))	2001 = 100	133	133
Consumer price index numbers for agricultural labourers	1986–87 = 100	408	410
Consumer price index numbers for rural labourers	1986–87 = 100	408	410

TABLE 16.18 Modifications made in calculation of DA

Basic	Rate of neutralization
Up to ₹5,000	100% of basic pay
Between ₹5,001 and ₹7,000	80% of the basic pay or 100% of ₹5,000, whichever is higher.
Between ₹7,001 and ₹9,500	70% of basic pay or 80% of ₹7,000, whichever is higher.
Between ₹9,501 and ₹12,500	60% of basic pay or 70% of ₹7,001, whichever is higher.
Above ₹12,500	50% of basic pay or 60% of ₹9,501, whichever is higher.

The Supreme Court of India has laid down certain criteria for regulating the payment of DA, which are as follows:
1. capacity to pay
2. rates prevailing in comparable concerns in the region
3. extent of neutralization of price rise

The views of National Labour Commission are as follows.
1. The basic wage in all cases should be adjusted to a common base year.
2. DA should be adjusted every time there is a five-point change in the CPI.
3. Neutralization should be allowed at the rate of 95 per cent in non-scheduled employment.
4. Capacity to pay is irrelevant for payment of DA at the minimum level.

Table 16.18 shows important modifications made in the calculation of DA. It illustrates the modifications made by the Supreme Court of India in calculations of DA.

DA payment formula after neutralization is determined as per the following formula:

$$\frac{(\text{AICPI for the quarter ending}) - (\text{AICPI for the previous quarter})}{(\text{AICPI number for the previous quarter})}$$

Apart from these, other allowances commonly offered by organizations as part of salary are city compensatory allowance, conveyance allowance, and house rent allowance. However, the nature of perquisites varies from one organization to another, with a specific focus on executive compensation.

INCENTIVE DETERMINATION

This section discusses the determination of incentives using various incentive plans such as the straight piece method and differential piece rate methods.

Straight Piece Rate Method

The straight piece rate method considers a fixed rate per piece, which remains constant for different output levels. Under this system, workers get paid strictly on the basis of their output. Most of the organizations follow this method as a substitute for time rate. The major difficulty in this system is that workers do not get any guaranteed payment for their work except for a basic hourly rate, which again depends on achieving some fixed level of output. We can illustrate this using the following formula:

$$\text{Work piece rate} = \frac{\text{Adjusted hourly rate}}{\text{Average production per hour}}$$

Using this formula, let us consider the day's earning of a particular worker in the following case:

Example

A company pays a worker for a given job as per Table 16.19.

TABLE 16.19 Day's earning for a particular worker

Basic hourly rate	₹6
Increase in rate	25%
Standard hourly output level for the job	800 Units

Suppose the worker in a particular day of 8-hour work produced 7,000 units. Compute the day's earning for the worker.

Solution

Basic hourly rate = ₹6
Increase on rate = 25%
Adjusted hourly rate = 1.25 × 6 = ₹7.50
Average output per hour = 800 units
Therefore, hourly work
Piece rate = Adjusted hourly rate/Average output per hour
= 7.50/800 = 93.75 × 10^{-4}

Hence, for producing 7,000 units in a 8-hour work day, the worker will receive incentive as per the following calculation:

Day	Day's production	Wort piece rate	Day's earnings
1	7,000	93.75 × 10^{-4}	₹65.63

Differential Piece Rate Methods

This section discusses the various differential piece rate methods such as Taylor's method, Merrick differential piece rate, Gantt Task system, Emerson's efficiency plan, Rowan premium plan, and Scanlon plan.

Taylor's method

In Taylor's method, no minimum wage is guaranteed. Workers are required to produce at 100 per cent efficiency in a specified standard time limit. There are two piece rates specified for each job. A lower piece rate is applicable for performance below the standard level and a higher piece rate is applicable for performance higher than the standard level.

Example

A company, using time study, fixed the standard output level per hour for a given job as 125 units. Hourly labour rate is ₹7. The company applies two differential rates for determining earnings of a worker. Workers get 80 per cent of the standard piece rate for below standard level of performance and 120 per cent of the standard piece rate for above standard level of performance. Calculate the earnings of a worker in the following cases for two different days:

1. In an eight-hour workday, the worker produces 900 units.
2. In an eight-hour workday, the worker produces 1,200 units.

Solution
The calculation is given in Table 16.20.

TABLE 16.20 Standard time calculation

Standard output per hour	125 unit
Labour rate per hour	₹7
Standard piece rate	7/125 = 0.056
Lower piece rate	0.056 × 0.8 = 0.045
Higher piece rate	0.056 × 1.20 = 0.067
Earning of the worker in day 1	900 × 0.045 = ₹40.5
Earning of the worker in day 2	1,200 × 0.067 = ₹80.4

In the first case, the worker produced less than the standard level. With 125 units per hour, the standard output level for 8-hour work in a day should have been 1,000 units.

Merrick differential piece rate

In this method also, there is no guaranteed minimum wage. A standard time is established for each job and workers are paid the following differential rates.

Example

In a particular week, a worker has produced an item as given in Table 16.21.

TABLE 16.21 Merrick differential piece rate

Day	Quantity produced
1	170
2	185
3	210
4	195
5	220
6	198

Standard output per day of 8-hours work is 190 units and hourly rate is ₹5. Calculate the earnings of the worker for different days of the week using Merrick's differential piece rate method.

Solution

Standard Output per day of 8 hours week = 190 Units
Labour hourly rate = ₹5
Rate differentials
- For output up to 83%: Basic rate
- For output up to 83% and up to 100%:
  Basic piece rate + 10% of hourly rate as bonus
- For output above 100%:
  Basic piece rate + 20% of hourly rate as bonus

Standard output per hour = 190/8 = 24 units
Basic rate per piece = 5/24 = ₹0.21

We can now tabulate the earnings of the worker for the entire week as shown in Table 16.22.

TABLE 16.22 Earnings of the worker

Day	Standard output	Actual output	Output performance	Rate applicable	Day's earning (Quantity × Rate) (in ₹)
1	190	170	89%	BR + 20%	170 × 1.10 × 0.21 = 9.27
2	190	185	97%	BR + 20%	185 × 1.10 × 0.21 = 42.74
3	190	210	111%	BR + 20%	210 × 1.20 × 0.21 = 52.92
4	190	195	103%	BR + 20%	195 × 1.20 × 0.21 = 49.14
5	190	220	116%	BR + 20%	220 × 1.20 × 0.21 = 55.44
6	190	198	104%	BR + 20%	198 × 1.20 × 0.21 = 49.90

Gantt task system

The only difference between this system and the earlier systems is that this system provides minimum guaranteed wage even if the performance is below the standard level.

Example

The hourly wage rate for a worker is fixed at ₹5. The standard time set for the job is 12 minutes per unit. The worker receives a 20 per cent bonus on receiving the standard output level. The rate for the job above the standard level is ₹1.70 per unit. Assume the worker has produced output for the entire week as per the figure given in the actual output column in the table. Compute daily earnings of the worker for the week.

Solution

Standard output per day = Standard time per unit × 8 hours (assuming 8 hours work per day)

Standard time per unit = 12 minutes
Standard output per hour = 60/12 = 5 units
Standard output per day = 5 × 8 = 40 units
Daily earnings of the worker is give in Table 16.23.

TABLE 16.23 Wage rate

Day	Actual output	Actual output as percentage of standard	Payment rate	Day's earnings (in ₹)
1	36	90	Day wages	5 × 8 = 40
2	44	110	High piece rate	44 × 1.70 = 75
3	56	140	High piece rate	56 × 1.70 = 95
4	50	125	High piece rate	50 × 1.70 = 85
5	40	100	Day wages + 20% Bonus	1.20 × 5 × 8 = 48
6	50	125	High piece rate	50 × 1.70 = 85

Emerson's efficiency plan

Under this plan, efficient workers are rewarded at an increasing rate with the increase in their performance, measured in terms of saving of time. The main features of the plan are as follows.
1. Guaranteed day wages are paid irrespective of performance.
2. Standard output is determined based on past performance, which is taken at 100 per cent efficiency.

3. Performance of the workers is measured in terms of the efficiency achieved, comparing actual output with the standard output, using the following formula:

$$\text{Efficiency percentage} = \frac{\text{Acutal output}}{\text{Standard output}} \times 100$$

Incentive bonus is paid if the worker's efficiency exceeds two-thirds (66.67 per cent) of the standard performance (taken as 100 per cent). Incentive rates vary with the increase of performance beyond two-thirds (66.77 per cent) at an increasing rate (Table 16.24).

TABLE 16.24 Efficiency rate and remuneration

Efficiency rate	Remuneration
Below 66.67%	No incentive bonus only time wages
Over 66.67% but up to 100%	Time wages + proportionate Bonus for Incremental output percentages, rising up to 20% at 100% level of efficiency
Over 100%	Time wages + 20% bonus + 1% Bonus for each 1% increase in efficiency beyond 100%

Example

A worker is assigned different jobs in a day and for each job unit the company has fixed a standard time. Based on the tabulated information, compute the total earnings for the day.

Job code	Quantity produced	Standard time set per unit (in hours)	Time taken (in hours)
A–1	2	1/2	1.25
B–3	4	1/2	1.75
C–1	20	1/3	5.00

Solution

Bonus for each job has to be computed separately. The calculation is shown in Table 16.25.

TABLE 16.25 Calculation of bonus

Job code	Standard time for the job (in hours) — Quantity × Standard time per unit	Time taken (in hours)	Bonus earned, if any (@ 50% of time saved) (in ₹)
A–1	2 × 1/2 = 1 hour	1.25	Nil
B–3	4 × 1/2 = 2 hour	1.75	0.625
C–1	20 × 1/3 = 6.67 hour	5.00	4.175
		Total	₹4.8

Total earnings for the day = (8 × 5) + 4.8 = ₹44.8

Rowan premium plan

Rowan premium plan is different from Halsey premium plan with respect to computation of incentive bonus payable to worker. As per Halsey plan workers are paid at the time rate when actual time taken by them to complete the job is equal to or more than the standard time. But when the worker is able to complete the job taking less than the standard time, the worker gets 50 per cent of the time saved as bonus. Incentive bonus as per Rowan plan is not calculated as a fixed percentage of time saved. It is the ratio of the actual time taken to the standard time of the job. Therefore, incentive bonus is computed using following formula:

$$\text{Incentive bonus} = \frac{T(S-T)}{S} \times R$$

where T = Actual time taken by the worker; S = Standard time set for the job; (S–T) = Difference between standard and actual time; R = Hourly rate of wages

Example

In a factory, standard time set for a job is 8 hours and the basic wage rate is ₹3 per hour. The workers receive normal wage for their actual work and incentive bonus at a fixed proportion of the time saved. Compute incentive bonus payable to workers for different levels of actual time, as mentioned in the Actual time taken column:

Solution
The calculation is shown in Table 16.26.

It is evident from Table 16.26 that when time saved is beyond 50 per cent of the standard time, workers get bonus at a diminishing rate. This is a major defect

TABLE 16.26 Incentive bonus for different levels of actual time

Acutal time taken (T)	Standard time (S)	Time saved (S–T)	Incentive earned $\frac{T(S-T)}{T}$
8	8	0	0
7	8	1	2.625
6	8	2	4.5
5	8	3	5.625
4	8	4	6.0
3	8	5	5.625
2	8	6	4.5
1	8	7	2.625

of the scheme as it discourages workers from saving more than 50 per cent of the standard time.

Scanlon plan

It is a popular group incentive scheme, which relates labour cost to the total sales value to measure labour effectiveness. Incentive bonus is paid to the workers based on the percentage reduction in the labour to sales ratio, determined by comparing base period and assessment period. The formula for computing percentage reduction in labour index is as follows:

$$\text{Percentage reduction in labour index} = \frac{\frac{L_b}{R_b} - \frac{L_a}{R_a}}{\frac{L_b}{R_b}} \times 100$$

where L_b = Total labour cost for the base month; R_b = Total sales value for the base month; L_a = Total labour cost for the assessment month; R_a = Total sales value for the assessment month; L_b/R_b = Standard labour to sales ratio for the base month; L_a/R_a = Actual labour to sales ratio for the assessment month.

Example

A company employs 150 workers. Sales during the base month was ₹15 lakh. For the same period, labour cost was ₹2.5 lakh. Compute the group incentives payable, if any, to the workers in the following two situations:

(a) Sales value is ₹16 lakh against labour cost of ₹2.25 lakh
(b) Sales value is ₹16 lakh against labour cost of ₹2.8 lakh

Solution

(a) Labour cost during the base month (L_b) = ₹2.5 lakh
Sales value during the base month (R_b) = ₹15 lakh

$$\text{Standard Labour to Sales ratio} \left(\frac{L_b}{R_b}\right) = \frac{L_b}{R_b} \times 100$$
$$= 2.5/15 \times 100$$
$$= 16.67\%$$

Labour cost for the assessment month (L_a) = ₹2.25 lakh
Sales value for the assessment month (R_a) = ₹16 lakh

$$\text{Actual labour to sales ratio during the assessment month} = \frac{L_a}{R_a} \times 100$$
$$= 2.25/16 \times 100$$
$$= 14.06\%$$

Here the actual labour to sales ratio is lower than the standard labour to sales ratio. Therefore, employes would be entitled to receive incentive bonus as follows:

$$\frac{\frac{L_b}{R_b} - \frac{L_a}{R_a}}{\frac{L_b}{R_b}} \times 100$$

= 16.57 − 14.06/16.67 × 100
= 2.61/16.67 × 100 = 15.66% (approximately)

(b) In situation (b), this would be as follows:

L_a = ₹2.8 lakh
R_a = ₹16 lakh
$\frac{L_b}{R_b} \times 100$ = ₹17.5%

In this case, since actual labour to sales ratio is higher than the standard labour to sales ratio, workers would not be entitled to receive any incentive bonus. Hence their wages would be restricted to fixed rate.

Bedeaux point plan Under this plan, minute is considered as time unit. For each job, standard time in minutes is determined. Unit of measurement under Bedeaux point is named as B. Therefore, if standard time for a job is 6 hours, it is expressed as 360 Bs. If the workers fail to complete a job within the standard time or just finish the same within the standard time, they are paid just the normal time rate. If, however, they can complete their work earlier, they receive incentive bonus equal to the wages for the time saved, measured in terms of excess of B points over the actual time taken. Incentive bonus is paid to the workers normally @ 75% of the time saved. Rest 25 per cent goes to the supervisors.

Let us explain the plan using the following illustration:

Hourly rate for workers (R) = ₹6
Standard time for the job (S) = 360 Bs (6 hours)
Actual time taken by the workers for the job (T) = 300 Bs (5 hours)
Value of time saved = 360 − 300/60 × 6 = ₹6
Total wages payable = S × R + 75% of the value of time saved
= 6 × 6 + (75/100 × 6)
= 36 + (0.75 × 6)
= 36 + 4.5 = ₹40.5

Priestman production plan This is also a popular group incentive plan, where employees are paid a guaranteed time wage and incentive bonus for increase in productivity in proportion to the increase in per capita output. Under the scheme, a standard output level is determined on mutual agreement between the employer and the employees. Then actual output is compared with the standard output to decide about incentive bonus.

Percentage of productivity bonus payable to each employee is determined as per the following formula:

$$\frac{\frac{P_a}{W_a} - \frac{P_b}{W_b}}{\frac{P_a}{W_a}} \times 100$$

where P_a = Actual production during the assessment month; W_a = Number of workers in employment during the assessment month; P_b = Standard production in the base month; W_b = Number of workers in the employment during the base month; P_a/W_a = Actual production per worker during the assessment month; P_b/W_b = Standard production per worker during the base month.

Example

A steel plant employs 500 workers. The standard output of steel is fixed at 1,000 tonnes per month. As per the agreement, each worker is entitled to get productivity bonus for percentage increase in production over the standard output level. Compute bonus payable, if any, to workers in the following two situations:

(a) Output has increased to 1,200 tonnes but number of workers engaged during the corresponding period increased to 550.
(b) Output is 1,100 tonnes and the number of workers engaged is 520.

Solution

Standard output in the base month (P_b) = 1,000 tonne

Standard output per employee $\left(\dfrac{P_b}{W_b}\right)$ = 1,000/500 = 2 tonnes

(a) Output during the assessment month (P_a) = 1,200 tonnes
Number of employees during the assessment month (W_a) = 500
Output per employee during the assessment month

$$\left(\frac{P_a}{W_a}\right) = \frac{1,200}{550} = 2.182$$

Percentage increase in production per employee

$$\frac{P_a}{W_a} - \frac{P_b}{W_b} \times 100 = \frac{(2.182 - 2)}{2.182} \times 100$$

$$\frac{P_a}{W_a} = 8.34\%$$

Hence in this case all workers would receive a productivity-linked bonus of 8.34% over their basic pay.

(b) In situation (b) output per employee during the assessment month $\frac{P_a}{W_a}$ is 1,100/520 = 2.12

Percentage increase in production per employee
$$= (2.12 - 2)/2.12 \times 100 = 5.66\%$$

GROUP INCENTIVE PAYMENT PRACTICES IN ORGANIZATIONS

Payment of group incentives as a practice is followed by many organizations, based on their self-designed formula. One such practice is illustrated below, which designs productivity-linked incentive as follows:

This is for one of the plants manufacturing wheels and axles for railways.

1. Define the plant capacity and standard man-hours:
   Plant capacity for wheel = 8,800/month
   Plant capacity for axles = 4,500/month
   Standard man-hours:
   – Wheel shops = 87,414
   – Axle shops = 41,724
2. No bonus up to 83% plant capacity.
3. Incentive rates based on the minimum of the pay scale
   – Wheel shops = ₹0.55/wheel
   – Axle shops = ₹1.07/axle
   Incentive for wheel shop = (0.55 × Eligible production in the month/base output) × (100 – Actual absenteeism % in the month)/84
   Incentive for axle shop = (1.07 × Eligible production in the month/base output) × (100 – Actual absenteeism % in the month)/84

OVERTIME WAGES

Overtime wages are calculated on the basis of the working hours prescribed to the several types of workers. If 36 hours a week are prescribed as working hours, the company should pay extra wages to workers if they are required to work beyond 36 hours. Usually the rate of wages for period beyond 36 hours should be at the ordinary rate, while the rate should be double if the workers are required to work more than 48 hours a week for the period beyond 48 hours. However, where wages are paid on a piece-rate basis, the state government, in consultation with the employer concerned and the representatives of the workers, shall fix the time rate as much as possible, considering average rate of earnings of those workers and the rates so fixed shall be deemed to be the ordinary rate of wages of the workers and hence, overtime rate should be decided following the aforesaid principles.

MERIT MATRICES

According to merit pay system, an increase in compensation is based on the level of job performance of employees. Hence, to introduce merit pay, organizations align their performance management systems with the compensation grades and ranges. Once the merit pay system is introduced, the organization has to develop a merit matrix tool to determine the appropriate increase in pay for all grades of employees. Based on the past experiences, HR managers draw a merit budget to assess the possible fund requirement to accommodate pay increase. Merit matrices should be understandable and manageable for all cross-sections of employees, which should be capable of recognizing and relating performance differentials with the merit increase differentials.

ECONOMIC VALUE-ADDED (EVA)

EVA-based compensation is much discussed now in the corporate world. It measures internal and external operating performance of the company, funds the credit initiative, constraints, and challenges. It can be tied to evaluating employee performance and success by developing a goal-oriented compensation package based on an incentive reward system that links cause and effect accountability. The EVA results should be made available to all managers and employees to be used as a performance measurement and management that is directly calculated and applied. Earnings, operations performance, and return on capital invested are measured and compared to profits. They are then compared with the cost of debt and equity to fund operations.

EVA = Net operating profit after tax (NOPAT) − Capital charge (Invested debt and equity × Weighted average cost of capital (WACC))
NOPAT = Operating income − Operating expenses + Interest expense + Taxes
WACC = Cost of equity (equity) + Cost of debt (debt)

An excess of EVA equals profit. The initial implementation of EVA values current operations and then subsequent new projects are measured with decision being made on whether the accounting numbers are justified for continuing with the project. If the cost of the project exceeds the value added, the project should not be undertaken since adding shareholder value is the primary goal of the company. EVA originated from the Stern Stewart company in 1982. The Stern Stewart 'four Ms' are:

Measurement Designing a measure of value creation that best reflects economic reality in a particular industry

Management Developing policies, procedures and tools, which link decision-making to the measure of value creation

Motivation Establishing incentive plans that simulate ownership by giving managers a share of value created

Mindset Increasing the business literacy of employees through training and communication

Therefore, EVA measures the change in financial performance through operating performance, focusing at the unit management level, and at an employee level. The main drivers of EVA are operating revenues, operating expenses, and capital charges. EVA-based compensation aligns the interests of management and employees with the shareholders. In Chapter 3 on Employee compensation and the labour market, the EVA practices in compensation design of the Tata group are discussed.

SUMMARY

Compensation research is now one of the strategic priorities for organizations. In developed countries, the cost of employee compensation is either first or second in order of cost burden to the organizations. Even Indian organizations are now losing their competitive strength due to high cost of employee compensation. On one hand, there is need for optimization of compensation cost; whereas on the other hand, compensation designing should be competitive to retain talent. Often cost optimization is done by outsourcing non-core and at times even core activities to keep compensation cost competitive.

There are four levels of measurement: nominal, ordinal, interval, and ratio. These constitute a hierarchy where the lowest scale of measurement (i.e., nominal) has far fewer mathematical properties than those further up in this hierarchy of scales. Nominal scales yield data on categories; ordinal scales give sequences; interval scales reveal the magnitude between points on the scale, and ratio scales explain both order and the absolute distance between any two points on the scale.

Compensation is a methodical approach to assign a monetary value to employees in return for work performed. It may include any or all of these: base pay, overtime pay, commissions, stock option plans, merit pay, profit sharing, bonuses, housing allowance, vacations, and all other benefits. Compensation is a term used to describe not only employee salaries, but also all other benefits received. Human resource management approach makes compensation issues a prerogative of managers as they can make use of compensation as a tool to enhance performance of employees at the workplace to sustain an organization's competitive advantage. The strategic use of rewards to regulate behaviour and performance has led to the concept of compensation management or reward systems. Remuneration refers to monetary rewards, which are seen as one arm of total compensation.

Compensation is a more holistic term. Traditional wages and salary administration has now started losing ground because compensation has to be designed in a way that it is a reward for the employee rather than a monthly salary for the job done. To do so, HR researchers have to understand various aspects of compensation management. Minimum theoretical inputs in the chapter are intended to appreciate the changing concepts in compensation management. Just complying with statutory norms and expecting employees to deliver results are not enough in today's competitive scenario. Organizations need to emulate best practices, continuously benchmarking their compensation designs and understanding, which compensation design is suitable for them. Even decisions on fixed and variable components of compensation must be taken, while taking into account numerous factors such as nature of the job, company's business goals, product life cycle, and performance management systems. There are various short-term and long-term incentive schemes available to the organizations. Taking into account its human resource strategy, an organization has to choose from among these different alternatives. Choosing right incentive plans is again another important area. Various incentive schemes have been discussed in this chapter. Salary determination, fixation, pension and gratuity payment issues, provident fund, dearness allowances, and stock options are all discussed both in the context of theory and practice. It depends on the HR researcher to choose the right mix. The efficacy of various incentive schemes can be tested, making use of statistical tests like ANOVA.

HR researchers would be able to tackle compensation research issues successfully using the quantitative tools discussed in this chapter.

Key Terms

401(k) plans These are popular retirement benefit plans and used as an alternative to fixed pension plans. Employees can choose where to invest their funds from among several investments options (usually more than seven) and can see their investments grow.

Beadeaux plan Under this plan, minute is considered as time unit. For each job, standard time in minutes is determined. Unit of measurement under Bedeaux point is named as B.

Compa-ratio It is a percentage representation of a company's pay levels as they compare either to the company's own structure or to competitive levels.

Employee stock option (ESOP) Under this scheme, an employee is offered a specific number of shares, which can be exercised (bought) at some specified time in the future.

Maturity curve This curve plots salary (y-axis) against years of work or years since degree (x-axis) to track the career progression opportunity of employees.

Percentiles These are arbitrarily selected units determined by dividing a whole into a distribution of 100 equal parts. A percentile distribution is based on the number of observations constituting a given percentage of the total number of observations in the distribution. Percentiles are frequently used to determine what proportion of the compensation distribution falls below a given level.

Priestman production plan This is a popular group incentive plan, where employees are paid a guaranteed time wage and incentive bonus for increase in productivity in proportion to the increase in per capita output.

Scanlon plan A popular group incentive scheme, which relates labour cost to the total sales value to measure labour effectiveness. Incentive bonus is paid to the workers based on the percentage reduction in the labour to sales ratio, comparing between base period and assessment period.

Semantic scales These scales are used extensively to track the feelings of the respondents in bipolar adjectives form in a salary survey.

Exercises

Concept Review Questions

1. What are the different theories of compensation? Do you recommend applicability of all these theories for all levels of employees in an organization? Justify your answer.
2. What are the various concepts of compensation? How does economic theory help in making decision about employee benefits?
3. Discuss the concept of productivity-linked compensation. Which model would you recommend for an automobile manufacturing unit run using team-work systems? Justify.
4. Discuss basic concepts of variable pay systems.
5. Explain what a semantic differential scale means and how it can be used in compensation research.
6. What are the major limitations of nominal scaled data?

Critical Thinking Questions

1. Discuss important points to be considered, while designing a compensation model for top executives.
2. Write a detailed note on ESOP. How ESOP valuation can be done in an organization, which mostly employs knowledge workers?
3. Illustrate a case of salary increase decisions for supervisors of an FMCG company.
4. Discuss in detail the Scanlon plan. How is it different from Priestman production plan?
5. Critically evaluate compensation management practices in India.

Oxicom's Compensation Dilemma

CASE STUDY

Compensation discrimination is a serious flaw in compensation design in organizations. Many organizations often ignore the diversity issues and compensation is gender based. Oxicom is a computer hardware assembler in Kolkata. Computer hardware semis are procured by the company from Southeast Asian countries and assembled in a plant in a suburb of Kolkata, where representation of male and female employees is 60:40. Computer hardware assembling jobs are very mechanical and hardly require any special skill input. Hence, job evaluation and compensation designing perspective is literally redundant in this case. Oxicom recruited candidates who have passed the SSLC examinations with high marks in science and mathematics subjects, and who can understand the basic circuit designs and soldering jobs. All newly recruited employees are required to undergo one week training and then are placed in the job, which is segmented into various stages. The final stage of the job, that is, stage four is allocated to diploma engineers, who are highly skilled. There job is to test the functionality of the assembled computers. They also make good the errors, if any, left due to bad workmanship in earlier stages. From this level onwards, the company follows

(Contd)

CASE STUDY (Contd)

scientific compensation designs based on job evaluation and several performance criteria. Table 16.27 shows the gender specific distribution of compensation.

At the workers' level, the company negotiates the wages individually and based on the negotiated figure decides the compensation package. Female employees alleged that they are being paid less by the company. The management has never considered compensation disparity as an issue. However, with the increased awareness about workers' rights and privileges, female employees formed an independent union to persuade the company to enforce pay equity with their male counterparts. Based on their complaint, a prima facie charge of disparity has been framed against the company by the Ministry of Labour and they have been asked to clarify the charges before issue of any stricture by the government for such discriminatory compensation designs.

You have been given the following wage data by the company and then asked to analyse whether there exists any such discrimination, traceable to gender-biased employment practices followed by the company.

Discussion question

Statistically determine, whether there exists any significant differences between the wages of male and female employees. And if such a differences exists, can it really be attributed to gender bias in compensation designing?

Hint: Compare expected (the median value) and actual salaries of female employees and then find out statistically the degree of differences. The chi-square test is recommended.

TABLE 16.27 Gender specific distribution of compensation

No.	Employee ID	Gender	Salary per year (in ₹)	
1	1-23-46	Female	22,100	
2	1-23-17	Male	22,200	
3	1-23-19	Male	22,300	
4	1-23-27	Male	22,400	
5	1-23-44	Female	22,500	
6	1-23-47	Female	22,600	
7	1-23-48	Female	22,700	Median value
8	1-22-12	Female	22,800	
9	1-22-15	Female	22,900	
10	1-22-18	Female	23,000	
11	1-23-55	Male	23,200	
12	1-23-68	Male	23,500	
13	1-22-25	Male	23,600	
14	1-23-72	Male	24,000	

References

Balkin, D.B. and L.R. Gomez-Mejia (1990), 'Matching compensation and organizational strategies', *Strategic Management Journal*, vol. 11, no. 2, pp. 153–69.

Barkema, H.G. and L.R. Gomez-Mejia (1998), 'Managerial compensation and firm performance: A general research framework', *The Academy of Management Journal*, vol. 41, no. 2, pp. 135–45.

Bhattacharyya, D.K. (2006), *Human Resource Management*, Excel Books, New Delhi.

Bhattacharyya, D.K. (2007), *Human Resource Research Methods*, Oxford University Press, New Delhi.

Ellig, B.R (1982), *Executive Compensation – A Total Pay Perspective*, McGraw-Hill, New York.

Galbraith, G.S and G.B. Merrill (1991), 'The effect of compensation program and structure on SBU competitive strategy: A study of technology-intensive firms', *Strategic Management Journal*, vol. 12, no. 5, pp. 353–70.

Gomez-Mejia, L.R. (1994), 'Executive compensation: A reassessment and future agenda', *Research in Personnel and Human Resources Management*, vol. 12, pp. 161–222.

CHAPTER SEVENTEEN

International Compensation Management

Learning Objectives

After reading this chapter you would be able to:
- understand the concept and issues in international compensation design
- examine culture and its impact on international compensation
- assess different components of international compensation
- understand repatriation and immigration issues in international compensation
- study the process of designing international compensation
- analyse cross-country differences in international compensation practices

Base

HRA

EPF

Gratuity

Variable

Bonus

LTA

Conveyance

Medical

OPENING CASE

International Compensation Practices of the Lata Group

Globalization has different business perspectives. From an HR perspective, what differentiates a global company from others is its ability to access and deploy people, and connect them to customers in different segments and markets in different geographies through best in class processes. The basic question is *how do you do it better*. This is related to the capability embedded in the company's fabric. For example, the engineering capability Tata group possesses in companies such as Tata Motors, TACO, Tata Technologies, and Tata Consultancy Services is phenomenal. However if it is looked at as a bundle of capabilities, it is about pulling the right kind of resources on a global basis, making meaningful propositions to global customers, and managing the delivery. As a group, several initiatives have been undertaken by Tata's to embed and cultivate the global mindset in people's approach and thinking. Starting with the work that the Tata group of companies began on initiatives like cost competitiveness, it continues to work along with thought leaders and faculty from top universities such as Harvard Business School, INSEAD, CEDEP, and Michigan Business School to progress along these lines.

The company focuses on figuring out how to manage a global business, which involves defining and adopting a common set of principles and approaches to be utilized when operating globally. For instance, how does one define and design a global compensation policy that takes care of people movement seamlessly within the company across various geographies? A global compensation programme has to be flexible enough to address unique nuances and at the same time should have common underlying principles. This can be an intense technical exercise and is just one of the many processes that a company needs to define. In addition, the company needs to develop and inculcate a comfort level of working with a multi-ethnic workforce in a global business environment.

From a senior management perspective, the fundamental challenges involved in building global companies do not change. What changes is the magnitude of global organizations. One of the key attributes is for people to buy into the global vision. The vision should not be too generic nor should it be too codified. The vision should ideally be crafted in the form of a compelling story in which individuals can write themselves in as heroes and heroines. It is important to engage people. The critical challenge for a global company's leadership is to engage with employees with the same level of intensity and seriousness as it does with capital investments or business strategy.

The Tata Group has set itself on a path to become truly global. However, the path would not be without bumps. There are many lessons that need to be learnt; many challenges need to be overcome.

INTRODUCTION

From a business organizations perspective, globalization has exerted two key influences—market globalization and the need for reducing the cost of production. A large number of companies now sell their products and services globally. With the easy availability of latest state-of-the-art communication technology, globalization has increased the demand from across the borders. In addition, people have the option of best bargain for products and services, irrespective of the country in which they are produced. To reduce the cost of production, organizations are now taking many initiatives including relocating their production facilities to low labour cost countries. However, relocating the production facilities to low labour cost countries may not always be feasible as it may put the organizations in a relatively disadvantageous position due to lose of market proximity. The relocations require the organizations to expand their plant and offices all around the world, recruit people from local markets, and depute their own employees to these countries as expatriates. Compensation design both for the local country nationals (LCN) and for the expatriates (i.e., third country nationals (TCN)) is a big challenge. Organizations have to frame compensation strategically so that the compensation cost discrepancies do not defeat their business goals in global markets.

Expatriates can be assigned an international position both for a short term (less than a year) as well for a longer duration. In US, international assignments may be spread over a period of two to three years. In Japan, such assignments are for longer duration, usually five years. However, the period of assignment from such trends can be for a specific time-frame. For short-term assignments, there is usually no change in the compensation structure. Expatriates in such cases are given their usual salaries plus some living expenses to meet their additional expenses in international assignment. However, in case of long-term assignments, the organization needs to design a suitable compensation structure.

INTERNATIONAL COMPENSATION

Globalization is now a reality for organizations. Globalization has enhanced the level of awareness through free flow of information across nations, thus influencing the market and the people. It also has bearings on compensation management. Internationally equitable compensation across nations is now common for companies having presence in the global market. International compensation management is a complex function because of cross-cultural issues, difference in organizational practices, labour costs, etc. Therefore, for an organization that operates in a multinational environment, it is important to understand international compensation practices. Problems of international compensation become more serious when expatriated employees return to their home countries.

Before issues involved in international compensation are clarified, it is important to clarify certain terms. Designing compensation for an expatriated employee is a challenging task for organizations. An expatriate is a citizen of the country, where their organization is headquartered. For example, an Indian working for the subsidiary of an Indian organization in the US is an expatriate. International assignments are common in IT and ITeS companies as they are used to optimize the utilization of expertise or to restructure the manpower, or even to train the employee. For instance, overseas assignments for training and development become necessary in case of technology transfer.

Today's workforce is mobile. For international assignments, workforce is classified as short-term transferees, permanent transferees, expatriates (TCNs), glopats, etc. Compensation systems largely depend on the nature of the assignments and the workforce. Organizations send workers to international assignments with definite goals and objectives. Alignment of international compensation with defined goals and objectives is very important.

A short-term transferee is temporarily assigned to work abroad for a period of 2–12 months. An expatriate is usually transferred to an international assignment to work for a period of 3–5 years. They are also known as assignees. A glopat is a worker who is sent from one international assignment to another. Third country nationals are workers, who are neither from the country their organization is headquartered, nor from the country where they are working. They are from a third country, that is, different from the one where they are working and also different from the one where their companies headquarter is located. For example, Chinese workers working for Infosys's software development projects in the US represent TCNs.

CULTURAL ISSUES

International compensation design also requires consideration of cultural constructs of the countries. Most important among such issues are collectivism and individualism. In countries such as China, Israel, and Japan, group-based compensation needs to be designed following the principles of equity. Recognition of individual merit and giving rewards accordingly cannot be allowed because of their collectivist cultures. On the contrary, in countries such as the US and in the UK, designing compensation based on individual merit is very important because of their individualistic cultures. Earley and Erez (1997), Wagner (1995), and Trompenaars (1994) analysed the effects of cultural diversity (variability in individualism—collectivism, risk aversion, and power distance) between and within the nations. The most interesting part of their studies is that even within a nation, workers may have different views about compensation. Some may prefer individualistic compensation, whereas others may prefer group-based compensation. They observed this trend even in the US. Hence, cultural differences, both between and within the countries, need to be studied very seriously before designing compensation.

Cross-cultural issues are also taken into account in compensation designing (Bhattacharyya 2010). According to Hofstede (1983), management in any organization is culturally dependent. For this reason, when organizations spread their activities beyond their countries of origin, they adapt themselves to local cultures for sustenance. A failure to do so raises the prospect of their losing out to competition. In compensation management practices, cross-cultural issues are particularly important. For example, designing performance-related pay (PRP) with more focus on individualization agenda may be a right strategy for countries where the national culture emphasizes individualism. However, it may not be the right strategy for countries where the culture puts more emphasis on collectivism. Reviewing the PRP models of public sector enterprises in India discussed in Chapter 9 on Performance-related compensation, it is evident that weight on individual performance has been kept significantly lower than the weight on organizational performance.

Studies made by Freeman and Lawrence (1994) show highly decentralized and less government interfered compensation systems in countries such as the US, UK, and Canada. In these countries compensation is heavily dependent on negotiation at the individual level and varies widely across the organizations. On the contrary, the compensation system in countries such as Japan, Germany, and Spain is highly sector-specific and moderately centralized. High degree of centralization with maximum government interference is evident in countries such as Sweden, Denmark, and Belgium. In India, we find moderate to high influence of centralization and government interference in compensation.

CONCEPT OF VARIATION

Variation in international compensation denotes the degree of heterogeneity in wage-related laws in different countries. Like in India, wage-related laws in a number of countries vary from region to region. Such variation influences the compensation design, particularly true in case of multinational organizations. This is more applicable in designing employee stock options. The US laws permit a mix of options, whereas Chinese laws offer fewer options. Multinational organizations structure the compensation taking into account such variability. Another form of variation, which affects the compensation design, is social norms. A good example of it is vacation allowances. In many countries, vacation allowances are allowed as social norms even without the existence of law related to vacation days. For example, a minimum two week vacation is a common social norm in the US, which organizations commonly comply with.

An analysis and comparison of national compensation systems of countries such as Japan, Germany, and the US reveals that though compensation designs largely follow a national standard, multinationals vary their compensation structure to fit their specific organizational requirements. Therefore, variability in international compensation design is more evident in such organizations.

COMPONENTS OF INTERNATIONAL COMPENSATION

International compensation components vary widely across nations. Some common international compensation components are base salary, indirect monetary compensation (benefits), equalization benefits, and incentives. Although these terms are common for general compensation design, they may have different meaning from an international perspective. For example, base salary in international compensation has two dimensions: determination of base salary for the expatriate in accordance with the policies and procedures of the parent country from where the company originates; and determination of base salary following the policies and practices of the country in which the expatriate works. Since many international assignments are for short durations, usually for three to five years, it may be wise to keep base salary aligned with salaries in the home country. Doing so makes the transition back to the home country less complicated as major salary changes do not have to be made.

Although, non-monetary compensation or benefits for expatriates are normally made compatible with the home country by aligning them with the country-specific practices, organisations are often compelled to vary them in accordance with practices followed in the country where the expatriate is posted. For example, in France employers are required by law to provide every employee with 25 days of vacation. Although a US citizen working for a US company in France is not legally entitled to such a vacation, the organization may want to follow this practice to avoid morale problems with expatriates. Other countries have different retirement, disability, and termination policies.

To provide transitional support to expatriates, equalization in benefits is practised in international compensation as a part of social adjustment assistance. It is practised to ensure that their financial condition remains stable, that is, the state they were in before accepting the overseas assignments. Some of the areas where equalization is sought are housing allowance, educational allowance for children, foreign service premium, assignment completion bonus, emergency leave, home leave, language training, domestic staff, club membership, employment for spouse, etc.

In international compensation, design of incentives for expatriates is also a crucial issue. Various cash bonuses, stock options, and performance-related payments are used as incentives. The compensation structure should be strategically designed keeping in view the nature of assignment, its duration, and hierarchy of employees.

EXPATRIATE AND REPATRIATE COMPENSATION

Globalization has enhanced the cross-country movement of labour force. While we have elaborately discussed the complexities involved in designing compensation for the expatriates, the complexity involved in designing compensation for repatriates too are increasingly becoming complex. Like expatriates, repatriates also suffer after they are back to their home countries from foreign postings. For many organizations, particularly those who are operating at a global scale, the number of repatriates is increasing day by day. While organizations have specific compensation plans and policies for expatriates, they hardly have anything for repatriates. However, this is changing gradually. Retaining repatriates, who are talented and more matured after their foreign assignments, is slowly becoming an important priority for organizations. Many organizations now provide financial support to repatriates, at least for the initial period of six months to one year (the period of settlement) and career counseling. In addition to these, organizations may also have some specific strategies to help the repatriates integrate with their jobs such as assigning them some meaningful functions, arranging for mentoring, and extending support to their family.

Many studies like Baruch (2004) observed that compensation issues are very significant for expatriates in accepting their international assignments. Irrespective of the location, organizations globally come out with special compensation packages to motivate expatriates. As we have discussed these issues separately under the heading international compensation design and approaches to international compensation, we will now focus on the issues related to repatriation.

ISSUES RELATED TO REPATRIATION

Overseas assignments may not always be sought after by employees. It requires transparency in repatriation policy, information on career progression path, degree and support from the organization during international tenure, etc. It is important to instill confidence in the minds of the employees so that they volunteer for such assignments. Many organizations develop documented guidelines for overseas assignments. These help employees in developing an understanding of the issues involved, before they are employed on overseas assignments.

Assignment policy covers issues related to benefits for employees. Information on salary and benefits spell out the ratio of salary component that can be retained by the employees in their host country and the quantum of salary that they will be compensated for any additional expenses incurred when they move to a country with higher cost of living.

Similarly information on pensionary benefits (if applicable), housing costs support, travel expenses, medical expenses, children's education, and living allowance along with the relevant data of the country where they are being posted is also important.

Immigration

Immigration related issues for expatriates are largely governed by immigration laws and procedures of the land. Although immigration issues have been simplified under World Trade Organization (WTO) regulations, they are still largely influenced by local regulatory norms. For member countries of European Economic Communities (EEC), such issues are quite relaxed in pursuant to EEC resolutions, as it now allows free flow of goods and people. Member countries have now made their border free for such purpose. Such movements are still restricted in many East European countries. Many countries do not issue work permits even for Indian expatriates. Such immigration norms hinder the best utilisation of talent. These issues are likely to get resolved in the near future, with an increase in the magnitude of globalization and consolidation of WTO powers. Even though, immigration issues, per se, may not exert direct influence on international compensation, they have some ramifications in expatriates pay differentials, thus creating a problem with respect to the availability of quality manpower.

Taxation

In international compensation, the biggest challenge is to accommodate tax issues. Tax regulations are quite different across the nations, thus creating problems of tax equalization for the expatriates. In many overseas assignments, expatriates have to pay higher tax, which often nullifies their increased compensation and benefits. In this context, it is important to mention that Indian tax laws are expatriate-friendly. There is hardly any difference between tax liabilities of an Indian employee and an expatriate.

Social security

Payment of social security contributions in host countries often becomes a major problem for expatriates. For many expatriates, social security contributions often become dual as they have to contribute in the host countries where they get posted as well as in the country of origin, that is, where their parent organization operates. Designing compensation for such international assignments becomes a serious issue as contribution to social securities is regulated by legal norms. For operational flexibility, it is desirable to subject the expatriates to the social security legislation of the countries where they work, but there are exceptions to this too. However, in cases where the expatriates are posted to host countries for more than five years, it is not just desirable but also practical that they be brought within the scope of the host country's social security system.

Secondment agreements

Secondment refers to the temporary assignment of worker in another job. For international assignments, this term is used as an extension to a job in another country. Most of the employers prefer to sign secondment agreement with the employees to validate their existing terms of contract of employment in their home country. This is done to ensure that all the terms and conditions of their current contract of employment with the employer remain otherwise unaffected during the secondment.

Usually the secondment agreement put the following obligations on the employee:
- carry out the duties assigned by the secondee company
- comply with the standards of conduct and performance and rules and procedures of the secondee company
- comply with any relevant local law or practice

- devote all of their time and attention to the secondee company
- ensure that the secondee company's confidential information and trade connections are adequately protected per the contract terms

Apart from these, it specifies the employee's reporting line at the secondee company. It also specifies the method to rate employee's performance and the manner in which disciplinary or grievance issues are to be addressed, while on secondment. Administration issues, tax and social security payments, holiday entitlement, returning to work with the employer after repatriation, etc. are other important areas covered in the secondment agreement.

FOREIGNERS WORKING IN INDIA AND RELATED STATUTORY COMPLIANCES

Before a foreign national is engaged for employment in India, he must obtain an employment visa. Such employment visa is issued only if the foreign national would be drawing a minimum annual salary of US $25,000. This is what we call the floor limit of compensation for foreign nationals engaged in India. However, there are some exceptions to the floor limit. For example, it is not applicable for ethnic cooks, language teachers or translators (other than English), and staff for the embassy or high commission.

Under the Income Tax Act, in India an individual is taxed on the basis of his residential status. Residential status is determined on the basis of physical presence of the individual in a particular financial year. Residential status could be *resident and ordinarily resident* (ROR), *resident but not ordinarily resident* (NOR), or a *non-resident* (NR). A ROR is liable to pay tax on his global income. NOR is liable to pay tax on income sourced from India, or income derived from a business controlled or set up in India. For a NR, the tax liability is only on income sourced from India. A foreign national gets exemption from the payment of income tax if his stay in India does not exceed 90 days. For details about the taxation rate, etc. students are advised to refer to latest provisions of the Income Tax Act.

INTERNATIONAL COMPENSATION DESIGN

In the global market place, strategic flexibility is assigned more weightage than national culture while determining compensation. Employment practices vary worldwide. Even after globalization, the influence of local practices has hardly diminished. For example, life-time employment in Japan and industry-wide bargaining in Germany are still practiced. These influences weaken the case of bringing uniformity in international compensation design. In this situation it is important to look for of international compensation designs, which can keep the expatriates *economically whole*.

International compensation design requires a global mindset. With the right global mindset, organizations can balance the corporate, business unit, and functional priorities on a global scale. In words of Jack Welch, the former CEO of General Electric, 'The aim in a global business is to get the best ideas from everyone, everywhere.' To compete successfully in a global market, it is essential for organizations to not only design their international compensation with a global mindset, but also to understand the economic, social, and political realities of the countries they operate in. The global mindset helps the organizations become flexible in designing compensation for the expatriates. For example, in China, local labour costs for state-owned enterprises (SOE) and private or foreign organizations are different. The compensation costs are quite high in SOEs, whereas they are low for other organizations. Most global organizations have relocated their manufacturing units in China to reap the advantage of low labour cost. In Japan, employee compensation depends largely on the organization's size, degree of unionization, capital–labour ratio, degree of global competition, and above all the profitability; whereas in Korea, compensation depends on labour market issues, customer–supplier relations, economic situation, and technology level. Political, economic, and institutional forces play more important role when it comes to organizational compensation decisions in Hungary and the US. In India, employee compensation issues are regulated largely by the labour laws, with little room for variation and flexibility to accommodate organizational needs. Country-wise norms on fixed and variable pay vary widely.

APPROACHES TO INTERNATIONAL COMPENSATION

Two main approaches to international compensation are the *going-rate approach* and the *balance sheet approach*. The going-rate approach is basically designing compensation based on the market rate. The balance sheet approach is a build-up approach as under this method compensation is designed based on living standards in the home-country. Considering home country pay and benefits as the basis, some extra financial inducements are provided while designing compensation using this approach.

Going-rate Approach

As already explained, the basic characteristic of this approach is linking compensation of the expatriates to the compensation structure in the host country. For this purpose, organizations need to first decide the basis of benchmarking their compensation structure. The appropriate market rate is decided based on compensation surveys conducted locally. After this organizations decide whether host country nationals (HCNs, i.e., local), expatriates who are actually the citizen of host country and the expatriates of other countries should be treated alike. To clarify this point further, while benchmarking the market rate, it is important for an Indian white goods multinational company (MNC) operating in South Africa to decide whether the reference point would be the compensation structure of South African competitors of Indian MNC in South Africa, or all the other white goods companies operating in South Africa. Most of the MNCs operating in India pay expatriates a higher salary as India is a low labour cost country when compared to developed countries of the world. They supplement the base pay of such expatriates with additional perks and benefits.

Some advantages of the going-rate approach are equality, simple administration, simple to understand, and the overall sense of identity to the expatriates as they can relate them with the host country. The disadvantages are compensation variation when the same employee as expatriate works in different countries with different assignments. This may lead to employees accepting assignments and postings, which give them better compensation. Hence, this type of compensation plan can unnecessarily set off competition among employees for foreign assignments, which increases their chance of an increased compensation.

Balance Sheet Approach

As already explained, this type of approach provides for some extra financial benefits to adjust the home country's living standard. Home-country pay and benefits are the basis of this approach. This approach links the base salary for parent country national (PCN) and TCN to the compensation structure of the home country, that is, the country where the organization is headquartered. Top-ups, that is, financial benefits, are provided in alignment with the living standards in the host country. An Italian expatriate, working for an Italian company in India will certainly not feel comfortable with the Indian level of compensation. His base salary would be of Italian standard, that is, at par with the home country rate. In India, that is, the host country, the expatriate may be provided some extra financial incentives. The basic purpose of this approach is to equalize the purchasing power of expatriates in the host country to the home country.

The main advantages of the balance sheet approach are to reduce the compensation gap between foreign postings and the home country for smoothening the repatriation of expatriates for principles of equity. This type of compensation package is also easy to communicate. The main disadvantages are disparities between PCNs and HCNs and the dissimilarities in taxation rates. ESOP is now considered as one of the important compensation variables. To understand the cross-country difference in compensation practices, the practice of ESOP across the world is illustrated in Table 17.1.

TABLE 17.1 ESOP across the world

Country/Region	Features
United States	• More emphasis on incentives and ownership • Relatively higher dilution level, which oilers more benefits to the ESOP holders • Hardly any performance conditions are attached
UK	• Less preferred as more emphasis on fixed pay component • Performance conditions are imposed
Europe	• ESOP is used sparsely and for only a few people • More tax-friendly
China	• Highly regulated • Offered only to key senior managerial people
Hong Kong	• Used extensively as LTIs (long term incentives) • Maximum income tax rate is 15%
India	• Regulated by the Securities and Exchange Hoard of India (SEBI) • As LTI, ESOPs arc gaining importance • Aligned with the broad-based plans • Becoming more tax-friendly
Other Asian countries	• Mostly offered by multinationals • Offered only to a privileged few • Legal complications still dissuade many organizations from issuing ESOPs

INTERNATIONAL COMPENSATION STRATEGIES FOR TALENT ENGAGEMENT

With McKinsey's study on 'Ware for Talent' (1998), organizations globally started renewing their focus on talent engagement and retention through effective compensation strategies. In practice, organizations follow two approaches to manage talent; differentiating and inclusive. *Differentiating approach* means organizations focus only on those employees who are indentified talent, that is, who are identified as having higher value and potential over others. Such identified talents, gets more attention in terms of resource support, training, increased compensation, etc. However, we also find organizations, who adopt inclusive approach, that is, they focus on all cross-sections of employees. In the first case, organizations try to achieve excellence through top performers; whereas in the second case, organizations try to institutionalize the culture of performance making every one competent through effective talent management activities. Differentiated approach to talent management were initially practiced by GE. Today, we find that many organizations across the globe practice this. Globally companies like Shell and in India Murugappa Group follow this inclusive approach.

Whatever may be the approach to talent engagement, international compensation strategies focus on the following principles:
• alignment of the compensation plan with business strategy of the organization

- valuing internal equity
- valuing culture
- top-down approach
- balancing between global and local needs
- focus on organizational branding for talent attraction

These are generic principles for talent engagement at international level, through compensation strategies. Firms may utilize their own tools and techniques to engage talent using other human resource management practices.

SUMMARY

Design of international compensation is a key issue in the current globalized business environment. It is complex as differences exist in compensation levels across nations. When an organization develops compensation plans for expatriates in tune with its strategy and culture, it also needs to consider country-specific issues to remain competitive in the local market. Demotivation due to below market level compensation, loss of productivity, problem of retention, and at times refusal to take up foreign assignments are some of the issues that can be attributed to ill-designed international compensation systems. Major variation in international compensation is due to the differences in taxation and the purchasing power. Along with this, other challenges that need to be taken care of are exchange rate variation and the inflation levels.

Apart from the external factors, the most important factor that influences an organization's international compensation structure is its own strategy. International compensation strategies of an organization are framed to attract, retain, and motivate the talented expatriates who are mostly experts in their respective areas of specialization. The compensation designs should emphasize on consistency and follow the principles of equity, while keeping the compensation level competitive. Two main approaches followed by the organizations while designing the international compensation are the going-rate approach and the balance sheet approach. The choice of the approach depends on organizational strategies.

Key Terms

Balance sheet approach This approach links the base salary for PCNs and TCNs to the compensation structure in the home country, where the organization is headquartered. Top-ups, that is, financial benefits are provided, keeping pace with living standards.

Going-rate approach Basic characteristic of this approach is linking compensation of the expatriates to the compensation structure in the host country. For this purpose, organizations need to first decide the basis of benchmarking their compensation structure.

Repatriation It is a return of employees earlier sent for foreign deputation.

Secondment agreement It is a temporary assignment of a worker to another job. For international assignment, this term is used as an extension to a job in another country. Most of the employers prefer to sign secondment agreement with the employees to validate their existing terms of contract of employment in their home country. This is to ensure that all the terms and conditions of the employee's contract of employment with the employer remain otherwise unaffected during the secondment.

Exercises

Concept Review Questions

1. Explain the genesis of international compensation. How can cultural issues influence international compensation design?
2. What is the concept of variation in international compensation? How does this concept alter the components of international compensation?
3. How do repatriation and immigration issues influence international compensation design?
4. Explain the concept of secondment agreements. To what extent such agreements can influence international compensation practices?

Critical Thinking Question

What are the different approaches to international compensation computation? Which approach do you recommend for an Indian consumer electronic MNC for its units in the US? Justify your answer.

Differential Pay Policy of Nita International

International organizations believe in aligning pay and performance. This makes a difference in compensation payouts to executives between low-performing and high-performing organizations. The gap can even extend to 75 per cent or more according to a Watson Wyatt study conducted in 2007. Executives in high-performing organizations also get the benefit of increased stock price under stock options, leading to huge retention problems in low-performing organizations. Nita International has cross-border operations, specializing in aluminum fine blanks, with manufacturing units in 10 different countries. The company is headquartered in New Delhi and believes in following an ethnocentric approach in compensation practices across the nations. Uniform compensation policy with 80 per cent fixed pay and 20 per cent variable pay is followed. Earning 20 per cent variables by the employees is simple as it requires 100 per cent attendance and simple compliance with the production plan.

Nita's HR department is responsible for developing compensation practices that would help the organization remain competitive in the labour market, to attract talent to the organization, and finally to retain the best performers. With the present structure of compensation variables, 100 per cent of the Nita's incentives are paid as additional wages. Nita continues to review its compensation strategies and practices to attract, motivate, and retain qualified personnel and to reward employees with the potential to assume responsible positions within the organization. Manufacturing of fine blanks is a highly profitable activity as it is technology-driven and provides up to 98 per cent

(Contd)

CASE STUDY (Contd)

realization of the product from core raw materials. The company is a world leader in the field and is able to meet the market demand with non-stop production in all the units spread across ten countries.

To remain competitive, Nita's current compensation practices aim to achieve the following objectives:
- attract qualified and talented applicants
- provide flexibility to respond to departmental needs
- ensure consistency and fairness in compensation administration
- improve employee morale
- motivate a knowledgeable and innovative workforce
- support a healthy work environment by providing promotional opportunities
- maintain salaries that are externally competitive and internally equitable
- ensure retention of talented staff
- be fiscally responsible

The company realizes its main compensation goals of attracting, motivating, and retaining qualified employees by using compensation tools such as structured job evaluation system, salary structure, performance management system, spot award programme, and market pricing system for the current, new, and restructured jobs.

The global HR head of Nita, while explaining the compensation policies, focuses on the following areas:
- maintain salary ranges that are not only competitive, but also consistent with the economic requirements of the organization
- provide equal pay for equal work under comparable working conditions without regard for race, color, religion, marital status, sex, age, national origin, disability, sexual orientation, or status as a veteran
- establish salary rates that reflect the value of various jobs in the labour market as determined by a system of continuing job evaluation and market pricing
- react to shifts in the competitive labour market
- adjust pay ranges when warranted by changing economic and competitive factors, as determined by salary surveys
- develop employee knowledge regarding compensation policies, procedures, practices, and guidelines
- provide employees access to job descriptions and salary grade structures
- reflect a direct relationship of pay to individual job performance
- ensure compliance with state and federal employment laws regarding compensation

Nita pursues a differential compensation policy for senior executives and managerial employees of the organization. Executive compensation is broad-based with stock options rendering huge intrinsic benefits. Apart from this, periodic pay-outs of organizational performance-linked bonus benefit all the executives make it possible for them to get additional 20–25 per cent of their gross compensation. Nita's Detroit factory suddenly earned the displeasure of the corporate governance body, which questioned Nita's differential compensation practices. The Detroit unit largely employs American workers, who are unionized. Taking a cue from the corporate governance body, the unions also issued similar notices to the company headquarters asking for pay equity.

Discussion question

As a compensation specialist, suggest how would you resolve this crisis?

References

Baruch, Y. (2004), *Managing Careers: Theory and Practice*, Harlow, FT Prentice Hall.

Belcher, D.W. and T.J. Atchison (1987), *Compensation Administration*, 2nd edn, Prentice Hall, Englewood Cliffs, New Jersey.

Bhattacharyya, D.K. (2006), *Human Resource Management*, 2nd edn, Excel Books, New Delhi.

Bhattacharyya, D.K. (2008), *Manpower Development for Technological Change*, Excel Books, New Delhi.

Bhattacharyya, Dipak Kumar (2010), *Cross-cultural Management: Text and Cases*, PHI Learning, New Delhi.

Chambers, E.G., M. Foulon, H. Handfield-Jones, S.M. Hankin, and E.G. Michaels (1998), 'The War for Talent, McKinsey Quarterly, 3, pp. 44–57.

Dowling, P.J., D.E. Welch, and R.S. Schuller (2002), *International Human Resource Management: Managing People in a Multinational Context*, Thompson South Western, Cincinnati.

Earley, C. and M. Erez (1997), *The transplanted executive*, Oxford University Press, London.

Freeman, R.B. and F. Katz Lawrence (1994), *Rising wage inequality: The United States vs. other Advanced Countries*, in R. Freeman edited, *Working Under Different Rules*, New York, Russell Sage Foundation and NBER, pp. 29–62.

Hibbitt, W.J. and T. Dwyer (1996), 'Keeping expatriates out of danger', *International HR Journal*, Fall.

Hofstede, G. (1983), 'The cultural relativity of organizational practices and theories', *Journal of International Business Studies*, vol. 14, pp. 75–89.

Kates, S.M. and C. Spielman (1995), 'Reducing the cost of sending employees overseas', *Practical Accountant*, vol. 28, pp. 50–5.

McGoldrick, F. (1997), 'Expatriate compensation and benefit practice of US and Canadian firms: Survey results', *International Human Resource Journal*, pp. 13–17, Summer.

Stone, R.J. (1986), 'Compensation: Pay and perks for overseas executives', *Personnel Journal*, p. 67, January.

Trompenaars, A. (1994), *Riding the waves of culture: Understanding diversity in global business*, Burr Ridge, IL: Irwin.

Wagner, J. A., III. (1995), 'Studies of individualism-collectivism: Effects on cooperation in groups', *Academy of Management Journal*, vol. 38, pp. 152–72.

Index

Base pay calculation   25–26
Benefits   107
   employment security   109
   medical and health care   109
   non-monetary   107–8
   of reward and recognition programme   313–4
   old age and retirement   109
   statutory   110
      bonus   110
      employee security   110
      lay-off   111
      retrenchment compensation   110
      safety and health provisions   111
Broad band pay plan   45

Collective bargaining in India   345–7
Compensable factor   162–4
Compensation   2–3
   and talent management   9–10
   and Income Tax Act   327–8
   benchmarking   44
   decisions   40–1
   design and strategy   357–8
      strategy across levels   358–9
      tactics and strategy   359–60
   factors influencing   10–2
      external factors   12
      internal factors   11–2
   objectives of   6–8
   payroll and   8
   philosophy   26–7
   plan in India   50
   planning   27
   practices
      for talented employees   139
      in India   51
   tax implications of   327
   trends in India   45–7

Compensation decisions
   determinants of 42–3
   econometric application in   88–9
   principles for   42–3
Compensation design through skill-based
   programmes   244–5
Compensation determination   14–6
Compensation formulation   13–4
   determinants of wage rates   13–4
Compensation management and PMS   209–10
   performance-related pay   210–2
   problems in monitoring PRP   212–3
Competency-based
   approach   198–9
   pay   246–7
      performance guide charts   246
Concept of variation   429
Contribution-based sales compensation   300
Cost to company   23–4, 337–8
Criticisms of labour economics   68–9
Cultural issues   428–9

Deferred compensation   111–2
   non-qualified   112
   qualified   111
Definition of wages   324–7
   wage determination   326–7
Developing performance metric   228–32
   EFQM Excellence Model   231–2
   Malcolm–Baldrige criteria   231–2
   Shingo Prize Model™   229–30
Developing performance standards   226–7
   checklist   226–7
   guidelines   226

Economic theories of wages   78–81
   bargain theory   79
   classical school   80

Keynesian school 81
marginalist school 81
marginal productivity theory 79
Marxian school 80
neoclassical economic theory 80
neoclassical school 80
Philips curve 81
residual claimant theory 79
subsistence theory 79
surplus value theory 79–80
wage fund theory 79
Economic value-added 223–4, 418–9
Effective performance modelling 232–3
customer-focused metrics 233–4
designing metrics 233
Effective PMS 234–5
Effective sales compensation plan 300–2
Employee benefits 106, 108–10, 401–7
alternatives to 114–5
dearness allowance 405–7
fringe benefits 106–12
need for 113
objectives of 114
golden parachute 109
gratuity computation 401–3
income tax issues in payment of gratuity 403–4
labour markets and 87–8
perks 106
perquisites 106
provident fund 404–5
salary sacrifice 106
tax obligations 108
Employee compensation
economic theories 81–2
significance of 30–3
trade-offs and 82
valuation of 82–3
Employee reward system in India 47–9
aims of 49–50
elements of 48–9
employee stock options 49
Equity in employment benefits 88
Ergonomics 191–2
and work study 192
Ergonomics and management 193
human engineering 195–7
and machine design 196

motion economy 194–5
value analysis 197–8
working areas 193
Ethical issues in
compensation 33–4
rewards and recognition 318–9
Executive compensation 266–7
calibration of 268
components of 45, 267–8
criteria of 281–3
behaviour 283
individual characteristics 282
market 283
peer compensation 283
performance 282
role or position 282
size 283
strategy 281–282
organizational strategy 278–81
organization level practices 279–81
recent studies on 283–5
say on pay 284–5
design 272–6
context of 274–5
culture and 275
decision context 275
use of performance criteria 274
theories 269–72
agency theory 271
balance sheet approach 271
cafeteria plan 272
competency-based pay 272
golden handcuffs 271
golden parachutes 272
headquarters-based pay 271
profit-sharing plan 272
social comparison theory 271
tournament theory 271
transparency in 268–9
Expatriate and repatriate compensation 430–1

Foreigners working in India 433–4

Group incentive payment practices in organizations 417

Incentive determination 407–17
differential piece rate methods 409–17

Bedeaux point plan   415
Emerson's efficiency plan   411–2
Gantt task system   411
Merrick differential piece rate   409–10
Priestman production plan   415–7
Rowan premium plan   413–4
Scanlon plan   414–5
Taylor's method   409
straight piece rate method   408
International compensation   427–8
approaches to   434–6
balance sheet   435
going-rate   434–6
components of   429–30
design   433–4
strategies for talent engagement   436–7
Issues related to repatriation   431–3
immigration   431–2
secondment agreements   432–3
social security   432
taxation   432

Job assessment   182–8
method study   184–8
pricing job value   182
work study   183–4
Job description   159–61
job specifications   161
transparency   161–2
Job design   146–9
characteristics of   149
components of   152–62
assessment centres   158–9
job analysis   153–8
job information   152–3
strategies and techniques of   150–2
autonomous work groups   151–2
job enlargement   150–1
job enrichment   151
job rotation   150
sub-contracting   152
Job evaluation   172–3
Job evaluation techniques   173–80
classification   174
factor comparison   179
Hay's method   177–9
limitations of   182

other methods   179–81
graded pay structure   180–81
points rating   174–6
compensable factors   176
Hay's profile method   176
ranking   174–5

Labour market
changes and trade unions   69–71
internal   63
macro economics of   59–60
neo-classical microeconomics of   63
policies in India   71–2
unemployment and its impact on   60–3
Labour welfare administration   72–3
Legal interpretation of wage fixation   338

Mechanism of motivation   124–6
Merit matrices   418
Mistakes in compensation designing   51
Motivating generation Y   138
Motivation   120–3
and compensation   126–7
and morale   136–7
objectives of   124
Motivational research   137–8

National wage policy in India   23
Neo-classical microeconomic model   64–8

Overtime wages   417–8

Pay-at-risk   338
Pay grades and pay bands   28–30
Payroll management   381–2
Performance indicators   225–6
Performance management system (PMS)   208–9
and 360-degree appraisals   240–2
and compensation broad banding   243
assessment centre method   238–239
bars   239–240
behavioural observation scales   240
human asset accounting method   238
organizational strategy   235–6
balanced scorecard   241–3
mixed-standard scale   239

through management by objectives 237
Performance measurement in executive incentive programme 276–8
Performance objectives 225–6
Perquisites 328–37
  home loan and tax planning 331–3
  leave travel concession 331
  medical insurance 331
  motor car 329–30
  rent-free residential accommodation 330–1
  tax on non-monetary perquisites 333–6
  treatment of special allowances 337–8
Pricing of employee stock options 83–87
  Black–Scholes model 85–86
  legal perspective 84–85
  problem of expensing 86–87
  regulatory framework 84
Productivity-linked employee benefits 89–100
  employee benefits and productivity 95–7
  factors to improve productivity 91–3
  organizational level data support 97–8
  productivity 90–1
  productivity and quality 95
  productivity bargaining 98–100
  productivity measurement 93–4
    omni factor model 94
    surrogate model 94
    for knowledge workers 95
PRP in CPSEs 213–6
  PRP scenario in CPSEs 216–8
  sample KRA and KPI 218–22

Quantitative analysis 382–401
  alternate techniques 388–92
  compa-ratios 395–8
  compensation metrics 400–1
  cost–benefit analysis 398
  interval measurements 384–5
  levels of measurement 383
  Likert scale 387–8
  maturity curves 393–5
  nominal measurements 383
  ordinal measurements 383–4
  pay structure formation 392–3
  ratio measurement 385–6
  salary increases 398–9
  scaling techniques 386–7
  semantic scale 387

Relating sales compensation plans with organizational life cycle 302
Relationship between fixed and variable pay 276
Retirement plans 378–81
  401(k) plans 380
  health and welfare plans 380–1
  pension plans 378–80
Rewards
  changing views toward 315–7
    total rewards strategy 316–7
  compensation and 312–313
  definition and concepts of 310–2
Rewards and recognition policy 317–8

Sales compensation constructs 302–4
Sales compensation design and administration 296–9
  compensation method 297–8
  components of 298–9
  controllable and measurable elements of sales function 297
  designing effective sales compensation plan 296
  level of compensation 297
  non-cash incentives as sales compensation 299
  pilot testing 298
  rollout of the plan 298
  understanding sales job descriptions 297
  understanding objectives of 297
Sales compensation issues 293
  sales goals 293
Sales compensation plan 294–6
  sales cycle 296
Sales incentives and motivation 299
Strategic compensation
  and talent issues in global hiring 365
  design 362–4
  policies 364
Strategic planning 361–2
  mission 361
  objectives 362
  vision 361
Strategy 354–7
  descriptive schools 355
    cognitive school 355
    configuration school 356–7

cultural school   356
entrepreneurial school   355
environmental school   356
learning school   356
power school   356
prescriptive schools   355
   design school   355
   planning school   355
   positioning school   355

Team-based compensation   254–8
   effective design of   259–260
   employee evaluation system   256–7
   gainsharing plan   258
   group incentive plans   257–8
   problems in rewarding teams   258
   recent trends in   260
Theories of motivation   127–36
   attribution theory   133
   content theories   134
   equity theory   131
   expectancy theory   131
   job characteristic model   129–30
   locus of control   133
   need hierarchy theory   128
   performance satisfaction theory   132–3
   perspective theories   134
   process theories   134
   two-factor theory   128–9
Theories of wage determination   14–6
   theory of negotiated wages   14
   traditional theory   14
Total rewards concepts and strategies   314–5

Types of wages   16–20
   fair wage   20
   living wage   19–20
   minimum rate of wages   16–8
   need-based minimum wages   18–9

Understanding sales function   292–3

Variable compensation   375–8
   alternative pay   377
   bonus or incentive plans   376
   employee goals and organizational goals   376
   gain-sharing plans   377
   lump sum merit awards   377
   motivated employees   376
   profit-sharing plans   376
   spot bonuses   377
   stock plans   377–8
   variable compensation plans   375–6
Various dimensions of performance   236–7
VIE theory and compensation   43

Wage borders   20–1
Wage components   5–6
Wage fixation through collective bargaining   338–41
Wage policy   21–3
Wages and compensation   3–4
   differences between   4–5
Work measurement   188–91
   time study   188–90
   other techniques   190–2

About the Author

Dipak Kumar Bhattacharyya is a Professor, Organizational Behaviour and Human Resource Management, at the Xavier Institute of Management, Bhubaneswar (XIMB). He has done Masters in Economics from Jadavpur University and doctorate in management from the University of Calcutta. He started his career in the industry before turning to academia in 1988. He has worked with several prominent institutes including Institute of Management Technology (IMT), Ghaziabad; All India Management Association (AIMA); Indian Institute of Social Welfare and Business Management (IISWBM); and Institute of Engineering and Management, Kolkata (IEM).

In addition to the above, Prof. Bhattacharyya has been involved in preparing the Entrepreneurship Development Programme at IISWBM conducted in association with Entrepreneurship Development Institute of India (EDII), Ahmedabad. He has been a visiting faculty at Xavier Labour Relations Institute (XLRI), Jamshedpur and Indian Institute of Foreign Trade (IIFT), Kolkata. He has been attached to several universities including the external programmes of foreign universities such as the University of London and the DeSales University.

Prof. Bhattacharyya has over 35 years of experience in academia and industry across various domains of management including total quality management, quality circles, statistical quality control, and human resource management. He has published 25 books including *Organizational Behaviour*, 2e (2014), *Organizational Change and Development* (2011), and *Human Resource Research Methods* (2007) all published by OUP; and has more than 100 research papers in prominent national and international academic journals to his credit. He continues to pursue research areas such as human resource development, cross-cultural management, six-sigma practices, human resource control systems, and organizational systems.

Prof. Bhattacharyya also provides consultancy services and conducts management development programmes (MDPs) in several organizations. Previously, he was a member of Industrial Relations Committee of the Bharat Chamber of Commerce and the Department of Labour, Government of West Bengal.

Related Titles

Industrial Relations [9780195671087]

C.S.Venkata Ratnam

The text provides an in-depth coverage of the four key components of industrial relations: the conceptual foundations, the institutional structure and policy framework, the role of government, and industrial relations in unionized organizations.

Key Features

- Explores the emerging issues in industrial relations, such as labour law reform, employment security and management of redundancies, and technological change and industrial relations
- Examines the challenges faced by business organizations in industrial relations

Performance Management [9780195693379]

Tapomoy Deb, *Jamia Milia Islamia, Delhi*

Performance Management is a comprehensive textbook designed to meet the long-felt need of management students for a book on performance appraisal and management. Oriented towards managerial decision-making, the book provides a strong theoretical framework while emphasizing the application of concepts through real-life examples, illustrations, caselets, and case studies.

Key Features

- Combines sound theoretical concepts with real-world organizational experience covers contemporary perspectives as also futuristic possibilities in performance management
- Includes many exhibits, diagrams, illustrations, and cartoons to facilitate easy grasp of the concepts
- Includes case studies that explore the concepts discussed to enable students hone their diagnostic/application skills
- Provides practice-based tools such as performance management proformas, templates, and checklists

Cross-Cultural Management [9780198066293]

Shobhana Madhavan, *Amrita School of Business, Amrita Vishwa Vidyapeetham, Coimbatore*

Cross-Cultural Management—Concepts and Cases is a comprehensive textbook designed for postgraduate degree/diploma students of business management and practicing managers. It explains how culture impacts international management in the areas of communication, negotiations, organizational behaviour, and human resource management.

Key Features

- Discusses cross-cultural management in today's corporate India with a wide variety of Indian/Asian examples—making this text relevant to today's global India
- Provides important tips on business etiquette and key information regarding doing business in several countries, ranging from Brazil to Nigeria

Organizational Change and Development [9780198066460]

Dipak Kumar Bhattacharyya, *Xavier Institute of Management, Bhubaneswar*

Organizational Change and Development is aimed at postgraduate students specializing in human resources (HR) and strategy. Providing a strong conceptual foundation of the subject, the book takes the readers through all the processes and stages of change, as seen and experienced.

Key Features

- Discusses organizational development experiences in several Indian and international organizations such as Wal-Mart, Lehman Brothers, Godrej, and Indian Ordnance Factories
- Provides appendices on guidelines for organizational change, sample of a dashboard, and organizational health survey

Other Related Titles

ISBN	Author: Title
9780195683592	**Agarwala:** *Strategic Human Resource Management*
9780195689105	**Bhattacharyya:** *Human Resource Research Methods*
9780198074113	**Jyothi & Venkatesh:** *Human Resource Management, 2/e*
9780195698718	**Haldar:** *Human Resource Development*